D1447549

A HANDBOOK
OF GREEK LITERATURE

By the same author

A HANDBOOK OF GREEK MYTHOLOGY
A HANDBOOK OF LATIN LITERATURE
GODS AND HEROES OF THE GREEKS
OUTLINES OF CLASSICAL LITERATURE

A Handbook
of Greek Literature

FROM HOMER TO THE AGE OF LUCIAN

H. J. ROSE

M.A., LL.D., F.B.A.

βραχύ μοι στόμα πάντ᾽ ἀναγήσασθαι

METHUEN & CO. LTD LONDON
E. P. DUTTON & CO. INC. NEW YORK

First published 14 June 1934
Second edition 1942
Third edition, revised, 1948
Fourth edition, revised, 1951
Reprinted with minor corrections, 1956 and 1961
Reprinted 1964
Reprinted by lithography in Great Britain
by Jarrold & Sons Ltd, Norwich
Catalogue No 02/3333/31
4.4

TO
MY TEACHERS

PREFACE

WHEN so many manuals of Greek literature have already been written, the author of a new one may reasonably be asked to justify himself. My explanation is, that I do not find any book in English and at present in print which covers the whole field, is of moderate length yet not so short as to include the principal authors only, and takes account of the latest results of investigation. I have tried to meet those requirements in the present work.

As in my *Handbook of Greek Mythology*, I have used different sizes of print for different paragraphs. Those in larger type assume no knowledge whatever on the student's part save the alphabet of Greek, which he may learn in half an hour. They attempt a continuous account of all those movements which are of importance to the literature of Greece or of the world generally. Less important authors, and especially those whose works are lost, are dealt with in the smaller type. These parts are also a little more technical and presuppose a little acquaintance with the subject. Details, however, of chronology, the genuineness of works assigned to a particular author, and such things interesting mainly to the specialist, are in the footnotes, which are meant to guide those who wish to pursue their studies further, or to judge for themselves of the value of statements which, for brevity's sake, it has often been necessary to make in a dogmatic form.

Brevity has also been sought by cutting down aesthetic criticism to the barest minimum. Furthermore, the vast Christian and the considerable Jewish literature written in Greek have been wholly omitted, not that they lack importance, but that they represent a different spirit from that of the Greeks themselves, and are best handled in separate works. Some space has been saved by assuming that the reader has access to a History of Greece, of which there are many, and by referring to the author's little works on Mythology for explanations touching that subject.

Greek names, with a very few easily understood exceptions, have been simply transliterated, not given in their Latinized forms. On the other hand, the Latin titles of many Greek works have been so long familiar that they have been retained, save for writings which are now lost. Therefore the reader will find Oidipus mentioned, but the *Oedipus Tyrannus*, and the *Hellenica* of Xenophon, but the *Hellenika* of Anaximenes.

H. J. ROSE

St. Andrews
New Year's Day, 1934

A fourth impression being called for, the author has taken the opportunity to make a number of minor additions and improvements.

H. J. ROSE

St. Andrews
January, 1950

Every handbook needs constant revision, as knowledge progresses. This imprint contains such alterations as seemed desirable and technically possible; several would have been made earlier but for the Second World War and its aftermath, which cut British scholars off from their Continental colleagues for some time.

H. J. ROSE

St. Andrews
November, 1955

Between 1950 and 1960 some important and many minor discoveries have been made; I have tried to include as many as possible of these in the fifth impression.

H. J. ROSE

St. Andrews
March, 1960

CONTENTS

A HANDBOOK OF GREEK LITERATURE

CHAPTER I

PEOPLE AND LANGUAGE : WRITING

A T an unknown, but fairly early date, perhaps towards the end of the third millennium B.C., a tall, fair-haired people was making its way southward down the Vardar valley and, farther east, across the Dardanelles into Asia Minor. The more westerly section of this migration in time conquered and occupied that country which was afterwards known as Hellas, but is generally called by us Greece. There, the invaders, who probably were not very numerous and certainly were not under one central command, found a people whom they, at least in historical times, termed Pelasgians ; a convenient modern name, which begs no questions as to their origin or ethnology, is Helladics. These were not savages ; they had attained some degree of culture of their own, and both they and the new-comers were profoundly influenced by the great and ancient civilization—we call it Minoan—of the island of Crete. The result was the formation of a new culture, the Mycenaean, containing elements from the northern and the southern constituents of the mixed population, but ruled by chieftains of the invading stock. The language was, or at least ultimately became, that of the northerners ; in historical times but a few small districts still kept remnants of the Helladic or Pelasgian speech.[1]

The more easterly group likewise founded new kingdoms, in Asia Minor, where they seem to have led a somewhat turbulent existence as unruly vassals of the Hittite empire, or as principalities more or less independent, maintaining relations, friendly or other, with the native powers. We hear of one such principality in

[1] See Herodotos, i, 57.

particular, that of the district known to us as Troy, or the Troad, where a dynasty probably partly northern in origin seems to have borne sway for many years, till finally its power was broken by a united effort of the settlers in Greece itself, traditionally led by their great king Agamemnon. After this, Greece was disturbed by a new immigration ; a belated and culturally rather backward section of their own kin, known to us as the Dorians, swept down into the Peloponnesos, perhaps about the eleventh century B.C., and drove out the earlier comers, who seem to have called themselves Achaioi. Bereft of their possessions in Greece, many of these passed across the sea to Asia Minor, where in time they formed a long line of coastal settlements, collectively known as Ionian and their inhabitants as Iones, Ionians, the Yawan (Javan) of the Old Testament. These settlements, founded by fairly civilized people close to ancient seats of civilization, rose with some rapidity to a brilliant culture, while the people of Greece proper remained for a while comparatively backward. With Ionia, therefore, the history of Greek literature begins.[2]

But, since all Greek literature has certain characteristics in common, it is well to ask what the new-comers brought with them and what they found when they came. The Achaians, so to call them, appear to have been a race of hardy, intelligent, courageous folk, of independent character, respecting more, perhaps, than most peoples in the stage of culture they had attained the rights of the individual. They might be loyal subjects of a ruler who understood them, exceedingly turbulent under one who did not, but hardly the slaves or contented underlings of any man. Their material culture was not very high as yet, but they were willing and able to learn. Their religion, so far as we can say anything about it, included the worship of a sky- or weather-god, Zeus, the one certainly common feature in the cults of all Wiros.[3] Probably they also reverenced a corn- or earth-mother, the later Demeter. The Helladics were less

---

[2] For details of this early history, see *C.A.H.*, vol. ii. p. 431 *sqq.*; iii, p. 527 *sqq.*; Meyer, i, p. 771 *sqq.*; ii, p. 162 *sqq.*; Myers, *Greeks, passim*. Certainty is still a very long way from being reached ; I have given in outline what seems to me the most probable view.

[3] I prefer to use the name ' Wiro ' for those peoples, or that people, which originally spoke the language from which the existing tongues, ancient and modern, more commonly known as Indo-Germanic, Indo-European and Aryan are descended ; also for their language. In the former sense, the term is due to Dr. Giles, and avoids begging any questions of habitat or race, merely denoting the existence of a widespread word for *man*, Lat. *uir*, mod. Welsh *gwr*, Eng. *wer* (-*gelt*, -*wolf*), declined with an o-suffix (as in the so-called second declension of Latin).

valiant and independent, but more skilful of hand, not slow of wit, and capable of influencing and being influenced by the new-comers. Their religion is obscure enough, but seems to have included a number of cults of powers who could bestow fertility on the land and all that lived in it ; some at least of these were female.[4] Of their language we can say very little, for the tongue of the invaders won the day.[5] Of this tongue, the Greek language. it is necessary to say something.

The Achaians, if we may use that name for the new-comers generally, had as their common heritage one of the languages of the great Wiro or Indo-Germanic family. It was rich, varied, melodious [6]

[4] No account of Greek religion can be given here. A good short sketch is provided by Farnell, *Outline History of Greek Religion*, London, Duckworth, 1920 (a reprint of his article, *Greek Religion*, in Hastings, *Encyclopaedia of Religion and Ethics*). Somewhat longer, and to be recommended, is Nilsson, *History of Greek Religion*, Oxford, Clarendon Press, 1925. The same author deals with pre-Greek cults in his *Minoan-Mycenaean Religion*, Lund, Gleerup (London, Milford), 1927. Much that is excellent will be found in Wilam., *G.d.H.*

[5] Details of this process will be found especially in Huber, Kretschmer, and here and there in Kühner-Blass. These works, together with Kieckers (short account of the whole subject) and Meillet, *Aperçu*. should be consulted for the history of the language in general.

[6] It is much to be regretted that, in English schools especially, a conventional pronunciation is still heard which is ugly and unlike anything Greek. The following facts concerning classical pronunciation are fairly certain (see Kühner-Blass, i, pp. 46–322 ; Pernot, pp. 98–180). α, whether short or long, was an Italian *a* : ε, a narrow sound approximating to French *é* ; it is regularly short, and when long is conventionally written ει. η, a much broader sound, resembling Fr. *è*, and always long. ι, like *i* in *machine*, not as in *mine* or *it*. ο, a narrow sound, approximating at times almost to *u* ; when long, it is conventionally written ου. ω is much broader, and always long. υ, originally like a German or It. *u* (Eng. *oo* in *moon*), was in classical times, for most dialects, like Fr. *u* or Germ. *ü*, save in diphthongs, where it kept its original signification. Of the diphthongs, αι was like Eng. *ai* in *aisle* ; αυ, like Germ. *au*, Eng. *ow* ; ει, when not the conventional writing of a long ε, had a sound approximately like Eng. *ay* in *lay* (never like *y* in *try*), at least originally, but confused with it with *é* ; ευ and ηυ had simply the sounds of the component vowels pronounced in one breath :· οι, like Eng. *oi* in *boil* ; ου, at least in the developed Attic pronunciation, apparently *u* (Eng. *oo* in *moon*) ; υι, much like Eng. *we*. ᾳ (āι), ῃ (ηι), ῳ (ωι), a combination of the long vowels with a slight *i*-sound following. The unaspirated mutes (π, τ, κ ; β, δ, γ) were pronounced as in French, *i.e.*, with no perceptible emission of breath ; the aspirates (φ, θ, χ) had a distinct emission of breath accompanying them, *p-h, t-h, k-h*, not as in Eng. *Philip, thin,* and Scots *loch*. The other consonants were practically as in English, but ξ everywhere *ks*, even at the beginning of a word, ζ a combination, probably varying locally, of the sounds of *d* and *z* or *s*, possibly like *dz* in *adze*, not like Eng. *z*. Cf. Sturtevant, also Cessi, pp. 154–67.

and highly inflected.[7] Maintaining its structure almost if not quite unimpaired by the native speech, it nevertheless borrowed from it a number of words, especially names of plants, animals and above all of the unfamiliar sea-fish. Thus strengthened it became an admirable vehicle, perhaps the most admirable yet evolved, for the expression of thought ; and thought the people had in abundance, together with keen observation (they were, to use a technicality now in fashion, predominantly extroverts), a critical faculty which developed early, a keen sense of the beautiful in all forms, and a wholesome love of a good story, well told.

Since not all the Achaians settled in the same district, and both Greece and, to a less extent, the coast of Asia Minor abounds in natural barriers, the new-comers necessarily broke up into small and scattered groups. Being thus deprived of close inter-course with each other, their language naturally divided in time into a number of dialects.[8] Many of these remained mere local patois ; others never produced any literature ; but four evolved into standardized literary forms, and are recognized by the ancient grammarians. They are

1. DORIC, the speech of the latest comers into Greece. This, while very far from being identical with primitive Greek, retained certain rather old-fashioned features, the most obvious and notable being the preservation of the long *a*-sound in words which had originally had it. Thus, the word for ' mother ', pronounced and written μήτηρ in Ionic and Attic, remained in Dorian mouths μάτηρ, as in Latin. Of the phonetic changes to which this dialect like all others was subject, one especially persisted till a late date in the variety of Doric spoken at Sparta, when most forms of Greek had ceased to be affected by it. The sound of *s*, when it occurred singly between two vowels, had anciently a very strong tendency to be dropped. Thus a whole series of nouns whose stems ended in σ lost that letter when the ending began with a vowel ; for example, the dative case of the common word signifying a clan was originally γένεσι, but by the operation of this law it became γένεϊ and then γένει. In time, this dis-like of a single *s* between vowels passed away, but persisted in Sparta, which thus pronounced the common and familiar name

---

[7] The inflections will be found in the various works on grammar, as Kühner-Blass, Gildersleeve, &c. : they cannot be discussed here, though occasional mention of them may be necessary.

[8] For a full and scientific account of the dialects and their peculiarities, see the various modern works on the subject. There is also a long discussion of them in the appropriate sections of Kühner-Blass, vol. i.

of the Muse *Mῶ‘a* (*mō-ha*), when the rest of Greece said *Moῦσa* or *Moῖσa*.

2. AIOLIC, again a dialect with certain features of great antiquity. Like Doric, it preserved the original long *a* ; but more tenaciously than Doric it clung to the sound represented by Eng. *w*, in Greek written ϝ and called *wau* or, in later times and by most moderns, *digamma*. Aiolic had also a peculiar habit of shifting the accent nearer the beginning of the word than was the custom in other dialects ; and it resisted one phonetic change, the passing of *p* into *t* in certain combinations, saying for example πίσυρες for ' four ' when the usual word was τέσσαρες, πήλυι instead of τηλόθι for ' at a distance '.

3. IONIC, with which it is usual, though not strictly scientific, to class the so-called Epic or Homeric dialect. This also had at least one somewhat old-fashioned feature, in that it often did not contract its words ; *i.e.*, if two vowels came together, it was more apt than most forms of Greek to pronounce them as two distinct syllables, instead of running them together into a diphthong. Thus the common word for ' sheep ', which in Athens was a monosyllable, οἶς, was a dissyllable in Ionic, ὄϊς. This dialect lost its digamma quite early, and consistently made its long *a* into a broad *e* (*η*).

4. ATTIC, the dialect of the territory of Athens. This became by far the most famous and important of all, and in a somewhat debased form, known as the Common Dialect or κοινή, it was the ordinary speech of most civilized men for some centuries after Athens had ceased to be of political importance or even a great cultural centre. To this result the large and admirable Attic literature contributed greatly. It was apparently a development of Ionic, affected also by other forms of Greek ; in its vocalization it carried out the change of long *a* to *e* much less consistently, and certain combinations of vowels were invariably contracted.

But all the invaders seem to have had, even at the moment of their entry into the territories they were to occupy, rudiments of what, in some cases, was to become a great literature, the only European literature that is wholly native and original, for a long time the only one existing on this continent, and in a sense the parent of all the rest.

One of these was no doubt the possession of certain folktales, or *märchen*,[9] or at all events the themes of such. We are, it is true, in the dark as to many things concerning these tales, widespread in later ages and reported from many areas of the world ;

[9] See Rose, *Myth.*, Chapter X ; W. R. Halliday, *Indo-European Folk-Tales and Greek Legend* (Cambridge, 1933).

but sufficient traces of them remain in the literature of Greece to make it almost certain that they were never entirely absent. That more were borrowed from the native population is highly likely, although we cannot prove it.

We can say with rather more definiteness that the invaders had a kind of metre in which to express their thoughts when, as commonly happens in the unwritten beginnings of a literature, these took poetical form. The fact on which this statement is based is the resemblance which has been noted between Greek and Indian metres,[10] suggesting that the rudiments of them at all events are a common inheritance from the so-called pre-ethnic period, prior to that series of emigrations which spread the original Wiro tongue from its primitive centre, wherever that may have been, to the regions where its various descendants appear in historical times.

In Sanskrit and Prakrit are to be found several types of verse, whereof some have a fixed number of syllables, the quantity of which is subject to no very constant law, although a tendency is seen to have long syllables in some places, short in others; some again have a fixed number of times, *i.e.*, are equivalent in all cases to a certain given number of short syllables, but make up this number by sundry combinations of long and short, often very like the ' feet ' which later metricians recognize in Greek poetry. Corresponding roughly to these phenomena, we have in Greek certain lyric lines not all of whose syllables are of a determinate quantity, especially those at the beginning of the verse, but the total number of syllables is constant ; thus the verse known as the Glyconic has always eight syllables, but in Greek usage the first two may be of any quantity, while on the other hand the hexameter, Homer's metre, may vary in length from twelve to seventeen syllables, but has, with the rarest exceptions, a total value of twenty-four short syllables, one long counting as equal to two shorts and the slight pause at the end of the line being allowed to make up for any lack of length the final syllable may have.

Be that as it may, the Greeks had developed, in the earliest days of which we can find any record, a system of metre depending entirely upon the quantity of syllables ; that is, upon the difference between a syllable containing a long (slightly drawled) vowel, or a diphthong, and those whose vowels were short, *i.e.*, somewhat clipped in pronunciation. Syllables which contained a short vowel, but had more than one consonant intervening between it and the next vowel, were regarded as long, save in certain well-defined cases.[11] The rhythm depended wholly

[10] See Meillet, *Origines* ; Leumann.
[11] Abundant details will be found in Wil., *Verskunst* ; White, *Verse* (contains bibliography of older works) ; short account in Hardie.

upon regular recurrences of these two elements ; we have no proof that any syllable anywhere in the verse was ever stressed in reciting or singing, and indeed the only accentuation we can prove classical Greek to have had under any circumstances (that conventionally marked by the signs ', ` and ^ over certain vowels in our texts, which follow on the whole the usage of ancient grammarians in this matter [12]) was a difference in the pitch of the voice, not in the intensity with which the sound was pronounced. In any case, it was totally disregarded in metre throughout the classical epoch.

What beginnings of literature the Helladics possessed, or if they had any, we cannot now tell ; but it is fairly certain [13] that the Mycenaean civilization, which as already (p. 1) mentioned resulted from a mixture of the immigrants with the natives and the influence of Cretan civilization upon both, produced several great cycles of saga and had more than a little to do with the formation of myths.[14] The most noteworthy of the hero-tales current from Homer down are concerned with the exploits of kings and nobles living on Mycenaean sites, and the gods, to whatever stratum of the population they may have belonged originally, are organized in a community of their own very like what we may suppose the entourage of a Mycenaean lord to have been.

And now another factor of very great importance for the development and survival of Greek literature must be mentioned. At their first coming into Greece and Asia Minor, the Achaioi were doubtless illiterate ; but they entered an area in which writing of one sort or other had long been known. We have still extant actual documents (not copies) written in Egypt, Babylonia (from which the Hittites adopted a system of writing) and Crete not later than 2000 B.C. and in some cases earlier. These are all apparently (most Cretan scripts are undeciphered) ideographic, like the present Chinese system ; that is, their characters for the most part represent words, not letters nor syllables.[15] Hence from the moment of their arrival, or not long after, the Achaioi might have written what they thought worth preserving, for Cretan script at least was known, though it would seem not very much used, on the mainland of Greece in Mycenaean times ; how

---

[12] Accentuation is well discussed in Postgate, *Guide* (contains short bibliography).

[13] See M. P. Nilsson, *Mycenaean Origin of Greek Mythology*, Berkeley, California, Univ. of Cal. Press, 1932.

[14] For definitions of these terms, see Rose, *Myth.*, Chapter I.

[15] Brief account in Kenyon, *Books*, pp. 4-16. See pp. 14, 422.

much Greek poets used it, or if they used it at all, we cannot say. Much more important was the adoption, with successive modifications, of that North Semitic alphabet which the Greeks called the Phoenician letters.[16] This, save for some differences in the shape of the characters, was the same as the Hebrew alphabet, *i.e.*, it consisted of a series of symbols each representing a consonant. With characteristic felicity [17] the Greeks made the improvement that was needed to express perfectly a language like their own. They used as signs for the vowels certain characters which represented Semitic sounds not existing in Greek, supplemented these with newly invented characters, or perhaps adoptions from other sources, and so in time produced, with various local modifications,[18] the alphabet known to us, the parent of the Roman and hence of our own.

Once this was done (and a practicable system of Greek writing certainly existed as early as the eighth century B.C., very likely a good deal earlier), the Greeks had ready to hand a method of preserving their literature which they never lost through all the vicissitudes of their history. Besides permanent records in the shape of inscriptions on stone, metal, &c., obviously not well adapted to literary purposes, they seem to have used prepared leather,[19] a less efficient form of the later parchment, which is also a Greek invention. No doubt use was also made from early times of the material which Homer names in his one mention of writing, a ' close-folded tablet ' presumably of wood, perhaps overlaid with wax, as in classical times.[20] But for longer documents, to be conveniently read, they adopted the book-roll, made of Egyptian papyrus-paper when it could be had. This was simply a long strip of papyrus, made by gumming together a number of smaller pieces. On one side of this was written the work it was desired to preserve, in a series of columns, running down the width of the roll. The reader held the roll in his hands, unwound a part from the beginning, read what was written on it, and then unwound more, winding up what he had already read.

[16] γράμματα Φοινικήια, Herodotos, v, 58, 2. For details, see Roberts-Gardner, i, p. 4 *sqq.*; Kühner-Blass, i, 39 *sqq.*

[17] ' Whatever ' says the author of the *Epinomis*, 987 e, ' the Greeks borrow from the barbarians they improve upon in the end.'

[18] One of the most noteworthy was that the Western Greeks, including the settlers in Italy, used X as the Romans did and we do ; the Ionians used X for the sound *kh*, representing that of our *x* by Ξ.

[19] Herod., *l.c.*, 3, says that διφθέραι (' hides ') was an old Ionic word for ' papyrus rolls ', ' because once they used hides of goats and sheep for lack of papyrus.'

[20] σήματα λυγρά, γράψας ἐν πίνακι πτυκτῷ, Il., vi, 168-9.

Often a round stick, like a ruler, was gummed to one end of the roll to facilitate this. In the earliest rolls, we may conjecture, he would start at the right-hand end of the volume (*uolumen*, ' thing that is rolled ', the Latin term for it ; the Greeks usually said βύβλος, which is simply another name for the papyrus plant itself, βυβλίον, or less correctly βίβλος, βιβλίον), for the earliest script ran from right to left, after the Semitic fashion ; but we have no rolls so early as this, and all our specimens are to be read from the left-hand end. The amount of text must be but moderate, or the roll would be unwieldy ; hence the conventional division into ' books ', *i.e.*, rolls, of epic poems, histories, romances and so forth. Hence also the amount of space needed for a library in antiquity was much greater than for one of the same size to-day ; thus, the *Anabasis* of Xenophon, printed in Greek type of ordinary size and on a page somewhat smaller than this, is about half an inch thick in the Oxford edition ; in antiquity, written in a small and neat hand, it would still require seven rolls, each containing about a dozen yards of papyrus some eight or nine inches wide.[21]

The unhandiness of the Greek book was the less felt because classical Greek students used their eyes much less, their ears and their memories far more than moderns do. The normal way to become acquainted with a new work, at least up to the fifth century or even the fourth, was to listen to it when read or sung, by the author or someone else. We need hardly doubt that professional reciters, to say nothing of authors, possessed copies of such works as the Iliad, or at least parts of it, from quite early times, to consult when their memories failed them or they wished to increase their répertoire. School-boys, much of whose education consisted in memorizing poems, must have had copies of some sort available to learn them from ; at least the master must have one himself. Pindar, in an ode written about 472 B.C., urges its recipient not to ' hush the tale of his father's virtue nor silence these hymns of mine '.[22] It is absurd to suppose this to mean ' do not refrain from letting this ode be performed ', since a performance was the avowed reason for writing it at all ; it must surely imply ' do not refrain from letting copies of it be circulated '. Yet for one such hint at publication, and a few mentions, much later in the century, of people owning and habitually reading books,[23] we have many which assume that the

---

[21] See Kenyon, *Books*, Chapter II ; more details will be found in the various manuals and encyclopaedias of antiquities.

[22] Pindar, *Isthm.*, ii, 45 (Farnell's trans.).

[23] As Eurip., *Hipp.*, 954 ; Ar., *Frogs*, 1400

writings in question are to be heard, rather than read ; Theognis in the sixth century [24] declares that his poems will bring fame to the youth he addresses because they will be sung, and Aristophanes, in one of his latest plays, still, in the fourth century, talks of shaming cowards by recitations of poems written about them.[25]

It is therefore not surprising that there were no large libraries until after the foundation of Alexandria, of whose famous collection we shall have occasion to speak later ; and it is very probable that by that time a great many works had already perished. A few enterprising cities like Athens might keep records, even copies, of plays and other poems which had competed at public festivals ; some had issued editions of Homer (see below, p. 388) ; the birthplace of a famous author might preserve piously an old copy of his writings, or of part of them, such as the ancient and damaged MS., written on lead, of Hesiod's *Works and Days* which Pausanias was shown at Mount Helikon ; [26] but there was no general system of storing or preserving even those pieces which were most generally esteemed, and the majority of the copies in existence were in private ownership, subject to all the accidents which private property is exposed to in troubled times. However, it may be supposed that at least the great bulk of such authors as then existed passed into the Alexandrian collection, and there were studied and catalogued. From then till towards the close of ancient history much was added and little lost. But as ancient civilization declined and even the studious were more attracted to theology than literature, the great inheritance was neglected, and much of it was allowed to perish from neglect. There is indeed little or no evidence that any of it was deliberately destroyed. The famous burning, on theological grounds, of the library of the Alexandrian Museion by the Arab conquerors is a fable many times refuted ; the library was no longer in existence when they came, for it was destroyed in 272. No doubt much was lost when a mob of fanatics, calling themselves Christians, destroyed the Serapeion, which had a large library attached to it, in 394; but their quarrel was rather with the ancient sacred building than with the books as such. When S. Chrysostom says [27] that most pagan works have long ago perished, being destroyed as soon as they were found, save for a few copies in the hands of Christians, the context makes it clear that he means controversial writings directed against Christianity, such as that

---

[24] Theogn., 241–3.   [25] Ar., *Eccles.*, 680–1.   [26] Paus., ix, 31, 4.
[27] Chrysost., *de sancto Babyla*, 2 (vol. ii, p. 539 D, edit. Bened.).

of Celsus, and not classical literature. State suppression of books thought disloyal was neither frequent nor very efficient ; classical instances are the suppression of the *Annals* of Cremutius Cordus under Tiberius, and the *Notebooks* of Fabricius Veiento under Nero, which resulted in the former case in surreptitious publication, in the second gave the author an undeserved advertisement until the ban was removed and his works forgotten.[28] Tacitus assures us that similar ill success met other attempts to suppress books ; we may remember the complete failure of Diocletian's edict for the destruction of the Christian Scriptures.[29] Far more damage was done by the neglect resulting from changes of fashion—the classicizing movement under the Roman Empire is one great cause of the loss of nearly all the Alexandrian literature—and worse still, the rapid decline in taste, energy and interest as the end approached. Speaking broadly, we may say that the surviving books are for the most part either such as were used in schools, and in such cases we have as a rule no more of each author than would fill one folio parchment volume (*codex*), of the shape we now use and manageable size ; or else those which continued to enjoy so great a reputation both for style and contents that only a total destruction of all intellectual and literary interest would suppress them. Of the latter, the best example is perhaps Plato, one of the very few authors who have come down to us complete from either Greece or Rome. But selections were commonly made from all the bulkier writers of literary merit, whether in verse or prose ; those who were interesting for their contents only, especially the more technical and difficult, were replaced by compendia and excerpts, or by the miscellanies and anthologies which were increasingly popular ; thus not a single work of the great Alexandrian medical school has come down intact, the bulky writings of the Stoics, including such important figures as Chrysippos and Poseidonios, are known only from quotations and references, while poets of the rank of Stesichoros and Alkaios have vanished, save for fragments in later authors and occasional finds of a tattered scrap of a copy in Egyptian rubbish-heaps. By a curious and ironical chance, the most important works of Aristotle were lost for a while in antiquity and afterwards recovered, while much more of his writings, known and admired by Cicero, has now disappeared.[30]

But with all these losses, a not inconsiderable fraction of

[28] Tacitus, *Annales*, iv, 34, i, 35, 5 ; xiv, 50, 1–2.
[29] Eusebios, *Hist. eccles.*, viii, 2.
[30] For a fuller account of these matters, see the discussion in this work of the authors referred to.

Greek literature made its way to Constantinople, which although its intellectual activities were at first largely legal and theological never quite neglected letters. To the Byzantines we owe the preservation of most of what we now have ; for it is no fault of theirs that a great deal perished, not so much at the hands of the Turks in 1453 as by the wanton and senseless ravages of the pious brigands of the Fourth Crusade, in 1204.

What did not perish, because it never existed, was any ancient attempt at a complete and systematic history of literature. It was not customary, in the greatest ages of antiquity, to write biographies, literary or other ; these seem to have had a pioneer in Ion of Chios, in the fifth century, who had a good deal to say about his contemporaries, and to have begun seriously with Aristotle and his followers, whose zeal for knowledge extended to all departments and who rightly perceived that the first necessity for scientific mastery of any subject was the most extensive possible collection of facts. These same men, the Peripatetics, were likewise active in what had already begun before their time, aesthetic criticism, which can hardly be carried out without some consideration of historical facts, such as the age in which the writers under discussion lived, or their social standing and the process by which they became known. But it was then already too late to get accurate information about many of the older poets ; Homer and Hesiod were as misty figures to Aristotle as they are to us. The example set by the Peripatetics was followed by the Alexandrians, and from the end of the fourth century B.C. on there came a long succession of lives of authors, aesthetic and textual commentaries, chronological works, editions, *catalogues raisonnés*, discussions on the genuineness of works ascribed to particular writers, and so forth ; in fact, valuable preliminary studies for a complete and exhaustive history of the literature, had any one undertaken to write it. Of all this mass of research, only remnants have come down to us, but they are by no means without value. The great commentaries were excerpted by later generations to form those marginal notes which we find in many MSS. and call scholia ; the chronologers were much used by Christian writers, to set forth their views of the religious and secular history of the world, and thus considerable fragments of them, including many dates of importance to literature, have reached us ; the biographical works form the ultimate basis of the many notes on authors which we find in Byzantine lexicons, such as those of Hesychios, Photios, Suidas [30a] and others, also for the short lives of sundry writers which are often prefixed to MSS. of their works ; and

[30a] See p. 422.

best of all, a few ancient treatises survive more or less complete, and will be dealt with later on. This material we are able to supplement here and there, not only by occasional finds of papyri giving us hitherto unknown scraps of Alexandrian learning, but by such things as inscriptions, as for instance the famous Marmor Parium or chronicle-inscription of the island of Paros, now at Oxford, which consists of a long series of dates, all in the form ' from such and such an event (to the present day), so many years '. Besides, we have, in the ancient texts themselves, some part of the evidence the Alexandrians had, and thus can check a certain number of their conclusions.

Two advantages we have over our ancient colleagues, namely more convenient ways of arranging our material (to name but one point, the ancients could never give a page-reference to any author, for they had no way of producing two uniformly paged copies of the same book, to say nothing of a whole edition exactly alike), and a better philological method. It is true that we lack that exquisite sense of style [31] which some of the best of them had, for we have not spoken Greek from our cradles ; even the modern Greeks are scarcely, if at all, better off than the rest, owing to the profound and radical changes the language has undergone ; but to balance this, we have scientific etymologies to help out our lexicography, in place of more or less ingenious guesses ; our historical technique is much in advance of theirs, especially since the great scientific historians of the nineteenth century ; and we command delicate methods of linguistic analysis undreamed of by them, which go far to replace, and on occasion

[31] Of the high development of the ancients' sense of style, two examples may be given. Dionysios of Halikarnassos (see p. 398 *sqq.*) testifies (*de Lysia*, 12 ; p. 30, 9–15, Usener-Rademacher) that there are ' many speeches attributed to Lysias, and vulgarly supposed to be most certainly genuine ' which he has suspected to be spurious, because ' although meritorious enough in other ways, they do not display the charm of his style nor his felicity of diction ', and that after finding them wanting in this respect, he has then confirmed his judgement by external evidence ; thus, two speeches said to be composed by Lysias for cases in which the celebrated general Iphikrates was concerned appeared to him not to have the true Lysian flavour, and on computing their dates, he found them both posterior to the orator's death. Galen (περὶ τῶν ἰδίων βιβλίων, vol xiv, pp. 8–9 Kühn, p. 91 I. Müller) tells how he was one day at a bookshop in Rome and heard a dispute over the genuineness of a book which had his name on its title. The argument was settled by a critic who, after reading but two lines, declared that the style was not Galen's, and threw the book down. Galen implies that the detector of the forgery was not a distinguished scholar, but simply one who had had the advantages of what the physician regards as a respectable preliminary education, such as was open to any Greek boy decently brought up.

even surpass, the instinctive insight of native speakers which no foreigner can ever quite attain.

But when all is said and done, a complete history of Greek literature can never be written now. We are not cleaning a darkened picture, but trying to form an idea of what a mutilated statue looked like before one accident robbed it of its head and another broke the body into a dozen fragments, several of them now lost. All that we can hope for, and the hope is not immodest or unreasonable, is to put together a sufficiently correct restoration for a sympathetic student to form an idea, incomplete indeed but not contrary to the facts, of what manner of things Greeks wrote, heard and read, and how they came to write in that manner and no other.

ADDITIONAL NOTE

The script known as Linear B has of late been interpreted, by the efforts especially of the late Michael Ventris, as a clumsy and ambiguous method of writing archaic Greek. His results, for which see M. Ventris and J. Chadwick, *Documents in Mycenaean Greek*, 1956, are generally accepted, though severely criticised in some quarters. Assuming them to be correct, they throw a most interesting side-light on many details of Mycenaean culture.

CHAPTER II

HOMER AND THE ANCIENT EPIC

FOR us as for the ancients, the oldest Greek book is HOMER. As his works are also among the sublimest in any language, indeed supreme in their kind, and exercised an enormous influence on subsequent writers of all sorts, they form in every way a fitting start for a history of Greek, or indeed of European literature, and we shall do well before going further to give a brief account of their nature and contents, proceeding then to discuss the chief problems connected with them.

Owing to the excessive admiration for Homer, which passed into sheer idolatry and represented him as a sort of compendium of all knowledge and excellence,[1] there was naturally a reaction, much like those which have from time to time occurred in the case of Shakespere. One form which this took was theological ; the strange authors known as the Orphics, whose literature will be discussed later (p. 71), put forward a claim that their writings, the supposed productions of Orpheus himself and of his associate Musaios, were of older date than Homer, and that the latter had borrowed from them freely. Hence it is, for example, that the genealogy of the poet given by Suidas (*s.u.* "Ομηρος) on the authority of Chares, a writer of the fourth century B.C., includes the names of several elder poets, Linos, Orpheus and Melanopos. The Apolline clergy also put in a claim for the seniority of certain ancient servants of their god ; a local Delphic poetess, BOIO, declared that an old hymn-writer, OLEN, was the first to use the hexameter ; others gave the credit for this invention to the Pythian prophetess Phemonoe ;[2] Melanopos seems to have been claimed, as the genealogy already quoted shows, as pre-Homeric ;[3] while a local tradition of Troizen alleged that a certain OROIBANTIOS

---

[1] See, for example, Plato, *Ion*, 539, d, e (he who thoroughly understands Homer knows all manner of arts perfectly), and the very curious work of Herakleitos, *quaestiones Homericae* (see p. 355), which sets forth that if Homer is rightly, *i.e.*, allegorically interpreted he is a store-house of piety and philosophy.

[2] Pausan., x, 5, 7.   [3] Paus., v, 7, 8.

of that town had written an epic before Homer's days.[4]   It need hardly
be said that these allegations, where we can check them, are plainly
unhistorical. [Cf. Cessi, p. 825.]

We have, then, two poems attributed to Homer by the consensus of the best criticism of antiquity, which we shall see reason
to suppose correct in this matter : they are the Iliad and the
Odyssey.

The former of these, despite its title,[5] does not deal with the
entire Tale of Troy, which indeed it supposes known, at least
in general outline, to its readers or hearers, but with an episode
of the tenth year of the war, the Wrath of Achilles.   The outline
of the poem is as follows :

Book I.[6] Agamemnon, commander-in-chief of the Greek
army before Troy, offends a priest of Apollo, Chryses, by refusing
to let him ransom his daughter Chryseis, Agamemnon's slave.
Chryses prays to Apollo to punish the Greeks ; the god sends a
plague.   On the tenth day, Achilles summons an assembly, and
Kalchas, the seer, declares that the girl must be restored to her
father and an offering made to Apollo.   Agamemnon sulkily
assents, but insists on compensation ; angered by a sharp speech
from Achilles, he seizes Briseis, the latter's slave-concubine.
Achilles withdraws his allegiance, refuses to take further part in
the war, and appeals to his divine mother, Thetis.   She persuades
Zeus to exact vengeance for her son.

[4] Aelian, *uar. hist.*, xi, 2, who also mentions the Dares Phrygius so
important later for the medieval Troy saga.

[5] For some speculations on the original meaning of the title ('Ἰλιάς,
sc., ποίησις, ' the poem concerning Ilion ') see Schmid-Stählin, i, p. 93,
n. 5.   The story of the Trojan War is told in Rose, *Myth.*, pp. 230–48,
and in many other handbooks.

[6] How old the traditional division into 24 books of the Iliad and
Odyssey is we do not know ; it may be due to Zenodotos (Schmid-
Stählin, i, p. 132).   The number and the fact that each of them is lettered,
from *A* to *Ω* (it is customary now to refer to books of the Iliad by capitals,
books of the Odyssey by minuscules, *e.g.*, Z is Iliad vi, ψ is Od. xxiii)
suggest that it was at some date after the common adoption of the familiar
alphabet of 24 letters.   It is noteworthy that they are usually called
ῥαψῳδίαι, or recitations, and it may very well be that several at least
begin and end at traditional points for the rhapsodes or professional
reciters to do so.   Thus, Il. i ends and Il. ii begins with conventional
and mutually contradictory formulae (' Zeus went to sleep . . . every
one else was asleep, but Zeus was awake '), and much the same is true
of Il. ix and x ; Od. v retells briefly the story of the council of the gods
with which Od. i began.   These and other like phenomena strongly
suggest devices of reciters, possibly as old as the poet himself, corresponding to the synopses of earlier chapters prefixed to instalments of our
continued stories in journals.

Book II. Zeus, to bring harm upon Agamemnon and his followers, sends him a deceitful dream which assures him that he will take Troy immediately. Agamemnon confides the dream to the principal chieftains, and then proposes to test the army by proposing to them to return home at once.[7] To his horror, the rank and file take him seriously and rush to prepare for departure.[8] With difficulty Odysseus, inspired by Athena, restores discipline, and after a comic episode in which Thersites, an insignificant and foul-mouthed fellow, the first demagogue in Greek literature, abuses Agamemnon and is beaten into silence by Odysseus,[9] the host is persuaded by the latter, together with Nestor [10] and Agamemnon himself, to arm and set out. Here is inserted, whether by the poet or some one later, a catalogue of the Greek and Trojan forces, certainly a very old document, giving a probably correct account of geographical and political conditions in Mycenaean days.[11]

Book III. The two armies advance to meet each other,[12] when the fight is checked by a proposal from the Trojan side,

[7] The character of Agamemnon is drawn with the utmost skill and consistency. He is a weak and irresolute man, physically brave enough, but wholly lacking in moral courage and especially unwilling to accept any avoidable responsibility. Here he clearly would have the attack on Troy appear the army's own wish ; see Sheppard, *Pattern*, p. 27.

[8] It is to be remembered that they had been campaigning for some nine years ; Homer understood soldiers' psychology and their liability to *cafard*. With glorious effrontery, Odysseus (ii, 303) tells them it is only ' a day or two ago ' (χθιζά τε καὶ πρωίζα) that they were at their rendezvous in Aulis.

[9] Odysseus is throughout the man of cool, on occasion unscrupulous and hard, common sense ; an admirable foil to Achilles, Agamemnon, Nestor and Diomedes.

[10] Nestor may perhaps best be described by saying that he is a Polonius, drawn with more affectionate sympathy and scarcely less humour. He has been in his time a great warrior, and still retains remarkable vigour for his seventy years or so. Universally respected for his wisdom, he is fond of dealing out sage advice, in season and out of season, and of falling into long reminiscences of his youthful exploits.

[11] See T. W. Allen, *The Homeric Catalogue of Ships*, Oxford, Clar. Press, 1921.

[12] The fact that the Trojans advance is in itself a sign that all is not going well with the Greeks. Their normal tactics had been merely to defend the walls, Il., vi, 433 *sqq.* As they are in no way besieged, but only cut off from the sea and hindered in their movements by Agamemnon's army, they can in the long run afford general engagements better than the latter, who are far from their home base and strategical reserves, while the Trojans have the hinterland and Thrace to draw upon for supplies and men. That they should come out of their own accord to meet the Greeks shows that the moral superiority established by the latter in the preceding years is vanishing with the defection of Achilles.

made by Hektor and Paris. Paris and Menelaos are to fight a duel. If the former wins, he is to keep Helen and the Greeks to go away ; if the latter, Helen and all her property are to be returned, and peace made. Priam comes to the walls of his city, where he meets Helen and has the principal Greek chieftains pointed out by her.[13] He goes thence to the armies and joins in the ceremonial oath-taking which ushers in the truce. Paris then fights Menelaos and is defeated ; Aphrodite saves him and takes him back to Troy.

Book IV. After some discussion, the gods decide to let the truce be broken, as Hera is implacably hostile to Troy. Athena, in disguise, persuades Pandaros, one of the Lykian allies of Troy, to shoot an arrow at Menelaos. This he does, wounding him slightly and incidentally giving Agamemnon a chance to display the real, if somewhat fussy affection for his brother which is one of his amiable features. The truce being thus broken, Agamemnon hastily reviews his army, showing abundant absence of tact in the manner of his address to some of them, notably Diomedes.[14] A fierce fight begins.

Books V and VI. Favoured and helped by Athena, Diomedes performs wonders, finally, at the goddess's instigation, scratching with his spear the wrist of Aphrodite herself as she tries to rescue her son Aineias, and even laying Ares low as he rallies and assists the Trojans. Hektor goes to Troy to ask his mother Hekabe to make an offering to Athena for her favour.[15] Reaching the

[13] This is of course illogical, for Priam would have had abundant opportunities of learning what the principal Greeks looked like. But it is poetically understandable enough, since this is the first opportunity in the poem of introducing Helen and giving some description of Agamemnon, Aias and others.

[14] Diomedes is perhaps so drawn as to give an idea of what Nestor was when he was young, or Achilles might have been if less impulsive. He has all the valour of his father Tydeus without his savagery ; at the same time, he gives, especially in the second half of the poem, much shrewd advice. His attitude towards Agamemnon is an admirable mixture of deference in public and resolute opposition, when necessary, in private.

[15] The motivation, here and in Book vii, of Hektor's actions is unsophisticated ; there was no particular reason why some inferior man should not take the message to the queen, and little to be gained by the challenge. But the poet clearly wishes to show Hektor, one of the finest characters in the whole poem, in several different relationships, as son, husband, father and finally as champion. He is the defender of a cause which he knows to be hopeless ; ' I know well ', he tells Andromache, ' in mind and heart that there shall come a day when holy Ilion shall perish, and Priam, and the folk of Priam that good warrior ' (Il. vi, 447–9). Yet he perseveres, hoping against hope, till finally he is slain by Achilles.

city, he interviews her, exchanges a few words with Helen, sends
an urgent message to Paris to arm and come forth, and finally
sees and speaks to his wife Andromache and his little son
Astyanax. Meanwhile, Diomedes' career has been checked by
encountering Glaukos the Lykian, in whom he discovers a guest-
friend (ξένος) of his own family. They exchange armour in
token of friendship, and agree to avoid each other in battle.

Book VII. Hektor and Paris now return to the battlefield,
and the former issues a challenge to any Greek to meet him in
single combat. Aias, son of Telamon, is chosen by lot, and a
sharp encounter ends indecisively, Aias having a little the better
of it. The champions exchange presents and a truce for the
burial of the dead is agreed to. A further proposal of the
Trojans, that Paris be allowed to keep Helen on surrendering
her wealth, is indignantly refused by the Greeks. On Nestor's
advice, the latter fortify their camp.

Book VIII. Zeus forbids the other gods to take part in the
fighting. He encourages the Trojans, and the Greeks, after a
day's indecisive battle, retire to their camp. The Trojans
bivouac on the plain.

Book IX. Agamemnon, much discouraged by the turn of
events, calls a council and, on Nestor's advice, sends Aias, son
of Telamon, and Odysseus, accompanied by Phoinix, an old
retainer of Achilles, to offer the return of Briseis, an enormous
present by way of compensation for the insult received, and the
hand of one of Agamemnon's daughters in marriage, if Achilles
will join in the fighting again. After speeches from the three
envoys and replies from Achilles, Odysseus and Aias return,
bearing Achilles' definite and contemptuous refusal of all reconciliation. Phoinix remains with him, as he is playing with the
idea of setting sail for home on the next day.[16]

Book X. Agamemnon, unable to sleep, rises and collects
some of the principal chieftains. They go to visit the outposts,
and Nestor suggests that some one should volunteer to scout
towards the Trojan position and learn what they are doing.
Diomedes volunteers and asks for Odysseus to accompany him.

[16] Achilles is a passionate and generous young hero, a kind of Harry
Hotspur, whose guiding principle is his boundless thirst for personal
honour ; next to that comes his deep and lasting affection for his friend
Patroklos. His refusal to accept Agamemnon's terms puts him definitely
in the wrong ; he shows neither proper respect to one in some sense his
overlord, nor consideration for the need of his brothers in arms. What
was justifiable resentment has now passed into ὕβρις, disregard for everyone's rights and wishes save his own. See Murray, *Rise of the Greek
Epic*, p. 81 ; Lang, *World*, pp. 124–5.

On the way, they capture a Trojan scout, Dolon, who tells them that a newly arrived Thracian force under its king, Rhesos, is bivouacked on the Trojan flank. Stealing upon these in the darkness they kill Rhesos and twelve of his followers and capture his horses, which they ride back to their own camp.

Book XI. In the morning, the Greek army advances once more, and is met by the Trojans.[17] At first, Agamemnon does valiantly, but presently he is wounded and has to leave the fighting ; several other men of note are hurt, among them Diomedes and Odysseus, and the whole army falls back upon the entrenched camp. Achilles sends Patroklos, his closest friend, to the hut of Nestor, who has just returned in his chariot with Machaon, one of the casualties, to ask who has been wounded. Nestor bewails the hard-heartedness of Achilles and suggests that Patroklos ask him, if he will not move himself, at least to send his men and to lend Patroklos his own armour, in hopes that the Trojans will think Achilles himself is back in the fray. Patroklos starts to return, but is met by another wounded man, Eurypylos, badly in need of attention, and spends some time dressing his hurt.

Book XII. The Trojans form five storming columns and attack the camp, with varying success. At last Hektor smashes in a gate and the wall is taken.

Book XIII. Desperate fighting goes on at the ships, drawn up along the beach, which form the Greeks' second line of defence. Poseidon appears, disguised in human form, and encourages them to resist. Idomeneus of Crete distinguishes himself, and Aias, son of Telamon, keeps Hektor in check.

Book XIV. Hera, getting from Aphrodite a charm which will render her irresistibly lovely, distracts the attention of Zeus, who is watching the battle from Mount Ida. He falls asleep in her arms ; Poseidon increases his efforts and the Trojans are driven out of the camp, Hektor being stunned by a stone hurled by Aias.

Book XV. Zeus, awaking, furiously rebukes Hera, sends Iris with orders to Poseidon to withdraw at once, and bids Apollo restore Hektor. The Trojan attack recommences, and the Greeks are driven past the wall to the ships. Patroklos, hearing the uproar, hastens to Achilles,

---

[17] Although Homer does not say so, he clearly means us to understand that the minor success of the night-raid has heartened the army, and not least Agamemnon. By xiv, 74, the latter is again so discouraged that he hopes only to fight a rear-guard action until evening and then sail away. See, for full discussion of Bk. x, Shewan, *Lay.*

Books XVI, XVII, whom he persuades to lend him his armour and let him lead forth the Myrmidones. The Trojans, who have just set fire to a ship, are thus driven back, Patroklos killing many, including Sarpedon. Neglecting Achilles' express command, he pursues the Trojans to the city walls, from which Apollo in person thrusts him back. Shortly afterwards he is stunned and disarmed by Apollo, wounded by Euphorbos and dispatched by Hektor, who strips the armour off him and puts it on. The Greeks, fighting desperately. retreat with Patroklos' body towards their camp.

Book XVIII. Achilles, hearing of the death of Patroklos, is half-mad with grief. Thetis comes from the sea to comfort him, and promises to get him new arms from Hephaistos. Iris, sent by Hera, encourages Achilles to go to the trench outside the camp, where he frightens the Trojans away with his battle-cry. The body is carried into the camp. Hektor, now over-confident, bivouacs once more on the plain, against the advice of Polydamas his kinsman. Thetis fulfils her promise ; the making of the arms, and especially of the shield, is described.

Book XIX. Next morning Achilles, though Thetis has warned him that he cannot live long after Hektor, is anxious to go forth to battle at once. Odysseus, however, insists on a formal reconciliation with Agamemnon, when the gifts promised are handed over [18] and the army is given time to breakfast. Agamemnon excuses his conduct in an elaborate speech, declaring that he was possessed by Infatuation (Ate). The women lament around Patroklos ; Thetis supports Achilles, who will not eat, by putting nektar and ambrosia in his bosom, at the suggestion of Athena. He arms, and Xanthos, one of the immortal horses of his chariot-team, foretells his death.

Book XX. Zeus summons all the gods to council and gives permission to them to take what part in the fighting they will. They descend to earth. Meanwhile Achilles advances on the Trojans, who give way before him. Aineias is encouraged by Apollo to face him, and when likely to be killed, is snatched away by Poseidon, because it is fated that his descendants shall be lords of Troy. Hektor also withstands Achilles for a moment,

---

[18] Achilles, having been inconsiderate of others' claims, has now become careless of his own rights, in the revulsion of feeling arising from the death of his best friend. To omit the formal reconciliation and payment of the honour-price would be to put himself in the wrong as regarded the whole quarrel ; the payment was part of the apology due to him as a gentleman of high rank. Odysseus saves him from this offence against the traditions and feelings of his order. Cf. Lang, *World*, p. 243.

and is rescued from him by Apollo. Many of the others are slain by Achilles in the retreat.

Book XXI. The flight of the Trojans is hampered by the fords of the river Xanthos, or Skamandros. Achilles, despite the river's protests, fills the water with dead bodies. The river rises against him, and he is in danger of drowning. At the command of Hera, Hephaistos checks the water with his fire. The gods now engage each other ; Poseidon and Apollo, Hermes and Leto, at once make peace, but Athena strikes down Ares with a great rock and afterwards thrusts down Aphrodite as she leads him away ; Hera snatches Artemis' bow and beats her with it.[19] Apollo saves Antenor from Achilles and, himself taking the former's shape, flees from him away from the city ; the rest make good their escape thither.

Book XXII. Apollo, having drawn Achilles sufficiently far away, reveals himself ; Achilles returns towards Troy, to find only Hektor outside the walls, ashamed to enter after the failure of his plans, despite the appeals of his parents. But as Achilles approaches, his courage fails him and he runs three times around the walls, hotly pursued but not overtaken, Apollo helping him for the last time and giving him speed equal to that of his enemy, Achilles ' Swift-foot ' (πόδας ὠκύς, ποδάρκης, his standing epithet). At last Athena intervenes ; taking the form of Hektor's brother Deïphobos, she bids him stand and promises help. Both heroes cast their spears without effect, but Athena gives Achilles' spear back to him. Hektor realizes that he is alone and that the seeming Deïphobos was a trick of Athena. Making a desperate charge upon Achilles, he is mortally wounded, and his dying prayer to have his body returned for burial is contemptuously rejected. Achilles fastens the corpse to the rim of his chariot and drives back to the camp, dragging it behind him, in full view of those on the walls, including Andromache, who had not yet heard that Hektor was outside.

Book XXIII. During the night, the ghost of Patroklos appears to Achilles and begs for speedy burial, that it may enter Hades. The next day a most elaborate and splendid funeral is

---

[19] This whole episode of the skirmish between the pro-Greek and pro-Trojan gods is the poorest thing in the Iliad, especially poor after the majestic description of their descent to earth, xx, 54 *sqq.* It has no organic connexion whatever with anything else in the poem, but forms a pendant to the preceding episode, the overcoming of the river by Hephaistos. In my opinion, it is one of the few places in Homer where we may confidently look for an interpolation ; some stupid Homerid has tried here to make more use of the divine machinery introduced by the master.

given his body ; twelve prisoners of war are killed on the pyre,[20] together with horses and dogs. Athletic sports are then held, including chariot and foot-races, archery and other contests, boxing and wrestling. Achilles presides and distributes prizes to all competitors, showing especial courtesy to Agamemnon and Nestor.

Book XXIV. After the body of Hektor has lain unburied and daily dragged around the tomb of Patroklos for eleven days, the gods decide to intervene. Apollo has saved the corpse from corruption and mutilation ; Thetis is now sent to bid Achilles let it be ransomed, and Iris to tell Priam to take treasure and go by night into the Greek camp. He is guided thither by Hermes in the form of a young Myrmidon. Reaching the presence of Achilles, he finds him in a mood in which his natural kindness of heart, when not excited to anger by opposition or a slight, has full scope. He treats the old king with sympathy, remembering his own aged father, Peleus ; Priam is his guest for a few hours, and departs unmolested before dawn. The poem concludes with a brief mention of Hektor's funeral, preceded by a longer account of the lamentations over his corpse.

It will be seen from the above analysis that the pivots of the whole story are the first book, which provides a motive for the entire action ; the ninth, in which Achilles, hitherto entirely in the right, puts himself also in the wrong, thus providing the ideal tragic situation, a conflict between two parties, neither unsympathetic and neither entirely blameless ; the sixteenth, in which the stubbornness of Achilles brings about, indirectly, its own punishment ; and the catastrophe in the twenty-second. The functions of the other parts of the poem are various ; some, as the third book, keep the interest in suspense by creating a possible escape from the coming disasters ; others, as Hektor's visit to Ilion, are episodes, varying and enriching the whole , others again, as the tenth, supply motives for parts of the action— the slaying of Rhesos and his followers dispels the atmosphere of defeatism which was prevalent in Agamemnon's camp the evening before—or develop one or more of the characters ; thus, the twenty-third book gives occasion for brilliant pictures of the temper and behaviour of the various Greek chieftains under less

---

[20] These are the only human victims in Homer and this is the only hint that a dead man may need a retinue in the next world, or indeed enjoy anything more than a dreary shadow-existence there. Both facts are intelligible when we note that Achilles, a Thessalian, has more than one uncivilized trait, contrasting with the more polished manners of the other nobles.

trying conditions than battle or hasty councils of war, and the twenty-fourth makes the wrath of Achilles stand out the clearer by contrast with his mercy when not angered.

The Iliad is based on saga ; the Odyssey approaches more nearly to *märchen*. In form it is one of the many legends, which were widely popular, explaining how the various heroes came home again after the war of Troy (see below, p. 50). But its main plot is a well-known folk-tale, the story of how a hero came back after a long absence just in time to prevent his wife from assuming his death and marrying some one else. Upon this are superimposed many more such themes. The whole poem is much shorter than the Iliad (11,670 lines against 15,693), but like it, is conventionally divided into twenty-four books. The outline of the story is as follows :

Book I. The gods, in the absence of Poseidon, meet in council and Athena asks that Odysseus be sent home. Zeus agrees ; Athena goes to Ithake to rouse Telemachos to get himself a good name by trying to dismiss his mother's wooers and by searching for news of his father. She appears to him in the form of a guest-friend of Odysseus, by name Mentes.

Book II. Acting on her advice, Telemachos calls a folk-moot and bids the wooers depart. They refuse ; Telemachos prays for help to the unknown god who had appeared to him the day before. Athena appears, this time in the form of Mentor, an Ithakesian. In this shape she borrows a ship for him and collects a crew, and they leave the island together.

Book III. They arrive at Nestor's city of Pylos on the mainland ; Athena disappears in bird-form. Nestor makes sacrifice to her, and, as he has himself no news of Odysseus, sends Telemachos on to Lakedaimon, lending him a chariot and one of his sons, Peisistratos, as escort.

Book IV. Arrived at Lakedaimon, they interview Menelaos, the last of the Greeks so far to return. He says that when weatherbound on the island of Pharos he had an opportunity to question Proteus, the shepherd of the flocks of the sea ; this deity, besides giving him advice concerning his own affairs, told him of the adventures of other heroes, including the drowning of Aias the Lokrian and the murder of his own brother Agamemnon. Odysseus, he said, was not dead but captive on an island, the prisoner of the nymph Kalypso, who wished to marry him. Meanwhile in Ithake, the wooers plot to ambush and kill Telemachos on his way home, while Penelope his mother is comforted by a reassuring dream sent by Athena.

Book V. Zeus sends Hermes to bid Kalypso let Odysseus go.

She gives him tools and materials to build a large boat, in which
he sails away from her island. As he nears land, Poseidon sees
him and wrecks his boat with a great storm. Ino-Leukothea
takes pity on him and lends him her veil, with which he cannot
be drowned. On the third day he draws near an unknown coast
and contrives to land. Being naked, he crawls into a hollow
full of leaves and there goes to sleep.

Book VI. Athena comes in a dream to Nausikaa, daughter
of Alkinoos, the king of the Phaiakians, in whose country,
Scheria, Odysseus has come ashore ; she urges her to take the
family linen to the river-mouth the next morning, to wash it
there. Odysseus, asleep near by, is awakened by a shout from
one of Nausikaa's maids, and, hastily contriving a loin-cloth out
of a leafy branch, comes out and begs her to relieve him. She
gives him food and clothing, takes him to the outskirts of the
town, and tells him how to find her father's palace, and how to
conduct himself there.

Book VII. Odysseus, made invisible by Athena, reaches the
palace unmolested and sits as a suppliant on the hearth. He is
kindly received by the queen, Arete, and afterwards by Alkinoos,
who grants his request to be sent home in one of the Phaiakian
ships, the swiftest in the world.

Book VIII. Alkinoos invites the nobles of Scheria to a feast
and games in honour of Odysseus. At the games, Odysseus,
being annoyed at a tactless remark from a young Phaiakian,
astonishes them all by hurling a heavy discus an immense way.
Sure now that he is some notable man, they treat him with distinguished respect. After a dance, and a song by the blind
minstrel Demodokos concerning the loves of Ares and Aphrodite,[21]
they go to a banquet at Alkinoos' palace ; here the king notes
that his guest weeps when the minstrel sings of Troy. He asks
him his name.[22]

Books IX–XII. Odysseus declares who he is and is further
questioned about his adventures. On leaving Troy, he went on

[21] The tone of this episode is hardly Homeric, reminding one rather
of later compositions like the Hymn to Hermes (see below, p. 54). It is
not organically necessary to the poem, and may very well be the addition
of some Ionian poet of later date than Homer. There are a few peculiarities of language in it ; the Sun is called Ἥλιος (elsewhere Ἠέλιος),
and the verb εἴσατο has the elsewhere unexampled meaning ' made a
pretence ' of doing something.

[22] That he had not asked him before is a piece of Homeric etiquette;
Any stranger, as such, had a right to hospitality, with no questions asked.
After he had had his wants seen to, he might be interrogated, but not,
it would appear, before.

a piratical raid to the land of the Kikones (in Thrace), but was driven off with loss. Then a storm drove him to the land of the Lotos-Eaters ; here some of his men, eating the fruit of the lotos, were affected by it with a desire to remain there permanently, and had to be taken away by force. Next they arrived at a little island near the land of the Kyklopes, and next morning Odysseus with his own ship crossed over the intervening strait to explore the country. He and some of his men were taken prisoners by the Kyklops Polyphemos, who shut them in his cave, closing the entrance with a huge rock, and ate two of them that night and two more the next morning. While he was away tending his flocks, the survivors made ready a great pointed stake, and having made Polyphemos drunk, they blinded him with it in the night. He called for help to his fellows, but they, hearing him say that Nobody ($Oὖτις$) was hurting him (Odysseus having told him that that was his name), went away again, and the next morning the prisoners escaped among the sheep as they left the cave. Polyphemos, taunted by Odysseus from his ship, prayed to his father Poseidon for vengeance. Odysseus now arrived at the island of Aiolos the wind-god, where he was hospitably received and given, as a parting present, all the winds tied up in a great bag, except the one that was to bear him home. When in sight of Ithake, his men opened the bag, which they supposed to contain treasure, and were carried away by the winds, first back to Aiolos, who would have no more to do with them, and then to the land of the Laistrygonians, cannibal giants who caught and devoured them all except Odysseus' own ship and crew. He made his way to the island of Aiaie, inhabited by the goddess Kirke, who turned half his crew into swine by magic. Meeting with Hermes, Odysseus was given the herb moly, which overcame Kirke's spells, and forced her to restore his men to their proper form. On this island he lived for a year, and then asked to be sent home. Kirke informed him that he must first visit Hades, to inquire of the soul of Teiresias the great Theban prophet. By her directions, he sailed to the other side of the stream of Ocean, evoked the ghosts, was told much concerning his future adventures by Teiresias, and then saw something of the other spirits, including those of his mother and of his old comrades.[23] Returning to Aiaie, he set out again and, by following Kirke's instructions, safely passed the island of the Seirenes, whose song lured all passers-by to shipwreck (he had stopped the

---

[23] Also, in the text as we have it, a number of the older dead ; but the tone here is rather that of Hesiodic catalogue-poetry (see p. 63) than of Homeric epic, and interpolation is not unreasonably suspected.

ears of his crew with wax and had himself bound to the mast), then the strait between the monster Skylla, who seized six of his men, and the more formidable whirlpool Charybdis, and so to the island Thrinakie, where lived the cattle of the Sun. Here he was weather-bound, and his men, without his knowledge, killed some of the cattle when provisions ran out. When they left the island, their ship was caught in a storm and destroyed by a thunderbolt, in punishment of the sacrilege. Only Odysseus escaped drowning and was carried to the island of Ogygie, where Kalypso had kept him for the seven years prior to his arrival in Scherie.

Books XIII–XIV. The Phaiakians make Odysseus rich presents and send him to Ithake in one of their ships, which however Poseidon turns into a rock on its return home. Odysseus, who has been landed while asleep, does not at first know where he is, but is met by Athena, in the shape of a young man, learns from her the name of the country, and answers her questions about himself with an improvised tale of adventure. She makes herself known, advises him that he must overcome the wooers by stratagem, and changes his appearance into that of an old beggarman. She then goes to Lakedaimon to fetch Telemachos, while he goes to the house of his thrall Eumaios, the chief swine-herd. There he is hospitably received, professes to know something of Odysseus, who he says will return shortly, and answers Eumaios' questions about himself with more inventions.

Books XV–XVI. Athena appears in a dream to Telemachos, advises him to return at once, and warns him to take a different route home, to avoid the wooers' ambush. He arrives safely, picking up on the way a seer, Theoklymenos of Argos, who has had to leave home on account of a blood-feud and asks him for shelter. He reaches the house of Eumaios, and there sees the supposed beggar. When they are alone together, Odysseus is restored by Athena to his true shape, and father and son greet each other and plan vengeance against the wooers. Odysseus is to go to the palace as a beggar and so spy out the condition of affairs for himself.

Book XVII. Telemachos returns to the palace, where Theoklymenos prophesies to Penelope that her husband will come back very soon, if he is not already in the country. Odysseus, on his way to the palace, meets the goat-herd Melanthios, who strikes and reviles him. On his arrival, he is recognized by his old hound Argos (Swift), who dies after feebly trying to greet him. Begging from the wooers, he is struck by their leader, Antinoos.

Book XVIII. The wooers oblige Odysseus to fight another

beggar, one Iros. Fearing to make himself known, he gives the
man but a gentle tap, which breaks his jaw. Iros is thrust out
of the hall, and Odysseus takes his place as a tolerated hanger-on.
Amphinomos, one of the wooers, speaks kindly to him, but does
not understand a covert warning which the hero tries to give
him. Penelope, who has been made marvellously beautiful by
Athena, appears in the hall and is given rich presents by the
wooers. After her departure Eurymachos, one of the wooers,
throws a stool at Odysseus, but is sharply rebuked by Telemachos.

Book XIX. Odysseus and Telemachos, after the wooers are
gone, remove the armour which hangs in the hall.[24] He then
has an interview with Penelope and warns her that her husband
will certainly return before long. She is much moved by his
speech and a tale he tells her concerning himself, and bids her
old nurse Eurykleia wash his feet. In doing so, the old woman
recognizes a conspicuous scar on his thigh, and is stopped just
in time from revealing his secret. Penelope tells him that she
has at last decided to make a choice between her wooers ; she
will bring out Odysseus' bow and promise to marry whoever
can string it and shoot ' through the twelve axes '.[25] He advises
her to do so without delay.

[24] A very suspicious episode. In xvi, 281 *sqq*, where this plan is
first mooted, Odysseus directs Telemachos to leave two swords, two
spears and two shields in place ; but in xix nothing is said of this, and
in xxii arms are fetched for Odysseus and the thralls from the store-room ;
Telemachos is wearing a sword, as Homeric gentlemen regularly do, and
has one spear at hand. Now it is against the Homeric manner for a plan
to be tacitly altered in this way. Moreover, in xix, 36, Athena comes to
light them at their task, holding a lamp ($\lambda\acute{\upsilon}\chi\nu\sigma\varsigma$). But neither the word
nor the thing occurs elsewhere in Homer, light being provided in all
other cases by a hearth-fire or torches. Besides this, Odysseus in speaking
of the arms calls them ' iron ', $\sigma\acute{\iota}\delta\eta\rho\sigma\varsigma$, xvi, 294 and xix, 13. See Lang,
World, pp. 100–104 ; Bérard, *Odyssée*, vol. iii, p. 70a. The passage in
xvi has been excised by many critics since Aristarchos ; I personally
consider both due to a rhapsode, a tolerable poet, who wanted a reciting
version somewhat shorter than the existing Odyssey, and so wrote these
lines as a substitute for the whole episode of the visits to the store-chamber
in xxii. See p. 422.

[25] A standing puzzle. The axes are stood up on their helves and the
arrow shot ' through ' them. Now Homer, although he represents his
heroes as much stronger than his contemporaries, attributes no such
formidable exploits to them as shooting an arrow through twelve iron
blades, any one of which might turn a modern rifle-bullet. The solution
which seems least unlikely, and has some little archaeological evidence to
support it, is that each blade had a hole pierced through it at the broadest
part, to lighten it or to save iron in the making of it ; these holes would
form a sort of tube through which a skilled archer, with a bow strong
enough to give the necessary flatness of trajectory, might possibly shoot

Book XX. Tossing sleepless, Odysseus prays for favourable omens, and is granted them by Zeus. In the morning, he meets Philoitios the cattleman, and on speaking to him of the certainty that vengeance will fall upon the wooers, finds that he is faithful to his master. While feasting, Ktesippos, a wooer, throws a bone at Odysseus.[26] Soon after the second sight comes upon Theoklymenos, and he foretells the destruction of the wooers. They laugh at him, and he leaves the hall.

Book XXI. Penelope brings out the bow and proposes her terms. One by one the wooers fail to string it ; Telemachos tries, but purposely fails on a nod from his father. Finally Odysseus, who in the meantime has revealed himself to the two herdsmen, asks to be allowed to try. Getting the bow, after much opposition, he strings it easily and shoots the arrow through the axes. Telemachos quietly slips on his sword and takes a spear.

Book XXII. Odysseus throws off his rags and springs upon the threshold [27] of the hall. Promising to try his skill at a mark never shot at before, he hits Antinoos and kills him. He reveals himself to the rest, and rejecting offers of composition, proceeds to shoot them down. They resist as best they can with their swords, using the tables as shields.[28] Telemachos fetches equipment for his father, himself and the two herdsmen from the store-room ; Melanthios manages to do the same for the wooers, but after he has armed twelve of them, the herdsmen catch him in the store-room and bind him. Helped by Athena, who turns their enemies' spears so that they miss or barely graze them, the four kill all the wooers. Then those maids who had been the wooers' mistresses are forced to carry out the bodies and

an arrow. The bow is manifestly of what was afterwards called the Scythian type, composite and strongly reflexed, needing both strength and skill to string it. See Balfour in *J.R.A.I.*, li (1921), pp. 289–309. Penelope's decision has been declared inconsistent both with her declaration earlier in the book that she does not know what to do and with xxi, 1, which states that Athena suggested the trial of the bow to her. Both criticisms are pointless. She suddenly makes up her mind after long indecision, and it greatly heightens the interest of the story for Odysseus to intervene after the last shred of her resistance to the wooers has gone ; Athena prompts her simply to put her plan into immediate effect.

[26] This episode is rejected by some as a mere repetition of the affair of Eurymachos in xviii ; but Greeks of all ages are fond of threes, and this makes three principal wooers insult Odysseus.

[27] Immediately outside the hall was a barnyard ; the threshold was a high stone platform, protecting the earthen floor against filth and rainwater from without.

[28] They were small and light, something like our ' occasional tables '.

clean the hall ; they are then hanged and Melanthios horribly mutilated.[29]

Book XXIII. Penelope, who has been cast into a deep sleep by Athena, is told the news, but at first will not believe that the stranger is really Odysseus. She enters the hall, where a pretence of dancing and feasting is kept up to deceive casual passers-by. At last Odysseus persuades her of his identity by mentioning a secret in the construction of their marriage bed which only he and she and one serving-maid know. They retire for the night and tell each other of their adventures and sufferings.

Book XXIV. Odysseus goes into the country and reveals himself to his aged father Laertes. They gather what men they can to resist the vendetta of the wooers' kin ; the ghosts of the slain have meanwhile been taken to Hades by Hermes. The avengers are headed by the father of Antinoos, Eupeithes, whom Laertes kills, his youthful vigour being supernaturally restored for the occasion. Zeus now hurls a thunderbolt between the combatants, and peace is made.[30]

These two great epics, according to the usual opinion of antiquity and the most modern views of to-day, were the work of one poet, conventionally called Homer ($"O\mu\eta\varrho o\varsigma$), whatever that name may mean.[31] The language and metre alike show that he has behind him a long artistic tradition. The former is composite ; in it are to be found side by side, not only forms which in historical times belong to different dialects (that might be explained either by supposing that the differentiations between, say, Ionic and Aiolic as we know them were of later date than the poems, or by placing their composition in some region of mixed population) but to different ages.

To take but one instance out of many ; the genitive singular of masculine nouns in the so-called first declension primitively ended in *asyo*. By regular Greek phonetic changes (loss of the sound of our consonantal *y* and disappearance of the *s* between vowels) this became

---

[29] This is the one instance of mutilation, usually an Oriental punishment, in Homer ; but it is also the one case of deliberate betrayal of his lord by a thrall.

[30] A modern would have ended at Book xxiii ; Homer could not leave his hero with an unsettled blood-feud hanging over him.

[31] It sounds like the Greek for ' hostage ', and the ancients noted this and made up a story or two to account for it ; again, some etymologist declared it to be derived from $\dot{o}$ $\mu\grave{\eta}$ $\dot{o}\varrho\tilde{\omega}\nu$, ' he who sees not ' and referred it to the poet's traditional blindness. Needless to say, neither of these fancies deserves serious attention. See the various ancient lives of him (collected in Allen, *Homeri Opera*, vol. v, Oxford Class. Texts) and Eustathios *ad Iliadem*, p. 4, 25.

-āo, and this form is certainly common in Homer, probably to be restored in many passages where the MSS. do not give it. But -āo, or in Ionic -ηο, was subjected to another change, the so-called *metathesis quantitatis*, and thus became -εω, often pronounced as one syllable. Now this form -εω, or even -ω, is likewise found several times where the metre guarantees it, and is very often given by the MSS., *i.e.*, by ancient tradition, it being far the more familiar form, where it may be wrong. When this sort of thing occurs sporadically all over the poems, the natural assumption seems to be that we are dealing with a poetical diction which deliberately retains many archaic forms.

The metre is likewise far from primitive. It is the hexa-meter (five dactyls, $\bar{\ }\cup\cup$, for any one of which a spondee, $\bar{\ }\bar{\ }$, may be substituted, and a sixth foot which may be $\bar{\ }\bar{\ }$ or $\bar{\ }\cup$), perhaps the offspring of two shorter verses united into one. This is handled with such a wealth of variety in the pauses, such euphony, and such obedience, conscious or otherwise, to a number of minute rules as could arise only from generations of experience, at least as many as went to the perfecting of English blank verse.

The style, apart from mere linguistics, I need not characterize, for that has been done, for all English readers, by Matthew Arnold.[32] I do but note that there are embedded in it many formulae, epithets and turns of expression which strongly indicate, indeed practically prove, the existence of an age of balladry before the date of the epics. For instance, Achilles is regularly ' swift-foot ', Odysseus scores of times ' much enduring ' and not infrequently ' sacker of cities ' ; Patroklos again and again ' horseman ' and Nestor ' Gerenian horseman ', the sense of the adjective being extremely doubtful to us and probably to Homer also. Very numerous speeches are introduced by the line ' and in answer to him spake ' (the name of the speaker and an epithet follow), or ' and addressing him he spake winged words ' ; half the dead are slain ' by the pitiless bronze ', and several short descriptive passages, comparable to ballad-stanzas, recur a number of times each.

The society described may be called feudal ; each prince or baron (βασιλεὺς) has an estate and vassals of his own, which he governs, by the aid of a sort of council of elders and on occasion an assembly of all free men, according to certain traditional, unwritten laws or ' dooms ' (θέμιστες), which it is his duty to preserve.[33] There is no central government, although the

[32] *On Translating Homer.*
[33] For fuller details on all these points, see Chadwick, *Heroic Age* ; Lang, *World.*

supremacy of Agamemnon over the others in the Iliad is probably
a reminiscence of days when there was one, an empire in fact on
a small scale.   The culture is transitional between bronze and
iron ; the latter is well known, but apparently the art of tempering
it is still to be discovered, therefore it is used only for the rougher
sort of implements, such as axes and hoes, while anything like a
sword or spear, which needs a keen edge, is of bronze.   In many
other ways also a mixture of old and new is to be seen, as the
co-existence of bride-price and dower, much as in Albania at the
present day.   Homer feels that degeneracy has in some respects
set in ; the men of old were more powerful than those of his own
time.   The picture does not correspond to what archaeology tells
us of the Mycenaean age, but we can very readily imagine it
being true of a condition of affairs growing out of that age, when
the influence of Crete had weakened and a certain retrogression
in material culture had set in.

All these facts forbid us to suppose that Homer is either
primitive or a poet of the earliest age of the Greek people.   Assuming for the present that he is a reality, *i.e.* that there was a single
great poet who composed the two epics, let us try to determine
his approximate date.[34]

We have seen that he is later than the Mycenaean epoch,
that is, well after the middle of the second millennium B.C.   He
is also long after the War of Troy, a historical event, however
glossed by popular and poetic imagination, which ancient chronology and modern archaeology concur fairly well in placing not
far from 1200 B.C. of our reckoning.[35]   We may not unfairly
postulate [36] something like 150 to 200 years as the time necessary
to make solid fact pass into a tradition largely unhistorical, and

[34] The ancients had a number of conjectures on that subject, see
Schmid-Stählin, i, p. 85 *sqq.*   They put him at all manner of dates, from
that of the Trojan War itself down to the seventh century B.C. of our
reckoning (contemporary with Archilochos, Tatian *contra Graecos*, 31),
this last by identifying the ' land of the Kimmerians ' in Od. xi, with
that of the historical Kimmerians who invaded Asia Minor at that epoch.
A neglected point in modern times is the astronomy of the poems ; if
Homer is accurately describing contemporary conditions (the Great
Bear never sets at night and there is no polestar), he cannot possibly be
later than about the tenth century, see D'Arcy W. Thompson in *Proc.
Class. Ass.*, xxvi (1929), pp. 28–9 ; but it is possible, though in my opinion
unlikely, that he is repeating traditional statements about the stars.

[35] For a judicious and brief account of the historical background of
the Trojan War, with some mention of modern authorities on the subject,
see Bowra, *Tradition*, chapter viii.

[36] See A. van Gennep, *La Formation des légendes* (Paris, Flammarion,
1910), p. 163.

the interval may of course be longer. Moreover, it appears that he wrote in Ionia, for not only were his poems and the tradition of epic preserved there, but his geographical references are on the whole more accurate for northern Asia Minor than for Greece proper. Yet his whole point of view is that of a native of Greece ; all his chief Greek heroes live there, not in Ionia, and his gods on the Greek Olympos. The natural conclusion is that he composed for those Achaians who were driven from Greece by the incoming of the Dorians. Now there were Dorians in full possession of Menelaos' old kingdom of Lakedaimon (Sparta ; but the Dorian settlement was the other side of the river from the old town) at some date not far removed from 900 B.C.[37] It seems very natural to suppose that they would be busy driving out the Achaians from more northerly districts of the Peloponnesos, which they probably entered from the north-west, in the neighbourhood of 1000, if not earlier. About the tenth century therefore appears again to be a reasonable date for poems which, on the whole, ignore the Dorians in a way hardly possible if they had been long established in the sites they held in historical times.

Thus we see that in the tenth century B.C. the conditions necessary to produce a Homer existed. If we ask whether as a matter of fact the poems were composed as early as that, we have evidence pointing in the same direction. Hesiod, as we shall see later, can hardly be brought further down than the eighth century ; but he and his school manifestly have behind them not only Homer but other epics as well. Now the other epics, so far as we know, are later than the Iliad and Odyssey, at least for the most part, since they centre around them ; and for the development of so large a body of literature and the spread of its influence from Ionia to the mainland we can scarcely allow less than a century, and might allow more. The evidence of Homeric and other epic influence on the earliest lyric poetry is of less importance, for this is not older than the seventh century.

Putting all our evidence together, we may be disposed to agree with Herodotos,[38] who, taking Homer and Hesiod to be contemporaries,[39] gave it as his opinion that they had lived four hundred years before his own day, i.e., about 850, with the

[37] The ivories found on this site go back to about the ninth century, and the shrine of Orthia to about the tenth, see *Artemis Orthia*, ed. R. M. Dawkins, London, Macmillan. 1929, pp. 1, 18, 203.

[38] ii, 53, 2.

[39] Cf. note 34. Herodotos probably derived his opinion from the curious and puzzling statement ascribed to Hesiod (frag. 265 Rzach) that he and Homer sang hymns in honour of Apollo at Delos.

modification that the former may well be anything up to a century older, the latter perhaps as much as a century younger than that date.[40]

Hitherto I have deliberately ignored the famous ' Homeric Question '. It is my considered opinion that the theories put forward within the last few generations concerning the authorship of the poems are now mainly of interest to students of the history of scholarship, while the learner who wishes to acquaint himself with the facts of Greek literature need not trouble about them. Nevertheless, it would be impossible not to mention views so famous and urged by such excellent scholars with such abundance of learning and ingenuity ; so the following paragraphs contain a bare outline of them and of the reasons for rejecting them almost wholly.

In antiquity, criticism mostly accepted without question the authorship of Homer for the two poems ; a few critics (see below) suggested that the Odyssey was not by the same poet as the Iliad, and a number of passages, some of them of considerable extent,[41] were supposed by one authority or another to be spurious additions. Also, the Alexandrians and to some extent earlier scholars (see p. 388) successfully distinguished between the Iliad and Odyssey and the numerous other works ascribed to Homer but really of considerably later date (see p. 47 *sqq.*). Further, there was a theory put forward, it would seem, about the first century B.C.[42] to the effect that Homer

---

[40] Nilsson (see Bibliography) finds archaeological evidence pointing to the eighth century. I prefer to suppose some slight additions to have been made then.

[41] Aristophanes of Byzantion and Aristarchos believed that the Odyssey ended at xxiii, 296 ; see the scholiasts there and Eustathios, p. 1948, 49. The latter objected especially to the opening episode of Od. xxiv, see schol. on xxiv, 1, who gives a list of his principal arguments and tries to refute them. Il. x, was added by Peisistratos (see next note), see the schol. of the Codex Venetus at the beginning of that book, and Eustath., p. 785,.41. Excisions of single lines or short passages are very humerous ; see any critical edition of Homer.

[42] The earliest datable passage is in Cicero, *de oratore*, iii, 137 (written 55 B.C.), who says that Peisistratos ' is stated to have arranged the books of Homer, formerly in a state of confusion, in the order in which we now have them '. A similar statement is made by Aelian, *uar. hist.*, xiii, 14, some three centuries later, also by an epigram of unknown authorship and date (Anth. Pal., xi, 442, 3, cited also in the fourth and fifth Lives of Homer [Allen, *Homeri opera*, vol. v] and in Bekker's *Anecdota*, p. 768). The theory is referred to by Pausanias, vii, 26, 13, and by the commentators on Homer, see last note, besides several more passages in late authors of no independent value. It seems to be a development of the probably true statement that either Solon or one of the family of Peisistratos made a law obliging reciters of Homer at the Panathenaia to recite ἐξ ὑπολήψεως ἐφεξῆς or ἐξ ὑποβολῆς, *i.e.*, one beginning where the last left off (which in

himself composed the various parts of his poems separately and never issued a complete edition, which was done much later by Peisistratos of Athens. This still said nothing of the authorship of the poems, beyond assuming the existence of the traditional Homer; whoever was responsible for it was plainly a bookman, with his mind running on collected editions of writers and the activities of scholarly librarians and enlightened princes, such as those of Alexandria and Pergamos. In modern times, since the Revival of Letters, this theory was taken up again and distorted, first, it would seem, by Charles Perrault, one of the most fatuous writers in the notorious controversy of the Ancients and Moderns which occupied so much of the seventeenth century. Being an outspoken partisan of the Moderns, he attacked Homer with all the vehemence of one who had never read him, and in particular, declared that many excellent critics denied his very existence.[43] His supposed works were a collection of shorter pieces by a number of different authors, hence the name ' rhapsodies ', or stitchings together of poems. A more important work was the *Conjectures académiques ou dissertation sur l'Iliade* of Abbé François Hédelin d'Aubignac, written in 1664 and apparently circulated to some extent in MS., but never printed till 1715, after the author's death. He declared the Iliad too full of inconsistencies and irrelevancies to be the deliberately constructed work of a single poet, and supposed that a number of shorter pieces, composed for festivals comprising poetical compositions, had been collected by some unknown person under the general title of *Ilias*.[44] He concluded that this collector, or editor,

itself presupposes a more or less standard text of the poems), which was improved upon by one or two writers either into crediting Peisistratos' son Hipparchos with being the first to bring Homer to the mainland of Greece (pseudo-Plato, *Hipparch.*, 228 B), and also, by Megarian writers especially, into a statement that Solon or Peisistratos interpolated the Iliad by adding ii, 558, or the whole passage ii, 546 *sqq.*, to use as a proof-text against Megara in support of the Athenian claim on Salamis. See, for the law, [Plat.], *loc. cit.*; Diogenes Laertios, i, 57, with the vaguer allusions in Isokrates, iv, 159; Lykurgos, *c. Leocratem*, 102; for the alleged forgery, Plut., *Solon*, 10; Diog. Laert., *loc. cit.*, and *ibid.* 48; Strabo, ix, 1, 10; Quintilian, *Instit. orat.*, v, 11, 40; and the schol. on Il. ii, 557. Eustath., p. 284, 40 *sqq.*, copies Strabo. The whole tale of the services to the text done by Hipparchos, or Peisistratos, seems a later pendant to the story, which possibly goes back to Ephoros in the fourth century B.C., that Lykurgos got hold of a complete copy while he was on his travels, the poems having been previously known only in fragments, Plut., *Lyc.*, 4; Aelian, *loc. cit.*; and more briefly, [Herakleides Pontikos], *de rep. Laced.*, 2 (Müller, F. H. G., vol. ii, p. 210) and Strabo, x, 4, 19. See further Cauer, *Grundfragen*, pp. 111–16; Schmid-Stählin, i, pp. 159–62.

[43] See, for Perrault, Finsler, *Homer*, p. 189 *sqq.*

[44] See Finsler, p. 208. Wolf had read d'Aubignac and Perrault (*Proleg.*, note to c. xxvi, p. 69), but had so poor an opinion of both, especially the former, that he hesitated a long while to publish his own theory, because it resembled theirs.

was Lykurgos, the Spartan legislator. Bentley also, in an *obiter dictum* very characteristic of him, declared that Homer wrote a series of disconnected pieces which were put together five hundred years later by Peisistratos.[45] He did not, however, follow this up with any systematic argument.

The first important and thorough handling of the question by a professed Homeric scholar of learning and ability was the *Prolegomena ad Homerum* of F. A. Wolf, 1795,[46] in memory of whom it is not unreasonable to call this form of the separatist theory the Wolfian hypothesis, although, as we have seen, he was not its actual originator and naturally cannot be held responsible for the shape it assumed after his death, in other hands. His essay was an introduction to a critical edition of Homer, and deals largely with matters of textual criticism and the history of the Alexandrian editions and commentaries. The theory now to be stated occupies less than half, chapters xii–xxxv inclusive. He starts from the argument that writing, if not entirely unknown, was a strange and very rare art in Homer's Greece, not common or convenient enough to make the recording of a long poem possible. Here he reasons acutely from the materials available to him, and cannot be blamed for not foreseeing archaeological discoveries made generations later. He then denies that any man, without the aid of writing, could compose poems so long and on the whole so admirably constructed as the Iliad and Odyssey ; or if he did, that they could survive in an illiterate age.[47] And supposing (p. 77) that by some miracle they were constructed and did survive, why did the authors of the Cyclic epics (see p. 47) not learn the art of constructing a poem from them, instead of producing, as we know from Aristotle that they did, works lacking in unity ?[48] He concludes, then, that behind the poems as we have them there must lie a number of short pieces, rhapsodies or lays of moderate compass, which were afterwards collected, joined together by very able editors or diasceuasts,[49] and written down in more or less their present form. In support of this he cites a few passages (Il. xviii, 356–68 ; Od. iv, 620 *sqq.*) which he holds to show a rather clumsy join between two distinct lays. Moreover, ancient and modern critics have declared unhomeric certain passages essential to the story, or at least highly desirable, as the conclusion of the Odyssey (see note 41, and cf. note 30 ; Wolf gives the same reason for not ending the Odyssey earlier), and the last book of the Iliad (rejected by Dawes, *Miscell. Crit.*, p. 152 = p. 257 of ed. 4, Camb., 1817).

[45] *Remarks upon a late Discourse of Freethinking,* 7. It is little more than a paraphrase of what Suidas says, *s.u.* Ὅμηρος (p. 771 *b*, Bekker).

[46] I cite from the edition of 1871 (Calvary, Berlin), which has some additional notes taken from the margins of Bekker's copy.

[47] It should be noticed that he never denied the possibility of learning the poems by heart once they were written, a feat which has been achieved in both ancient and modern times.

[48] See Arist., *Poetics,* 1451a, 19 *sqq.* ; 1459a, 30 *sqq.*

[49] See note 51.

Now if important parts of the poem are additions to what the original Homer composed, why not less important ones ? However, this question needs careful investigation, for the additions are the work of able rhapsodes, not very much later (he supposes a century or two) than Homer himself, and therefore closely resemble the genuine parts in style. The actual putting together was done by, or rather under the direction of Peisistratos, who had at his court several notable poets.[50] He, however, did not finally settle the text, as we may see from the numerous divergences between our MSS. and scholia and the quotations from Homer in sundry authors later than Peisistratos but earlier than the Alexandrians. That some knowledge of these changes survived may be gathered from occasional mention in the scholia of διασκευασταί, arrangers or makers-over of the poems.[51]

Wolf, having stated his case with learning, moderation and good sense, deserved and got a hearing from scholars, especially in Germany. With literary men, and particularly the foremost of his time and country, he found less favour. Schiller, who though no great classic had Greek enough to read Homer in the original and was an enthusiast for antiquity, attacked him and his theories vigorously ; Goethe, at the time when he wrote *Hermann und Dorothea*, was a declared Wolfian, and went further than Wolf ; for the latter consistently upheld the reality of Homer, whom he supposed to have lived in the tenth century B.C. and to be the author of lays which in the end formed a great part of the Iliad and Odyssey (*Vorlesungen*, pp. 4–5, 11), while Goethe supposed a number of Homeridai, whose collective efforts had finally led to the genesis of the poems. But later, while working at his *Achilleis*, he became more and more fully convinced of the unity of Homer. Wieland testified from his own experience in writing *Oberon* that a poet need not lay down a plan beforehand to compose a work having sufficient unity. Why should not Homer have simply been led on by his poetical instincts to compose more and more, until his productions of themselves fell into the framework of unified poems ?[52] But the great critic Schlegel strongly supported Wolf,

---

[50] He instances Orpheus of Kroton (Suidas, *s.u.* Ὀρφεὺς Κροτωνιάτης), Anakreon and Simonides ([Plat.], *Hipp.* 228c). The whole passage shows a curious absence of Wolf's usual critical abilities. He actually accepts this late story as the ' voice of all antiquity ' (*uox totius antiquitatis*, p. 86), and reads into his authorities, what they nowhere say, that Peisistratos was the first to put Homer into writing (*primum consignasse litteris*). It should, however, be remembered that the minute analysis of historical sources was far less developed and familiar, even among professional scholars, then than now.

[51] The words διασκευαστής, διασκευάζειν, occur several times in the Venice scholia, for example on Il. vi, 441 ; viii, 73–4 ; ii, 807 ; iv, 208. But in all cases they seem to mean no more than ' editor ', ' edit ', and to refer, not to any process of interpolating or re-writing the poems, but to the readings and critical opinions of an earlier Alexandrian edition than the one (that of Didymos) to which these scholia in the main go back.

[52] Finsler, pp. 466–8.

and his own colleagues, the classical specialists, followed the lines he
had laid down in a long series of investigations, characterized by
greater learning and diligence than insight.

As a result of much analysis (Lachmann, for example, dissected
the Iliad, down to the death of Hektor, into sixteen lays),[53] a modification of Wolf's view began to grow up. We may conveniently call
it by the name of Grote, the historian of Greece, although he did not
actually originate it,[54] since his is the best-known statement of it and
aroused interest, not only in England but in Germany. In the twenty-
first chapter of his *History*, first published in 1846, he discussed Homer
at some length, and gave it as his opinion that the Odyssey was beyond
reasonable doubt the work of one poet. The Iliad, however, seemed
to him to show decided traces of multiple authorship, notably certain
inconsistencies between various sections,[55] and he proposed to account
for these as follows. After the primitive age of ballad-making there
had come a time when poets of more constructive talent (he rejected
the idea of the Peisistratean commission altogether) had emerged,
capable of constructing epics of moderate compass. One of these
works was an Achilleis, a poem on the Wrath of that hero, as promised
by the first line of the Iliad, and it was equivalent to the present first,
eighth, eleventh to twenty-second books of the existing poem. ' If
we take ', he said, ' those portions of the poem which I imagine to
have constituted the original Achilleis, it will be found that the series
of events contained in them is more rapid, more unbroken, and more
intimately knit together in the way of cause and effect, than in the
other books.' He rejected several theories which would further
subdivide this supposed kernel of the poem.

This theory had a considerable success, not least in the author's
own country, and has found its way into many non-specialist works,
for example into school editions of the Iliad. Modifications of it were
put forward from many quarters, some dealing merely with details of
the supposed structure of the original poem, but one in particular,

[53] K. Lachmann, *Betrachtungen über Homers Ilias*, first issued in book
form 1847.

[54] Wolf himself had supposed (*Proleg.*, c. xxviii) that the narrative of
Odysseus to Alkinoos, Od. ix–xii, quite a little epic in itself, might have
always been one continuous poem. But views more nearly resembling
Grote's had been put forward as early as 1831 by G. Hermann, and in
1836 by W. Müller. See Schmid-Stählin, i, p. 135.

[55] He especially found fault with the alleged discrepancy between
xi, 609, in which Achilles says he expects the defeated Achaians will
now come as suppliants to him, and the ninth book, containing their
appeal. But as a matter of fact there is a wide difference between the
two situations. In ix, an embassy arrives, making a handsome acknow-
ledgement that Agamemnon has been in the wrong and offering a large
compensation for Achilles' wounded honour ; there is nothing abject in
their words or actions. In xi, Achilles expects that the Greeks will
' stand about his knees ' as helpless suppliants, begging him to rescue
them, and not speaking as equals at all.

that of Kirchhoff,[56] which applied especially to the Odyssey, whereof indeed his book was an edition, with notes and excursuses setting forth his views. He supposed two poems, with an enlargement forming practically a third, whose combination had made the present work. Of these, one consisted of parts of Book i, followed by considerable sections of v–xiii, with the further complication, however, that originally the long narrative of Odysseus had been in the third person, not the first. It was, then, a Return of Odysseus. The second he supposed later ; it was the Vengeance of Odysseus, roughly, Books xiv–xxiii, 296, with omission of most of xv and some smaller excisions. Finally, some one had had the idea of providing Telemachos with a series of adventures of his own, and had therefore added a Telemacheia, consisting of all those scenes in which the youth plays any but a very subordinate part (the end of i, all of ii–iv, and xv). Last of all, these had been put together, but not so skilfully as to hide a number of clumsy joins.

The outstanding characteristic of this theory is its utter impossibility. Wolf and Grote had supposed things to happen which really have taken place in the history of literature. An editor of taste and poetical feeling has put together a selection of ballads into an epic ; Lönnrot made the Kalevala in this way.[57] An original shorter epic has been expanded by additions into a larger one ; this is the history of the Chanson de Roland.[58] What is known to have happened in Finland and France might have done so in Greece. But that any one possessed of tolerable poetic ability, to say nothing of a genius, should have written an epic without an end, like the supposed Return, or without a beginning, like the supposed Vengeance, still more one with neither end nor beginning, like the Telemacheia, is past belief altogether, and most of all past belief when Kirchhoff assigns some of his supposed shorter epics to an age of whose art we know enough to say that the characteristic Greek feeling for form and symmetry was rapidly developing.[59]

[56] A. Kirchhoff, *Die homerische Odyssee und ihre Entstehung*, Berlin, 1859, second ed.. 1879.

[57] See Comparetti, *The Traditional Poetry of the Finns*, trans. I. M. Anderton, Longmans, Green & Co., 1898, p. 6 *sqq.* The late N. G. Politis was of opinion that much the same relation existed between the mediaeval Greek epic of Digenís Akrítas and the numerous folk-songs relating to that hero ; see Λαογραφία, A', p. 169 *sqq.*

[58] See Murray, *Rise*, App. F. For acute criticism of the supposition that the Iliad could have arisen in this way, see A. van Gennep, *La question d'Homère*, Paris, Mercure de France, 1909, pp. 38–50. Briefly, the reason why none of these countries ever had an Iliad is that none of them ever had a Homer.

[59] The Telemachy was composed between the 30th and 50th Olympiads (Kirchhoff[1], p. vii, Kirchhoff[2], i, p. 290) or about 650–570 B.C., a time when archaic art was well under way. The characteristic of this which is perhaps the most striking is that it developed a fine appreciation of grouping, symmetry and architectonic arrangement before it mastered either drawing or modelling.

Apart from such absurdities—I can find no milder word—as these, the objections to the various forms of the separatist theory, Wolfian, Grotian or Kirchhoffian, are of a negative kind; viz., that the arguments used to support it are too weak to be capable of proving anything. They fall under three heads, linguistic, archaeological and literary. For it is plain that if the poems are composite and not all the product of one age, we should be able to detect differences in the accidence and syntax between the older and later parts, and also to find in the later allusions to customs, instruments, industries, laws and so forth inconsistent with what the older ones relate. Finally, it is not likely that any longer work could be put together from shorter ones so cunningly as not to show the joins here and there to a careful observer. Hence arguments of all three kinds have been used, but mostly of the third sort.

In a book such as this, linguistic arguments cannot be gone into in much detail; I will give only one or two examples, asking the reader, if he wishes for further information, to seek it in the works named in the Bibliography and in the footnotes to this chapter. One of the most famous weapons of the separatist is the digamma (see above, p. 5). That this is a sound occurring in primitive Greek is clear from comparative philology; thus the word for ' work ', ἔργον, is known to have been originally ϝέργον, precisely identical, save for a difference of vocalization, with its English equivalent. One of the commonest words for ' to see ', ἰδεῖν, was originally ϝιδεῖν, identical in root and vocalization also with Latin *uidere* and English *wit*. Now it is a known fact that this sound, and with it the letter expressing it, had vanished from Ionic in later times. It is also clear, from the scansion of many passages in Homer, that he often pronounced it, or at least allowed vowels to remain unelided before words beginning with it in primitive Greek, and otherwise showed a knowledge or a memory of its presence.[60] At other times, he treats such words as if they contained no ϝ. The suggestion was therefore fairly obvious, that if indeed the Iliad and Odyssey were produced from a number of poems of different dates, the earlier parts would neglect the digamma seldom or never, the late ones often. Statements to that effect have indeed been made; but closer examination shows them unfounded. If any part of the Iliad is original, it must surely be the first book, without which the story is quite unintelligible.[61] If any part of the

[60] A sound no longer heard, or scarcely heard, can prevent elision. Thus in French, the so-called *h aspiré* is almost inaudible, yet no one says *l'honte, l'homard*, but *la honte, le homard*. There is clear evidence (see Burnet on Plato, *Euthyphro*, 12 A) that ϝ was occasionally written in Epic texts as late as the fourth century B.C.

[61] It has indeed been to some extent dissected, for instance by Lachmann; but no Iliad, or even Achilleis, would be conceivable without the quarrel, the interview between Achilles and Thetis, and that between Thetis and Zeus. Similarly, that part of Od. xxiv which is considered, so to speak, yet more spurious than the rest is the episode of the arrival in the other world of the wooers' ghosts. The calculation has been made by Mr. A. Shewan; see *Revue des études homériques*, II (1932), p. 3 *sqq.*

Odyssey, universally or almost universally supposed to be the later poem, is a spurious addition, it is the end, from xxiii, 297 on. As these two passages are roughly of the same length (611 lines in the former case, 614 in the latter), there should be comparatively many digammas in the one, comparatively few in the other. The plain fact is, that the observances and neglects are nearly the same in number in both cases. On the assumption that both poems are of nearly the same date, and that the sound of the digamma was obsolescent in the language of their author, there is nothing here to cause the least surprise.[62] It is, moreover, recognized by the vast majority of students that a number of passages which apparently neglect the sound do not do so in reality,[63] but have been slightly modernized by reciters, copyists, or editors in antiquity. Indeed, it is fairly clear that the whole Homeric corpus, as was very natural in poems which were recited a thousand times for once that they were written down, has passed through a long period of unsystematic modernization, sometimes producing unmetrical lines and very frequently giving us late, even artificial forms, side by side with good old ones. An excellent example of this last is the phenomenon known to the Germans as *Zerdehnung*. In Greek, a number of verbs have stems ending in a vowel (*a, e* or *o*), which in the pronunciations usual in most places in historical times contracted with the endings. Thus, the ordinary word for ' seeing ' was to begin with ὁράων ; in Attic, for example, this is shortened to ὁρῶν. In Homer, the ending of this and many similar words is shown by the scansion to have a syllable more than in Attic ; but instead of appearing in the MSS. as ὁράων, etc., they assume the strange forms ὁρόων and the like, introducing a vowel which the stem never had. The reasonable explanation is simply this ; reciters unwittingly used the shorter pronunciation, to which they were accustomed in daily speech ; their ear told them that this left the word too short, and they therefore made good the deficiency by drawling the long vowel beyond its normal length ; when this came to be written down, the scribes indicated the conventional way of delivering the line exactly as they were accustomed to indicate a slur when writing the words of a song,[64] by writing the

[62] *Woman* and *'ooman, causeway* and *causey* alike exist in spoken English to-day ; it is mere accident that only one form in either case is of the literary language. If we imagine a population of mixed English and Swedish descent producing a literary language of their own and a great poet to write in it, there might well occur side by side *wonder* and *under, word* and *ord*. The digamma was still heard in Aiolic centuries after Ionic had abandoned it, and Pindar uses it when his contemporary Aeschylus, a few miles away across the Attic border, does not.

[63] For instance, a short word such as τε often occurs where it has no meaning ; sense can commonly be restored by writing ϝε, the old form of the pronoun of the third person in the accusative case, instead.

[64] *E.g.*, Aristophanes, *Birds*, 310, ποποποποποποῦ, *i.e.*, ποῦ, ' where ? ' sung to a long bird-like trill. It is as if we printed ' Flow gently, swee-eet A-afton, a-among thy gree-een brae-aes ', because it is sung in that manner.

vowel twice over, first short and then long. It is to be regretted that only a few modern editors return to the genuine way of writing such words, which is indeed preserved in somè passages even by the MSS.[65]

Another method, and a perfectly legitimate one, was to apply the discoveries of archaeology to the question. Again to take but a single example, Reichel made an interesting effort to tell old from new by investigating the armour of the Homeric heroes and comparing it with that found in Mycenaean works of art or restorable from fragments in tombs of that period. He established the fact that the shield of Mycenaean days, and indeed, apparently, for some time after in mainland Greece, was not the familiar round target of classical times, the *clipeus* of Roman writers, but a ponderous affair of leather, or more probably dried hide, more like a mantlet than a shield, having no handles, but attached to the wearer by a baldrick passing over the left and under the right shoulder.[66] A number of Homeric fighters, notably Aias son of Telamon, seem to use this type of shield, ' like unto a tower ' as Homer repeatedly says. Other scenes clearly presuppose the classical type of round shield, lighter and furnished with handles, which Herodotos [67] says was invented by the Karians and not known before. But no division of the poem into strata on these lines is practicable (Aias and Hektor have the older, Agamemnon the later form), and Reichel himself furnishes a sufficient refutation of his own theory when he points out that for some time the two shapes must have existed, indeed can be shown by archaeological evidence to have existed, side by side.[68] Homer was not a Mycenaean, nor learned in archaeology, and represented his heroes in the equipment of his own day, pretty obviously as mixed as his own dialect.

But the chief weapon of the separatists has always been literary criticism, and of this it is not too much to say that such niggling word-baiting, such microscopic hunting of minute inconsistencies and flaws

---

[65] Examples in Cauer, *Grundfragen*,[2] p. 79. The same author acutely observes that no possible division of the poems will break them up into sections having respectively older and later forms of the language. Thus, no one supposes Il. vi, 281 to be by two different authors ; yet there we must either read ἐθέλῃσ’ εἰπόντος, with the older form of the subj. and neglect of ϝ, or ἐθέλῃ ϝειπόντος, keeping the ϝ but getting a later form of the subj. Similar phenomena take place, for example, Il. xiii, 163, xxii, 454 ; Od. xix, 136 (Cauer, pp. 83, 85).

[66] Reichel, *Hom. Waffen*[2], p. 1 *sqq.* A synopsis of Reichel's views will be found in Leaf's *Iliad*, vol. i, App. B. In his first edition, Reichel had argued that the cuirass was not Mycenaean, and tried to get rid of all references to it in what he supposed to be the earlier parts of the Iliad. Later (*op. cit.*, pp. 93-4), he found that this was not so ; unfortunately, he died before he could develop this new piece of information.

[67] Hdt., i, 171, 6. That the Greeks in Asia heard of and adopted the new invention before those in Greece proper seems a reasonable supposition, supposing the tradition, or theory, recorded by the historian to be correct.

[68] Reichel, *op. cit.*, p. 45.

in logic, has hardly been seen, outside of the Homeric held, since Rymer and John Dennis died. No long poem and no long novel is ever likely to be without self-contradictions here and there, and indeed many shorter pieces contain them. In *Les Femmes savantes*, iii, 2, Philaminte says she has written no verse ; yet a little further on (iv, 2), Armande says to her ' et vingt fois . . . j'ai lu des vers de vous '. In *Othello*, the double timing is well-known. Bianca taxes Cassio with having neglected her for a week, iii, 4, 173 ; therefore he has been in Cyprus for something more than seven days. Yet the preceding scenes occupy the night of the day on which he arrives and the following day, less than forty-eight hours. No one supposes Shakespere or Molière to have written these plays in conjunction with any one else ; but when it comes to Homer, such arguments as the following have been offered, and taken, seriously. In Il. i, the gods are said to have gone away to the Ethiopians' feast the day before, 423 ; but during the assembly held on the preceding day Athena descended from and returned to Olympos, 221, cf. 195, and Apollo was still plaguing the Achaians with his darts of pestilence on the same day, 96. Hence these passages belong to different ' lays ' by different authors.[69] Menelaos vainly searches for Paris, who has been snatched away by Aphrodite, iii, 449 *sqq.* This must follow immediately on his disappearance in 380–82, for it is asymmetrical to have sixty-six lines explaining what he did after his escape between the two passages ;[70] the interview between him and Helen in these lines is by another author. Worst and most grotesque of all is the manner of Kirchhoff. Athena (Od. i, 271-97) gives Telemachos the following advice, in substance : ' To-morrow, call a folk-moot and publicly bid the wooers begone, adding that your mother, if she wishes to marry again, must go home to her father and be re-married from his house in due form. Then take ship and go to look for news of your father. If you hear he is still alive, come home and wait for him ; you can still hold out for a year. If you learn that he is dead, perform his funeral rites, marry your mother to a new husband, and plot vengeance against the wooers for devouring your substance '. Because Homer does not say in so many words that the search for news and the vengeance are to follow if the wooers will not go away, Kirchhoff devotes half a score of pages to denouncing the illogicality and other gross faults of this simple passage, and puts it among the late additions to the poem.[71] Other examples of this kind of thing could be multiplied from the writings of scholars, by no means the worst of their schools, who have dissected the two poems. If they wished to prove multiple authorship by a sound criterion, evidence of the smoothing away of inconsistencies would be more to the point ; for

[69] Lachmann, *Betrachtungen*, p. 6. Sir M. Bowra, with good insight, says (*Tradition*, p. 225), ' This (the visit to Ethiopia) is mere story. The religious consciousness knows better.'

[70] *Ibid.*, p. 15.

[71] Kirchhoff,[2] pp. 240–54.

such things are much more clearly evident to readers, especially perhaps to persons who are getting the poem by heart, than to the author.

The fact is that the separatist doctrine sprung from a very pardonable misapprehension, and was later supported by another. Wolf, as we have seen, began by stressing the great difficulty, if not impossibility, of composing or learning such works as the Iliad and Odyssey without the aid of writing. Difficult in the extreme it no doubt would be for a modern, for we generally commit but little verbatim to memory, contenting ourselves with remembering the substance of whatever scientific and literary works we have mastered and recollecting where to go for more accurate information. It was not so in Homer's time, nor for that matter in classical Greece. To know by heart 15,000 lines or so was probably not a rare accomplishment then, any more than it seems to have been in Finland; [72] much more remarkable feats are reported of Arabian story-tellers. [73] In an age nearly as dependent upon the written word as ours is, the elder Seneca was able to compose a whole treatise, packed with long quotations, from memory alone. [74] What others are known to have done, it is reasonable enough to suppose Homer doing. But all such speculations are needless, since, as has already been pointed out, writing had been known in that region for long before he or even his people arrived there. On top of this misconception came the theory that was for a while prevalent in the nineteenth century, that much literature and art had grown up, not from the efforts of individuals, but from the people in general. The truth, as we now see it, is that a people can and do condition an art (there could have been no English poetry but for the English language, the creation of the people at large, and certain generally shared ideas as to what constitutes verse), but that art is always and everywhere the creation of individuals, the so-called popular poems, such as ballads, being simply the works of writers, or other composers, so obscure that their names have remained unknown. Nothing remotely like an epic has ever taken shape without a poet to shape it.

It remains to discuss the oldest form of separatism and ask whether the Iliad and Odyssey are by one author or two. That they were by different authors was asserted by a minority of the Alexandrians, [75] and is often assumed in modern times; but the proofs for it are feeble. There is certainly a difference of tone between it and the Iliad, as

[72] Comparetti, *op. cit.*, p. 336; see *ibid.*, p. 70, for the manner in which unwritten Finnish poems were passed from one singer to another.

[73] See van Gennep, *op cit.*, p. 50 *sqq.* For Greece, see, *e.g.*, Xenophon, *Symp.*, iii, 5. Modern instances of a memory capable of containing long works verbatim are fairly plentiful.

[74] Seneca rhetor, *Contr.*, i, praef. 2–3.

[75] Seneca, *de breuit. uit.*, 13, 2; one of the vanities of grammarians is to discuss *prior scripta esset Ilias an Odyssia, praeterea an eiusdem essent auctoris.* Mention of arguments of the chorizontes (so upholders of this theory were called; see further, below, p. 388) schol. Od. xix, 28; Ii. ii, 356, 649; x, 476; xii, 96.

great, say, as that between *Coriolanus* and *The Tempest*. There is some difference in vocabulary, rather more abstract nouns occurring in the Odyssey, for example. There are differences in mythology; Hephaistos is wedded to Aphrodite, not to Charis, and the gods live in the sky, not on Olympos (a distinction without a difference, for the great mountain is a sort of vestibule to heaven; thus Athena in Il. i, 195 comes down 'from heaven' and presently (221) returns 'to Olympos'). There are some few doubtful archaeological differences, such as the passage, discussed above, note 24, in which 'iron' means 'a weapon'. Applying the microscope, more divergences of this sort can be found; yet the general impression is one of uniformity with the Iliad in language, artistry and tone. It is a question of probabilities. Which is likelier, that there should have been one great poet whose two chief, perhaps only, works differed somewhat from each other in choice of plot and consequent minutiae of treatment, or that there were two of about the same age, so like one another that only very close inspection can detect the difference? To the present writer, there can be but one answer; Homer is one, both poems are his, and the changes in manner, such as they are, can be easily explained by supposing the two works to have been written some years apart. Had there been another writer great enough to produce the Odyssey, he would have had a style of his own, differing from Homer's at least as much as that of Sophokles does from Aeschylus.

Having thus rejected separatism in all its forms, we may ask whether any results of value have come from this long aberration of scholarship. The answer is that, like all honest research, that of the separatists has done good to the subject. Not only has it interested many who were not professional scholars (Grote, Schliemann, Bérard, Lang, Shewan), but it has drawn attention to a vast number of details, literary, aesthetic, grammatical, metrical and archaeological, comprehension of which adds greatly to an intelligent reader's enjoyment of these masterpieces. Also, it has given us a far clearer picture than before of the manner in which the epics were composed and published. We have left behind us the picturesque figure of the blind bard, chanting his inspired lays in the childhood or youth of the world. We have instead the more intelligible figure of the Ionian man of literature, probably of letters also, working upon traditional material, taking a legend here, a phrase there, again perhaps a line or two, from the earlier poems with which his memory was stored, and possibly also from rolls jealously guarded as the sacred property of his gild. We can picture him reciting, lyre or staff in hand,[76] before the nobles of his day or at public festivals. We can imagine him instructing pupils to do as he had done. No one is likely to suppose that he sat down

---

[76] Homer himself represents minstrels as carrying a little harp or lyre, φόρμιγξ; in Hesiod, *Theog.*, 30, the Muses meet him and give him a laurel staff to carry. That this represents a transition from sung to recited poetry I do not believe; rather, the epics seem to me to have been delivered in a kind of recitative. like some Highland narrative poems.

and, beginning at Il. i, 1, wrote steadily on till he reached the end of the Odyssey. Nor does any one imagine that a *ne uarietur* edition of his words, too sacred to have a single letter altered, passed into the hands of those who came after him. On the contrary, it is highly probable that small alterations and insertions were made here and there,[77] certain that the language was gradually modernized, as has happened to most English classics, by no means unlikely that one or two details were the work of pupils, not of the master himself. Substantially, we have Homer complete and perfect ; in detail, we must count on retouchings and allow for them to the extent of our knowledge and ingenuity in restoration.

The poems, when composed, seem to have become the property of a gild or clan, the Homeridai,[78] who gave them the only form of publication usual or indeed possible in that age, by recitation. These men were, in some cases at least, themselves poets. It is

[77] For what they are worth, I record my guesses concerning interpolations, apart from short additions of a line or two. Iliad : ii, 484–877 may be from another document ; xii, 19–23 contain a list of river-names largely unknown to Homer and the unhomeric word ἡμίθεοι, ' demigods ', applied in Hesiodic manner (*Op. et Di.*, 159–60) to the heroes of Homer's poems ; the rivers also recall a similar list, *Theog.*, 340 *sqq.* I am inclined to excise the whole passage, 10–34, supposing it to be the insertion of an archaeologically minded rhapsode, who wished to explain why there was no trace of the Greek wall left in the Troad. If this is so, he altered 35 slightly to fit his insertion. xiv, 315–27, the ' Leporello-catalogue ' of the former loves of Zeus ; xviii, 39–49, the Hesiodic catalogue of sea-nymphs ; xxi, 383–514, see above, note 19 ; perhaps one or two of the minor ' events ' of the sports in xxiii. Odyssey : xi, 225–332, 566–632, as being mythological insertions of no particular point or utility ; the passages discussed in notes 21 and 24 ; perhaps the episode xxiv, 1–204. Needless to say, I am not the first to object to any of these passages, and many of them were suspected in antiquity.

An amusing parallel to the rise and fall of the separatist theories may be given from Middle English philology. In 1902, a theory was put forward and rapidly gained ground to the effect that *Piers Plowman* was the work of a plurality of authors ; see *Camb. Hist. Eng. Lit.*, vol. ii, p. 3 *sqq.* To-day, as my late colleague A. Blyth Webster informed me, scarcely a philologist of any eminence takes it seriously. In the case of Homer, the paradox has had a longer run.

[78] First named by Pindar, *Nem.*, ii, 1 ; how old they were in his time, we do not know. The scholiast on that passage says they were originally the actual descendants of Homer, ' and so the name passed to rhapsodes who no longer claimed such descent '. He names one in particular, Kynaithos of Chios (one of the places which claimed to be the birthplace of Homer, and often named in the tales concerning him ; it may well have been a principal centre of the Homeridai) who introduced the poems into Syracuse at a date too corrupted in the MSS. to be recoverable with even approximate certainty, and was said to have composed the Hymn to Apollo (see p. 53). More details in Schmid-Stählin, i, pp. 157–8.

largely, no doubt, to them that the comparatively modern form of much of Homer's text is due. At some period, perhaps the seventh century, the poems became well known in Greece proper, and by about the sixth it may be that written copies of them, besides any that the Homeridai themselves possessed, were by no means unheard of. In particular, Athens seems to have become active in passing on the written tradition, and to this fact we may well ascribe the fairly frequent occurrence of Attic forms, foreign both to Ionic and to the mixed dialect of Homer himself, in our text.[79]

Two results, both of considerable importance for literature, arose out of this state of things. Starting from the Iliad and Odyssey, it was natural that poets should wish to tell, and their hearers to listen to, the rest of the story of Troy. That poems dealing with it already existed is highly probable, but it is also quite likely that they were not full-length epics. At all events, we do not know of any long poem of epic character which is not later than the probable date of Homer himself.[80] Gradually, by the work of several hands, there grew up what later ages knew as the Cycle of Epic (ἐπικὸς κύκλος, or simply κύκλος) [81] consisting of the following works, now lost and known only by quotations and a jejune epitome.[82]

[79] Examples of this will be found in Cauer, p. 124 *sqq.* He adduces amongst others ἑωσφόρος, Il. xxiii, 226 (Ionic says ἠὼς and Aiolic αὔως for ' dawn ') ; βεβῶσα, Od. xx, 14 (Ionic would not contract) ; ἤντο, Il. iii, 153 (Ionic ἥατο). He is on less certain ground when he urges, p. 126, that the poems must have passed through a stage in which they were written in the old Attic alphabet, which used E for ε, η and certain occurrences of ει, O similarly for ο, ου, ω. That they were once in an alphabet of this kind is shown by such corruptions as ὠλεσίκαρπος (for οὐ—), περιώσιος (——ούσιος), ἔγρετο (ἤγρετο) in several parts of the poems ; but as our knowledge of the earliest Greek alphabets is still far from complete, it is rash to assume that such a method of writing was never used in Ionia.

[80] A possible exception is the cyclic *Thebais* ; see below, p. 51.

[81] The phrase (ἐπικὸς) κύκλος is found only in late writers, such as Proclus (see below, note 82) ; references in Schmid-Stählin, p. 196, note 3. But the adjective κυκλικός is certainly in Horace (*ars poet.*, 136), who draws upon Neoptolemos of Parion (see below, p. 399), and is to be found in Kallimachos (epigr. 30, 1 Mair) and other Alexandrians. Here, however, it is not clear whether it means ' belonging to the Cycle ', for it was also used in the sense of ' found on every hand, commonplace, trivial ', see Merkel, *Apollonii Argonautica*, Proleg., p. xxxi and Liddell & Scott (ed. 9), *s.u.* The fundamental discussion of the word is in Pt. i of Welcker, *Cyclus* : older views outlined *ibid.*, pp. 419–55.

[82] Proclus, or Proculus, who died A.D. 485, wrote a *Chrestomathia* or handbook of literature, including an account of the Cycle with epitomes of its various poems. It is likely that he did not read them for himself,

I. The *Kypria* (Poem of Cyprus ; the reason for the title is
not clear), divided in later times into eleven books. Zeus plans
to relieve Earth (Ge-Themis) of the burden of the too numerous
human race, by a great war. Arising out of the incidents of the
Apple of Discord and the Judgement of Paris [83] the Rape of
Helen takes place ; Helen's brothers, Kastor and Polydeukes,
have meanwhile passed out of mortal life as a result of the fight
with Idas and Lynkeus. Menelaos, informed of Helen's departure, takes counsel with Agamemnon and Nestor ; the fleet
assembles at Aulis, an abortive attempt to reach Troy is made,
ending with the descent on Mysia and subsequent withdrawal ;
the fleet reassembles, Iphigeneia is brought to sacrifice but rescued
by Artemis. Finally Troy is reached, Philoktetes being left
behind at Lemnos ; Achilles, who has had sight of Helen, restrains
the Greeks from departing. Several minor battles and sieges
take place. Palamedes is put to death. Zeus plans to ease
matters for the Trojans by detaching Achilles from the Greeks.

This poem, ascribed by many to Homer himself, was adjudged
by some critics to be the work of a certain STASINOS, or of
HEGESIAS, both very vague figures to us ; it is much to be
doubted whether they were less so to the ancients, or anything
was really known about them. The best writers give no name,
merely citing ' the author of the Kypria ', and similar anonymity
is observed for the other poems of the Cycle. [84] It is said, how-

but went to some older synopsis of their contents for his information.
His work is lost, but we have fairly copious extracts from it in the
Bibliotheca of the patriarch Photios and other Byzantine works. Thus
we read a shortened epitome of an epitome of the original poems. Such
as it is, it will be found in Allen, *Homeri Opera*, vol. v, p. 93 *sqq.*, followed
by the fragments. Welcker, *Cyclus*, pt. ii, contains a discussion of the
poems and their authors : for later work, see Schmid-Stählin, i, p. 195
sqq.

[83] These and the other tales will be found briefly told in Rose,
Mythology, chapter viii, pt. 2.

[84] Philodemos, Apollodoros, Pausanias (generally), Clement of Alex-
andria (generally), the best of the scholia, and earlier than any of them,
Herodotos, Plato and Aristotle, name no authors ; Pausanias names
Lesches several times, Agias once ; Clement names them both, also
Arktinos and Eugammon. Proclus and other very late compilers,
Eusebios, and of somewhat earlier writers, Athenaios name them more
or less frequently. The best authority to mention any of them is
Dionysios of Halikarnassos (see below, p. 398) who quotes Arktinos twice
(*Antiquit. Rom.*, i, 68, 2, 69, 3), as the oldest authority he knows on
certain legends connected with Troy. However, a few representations
on vases and other popular works of art mention names of the Cyclic
writers and date from early Hellenistic times. It would seem, then,
that these names are the fruit of some unknown literary researches about

ever, to have ended with a catalogue of the Trojan allies, and on this slender foundation has been built the conjecture, often stated as if it were a fact, that the Catalogue of the Ships (Il. ii, 484–877) was interpolated from the Kypria.[85]

II. Next came a sequel to the Iliad, the *Aithiopis*, ascribed to ARKTINOS of Miletos and noted for the event with which it opened, the coming of Penthesileia and her Amazons. There followed her death at the hands of Achilles, his slaying of Thersites for mocking him when he grieved for her, his purification from the guilt of blood, the arrival of the Ethiopian Memnon, who was slain by Achilles but given immortality by Zeus, and the death of Achilles himself at the hands of Paris and Apollo. The poem concluded its fifth and last book with the funeral of Achilles and the quarrel between Odysseus and Aias son of Telamon for his armour.

Little though we know of this work, the idea of purification for manslaying and that of immortality given to a man are non-Homeric and help us to assign a provisional date ; in or about the seventh century the cult of Apollo began its insistence (perhaps Oriental in origin) on purifications, and that of Dionysos, which seems to have held out hopes of a sort of deification, became well-known in Greece. This epoch may therefore be the time when Arktinos, or whoever it was, wrote his epic.[86]

contemporary with the beginning of serious Homeric study at Alexandria, but by no means so convincing as to be accepted without question. For more detail about them, see Welcker, *Cyclus*, pt. ii, and the relevant arts. in Pauly-Wissowa.

[85] What seems to me totally unbelievable is the idea that we have, here or elsewhere in Homer, insertions due to Athenian vanity (cf. note 79 for the influence of Athens on the text of Homer). That so proud a people, if they had an opportunity to foist interpolations into the poems, should have given their own ancestors so slight and insignificant a rôle as they play in the Iliad (the city is named twice and its inhabitants six times, never as accomplishing any noteworthy deed), and practically omitted them from the Odyssey (Athena once goes to Athens, Od. vii, 80), proves, if indeed these are the fruits of attempted alteration of the text, complete and utter failure, arising from the poems being already too well known and established for changes to be possible without detection ; far more likely they are the poet's own mentions of a city certainly in existence in his day and long before it.

[86] There is another faint indication of date. The François vase represents the marriage of Peleus and Thetis ; the Chest of Kypselos, described by Pausanias, v, 17, 5—19, 10, was decorated with a number of scenes comprising events from the whole Trojan War and the wanderings of Odysseus, *i.e.*, corresponding to the contents of the *Kypria, Aithiopis, Little Iliad* and *Sack*, besides the Homeric poems. These works of art being of the sixth century, the poems may very well have been known then, which makes the seventh a reasonable date for them ; but we are

III, IV. According to Proclus, the *Little Iliad*, ascribed to
LESCHES of Mytilene, was the next poem in the series ; it consisted of four books, carrying the story down from the Judgement of the Arms and the consequent madness and suicide of
Aias to the reception of the Wooden Horse into Troy. Then
came the *Sack of Ilion* ('Ιλίου Πέρσις), another poem by Arktinos,
in two books, containing the capture of the çity and the departure
of the Greeks with their booty, while Athena planned their
destruction at sea in punishment for the rape of Kassandra.
But the matter is not really so simple, for enough fragments
remain of the *Aithiopis* to tell us that the suicide of Aias was
mentioned in that. Hence it and the *Little Iliad* overlapped.
Various explanations are possible, one being that the *Little Iliad*
was a kind of synopsis of the *Aithiopis* and *Sack* ; but we have no
sufficient evidence.

V. There followed the *Nostoi*, or *Returns*, said to be the
work of AGIAS, or more properly HAGIAS,[87] of Troizen. It described, in five books, the various fortunes of Neoptolemos and
Kalchas, who went home by land, Nestor and Diomedes, who
sailed straight back across the open sea, and the others, who took
the usual coastal and island route and met with various disasters.
One prominent event was the murder of Agamemnon. Of
Hagias, if he really was the author of this poem, nothing is known ;
if it is true that he was a Peloponnesian, he probably is relatively
late, since the school of epic poetry must have taken some time
to spread from Ionia to the mother country ; that he should
represent a very old, pre-Ionian school of composition which had
survived the Dorian migration is most unlikely, for his name
shows that he was a Dorian himself. At all events, the few
fragments we have of his poem are in the usual epic dialect.

VI. Last of this series is the *Telegonia*, or story of Telegonos,
attributed to one EUGAMMON of Kyrene. If he was the author,
or if the poem contained any indication that it was written at
Kyrene, it can hardly be earlier than the sixth century.[88] The

not sure that the artists went to epics for their information, although it
is likely, nor can we say how long the poems had been in existence when
they were thus used.

[87] The Greek *h*, never very strongly aspirated, was dropped altogether
in the later forms of the language and does not exist in the modern speech.
Hence it has often to be restored.

[88] Kyrene was founded about 631 B.C., and did not become important
till the arrival of more colonists under its third king, Battos II. The
chronologists place the *floruit* of Eugammon in 566. See Clinton, *Fasti
Hellenici*, under these years. One object of the poem seems to have
been to connect the royal house of Kyrene with Odysseus.

plot continued the Odyssey. Teiresias (see above, p. 26) had told Odysseus that when he came home he must, after settling matters with the wooers, go away again inland, carrying an oar, until he met some one who took the oar for a winnowing-fan, among a people who ate no salt, and had never heard of the sea. There he was to make an offering to Poseidon, return home, sacrifice to all the gods, and settle down to await a quiet death ' from the sea ' in his old age. This gave the later poet an opportunity, first to send Odysseus on some rather pointless travels, next to introduce the very old motif [89] of the son who fights his unknown father. Telegonos, Odysseus' son by Kirke, had learned who his father was and went to look for him. Landing in Ithake, he was mistaken for a pirate and in the ensuing fight killed Odysseus with a spear pointed with fishbone, thus literally fulfilling the prophecy. Telemachos then married Kirke and Telegonos Penelope, Kirke making all the mortals concerned immortal. This rather fantastic tale occupied two books.

Apart from these supplements to Homer, several other ancient epics existed. There was (VII) a *Titanomachia*, obviously dealing with the accession of Zeus to the lordship of the universe ; it consisted of at least two books and was variously ascribed to ARKTINOS and to EUMELOS of Corinth [90]. (VIII) An *Oidipodeia* or Story of Oidipus was attributed to KINAITHON (a Lakedaimonian poet, of whom more will be said later) and extended to 6,600 lines.[91] A *Thebais* (IX), or *Epic of Thebes*, 7,000 lines long, told the story of the attack of the Seven and the events leading up to it. It was long ascribed to Homer himself, and Pausanias reckons it next best to the Iliad and Odyssey.[92] Continuing this was (X) the *Epigonoi*, *i.e.*, the story of the second and successful attack by the children of the Seven ; it was credited also to Homer, though as early as Herodotos' time some doubted this, or to ANTIMACHOS, which is absurd if it means the Antimachos dealt with below, p. 315, but much less unlikely if it is Antimachos of Teos, who is said to have lived in the middle of the eighth century B.C.[93] All that we can say with any certainty is that it is later than the *Thebais*, for it opened ' And now, ye

---

[89] An interesting collection of examples, with very hazardous explanations of the genesis of the story, in M. A. Potter, *Sohrab and Rustem*, London, David Nutt, 1902.
[90] See Allen, *Homeri opera*, v, p. 110.
[91] *Ibid.*, p. 111.
[92] *Ibid.*, p. 112 ; the passage of Pausanias is ix, 9, 5. The first line was Ἄργος ἄειδε, θεά, πολυδίψιον, ἔνθεν ἄναχτες, an evident imitation of the beginning of the Iliad.
[93] *Ibid.*, p. 115.

Muses, let us begin the tale of the younger men ', in obvious allusion to the story of their fathers, already told. Finally, three poems of which little or nothing is known were believed by some to be Homeric, though they are not reckoned as part of the Cycle, the *Departure of Amphiaraos* ('Αμφιαράου ἐξέλασις) (XI), if indeed this was not a part of the *Thebais*, imagined to be a separate poem by late writers who had never read either ; the (XII) *Capture of Oichalia*, variously attributed to Homer himself and to a figure of the legend concerning him, KREOPHYLOS of Samos, who had once received him hospitably ; and (XIII) a poem called the *Phokais*, of unknown content.[94]

This dry enumeration of lost poems and vague authors has been necessary because of the great influence the poems in question exercised on the later imaginative literature of Greece. Their surviving fragments do not give the impression that they were great works ; but their authors were in the Homeric tradition, at least to some extent, could write tolerable hexameters, and had hold of, or perhaps in some cases invented, a number of interesting legends. On these later poets drew as on a rich storehouse, from which came themes for choral lyric, tragedy, and other forms of composition, to say nothing of the use made of these venerable documents by historians and mythographers.

The other result of the Homerids' activities was the production of what are called the *Homeric Hymns*. It was a common custom to introduce a recitation of epic by an invocation, long or short, of a god, particularly the god at whose festival the rhapsode was displaying his powers. Given sufficient poetical talents, a Homerid might treat his audience, and the local deity, to a new poem of merit, before going on to the Iliad or the *Kypria* ; he might on the other hand content himself with a dozen or half a dozen pious verses of no great importance. Both these kinds of prelude (προοίμιον), as the hymns were often called, find a place in our collection, which is preserved more or less complete in a number of MSS. Out of a total of thirty-three, six are of more importance than the rest ; they are Nos. ii (to Demeter), iii (to Apollo ; really two poems patched together into one), iv (to Hermes), v (to Aphrodite), vii (to Dionysos) and xix (to Pan).

The others are : i, to Dionysos, fragmentary and manifestly of Alexandrian date ; vi, another address to Aphrodite ; viii, to Ares ; ix, to Artemis ; x, again to Aphrodite ; xi, tq Athena ; xii, to Hera ; xiii, to Demeter (three lines long) ; xiv, to the Mother of the Gods,

---

⁹⁴ See Allen, *Homeri opera*, v, pp. 144-7.

and therefore not earlier than the introduction of her cult, in the fifth
century B.C. ;   xv, to Herakles Lion-Hearted ;   xvi, to Asklepios ;
xvii, to the Dioskuroi ;   xviii, again to Hermes ;   xx, to Hephaistos ;
xxi, again to Apollo ;   xxii, to Poseidon ;   xxiii, to Ƶeus (four lines) ;
xxiv, to Hestia ;   xxv, to the Muses and Apollo ;   xxvi, again to
Dionysos ;   xxvii, again to Artemis ;   xxviii, again to Athena ;   xxix,
again to Hestia ;   xxx, to Earth the Mother of All ;   xxxi, to Helios
(perhaps for a festival in Rhodes, the only place which had a sun-cult) ;
xxxii, to Selene, the moon-goddess ;   xxxiii, again to the Dioskuroi.

The Hymn to Demeter is one of the best, a little epic in itself,
dealing in 495 really poetical and eloquent lines with the story
of Demeter's sorrows ; how Persephone was carried off by Hades
and searched for by her mother, who in her wanderings came to
Eleusis,[95] and after the restoration of her daughter inaugurated
her Mysteries there.   Since Athens is not mentioned in this
connexion, Eleusis must have been independent when the
Hymn was written. It was annexed somewhere about 610 B.C. ·
therefore a seventh-century date is consistent with this piece
of evidence, and not contradicted by anything else in the
poem.

The Hymn to Apollo of Delos (iii, 1–178) is perhaps the earliest
of all, for it tells a somewhat unusual legend, and says something
of its author.   The date cannot be exactly determined, but it is
a good deal later than Homer himself, for the writer has forgotten
how stiff the Homeric bow is ; in line 6, Leto unstrings Apollo's
bow for him, and even a Titaness would risk her fingers in handling
the divine counterpart of so formidable an instrument as that
which Pandaros and Odysseus use (see note 25).   Then, one of
the many Homeric passages which he imitates is the ' Leporello-
catalogue ' (see note 77) and one phrase seems taken from
Hesiod.   The story is that of the birth of Apollo, but the author
makes Artemis to be born several days before her brother, and
attributes Leto's difficulty in finding a place for her confinement
to the terror which the world feels, not of Hera's anger, but of
the new god's appalling power.   At the end of the poem, the
poet says that he is a blind man, dwelling ' in craggy Chios ',
a source, if not the source, of the later idea that Homer was a
blind Chian bard.   Perhaps if we suppose this ingenious poet,
for such he was, to have lived late in the eighth century, we shall
not be far wrong.

The Hymn to Apollo of Delphoi (iii, 179–end) is a later
composition, imitating the earlier to the extent of borrowing a

[95] For the hymn, see Allen-Halliday, pp. 2 *sqq.*, 108 *sqq.* ; for the legend,
Rose, *Mythology*, pp. 91–4.

line and some phrases from it. It is much poorer as poetry, but full of interest for the large number of mythological and geographical references it contains. Apollo chooses a site for his temple, fixes on Delphoi, kills the dragon (a female in this version of the myth), punishes the spring-nymph Telphusa for sending him to so dangerous a place, and brings a shipload of Cretans to be priests at his shrine. The author may well have been a Boiotian of Hesiod's school, for he clearly knew Boiotia well ; he pretty certainly wrote before 586, for he says nothing of the chariot-races which were then introduced into the Pythian Games, and he may be a good deal earlier. His hymn has been rather unskilfully stuck on to the end of that to the Delian Apollo.[96]

Hermes is honoured by a hymn (iv) which is thoroughly delightful and completely non-moral. The poet laughs with and at his god, telling the tale of how Hermes, the day he was born, invented the lyre and stole Apollo's cattle, and of the reconciliation between the divine brothers. The clearest indication of date is that the lyre has seven strings ; as this is said to have been the invention of Terpandros (see below, p. 104), who was alive in 676 B.C., we cannot put the poem earlier than his time, and it is likelier to be later, for the language has departed a great way from Homeric usage ; in particular, the digamma is much neglected. Of the author we know nothing.[97]

The Hymn to Aphrodite (v) is to the goddess's discredit, for it tells how Zeus, to punish her for the ravages she had made among the deities, made her fall in love with a mortal, Anchises the Trojan ; how she came to him in the guise of a mortal woman, and obtained her desire ; and how, having revealed herself to him, she foretold the birth of Aineias. Yet even so, she is not the conventional Venus of Ovidian poetry, but retains something of the dignity which belonged to her in the original myth (the mating of the Great Mother with a lover whose whole *raison d'être* was to render her fertile). The writer, whoever he may have been, was a good poet, and probably a fairly early one, though nothing like an exact date can be fixed.[98] His last line is one of the regular reciters' formulae ; we find ' I will make mention of thee and of another song also ' (αὐτὰρ ἐγὼ καὶ σεῖο καὶ ἄλλης μνήσομ' ἀοιδῆς) at the conclusion of several hymns,

[96] See Allen-Halliday, p. 183 ; Dornseiff, p. 1 *sqq.*, argues for the two hymns being really one.

[97] *Ibid.*, p. 267 *sqq.*

[98] *Ibid.*, p. 349 *sqq.* ; for the legend, see Rose in *Class. Quart.*, xvii (1924), 11 *sqq.*

while others, like this one, have ' Beginning from thee, I will pass to another chant ' (σεῦ δ' ἐγὼ ἀρξάμενος μεταβήσομαι ἄλλον ἐς ὕμνον).

Dionysos (vii) has also a hymn of unknown date and authorship, of which we can say only that it is not very late ; it tells the legend of the god's capture by the Tyrrhenian pirates and the miracle by which he turned them into dolphins. It is but fifty-nine lines long.[99] The hymn to Pan (xix) is even shorter, forty-nine lines, and probably not early, for Pan was scarcely known outside his native Arkadia till about the sixth century or later.[100] It has an original turn ; the legend, Pan's birth and his presentation to Olympos by his proud father Hermes, is not told directly by the poet, but put into the mouths of Pan's company, the mountain-nymphs.

Lastly, the Epic movement, as it grew old, produced a few trifles, including parodies. The most famous of these in antiquity was the *Margites*, apparently a mock-heroic tale of a rich and would-be clever man who ' knew many works, but knew them all ill ' (fr. 3, Allen), for ' the gods made him neither delver nor ploughman nor in any wise skilful, but he failed of every trade ' (fr. 2). He was so muddle-headed that he asked his mother whose child he was, hers or his father's (fr. 4). The life and adventures of this figure of folktale were set forth in hexameters mixed at irregular intervals with iambics (see Chapter IV), and Aristotle thought well of the poem, since he declares [101] that it is in the same relation to comedy as the Iliad and Odyssey are to tragedy. A less-known work was the *Kerkopes*, dealing with certain mischievous persons so named, who were turned into monkeys.[102] One poem of this class survives, the *Batrachomyomachia*, or *Battle of the Frogs and Mice*. It is rather poor fun. A frog drowns a mouse, and war breaks out in consequence. The gods consult, and resolve to remain neutral. But the fighting, in which frog-heroes with names such as Puff-Cheek (Physignathos), Mud-Lier (Borborokoites) and Leek-Green (Prassaios) are hard pressed by the champions of the mice, Cheese-Eater (Tyrophagos), Lick-Platter (Leichopinax), Snatch-Crumb (Psicharpax) and others, rages until Zeus puts a stop to it by sending an army of crabs which rout the mice. This and *Margites* were alike attributed by some to one PIGRES, a Karian of whom Suidas says that he was a brother of Queen Artemisia,

---

[99] Allen-Halliday, pp. 76 *sqq.*, 375 *sqq.*   [100] *Ibid.*, p. 402 *sqq.*

[101] Arist., *Poetics*, 1448ᵇ 38. For the remains of the poem, see Allen, *Homeri opera*, v, p. 152 *sqq.*

[102] See Allen, *ibid.*, p. 159.

who fought at Salamis,[103] and that he produced an Iliad turned into elegiacs by adding a pentameter to every line. If there is any truth in this, the poem was written about 500 B.C.; but certainly the text as we have it has been much interpolated, for not only does it contain a number of lines, excised by modern editors, of manifestly Byzantine workmanship, but its opening verses are a patent imitation of Kallimachos.[104]

Scattered up and down the Lives of Homer there are a number of short pieces, all in respectable epic verse and dialect, and so fairly old, said to have been composed by him on various occasions; they include an address to certain potters, invoking blessings on their work if they are generous to him, but a plague of pot-spoiling imps if they are not; an epitaph on one Midas, so contrived that it will make equally good sense whichever line one begins at; an Eiresione, or song to be sung by children bearing a sort of maypole from house to house and asking, according to old custom, for contributions of food and the like; and several other slight compositions, attributed to Homer simply because they were in hexameters and no one knew who had written them. They are collectively known as the Homeric Epigrams.

[103] Suidas, s.u. Πίγρης : he speaks of Artemisia as ' famous in wars ', which suits Xerxes' contemporary, but goes on to call her wife of Maussollos, the famous satrap in whose memory the Maussolleion (persistently miswritten Mausoleum in modern times, a barbarism comparable only to ' coliseum ' for colosseum) was built. His wife also was called Artemisia, and Suidas or his authority has confused the two women. Plutarch, de Herod. malig., 873 f., says simply Πίγρης δ 'Αρτεμισίας ; ἀδελφὸς has probably fallen out.

[104] See Pfeiffer in Hermes, 1925, p. 319. The resemblance is especially close between Batr. 3, ἣν νέον ἐν δέλτοισιν ἐμοῖς ἐπὶ γούνασι θῆκα and the fragment of Kallimachos, 1, 21-2 Pfeiffer, [καὶ γὰρ ὅτ]ε πρ[ώ]τισ[το]ν ἐμοῖς ἐπὶ δέλτον ἔθηκα [γούνασι]ν.

CHAPTER III

HESIOD AND THE HESIODIC SCHOOLS

THE poets we have dealt with thus far have all in common one characteristic. They are the spokesmen of deity, and their own personality counts for comparatively little. Their learning, and the inspiration which enables them to sing sweetly for the delight of men, comes from above, from the Muses, or a Muse, or from Apollo. This attitude never was quite lost [1] during the whole classical period, and has remained as a convention down to modern times ; but it was inevitable among a people so strongly individualistic as the Greeks that the poet's own thoughts and feelings should, sooner or later, be expressed as such. We have now to trace the result of a growing emergence of individuality in the utterances of poets.

The earliest who tells us something of himself and puts forward his thoughts as his own, not merely as the dictation of the Muses, is HESIOD ('Ησίοδος, in Aiolic Αἰσίοδος, in the later Boiotian orthography Εἰσίοδος ; the first spelling is that of the poet himself) of Askra, an insignificant Boiotian town at the foot of Mount Helikon, and therefore in the Muses' own region, for they had an ancient cult on the mountain. His father was a native of Kyme in the Aiolid, who left home to seek his fortune, it would appear,[2] settled in the new country, and there died, leaving his estate between two sons, Hesiod and Perses. The brothers did not agree ; Perses squandered his share of the inheritance and then tried, with what success we do not know, to get his brother's

---

[1] Hence the estimate of poets as late as the fifth century and beyond ; they are inspired (Plat., *Rep.*, i, 331e, Simonides is not only σοφός but also θεῖος), and therefore instructors of the rest of mankind (Aristophanes, *Frogs*, 686, where he speaks of his chorus as ' holy ' also, but that is because they are in the service of Dionysos ; 1030 *sqq.* ; *Wasps*, 1043, he half-seriously calls himself ἀλεξίκακος, or ' averter of evil ', properly a divine title, and καθαρτής, a purifier of the country ; cf. *Acharnians*, 648 *sqq.*, and many other passages).

[2] See *Works and Days* (hereafter abbreviated *W.D.*), 633 *sqq.*

as well, by bribing the local authorities, ' kings ' as Hesiod calls them, still using the Homeric name, barons as we might say, in whose hands lay the government of the country and the administration of justice. Hesiod therefore addressed to his brother a poetical remonstrance, coupled with much good advice, the first proclamation in Europe of what it has been the fashion to call the gospel of labour. ' No work is a reproach, idleness is a reproach,' is his text,[3] and the kind of work which he recommends is agriculture, the hard life of the peasant-farmer, which nevertheless has its compensations, for it keeps hunger and want away, and even its pleasures. This open letter, so to call it, must have been intended for recitation in public from the first, for there was no other way of circulating it ; it is in Homeric hexameters, for Hesiod knew of no other literary form, and had mastered that one, when and where we do not know, but certainly under Ionian influence, for he writes in the epic dialect with but little trace of Boiotian. It survives, not much damaged or altered, and reveals its author as a man, not indeed of the transcendent genius of Homer, but of great talent, coupled with a vigorous and bold tendency to think for himself, and an interest in ethics and the systematization of knowledge in which we can already see the germs of those qualities of the Greek genius destined to originate the philosophy, morality and science of the whole western world.

The contents of the poem are briefly as follows :

1–10. Invocation of the Muses to sing the praise of Zeus the almighty. Zeus, hear me, and grant justice. I will tell Perses a true thing.

11–41. Perses, there are two kinds of strife, one evil, the other good ; the good is emulation.

42–105. For it is the will of Zeus [5] that livelihood should be hard to find ; else a man might earn in a day enough to keep

[3] W.D., 311. It seems possible that the Boiotian gentry of that day were infected with the idea, prevalent at various times in Europe, and not unnatural in a warlike aristocracy, but not Homeric, that manual labour is degrading. Perses and Hesiod were of good family (δῖον γένος, 299) ; the former perhaps was trying to live in a manner suited to his ideas of his rank but above his resources.

[4] The fashion, once prevalent, of dissecting the W.D., has lost favour even with scholars who still hold the separatist theory of Homer. The only question now seriously debated is whether the ' Days ' are not a later addition to the poem. Small insertions here and there may reasonably be suspected. See, for recent discussion, Sinclair, pp. ix–xvi.

[5] Hesiod first says ' the gods ' and then ' Zeus ' ; a very interesting proof that to him the two expressions meant much the same. He was on the road to a philosophical monotheism.

him a year. Zeus was wroth when Prometheus stole fire, and so sent a woman, Pandora, created by Hephaistos and adorned with the gifts of all the gods.[6] Prometheus' foolish brother, Epimetheus, received her, and she opened the jar in which all evils were kept, letting them loose ; only hope remained, caught under the lid of the jar.

106–201. There have been five ages of the world ; first came the Golden Age, in which men lived without toil, never grew old, and died as if they were falling asleep. Kronos was king then. These men were turned by Zeus into good daimones, who walk the earth guarding mortal men and giving them wealth. Next came the Silver Age ; the people of that time were much inferior. They took a hundred years to grow up, and did not live long after reaching maturity. Zeus destroyed them, because they were unjust to each other and neglected the worship of the gods ; but they too became daimones, living underground. Next, in the Bronze Age, all was strife ; they were a mighty race, who fought and in the end destroyed one another with bronze weapons, for they had no iron. Zeus then created the race of heroes, which was better and more righteous ; they were demigods, and having died in the great wars at Thebes [7] and Troy, they went to the Islands of the Blessed. Would I had died sooner or were not yet born ! [8] for now is the Age of Iron, which is very vile and will grow steadily worse.

202–212. A fable for princes : a nightingale was caught by a hawk, and lamented ; but the hawk said ' Why lament ? Might is right '.

213–247. Perses, seek after righteousness and flee iniquity

---

[6] This is one of the most puzzling passages in Greek. Pandora is the All-Giver, *i.e.*, the earth-goddess ; Hesiod implies that she is the receiver of ' all gifts ', which is doing violence to the etymology to fit his story. She appears as a sort of Eve, the first woman, apparently, and the bringer of evil into the world. The allegory is confused; is hope thought of as an evil ? if not, why should it be in the jar (which by the way is not a ' box ', and is not said to have belonged to Pandora) ? A recent discussion of the story, with numerous references to earlier work, has been published in *Bullet. Assoc. G. Budé*, avril 1929, pp. 3–36 (L. Séchan). Cf. S. M. Adams in *Class. Rev.*, xlvi (1932), pp. 193–6, and for a different view, Sinclair on *W.D.*, 96. See p. 79.

[7] Not, however, the familiar War of the Seven, nor that of the Epigonoi ; they were slain ' fighting for the sheep of Oidipus ' (163), a form of the story not otherwise known.

[8] If this is to be pressed, Hesiod believes that a better time (a recommencement of the whole cycle ?) is coming, a doctrine very familiar in later days, see Seeliger in Roscher, *Lex.*, art. *Weltalter*, for detailed discussion.

and frowardness ; for heaven sends prosperity to the righteous, but ruin upon the wicked, both themselves and their city.

248–274. Princes, beware ; the gods see the ways of men, Zeus has innumerable [9] unseen emissaries who observe our doings ; Justice is his own daughter, and he hears her complaints ; also his eye sees everything.

275–285. Therefore, Perses, listen to Justice ; beasts have none, it is the attribute of men, given them by Zeus, who will bounteously reward the just.

286–380. Hear, Perses ; it is easy to be evil, hard to be excellent ; therefore listen to my good counsel, cast aside false shame, work, and shun dishonest ways. (Here follows a series of proverb-like sayings, or gnomes, recommending caution, economy and moderation.)

381–764. If you would know how to work, this is the way. Reap when the Pleiads rise,[10] plough when they set ; do not spare your labour. Get a house, a wife and a plough-ox ; provide necessary implements, do not borrow them, for that loses time. Get in timber after midsummer, and make your utensils, including two ploughs of different kinds. Plough when the cranes cry, at the beginning of autumn ; if you wait for winter you will probably get no harvest worth speaking of. Plough again in spring. Do not lounge in the smithy. Prepare in summer for the biting winter cold, when thick clothes are wanted. Here follows an account of the proper seasons, dated by the heliacal risings of constellations and other natural phenomena, for various farming operations. It is diversified by a picture, 582–596, of a picnic under the shade of a rock in the heat of summer, and an excursus, 618–694, on navigation. This section of the poem ends with another series of miscellaneous precepts, on the right age for marriage, prudence in money and family matters, decency and the observance of certain tabus.

765–928, a calendar of lucky and unlucky days of the (lunar) month.

Hesiod's poem looks at life through the eyes of a peasant, not of a noble, and its ethics are narrow, leaving but little room for generosity, charity, or sympathy with the weak and unfortunate. It countenances childish superstitions which Homer has outgrown. Yet it does insist, with an earnestness which he lacks,

---

[9] Literally ' thrice ten thousand ' ; but as μυρίοι commonly means ' innumerable ', ' incalculably many ', this is not 30,000 but ' far beyond all counting '.

[10] *I.e.*, when they and the sun rise together, the heliacal rising ; the usual meaning in dates of this sort.

on the existence of justice as a universal principle, the especial care of the greatest god. It also is more reflective, and shows that not uncommon mark of the beginnings of reflection, pessimism of a much deeper kind than his. Its attitude towards women is decidedly more illiberal than that of epic ; a good wife is indeed the best prize a man can win (702), but a bad one is the greatest curse ; generally speaking women are a snare and a temptation (373–5), and Pandora was the origin of all our woes. The view of society has analogies to that of *Piers Plowman* ; the present state of things is bad, but Hesiod has no political scheme for putting it right. His remedy is rather that the existing governors should do their duty, namely to practise justice and so win the approval and favour of Zeus, while the lower orders devote themselves to honest hard work.

It was the local opinion, at any rate in Hadrian's days, that Hesiod did not compose the other poem attributed to him, the *Theogonia*, or *Generation of the Gods*.[11] It is undoubtedly in a style like that of the *Works and Days*, allowing for the large difference in vocabulary which must exist between a poem dealing with agriculture and moral precepts and one which is the first systematic treatise on mythology and cosmogony. A passage near the beginning of the *Theogony* seems to claim it as Hesiod's work, although the wording is a little ambiguous. The Muses, says the poet,[12] ' taught Hesiod a fair song, as he pastured his sheep under holy Helikon ; and this was the first word the goddesses said to me '. One might conceivably understand the ' fair song ' as being the *Works and Days*, and take the author of the *Theogony* as contrasting himself with Hesiod ; but it is far more natural to suppose that he refers to himself throughout, first by name and then by the pronoun. When to this we add the almost universal verdict of ancient critics that Hesiod wrote both poems, the general resemblance in style and manner, and the fact that the myth of Prometheus is told half in one poem and half in the other, the likelihood of the two works having one author seems to amount almost to certainty.

The contents of the *Theogony* may be briefly stated as follows : 1–35, introduction ; invocation of the Muses and account of the poet's meeting with them. Here we have the first literary

---

[11] See Pausanias, ix, 31, 4, ' It is the traditional belief of the Boiotians who live about Helikon that Hesiod never wrote anything else than the *Works* ; and even from this they excise the prologue to the Muses (1–8) and allege that the beginning of the poem is the passage about the Strifes (9, or 11) '.

[12] *Theog.*, 22–4.

manifesto in Europe : the Muses say to him ' we know how to tell many lies like to truth ; and we know, when we choose, how to speak truthfully '. The first half of this [13] is taken almost unaltered from the Odyssey ; it seems that Hesiod is declaring himself the representative of a new school of poetry which shall not be concerned with doubtful legends of the heroic past, but with facts, whether of religion, morals or daily life. They then give him a laurel staff and ' breathe wondrous song ' into him.

36–115, second prologue. Let us begin from the Muses, the daughters of Zeus and Mnemosyne (Memory), who sing of all things in heaven and earth.

116–153, the beginnings of things, from Chaos. The marriage and offspring of Heaven and Earth. [14]

154–410. The children of Heaven and Earth, the Titans, rise against their father (Heaven), whom they mutilate and sever from Earth. The marriages and offspring of the Titans.

411–452, an episode ; hymn in honour of Hekate, daughter of the Titan Koios and his wife Phoibe. She is especially favoured of Zeus, and can bring men all manner of blessings. [15]

453–506. The children of Kronos and Rhea. Zeus, the youngest son, rises against his father and ousts him from the sovranty of the universe.

507–616. The birth of Prometheus, son of the Titan Iapetos. He deceives Zeus in apportioning the sacrificial victim between gods and men. He steals fire from heaven. Zeus, in wrath, sends Pandora, the ancestress of women, among men. Prometheus is bound.

617–819. The fight between the children of Kronos and the Titans ; victory of the former.

820–880. Earth bears one more child, the monster Typhoeus, whom Zeus overthrows with his thunderbolts.

881–955. Their enemies being all defeated, the gods, by the advice of Earth, choose Zeus to be their king. His successive marriages and those of the other chief deities.

956–1022. The mortal children of the Sun. The mortal mates and children of goddesses. Transition to the *Ehoiai* (see below).

[13] Line 27, ἴδμεν ψεύδεα πολλὰ λέγειν ἐτύμοισιν ὁμοῖα : cf. Od. xix, 203, ἴσκε ψεύδεα πολλὰ λέγων ἐτύμοισιν ὁμοῖα. See Schmid-Stählin, i, p. 250. Cf. p. 422.

[14] For the myths involved, see Rose, *Mythology*, Chapter ii.

[15] Why Hekate in particular, who is usually an insignificant goddess apart from her much later popularity with sorcerers, is not clear. The scholiast supposes that she was especially worshipped in Boiotia, but we have no evidence of this. The authenticity of the passage has been seriously doubted, but cf. F. Solmsen, *Hesiod and Aeschylus* (Ithaca, N.Y., 1949), 51 n. 169.

It is plain that we have here at once a theological or mythological treatise and a sort of introduction to universal history.
The poem is less interesting than the *Works and Days*, by reason
of the long enumerations of names which fill a great part of it
and are the earliest examples of the ' catalogue-poetry ' characteristic of the Hesiodic school. There is truth in the complaint
of Quintilian,[16] that ' Hesiod seldom reaches any great height,
and much of his work is taken up with names ', or at least it will
seem so until we realize that he is not trying to entertain, but
rather to edify. Like his contemporary Amos, he is a prophet,[17]
but unlike him, he is trying to set forth in something like a systematic form his idea of the structure and divine government of
the universe. To do this, he uses the names and legends of the
gods worshipped by his people ; to what extent he believed in
the literal truth of their history, how much, if any, was allegory
to him and how much he himself altered or invented, we cannot
know, since we have no other evidence for early Greek thought
except Homer. He supplements the traditional gods at any
rate with others less known (it is doubtful what cult, if any, most
of his Titans received in Greece), and with a vast number of
abstractions, such as Strife and her children Toil, Forgetfulness,
Hunger, Pains, and a dozen more, all descended from Night.[18]
He seems to make concrete deities into abstract ones now and
then, as when he represents Love (Eros), who was a local god of
Thespiai in Boiotia, as a great cosmic power, child without
father of the primaeval Chaos.[19] To him, the very word ' god '
(θεός) had taken on an abstract meaning, for he even says that
rumour (φήμη) ' is not altogether made of none avail when many
people speak it ; surely, it also is a god '. In other words, what
we call public opinion, for which no individual seems to be
responsible, is another manifestation of divine power working
in and through men.[20]

A third work was attributed to Hesiod in antiquity by nearly
universal consent [21] ; this was the *Catalogue of Women* (κατάλογος

---

[16] *Inst. orat.*, x, 1, 52, echoing conventional Greek criticism of a purely
stylistic and rhetorical kind.

[17] The comparison is made by Kern, *Relig. d. Gr.*, i, p. 266 (see the whole
chapter for sympathetic comment on Hesiod as a religious teacher),
following Wilamowitz-Möllendorff, *Antigonos von Karystos*, p. 314.

[18] *Theog.*, 226 sqq.   [19] *Ibid.*, 120 sqq.

[20] *W.D.*, 763–4 ; is this the ultimate origin of *uox populi uox dei* ?

[21] It is rejected by Pausanias (see note 11) and the scholiast on Pindar,
who once cites frag. 123 Rzach as by Hesiod ' they say ', and once as
' attributed to Hesiod ' (Pyth., iii, 52 ; 14). For the title, see Hesych.
s.u. (᾽Ηοῖαι· ὁ κατάλογος ῾Ησιόδου) and *Etymolog. Gudianum s.u.*

γυναικῶν), otherwise known as the Ehoiai ('Hoῖαι), from the fact that each section of it began with the words ἢ οἵη, ' or such as (was Alkmene, Alphesiboia or some other heroine) '. The framework of the whole poem may have been ' Many women of old were exceeding fair and won the love of the gods, such as (name of the heroine) ', and then an account of the adventures of the lady herself, or her son, or both. Clearly this would result in a very loosely constructed composition with no central theme or unity of interest, a sort of handbook of saga in verse. Why its author preferred to make women the leading figures is not known.[22] We are told [23] that it extended to five books ; judging by the number of the fragments and the length at which some at least of the stories were related,[24] this seems a decided understatement. Whether it was really by Hesiod cannot be certainly determined. The style of the fragments is not unlike his, but verses of this sort, much below the highest level of epic, might be achieved by a competent pupil imitating the manner of the founder of the school. The fact that the *Theogony*, as we have it, ends with a passage leading up to the *Ehoiai* proves nothing ; the latter poem was certainly meant as a continuation of the former, and adjustments might be made, as we know was the case with the Iliad, to join them closely together, regardless of authorship.[25]

Of Hesiod's date we have no exact knowledge. We have already seen (p. 33) that Herodotos supposed him to have lived about 850 B.C., and to have been contemporary with Homer. This latter supposition is certainly wrong. Homer, as already mentioned (p. 32), lived in a transitional age between bronze

---

[22] It has been suggested that the Lokrians somehow influenced the author, and that the Lokrians were or had been matrilineal. Even if the first statement were not doubtful and the second false, this would be an inadequate reason. See Schmid-Stählin, i, p. 267 ; Rose in *Folk-Lore*, xxxvii (1926), pp. 237–8, 244.

[23] Suidas, *s.u.* 'Ησίοδος.

[24] The *Aspis* (see below, p. 67) begins with an extract from the *Ehoiai*, which extends to 56 lines ; frags. 94 and 96 Rzach, both belonging to the same episode (the wooers of Helen), occupy over 150 lines, though much has been lost owing to the damaged state of the papyri on which they were found. Five books, *i.e.*, some 3,000–4,000 lines, would not allow of many stories on this scale. Suidas' figure (ε') is perhaps a copyist's error for ιε' (15) or κε' (25).

[25] The last line of the Iliad is ὣς οἵ γ' ἀμφίεπον τάφον "Εκτορος ἱπποδάμοιο. The scholiast of the Codex Victorianus tells us that some read

ὣς οἵ γ' ἀμφίεπον τάφον "Εκτορος·ἦλθε δ' 'Αμαζών,
"Αρηος θυγάτηρ μεγαλήτορος ἀνδροφόνοιο,

leading to the *Aithiopis* (see above, p. 49).

and iron ; Hesiod, in speaking of the men of the Bronze Age
(see p. 59), mentions it as one of their peculiarities that their
arms were of bronze, implying that iron was used in his own time.
The transition, then, was over, and he must consequently be a
good deal Homer's junior, as indeed is· rendered very likely by
the fact that he borrows words, phrases, epithets, even whole
lines, freely from the Iliad and Odyssey.   On the other hand,
we must not put him too far down, for the oldest Homeric hymns
borrow from him, and, as we have seen (pp. 26, 46), there are interpolations in the Homeric epics themselves which seem to be due
to members of his school.   These can hardly be late, as their
genuineness is attested by all MSS. evidence, so far as we know,
both ancient and modern,[26] and they are condemned on internal
evidence alone.   Again, although one gathers from his poems
that the Homeric system of government has degenerated, and,
more clearly, that the various parts of Greece are passing into
that stage of political isolation from one another in which they
were in historical times, no new form of government has yet
sprung up ; we hear, for instance, nothing of tyrants and little
of merchandise or industry.   Perhaps the scanty data are best
accounted for if we suppose that he lived in the eighth century.[27]

What is certain is that he had a following, whether in his own
lifetime or not.   A number of poems, not now extant, circulated
in antiquity, sometimes ascribed to him and sometimes to other
writers, named or unnamed.

Of these, two seem to have been extensions of genuine works of
Hesiod ; they were known respectively as the *Great Ehoiai* and the
Great ' Works '.   But few fragments remain of either (it is no doubt
possible that some remnants generally assigned to the *Ehoiai* proper
really belong to the *Great Ehoiai*), but from the little we have it is
plain that the former poem dealt with heroic genealogies and used the
formula ἢ οἵη, while the latter contained gnomic sayings like those
which fill two large sections of the genuine *W.D.*   Other poems were

---

[26] By ancient evidence I mean that which we gather, from our oldest
papyrus fragments of Homer and from the statements of scholiasts and
grammarians, to have lain before the Alexandrian critics.   By modern
evidence is meant that of the existing MSS., all mediaeval, together with
such scraps of the text as are earlier than these but later than the great
grammarians.

[27] Astronomical data help us a little, but not much.   Hesiod says
(*W.D.*, 564-7) that Arcturus rises in the evening twilight 60 days after
the winter solstice.   His acronychal rising is now 57 days after the
solstice.   If Hesiod is speaking accurately, *i.e.*, not giving a round
number, and if his observation or that of his authority is accurate, the
very earliest possible date is about 850 ; a later date is likelier.   See
T. W. Allen and A. A. Rambaut in *J.H.S.*, xxxv (1915), pp. 85-99.

of mythological content ; one was the *Marriage of Keyx*, and, it is to be supposed, dealt with some part of the tale of Keyx and Alkyone [28] ; another, the *Melampodeia*, treated of the adventures of the famous legendary prophet Melampus ; a third was the *Idaian Daktyloi*, and gave some account of these curious and little-known beings ; [29] while a fourth, the *Aigimios*, was at least two books long, and was ascribed by some to a certain KERKOPS of Miletos.[30] It was apparently an interesting attempt of the Dorians, who had but few sagas of their own, to claim a share in the legendary past, already long, of the country they had conquered. This Aigimios was an ancient Dorian king ; the poem seems to have told a story [31] of how, being hard pressed in a war, he invited Herakles to help him. The intervention of the hero brought success to Aigimios, who in gratitude adopted Herakles' son Hyllos. Besides these quasi-historical poems, there existed one called *Astronomia*, whose title sufficiently indicates its contents ; it is cited more than once as authority for a star-myth, and is for that very reason rather suspicious, for certainly the great majority of Greek legends about the stars are of comparatively late date, hardly becoming well-known till Alexandrian days. It is noticeable that the not over-critical Pliny [32] says only that the poem was ascribed to Hesiod. Ephoros (see below, p. 310) had read a geographical work, γῆς περίοδος, from which he quotes a line, cited from him by Strabo, vii, 3, 9. There was also a poem called the *Maxims of Chiron* (Χίρωνος ὑποθῆκαι), of which we know three things ; that it contained, probably near the beginning, the advice ' first of all, when thou comest to thine house, to sacrifice to the everlasting gods fair

---

[28] The fragments of this and the other works mentioned will be found in Rzach's edition. It may be that the *Marriage* is simply the separate title of part of the *Ehoiai*. For the story of Keyx, see Rose, *Mythology*, p. 257.

[29] See, for the Daktyloi, Rose, *op. cit.*, p. 166 *sq.*

[30] So Athenaios, xiii, 503d. This Kerkops is also said to have written part of the Orphic literature, for which see Chapter iv, by Suidas, *s.u.* Ὀρφεύς (f), who there calls him a Pythagorean. That the same Kerkops is meant would seem to follow from the fact drawn attention to by Wilamowitz, *Il. u. Hom.*, p. 412, n. 1, that a verse of the *Aigimios* is cited by Hermias the neo-Platonist as by Orpheus. In other words, the ' Orphic ' writers drew upon this poem, as on much else of the Hesiodic school. If Kerkops was really a Milesian, it indicates the backwardness of the Dorians that they had to employ a foreigner to write their propaganda. He is called a rival of Hesiod by Aristotle, frag. 65 Rose, which may be a deduction from the fact that the *Aigimios*, possibly other poems also, was attributed sometimes to one and sometimes to the other. As the tendency would be to ascribe to Hesiod any ancient hexameter poem which did not belong to the Homeric school, Kerkops is much the likelier author here, supposing that any reliable tradition on the subject survived at all.

[31] See the art. *Aigimios* in Roscher's *Lexikon*.

[32] Pliny, *N.H.*, xviii, 213 (*huius quoque nomine exstat astrologia*), copied by schol. Strozziana on Germanicus, *Arat.*, p. 209, 12 Breysig.

offerings'; that it said a child should not learn to read till he was seven years old; and that it stated the life of Nymphs to be 9 × 4 × 3 × 9 × 10 times as long as a man's.

More interesting to us, if only because it survives complete, is the poem called the *Shield of Herakles* ('Ασπὶς 'Ηρακλέους; generally shortened to either ' Shield ' or ' Aspis ' in modern quotations), a sort of epic ballad, 480 lines long. The first 56 of these are from the *Ehoiai* [33] and deal with Alkmene and Amphitryon and the birth of the twins, Herakles and Iphikles. The rest treats of an adventure of Herakles, who encounters the formidable brigand Kyknos, son of Ares. Herakles' arming for the fight is told at considerable length, 178 lines being devoted to a description of the figures on his shield, in obvious imitation of the shield of Achilles in the Iliad. With the help and advice of Athena, he kills Kyknos and wounds Ares. The poem suffers from comparison with the passages of the Iliad it imitates, and is at times guilty of ranting, over-accumulation of similes, and other lapses from good taste ; still it is by no means contemptible, but a brisk, lively telling of an interesting story. Who wrote it we do not know ; if it was used by Stesichoros (see note 33), it is obviously earlier than he. The earliest surviving imitation of it is in Sophokles. [34]

Hesiod may be regarded as the founder of a school, although much less extensive and important than the Homeric group of poets. He was perhaps regarded as the poet of the poorer and lower classes, which were now rapidly gaining importance as the governments of the Greek cities tended towards a democratic, or at all events a non-aristocratic type. In Boiotia itself, as it happens, we hear of but one name, that of the obscure CHERSIAS of Orchomenos, of whom Plutarch knows that he was contemporary with Periandros tyrant of Corinth, and therefore must have lived about 620 B.C., and Pausanias quotes two lines of his work at second hand, remarking that the poems were quite lost and forgotten in his own day (the second century A.D.). [35] A more important centre appears to have been Corinth, now coming rapidly to the fore as one of the leading states of Greece. Here was written a poem generally known as the *Corinthian Epic* (Κορινθιακὰ ἔπη), ascribed to EUMELOS, a member of the ruling family of the

---

[33] 'Υπόθεσις A to the *Shield*, which says that Aristophanes of Byzantion suspected the poem was not Hesiod's, while Megakles of Athens and Apollonios Rhodios thought it genuine and Stesichoros said it was by Hesiod, *i.e.*, presumably, imitated or adapted some part of it in one of his odes, naming Hesiod in connexion with it.

[34] Soph., *El.*, 167, δάκρυσι μυδαλέα, from *Aspis*, 270, word for word save for difference of dialect.

[35] Plut., *septem sapientium conuiu.*, 158e *sqq.* ; Paus., ix, 39, 9–10.

Bakchiadai. Enough survives of this work[36] to show that it dealt, apparently in considerable detail, with the legendary history of the city. Medeia was one of the characters, and the adventures of the Argonauts formed, it would seem, an episode. Like much of the epic of this school it became a quarry for the early historians (see Chapter IX), which explains why Pausanias cites as perhaps by Eumelos a prose work called the *Corinthian History* (Κορινθία συγγραφή), and Clement of Alexandria calls him a prose writer.[37] The later work which used and named him was confused with his own writings. His date is uncertain ; Pausanias several times [38] mentions him as having lived in the eighth century, but as he also doubts that he wrote anything but an ancient hymn for the festival of Apollo at Delos, whereof he cites two verses written in Doric, this does not help us to determine when the epic was produced. The scholiast on Pindar (*Ol.*, xiii, 31) says ' there were very notable poets in Corinth, including AISON, whom Simonides mentions '. If the name is not corrupt, this is the sole trace now surviving of this once ' notable poet '. To this Corinthian group perhaps belonged a poem, *Europia*, which some ascribed to Eumelos ; [39] it dealt no doubt with the story of Europa and the bull, but the three fragments that survive deal respectively with Dionysos, Apollo and Amphion. Farther south, Sparta had an epic poet of her own, by name KINAITHON,[40] whose date is given by S. Jerome in his translation of Eusebios' chronicle as the fourth Olympiad, *i.e.*, about 760 B.C., suspiciously early. He was credited by sundry ancient writers with the authorship of the *Little Iliad, Oidipodeia* and *Telegonia* ; but not a line that can definitely be ascribed to him has come down to us, only a few references. A little more is known of a work called the *Poem of Naupaktos* (Ναυπάκτια ἔπη), ascribed by some to a Milesian, by others to a certain KARKINOS of Naupaktos (Lepanto) on the Corinthian Gulf.[41] It was apparently something like the *Ehoiai* in plan, for it dealt with famous women of legend ; one story which seems to have been treated at considerable length was that of the Argonauts. That the interest in genealogical and quasi-historical writing was not confined to the mainland is shown by the occasional mentions of ASIOS of Samos, whose work, to judge by the little that is quoted from it, dealt largely with the relationships of ancient hero-

---

[36] His fragments and the ancient notices of him are in Kinkel, *Ep. graec. frag.*, p. 185 *sqq*.

[37] Paus., ii, 1, 1 ; Clem. Alex., *Strom.*, vi, p. 752, Pott.

[38] Paus., iv, 33, 2 ; iv, 4, 1 ; v, 19, 10, Eumelos perhaps wrote the verses on the Chest of Kypselos (see above, Chapter ii, n. 86) ; this does not mean that he supposed the poet to be of the sixth century, but that he imagined the Chest to be of the eighth. Cf. Clem. Alex., *Strom.*, i, p. 398, Pott., Eumelos contemporary with the founding of Syracuse (734 B.C.).

[39] See Kinkel, p. 192. [40] *Ibid.*, pp. 196–98.

[41] *Ibid.*, pp. 198–202. Pausanias, x, 38, 11, who himself prefers the opinion of Charon of Lampsakos, that Karkinos wrote it, else why is it called Naupaktian ?

ines,[42] though one passage contained a lively description of his fellow-countrywomen going in their finest dresses to a festival of Hera. Apparently Athens had a share in this movement also, for Pausanias once quotes at second hand, from HEGESINUS, who he says wrote a poem on Attica (*Atthis*), a few lines dealing with the legendary history of Hesiod's town of Askra.[43] Who wrote the *Phoronis* we do not know, but may conjecture that he was an Argive, since Phoroneus, its hero, was son of Inachos the river of the Argolid.[44] The *Minyas*, which would appear to have dealt with the capture of Orchomenos by Herakles, was a little less anonymous, for some said it had been composed by PRODIKOS of Phokis, of whom we know nothing.[45] Vaguer still are the various poems concerning Herakles and Theseus of which we can only say that they existed,[46] and scarcely more is known of the *Danais* than of these ; it dealt with the adventures of Danaos and his fifty daughters and extended to the considerable length of 6,500 lines.[47]

As in the last chapter, these works are mentioned solely because of the considerable influence which their contents were to exercise. Two classes of writers seem to have read them diligently ; the early prose chroniclers of whom we shall speak later, and the poets of the sixth and fifth centuries, who drew upon them for material. Mythology was and for a long time continued to be the most popular subject for literary compositions of all kinds,[48] and therefore a good knowledge of it was essential to a poet, or even an orator or historian. The minor epic writers just enumerated were the mythological handbooks of the later authors, and were superseded by them.

There is one more development of the movement inaugurated by Hesiod which is worth attention before we pass to other and later forms of poetry. He had uttered his views concerning religion and morality in hexameters ; the same vehicle came to be used, in the sixth and fifth centuries especially, for works of religious propaganda and philosophical theory.

[42] Kinkel, pp. 202–06.   [43] Paus., ix, 29, 1–2.
[44] Kinkel, pp. 209–12.   [45] *Ibid.*, pp. 215–17.   [46] *Ibid.*, p. 217 *sqq.*
[47] *Ibid.*, p. 78. Another anonymous epic, the *Alkmaionis*, has left us a few fragments (*ibid.*, pp. 76–7).
[48] See for example Thucydides, i, 22, 4 (his work will not make popular reading because the lack of anything μυθῶδες will make it seem dull) ; Isokrates, ix, 6 (our poets spend all their energies on the War of Troy and its heroes, neglecting equally notable deeds of to-day) ; ii, 48 (to be popular, a writer must deal in myths, not wholesome advice) ; Arist., *Poet.*, 1451ᵇ 15 *sqq.*, 1453ᵇ 22 (original plots in Tragedy are rare, and most plays deal with the fortunes of a few legendary houses). Later (Verg., *Georg.*, iii, 6 *sqq.* ; anon., *Aetna*, 9 *sqq.* ; Juvenal, *sat.*, i, 7 *sqq.* ; Martial, *epigr.*, iv, 49) it becomes a commonplace that the mythological themes are worn out and stale.

The seventh and sixth centuries were times of upheaval and unrest for the whole Greek world. The lower classes grew discontented, not without cause, and sought to better their condition by demanding a share in the government of their states. To achieve their ends, they usually rallied under some able leader, often an aristocrat, who having overthrown the aristocracy made himself tyrant, in other words assumed the position of dictator without constitutional sanctions or safeguards. Usually these tyrants were in turn soon overthrown, and a new form of government introduced, which whether oligarchic or democratic was constitutional, depending on a code of laws reduced, then or later, to writing. But during the long periods of change and even anarchy it was but natural that the general discontent should spread to other spheres than politics and economics. Men grew ready to question such fundamentals as the justice of their gods and the instinctive feeling that life is worth living. Of the many results of this, two are of importance for literature ; the emergence into prominence of cults, hitherto foreign or plebeian, which promised recompense in another life for the woes of this one, and the rise of a new kind of thought, more or less independent of religious sanctions and limitations, which began to investigate the whole structure of the universe and of human society. Between these two, and between one or both of them and the established religious forms, all manner of contacts ensued, the most notable being the compromise effected between the long-standing cult of Apollo at Delphoi and the newer worship of Dionysos, which resulted, some time during this period, in the temple being shared between the two deities,[49] and the union of a ceremonial and mystic religion with vigorous philosophical activity in the Pythagorean sects of Magna Graecia.

Among a people possessed already of a not inconsiderable bulk of literature, it was inevitable that this in turn should produce new writings, setting forth the new views. So far as the most vocal of the religious movements was concerned, these were anonymous, or rather ascribed themselves to imaginary authors of remote antiquity. Orphism professed to derive its tenets, never very definite or regulated by any strict standard of orthodoxy, from the inspired works of Orpheus himself, who so far as he could be dated at all was made out to be contemporary with the Argonautic adventure, a generation before the War of Troy. It was very natural that a new movement, appealing especially,

---

[49] There is no conclusive evidence for the date of this important event, see Farnell, *C.G.S.*, v, p. 112 *sqq.* Nilsson, *Hist. Gk. Rel.*, p. 208, believes it to have taken place by the seventh century.

it would seem, to the lower classes, should thus give itself an aristocratic ancestry, appealing to an authority older and of higher rank than the aristocratic Homer (see above, p. 15). An echo was heard, many centuries later, in the amusing attempts of the various competing religions, Christian and pagan, to outdo each other in length of ancestry.

The history of Orphism and of its literature is a mass of obscurities, and the modern accounts of it necessarily contain a large proportion of conjecture. The activity of the sect, if it can be called one, extends over some thousand years, from the sixth century B.C., or possibly a little earlier, to the fourth or fifth A.D. During all this time there seems to have been no recognized authoritative text or body of literature, corresponding to the Bible or the Quran, to which final appeal could be made ; the name of ORPHEUS and that of his companion, son, or other associate MUSAIOS covered all manner of forgeries, which began early and continued late. Hence it is extremely difficult to say what was taught or commonly read in Orphic circles at the period we are dealing with.[50] To judge, however, by such fragments of the literature as we can date with some definiteness and by the prominence in the later and fuller documents of certain doctrines, we may say that the followers of this religion had a mythology of their own including several deities not in the ordinary Greek pantheon, of whom one of the most important was Zagreus, son of Zeus and Persephone, who was killed and devoured by the Titans. From the bodies of his murderers, slain by the thunderbolts of Zeus, sprang man. Thus man is partly divine and partly Titanic, *i.e.*, evil, and should endeavour, by observance of an ascetic discipline, to get rid of his Titanic part and so qualify for a divine and blissful life after death. The whole question is further complicated here by the presence in Pythagoreanism of something not unlike this doctrine of original sin and also of a minutely regulated, almost monastic ascetic life ; where Orphism ends and Pythagoreanism begins is often impossible to say.

[50] The best collection of the fragments of Orphic literature is that of Kern (see bibliography), which supersedes Abel's (*ibid.*) ; the latter, however, is still useful for the text of several complete works of late date. The first scientific account of the whole doctrine and literature was given by Lobeck in 1828 (see bibliography), whose *Aglaophamus* is still valuable, though now in need of supplementing from later works. The best-known later treatise is perhaps Rohde's *Psyche* ; one of the most readable accounts is given in Miss Harrison's *Prolegomena to the Study of Greek Religion*, Chapter x and appendix. For a fuller list, see the bibliography of Kern, *op. cit.* See p. 422.

The Orphic literature, so far as we know, begins in the sixth century.[51] At the court, apparently, of Peisistratos, certainly at that of his son Hippias, there existed a collection of oracles ascribed to Musaios, and an expert on prophecies, ONOMAKRITOS, was banished for having been caught adding oracles of his own forging to those which he was charged to edit and arrange.[52] This incident apparently lies behind the theory of certain grammarians, among them EPIGENES (of unknown date but old enough to have been mentioned by Kallimachos),[53] that Onomakritos was himself the author of the Orphic poems, including Musaios'

[51] The earliest mention of Orpheus in literature is Ibykos, frag. 17 Diehl, ὀνομάκλυτον ᾿Ορφήν. In what context he spoke of him or how much he knew of him we cannot tell. The earliest surviving appearance of his picturesque figure in art is on a metope of the Sekyonian treasury at Delphoi (Kern, p. 1). There is good evidence in the literature and also in art that he was associated with Dionysos, although his religion of purification was claimed by the great god of purifications in the official religion of Greece, Apollo, and consequently he is said to have been an ardent worshipper of Apollo (see [Eratosthenes], catast., 24, from which derive by one route or another Hyginus, poet. astron., ii, 7, and schol. German. Arat., pp. 84, 151 Breysig), or even his son (authorities in Kern, p. 8, to which add Ovid, Amores, iii, 9, 21 sqq.). That he is said to have met his death at the hands of Dionysiac maenads (first, apparently in Aeschylus, cited in the above-quoted passage of pseudo-Eratosthenes) is no objection ; we know little of the Thracian worship of Dionysos, but there is nothing to show that it might not include the killing of a priest or other person who incarnated the god, a proceeding familiar from Frazer's Golden Bough, and a certain amount of indication that it did do so.

[52] Herodotos, vii, 6, 3–4 ; he calls the successor of Peisistratos Hipparchos in accordance with the usual popular account, controverted by Thucydides, vi, 54, 2, and incidentally mentions that the discoverer of the fraud was Lasos of Hermione (see below, p. 107). For editing Orphic literature the Peisistratidai had a good political reason ; like all tyrants, they counted on popular support, and therefore may very well have thought it advisable to have under their control the documents of a religion rather popular than aristocratic.

[53] Kallimachos is said by Harpokration, s.u. ᾿Ιων, to have attributed to this Epigenes the Triagmoi of Ion of Chios ; hence Epigenes must have been at least an older contemporary of Kallimachos. For his theories of the authorship of the Orphic works, see Clem. Alex., Strom., i, p. 397 Pott., cf. p. 675 Pott. : Clement's language is inconsistent, for he shifts from definite mentions of Epigenes to a vague λέγουσι, but the general sense is that Onomakritos wrote the Oracles of Musaios, or generally, all the Orphic poems (τὰ εἰς ᾿Ορφέα ἀναφερόμενα), ZOPYROS of Herakleia the Krater (fourth century B.C. ?), PRODIKOS of Samos the Descent into Hades (a poem, or poems, on this theme certainly existed, and may have furnished Vergil and Lucan with subject-matter), which also was ascribed, this time definitely by Epigenes, to KERKOS the Pythagorean, together with the Sacred Legends ; while the Peplos (probably ' the miscellany ') and the Physics were credited to a certain BRONTINOS.

oracles, an unlikely idea, for he could hardly have hoped to pass off his forgeries unless there were some supposedly genuine works for him to add to. Besides these oracles, of which we know nothing definite, we may name as old Orphic works certain books dealing with ritual and containing hymns and some account of the fate of the human soul after death ; [54] a poem, or poems, concerning Demeter and Kore, whereof one, an adaptation of the Homeric Hymn to Demeter, is preserved to us, in a very fragmentary form, on a papyrus now at Berlin ; [55] and certain parts, though by no means the whole, of a long work in twenty-four books known to later ages as the *Sacred Legends* (ἱεροὶ λόγοι).[56] But this scanty list is far from exhausting the early literature ; in the latter half of the fifth century there were ' many books ' which an adept might be supposed to have read, whereof some dealt with medicine, others apparently with ritual, including the fundamental practice of abstinence from animal food.[57] In general we may say of what little is preserved verbatim that it closely imitated Hesiod, owed much to Homer and the Homeric hymns, and borrowed whole lines or even whole sections with but slight changes, impudently asserting, at least in later days, that it was Homer or Hesiod who was the plagiarist.[58]

About contemporary with early Orphism was the strange figure of the SIBYL, or the Sibyls,[59] to whom, and also to a certain BAKIS, were ascribed a large number of prophecies in hexameter verse, the natural fruits of the disturbed state of affairs in those turbulent centuries, among a people who still believed firmly in divination, both by methodical observation of signs and by direct inspiration or posses-

[54] The most famous fragments of this part of Orphic literature are some tablets (see Murray in Harrison, *Prolegomena*, Appendix, Kern, pp. 104–09, who names earlier editors), discovered at Petelia (Strongoli), Eleutherna (in Crete), Thurioi and Rome. They are of very thin gold, and the writing difficult to read ; the dates vary from about the fourth century B.C. to the second A.D., but the documents on which they draw may have been much earlier than the earliest of them. They describe the arrival of the soul at a place in Hades where it is given a drink from the well of Memory, and greets and is welcomed by the guardians of the well, as they appear to be. No doubt the *Descent into Hades*, which treated of Orpheus' search for Eurydike, handled some of this material.

[55] Frag. 49 Kern ; another scrap of this or a similar poem was found on a gold tablet at Thurioi, similar to those mentioned in the last note, see Kern, frag. 47, p. 117 *sqq.*

[56] See Kern, pp. 140–248.

[57] See Euripides, *Alc.*, 966 *sqq.*, *Hipp.*, 952 *sqq*

[58] For one example of many, see frag. 48, Kern, p. 119.

[59] For the Sibyl (Σίβυλλα), or Sibyls, see Rose, *Myth.*, p. 138 and the authorities quoted *ibid.*, n. 9.

sion by a god. Here again we have, as in Orphism, an earlier and a later stratum. There survive no oracles which can be certainly dated earlier than about the end of the fifth century B.C., but a few which are of various dates between that and the principate of Nero, to judge by the events to which they allude. All are in hexameters, mostly indifferent, and some are taken from the famous Roman collection, one at least apparently from the older one, supposed to date from the time of the Tarquins, *i.e.*, from the sixth century ; if we make the very large assumption that it is genuine, it is the oldest fragment we have. It contains elaborate directions for purificatory ceremonies to be held on the occasion of a hermaphrodite birth. The language suggests that it is not much older than the year in which it is said to have been published, 125 B.C., and it may even be a forgery of later date.[60] But there is, in addition to these scraps of an older tradition, a large collection, in fourteen books originally, whereof we now have twelve surviving in various MSS. This is what is usually meant when reference is made to ' the Sibyl ' in modern literature ; it is a most patent Judaeo-Christian forgery, largely drawn upon by early Christian apologists, who seized on it as eagerly as their opponents did the Orphic literature to find evidence for their views. Here and there some fragment of older Sibylline work may be perhaps found in this mass of deplorable and often unmetrical verses ; but as a whole it lies outside the scope of this book.[61] Of the other prophets of the seventh and sixth centuries nothing survives that is worthy of remark, save only the name of EPIMENIDES the Cretan, who wrote, according to later authors, not only oracles but also a book, presumably in hexameters, on purificatory rites (καθαρμοί), a *Theogony*, an account of the Argonauts, and other poems on mythological or theological subjects. Of all this, very little survives, the most famous fragment being that quoted in the Epistle to Titus, ' The Cretans are alway liars, evil beasts, slow bellies ' (Κρῆτες ἀεὶ ψεῦσται, κακὰ θηρία, γαστέρες ἀργαί), which incidentally has given rise to the amusing logical puzzle regarding the consequences to be drawn from the

---

[60] There is a convenient collection of oracles in the Didot edition of the *Anthology*, vol. iii, pp. 464–561 (Appendix, caput vi). Those attributed to the Sibyl are Nos. 208–219. Of these, remembering that they contain prophecies after the event, we may assign No. 210 to about the end of the fifth century B.C., 212 to the fourth (Battle of Chaironeia and murder of Philip of Macedon), 219 to the same period (it is cited from Herakleides Pontikos, and is therefore not later than his time). The one discussed in the text is No. 216, is preserved by Phlegon (time of Hadrian), *de mirabilibus*, 10 (p. 133 *sqq.*, Westermann). For the Roman collection of oracles, see the works on Roman religion and history, *e.g.*, Wissowa, *Religion und Kultus der Römer*, ed. 2, p. 542 *sqq.*, with short bibliography, p. 549.

[61] The later Sibylline oracles have been several times edited, notably by Rzach, Prague, Vienna and Leipzig, 1891,' whose preface contains a brief account of the earlier editions. For more information, see the relevant articles in the classical dictionaries and encyclopaedias.

statement of a Cretan that Cretans always lie. The author, whose history is clouded by a mass of legends concerning his miraculous powers, would seem to have been a professional diviner and expert on purificatory ceremonies, who lived some time in the seventh and sixth centuries.[62] We have no evidence that he belonged to the Orphic or any other sect.

Much more is known of the philosophico-religious poetry of EMPEDOKLES of Akragas, and the poet himself is a far more definite figure to us in consequence. It would seem also that he deserves to be better known than the Cretan, being not only a prophet held in more than human respect in his own day, and a great physician (medicine was in his time a rapidly developing art in Sicily and Southern Italy), but a poet of such merit as to appear *uix humana stirpe creatus* to Lucretius,[63] despite the latter's disagreement with his scientific opinions, and besides this one of the greatest names in the early history of philosophy. His fairly abundant fragments, amounting to some 500 lines in all, that is to say about one-tenth of what he wrote and published, belong to two poems, the *Purifications* (καθαρμοί) and the *Physics* or *System of Nature* (περὶ φύσεως); the allocation of particular passages to one or the other poem is not always certain. The former poem, perhaps the earlier, was an address to his friends, in which he boldly declared that he was himself ' an immortal god, no longer a mortal ', and spoke of his own high reputation in a way which would have been intolerably conceited in a lesser man, but in him might be held to spring from a proud consciousness of real greatness. After lauding the wisdom of Pythagoras, it recommended his philosophy, especially the doctrine of rein-

[62] His fragments are in Kinkel, pp. 230–38; Diels, ii, p. 188 *sqq*. The only important evidence for his date is that he performed purificatory ceremonies in Athens after the affair of Kylon, about 596, see Suidas *s.u.* 'Επιμενίδης and the authorities cited by Clinton, *Fasti Hellenici*, on that year. Besides Epimenides, we hear rather vaguely of two other poets, or poet-prophets. ARISTEAS of Prokonnesos, of the seventh century (Herodotos, iv, 15, 1 ; his ghost had appeared in the historian's own day, about 440 B.C., and this was 240 years after he had disappeared), of whom numerous and curious legends seem to have been told, was real enough to be the author of an epic, the 'Αρισμάσπεια ἔπη, dealing with the fabulous Arismaspeians, and a *Theogony*, said by Suidas to have been in prose ; the former poem professed to describe the writer's own experiences when divinely conducted to those regions under the influence of Apollo. ABARIS was also a servant of Apollo and a diviner, to whom were ascribed oracles and a poem on the Hyperboreans, another fabulous people, said to live in the north and to worship Apollo. Fragments and *testimonia* of both these in Kinkel, pp. 242–47.
[63] Lucretius, i, 733.

carnation which he had taught, with its corollary of abstinence from all flesh food, lest the seeming beast should be simply a human being in a new form, perhaps a near relative, and gave directions, often quite minute, for rites of purification. The object of these was probably not to avert ordinary evils, but to regain the divine condition from which, according to him, human souls have fallen ; elsewhere, in a passage assigned by Mullach to the *Physics* and by Diels to the *Purifications*, he explained that a supernatural being guilty of sin was banished for ' thrice ten thousand seasons ' (the Hesiodic reminiscence is patent, compare note 9) into the miserable world of change in which mortals live. He was himself one of these beings, ' a fugitive and a wanderer from deity '. Presumably his claim to be ' no longer a mortal ' meant that he had nearly won his way back to the blissful state from which he had set out ; he declared that he had already passed through a number of incarnations, ' youth and maid, bush and bird, and dumb fish in the salt sea '. Meanwhile, being in this world, he gave an explanation of it ; it is composed of the four elements, earth, air, water and fire, which he sometimes called by their names and sometimes personified as Aïdoneus (Hades), Hera, Nestis and Zeus. These are everlastingly combined and separated by two forces, Love and Hate (in other words, attraction and repulsion), of which sometimes one and sometimes the other gets the better, in endless alternation. All this, involving frequent use of comparatively technical language and close argument, is set forth in verse so often eloquent and genuinely poetical and so seldom lame or stiff that Lucretius' admiration is the more easily explicable, seeing that he was successfully attempting a like task in Latin. That so original and forceful a personality as his (for he seems to have added political activities to his philosophy and the practice of medicine) should be admired in his own day and afterwards is no way remarkable. It hardly need be added that legends grew up around him, which make it difficult to arrive at the real facts concerning his life and date. But it is probable that he lived, roughly speaking, through the first three-quarters of the fifth century.[64]

[64] The fragments are in Mullach, *F.Ph.G.*, i, pp. 1–14, followed by a commentary and accompanied by a Latin version ; Diels, *F.d.V.*, i, p. 308 *sqq.*, with a German translation. The chief source of information concerning his life and teachings is Diogenes Laertios, viii, 51–77 ; the last few sections, from 68 onwards, contain some of the legends about him. His exact date cannot be determined ; he was almost certainly dead by 415, Apollodoros *ap.* Diog. Laert., 52, and he was sixty years old when he died, Aristotle (frag. 60 Rose) ; he might so far as that goes have been born about 480. But Gorgias was his pupil, Diog. Laert. 58, and

I have mentioned Empedokles a little out of his chronological order, partly because he is nearest in spirit to the theological poets just discussed, partly because his comparatively abundant remains make him rather more important for us, at least in considering literature only.   Older in date and, in one case, occupying a larger place in the history of thought were two other writers, both resident in Italy.   The first was XENOPHANES, a native of Kolophon, who migrated to Elea, apparently when twenty-five years old,[65] and may therefore, if he was one of the original settlers of that colony, have been born in 565.   The sixth century, which saw the rise of Persia, sent many Ionians away from their threatened country to the west, to seek their fortunes or at least avoid so formidable a neighbour.   ' How old were you when the Mede came ? ' was, according to Xenophanes himself, one of the regular bits of small-talk to a new acquaintance.[66]   He was a professional poet, a rhapsode who declaimed his own works and, likely enough, those of others as well.   In temperament he was perhaps a little like Samuel Butler, not a great constructive thinker, but a shrewd critic of established views and possessed of enough powers as a philosopher to stimulate others.   He seems, to judge by a pretty description of a dinner which he has left us, to have had simple and at the same time fastidious tastes.[67] Among his miscellaneous writings, which included an account in verse of the founding of Kolophon and another, if it was not part of the same poem, on the emigration to Elea, there were a series of attacks, in hexameters, iambics and elegiacs, on Homer and Hesiod, for attributing unworthy actions to gods.   These were called, at any rate in later days, *silloi*, and Timon (see p. 358) hailed Xenophanes as a pioneer.   Finally, perhaps in his old age, he turned to constructive thought and wrote a philosophic poem in which he tried to explain the true nature of the universe and of God.   As an expositor he was, says Aristotle, somewhat rustic (ἀγροικότερος), but he was capable, evidently, of setting others thinking and the little that is left of the work suggests that it was not deficient in poetical merit.[68]

Gorgias died at 99, or even older, somewhere about the end of the fifth century ; he was born therefore probably not long after 500. The teacher can hardly have been much younger than the pupil, and therefore we may suppose Empedokles to have been born between 500 and 490 and to have died between 440 and 430.

[65] Xenoph., frag. 8, 3 Diels ; something of importance happened to him at 25.   See Diels, p. 113 *sqq.*, for the other materials for his life.

[66] Frag. 22, 5 Diels, 17 Mullach.

[67] *Ibid.*, 1 Diels, 21 Mullach.

[68] Arist., *Metaph.* A, 986ᵇ 27.

Xenophanes was regarded as the founder of the Eleatic school of philosophy, whose leading tenet was that reality was one and indivisible, change and plurality not being real, but only apparent to the uncritical senses of men ; as we might now say, phenomenal. Clearly, such a view as this, involving close and technical dialectic for its exposition, was ill suited for poetry, and the next to attempt it, PARMENIDES, while making a deserved reputation for himself as a thinker, produced but sorry verses. Of the fragments which remain of him, one, the prologue to his poem, in which he rides on a mystical chariot to the gates of Day and Night, the Daughters of the Sun receive him and Justice promises to expound the mind of Truth to him, has some right to be called poetry ; of the rest one can hardly say more than that it scans, and not always that, for any one whose ear has been trained on Homer. His date can be approximately determined. He was in his prime about 500 B.C., according to Diogenes Laertios (ix, 23), which means that he was born about 540, and was of a likely age to be influenced by Xenophanes and influence Empedokles.[69]

In conclusion, we may name PHOKYLIDES, who seems to have written pithily enough, somewhat in the style of the *Maxims of Chiron* and of the numerous sententious sayings scattered up and down Hesiod. He did not, says Dion of Prusa, indulge in any long flights, but confined his poems to two or three verses, and put his name to each maxim.[70] To this the surviving quotations from him bear witness, for example

Καὶ τόδε Φωκυλίδεω· πόλις ἐν σκοπέλῳ κατὰ κόσμον
οἰκεῦσα σμικρὴ κρέσσων Νίνου ἀφραινούσης (frag. 4, Diehl).

' This also is of Phokylides. A little town set on a crag, well-governed, is better than Nineveh, if Nineveh be foolish '.

Incidentally, this raises the problem of date. Nineveh fell in 612, and Phokylides speaks of it as the very type of a great and prosperous city.[71] Either, then, he wrote this before 612 or else long after, when the misfortunes of the city were sufficiently ancient for its prosperity to be once more proverbial. The latter agrees well enough with Suidas' statement (*s.u.* Φωκυλίδης) that he lived in the 59th Olympiad, *i.e.*, 544–541.

[69] See Diels, i, pp. 217–27 ; Mullach, i, pp. 109–30.
[70] Dion Prusias, *orat.* xxxvi, 12, von Arnim.
[71] By a slip, Schmid-Stählin (i, p. 299) makes him allude to the fall, not the prosperity, of Nineveh.

Much later, some person, probably a Jew, certainly acquainted with the Old Testament, wrote a long series of maxims in hexameters which he ascribed to Phokylides. These are usually known as the *Pseudo-Phocylidea*, and are published at the end of the genuine fragments in Bergk.

ADDITIONAL NOTE

P. 59, note 6; for further discussions of this difficult passage, see O. Lendle, *Die 'Pandorasage' bei Hesoid* (Würtzburg 1957), p. 108 : G. Méautis, *La mythologie grecque* (Paris 1959), p. 48 *sq.*

CHAPTER IV

PERSONAL POETRY : ELEGIACS, IAMBICS, SOLO LYRICS

IN the last chapter the reader will have noticed that a large proportion of the authors named were not Ionians. We now have to return to Ionia, and also to retrogress somewhat in time, in order to trace a new movement, full of important consequences for literature.

The poets hitherto dealt with used, almost without exception, the hexameter only. This metre, although very supple and capable of being employed for a wide range of compositions, still retains a certain stateliness which makes it unsuitable for the more personal kinds of expression and also for trifling, comic or satirical writings, unless these have an element of parody and mock-heroic. Furthermore, it is associated with a vocabulary founded on the serious epic narratives, and for that reason alone it is less adapted to speak of common life or of feelings strongly experienced by an individual. For like reasons, the range of subjects which an English author can treat in Miltonic blank verse is limited. Hence, as the subject-matter of literature widened, it was inevitable that new media of expression should grow up. One of these, namely prose, we shall have to consider later ; at present I will deal with three new types of metre.

Of these, one was derived either from the hexameter itself or else from one of the shorter verses out of which it is generally supposed to have developed. It is common for a hexameter to have a caesura in the middle of its third foot, thus, $-\cup\cup-\cup\cup-\,|$; such a succession of syllables is often called a *hemiepes* or half-verse. Two of these combined produced a line shorter and less sonorous than the hexameter itself, known generally as a pentameter (which it is not), because its total length is equal to five dactylic feet. By alternating this verse with ordinary hexameters, the so-called elegiac couplet was produced. This, from the mere fact that it was a couplet, broke the sweep and rush of the hexameter used by itself ; it corresponded to the rhythm of Pope's verse as compared to Milton's. It was therefore a very good metre for a plain story, to be told in fairly short sentences with no great affectation of eloquence, or for expressions of personal opinion, which should not be too grandiloquent ; also for epigrams, proverbial maxims, and so forth. Its range was wide, and various poets used it for all manner of works ; warsongs and laments, good advice and love-poems, epitaphs and political pamphlets. It seems probable that originally at least all these compositions, except perhaps the epitaphs, were meant to be sung.

The ancients themselves associated the elegiac metre (ἔλεγος) with flute, or rather oboe-music, which was Oriental and not Greek. Some of them also appear to think that it should properly be used for mournful compositions, and even derive its name fancifully from ἒ ἒ λέγειν, ' to say, alas, alas ! ' [1] But the wide range of subjects for which it actually was used from early times lends no support to this idea ; that elegiacs were sung to the music of wood-winds and airs written in modes originating in the Near East is a statement of historical fact which we have no grounds for rejecting.

The elegiac metre, however, was still far removed from the speech of every-day life by its rhythm. Greek, as Aristotle observes and as extant Greek prose amply proves, had a tendency to fall into quite another kind of metre, the iambic.[2] This does not as a rule signify pure iambics, *i.e.*, long successions of the foot called an iambus (ἴαμβος), ◡—, which would have become extremely monotonous. The Greek ear felt that so short a foot could not stand alone, but always treated it as one of a pair (called a *metron* or measure), of which the first member might be a spondee, ——, while to a moderate extent the privilege might be exercised of replacing one long syllable by two short ones. The result was a number of different lines (of which the most

---

[1] See Suidas, *s.u.* ἔλεγος, wιτη which cf. [Plut.] *de musica*, 1134 a, ἐν ἀρχῇ γὰρ ἐλεγεῖα μεμελοποιημένα οἱ αὐλῳδοὶ ᾖδον· τοῦτο δὲ δηλοῖ ἡ τῶν Παναθηναίων γραφὴ ἡ περὶ τοῦ μουσικοῦ ἀγῶνος. Plut., *de E apud Delphos*, 394 c, τὸν δὲ πρῶτον χρόνον (ὁ αὐλὸς) εἵλκετο πρὸς πένθος. So Ovid (?), *Heroid.*, xv, 7 *elegiae flebile carmen*, where see Palmer ; cf *Amor.* iii, 9, 3-4.

[2] Arist., *Poet.*, 1449ᵃ 24 ; *Rhet.*, 1408ᵇ 33, where see Cope-Sandys, 1404ᵃ 31. The first speech of Lysias, which is in a designedly plain and familiar style for the most part (the speaker is represented as a simple honest man, grievously wronged), shows in 30 lines of the Oxford text (sections 15-18) 19 fragments of iambic trimeters of comic type, and we may be sure that actual speech would contain a higher proportion, for Arist. says, *ll. cc.*, that whole trimeters were often undesignedly uttered. Similarly in English, a careless prose style often runs into rough blank verse, a conspicuous fault in Dickens, for instance.

popular, the trimeter, consisted of six feet or three *metra*), all capable of a good deal of variety, yet none very far removed from the cadences of ordinary conversation. It thus was admirably suited for poems meant to be recited, not sung, and for compositions having a familiar tone and deliberately imitating ordinary speech, such as simple stories, fables, personal addresses to individuals, lampoons and satires, and so forth.

A poet could, if he saw fit, depart a little from this tone of composition and yet not be too elevated or poetical, by using the trochee, — ◡, instead of the iambus as the base of his metre. This also admitted the use of spondees, but at the end, not the beginning of each metron, and the other licences which iambic metre enjoyed. To the Greeks, the effect of such lines was rapid.

Finally, a number of song-metres were cultivated, particularly by a little group of poets native to the island of Lesbos, for all the purposes of personal lyric, in other words for solos. There arose, or more likely there was developed out of popular rhythms long in use for simple ballads and songs, a whole group of metres, which may conveniently be referred to collectively as Aiolic, from the dialect spoken at Lesbos, and these were the chief vehicle of the ideas of an important class of writers. It is to be remembered that in this age and for some time after a poet was regularly a musician also, and probably composed words and air together ; the accompaniment would be very simple, for what we call harmony remained unknown, or almost unknown, to Greek music of all periods.

The varieties of Aiolic metre cannot be detailed here, and the reader is referred to the works cited in Chapter I, note 11.

The earliest ELEGIAC writer of whom we have any knowledge is KALLINOS, author of some rousing verses inciting his countrymen to take arms against a common enemy. Two or three lines survive of another poem, an address to Zeus, which give his date and nationality ; as he prays for mercy on Smyrna, that was presumably his city,[3] and since he says the Kimmerians

---

[3] The fragments of Kallinos are in Diehl, *Anthol. Lyr.*, i, pp. 3–4, so far as they consist of verbatim quotations : Bergk gives also those which, being merely references, cannot be fully restored. The same applies to all authors cited in this and the next chapter whose complete works are not preserved. For the dates of Kallinos and Archilochos, see Hudson-Williams, *Elegy*, 9 *sqq.*, and for bibliography of the elegiac poets, see *ibid.*, pp. 35–7. Strabo, who preserves two small scraps of the address to Zeus, uses them as part of his proof (xiv, 1, 4) that Smyrna is the old name of Ephesos. The longer fragment (1 Diehl) mentioned in the text is found in Stobaios, *Floril.*, li (xlix), 19, among a series of passages from various authors dealing with courage.

are coming against them, we may put him contemporary with the invasion of the people whom the Greeks knew by that name, *i.e.*, about the first half of the seventh century B.C. No more is known of him. Less ancient is MIMNERMOS of Kolophon, who lived in the second half of the same century.[4] His fame rested chiefly on an amatory poem, or collection of such poems, entitled *Nanno*, which was presumably the name of the real or imaginary object of his somewhat sickly affections. The greater part of the fragments which we have consist in pessimistic reflections on the shortness of life and its miseries once youth is over. It is noteworthy that he addresses an Oriental, not a Greek woman, a good example of the mixed character of Ionian civilization in that age, when it was yielding to the influence and passing under the empire of the Lydians.

It has already been mentioned (above, p. 77) that XENOPHANES wrote elegiacs. Some were also attributed to PHOKYLIDES (p. 78), whereof one couplet survives.[5] An old, but very dim figure is DEMODOKOS, of whom we have a few detached couplets, and one little epigram of six lines, to the effect that all Kappadokians are great rascals, become worse if they prosper, and will ' Kappadokianize ' the whole universe unless a kindly Providence intervenes.

But so far as our acquaintance with them goes, the chief elegiac poets were of Greece proper. It is noteworthy, however, that all of them write in a more or less correct Ionic, neither Tyrtaios nor Theognis using Doric for this kind of composition. Here we have an early and clear example of a usage which prevailed throughout Greek literature. Once a *genre* had established itself, it might and generally did spread beyond the district of its origin ; but writers of other nationalities would adopt the dialect of the earliest models, or at least give their own dialect a flavour of it. In the case of poetry so closely related to the

---

[4] His date is the 37th Olympiad (632–628 B.C.), according to Suidas, *s.u. Μίμνερμος*, who says he was ' of Kolophon, or Smyrna, or Astypalaia '. The date, which is presumably that of his ἀκμή, or prime, usually put by ancient chronologists about the fortieth year of life, agrees well enough with the fact that Solon quotes him (frag. 22 Diehl, cf. Mimn. frag. 6), also with the statement of Plutarch, *de fac. in orbe lunae*, 931 e, that he somewhere mentioned an eclipse of the sun ; there was one on April 6, 648 B.C. He was a professional flute-player, which at that time and place means low rank : see Wilamowitz, *S.S.*, p. 278.

[5] It runs (frag. 1 Diehl), καὶ τόδε Φωκυλίδεω· Λέριοι κακοί, οὐχ ὁ μὲν ὃς δ' οὔ, / πάντες, πλὴν Προκλέους, καὶ Προκλέης Λέριος, a conceit which reappears twice in slightly different forms in Demodokos (frags. 2, 3 Diehl), and is imitated in Porson's famous epigram ' The Germans in Greek '.

hexameter, and therefore to epic, as the elegy, constant imitation of the Homeric style, including the adaptation of whole phrases, borrowings or citations of parts of lines, whole lines and so forth, was almost the rule, and Hesiod likewise was laid under contribution. But it should be noted that the influence of Homer extended further than this, and phrases, words and word-forms borrowed from him may be looked for in almost any kind of poetry, however widely it differs from him in its dialect or its general style. No other poet ever had such wide-reaching effects on later writers as this.[6]

The earliest of these poets of Greece proper was TYRTAIOS of Sparta,[7] who was contemporary with the Second Messenian War (traditionally 685–668 B.C.) and had a great deal to do with the reorganization of the Spartans in face of the formidable dangers of that life-and-death struggle. A sorely battered, but venerable papyrus, dating from the third century B.C., preserves a little of what seems to have been a stirring poem enough, calling on the members of the ancient Dorian tribes, Hylleis, Pamphyloi and Dymanes—in other words, on all true Spartans—to stand fast in their ranks, putting their trust in the gods and the steadiness of their leaders, and then reminding them of the legendary past of their race. There seems to have been a collection of his works under the general title of *Eunomia*, or *Law and Order*; it had, to judge by the fairly abundant fragments, much the same tone, if indeed the papyrus does not simply contain a part of it. It is significant that the kind of valour it praises in good Homeric phraseology is no longer that celebrated in Homer; we hear nothing more of knightly champions dashing about the field in chariots, but of burghers on foot, standing shoulder to shoulder with their spears forward. The tactics and the politics of the times had changed together, and the government was in the hands of what we should call the middle class,

---

[6] Thus, to instance but a small point, the poets now under discussion do not follow Kallinos in the use of κῶς, κότε and so forth, but use the Homeric forms, which were also those of Attic and most literary dialects, πῶς &c.

[7] No attention need be paid to the absurd Athenian story (first in Plato, *Laws*, 629 a) that he was an Athenian, still less to the absurder one (Paus., iv, 15, 6 and schol. on Plat., *l.c.*) that he was a lame Athenian schoolmaster. The discoveries of the British School at Sparta show considerable influence of Asia Minor on Spartan art till the end of the seventh century; if Phoenician nicknacks could find their way there (see Dawkins in *Artemis Orthia*, p. 245), certainly Ionian metres and knowledge of Homeric style might. We have no real reason to call Tyrtaios anything but what he calls himself (frag. 4, Diehl), a Spartan, though it is no doubt possible that he was naturalized.

including all those who, if not rich enough for such expensive luxuries as horses, could provide themselves with a serviceable infantry equipment of body-armour, shield, spear and sword ; in the Greek phrase, could be enrolled as hoplites (ὁπλῖται) or men-at-arms.[8] To influence such a class, some kind of propaganda was necessary, and we may regard Tyrtaios, Solon and others like them as a sort of equivalent of the eighteenth-century pamphleteers and the modern leader-writers, although their literary value was incomparably higher.

Tyrtaios, besides his elegies, wrote war-songs in which he used the Doric dialect and an anapaestic metre ; at any rate, a few scraps of such songs have come down to us, and one of them is attributed to him,[9] but it is to be remembered that works of unknown authorship were and are apt to be ascribed to known authors of about the right date or style.

Passing from Sparta to Athens, we have fairly considerable remains of SOLON, the great statesman and reformer of the sixth century (traditional dates 634–560 or 554 ; these are not to be taken too seriously, for the mere fact that he expresses a hope [10] that he will live to be eighty would be quite enough to set going a story that such was the actual length of his life), who used verse freely to set forth his ideas. We have, preserved in various quotations, an address to the Muses, very likely the beginning of his series of elegies,[11] praying for prosperity, good fame and wealth, but not such wealth as comes by unrighteous means, a theme on which he moralizes at some length ; also passages dealing with the condition of Athens and with his own reforms, and a scrap of the famous poem which, according to the story told in later times, he recited publicly in the guise of a madman,

[8] See M. P. Nilsson in *Klio*, xxii (1928), p. 270 *sqq.* ; *J.R.S.*, 1929, p. 1 *sqq.* ; *Nordstedts Världshistoria*, vol. ii (*Hellas och de hellenistiska rikena*), p. 140 *sqq.*

[9] Fragments, &c., in Diehl, *Anth. Lyr.*, ii, pp. 197–8.

[10] In the fragment referred to above, n. 4 ; Mimnermos having expressed a wish not to live beyond sixty (ἐξηκονταέτη μοῖρα κίχοι θανάτου), Solon bids him correct his line and write rather ὀγδωκονταέτη. The fullest account of Solon in English is Linforth's (see Bibliography) ; for the poem to the Muses, see Wilamowitz, *S.S.*, p. 257 *sqq.* ; more references in Schmid-Stählin, i, p. 371 and in the notes on the preceding pages. Add I. Harrie, *Athenare* (Stockholm, Geber, 1927), pp. 9–49 (in Swedish).

[11] Frag. 1 Diehl ; the suggestion that it began the collection was made by Heinemann, *Studia Solonea*, Berlin, 1897, pp. 34, 37 *sqq.* The general title was simply ἐλεγεῖαι. To what extent the arrangement of the poems was due to Solon himself it is impossible now to say.

to rouse the state to go to war with Megara and make good the Athenian claims on Salamis [12] ; personal addresses to one or two friends, and several pieces of general reflection. A score of lines survive of a poem in trochaic tetrameters, addressed to a certain Phokos, in which he proudly records his own moderation as a reformer and his superiority to vulgar ambition. There is also a passage of about the same length, in iambics, on the services he had done in rescuing citizens from debt-slavery by his economic measures, and a few smaller scraps in the same metre, of which one seems to describe a time of prosperity and feasting, possibly the good days which he hoped the city would now enjoy. The general impression is of the utterance, not of a great poet, although his diction is capable of rising above the commonplace at times and his command of metre is good, but rather of a sane and moderate man, honestly conscious of having done his intelligent best for a sorely tried state.

A lesser man, but a more considerable poet, was a nobleman of Megara, by name THEOGNIS, to whom is ascribed a collection of gnomic poems in elegiacs, nearly 1,400 lines in all. That the whole of it is by him is very unlikely, however, especially as these poems now and then contradict each other in a way scarcely conceivable if they are all from the same hand, and several passages seem to come bodily from other poets, Solon, Tyrtaios, and the obscure EUENOS of Paros. [13] On the other hand, there is no reasonable doubt that a large amount of the collection is really the work of Theognis, especially those parts which are addressed to a young friend, Kyrnos son of Polypas or Polypaos. From these we gather that the author was a stubborn conservative, who saw in the troubles of his day nothing but the madness and degeneracy of men, especially of the lower orders. Hence his ethical advice has throughout a political tinge; Kyrnos is

---

[12] The story is well known from Plutarch, *Solon* 8 ; it being forbidden on pain of death to propose any further attempt to recover Salamis, Solon spread a rumour that he was mad, wrote a poem entitled *Salamis*, which Plutarch says was a hundred lines long and admirably phrased, and rushing out, recited it publicly.

[13] Besides mere resemblances, which prove nothing, Theogn. 153-4 =Solon frag. 5, 9 Diehl; Theogn. 227-9 is almost word for word from Solon frag. 1, 71-3 Diehl; the other borrowings are listed by Schmid-Stählin, i, p. 377, n. 1. As to contradictions, it is hardly likely that the vehement hater of tyranny that Theognis shows himself would give the advice in 847 *sqq.*, to trample on the people and goad them, *i.e.*, to become a pitiless and despotic ruler, unless indeed this is a piece of bitter irony. Nor does one see how the Megarian Theognis would have vineyards on Taygetos (879), or be especially interested in the Corinthian Kypselidai (894).

admonished, for example, to consort only with the ἀγαθοί or ἐσθλοί, but both words mean at once morally good and socially respectable, *i.e.*, belonging to the old land-owning nobility. Within this limitation, imposed by his class and his narrow outlook, Theognis gives typically Greek advice. The great crime, or rather sin, is ὕβρις, wanton, unrestrained frowardness which knows no measure and recognizes no rights in others. It is the greatest evil heaven inflicts on man (151) ; it brings ruin ; it has destroyed many great cities and threatens to destroy Megara (44 ; 541 ; 604 ; 835). Its consequence in the state is tyranny (40), which is the last stage of public calamity. There is no better bequest for a man to leave his children than the opposite of ὕβρις, namely αἰδώς, the nearest classical equivalent to the Christian virtue of humility (409) ; the greatest of all blessings is γνώμη, sound sense or prudence which will keep men from follies and let them follow the safe and moderate path (cf. 219 ; 335). One ought to practise piety towards father and mother (131), towards strangers and suppliants (143), above all towards the gods (see 805–10). He should be honest and truthful (87–92), a faithful friend and steadfast in all things (319 *sqq.* ; 811), and show a wise mistrust before he gives any one his confidence (75 ; 213 *sqq.*), but not be too mistrustful or ready to think evil (323 *sqq.*), for after all, no one is perfect and only the gods never mistake (327). These virtues, Theognis implies, are characteristic of his own class, the ἀγαθοί, when true to their traditions ; the more reason, then, for not marrying out of it (183–192). Wealth in itself is nothing of any great value, if piety and righteousness do not go with it (145–150), and it is to be remembered that chance or fate will have the last word (130 ; 817).[14]

As to the rest of the verses which make up the collection, no agreement has yet been reached [15] as to how they were added, or on what principle. The quotations from other authors which we can trace (see note 13) suggest that some unknown editor intended to make an anthology of early gnomic poems in elegiacs ; this is supported by

[14] All the above examples are taken from the passages most certainly Theognidean, those in which Kyrnos is addressed by name. Theognis says (19 *sqq.*) that he has set a ' seal ' on his work to prevent it from being counterfeited ; and the most reasonable interpretation of his words seems to be that the ' seal ' (= imprint of a signet) is the name of his young friend.

[15] A summary of attempts will be found in Hudson-Williams, p. 12 *sqq.*, whose attitude of skepticism I share. E. Harrison, *Studies in Theognis*, 1902, argues for Theognis as the author of practically the whole collection ; I should be willing to admit that he may have written much besides the Kyrnos-poems, but certainly not all.

such facts as the presence in the beginning of the first book of no fewer than four addresses to different deities, apparently the prologues to separate works, whereof the fourth, to the Muses and Charites, breaks off in the middle of a sentence. But it remains a puzzle how and when the poems we have were put together, still more why so erratic a collection was made. The last 150 lines, however, found in one MS. only and printed by most modern editors as a second book, have at least a common subject. They are all more or less distinctly amatory and all deal with the romantic affection for boys which was characteristic of the Dorian nobility especially, with results which ranged from a high and noble friendship to a peculiarly disgusting form of vice. Some of the little poems which occur here are addressed to Kyrnos, a few can be traced to authors other than Theognis.

Theognis himself would appear to have written in the latter half of the sixth century. We know the troubled history of Megara but imperfectly ; it is fairly certain, however, that a tyrant, by name Theagenes, established himself for a time about 525, his rule forming an interlude in a series of violent revolutions.[16] Theognis' frequent references to the insolence of the lower orders, their attempts at governing and the imminence of tyranny would fit this period very well ; we may therefore suppose him to have written from about the middle of the century till some time previous to Theagenes' usurpation of power, since no passage unambiguously states that there is a tyrant in Megara. This also fits with the opinion of the ancients, as reported by Suidas,[17] that he lived in the 59th Olympiad, *i.e.*, was in his prime 545–541 B.C.

Before leaving the elegiac poets it should be mentioned that during this period, and especially as the fifth century approaches, the practice of writing epigrams begins, a subject which will be discussed more fully in dealing with the Alexandrians. To inscribe a brief memorial of some kind on stone or metal (for instance, the name and country of a dead man on his tomb, those of a dedicator on the object dedicated, and the like) has been the custom of many nations. The Greeks, with their usual artistic sense, preferred to have the inscription as well phrased as possible. Hence it early became customary to inscribe a line

---

[16] Some good remarks on this subject in Halliday, *Q.G.*, see his index under *Megara*.

[17] Suid, *s.u.* Θέογνις. The critics to whom his note must ultimately go back had before them more verses ascribed to Theognis than we have ; besides an ' elegy addressed to those of the Syracusans who survived the siege ', which can hardly be by Theognis of Megara, he gives the length of his γνῶμαι δι' ἐλεγείας as 2,800 lines ; we have about half that number.

or two of verse containing the desired information, and for this purpose the elegiac couplet was found very suitable, though it was never the only metre in use. But to state plain fact simply yet not dully, without omitting anything essential or adding any superfluous ornament, while paying due attention to metre and poetic diction, is far from easy, and the services of a professional poet were not seldom called upon. It therefore is not surprising that many of the best writers mentioned in this and the next two chapters are credited with the authorship of epigrams, in this, the original, sense of the word ; Simonides in particular is supposed to have written a considerable number, no doubt including some which he did not write and others which do not belong to his age at all.

The IAMBIC POETS begin with one of the most interesting figures in Greek literary history, and one the loss of whose works we have most cause to regret. Not long before the year 700, the rocky and barren island of Paros (not yet deriving a revenue from its famous quarries, for Parian marble did not become fashionable among architects and sculptors till considerably later) sent out a colony to Thasos, a fertile and wooded island off the Thracian coast. One of the settlers was a man of noble family, by name Telesikleides (Tellis for short).[18] His grandson and namesake, following a practice not uncommon and tolerated by public feeling, took a slave-woman, by name Enipo, as his concubine, and had a son, perhaps also a daughter, by her.[19] The son was given the aristocratic name of ARCHILOCHOS (captain, leader of a company), and would occupy a recognized place in the family, though decidedly inferior to that of a legitimate child. He grew up something of an adventurer, willing to take risks to mend his fortunes (like his great-grandfather he also went to Thasos), and apparently inherited the enterprise of his father's family together with the bitter feelings of a *déclassé*, and added a poetical gift which was all his own. It would seem that he took delight in flouting the conventions of the aristocracy,

---

[18] Pausanias says (x, 28, 3) that Polygnotos' famous picture of Hades showed Tellis crossing the Styx in Charon's boat, and that he is represented as a youth ; he cannot, therefore, have had a long life. His date is got approximately by reckoning back from the datable events in the poet's life, who probably (but see Hudson-Williams, *Elegy*, pp. 9–12) saw the eclipse of April 6, 648 B.C., and was then in Thasos, for it was not visible at Paros, knew of Gyges king of Lydia, who died about 652 (frags. 22 and 74 Diehl), and therefore must have lived about the middle of the seventh century.

[19] The poet had a sister (Plutarch, *quomodo adulescens*, 23 b), but she may have been his half-sister and a legitimate daughter of Telesikleides.

that he was a rebel against their decencies and especially that he had few reticences. His doubtful birth, his personal loves and hatreds, his poverty and his adventures were all made themes of his poetry, to such an extent that his verses were largely auto-biographical and what we know of him almost certainly comes from no other source.[10]   His final offence was against the conventions of military honour.   The heavy shield was, to a Greek hoplite, almost as completely the embodiment of his title to be called a man of courage as was the sword to an old-fashioned Spanish nobleman.   The Spartan tradition was to ' carry it back or be carried back on it '.   In Athens, to tell a man that he had thrown his shield away was very serious slander, and Solon's laws punished it accordingly.   Now Archilochos was a soldier and probably did not lack courage ; [11] but in an unsuccessful battle of the Thasians against a tribe of Thrace, the Saioi, he threw his shield away in the rout.   Instead of carefully concealing this disgraceful fact, he published and made fun of it in a poem whereof the horrified interest of later times has preserved us a fragment.[12]

If he lacked reverence for established standards of conduct, he certainly lacked restraint where his personal feelings were concerned.   He fell, it would seem, violently in love with a girl named Neobule, and sought her in marriage.   Her father, Lykambes, seems to have agreed to the match and then broken it off.   Archilochos so lampooned the father and daughter alike that, according to later tradition, they both hanged themselves.[13] The vigour and zest of some abusive passages which survive among his fragments make the story, though there is no proof that it is true, certainly plausible.

It is characteristic of the poet that he sought other than the respectable dactylic measures wherein to express himself.   Some of his poems were indeed in elegiacs, but the bulk seem to have been in various iambic metres, trochees, and original com-

---

[10] The above genealogy is put together from Pausanias (cited in n. 18), Aelian (?) *ap*. Suidas *s.u.* 'Αρχίλοχος, and Kritias *ap*. Aelian, *Var. Hist.*, x, 13 (frag. 44 Diels) ; all probably go for the facts to Archilochos himself, directly or indirectly.

[11] To judge from frags. 1, 2, 7 Diehl.

[12] Frag. 6 Diehl.

[13] The story is told by Cruquius' commentator on Horace, *epod.*, vi, 13 (Lykambes and Neobule hang themselves), and the authors (all late) of *Anth. Pal.*, vii, 69, 70, 71, 351, 352 (Neobule and her sister or sisters hang themselves, because A. had falsely asserted they were unchaste). The following fragments certainly or probably relate to this affair : 24, 25 (?), 71, 72 (?), 74, 79, 88 *sqq.* ; 66 consists of the grim statement that A. knows one great art, to speak ill of whoever uses him ill.

binations in which the aristocratic dactyl and the plebeian iambus were strangely mated. Of the miserable handful of fragments which, by ill luck, are all we have left of this notable writer, admired by some in antiquity as almost on a level with Homer himself,[24] a large proportion come from metricians who cite them as examples of unusual rhythms, or as the earliest instances of metres afterwards popular. Another characteristic feature is that he used that typically popular form, the beast-fable, which thus makes its appearance for the second time in European literature.[25] There is just a possibility that he used his talent in a way which became respectable enough in the next century, by writing poems for those who would pay him for them ; that would at all events account for the presence of four items among his fragments very different from the personal tone of the rest, two epigrams (if they are really by him) and two hymns.[26] His end was violent, for he was killed in a battle against the Naxians by a certain Kalondas, surnamed the Crow ; in later days Paros was very proud of his memory, and it hardly need be added that a tale grew up to the effect that the Delphic oracle denounced Kalondas for killing a servant of the Muses.[27]

Roughly contemporary with Archilochos was another islander, SEMONIDES of Samos,[28] son of Krineas, who is said to have written

[24] See Quintilian, *inst. orat.*, x, 1, 60, some think *quod quoquam minor est, materiae esse non ingenii uitium* ; Cicero, *orator*, 4 (Homer, Archilochos, Sophokles and Pindar named together as the supreme poets of Greece). More examples in Schmid-Stählin, i, p. 389, n. 2.

[25] See Halliday, *Greek and Roman Folklore* (Longmans, Green & Co., 1927), p. 101 *sqq.*, for a good sketch of the Aesopic fable in Greece. Aesop (Αἴσωπος), if there ever was such a person, is said to have lived in the sixth century ; but Hesiod has the fable of the Hawk and the Nightingale, see above, p. 59.

[26] Frags. 16, 17, 119, 120 Diehl.

[27] The earliest authority for the fact and the legend is Herakleides Pontikos, in Müller, *F.G.H.*, ii, p. 214 ; *cf.* Galen, *Protrepticus* (vol. i, pp. 22–3 Kühn), also Suid., cited in n. 20. More refs. in Schmid-Stählin, i, p. 391, n. 8.

[28] See Suid., *s.u. Σιμωνίδης Κρίνεω*, for his works. His name is persistently confused in spelling with that of Simonides (see p. 111), an easy mistake, as η came to be pronounced with a narrower and narrower sound, till finally it became identical with ι, as in Mod. Gk. The only elegiac passage which there is reason to attribute to him (frag. 29 Diehl) has come down to us under the name of the better-known poet. The true spelling is preserved by the grammarian Choiroboskos in *Etym. Mag.*, 713, 17 (ἐπὶ μὲν τοῦ ἰαμβοποιοῦ διὰ τοῦ η γράφεται . . . τὸ δὲ ἐπὶ τοῦ λυρικοῦ διὰ τοῦ ι). As he was one of the founders of the Samian colony at Amorgos (Suid., *l.c.*), he is often called 'of Amorgos', especially by those modern writers who misspell his name.

elegiacs and other works, and certainly wrote iambics. Our principal relic of him is a very quaint poem, related in substance to the beast-fable, explaining that the minds of women were created from various beasts, sow, vixen, bitch, ass, stoat, mare, ape, and some also from earth and the sea ; the only satisfactory sort is made from bees. Another passage deals with the vanity of human hopes.[29]

About a century later than Archilochos [30] lived a man who may be regarded as a sort of exaggeration of him, HIPPONAX. To judge by his name, he was of good family ; all names compounded of ἵππος suggest nobility, since they allude to the breeding of horses for war or racing, which was a traditionally noble occupation. But, according to Suidas, he was banished from his native Ephesos by the obscure tyrants Athenagoras and Komas, and went to Klazomenai ; the latter fact, and probably the former also, is derived from his own works. In Klazomenai he seems to have fallen into great poverty, and whether for this or some other reason, he constituted himself the veritable bard of the gutter. Archilochos gives us glimpses of common life, and is on occasion coarse ; Hipponax, to judge by what we have left of him, was habitually foul and had a predilection for the worst doings of the lowest classes. One result of this was that he used most extraordinary words, many of them certainly not Greek and apparently Lydian, presumably to give the effect of the jargon spoken in Kolophonian slums. Another effect was the adoption of a strange metre, called by metricians the σκάζων (limping verse) or χωλίαμβος (lame iambus), which differed from the ordinary iambic trimeter by having a spondee in the last place, giving an odd, hesitant effect. But he also seems to have used spondees in other places where they may not come in legitimate iambic lines (the ends of the metra), unless indeed he was deliberately mis-scanning certain words, to reproduce a vulgar pronunciation.[31] He introduced a corresponding change into his trochaic verses. Two notable events of his life seem to have been a love affair with a woman called Arête, of whom we do not gather that she was conspicuous for either high station or

---

[29] Frags. 7 and 1 Diehl.

[30] He was contemporary with the capture of Sardis by Cyrus (Marmor Parium, ep. 43), i.e., 546 ; he lived during the 60th Olympiad (540–537), Pliny, N.H., xxxvi, 11. Cf. Suid., s.u. Ἱππῶναξ.

[31] He scans φαρμάκὸς five times, frags. 7–11, Diehl ; apparently κακομήχᾶνε, frag. 45, 1 ; either βάκτηρίᾳ, 14, 1, εὔωνον, 31, or illegitimate spondees in both cases ; ἡμίεκτον at the beginning of a scazon, 14, 2, may be a case of synizesis ; spondee in second foot, 28 ; scazon ends – ∪ ∪ – ∪ ∪ – –, 27.

virtue,[32] and a quarrel with two sculptors, Bupalos and Athenis. The story went that they made a caricature-statue of the poet's ugly face, and were so distressed by his furious lampoons against them that they committed suicide ; the former statement is highly unlikely, for realistic portrait-statues and caricatures do not belong to the art of the sixth century, and the latter is disproved by Pliny from the existence of works of theirs of later date than the quarrel. No doubt the story of Archilochos and Lykambes had something to do with this tale, but surviving fragments show that Bupalos was vehemently and coarsely attacked.[33] Polemon credited Hipponax with the invention of parody, and it is true that his fragments include the beginning of a poem in Homeric verse, making fun of one Eurymedontiades, a glutton, who seems to have been led through a mock-Odyssey of grotesque adventures.[34] Two decided merits Hipponax had, fidelity in his descriptions and concise vigour of style, and these brought him attention from later writers, not merely seekers after curiosities or improprieties, but the masters of Attic comedy and two of the most notable Alexandrians, Kallimachos and Herodas (see pp. 322, 339).

A much less conspicuous figure was ANANIOS, apparently about contemporary with Hipponax [35] and using the same metres. We have less than a score of lines of him and so can form no judgement of his powers ; as regards his subject-matter, we find him using a strange oath, 'by cabbage!', addressing Apollo and discussing the merits of various sorts of fish.

When we pass to SOLO LYRIC, we have to begin by lamenting a great loss, not simply to learned curiosity, but to the highest poetry of the world. The list of writers is headed by the name of a woman, SAPPHO, or more properly PSAPPHO, the Lesbian.[36]

[32] See frags. 15–22 Diehl. It would appear from 15 and 20 that Bupalos was Hipponax' rival.

[33] The story is mentioned by Suidas, *l.c.*, and several other writers, and discussed by Pliny, *N.H.*, *l.c.* See frags. 1, 13, 15, 20 Diehl. Hipponax fell foul of another artist, Mimnes the painter, frag. 45.

[34] Frags. 77, 78 ; for Polemon's views, see Athenaios, 698 b.

[35] He cites (frag. 1 Diehl) a saying of Pythermos, for whom see p. 102, and according to Athenaios, 282 b, was cited by Epicharmos. This puts him between about 550 and about 490. His fragments are in Diehl, i, pp. 286–7, to which add *Oxyrh. Pap.*, viii, p. 105, 56. Some named him as the inventor of the scazon, see Hephaistion, v, 5 (p. 33, Gaisford).

[36] Her name is properly Ψάπφω in her own dialect (voc. Ψάπφοι, frags. 68, 5 ; 144b Diehl ; Ψάπφ', frag. 1, 20 and 96, 6, the elided syllable being probably -οι). It is Σάπφοι (voc.) in Alkaios, frag. 63 Diehl, from a nom. Σάπφω, which would be accented Σαπφώ in most dialects. The genuineness of the fragment has been contested, *e.g.*, by Lobel, but

She was a contemporary and acquaintance of Alkaíos (see p. 98),
and, like him, lived through the very stormy times when the
democracy of Lesbos, led by several able and ambitious seekers
after power, Melanchros, Myrsilos and Pittakos the sage,[37] was
overthrowing the ancient nobility of the island. Probably therefore she was born about the middle of the seventh century ; if
the complaint of whitening hair and weakening limbs which a
fragmentary poem of hers contains [38] is spoken, as it probably is,
in her own person, she lived to a fairly advanced age. She
perhaps died in Sicily ; there is some evidence [39] that she took
refuge at Syracuse from the turmoil of Lesbian revolutions,
and certainly the Syracusans set up, in the fourth century, a
statue of her, a masterpiece of the artist Silanıon, which adorned
their town hall until Verres stole it.[40] Her native city was
Mytilene, though Eressos also claimed her.[41] That she was

there is nothing against it except the form of the name. Σαπφώ and Σαπώ
are also found, but are less correct. There was a biography of her in
antiquity, probably derived from her own works chiefly if not entirely,
and containing a number of quotations. Of this we have a résumé,
without quotations, in Suidas, s.u. Σαπφώ, and another, very fragmentary,
in *Oxyr. Pap.* 1800 (vol. xv, p. 138), while more can be recovered from
Ovid, or whoever wrote the *Epistle of Sappho* generally printed as No. 15
of his *Heroides*, and from Maximus of Tyre, *orat.* xviii (xxiv), 7 and 9,
besides occasional uses of it elsewhere. See Aly in Pauly-Wissowa, art.
Sappho, cols. 2360 *sqq.* See pp. 102, 422.

[37] For the events in question, see any history of the time ; all three
names are mentioned in the fragments of Alkaios. Pittakos is usually
reckoned among the Seven Sages.

[38] Frag. 65 Diehl.

[39] The Life does not seem to have mentioned this, but it has the
respectable authority of the Marmor Parium, ep. 36 (somewhere between
603 and 595 B.C.), where see Jacoby. Against it we may perhaps set the
fact that Ovid makes her regret she is not a Sicilian (*Sicilis esse uolo*, 52),
and says nothing of her going to Sicily. What is certainly unhistorical
is the tale on which his poem is based, that she loved a certain Phaon,
who left her and went to Sicily, and that she leaped off the Leukadian
Rock in an attempt to cure herself of this passion. The facts are well
given in Palmer's notes on the epistle ; Phaon was not a man, but a
daimon connected with Aphrodite. The story seems to appear first in
the comedy of the fourth century B.C. (as Menander 312 Koch), and may
not unreasonably be thought derived from a deliberate misinterpretation
of some passage in Sappho's own poems in which the beauty of the daimon
Phaon was dwelt upon, as it may well have been in a hymn to Aphrodite
or the like. Cf. Lisi, *P.G.*, pp. 33-43.

[40] Cicero, *in Verrem*, ii, 4, 126-7 ; for Silanion's date, see Pliny, *N.H.*,
xxxiv, 51 (Olymp. 113, *i.e.*, 326-323 B.C.).

[41] For Mytilene, see Herodotos, ii, 135 ; Eressos was named in the
Life, see Suid., *l.c.*, and its coins sometimes have her head on them.
She probably therefore had some kind of connexion with it.

married and had a daughter named Kleis is stated by ancient authorities and follows from the natural interpretation of one of the fragments.[42] All we know of her indicates that she was of a good family, and that is a fact of some importance.

We have no sufficient grounds for stating that the Aiolic dialect had as yet a literature of its own, though it is of course possible, even likely, that ballads, hymns and other such compositions existed.[43] But to form a literary language from a spoken dialect requires a process of polishing and selecting, which can take place in either of two ways. One is the handling of the dialect in question by writers of ability who gradually create a standard diction ; sometimes one great writer whose works are both extensive and popular will do this single-handed. The other way is the use of the dialect by a leisured and refined class, and not least by its women. Our evidence is [44] that Sappho wrote as she spoke, owing practically nothing to any literary influence, even that of Homer, except for certain classes of more formal compositions, and owing little to it even there. Hence she has, as we can see even from the pitifully small remnants of her verse that survive, the charm of absolute naturalness combined with most dainty refinement.

Her subjects are equally simple and natural—herself, her friends and their feelings towards each other. Men played very

[42] The daughter was mentioned and called Kleis in the Life (papyrus and Suid., cf. Ovid, 70, 120) ; frag. 152 runs ἔστι μοι κάλα πάϊς χρυσέοισιν ἀνθέμοισιν/ἐμφέρην ἔχοισα μόρφαν Κλεῦις ἀγαπάτα,/ἀντὶ τᾶς ἐγὼ οὐδὲ Λυδίαν παῖσαν οὐδ' ἐράνναν. . . . A difficulty, however, is that Sappho does not elsewhere use ἐστί, but πέλεται, for ' is ', see Lobel, A.M., pp. xxxviii–xxxix ; there is therefore the possibility that the passage is not hers. If it is not, the probable source of the statement in the Life disappears. Personally, I am of opinion that it is hers. I cannot agree with Aly, op. cit., col. 2361, 40, that her husband's name, Kerkylas, is an invention of comedy ; it is true it could be punned upon (Κερκύλας—κέρκος, with indecent implications), but if that were taken as a criterion, many names of real persons (Kinesias, for example) would have to pass out of history into fiction.

[43] That Aiolic elements exist in epic is of course not denied. There is a very ingenious theory of Fick (outlined in Cauer, *Grundfragen*, p. 164 sqq., q.u., for more details) that the Homeric poems in their original form were composed in Aiolic ; on the basis of the greater or lesser ease with which he found himself able to translate various portions into Aiolic he tried to establish a chronology of the poems. His theory, however, has not been generally accepted even by separatists ; and in any case, neither he nor any one else supposed that the Iliad in its earliest form was in the dialect of Lesbos. Aiolic has many varieties.

[44] The dialect has been very carefully studied by Lobel, *opp. citt.*, introductions.

little part in her life ; she mentions her brother,[45] perhaps Alkaios,[46] and some lost passage may have spoken of her husband, for our authorities tell us his name, Kerkylas of Andros. But the foreground is filled with the bright figures of young women, towards whom Sappho, by her own account, felt, not sisterly or motherly affection, but passionate love,[47] the counterpart of the men's romantic attitude towards the beauty of younger men. One poem seems to have told the story of her relations to an especial favourite, Atthis, for two stray lines of it say simply ' I fell in love with you long ago, Atthis ' and ' I thought you an undersized child and without charm '.[48] One of the most famous passages,[49] preserved through the just admiration felt for it by that admirable critic, the so-called Longinus (see p. 400), declares that the husband of one of these friends is as enviable as a god, for Sappho herself cannot even see her without almost fainting from emotion. That this is an abnormal condition is very clear ; but that it involved any uncleanliness is an idea wholly without support from our evidence and contradicted by the respect with which the best ages of antiquity uniformly mention Sappho.

An unfortunate result of Sappho's strange temperament and high

[45] Notably in frag. 25. We know from Herodotos, *loc. cit.*, what the occasion of this ode was ; Charaxos, as he was called, had gone to Egypt and there fallen in love with and purchased the freedom of a hetaira, whom Herodotos wrongly identifies with the famous Rhodopis (Sappho calls her Doricha, frag. 26, and Rhodopis was in her prime in the days of Amasis, Pharaoh 569–526, Hdt., ii, 134, 2, fifty years or so too late for Charaxos to have known her). Ovid 65–6 implies that Charaxos ruined himself over Doricha and turned pirate to retrieve his fortunes.

[46] The traditional interpretation of frag. 149 Diehl is that it is a reply to Alkaios, frag. 63. In Sappho, some one says, ' I have somewhat that I would say, but shame lets me,' and is answered, ' If your desire were for aught good and noble, and your tongue did not itch to say somewhat evil, shame would not fill your eyes, but you would speak concerning what is righteous.' We have the excellent authority of Aristotle, *Rhet.*, i, 9, 20 (1367ᵃ 9) for saying that the some one in question is Alkaios ; but this is no reason for connecting it with his fragment, which is in a different metre and consists of the courtly address ἰόπλοκ' ἄγνα μελλιχόμειδε Σάπφοι.

[47] Examples will be found *passim* ; some outstanding instances are frags. 2, 40, 137. A list of those who thought evil of Sappho will be found in Aly, *op. cit.*, col. 2361, 52 *sqq.* ; it is short, contains no name of authority in such a matter, and has against it the best opinion ancient and modern, from Alkaios through Maximus of Tyre to Wilamowitz, to say nothing of many others. A brief defence of Sappho, all the more interesting because written by a woman, will be found in Lisi, *P.G.*, pp. 51–62.

[48] Frags. 40 and 41.

[49] *Ibid.*, 2, preserved in the *de sublimitate*, 10, 2.

genius (she is the only woman who has yet written poetry of the first
order) is that her fragments are surrounded with a mass of speculation,
sometimes learned, sometimes merely imaginative, sentimental, or
even morbid. The most far-reaching theories have been spun out
of a few stray words, and fragmentary poems, especially those discovered on papyri, have been restored and emended often with great
ingenuity but also with no real evidence whatsoever for either the
language or the sense arrived at by the restorer. It is therefore most
advisable to start from Lobel, who contents himself with printing
accurately the modest amount of Sappho which we really have and
studying it from a purely philological standpoint. See p. 422.

Sappho gathered around her a group, how organized or if
organized at all we do not know, of friends, all of her own sex.
It is a not unattractive theory [50] that they were formally a cult-
organization or *thiasos*. This would agree with what is said in
frag. 99 Diehl, for example : ' these precious gifts, these kerchiefs
of bright purple sheen, Mnasis (a former member of the circle ?)
sends thee from Phokaia '. We know [51] that Aphrodite is
addressed here, and it may be that we have a fragment of a little
hymn of dedication. Be that as it may, Sappho certainly worshipped Aphrodite with fervent sincerity, and perhaps her most
famous remaining poem is the ode in which she invokes the aid
of the goddess to win some reluctant friend's love and praises her
for a former occasion on which she appeared in person and smil-
ingly promised her help.[52] That we hear also of the Charites
and the Muses is only what might be expected ; a little more
out of the common at so early a date is a scrap of a poem which
dealt with the story of Adonis.[53] But the bulk of the surviving
specimens of Sappho's nine books of verse [54] deal with personal
matters. She prays the Nereids to bring her brother safe home and
give him a better mind towards those who love him.[55] A dream
has come to her, bringing good hopes.[56] One of her friends
has left and forgotten her, pretending much sorrow at the part-

[50] See Aly, *op. cit.*, cols. 2377–8, where more references are given ;
add Lisi, *P.G.*, p. 30 : ' non è ardito il pensare che Saffo fosse una
sacerdotessa di Afrodite e riunisse atorno a sè giovinette di nobile famiglie,
perchè venissero educate '.

[51] Frag. 99, preserved by Athenaios, 410 d, e, who says it is addressed
πρὸς τὴν 'Αφροδίτην.

[52] *Ibid.*, 1.   [53] *Ibid.*, 107 Diehl.

[54] Or eight, see Lobel, *Σ.M.*, pp. xiii–xiv.

[55] Frag. 25 ; cf. n. 45.

[56] *Ibid.*, 67 ; in frag. 28 the poem begins with a vision of Hera in a
dream, and at once proceeds, by a rather abrupt transition, to speak of
the War of Troy. Possibly, as in 27, this may have led, via the beauty
of Helen, to the beauty of one of Sappho's friends.

ing.[57] Another, Arignota, is married to some one in Sardis, and Sappho pictures her, the most beautiful woman there, regretfully thinking of old days with Atthis.[58] Atthis has deserted her for Andromeda, a rustic creature who cannot dress properly.[59] Other poems are on more general subjects. Epithalamia or marriage-hymns seem to have filled one of the books ; [60] perhaps it was the custom of the circle to write and sing one when a member left to marry. A poem of which a considerable part is left deals with an allied subject, the wedding of Hektor and Andromache,[61] and another, very fragmentary, had a good deal to say of the Trojan War.[62] But the key-note almost everywhere is struck by Sappho's own feelings ; and it would be difficult to imagine a more suitable subject for personal lyric than the thoughts, joys and sorrows of this strange and brilliant woman, nor a better medium than her perfectly simple language, put into perfect metre.

Compared with Sappho, ALKAIOS was a much simpler character, although an excellent poet within his somewhat narrow range of subjects. That so good a judge as Horace took him for a model and obviously admired him greatly is evidence of his worth, and he also gives a good summary of Alkaios' themes ; he was a warrior and a wanderer, but in the pauses of his fighting and voyaging he was ready to sing of wine and love.[63] The fragments, for not one poem of Alkaios has come down to us complete, bear Horace out. We find several manifest references to the distressed state of the country : the ship of state is making heavy weather ; [64] ' this man who desires great power will capsize the city ere long ' another fragment puts it, more plainly.[65] He is himself in exile, and his party have been helped with money

[57] Frag. 96, one of the longest and best preserved. It has been conjectured that the unfaithful friend was Atthis.

[58] Ibid., 98 ; we have five stanzas complete and parts of two more.

[59] Ibid., 137, 61 ; the latter is preserved by Athenaios, who tells us (21 b) that Andromeda is referred to. She was probably the head of a similar circle to Sappho's own.   [60] The eighth or ninth.

[61] Frag. 55 ; in view of the good external evidence for Sapphic authorship, I do not agree with Lobel's rejection of this poem on linguistic grounds, Σ.M., p. lxv, A.M., xvii. There is always the possibility, however, that some poems of the collection were written by other members of the circle, not necessarily Lesbians, under Sappho's guidance.   [62] Ibid., 70.

[63] Hor., carm., i, 32, 6–12 ; cf. carm., ii, 25 sqq. ; both Sappho and Alkaios are heard with delight among the shades, but especially Alkaios, who can charm the very monsters of Tartaros with his ' fuller ' strains.

[64] Frags. 30 and 46 Diehl (that they belong to the same poem is not certain, but likely ; it has been doubted that the storm is metaphorical, see Diehl's notes) ; cf. Hor., carm., i, 14.   [65] Ibid., 31.

by the Lydians.[66] Again, he is wild with joy, for the tyrant Myrsilos has been killed ; [67] the good news is a sufficient excuse for drinking heavily—not that Alkaios ever needed very elaborate reasons for so pleasant an exercise. Elsewhere, plans for some enterprise are evidently made, for a ' great house ' is full of arms and armour.[68] The poet's own part in the fighting was not always very distinguished, for he, like Archilochos, had the misfortune to lose his shield, not in the constant civil brawls, but in a war with Athens for the possession of Sigeion in the Troad.[69] However, the general impression one receives is that he was bold enough. Of political theory he had little, save vigorous hatred of all democrats and their leaders, the tyrants in the making ; his general view of society was apparently that in these days nothing but money counts for very much,[70] and his usual moral was, that wine is a good cure for all manner of ills.[71] Of his lovemaking we hear a certain amount in the surviving fragments,[72] though it so happens that the beautiful boy Lykos whom Horace says Alkaios celebrated does not appear in them.[73] In addition to these themes, there are several remnants of hymns to various deities and heroes, Apollo, Hermes, Athena, Eros, Hephaistos, Dionysos, the Nymphs, Achilles and Aias ; so far as we can judge from the little that is left, they were all solos, and the names chosen are natural enough for a writer concerned with war (Athena, Achilles, Aias) and poetry (Apollo, Hermes), a lover (Eros) and a drinker (Dionysos, the Nymphs, *i.e.*, wine and water together),[74] who lived near Asia Minor (Hephaistos). Throughout, there is something rather lovable in Alkaios, who creates the impression of having been a good friend, honest and impulsive, with more loyalty and vigour than prudence or depth.

[66] Frag. 42.   [67] *Ibid.*, 39.   [68] *Ibid.*, 54.

[69] *Ibid.*, 49 ; Herodotos, v, 94–5 ; Strabo, xiii, 1, 38.   [70] Frag. 101.

[71] *E.g.*, frag. 86 (after toil or misfortune, and in old age) ; 90 (because the weather is cold and stormy) ; 91 (because one must not brood over ill-luck) ; 94 (because the weather is very hot and dry) ; 96 (because wine is the good gift of Dionysos).

[72] As frags. 65, 68, 69, 99, and along with drinking in several passages ; 67 seems to be a dramatic lyric, the supposed speaker being a girl in sorrow of some kind.

[73] His name is to be found in frag. 58 Bergk, οὐκέτ' ἐγὼ Λύκον/ἐν Μοίσαις ἀλέγω, but on further examination this appears to be wrongly read and attributed ; it comes from schol. Pind. Ol., x, 15, but seems to be no more than a misunderstanding, or miscopying, of Alkman (see below, p. 104), frag. 1, 2 Diehl, οὐκ ἐγὼν Λύκαισον ἐγ καμοῦσιν ἀλέγω. The names of the two poets are not seldom confused.

[74] Alkaios was a heavy drinker, but not a sot ; therefore, being a Greek, he drank his wine diluted. Cf., for Dionysos and the Nymphs in this connexion, *Anth. Pal.*, ix, 331 (Meleagros).

His date is roughly determined by the events he refers to. He, Sappho, Stesichoros and Pittakos are all said to have ' flourished ' in the 42nd Olympiad (612–609 B.C.) ; [75] all four of them therefore would have been born not far from the middle of the seventh century. How long Alkaios lived and how he died we do not know.

The Ionian civilization, vigorous enough to begin with, passed into a period of degenerescence by the sixth century ; admixture with the local populations brought about a certain weakening of the true Greek spirit, and at the same time, the rapid expansion of the great empires, first of Lydia and then of Persia, made the little city-state become an anachronism in Asia Minor two centuries earlier than in Greece proper. Under these circumstances, there were two possible courses, apart from rebellion, which proved futile when attempted, because the rebels lacked organization and energy. One was wholesale emigration, the other, abandonment of political interests, coupled with attention to intellectual or voluptuous refinements. From intellectual activities, philosophy resulted ; from the voluptuous, ANAKREON. This poet has had the singular fate of becoming famous in modern times chiefly for poems which were not composed till centuries after he was dead. A native of Teos in Ionia, he left his native city for the colony of Abdera ; [76] thence he seems to have gone to the court of Polykrates, tyrant of Samos, and, on the fall of Polykrates, was sent for by Hipparchos, son of Peisistratos, to Athens.[77] His seems to have been a pleasure-loving nature, not degraded nor coarse, but hardly capable of anything involving much physical or mental exertion. The circles in which he moved represented in its perfection the ' Ionian way of life ', βίος Ἰωνικός, which the rest of the Greek world regarded much as England or Germany did the Paris of the Second Empire, with moral disapproval combined with

---

[75] Suidas, *loc. cit.* ; cf. Diogenes Laertios, i, 74, Pittakos overthrows Melanchros ; *ibid.*, 79, he ἤκμαζε in Olymp. 42 and died in Olymp. 52, 3 (569 B.C.). Pittakos was himself a poet, *ibid.*, and a skolion by him is preserved (Diehl, ii, p. 191).

[76] Suidas, *s.u.*, Ἀνακρέων, says it was ' owing to the revolt of Histiaios ' ; but this was the Ionian revolt (end of the sixth and beginning of the fifth century), in which H. took a prominent part. Suidas' authority has probably confused Harpagos the contemporary of Histiaios (Hdt., vi, 28, 2) with the better-known Harpagos who invaded Ionia about the middle of the sixth century, and so put Histiaios himself about 50 years too early ; cf. Schmid-Stählin, i, p. 430, n. 14.

[77] Strabo, xiv, i, 16 ; [Plato], *Hipparchos*, 228c ; the author does not say when this was, but that Polykrates was then dead is highly probable in itself.

admiration for its elegance. Anakreon wrote the ideal poetry for such hearers to appreciate. His taste is absolutely faultless ; the metre is as simple as the language, the thought as limpidly clear as its expression. A beginner in Greek could construe the fragments, and it is fortunate that a first-rate critic has taken the trouble to illustrate their perfection.[78]

Besides these little gems—songs of love and wine, addresses to gods whom nobody took very seriously, turning into compliments to human beings, pronouncements concerning the proper and civilized way to conduct a banquet [79]—we have a few compositions of Anakreon which show that there was something more in him than the favourite poet of a brilliant if rather corrupt court. One or two morsels of satire remind us that he came of the same race as Archilochos ; there are three utterances of regret for the loss of brave comrades in battle which show that he must have seen some fighting himself, probably against the Thracians, who were ill neighbours to Abdera ; once there is a skeleton at the feast, for Anakreon says that he is growing old, grey and toothless, and sobs with dread when he thinks of what comes after death. But it is not a very despairing sob ; neither he nor any Ionian was ever devil-ridden.[80]

Anakreon's verses often resembled what are generally called *skolia, i.e.*, after-dinner songs ; the relation of the name to the adjective σκολιός (crooked) is doubtful. Indeed, he and Alkaios were thought of as being the authors of some of the older pieces of this kind.[81] In good Greek society, the guests at a dinner, or rather at the *symposion* which followed the meal, oftener than not furnished their own entertainment, and one of the most popular forms of amusement was singing, either solo or chorus.[82] It is plain that some of the surviving fragments of Anakreon were intended for such an occasion, for example 5 Diehl. PRAXILLA was credited also with having written compositions [83] of this kind ; we know no more of her than that she is said to have been a native of Sekyon and to have lived in the middle

[78] Wilamowitz, *S.S.*, pp. 102–36.
[79] *E.g.*, frags. 4, 41, 43, 55, 69, 70, 91, 96 and a score of others.
[80] Frags. 54 ; 90, 100, 101 ; 44. Add also (if it is his, for the authorship is disputed, Timokreon of Rhodes being another claimant) the famous frag. 86, which became proverbial, πάλαι κοτ' ἦσαν ἄλκιμοι Μιλήσιοι.
[81] Aristophanes, frag. 223.
[82] Our chief account of this is in Athenaios, 693 f *sqq.*, who also gives us nearly all the skolia we have ; they are printed, together with what little survives from other sources, in Diehl, ii, pp. 181–90.
[83] Athen., 694 a ; her other fragments, which appear to belong to choral lyric, in Diehl, ii, pp. 129–30. Eusebios' chronicle gives her *floruit* as Olymp. 82 (452–459 B.C.). See further, Schmid-Stählin, i, p. 450.

of the fifth century B.C., but there survive, besides any claim she may have to some of the existing skolia, six lines, of which one is borrowed from epic, the other five show that she could write very prettily. No doubt scraps of many well-known poets were pressed into service, and no doubt, also, many of them on occasion wrote such trifles, as they on occasion wrote epigrams, which indeed are a sort of composition not very different from skolia in content. But those we have are in the Attic dialect for the most part, with here and there a flavour of Doric or Ionic ; they were especially popular in Athens, and we cannot, with our present knowledge, trace any direct influence of Anakreon upon them. Their contents are sometimes commemorations of historical events (the slaying of Hipparchos by Harmodios and Aristogeiton ; an unsuccessful attempt of the Alkmeonidai to overthrow the tyranny of Peisistratos), more commonly pretty erotic conceits (' would I were an ivory lyre, to be carried by fair boys—would I were a jewel of gold, to be worn by a fair woman '), or shrewd, proverb-like comments on life ; some are short hymns to various gods. The metres are always simple, such as an amateur singer could easily manage and a casual flute-player, hired for the occasion, accompany well enough.

Of Anakreon's metres, one of the favourites was of the form ⏑ (⏑)‿ ⏑ ‿ ⏑ ‿ ᴗ, and seems to have been regarded in later times as his characteristic verse, hence the name ' Anacreontic ' given to it. In this metre were composed, we do not know when or by whom, but certainly not before the Hellenistic age, a number of little pieces, generally known as the ANACREONTEA. We possess a collection of these, sixty in all, at the end of the MS. of the Palatine Anthology, and a few are given in other sources also ; of one we have three different forms. There are also two or three scraps of other such poems, not in the collection. The metre was popular in late antiquity, and indeed was already in occasional use in early Alexandrian times ; post-classical writers put it to remarkable purposes, including Christian hymns. The Anacreontea themselves are not all of one date, for while some of the earlier and better ones are polished in metre and language and at times almost rise to poetry, others, clearly later, are miserable performances which will not even scan or construe. But the remarkable thing is that some of them were passing current as genuine works of Anakreon (which the collection expressly disclaims), in the second century A.D., as we learn from Aulus Gellius.[84]

About contemporary with the real Anakreon, or perhaps earlier, would appear to be PYTHERMOS, of whom we know from Athenaios that he was a Teian, that he used the Ionic harmony, and that he wrote a skolion whereof one verse survives, ' Gold's the only thing in the world that matters ' (οὐδὲν ἦν ἄρα τἆλλα πλὴν ὁ χρυσός).[85]

---

[84] Gellius, Noct. Att., xix, 9, 5–6. The surviving Anacreontea, both the collection and later pieces, are printed in Bergk, at the end of the genuine fragments of Anakreon.

[85] Athen., 625 c ; one or two other references to him in Diehl, ii, p. 60.

Note 36: on Sappho's apparently Asian name, see G. Zuntz in *Museum Helveticum* viii (1951), pp. 12–25.

CHAPTER V

CHORAL LYRIC; TERPANDROS—BAKCHYLIDES

HITHERTO we have been dealing with literary movements whose headquarters are either Ionia (including the neighbouring islands) or else some region known to have been directly influenced from that part of the Greek world. Now we turn to a different race, the Dorians, and discuss their one great contribution to poetry.

To sing in chorus is natural to any people accustomed to sing at all ; we often find (as Il. i, 472) that Homer mentions it as a thing familiar in his day, and it continued to be a common practice wherever any kind of Greek was spoken. As Greek music was simple, and singing was as commonly taught as reading and writing, there was never any lack of men, boys, or girls to form a choir ; since, moreover, all Greeks seem to have had more or less aptitude for dancing, the three elements necessary to satisfy their idea of what choral song should be, viz., expressive and interesting words, suitable music and appropriate movement, were all ready to hand wherever a poet or other instructor existed. Generally, one professional was enough to ensure the success of the whole performance, and he was usually responsible for writing the poem, composing the music, training the choir, and eventually conducting and accompanying the performance. At most, he might perhaps have one or two assistants to play string or wind instruments while he directed the whole.

This being the case, there is no ascertainable reason why choral lyric should not have developed to the heights it actually reached in any place in the Greek world. As a matter of fact, however, the Dorians developed it and impressed their language upon it, although it is far from being the case that Dorian poets were the only great artists in this field. We have to describe two centres of the movement, the Peloponnesos and Sicily ; somewhat later, Boiotia contributed the greatest name of all, that of Pindar. Concerning the first beginnings of the rise of choral lyric, and especially the reason why the Dorian cities had so much to do with it, we are quite in the dark.[1] Plutarch, or whoever wrote the well-informed treatise *On Music* which is included among his works, says its first establishment (πρώτη κατάστασις) was due to TERPANDROS of Lesbos, and arose in Sparta ; a later, second form he associates with a number of persons, mostly from Greece proper, who are mere names to us. The music of the first kind was extremely simple ; indeed it is said, and there is some evidence from early art to show that the tradition is founded on fact, that the earlier form of the lyre had but four strings, which, since they were not stopped as those of a violin or lute are, meant that it had a range of one major fourth, and that Terpandros invented the seven-stringed form.[2] It would seem that the introduction of wood-wind music from Asia had a considerable effect on the development of stringed instruments also, and by the time we have any real knowledge of the subject we may assume the existence of music, extremely simple no doubt to our ears, but past the extraordinary monotony of the earliest kind. Since Terpandros is represented, for us, by some half-dozen lines of his verse and a few statements regarding his musical career, we must begin with ALKMAN, or, to give him the name by which he was known in his own country, Alkmaion.[3] This man was originally of Sardis, presumably not a native Lydian but an Ionian Greek, and came, whether by invitation or on his own initiative, to Sparta, which at that time (the traditional date is the 27th Olympiad, or 661–658 B.C.) was a city simple and poor indeed in comparison with those of Ionia, but not the armed camp which it was forced later to become, nor devoid of artistic interests.[4]

By a fortunate chance we have a papyrus, discovered in 1855[5] which preserves about half of one of Alkman's works, and from

[1] It might not be easy to say why opera originated in Italy and not in France, for instance, or England ; yet we know far more of the musical history of that time than we can ever hope to know of its development in early Greece.

[2] Plut., *de musica*, 6–10 (1133 b–1134 f). For the archaeological data, see Deubner in *Ath. Mitt.*, liv, pp. 194–200 ; representations of Greek stringed instruments earlier than 676–3, the date of Terpandros' victory at the Spartan Karneia, do not show as many as seven strings. For more details of this earliest period, see Schmid-Stählin, i, p. 452 *sqq*.

[3] 'Αλκμὰν is the Doric contraction of 'Αλκμαίων or 'Αλκμέων ; he calls himself 'Αλκμάων in frag. 51. For his date, see Suidas, *s.u.* 'Αλκμάν, who says he was a Lakonian of Messoa (was he perhaps naturalized and assigned to that district ?), but proceeds to give the correct account, from Krates. Cf., *e.g.*, Alexandros Aitolos in *A.P.*, vii, 709.

[4] Cf. *Artemis Orthia* (Macmillan, 1929), *passim*.

[5] See Bergk's notes : the poem is No. 23 in P.L.G.[4], No. 1 in Diehl.

this and other fragments are able to form a pretty definite opinion of his style and personal character. Although he writes for a chorus, he is nearly as communicative about himself as Anakreon or Alkaios, and we get the impression of a light-hearted and amiable man, completely at home in his new surroundings and not given to taking himself at all seriously. The surviving poem is a *partheneion*, or hymn to be sung by a chorus of girls, apparently in honour of the local Spartan goddess Orthia.[6] We learn that the choir consisted of eleven members, led by a certain Hagesichora (if that was really her name ; since it means ' choir-leader ', it is so very appropriate as to suggest that it is rather a title given her by the poet). After duly telling a heroic legend, the battle between Herakles and the Hippokoontidai,[7] the chorus fall to jesting with each other and elaborately comparing the beauty of Hagesichora with that of another of their number, Agido, while others again come in for briefer but complimentary mention. The whole atmosphere is that of a family party rather than a public festival, and indeed Hagesichora is referred to as ' my cousin '. A good deal of the poem must have consisted of either short solos or performances by parts of the chorus, not the whole. Shorter fragments show us the poet expressing his love for some one,[8] for he had in later times a reputation as the founder of amatory poetry, and also giving his views about eating and drinking, especially the former, since he complains that in a Spartan spring there are flowers enough but short commons,[9] and is concerned for a certain cooking-pot which is to be filled in due time with pea-soup.[10] Again, we catch glimpses of his love for nature, in an exquisite fragment on the stillness of night,[11] while another, quaint and pretty, expresses his desire to become a halcyon, that ' holy bird of spring, dyed with purple of the sea ' ; which, as the author to whom we owe the quotation makes clear, is not a Greek equivalent of ' oh that I had wings as a dove ', but an allusion to the supposed habits of the halcyon's mate, who was said to carry the male on her back when he grew old and feeble, as Alkman declares he is.[12] Altogether, we may

[6] For her cult, see *Artemis Orthia*, Chapter xii. Cf., however, Bowra in *Class. Quart.*, 1934, pp. 35–44. See p. 422.

[7] See Rose, *Mythol.*, p. 219.

[8] Frags. 101, 103 ; cf. 92. Archytas, cited by Athenaios, 600 f *sq.*, calls Alkman the ἡγεμών of amatory lyric, and says he was in love with Megalostrata, whom he mentions, frag. 102, in terms which render Archytas' conclusion that she was a poetess not unreasonable. Her poems, if any, are lost.

[9] *Ibid.*, 56.   [10] *Ibid.*, 49.   [11] *Ibid.*, 58.

[12] *Ibid.*, 94, from Antigonos of Karystos, *hist. mirab.*, 23 (27).

believe that he was well content in his adopted home, and a general favourite. He retained the perfectly simple style of his Ionian countrymen, transferred to the foreign dialect which, so far as we can judge, he had mastered thoroughly. If we find difficulties in him, they are not his fault, but due to the mistakes of copyists, allusions which were not meant for us, and our imperfect knowledge of seventh-century Spartan Doric.

As to what happened in Sparta after Alkman died, we know practically nothing ; tradition has preserved the names of three later poets, SPENDON, GITIADAS and DIONYSODOTOS,[13] but not a line that they wrote ; choral singing seems to have been the one fine art which did not die out in Sparta during her long struggle for empire and sometimes for existence, in the succeeding centuries.

Shortly after Alkman—some said he was Alkman's pupil, the regular statement to make of any writer of importance if his date is slightly later than that of another whom he in any way resembles—came ARION,[14] whose name is familiar chiefly because of the picturesque story telling how he was saved by a dolphin. But he has a more solid title to a place in any such book as this, although not one line of his poetry has come down to us ; for it was apparently he who gave its literary form to the dithyramb. That he was its inventor, as is alleged by Herodotos (i, 23), is, if taken literally, absurd ; Dithyrambos, a word of very uncertain meaning, is one of the oldest titles of Dionysos, and the songs in his honour which bear the same name may be as old ; but if we look at Pindar and his well-informed scholiast we get near enough to the facts. ' In days of old ', says the poet, ' the song of the dithyrambs crawled along in a straight-drawn marching-line ', and again, while singing the praises of Corinth, ' Whence (save from Corinth) were revealed the fair fashions of Dionusos' service linked with the Dithyramb that leadeth on the sacred

[13] Plut., Lycurg., 28 ; Paus., iii, 17, 2 ; Athen., 678 c. The last passage is a fragment of the lost work of Sosibios, περὶ θυσιῶν, and mentions that D. wrote paeans.

[14] Suidas, s.u. Ἀρίων, has a note which seems to consist of very badly made extracts from a good source. He gives Arion's floruit as Olymp. 38 (628–625 B.C.), says his native city was Methymna (in Lesbos) and his father's name Kykleus (' circle-man ', an obvious figment, from the ' circular ' [κύκλιος] chorus of the dithyramb), and that he ' kept the —ω even in the genitive ', i.e., apparently, wrote in Doric, which has that form of the gen. sing., decl. ii. For the story of his adventure with the dolphin, see Rose, Mythol., p. 300. A fragment attributed to him is printed by Diehl, ii, p. 5, but is recognized by him and every one else as spurious.

ox ? ',[15] on which the scholiast notes that ' the most important form of the dithyramb was first seen in Corinth . . . it was a circular chorus, and Arion of Methymna organized it '. In other words, it was once a processional song, probably very simple in character ; Archilochos boasted that he could ' lead off ' such a chant ' when his wits were thundersmitten with wine '.[16] Arion, however, rearranged it to be sung by a chorus standing in a circle about the altar of the god, and such a chorus had great possibilities, as we shall see later.

Some time after Arion comes LASOS of Hermione, of whom we are told four things of interest. He wrote poems which had no S in them, a feat which at least involves great technical skill, for a glance through the paradigms in any Greek grammar will show what a multiplicity of forms he was debarred from using, to say nothing of words (including his own name and that of Dionysos) which have an S in their stem. He was the first to write a prose treatise on music, a statement which at least means that he studied the subject and that some precepts of his were remembered in later times. He was in Athens in the days of Hipparchos, and there did much for the development of the dithyramb, in which he made some improvements, and apparently introduced public and regular performances of it. He was Pindar's teacher, a statement not impossible or unlikely, since Pindar was at Athens at a time when Lasos may still have been alive, but not necessarily true (see p. 117).[17]

We can therefore see that this important form of poetry, for so it evidently was, although we are but ill-informed concerning it, arose at an unknown date, was developed and made generally popular in the Peloponnesos during the seventh and sixth centuries, and was known in Athens before the year 500 ; for we learn from the Parian Marble that somewhere between 510 and 500 the first ' choruses of men ' were instituted (apparently any that the Peisistratidai may have held were not counted as official by the democracy).[18]

Having traced, in the scrappy and incomplete way which is all that our imperfect knowledge allows, the growth of choral lyric in Greece proper, we turn to the west, and are at once confronted with the great but baffling name of STESICHOROS. Con-

[15] Pind., frag. 79 Bergk (*Dith. for the Thebans*, 1) : *Ol.*, xiii, 18–19 (trans. Farnell).

[16] Arch., frag. 77.

[17] For Lasos, and the dithyramb generally, see Pickard-Cambridge, *D.T.C.*, Chapter i. Lasos' poems ; fragment and references in Diehl, ii, p. 60. Treatise on music, with some other facts about him, Suid, *s.u.* Λᾶσος ; the words γεγονὼς κατὰ τὴν νη' ὀλυμπιάδα apparently mean, not that he *floruit* Olymp. 58 (558–555 B.C.), but that he was born then. Stay in Athens, cf. chapter iii, n. 50. Pindar ; see below, p. 117.

[18] *Mar. Par.*, ep. 46 (p. 14 Jacoby ; see his note, p. 174).

cerning this poet we are offered such a variety of statements
as to his date and nationality that Wilamowitz-Moellendorff [19]
argued plausibly for the existence of two men of the same name,
one a native of Himera in Sicily, of early date, who died at an
advanced age about the middle of the sixth century, and the
other a Lokrian of Italy, who lived near the end of that century,
and was in Athens in 485/4. Be that as it may, there certainly
existed in antiquity a considerable body of poems, enough to fill
26 books, or more than the length of the Iliad, ascribed to him.
When we have subtracted one or two which even the little that
remains is enough to prove spurious, [20] and perhaps one or two
more which are doubtful, the rest is still an imposing amount,
and we have good cause to regret that for us it consists of about
50 lines, mostly in dactylic metres of simple type, eked out by a
number of references to him which tell us what he said, but not
how he said it ; for he is uniformly spoken of with respect, not
only as a venerable authority on mythology, but as a great poet,
a lyricist of epic breadth. [21] These statements we are forced to

---

[19] Wilamowitz, *S.S.*, pp. 233–42. The facts, so far as they are known,
are conveniently grouped by Vürtheim, *Stes.*, p. 99 *sqq.* They are, briefly ;
his father was any one of a number of persons, the oldest being Hesiod (!) ;
he was younger than Alkman, his dates being 632–556 B.C., approximately ;
he was a native of Himera, or at least was called so ; some said he came
from Pallantion in Arkadia (a wild suggestion, not yet satisfactorily
explained) ; he was buried at Katana, and a gate of the city was named
after him ; his real name was not Stesichoros (= choir-master), but
Teisias, Stesichoros being a name given him for his services to music
and poetry. The above are from Suidas, and apparently, like the rest,
they are due to either Chamaileon, Aristoxenos or Didymos (see pp. 354,
357, 390). His brother was called Mamertinos and was a geometer, *i.e.*,
probably, a Pythagorean (Suid.). He was a native of Matauros (Steph.
Byzant., *s.u.*), a Lokrian colony (Vürtheim points out, p. 104, that there
is some evidence that both Himera and Matauros were founded from
Zankle, and so the same family might have branches in both towns).
He came to Greece in the year of Aeschylus' first victory, 485/4 B.C.
(*Marm. Par.*, ep. 50). The great objection to taking the later date for
Stesichoros is that to Simonides (see p. 111) he is an old poet, to be named
alongside Homer, or rather the epic cycle : οὖτω γὰρ Ὅμηρος ἠδὲ
Στησίχορος ἄειδε λαοῖς, he says (frag. 32 Diehl) referring to an incident
of the funeral games for Pelias. To add to the confusion, there was yet
another Stesichoros, known from the Marmor Parium (ep. 73) to have
been in Athens in 369/8 B.C., and probably the person referred to in
Didymos' commentary on Demosthenes, *Phil.*, col. 12, 60, as author of
a poem on the Kyklops.

[20] For one of the most remarkable poems ascribed to him, see Rose
in *C.Q.*, xxvi (1932), p. 88 *sqq.*

[21] Stesichorus quam sit ingenio ualidus materiae quoque ostendunt,
maxima bella et clarissimos canentom duces et epici carminis onera lyra
sustinentem, Quint., *inst. orat.*, x, 1, 62.

take at second hand, though certainly nothing in the scanty
remains contradicts them ; we know that his subjects included
the funeral games over Pelias (ἆθλα ἐπὶ Πελίᾳ ; for some reason
this seems to have been a favoured topic) ; Herakles' reiving of
the oxen of Geryon, and his adventures with Kerberos and the
robber Kyknos ; the story of Skylla ; the Kalydonian boar-hunt ;
the rape of Europa ; the tragic tale of Eriphyle ; several incidents
of the Trojan War, including the murder of Agamemnon and the
revenge of Orestes, and two poems concerning Helen, of which
the second declared the first untrue, hence giving rise to a tale
that Helen blinded him for his impiety and was appeased and
moved to restore his sight by his ' palinode ' ; and some miscellaneous matters, among them, if we may believe late and inaccurate witnesses, the obscure Sicilian legend of Daphnis, who was
loved by a nymph and blinded because he was untrue to her.[22]

We know nothing of XANTHOS, who was older than Stesichoros
and used by him, once for a very bad pun on the name of Elektra
('Aλέκτρα—ἄλεκτρος, ' unwedded ', despite the different quantity of the
a in the two words).[23]

Thanks to a lucky discovery, we know rather more of IBYKOS
of Rhegion, who until recently was scarcely more than the central
figure of the picturesque folk-tale of the cranes,[24] though we had
two charming amatory fragments of him.[25] But a papyrus came
to light a few years ago,[26] bearing no name, but containing a

---

[22] The sagas involved will be found in Rose, *Mythol.*, pp. 204 (death
of Pelias ; the games were simply an episode), 214, 215, 217, 64, 258,
183, 190 and 194 (Eriphyle), 230 *sqq.* The story of Helen is told by
Isokrates, x, 64, and several later authors ; the opening words of the
palinode, οὐκ ἐστ' ἔτυμος λόγος οὗτος, became proverbial, see Cicero,
ad Att., ix, 13, 1, οὐκ ἐστ' ἔτυμος λόγος, *ut opinor, ille de ratibus* ; a
modern might perhaps write, ' as to that rumour about the boats, " the
truth is not in it ", I fancy '. For Daphnis, see especially Aelian, *uar.
hist.*, x, 18 ; the relations between the legend Stesichoros is said to have
told and the Daphnis of Theokritos (see p. 332) are anything but clear.
[23] The mentions of Xanthos are Athen., 513 a, Aelian, *uar. hist.*, iv,
26 ; Robert, *Bild und Lied*, p. 173 *sqq.*, points out that the obscure
Peripatetic Megakleides is the source of both passages, that his statement
is wholly unsupported, and that like charges of plagiarism (the whole of
Stesichoros' *Oresteia* is stolen, according to him, from this Xanthos) are
rife among such gentry. He supposes that Stesichoros mentioned some
one called Xanthos somewhere, and that that gave Megakleides a handle
for his charge. Cf., however, Dornseiff, p. 55.
[24] Best known from Schiller's poem ; for the ancient telling of it,
see Plutarch, *de garrulitate*, 509 f, Suid., *s.u.* ῎Ιβυκος.
[25] Frags. 6 and 7 Diehl.
[26] *Oxyrh. Pap.*, 1790 ; frag. 3 Diehl ; see Bowra in Powell 3, pp. 30–6.

large portion of a poem which is almost certainly his. Suidas
tells us that Ibykos ' was born at Rhegion, but went from there
to Samos in the days when Polykrates, father of the tyrant,
governed it ; this was in the time of Kroisos, Olympiad 52 ',
in other words, 572–569 ; the name should be Aiakes, not
Polykrates,[27] but Suidas has many worse blunders. He goes on
to say that Ibykos was quite mad with love of young lads,
invented a new sort of stringed instrument, and wrote seven
books in Doric. The papyrus presents us with a poem addressed
to a Polykrates, who is not likely to be other than the future
tyrant of Samos and patron of Anakreon. The metre is simple,
such as we have learned to expect from the earlier lyric poets,
and the dialect may be described as epic with a Doric accent,
very much the sort of language one might expect from a Dorian
who wished to be understood by an Ionian audience familiar with
Homer. But, and this is the most important point, the style,
while still simple, is beginning to take on the gorgeously artistic
forms which appear in their complicated perfection in Pindar.
' Love brought ruin to Troy ' is expressed by ' Ruin mounted
sore-tried Pergamon because of golden-haired Kypris '. ' Only.
the Muses can tell the whole tale ' becomes ' These matters the
Muses of Helikon, fulfilled of wisdom, could well mount on (the
chariot of) story '. Another point which shows us that we are
reading a poet of the days when lyric was developing fast is that
the author uses, for the first time so far as existing poems go,
the triadic structure. The solo lyricists, and Alkman too, to
judge by what we have of him, contented themselves with a series
of stanzas, all alike, as in a modern ballad or hymn. This did
well enough for a single performer, or for the steady movement
of a procession ; but Stesichoros is said to have been the first
to try something a little more complicated. He arranged his
stanzas in groups of three, whereof the first two (strophe and
antistrophe) were identical with each other in metrical form, but
the third (epode) [28] was different. In the next triad, the same
grouping would be repeated. This is exactly what we find in
the ode to Polykrates ; it is still timidly used, for all three
stanzas are very short and simple, but it is there. Of the

---

[27] *I.e.* in Suid., *loc. cit.*, for ὁ Πολυκράτης ὁ τοῦ τυράννου πατὴρ we
should read, or at least suppose to have stood in his source, Αἰάκης ὁ
Πολυκράτους τοῦ τυράννου πατήρ ; cf. Herodotos, ii, 182, 2. But see Bowra
in *Class. Journ.*, xxix, 375.

[28] στροφή, ἀντιστροφή, ἐπῳδός, *i.e.*, turn, counter-turn, after-song ;
the last word also means a refrain, or a shorter line following a longer
one (as in Archilochos, and Horace's imitations of him). They were
called ' Stesichoros' three ', and ' not to know τρία Στησιχόρου ' meant
' to be grossly ignorant '. See Suid., *s.u.* τρία Στησιχόρου.

other fragments of this poet, some at least may very well be solos.[29]

Twilight at best, often thick darkness, shrouds the history of Greece proper during the sixth century ; but we may in passing mention two names. Argos found time, during her struggles with Sparta, to cultivate poetry, particularly, it would appear, in connexion with the worship of Apollo and Artemis.[30] Of the poets of that time and place we can name one, TELESILLA, datable because she is said to have rallied the women of the city to its defence after the great defeat by Kleomenes ;[31] as this was not very long before the Persian War, she must have been born during the sixth century. Of her poetry we have one tiny scrap, which mentions Artemis (not, as usual, Arethusa) fleeing from Alpheios, and a few references. What it was like as literature we cannot tell. TYNNICHOS of Chalkis in Euboia is an even vaguer figure. He wrote nothing of any account in all his life save one paean, but that was so excellent that it was in every one's memory in Plato's time, while Porphyry preserves an anecdote to the effect that Aeschylus refused to write one, saying that Tynnichos' work was like a venerable old statue, and nothing later could hope to be so divine.[32] If this has any truth in it, Tynnichos was already an old writer in Aeschylus' day, and so the earlier part of the sixth century is a possible date for him.

But now we pass to a greater name, and one of which we know something fairly definite. SIMONIDES of Iulis in Keos, son of Leoprepes, was born in 557/6 B.C.[33] The island was apparently poor, certainly densely populated.[34] Simonides had great natural gifts for poetical expression, a sympathetic, rather pessimistic temper which did not demand too much from life, and sufficient insight to have but few illusions. Lyric poetry had now developed to an elaborate art, and the movement, unlike epic, had spread from west to east instead of in the reverse direction. He threw himself energetically into it, and proceeded to earn his

[29] See Wilamowitz, *S.S.*, pp. 121–26.

[30] References for their cult at Argos in Farnell, *C.G.S.*, ii, p. 603, iv, p. 440.

[31] The battle is described in Herodotos, vi, 76 *sqq.*, who says nothing of Telesilla ; her heroism is recounted by Plutarch, *de mul. uirt.*, 245 c *sqq.*, who says that the event took place on the 7th of the month, which is Apollo's day, Paus., ii, 20, 8 *sqq.*, who tells it a little differently, Suid., *s.u. Τελέσιλλα*, who follows Pausanias. The exact date is unknown.

[32] Plato, *Ion*, 534 d ; Porphyry, *de abstin.*, ii, 18.

[33] Frag. 77 Diehl, which is either by Simonides himself or some early and well-informed writer, gives his age as 80 in 477/6 B.C. Strabo, x, 5, 6, names his birthplace.

[34] It is hard to assign any other reason for the well-supported statement that men over 60 were put to death, Strabo, *loc. cit.*, citing Menander.

living by writing poems to order. The numerous anecdotes told of his avarice need mean no more than that he was a good man of business ; that his art was any the worse for his being feed may well be doubted. There is a difference between the hack who gets what he can by peddling a meagre talent and the artist of genius who confers at least as great a favour as he receives when he consents to exchange his works for an honorarium. The art which Simonides principally exercised [35] was not only complicated but capable of being applied to many subjects. As far back as the days of Terpandros the *nomos* or lyrical composition which, in his hands, dealt with the praise of Apollo or some other god, was already not simple ; it is stated that it consisted regularly of seven parts, [36] and if not then, certainly later, as we see from Alkman and Ibykos, it became customary in an ode of any length to include a mythological episode. This, in the hands of men like Stesichoros, gave, as we have seen, an opportunity to rival epic in its own field of dignified narrative ; and the triadic structure, which Simonides certainly used, [37] added something like dramatic vividness to a well-performed ode, with the movements of the choir to reinforce words and music. Moreover, the range of subjects had widened. Hymns were still in demand, but three new forms of ode were much sought after, dirges (θρῆνοι) to be sung at the funerals of notable persons, laudations (ἐγκώμια) of the living and odes of victory (ἐπινίκια), on the occasion,

---

[35] Not all his compositions were lyrics. Besides the ill-attested but not impossible statement that he wrote a tragedy (schol. Ar., *Wasps*, 1411, Aldine ed., rejected by Dindorf as interpolated from Suidas) or tragedies (Suid., *s.u. Σιμωνίδης Λεωπρέπους*), a number of epigrams were attributed to him (printed at the end of his lyrical frags. by Bergk and Diehl), whereof one is certainly his, others fully worthy of him, notably the famous epitaph on the Three Hundred at Thermopylai, and certainly of his age, while others again are doubtful and some evidently refer to events later than his death. A brief sketch of the criticism of this collection will be found in *J.H.S.*, liii (1933), p. 71, n. 1. See p. 422.

[36] Called ἀρχά, μεταρχά, κατατροπά, μετακατατροπά, ὀμφαλός, σφραγίς, ἐπίλογος. The Doric forms of these words, which are preserved in somewhat corrupted shape by Pollux, *Onomasticon*, iv, 66, would seem to indicate that they are at all events not late grammatical inventions. Very little is really known of them, although they have been much talked of in modern times, and in particular, an ill-judged attempt was made by Westphal to find them in the odes of Pindar (critique in the introduction to Gildersleeve, *Olympian and Pythian Odes*, p. xlviii *sqq.*) ; they show the existence quite early of relatively long and elaborate poems.

[37] We have no complete poem of his, but two fragments, the *Ode to Skopas* (4 Diehl) and the *Danae* (13) are long enough to show, in the former, an invariable stanza, in the latter, the end of an epode, the whole of a strophe and the beginning of the antistrophe.

especially, of success in one of the great Games.[38] There quickly
grew up a regular traffic in such works ; those who could
afford it supplied the necessary information and agreed to pay
a fee ; the poet did the rest, including as a rule the training
of the chorus.   Thus the smallness of the reading public was
compensated for.[39]

In such a market as this Simonides had abundant goods of
excellent quality to offer.   There is a tradition, not well supported
but quite possible in itself, that he visited Asia Minor, probably
in his early days.[40] It is usually held, but the combination on
which the statement is based is doubtful,[41] that his first datable
work was an ode in celebration of the famous boxer Glaukos of
Karystos, in 520.   Be this as it may, we are on firm ground when,
towards the end of the sixth century, we find him in Athens, one
of the group of literary men who surrounded Hipparchos.[42]
Later, probably after Hipparchos' murder in 514, the poet withdrew to Thessaly, where he found patrons in Skopas of Krannon
and the powerful house of the Aleuadai.[43] Here again his stay
was ended by a disaster, the collapse of a banqueting-hall which
put an end at one blow to the family of Skopas.[44] Simonides
would seem then to have returned, whether directly or not, to
Athens, now a republic, and to have been associated with Themistokles, far too shrewd a man not to realize that a poet would

[38] For good accounts of the Games, see E. N. Gardiner, *Greek Athletic
Sports and Festivals*, London, Macmillan, 1910, and *Athletics of the Ancient
World*, Oxford, Clar. Press, 1930.

[39] That Simonides was the first to write for pay (schol. Ar., *Peace*,
697, copied by Suid., *s.u. Σιμωνίδης λυρικός*) is merely a bit of folklore.
The fondness for naming some one as having been the originator of any
famous, or infamous, custom is a feature of all popular traditions, and
Greece in later times produced several writers ' on inventions ' (*περὶ
εὑρημάτων*), see M. Kremmer's dissertation, *de catalogis heurematum*,
Leipzig, 1890.

[40] It occurs only in Phaedrus, *fab.*, iv, 22, 4, in a story of a well-known
type, the wise man who is impervious to material losses because he ' carries
all his property with him ', viz., in his head.   Still, a moral tale may be
attached to a real event.

[41] See Rose in *Class. Rev.*, xlvii (1933), pp. 165–7.

[42] That Hipparchos invited him to Athens is stated by [Plato],
Hipparch., 228 c, and Arist., '*AΘ. Πολ.*, 18, 1.   The latter clearly implies
that it was during the tyranny of Hippias, and therefore after Peisistratos'
death (528/7).

[43] The earliest evidence for this, apart from Simonides' own poems
(frags. 4, 6, 7 Diehl), is Theokritos, xvi, 34 *sqq*.

[44] This was a famous disaster, for it was attached to a story, found
as early as Kallimachos, who presumably did not invent it, that Kastor
and Polydeukes rescued Simonides (Kall., frag. 64[c], 11 *sqq*. Pfeiffer ;
Cicero, *de orat.*, ii, 352 ; Quint. xi, 2, 11).   Its date is not known.

make a good agent for propaganda, especially as a poet of some reputation, Timokreon of Rhodes, was attacking him bitterly.[45] In Athens he remained for some time—naturally he may have left it occasionally for visits elsewhere—and so was in Greece during the Persian Wars, which gave him opportunity for some of his noblest poems.[46] But, not long after the end of the war, he went to Sicily, and there apparently ended his days at the court of the great Hieron of Syracuse.[47] His nephew, Bakchylides (see p. 123), accompanied or followed him, and the two won a high place in Hieron's court, at least equal to that enjoyed by Pindar if not excelling it.[48]

Simonides' reputation has undergone curious vicissitudes. In his own day it would appear that he was in great demand for occasional poems, notably epinikia and dirges or memorial odes. The fragments we have of the former contain one or two passages which hardly suggest very keen interest in athletics or chariot-racing, but rather a tendency to diverge into reflections on some quieter subject.[49] The latter, which were evidently much admired in later times,[50] are represented by one of the most beautiful passages in Greek, the song of Danae over her child as she drifts

---

[45] Plutarch, *Themist.*, 5 (association of Them. with S.), 21 (Timokreon).

[46] Notably frag. 5 Diehl. *See* Wilam., *S.S.*, 140, Bowra in *Class. Phil.*, xxviii, 277 *sqq*.

[47] The date is roughly determined by his relations to Hieron and Pindar.

[48] Something of the fluctuations in Hieron's favour may be gathered from the epinikian odes written for him. Pindar wrote the odes commemorating Hieron's victory with the saddle-horse at Olympia in 476 (*Olymp*. i) and with the chariot at the Pythian games in 470 (*Pyth*. i; *Pyth*. ii and iii, whereof the former refers to the same event, are hardly epinikians at all); but Bakchylides, whether at Hieron's request or on his own or his uncle's initiative, sent a poem (Bakch. v) from Keos, in celebration of the former victory. Bakchylides, no doubt Simonides' nominee, for it does not appear that Simonides himself wrote any odes for Hieron, was employed to write the ode for Hieron's most notable success at any games, the victory with the chariot at Olympia in 468 (Bakch. iii), and he, as well as Pindar, celebrated the Pythian victory of 470. Pindar therefore gradually lost ground; his rivals may very well have been better and more supple courtiers than he condescended to be, and also moreover stayed much longer in Sicily.

[49] See for instance frag. 20 Diehl.

[50] Quintilian says that Simonides is *tenuis* but correct and sweet in style, *praecipua tamen eius in commouenda miseratione uirtus* (*inst. orat.*, x, 1, 64), which no doubt represents orthodox Hellenistic opinion and suggests the θρῆνοι more than anything else, and Dionysios of Halikarnassos selects (*de compos. uerb.*, 26, pp. 278–80 Roberts, 141–2 Usener-Radermacher) the lament of Danae, which may come from a θρῆνος, for comment.

in the chest on the sea.[51] The epinikians were overshadowed by those of Pindar ; but Simonides' reputation as a man of wisdom almost outdid his renown as a poet, and we have a great number of anecdotes of his good sayings to Themistokles or Hieron, most or all of them probably coming from the life of him by Chamaileon (see p. 357). It so chances that we have nearly complete what might be described as a philosophical poem, an address to Skopas ; [52] it expounds the thesis that moral excellence is hard to attain, impossible to keep when attained, and the best man is simply he who is not voluntarily evil and does his best for his country. Finally, after enjoying a reputation first as poet and then as sage, he is familiar to modern readers largely as an epigrammatist, on the strength of the collection already mentioned (above, note 35) containing the only complete poems ascribed to him that have survived. It is a curious fact that Egypt has yielded no fragments of him ; clearly he was little studied towards the beginning of the Christian era and in its early centuries.

We have had occasion to make passing mention of another lyric poet of that age, apparently a good deal younger than Simonides, TIMOKREON of Rhodes. Hardly enough survives of this man's writings to tell us whether he was a good poet, but quite enough to show that he was a good hater. He was a native of Ialysos in Rhodes and was banished thence for his pro-Persian sentiments. Themistokles, who used his influence to secure the return of certain other exiles, would not do so for Timokreon, because, as the latter alleged, he was bribed not to. Hence the concentrated venom with which Timokreon assailed him, and the shout of triumph which greeted his banishment, condemnation, and flight to Persia. ' So there are other rascals in the world, and I am not the only tailless fox ! ' The bitterness and the use of beast-fable alike recall Archilochos.[53] He was an athlete as well as a poet,[54] and some one, said to be Simonides, composed an epitaph for him, which described his life as consisting of eating, drinking and abuse.[55]

[51] Frag. 13 Diehl ; see last note.

[52] *Ibid.*, 4 Diehl, preserved by Plato, *Protag.*, 339 a *sqq.* ; see for recent and good comment Wilamowitz, S.S., pp. 159–91.

[53] The chief fragments are preserved by Plutarch, *Themist.*, 21 ; see Wilamowitz, SS.., p. 146 and references there, Bowra in *Hermes*, lxix, 350–52.

[54] Athen., 415 f *sqq.*, who represents him as displaying his powers in boxing to the King of Persia, having surprised him by the vast amount that he ate. If there is any truth in this tale, he was still in his prime about the seventies of the fifth century, and may therefore have been born about 510 or so ; the visit to the Persian court would probably be during his banishment.

[55] πολλὰ πιὼν καὶ πολλὰ φαγὼν καὶ πολλὰ κάκ' εἰπὼν/ἀνθρώπους κεῖμαι Τιμοκρέων 'Ρόδιος. This is preserved by several authors, among them Athen., *loc. cit.* ; the *Anthology*, vii, 348, says it is by Simonides.

We have now to turn from the islands to Boiotia, which produced in this period an interesting minor poetess and the greatest of lyric poets. KORINNA was little more than a name to us, celebrated as having given Pindar some hints in his youth, until a papyrus, found in Egypt, at Ešmunen, and now in the possession of the Museum at Berlin, presented us with a long specimen of her poetry, written, not in the orthography she herself used, but in the reformed Boiotian spelling of more than two centuries later ; evidently she was preserved by the Alexandrian philologists more as an interesting specimen of the dialect than for any other reason.[56] Of her life [57] we hardly know more than that she was older than Pindar, and so may have been born about the middle of the sixth century. Her style is of the simplest ; she tells old legends of Boiotia in the plainest and most straightforward manner, with next to no ornament, in metres borrowed from Ionia and the Lesbians. We have part of a contest of song between Kithairon and Helikon, the spirits, that is to say, of the two famous mountains ; another, almost as completely a catalogue-poem as those of the Hesiodic school, dealing with the daughters of Asopos and the ancestry of other local worthies, demi-gods and heroes, some hardly known elsewhere, some famous in epic ; we know that she wrote a poem dealing

If this is true, it was written merely as a jest, for Timokreon survived Simonides, who was dead before Themistokles went to Persia. *Anthol.*, xiii, 31, a bit of metrical trick-work (the two lines of which it consists are both composed of the same words, but re-arranged to make different metres) is ascribed to Timokreon and seems to be an attack on Simonides ; but its genuineness is highly doubtful.

[56] Published for the first time in *Berliner Klassikertexte*, v, 2 (1907), p. 19 *sqq.* ; frags. 4 and 5 Diehl. See, for recent discussion, Bowra in Powell 3, pp. 21–30. Lobel, *Hermes*, lxv (1930), p. 356 *sqq.*, holds that Korinna is not of the sixth century, but wrote between 350–250 B.C. His arguments do not seem to me cogent, and are replied to by Bowra, *C.R.*, xlv (1931), pp. 4–5, Lisi, *P.G.*, p. 105 *sqq.* See p. 422.

[57] Suidas *s.u.* Κόριννα has very little to tell us, except that she was a native of Tanagra or Thebes (the former is correct, cf. Paus., ix, 22, 3), that her lyrics filled five volumes and that she was a pupil of MYRTIS or MURTIS ; *i.e.*, Murtis, whom Korinna mentions, to blame her for trying to rival Pindar (frag. 15 Diehl), was older than she. Of Murtis's poetry nothing at all has survived. Aelian, *uar. hist.*, xiii, 25, is as usual talking nonsense when he says that Pindar on one occasion called Korinna a sow ; the idea is probably due to a ridiculous misunderstanding of Pind., *Olymp.*, vi, 90. Cf. Lisi, *P.G.*, p. 101 ; Rose in *C.R.*, vol. xlviii, p. 8. He and Suidas agree, *i.e.*, some lost work on literary history said, that she defeated him five times, presumably in local contests of poetry. Not knowing the source of this statement, we can form no certain opinion of its truth ; Paus., *loc. cit.*, seems to have heard of but one victory. Signorina Lisi, *loc. cit.*, regards it as wholly false.

with the Seven against Thebes.[58] That she was very popular in her own country we may easily believe, but she enjoyed hardly more than a local reputation.

A very different figure is Korinna's fellow-countryman and younger contemporary, PINDAR (*Πίνδαρος*) of Thebes ; and here we are in the fortunate position of having a large amount of his work to judge from. He was a man of good family and strongly aristocratic sympathies, proud of his real or supposed connexion with noble houses of Sparta and Thera. The date of his birth was either 522 or 518 B.C. He went, while in his 'teens, to the nearest cultural centre, Athens, where he is said to have been taught by Lasos of Hermione. What is more important is that he came into contact with the brilliant music and poetry which, under the Peisistratidai, had come in from both Ionia and the Peloponnesos, and continued to flourish under the still moderate democracy founded by Kleisthenes.[59] Here also he would learn something of what we call the archaic art of Greece, now long past its beginnings and capable of great beauty of form and of a somewhat rigid majesty, combined with daring brightness of colour.[60]

[58] Frag. 7 Diehl.

[59] The material for Pindar's life is firstly his own works, especially the epinikian odes, eked out by the existing scholia, which go back to well-informed Alexandrian commentaries ; next, an ancient life of him, preserved in several different forms (in the Codex Ambrosianus of his odes ; in a metrical paraphrase, cited by Eustathios in his commentary on Pindar ; in synopses by Thomas Magister and Suidas ; finally, interspersed with much nonsense, in the rambling biography in Eustathios). There is a good short life of him at the end of Farnell's first volume ; the standard modern work is Wilamowitz, *Pindaros*. For his rank, see Pyth., v, 73, in which he claims descent from the ancient house of the Aigeidai and says that members of that clan went from Sparta to Thera. His birth-date is given as Ol. 65 (520–517 B.C.) by the Life (Suid.), and he himself says (frag. 193 Bergk) that he was born in a Pythian year, which is the third year of an Olympiad ; thus the Life supports the date 518 B.C. On the other hand, his earliest known work, the tenth Pythian, was written Pythiad 22, which is 498 B.C. if we reckon from the first celebration of the Pythian games in 582/1, or 502 if we count from the doubtful date 586/5, see Jacoby's edition of the Marmor Parium, p. 166, for a discussion of the matter ; the former date is the likelier, for though it is a comparatively crude work, it is hardly possible that a lad of sixteen produced it, and even for a young man of twenty it shows remarkable technical skill. Since Pindar is said to have been at his *ἀκμή* about 480 (Suidas, Thomas Magister, Diodorus Siculus, xi, 26, 8), *i.e.*, to have been about 40 at that time, we must allow the possibility of his having been born in 522, the next Pythiad before 518, but it seems on the whole a rather less probable date. The Life is the authority for his visit to Athens.

[60] It must be remembered that the Greeks, at all events in the period of archaic art, did not see the coldly white statues of our collections, but painted them in bright colours, as they also did their stone buildings.

One acquaintance he certainly made, a poet as great as himself, for there can be little doubt that he knew and appreciated Aeschylus.   But if foreign art and letters influenced him, foreign philosophy, also coming from Ionia, did not, and he remained a devout, even old-fashioned worshipper of Apollo and of the local deities of Boiotia.[61] During the Persian Wars he had the misfortune to find his city on the wrong side ; what part he played in the conflict, or if he played any, is not known.   Soon after its conclusion, about 476, he went to Sicily at the invitation of Hieron, and there remained, as has already been indicated, for something over a year ; those poems of his which can be dated later than 474 seem to have been written in Greece.   A zealous lover of Dorian ways, he found his warmest friends, outside his own immediate circle, largely in Aigina ; at home he was not always popular,[62] though a good patriot.   The later years of his life had much to sadden them, in the conquest of Aigina by Athens and the wars between the latter state and Boiotia.   He died when about 80 years of age,[63] in Argos, according to fairly good authority ; his latest work that has survived can be dated about the middle of the century.[64]

It is said that his poetry filled seventeen volumes, i.e., in the Alexandrian edition.[65] We have therefore about a quarter

[61] He speaks of philosophers as plucking ' the unripe fruit of wisdom ' (ἀτελῆ σοφίας καρπόν), frag. 209 ; it is significant that for him an eclipse of the sun is a portentous event, frag. 107.   For his religion, see p. 121.

[62] We may cite, for his patriotism, such glowing passages as Isth., i, 1 sqq., and for his occasional unpopularity, the story in the Life (Thomas Magister) of his having been fined for his complimentary references to Athens, which probably has some fact behind it.

[63] The place of his death is given as Argos in the epigram at the end of the Life (Ambros., Thom. Mag.), which I conjecture to be of the third century B.C., see C.Q., xxv (1931), p. 121 sqq. ; the date is uncertain, but the Life says he was 80 years old (Eustath. and Thom. Mag. give another account as well, that he was 66, which is absurd, and Suid. says 55, which is so manifestly wrong that it is probably a corruption in his own text or that of the authority he was copying) ; this would make the year either 442 or 438.   Suid. records a pretty story that he died with his head on the knees of a youth, Theoxenos, whom he loved.

[64] Olymp. iv and v were written in 452 ; if we could believe the scholiast, Pyth. viii was composed in Pythiad 35, i.e., 446 or (less probably) 450, but the modern editors rightly point out that this is a mistake, or a corruption in the scholiast's text, for the poem speaks of Aigina in terms which imply that it is a free state, whereas it was conquered and made tributary by Athens in 456.

[65] They included. besides the epinikians, paeans, of which we have now several important fragments though still no complete poem ; partheneia, dithyrambs and several other sorts of ode, such as prosodia (processional odes).

of it, namely the four books of his epinikian odes, named after the four Great Games, Olympian, Pythian, Nemean and Isthmian, but including some odes written for none of these and some which are not epinikians at all, and the recently discovered paeans, together with numerous fragments of his other works. We can therefore estimate his worth in a manner impossible for Simonides or Alkaios ; and the consensus of critics ancient and modern is that he is a poet of the first rank.

To judge, then, by what we have, his finest work is shown in the epinikian odes, despite the nature, at first sight unpromising, of the subject. For the data of such an ode must always be essentially the same. Some one has gained the victory in racing, boxing, or some other event at an athletic festival ; he must be duly praised, his family complimented if possible and any former successes, especially in athletics, of himself or his kin must be mentioned. In the hands of any but an ingenious author this would result in a deadly monotony, and none but a great poet could elevate such subjects above ingenious or pretty commonplaces. Pindar made great poems of them. To do this he was helped to a certain extent by the traditions of his art. We have seen (p. 112) that it had become customary to insert a myth or legend of some kind ; we have seen also that a certain ornateness of language was practised by some at least of the Dorian composers ; we know that the hymn was one of the earliest forms of lyric, probably the earliest of all, and therefore a lofty tone would be felt to accord with the general style, even if the subject was not a god. But when all this, and our very imperfect knowledge of the history of choral lyric before Pindar, has been allowed for, we still must name as the chief reason for the magnificence of his work his own genius.

Genius cannot be analysed, but it is possible to see what tools it uses, and therefore it is profitable to glance at the structure of a Pindaric ode ; more than a glance is not possible in a book of this size. The first Nemean will do as well as another for our purpose. It is addressed to Chromios of Aitna, who had won a chariot-race in the Nemean festival, about 473 B.C. Starting from the praises of Syracuse (Hieron of Syracuse had founded Aitna not long before), and of Chromios himself, it continues with a mythical reference : Pindar will ' scatter glory ' on Sicily, which Zeus gave to Persephone and promised that it should always be fertile and always a home of brave men. This easily brings him back to Chromios again ; Chromios is not brave only, but hospitable and wise in counsel ; he uses his wealth as it should be used, and so wins reputation and friends, whom he can and does benefit : ' for in companionship lie the hopes of men that toil sore '.[66]   Now comes a sudden and characteristic transition, suggested apparently by the adjective ' sore-toiling ' (πολυπόνων). Pindar launches at once into a tale of the sturdiest of all toilers, Herakles.   The rest of the ode, some forty long and sonorous lines, contains the legend of his infancy, how Hera sent serpents to attack him in his cradle, and he strangled them with his baby hands, whereat his parents consulted Teiresias and heard of his future greatness, and of his final deification.   For the myth to be left thus to convey its own moral is not very common ; it is usual for him to point the lesson with a few short, pregnant utterances.   The legend may be a saga relating to the country or family of the man in whose honour the ode is composed ; thus, the many epinikians written for Aiginetans regularly contain some episode of the long history of Aiakos and his descendants ; while in many of the shorter odes there is no myth, or at most but the hint of one.   Again, the connexion between the story and the general subject of the ode may be so slight as to be almost unde-tectable ; thus, in the ninth Pythian,[67] it is a moot point why the poem should end with an obscure story of the manner in which a legendary native chieftain of the African town Irasa chose a husband for his daughter ; probably if we knew the persons concerned as well as Pindar did we should see the reason. Often the story is told rather for the sheer joy of telling it well than because it is either apposite or particularly instructive. Sometimes there is apparently no connexion whatever ; the crudest instance of this is the Tenth Pythian, in which, after saying that no man can reach the country of the Hyperboreans, he proceeds to explain that Perseus did so, and to tell something of what he saw in that land of marvels.

Pindar's moral and religious reflections, which are many and never platitudinous, do not need a myth to introduce them, however.   The Twelfth Olympian is one of those that have no myth at all.   The Second Olympian tells a myth and then goes on to another topic, appropriate in an ode addressed to a sick man, as its recipient, Theron, tyrant of Akragas, was at the time. Theron would seem to have been interested in the Pythagorean, or Orphic-Pythagorean, doctrines of the after-life, and certainly Pindar was, though we have no right to say that he ever belonged to that sect.   Wealth rightly used—it is one of his favourite

---

[66] This I take to be the meaning of the curious phrase κοιναί γάρ ἔρχοντ' ἐλπίδες πολυπόνων ἀνδρῶν, 32.   But in Greek the hopes, being half-personified, are said to ' come '.

[67] See Rose and Farnell in C.Q., xxv (1931), p. 156 sqq.

themes—brings much honour in this world, says the poet, and then, with one of his sudden transitions, he adds ' if indeed a man possessing it knoweth of the life to come ',[68] and there follows a veritable Apocalypse of the bliss of the righteous in another world, and the higher beatitude yet which awaits any who pass unspotted by guilt through a sixfold probation, three lives here and three in the other world. But this is not his normal tone, although he returned to the theme again to comfort some one in bereavement.[69] His was the orthodox religion, if we may call it so, of the older generations of Greece. The gods of his worship are alone immortal and wholly happy, and no man may think to attain to such bliss as theirs ;

' Men and gods are of one race,
And both from the self-same mother we draw our breath.
But measureless difference of power divideth us ;
For the one is a thing of naught,
But of the other the adamantine firmament abideth the unshaken
dwelling-place for ever.' [70]

As with all thoughtful Greeks from Hesiod, or even Homer, onwards, his polytheism is moving towards monotheism, and Zeus is supreme over all the rest, on his way to become simply ' God ' ; but naturally, as a poet dealing in myths, he does not consistently maintain this or any other theological system. Two things he had very much at heart, the majesty and justice of Apollo, whose servant he was,[71] and the righteousness of the gods in general. For this reason he more than once refuses to believe, or dismisses as a thing too hard for him, a myth derogatory to them.[72] But his ethics, like his religion, are somewhat old-fashioned, and open to criticisms that were raised during his lifetime, although not against him in particular. The gods are not bound by the same laws of conduct as mortals, but resemble rather the nobles of Homeric and later tradition ; especially, there is no cause of offence in the numerous stories of their loves for mortals. To be subject to so mighty a power as Aphrodite is no disgrace even for one of her fellow-deities ; and as to the mortal women on whom a god condescends to look, they neither incur blame nor give evidence of frailty in yielding to so exalted a wooer.[73]

[68] *Olymp.*, ii, 56 (trans. Farnell).
[69] See frags. 129, 130 Bergk (from a θρῆνος). [70] Nem., vi, 1–5.
[71] The latest discussion of this is in Farnell, ii, p. 462.
[72] As *Olymp.*, i, 52 *sqq.* ; *Olymp.*, ix, 35 *sqq.*
[73] I have discussed this subject at more length in a pamphlet, *Modern Methods in Classical Mythology*, St. Andrews, Henderson, pp. 12–17.

Pindar's myths, ethics and religion are set forth in a style whose genesis we can no longer trace, though we may conjecture that, besides what is original in it, he owed something to the conventions of earlier masters of choral lyric, including the dithyrambic poets. The chief and most striking feature is its extraordinary colour and vigour. This never degenerates into bombast, or obscurity for obscurity's sake, for Pindar's taste is as good as that of any Ionian ; but it often results in somewhat contorted diction, lacking in clearness, though never in force, and here and there in a strained construction, hardly to be brought into line with the normal, or even the poetical syntax of Greek. Metaphors are used with reckless profusion ; to take a random instance, one stanza of the Sixth Olympian has five in its seven lines.[74] Sometimes they are far-fetched and difficult to understand, and not seldom they are so piled one on another as to be mixed. Besides this, epithets are as numerous as they are brilliant and picturesque ; his own city's legendary namesake, the nymph Thebe, is a ' charioteer ' (literally, smiter of horses, πλάξιππος) in one passage, ' golden-shielded ' in another ; [75] songs are ' lords of the lyre ' (ἀναξοφόριμγγες) ; race-horses are ' whirlwind-footed ', the casualties of a great battle a ' sleeting rain of blood '.[76] At the same time the structure of the sentences is usually simple and even archaic. A like simplicity of arrange-ment extends to the thought ; Pindar seldom indicates, by such devices as the use of particles, what connexion there is between one part of an ode and the next, but leaves us to discover it for ourselves. It may be that when his work was sung and danced before an audience accustomed to expressing themselves largely by gesture, this deficiency was in some measure supplied ; but we know so little of Greek dancing that any such conjecture must remain unsupported.[77]

The dialect in which the poems are written is, as we have it in the good and reliable MSS., mostly Doric, with the usual sprinkling of epic forms, which, long before Pindar, were so well

---

[74] *Olymp.*, vi, 71–77 : wealth or prosperity ἕσπετο, followed (like a faithful attendant) ; the Iamidai ἐς φανερὰν ὁδὸν ἔρχονται. Everything τεκμαίρει, bears witness ; blame κρέμαται, hangs around the necks of their ill-wishers ; Charis lets glory ' drip ' upon them, ποτιστάξῃ.

[75] *Ibid.*, 85, and *Isth.*, i, 1.

[76] *Ol.*, ii, 1 ; Nem., i, 6, αἰνον ἀελλοπόδων μέγαν ἵππων (Simonides had used the epithet already, frag. 19) *Isth.*, iv (v), 49–50, Διὸς ὄμβρῳ/ ἀναρίθμων ἀνδρῶν χαλαζάεντι φόνῳ.

[77] The surviving descriptions of it are very much later than Pindar, and art of necessity shows us only isolated poses and gestures, not series of significant movements.

known that they might almost be regarded as a poets' *lingua franca*. In addition, there are occasionally words whose form reminds us that we have not a Dorian writer to deal with, but a Boiotian, whose native language was a form of Aiolic.

From the poems—the little anecdotes of him which are to be found in the lives are of much less authority—we can deduce something of his character, and it is one easily grasped, at all events by an English reader. Let him picture a particularly fine specimen of the old-fashioned English country gentleman, having developed to the very best the virtues of his class, such as courage, patriotism, loyalty, keenness in every manly sport and exercise. Let him further credit him with a full share of the limiting but not ignoble prejudices of his order. Then let him suppose this man endowed, firstly with more articulateness than is usual in Englishmen of that type, secondly with poetical gifts not usual in any type. Perhaps, if Sir Timothy Shelley had had a son who was not only a great lyric poet but also a fervent supporter of all that his father most respected, instead of a rebel against the orthodoxies of his day, the result would have been something like Pindar. But even so, we must allow for the differences between the finest type of old-fashioned Greek aristocrat and even his nearest analogies in any modern society.[78]

The Alexandrian critics drew up a canon of nine lyric poets, Alkman, Alkaios, Sappho, Stesichoros, Ibykos, Anakreon, Simonides, Pindar and BAKCHYLIDES. Of the last two the excellent critic who wrote the treatise *On the Sublime* (see p. 400), says : [79] ' In lyric poetry would you prefer to be Bakchylides rather than Pindar ? And in tragedy Ion of Chios rather than— Sophokles ? It is true that Bakchylides and Ion are faultless and entirely elegant writers of the polished school ($\dot{\alpha}\delta\iota\dot{\alpha}\pi\tau\omega\tau o\iota$ $\kappa\alpha\dot{\iota}$ $\dot{\epsilon}\nu$ $\tau\tilde{\omega}$ $\gamma\lambda\alpha\varphi\upsilon\varrho\tilde{\omega}$ $\pi\dot{\alpha}\nu\tau\eta$ $\kappa\epsilon\kappa\alpha\lambda\lambda\iota\gamma\varrho\alpha\varphi\eta\mu\dot{\epsilon}\nu o\iota$), while Pindar and Sophokles, although at times they burn everything before them as it were in their swift career, are often extinguished unaccountably and fail most lamentably. But would any one in his senses regard all the compositions of Ion put together as an equivalent for the single play of the *Oedipus* ? ' How just he is to Ion, whose works are now lost, we cannot say ; but without disparaging a poet of merit, we may complete the sentence with ' or all the newly-recovered works of Bakchylides as equal to the First Pythian '.

[78] *E.g.*, a modern's ideas of propriety would forbid him praising himself ; Pindar's do not ; and a modern, while he might warmly commend some promising young athlete, would not speak of loving him ; Pindar does.

[79] [Longinus] $\pi\epsilon\varrho\dot{\iota}$ $\ddot{\upsilon}\psi o\upsilon\varsigma$, 33, 5, trans. Rhys Roberts.

Until 1897 Bakchylides' name was hardly more familiar than Timokreon's or Pratinas' is now, even among students of Greek lyric poetry ; but in that year a large papyrus, discovered in Egypt and sent to the British Museum towards the end of 1896, was published by Dr. (later Sir) Frederic Kenyon, and at once aroused interest in every civilized country, for it contained, in fairly good condition, a number of the poet's odes—thirteen epinikia and six dithyrambs, the latter in alphabetical order of the first letters of their titles, the former arranged on no discoverable principle.[80] We are thus able to judge of Bakchylides for ourselves, and at the same time, from the very fact that he is not a poet of the first order, to see how far talent, industry and good training could take a man of that age, and so to realize how highly developed an art choral lyric had become.

In the surviving odes, his subjects are the same as Pindar's ; indeed, as already indicated, they occasionally celebrate the same events (see note 48). The difference which perhaps strikes a modern reader soonest is the much greater ease with which the younger poet can be comprehended. His language is ornate, having something not unlike the Pindaric multiplicity of epithets, but it is everywhere simple and clear. A little further examination shows that the odes are easy to understand for another reason, namely that their thought is commonplace, although pleasantly expressed, their myths told plainly and straightforwardly, but seldom very impressively (a favourable instance is the meeting of Herakles and the ghost of Meleagros, which has something of the weirdness that should attend a scene in Hades),[81] and their learning, which is considerable, a trifle apt to degenerate into catalogues like those in Hesiod or Korinna. The many epithets show little originality, and are not always happily chosen. Thus, having to describe the victory of an athlete in the pentathlon, he mentions his skill in hurling the ' wheel-shaped discus '.[82] The epithet is taken from epic, and appears in a fragment, still preserved, of the *Alkmaionis* ; but there it is used in describing the murder of Phokos by his half-brothers Peleus and Telamon, a somewhat ill-omened passage from which to take an adjective for a scene wholly free from horrors of any

---

[80] A good summary of the available information concerning the papyrus and its contents will be found in the introduction to Jebb's edition. The date of the papyrus is the first or second century A.D. For works on Bakchylides since Jebb, see Schmid-Stählin, i, p. 540.

[81] v, 56 *sqq.* For the story, see Rose, *Mythol.*, p. 216.

[82] viii, 32, διϲκὸν τροχοειδέα ῥίπτων. For the *Alkmaionis*, see Chapter iii, n. 45 ; frag. 1 Kinkel begins ἔνθα νιν ἀντίθεος Τελαμὼν τροχοειδέι δίσκῳ/πλῆξε κάρη. For the legend, see Rose, *Mythol.*, p. 260.

kind. Often he sounds as if he were imitating Pindar, although it is of course possible that both were drawing upon a common source ; once he certainly takes a phrase from him, but this time there is point in it ; Pindar had said that ' by the grace of the gods he had an illimitable path on overy hand ' to sing the achievements of Melissos of Thebes, winner of a chariot-race at the Isthmian Games. Bakchylides, a couple of years later, says to Hieron, ' thus for me also (*i.e.*, no less than for Pindar) there is an illimitable path on every hand to chant the praises of your excellence '. In other words, given a good subject, such as Hieron and his kin, he will prove as good a poet as Pindar.[83] The passage is thus subtly clever, complimenting Hieron and his family, Pindar, and incidentally Bakchylides himself. Bakchylides indeed handles compliments very well, never descending to base flattery but always preserving his tone of urbane courtesy. He has also a sense of humour, a virtue which Pindar lacks ; a good illustration of this, for naturally heroic myths and the strenuous doings of athletes leave little room for it, is found in a poem of another kind, apparently a sort of skolion,[84] addressed to Alexandros, probably the Macedonian prince, son of Amyntas, and containing an amusing account of the grandeur and prosperity which a man dreams of when a little flown with wine.

The dithyrambs are puzzling, in that one can hardly see what the title (vouched for by our papyrus) has to do with the contents, for in them we have no wildness of language or metre, no extravagant epithets and no trace at all of anything Dionysiac.[85] They are rather of the nature of ballads ; thus, the third (the sixteenth of our collection of his poems), entitled Ἠΐθεοι ἢ Θησεύς, is almost wholly occupied in the story of an adventure of Theseus on his way to Crete, while only the concluding lines mention that the poem is sung by a chorus of Keians in honour of Apollo of Delos. The next of the series is nothing but a short dialogue between certain unnamed Athenians and their king Aigeus, in which he, in answer to questions from them, describes the exploits and appearance of an unknown young adventurer (to wit, Theseus) whose approach towards the city has just been announced to him. It is strangely like a scene or episode from some longer work, and yet we have no right whatever to suppose that it is not complete. Such phenomena remind us how little we

---

[83] Pindar, *Isth.*, iii, 19 (iv, 1), ἔστι μοι θεῶν ἕκατι μυρία παντᾷ κέλευθος. Bakch., v, 31, τὼς νῦν καὶ ἐμοὶ μυρία παντᾷ κέλευθος ὑμετέραν ἀρετὰν ὑμνεῖν.

[84] *Oxyrh. Pap.*, 1361, frag. 1 (vol. xi), eked out by frag. 27 Bergk.

[85] Save the mention of his birth, xviii, 49.

know of the literature of Bakchylides' day, and incidentally throw some light on the origin of drama.

Taking the poems as a whole, their chief merit is their competent handling of theme and medium alike, in fact their careful and conscientious art. It is not hard to see what Pindar meant when he called Simonides and Bakchylides ' a pair of glib learners, with busy tongues which chatter to no purpose, like daws, against the divine bird of Zeus ', nor to realize that the stricture of the greater poet was far too severe. Bakchylides was neaier right when, tacitly allowing Pindar to be the eagle, he claimed for himself the title of ' Keian nightingale '.[86]

Of his life little is known. He was the son of Simonides' sister,[87] and younger than Pindar, perhaps by about ten or twelve years.[88] He may have lived till the outbreak of the Peloponnesian War (431 B.C.).[89] His odes, being addressed to persons living in various parts of the Greek world (Keos, Aigina, Athens, Phlius, Thessaly, Macedonia, Syracuse, Metapontion), indicate that his reputation, at all events, travelled far. He himself certainly was in Sicily, possibly in Macedonia (see note 84 ; but the poem mentioned there may have been sent to Alexandros), and probably, having been for some reason banished from Keos, in the Peloponnesos, it is not known when nor exactly where.[90] With him ended the great age of lyric poetry ; the next chapter will deal with the forms which succeeded it.

[86] Pindar, *Olymp.*, ii, 87, see Jebb, *Bacch.*, p. 15 *sqq.*, but *contra*, Farnell *ad loc.* ; Bakch., iii, 98. Süss (*Bacch. Carm.*, *praef.*, p. xix) says very reasonably, *nihil certe opus est Pindari comparatione minorem poetam, sed tamen poetam, urgere atque deprimere uelle*.

[87] For the facts of his life, see Jebb, *op. cit.*, p. 1 *sqq.*, to which add A. Severyns, *Bacchylide*, Paris, Droz, 1933. His grandfather's name was the same as his own, Suid., *s.u.* Βαχχυλίδης, and therefore his father Medon, Meidon or Meidylos cannot have been the brother of Simonides son of Leoprepes. That he was Simonides' nephew we know from Strabo, x, 5, 6.

[88] Eusebios' chronicle puts his ἀχμή at Olymp. lxxix, 2 = 467 B.C., therefore he may have been born about 507.

[89] He ἐγνωρίζετο then, according to Eusebios ; if this is not a mere blunder, it can only mean, as Jebb suggests (p. 3), that he was *still* alive and famous.

[90] Plutarch, *de exsilio*, 605 d, names among authors who composed their best works in exile Βαχχυλίδης ὁ ποιητής ἐν Πελοποννήσῳ.

CHAPTER VI

ATHENS AND THE DRAMA

THE reader will have noticed that the name of Athens has occurred several times in the preceding chapters. Hitherto we have spoken of foreign influences making themselves felt there, during or shortly before the enlightened despotism of Peisistratos and in the first part of the tyranny of his son Hippias. We have now to discuss the contribution of Athens herself to the literature of Greece, in consequence of which she became for some two hundred years the centre of the whole nation's thought and expression, ' the Greece of Greece ' as a well-known epigram styles her.[1] Slowly at first, but more and more rapidly as the fifth century wore on, her writers became the leading authors of the Greeks, her speech (the Attic dialect) the literary language, displacing both Ionic and Doric, and the stamp of her approval the very hall-mark of literary worth. To this result three main factors seem to have contributed.

Firstly, the geographical position of Attica made it easy for the inhabitants to enter into relations at once with their kinsfolk in Ionia and with the neighbouring peoples of Boiotia and the Peloponnesos. If they had been a slow-witted people, or one merely imitative, this might well have prevented them having an original literature of their own ; as it was, it gave their writers useful lessons in technique and good models, which they improved upon and transformed to their own ends.

A second reason was the prevalence of competitive or agonistic festivals, especially in connexion with the very popular cult of Dionysos. At these festivals all manner of feats of physical and mental skill were performed for prizes of one kind or another. With the former we are not now concerned ; the latter included recitations, vocal and instrumental music, and especially various kinds of concerted performances, such as dithyrambs. To men

---

[1] *Ελλάδος 'Ελλάς, 'Αθῆναι, Anth. Pal.,* vii, 45, 3 (attributed to Thucydides, or to Timotheos the lyric poet ; supposed to be Euripides' epitaph).

eager for the applause of their fellows, as the Athenians certainly were, this acted as a constant stimulus, urging those who had any talent to make the most of it, and to draw attention to themselves by novelties ; while the native good taste which seems to have marked the Athenians even more than the generality of Greeks, together with a certain reverence for antiquity, which they shared with the rest of the nation, prevented the fondness for novelty from running to absurd lengths and neglecting all that the past had to teach. Doubtless many unfortunate experiments, of which we know nothing, were tried ; but one great and abundantly successful innovation resulted in the creation of drama.

But the third and greatest reason was the remarkable expansion of Athenian power and the rise of their state to a leading place in Greece. The downfall of the Peisistratidai was followed by the establishment of democracy, a form of government which above all others demands strong and wise leaders. It was the good fortune of the state that for eighty years such leaders never failed to appear ; Kleisthenes, Aristeides, Themistokles, Kimon, Perikles and half a dozen more scarcely inferior to these contrived to unite a degree of personal liberty in thought and speech such as had never before existed in a civilized and orderly State with a firm and, on the whole, equitable rule, Perikles in particular combining, as Thucydides says in a much-quoted passage, nominal democracy with actual dictatorship.[2] Given the courage and enterprise of the people, and also the supreme opportunity, admirably used, of appearing as the champions and organizers of Greece against the Persian menace, this brought Athens to an unprecedented pitch of greatness and gave her a reputation which the misfortunes and misgovernment of that unhappy century intervening between the death of Perikles and the last struggle for independence against Antipatros could not quite abolish. It is a commonplace that when great and inspiring political events befall any State, her art and literature usually flourish ; and this certainly was true of Athens throughout the fifth century, while the reverberations of that great period did not die away till the end of the fourth.

As already mentioned, the new creation which enabled Attic poetry to rise to such heights (for a new impulse in literature inevitably calls for new forms and cannot content itself with the old) was drama. Concerning the origin of this we are reduced to speculation ; to begin with Tragedy, the chief theories of its genesis are as follows.

[2] Thuc., ii, 65, 9, λόγῳ μὲν δημοκρατία, ἔργῳ δὲ ὑπὸ τοῦ πρώτου ἀνδρὸς ἀρχή.

1. Aristotle, who has been followed by many modern writers, held that it arose out of dithyramb.[3] This can hardly be regarded as more than a hypothesis, for we have no reason to suppose that there were any records of the earliest plays, which seem to have been extempore, or at least never written down for publication or otherwise preserved once they had been acted. Therefore even his unrivalled knowledge of the history of drama can have had no material to work upon until near the beginning of the fifth century, when Tragedy, though far from its full development, was already a recognized literary form. But that it is a reasonable hypothesis no one will deny. We have seen (p. 125) that dithyrambs were sometimes dramatic in form, with dialogues replacing narrative. This being so, it would be no very revolutionary step to let one of the principal singers appear in costume, or at least sustain a part consistently throughout ; or again, to let him go out and come in again in another character. In the dithyramb of Bakchylides already referred to (p. 125) we have seen that Aigeus gave the chorus an account of what he had heard concerning a mysterious young hero who was approaching Athens. Let the story be carried on further, by performers in costume, and we should have a somewhat primitive form of play.

But Aristotle's theory suffers from grave defects. Formally, it does not explain why the chorus of Tragedy as we know it differed in numbers and in arrangement from that of the dithyramb. Materially, it does not tell us why Tragedy should commonly be tragic, containing an account of some event resulting in disaster, or at least a narrow escape from disaster, for the principal characters. And, a lesser point perhaps but not without its importance, it does not tell us why it is called Tragedy, τραγῳδία, ' goat-song '. These are not insuperable objections, but they are sufficiently serious to warrant us in looking for some other origin.

2. The late Sir William Ridgeway [4] put forward a very ingenious theory to account for two at least of the points which that of Aristotle does not clear up. He suggested that Tragedy had originally nothing to do with Dionysiac dithyramb (for he imagined that the dithyramb had no original connexion with Dionysos), or with the cult of the god, but arose from perform-

---

[3] ἀπὸ τῶν ἐξαρχόντων τὸν διθύραμβον, Poet., 1449ᵃ 10. ἐξάρχειν, a word not used elsewhere by Aristotle, seems to have been the technical term for ' leading off ' a dithyrambic chorus, cf. Archilochos, frag. 77 Diehl.

[4] *The Origin of Tragedy, with special reference to the Greek Tragedians*, Cambridge, Univ. Press, 1910 ; *The Dramas and Dramatic Dances of Non-European Races, in special reference to Greek Tragedy*, same pub., 1915.

ances of a mimetic character at the graves, or supposed graves, of heroes (ἡρῷα). He had no difficulty whatever in finding examples of performances of a dramatic character in connexion with the cult of the dead in many parts of the world, or in showing that these often involve imitation of the doings and appearance of the dead persons, who are represented by guisers. To show the existence of such a custom in Greece, he appealed to the testimony of Herodotos, who says that the Sekyonians used to ' honour Adrastos in various ways, but especially by tragic choruses having reference to what befell him (while alive), doing (this) honour not to Dionysos, but to Adrastos '.[5] From such mimetic performances, ' having reference to ', and therefore acting out with songs and dancing, the deeds of the local heroes, he supposed the Attic tragedies to have arisen. Such an origin would certainly go far to account for the serious tone of the performance and the frequency of plots which include the death of a leading character ; and Ridgeway sought a trace of it in the tomb which he alleged to be a normal feature of the stage-setting. However, as a tomb appears on the stage in less than half a dozen of the surviving tragedies, he was forced to the desperate expedient of supposing, in the face of classical usage,[6] that the altar (θυμέλη, βωμός) which was a constant feature was somehow a tomb.

His theory is generally and rightly rejected. It has the same difficulty as the first with regard to the name ; no reason can well be imagined for calling a mimetic performance in honour of the great dead a ' goat-song '. It has, further, two new difficulties of its own ; it does not explain why Dionysos was traditionally connected with Tragedy, so that it was performed at his festivals and not, for instance, at that of Theseus or some other Attic hero ; and it leaves quite unexplained those numerous plays in which no dead or dying man, no tomb and no funeral play any part. Further, the passage from Herodotos is far from proving all he would have it prove. Herodotos, speaking in the language of his own day, uses the term ' tragic choruses ' (τραγικοῖσι χοροῖσι) of a people who never acted tragedies, so far as we know, and a time before any such literary form existed. He cannot therefore mean it literally, but signifies that at the hero-shrine of Adrastos some kind of choruses gave a performance in some way resembling

---

[5] Herodotos, v, 67, 5.

[6] See especially Aristophanes, *Thesmoph.*, 886 *sqq.* ; Mnesilochos, in the character of Helen (see below, p. 237) says τόδ' ἐστὶν αὐτοῦ σῆμ' ἐφ' ᾧ καθήμεθα. He is sitting at an altar, and the old woman comments, κακῶς τ' ἄρ' ἐξόλοιο καξόλῃ γε τοι/ὅστις γε τολμᾶς σῆμα τὸν βωμον καλεῖν.

the tragedies which he and his readers knew.   How it resembled
them, whether in being mimetic or in the numbers or arrangement
of the chorus, the style of dancing, the costumes, the music or
some other respect, he does not say ; a chorus of a dozen persons
in the ' square ' formation used in the Attic theatre, singing some
kind of laudation of Adrastos and lamenting his misfortunes,
would justify his loose employment of the word ' tragic '.

3. The weaknesses of the two theories just described led Dr.
Farnell to put forward a third, highly ingenious and, in my
opinion, right in principle although mistaken in some details.[7]
He drew attention to two facts insufficiently noticed by other
writers.   One is, that to this day there exist, in the north of the
present State of Greece, mumming-plays of a type not unfamiliar
to British folklorists.   Without going into details, it may be
noted that in the neighbourhood of Viza in Thrace [8] certain
mummers, the chief of them disguised in goat-skins, perform, or
performed in 1906, a number of curious antics, culminating in
the pretended killing of one of them, preparations for his funeral,
and then his resuscitation.   That some such mummeries took
place in ancient Attica also Dr. Farnell tries to prove from the
legend of Dionysos Melanaigis.   According to the scholiasts on
Aristophanes and Plato,[9] who seem to derive their information
from Hellanikos (see p. 298), the Athenians and Boiotians were
once at war, and agreed to settle their differences by a single
combat between Xanthos, king of the Boiotians, and Melanthos,
the Athenian champion.   As they advanced towards each other,
Melanthos saw some one behind his opponent, and taxed him with
unfair dealing in bringing a second.   Xanthos turned around to
see who was behind him, and Melanthos took advantage of this
and killed him.   Such a tale, the combat of Fair-man ($\Xi\acute{a}\nu\theta o\varsigma$)
and Dark-man ($M\acute{\epsilon}\lambda a\nu\theta o\varsigma$) may quite possibly be the local version
of the almost world-wide combat between Summer and Winter.
The phantom which Melanthos saw wore a black goat-skin cloak,
$a\grave{\iota}\gamma\acute{\iota}\delta a$ $\mu\acute{\epsilon}\lambda a\iota\nu a\nu$, and hence Dionysos, for it was really he who
thus appeared, got his title.   If we suppose such a ritual combat
as this to have formed the subject of an Attic mummers' play,
it would give us the elements of seriousness, of association with
Dionysos, and incidentally of the wearing of a goat-skin by at

[7] In a paper read before the Hellenic Society, 11 May, 1909, and
reported in the *J.H.S.*, xxix (1909), p. xlvii ; see *C.G.S.*, v, p. 230 *sqq.*

[8] See Dawkins in *J.H.S.*, xxvi (1906), pp. 191–206.

[9] Schol. Ar., *Ach.*, 146, Plat., *Symp.*, 208 d ; the latter cites Hellanikos
in the first sentence of his long note, and probably means that the whole
of it rests on his authority : more references in Halliday, in *Class. Rev.*,
xl (1926), pp. 179–80.

least one actor,[10] thus fitting in very well with the characteristics of Tragedy.

Ingenious though it is, however, this theory is far from being certain. The modern evidence is of doubtful value. It is true that the performers at Viza were Greeks ; but they were living in Thrace, and it is very pertinently observed by Mr. Wace that such festivals are characteristic of the Balkans, and not of Greece proper at all.[11] In a region which has undergone such numerous invasions and consequent changes of population it is very rash to assume without confirmatory evidence that any custom has descended from either classical Greece or ancient Thrace and not been brought in by some much later arrivals. The legend of Dionysos Melanaigis again has been severely criticized, so far as its relevance to the present problem goes, by Principal Halliday (see note 9), who points out (a) that judging by one or two parallels of the story, Melanthos ought not really to have seen any one behind Xanthos, but merely have used a trick to make him look around ; (b) that if we are dealing with a mummers' play, the wrong man wins, for regularly it is Summer who defeats Winter. He suggests that the story is pure folktale, having no religious bearing, and also that the presence of Dionysos is intrusive ; the best source, Hellanikos as cited by the scholiast on Plato, does not mention him, and he may well have been added later when the story was pressed into service to explain certain features of the god's cult.

It thus appears that the theory, as originally stated, can hardly stand. Nevertheless, in a modified form it seems a reasonable hypothesis. We know very little of early Attic ritual ; but if we suppose that there existed some kind of rustic performance, connected with Dionysos himself or possibly with some similar god of fertility whom on his coming into Attica he absorbed, we can easily imagine that it involved a contest,[12]

[10] It must be borne in mind that the ' goats ' of Tragedy cannot be satyrs, for they are not goat-like in Attic art, but rather misshapen men with horses' tails.

[11] A. J. B. Wace in *Annual Brit. School Ath.*, xix (1912–13), p. 263.

[12] Pickard-Cambridge, *Dithyramb*, p. 162 and elsewhere, objects to all theories involving a contest as part of the original form of Tragedy that it would involve actors, and we are told there were none before Thespis. This is a serious objection, but not fatal. In Tragedy as we know it, the chorus often splits into two halves or semi-choruses ; the leaders of these might not unreasonably be supposed to represent antagonists, while the rest, grouped perhaps behind them, took the part of their followers or sympathizers.

I do not here discuss the elaborate and ingenious hypotheses of Prof. Murray and Dr. A. B. Cook (respectively set forth in Miss Harrison's

in which the power of fertility was for some reason killed (as deities of that kind often are, to rise again with the new vegetation of the next year, or the next crop of corn), or at least endangered by a formidable adversary (Summer fighting for his life against Winter, possibly). It is also very easy to imagine the country people who took part in such a mummery wearing the common country dress, goat-skin cloaks,[13] perhaps so arranged as to form a disguise, possibly chosen because of the fertility and lustiness of the he-goat. Such performers might quite as easily come to be called ' he-goats ' (τράγοι) as the Roman Luperci were,[14] and their performance, which included singing of some kind, consequently would be the ' he-goat-song ', τραγῳδία. It hardly seems possible to be more definite than this.

For our purposes, it is more profitable to consider what literary materials were ready to the hand of THESPIS when first he set out to give the ' he-goat-song ' some beginning of the regular form it afterwards assumed. He had, to begin with, the tradition of choral lyric, well developed by his time and associated with the service of the gods, not least of Dionysos. For his own great innovation, the introduction of a separate performer, the ' answerer ' (ὑποκριτής), or actor as we call him, who should speak to the chorus, replying to their questions, bringing them news and so forth, he had an equally appropriate vehicle in the metres, especially the iambic trimeter, which, as we have already seen (p. 81), imitated the cadences of ordinary speech. Thus the two parts of a tragedy, the dialogue (for there was nothing to prevent a member of the chorus speaking, instead of singing, when addressed by the actor) and the choral odes, already existed, albeit in an embryonic form, from the moment when his first play was ready to be rehearsed. For plots, there was no lack of material, for besides the abundant legends relating to Dionysos himself there was the entire wealth of mythology for him to draw upon, as the lyric poets had done and were doing ; and if he

---

Themis, ed. 2, pp. 341–63, and in *Zeus*, i, p. 645 *sqq.*), because (*a*) though differing widely in details from Farnell, they agree with him in postulating some kind of a ritual performance, or ' passion-play ' concerning Dionysos or a similar figure as the basis of Tragedy, (*b*) they have been well criticized by Pickard-Cambridge, *op. cit.*, pp. 185–218, (*c*) where they differ to any marked degree from Farnell, they appear to me to move away from the evidence we have and from probability, and therefore to be still more open to doubt than his view admittedly is.

[13] For goat-skins as typical peasant dress in antiquity, see Theognis, 55.

[14] They were popularly known as *creppi*, a dialectical or rustic variant of *capri* ; see Festus (Pauli), p. 49, 18 Lindsay.

did not take advantage of this treasury of good plots himself, his successors most assuredly did, as we shall see later.[15]

But we really know very little of Thespis ; [16] our notices of him are at best many generations later than himself, save for one passing reference in Aristophanes [17] which tells us nothing, and they are mixed with anecdote and bits of ancient theory to such an extent that it is hard to get at the few facts they contain, to say nothing of the singularly wild work which has been made of them by a number of moderns, from Boyle to the present day.[18] However, this much is reasonably likely, as representing the consensus of opinion among those authorities who seem to be the best informed. Thespis invented tragedy, *i.e.*, was the first person to compose it of whom any record could be found.[19] He was a native of Ikaria in Attica, a district which had an old cult of Dionysos.[20] He hit upon the idea of having an actor, ὑποκριτής, besides the chorus ; he himself was his own actor, at least at first, and used various simple disguises, as one might

[15] That the plots originally concerned Dionysos only was the ancient opinion, expressed in the various explanations of the proverb οὐδὲν πρὸς Διόνυσον, for which see Pickard-Cambridge, *Dithyramb*, p. 166 *sqq*.

[16] The notices concerning him are gathered and excellently commented on by Pickard-Cambridge, *Dithyramb*, p. 97 *sqq*.

[17] Ar., *Wasps*, 1478-9 ; old Philokleon (see p. 234), having got tipsy at dinner, comes back dancing τἀρχαῖ' ἐκεῖν' οἷς Θέσπις ἠγωνίζετο. The scholiast and Suidas preserve a grave note of some literal-minded scholar who declares that this cannot be the tragedian, but a harp-player of the same name. It is of course much the same kind of joke as that of the old soldier in *Punch*, who remembers being ' crimed ' for ' 'avin' a dirty bow an' arrow '.

[18] For Boyle, see Bentley, *Dissert. upon Phalaris*, p. 230 (258 of the Bohn ed.) *sqq*. Some of the more recent aberrations are considered and disposed of by Pickard-Cambridge, *loc. cit*.

[19] So most authorities say, including the damaged notice in the *Marmor Parium*, ep. 43, ἀφ' οὗ Θέσπις ὁ ποιητὴς [ἠγωνίζε?]το πρῶτος, ὃς ἐδίδαξε [δρ]ᾶ[μα ἐν ἄ]στ[ει, καὶ ἆθλον ἐ]τέθη ὁ [τ]ράγος, ἔτη (the number is illegible, but the date must have been something between 542/1 and 520/19 B.C., these being respectively the preceding and succeeding epochs). Pseudo-Plato, *Minos*, 320 e-321 a, gives it as the common opinion that Tragedy began ' from Thespis or Phrynichos ', and goes on to state a paradox of his own, that it was much older than they. A few late writers, one of them being Suidas, *s.u.* Θέσπις, say he was either the next or the seventeenth after EPIGENES of Sekyon, who was the real inventor of Tragedy. I agree with Pickard-Cambridge, *op. cit.*, p. 138, that this Epigenes may have composed some of the τραγικοὶ χοροί whereof Herodotos speaks, see note 5, and thus have been mistaken by a careless or ill-informed writer for a real tragedian.

[20] That he was an Ikarian we are told by Suidas ; for the latest discussion of its cult and legends, see Deubner, *Attische Feste* (Keller, Berlin, 1932), p. 118 *sqq*.

expect of a mummer—white lead, purslane shading or covering his face (perhaps hanging from his head-dress), then a kind of mask made of a piece of linen.[21] His date was the second half of the sixth century, and he received what looks like official recognition of some kind, presumably from Peisistratos, somewhere about 536 B.C.[22] There is no reason to suppose that any plays of his survived ; there are a few fragments and titles of dramas said to be his, but we are also told that Herakleides Pontikos (see p. 354) amused himself by writing plays to which he put Thespis' name, and of the fragments none suggests a date earlier than the fourth century.[23] A doubtful statement is that he took his plays about the country in waggons.[24] In any case, his scenic arrangements probably were of the very simplest ; an open space to give room for his chorus to manœuvre, some kind of vantage-ground from which spectators might look on, and the tent or marquee (σκηνή) in which, it would appear, the one actor changed his costume when necessary. Indeed, they cannot have been very elaborate, for who should pay for them if they were ? The system by which the State appointed *choregoi* to furnish what a poet needed was still in the future ; the prize, if we may believe our authorities, to be gained by a successful tragedian of Thespis' time was no more than a goat ; [25] and we have not a scrap of

[21] See Diog. Laert., iii, 56 ; Plut., *Solon*, 29 ; Suid., *loc. cit.* The account of the various ways of covering the face perhaps means that some tradition of disguises earlier than the developed mask of later Tragedy survived and so were attributed to Thespis. As white lead (ψιμύθιον) was used as a cosmetic, to make the skin look whiter, and as the bodies of women are regularly shown white, *i.e.*, not sunburned, in Greek art, those of men being brown, I suggest that this may have been the conventional make-up for a female part.

[22] See the *Marmor Parium*, cited in note 19 ; Suidas gives the date of Olymp. lxi, (536 B.C.) as the time when Thespis ἐδίδαξε, or produced a play ; this seems to refer to the same event as the other notice, and may well be a record of a contest of some kind at the Great Dionysia, which Peisistratos had much to do with.

[23] Titles in Suidas ; fragments in Nauck, pp. 832–3, to which add a citation of a single word in Photios (Reitzenstein, *Der Anfang des Lexikons des Photios*, p. 53, 10). For Herakleides, see Diog. Laert., v, 92, quoting Aristoxenos as his authority.

[24] Horace, *A.P.*, 275–7 ; but there is grave suspicion that he, or his authority Neoptolemos of Parion, has confused Tragedy, Comedy, and the jokes known as σκώμματα ἐξ ἁμάξης at certain Dionysiac festivals.

[25] So, for instance, the Parian Marble (see note 19), confirmed by the well-known epigram of Dioskorides, *A.P.*, vii, 410, and other passages, as Horace, *ars poet.*, 220. How much this tradition is worth is not known ; we may perhaps suppose that when Tragedy was in its infancy and still a mere mummers' play, the successful chorus was provided with a goat, the obvious material for a sacrifice to Dionysos and subsequent feast.

evidence either that Thespis was a wealthy amateur or that he had opportunity to make any large amount by charging for admission.

The next name of any importance is that of PHRYNICHOS.[26] As some seem to have considered him the inventor of Tragedy (see note 19), we may perhaps say with a certain degree of confidence that he was the earliest tragedian of whose work any considerable amount survived to later times. Aristophanes mentions him more than once, and always with respect,[27] especially as a composer of lyrics. His plots, to judge by the surviving titles, show a wide range of subjects, including not only very diverse myths but also one or two excursions into recent history, the *Persians* (if that is not the same as one or other of the next two), the *Sack of Miletos*, which treated of the disastrous overthrow of the Ionian revolt, and the *Phoinissai*, apparently the same or approximately the same in plot as the *Persians* of Aeschylus (see p. 149).[28] Besides this, we are told that his father's name was Polyphradmon or Polyphrasmon, and that he had a son, also called Polyphradmon, who like his father was a tragic poet ; that he won a victory, presumably his first, in 512/11, and was again victorious in 476, when Themistokles was his choregos ;[29] that he was the first to use female masks, or, for the word πρόσωπον is ambiguous, to introduce female characters into Tragedy.[30] So far the tradition is credible enough ; when Suidas tells us that Phrynichos invented the trochaic tetrameter, he is talking nonsense, although it is possible to guess what misled him.

[26] The facts are mostly in Suidas, *s.u.* ; modern discussions include Christ-Schmid, i, pp. 282–3 ; Haigh, *Drama*, pp. 42–5 ; Norwood, *Tragedy*, pp. 8–10 ; Pickard-Cambridge, *Dithyramb*, pp. 90–2.

[27] As *Birds*, 745, which mentions his ἀμβρόσια μέλη ; *Thesm.*, 164–7, where Agathon reasons that Ph.'s plays were καλά because αὐτός τε καλὸς ἦν καὶ καλῶς ἠμπίσχετο. The old men in the *Wasps* hum ' lovely honied Sidonian airs of old Ph.', ἀρχαιομελισιδωνοφρυνιχήρατα, 220, 269.

[28] The fragments are in Nauck, pp. 720–25 ; two new lines, *Oxyrh. Pap.*, ii, 221, col. 3, 4 *sqq.*

[29] Polyphradmon is not an Attic, but an Ionic name ; Polyphrasmon is the Attic form. The family, of which we know nothing, may have had Ionian connexions. The former of the two dates is in Suidas, the latter given by Plut., *Them.*, who gives the name of the archon, Adeimantos, known from other sources. The conjecture of Bentley, *Diss. on Phal.*, p. 257 (281 Bohn ed.), that the *Phoinissai* was the play acted then (or rather, one of the plays, see below, p. 145) is pretty, but has nothing whatsoever to support it.

[30] οὗτος δὲ πρῶτος ὁ Φρύνιχος γυναικεῖον πρόσωπον εἰσήγαγεν ἐν τῇ σκηνῇ, καὶ εὑρέτης τοῦ τετραμέτρου ἐγένετο, Suidas.

Aristotle says [31] that the earliest tragedies consisted of 'satyr-poetry', had a larger element of dancing than the later ones, and had short (or trivial) plots, dealing with satyrs, from which they did not change into the more serious form known to us until comparatively late (ὀψέ). With this change in subject came a change in metre, from trochaic tetrameters to iambics. That dancing played an important part in early Tragedy is not only very likely in itself but supported by Aristophanes' mention of old figures of dancing (σχήματα) associated with Thespis and Phrynichos, and by the tradition recorded by Athenaios that both these poets, and also Pratinas and Kratinos (sic : but the name is corrupt) were called 'dancers' and taught dancing to any who wished to learn.[32] The rest of Aristotle's remarks seems to be a corollary from his own theory of the origin of Tragedy. If it originated from dithyramb, it must have been Dionysiac ; the plots cannot have been long or elaborate ; satyrs were probably among the leading characters,[33] and dancing must have been a very prominent feature. Therefore the staider iambic metre would be unsuitable, and trochees, as fitter for persons dancing or running, would be employed. He certainly did not mean that anything as late as the work of Phrynichos had this character, for even the little we have left shows us that Phrynichos used iambics for his dialogue, indeed no trochaic tetrameters of his have come down to us ; while the same is true of the earliest play of Aeschylus (see p. 149).

Two other early tragedians are known to us by name. CHOIRILOS is said to have been an Athenian, to have composed 160 plays, and to have been before the public for a long time, 523–468 B.C., if we may combine the information given by several late and in no way impeccable authorities. Since there are left to us but one play-title (Alope), two short verbal quotations and one reference on a matter of mythical geography, we can hardly form an adequate opinion of him.[34] Of PRATINAS we know rather more, but what we know is

[31] Arist., poet., 1449ᵃ 14 sqq., where see the commentaries for details.
[32] Ar., Wasps, 1478–9 ; 1490–1 ; 1524–5 ; Athen., 22 a. For Κρατῖνος Bentley suggested Καρκίνος, for whom see p. 210 ; but he is rather late to be mentioned alongside of Thespis and Phrynichos.
[33] It is said of Arion (Suid., s.u.) that he ' introduced satyrs speaking in verse ' (σατύρους εἰσενεγκεῖν ἔμμετρα λέγοντας) See p. 106.
[34] Suidas, s.u. Χοιρίλος, who gives the sixty-fourth Olympiad (523–520 B.C.) as the date when he first began to exhibit (καθεὶς εἰς ἀγῶνας) and says that he won 13 victories with his plays. Eusebios' Chronicle puts him much later than this, floruit 482 ; while the Life of Sophokles prefixed to some MSS. of that poet, names him among those with whom Sophokles competed ; but this cannot have been earlier than 468, see p. 161. Since a minimum of fifty-two years is rather long for Choirilos' literary life, though not impossible, I am inclined to suppose the statement is a mistake due to misunderstanding Sophokles' work On the chorus, of which Suidas (s.u. Σοφοκλῆς) says λόγον (ἔγραψε) καταλογάδην περὶ τοῦ χοροῦ, πρὸς Θέσπιν καὶ Χοιρίλον ἀγωνιζόμενος, which I take to mean that

in one way somewhat puzzling. He appeared, says Suidas, as a competitor with Aeschylus and Choirilos in the seventieth Olympiad (499–496 B.C.). He was the first to write satyr-plays, and of his fifty dramas, thirty-two were satyric. Thus far Suidas; Pausanias, who visited Pratinas' native town of Phleius in the Peloponnesos and saw a monument to Pratinas' son ARISTIAS, says only that both father and son wrote the best-reputed satyr-plays of any except Aeschylus. Certainly the only long fragment of Pratinas we have, coming apparently from a satyr-play, indicates plenty of verve and abundant command of language ; it is a rollicking, vehement attack on the kind of music which was coming into fashion at the time.[35] It perhaps is true that, as Suidas says, Pratinas scored only one victory in his career ; his tastes were for the old style which was losing its hold on popular favour. But all the information concerning him is scrappy and dubious ; it seems to come from two works, Aristoxenos' Σύμμεικτα συμποσιακὰ and Chamaileon's Περὶ σατύρων, both much later (see pp. 354, 357) than Pratinas' own day. As for his satyr-plays, if he had lived about the middle of the fifth century it would be safe to assume a corruption in Suidas' far from impeccable text, or another of his numerous blunders ; but we have no exact knowledge of the date at which it became customary for every competitor at the Great Dionysia to present a quartette of plays, one being satyric.

Before giving an account of the three great tragedians, it is well to put together very briefly what little is known or conjectured of the manner in which the plays were produced during the fifth century. Here we are greatly handicapped, firstly by the loss of much of what the ancients wrote about the stage, by reason of which we are reduced to making what we can of statements in authors very much later than the great period of Attic drama, partly by the nature of our archaeological evidence.

it was a dialogue, the characters being Sophokles himself, Choirilos and, in despite of chronology, Thespis, representing three generations of Tragedy and disputing as to what the functions of the chorus should be. We may probably say, therefore, that Choirilos' literary life included the last two decades of the sixth century and an unknown part of the fifth.

[35] Suidas, *s.u.* Πρατίνας; Paus., ii, 13, 6 ; the frag. is preserved in Athen., 617 b, who calls it a hvporchema (a lively dancing-song ; the word commonly means a sort of ode and is mentioned several times along with the dithyramb ; I cannot find on what authority, if any, it is used, as by Jebb, to describe a joyous song of the chorus in Tragedy, as Soph., *Ai.*, 693 *sqq.*, *O.T.*, 1086 *sqq.*, *Ant.*, 1115 *sqq.*) ; but it is very reasonably explained (by Garrod in *Class. Rev.*, xxxiv, 1920, pp. 129–36) as being really part of a play, perhaps a satyr-play. The text is given in Garrod, *op. cit.* and Diehls, i, p. 124, besides the older collections of fragments and the editions of Athenaios. See also Pickard-Cambridge, *Dithyramb*, pp. 29 *sqq.*, 96. Of Aristias there survive half a dozen lines, see Nauck, pp. 726–8.

There are several Greek theatres in a very fair state of preservation, including the great Theatre of Dionysos at Athens itself ; but most of these are comparatively late, and the Dionysiac theatre was rebuilt more than once in antiquity ; consequently very little is left to tell us what its earliest form was.   This much is certain, that it had for its most essential feature the *orchestra* (ὀρχήστρα, dancing place ;   the word has undergone curious changes of meaning in modern times).   This was a circle, having at its centre the *thymele* (θυμέλη) or altar ; it is said that anciently there was a table beside it on which sacrificial victims were cut up, and that in the days before Thespis one member of the chorus used to mount on this to speak to the rest.[36]   Around some two-thirds of this circle the audience stood or sat ; we are told that originally temporary wooden structures (ἴκρια), presumably something like a grand-stand, were put up, but that on one occasion, in the days of Pratinas, these collapsed, and for that reason the Athenians built a (stone) theatre, *i.e.*, a horseshoe-shaped structure consisting of a number of tiers of seats rising above one another, as may still be seen in the ruins.[37]   The remaining third of the circle was almost touched by the stage-buildings (σκηνή), which in the theatres excavated by our archaeologists were substantial affairs of stone ; between the *skene* and the orchestra were passages (εἴσοδοι, πάροδοι) to right and left, through which the chorus entered.[38]

This is the Greek theatre ; a Roman theatre had a semi-circular orchestra, the diameter of which coincided with the front of the stage ; the orchestra was used for seating accommodation (our pit and stalls) and the whole performance was conducted on the stage.[39]

[36] See Pollux, iv, 123 ; it was called ἐλεός, or butcher's block.   Etym. Magn., *s.u.* θυμέλη, confuses it with the altar itself.   How true the tradition is, or on what it rested, we do not know ; see, for discussion, Haigh, *Theatre*, p. 80 ; Pickard-Cambridge, *Dithyramb*, pp. 118, 175.

[37] Suid., *s.u.* Πρατίνας ; for discussion of the theatre-buildings, see Haigh, *op. cit.*, p. 78 *sqq.*   The shape is a natural one, a concave hill-side with a piece of flat ground in front of it.   Many existing theatres, including the one at Athens, utilize the slope of an actual hill.

[38] They are commonly spoken of as πάροδοι by modern writers, and that is the name given them by late writers of antiquity, as Pollux, iv, 126.   The word also means the song of the chorus on entrance.   But the classical word seems to be simply εἴσοδος, or entrance, *e.g.*, Ar., *Clouds*, 327.

[39] See Vitruvius, *de archit.*, v, 6, 1.   There are several theatres of this form surviving in Italy, *e.g.*, a beautiful little example at Fiesole.   See Haigh, *op. cit.*, p. 82.   It should be noticed that the passages of Pollux and Vitruvius of which parts have been quoted are, besides archaeological discoveries and the text of the surviving plays, our chief materials for picturing the ancient theatre in its various forms.

With this form of building the present manual has nothing to do, as it belongs to a different culture and literature. In Greece, however, an approximation to such a theatre was made after the great age of drama was over.[40]

Archaeological evidence shows clearly that for at least the greater part of the fifth century there was no permanent stone *skene*. But that there was some kind of a back-scene is clear from the text of the surviving plays, which regularly assume either a building of some kind, or more rarely, some prominent natural feature, such as a hill or cliff, behind the actors. That this was represented with anything like the attempts at realism of a modern theatre is not to be supposed ; all that we know points to the acceptance by the public of a number of conventions and a use of the imagination such as no modern audience is called upon to make. Behind the actors was a wooden façade, probably (to judge by the analogy of the stone buildings which succeeded it and can be reconstructed with some approach to completeness from the remaining ruins) flanked by projecting wings, known as *paraskenia* or side-scenes,[41] within which there may have been dressing-rooms for the players. The façade was pierced by doors, probably three in number, as in later times, through which the actors generally entered, although not always ; for example, in the *Agamemnon* of Aeschylus, Agamemnon, Kassandra and their retinue drive in through the *eisodoi* and thence make their way to the stage on foot. The whole structure, although of wood, must have been substantial, for it had to support the weight of the ' machine ' ($\mu\eta\chi\alpha\nu\eta$), a strong instrument of the nature of a crane by means of which a god might be brought in flying through the air. That its weight was not trifling is shown by the *Prometheus*, in which the whole chorus enters in this manner. In addition there was, at least by about the year 425 or so, a kind of platform, the later ' gods' stage ' ($\theta\epsilon o\lambda o\gamma\epsilon\tilde{\iota}o\nu$), apparently fixed near the top of the *skene*, from which a god might speak. This is very clearly shown by the *Peace* of Aristophanes, in which Trygaios is seen flying up to heaven on the back of an immense beetle, and there meets and talks with Hermes. But the strangest convention was the

---

[40] See Vitruvius, v, 7 ; Haigh, pp. 112–39.

[41] In Dem., xxi, 17, Meidias' interferences with Demosthenes' chorus include τὰ παρασκήνια φράττων, προσηλῶν, *i.e.*, he blocked and nailed up the doors which led from the dressing-rooms in the *paraskenia* to the entrances ; that they were used as dressing-rooms or something of the kind (ταῖς εἰς τὸν ἀγῶνα παρασκευαῖς) is vouched for by Harpokration, p. 147, 18 Bekker. See Haigh, pp. 117, 379.

ekkyklema,[42] a contrivance used when it was desired to show something supposed to be happening inside the building which formed the back-scene. By the most natural interpretation of the evidence, one of the doors was flung open and an actor, or group of actors, thrust out through it on a wheeled platform ; then, their part done, the platform was wheeled back again and the door closed.

There has been hot debate as to whether the theatre of the fifth century had a stage, in our sense of the word, that is to say a raised platform upon which the actors stood. That it had in later times is quite clear from the remains of stone stages now in existence ; and the Vitruvian stage was quite high, ' not less than ten or more than twelve feet ' says that authority, who also explains that for a theatre of Roman shape, in which the orchestra was used for seating accommodation, it should be lower, five feet at most, or the spectators will not be able to see clearly what the actors are doing.[43] The archaeological evidence is, that even in the earlier stone theatres there was no stone stage between the *paraskenia*. Therefore, either the stage was of wood (perhaps removable to permit the theatre to be used for performances other than dramatic, when it would be an advantage to have the orchestra wholly unimpeded), or else there was none at all. The latter alternative has been warmly upheld by Dörpfeld, after being first propounded by Höpken.[44]

To begin with facts which, thanks largely to Dörpfeld's own researches, no one denies, it is not to be imagined that Aeschylus, Sophokles and Euripides wrote their plays for a theatre with a Vitruvian stage. The Greeks, as already mentioned, did not demand realism in drama, but they had a keen sense of the ridiculous, and would soon have exercised it upon the spectacle of an Antigone, for instance, appealing for sympathy to the chorus from the top of a twelve-foot wall, or an Agamemnon, in the heavy and elaborate tragic costume, climbing up a structure of that height to enter his palace. Not once but often the chorus comes into fairly close contact with the actors. Thus, in the *Agamemnon*, they are about to cross swords with Aigisthos' men when Klytaimestra intervenes ; in the *Medea* of Euripides, they speak of rushing into the palace to stop the murder of the children ; and there are several instances of a character coming in by the orchestra and then passing through one of the doors of the *skene*.[45] All this excludes a high stage, and moreover, it

---

[42] Haigh, pp. 201–09 ; see the whole chapter for various scenic devices.
[43] Vitr., v, 7, 2 ; 6, 2.   [44] Haigh, p. 144 *sqq.*
[45] See the analyses of the plays, pp. 154, 181. Cf. p. 422.

is perfectly possible to act a Greek play without any stage at all, as was shown, for example, by the Harvard performances, held in a stadium. The lowest seats of the audience being some little distance above the level of the orchestra, those occupying them can see over the heads of the chorus and thus get an uninterrupted view of the actors.

But in favour of a stage, though not a high one, very strong arguments can be urged. In the first place, no author ever hints at a time when there was no stage, and at least one suggests that in the fifth century there was a low one, built of wood.[46] If there was originally none at all, it is rather hard to see why there ever was a high one, and not merely a place at one end of the orchestra reserved for the actors. If now we look at the text of the plays, we find a number of passages which suggest that there was some slight barrier between chorus and actors, such as might be accounted for if we suppose such a stage, easily enough mounted (by a stair or inclined plane) by one person, but awkward for a dozen people to scale at once. Thus, in the passage already cited from the *Medea*, the chorus do not actually advance to the doors of the palace ; in the *Agamemnon*, again they do not rush into the palace at the moment of the murder, although they talk of doing so ; and in several plays they are clearly standing at some little distance from the actors. If we turn to Comedy, which often alludes to or makes fun of the setting of the plays, we have at least one passage which seems to necessitate an elevation of some kind for the actors to stand upon. The slaves of Demos, in the *Knights*, are in front of Demos' house, which is the Pnyx, or hill where the popular assembly met. The Haggis-Seller enters in the Agora, represented by the orchestra ; they call to him to ' come up ' to them, which he does.[47] Unless they are really on a somewhat higher level than he, this is hardly actable. A wooden platform, some four or five feet high, would suffice to meet all requirements, and it certainly would have the advantage of making the principal characters more conspicuous than if they were on the same level as the chorus. There is no need to assume that it was always of exactly the same pattern, or could not be changed for different plays, at least in the earlier period.

Stage or none, there was apparently no curtain or any similar device until Roman times, and as the whole performance took place in the open air, there could be no lighting effects. This is one reason for the numerous passages in which mention is made

---

[46] Hor., *ars poet.*, 279, *Aeschylus . . . modicis instrauit pulpita tignis* (on props of no great height).

[47] ἀνάβαινε, 149.

of the time ; the audience had to be told whether it was supposed to be day or night. As the scenery was of the very simplest, and devices for changing it primitive enough,[48] descriptions of things which a modern dramatist would leave the stage-management to show are also fairly common ; it must be made clear whether the wall behind the performers stood for a palace, a temple, or a cave. As also there seems to have been nothing corresponding to our programmes or play-bills, it was necessary often to explain who the characters were ; and as they were all masked, and so could not make any play with their features, an indication of the expression they were supposed to wear was often added.[49] This accounts, for example, for the chorus of the *Antigone* saying that they see Ismene coming out at the palace gate and weeping.[50] She obviously could not wear a

[48] It was not often necessary to change it during a play. The Unity of Place is indeed a figment of critics in modern times, since the Revival of Letters ; the scene shifts, for instance, once in the *Aiax* of Sophokles, twice in the *Eumenides* of Aeschylus ; but Greeks liked simple and concentrated effects, and therefore plays which were shorter than ours, with less movement and fewer incidents. When a shift was needed, the change in scenery was made, or rather indicated, by a simple device known as a περίακτος. There were two of these (see Pollux, iv, 126, cf. Vitruv., v, 7, 8) ; that on the right for ' scenery outside the city ' and that on the left for ' scenery within the city ' (τὰ ἔξω πόλεως, τὰ ἐκ πόλεως). Each was a large wooden prism, revolving on a pivot, fitted into an opening in the *skene* ; on each face of the prism was painted, or attached in some way, an indication of the scenery of the play, for example a tree to show that there was a grove in the background, a tent to represent a camp, or the like. Nilsson has shown excellently, by analogy with the art of the period, how absurd it is to suppose that anything like our full and elaborate changes of scenery were either possible or demanded ; see his article, *Die alte Bühne und die Periakten*, in *Från filologiska föreningen i Lund*, språkliga uppsatser iv, Lund, 1914, also the article of P. Gardner, *Scenery of the Greek Stage*, *J.H.S.*, xix (1899), p. 252 *sqq.*, which Nilsson cites.

Later authors called the periaktos a ' reversable scene ' (*scaena uersilis*, Servius on *Georg.*, iii, 24 ; cf. the phrase σκηνῆς περιφερομένης in Plutarch, *de esu carnium*, i, 996 b).

[49] For the various kinds of masks which were used in later times, see Pollux, iv, 133–54 ; how many of them were known in the early fifth century it is impossible to say. Aeschylus is said to have invented the tragic mask, Horace, *ars poet.*, 278, and Choirilos (Suid., *s.u.*) to have made some improvements in it and in the tragic costume generally. Sophokles (*Life*, 4) is credited with introducing a third actor, putting an end to the custom of the poet himself appearing in a part, and also (6) making some slight improvements in the costume. Here again we do not know how much of the tradition to believe ; that these poets introduced improvements of some sort is quite credible ; they were their own stage-managers.

[50] Soph., *Ant.*, 526 *sqq.*

mask showing a tear-stained face throughout her part. If we may judge by the practice of later times, the side from which a new arrival entered was significant, those coming in from the right being supposed to come from the neighbourhood (elsewhere in the city, if the scene was laid in one, the immediately surrounding country, or the harbour), while any one entering from the left was supposed to be a traveller from a distance.[51]

The actors were professionals and always men ; they were but three in number, distinguished, according to the importance of the parts they had to play, as first, second and third actor (πρωταγωνιστής, δευτεραγωνιστής, τριταγωνιστής). Hence it was often necessary for the same actor to fill several rôles ; for instance, while the protagonist would throughout appear as Oidipus in the *Oedipus Tyrannus* of Sophokles, the deuteragonist and tritagonist had between them to represent the priest of Zeus, Iokaste, Kreon, Teiresias, the servant of Laios and the two messengers. This was made possible by their being masked, and had the advantage that the total number of highly trained men, possessed of powerful and harmonious voices, required for the fitting performance of great plays before a critical audience, which did not hesitate to hiss or stamp, was not large.[52] Very rarely, and only towards the end of the century, a fourth actor was required, never for more than a short scene or two. Of mute parts there might be any number, for instance the attendants on kings and other great persons, children (one of Alkestis' children in the play of that name by Euripides has a short passage of lyric, how and by whom delivered we do not know ; Medeia's sons are heard to cry out in terror and entreat the chorus to rescue them, but this is done off the stage, and one of the regular actors probably recited the lines ; generally the children say nothing at all), and any other subordinate figures the poet saw fit to introduce. The general name for persons filling such minor rôles was παραχορηγήματα, literally ' additional expenses of the choregos '.[53]

In addition to their masks, the actors wore a special costume. In the time of Aeschylus, this apparently consisted of a long robe, a head-dress (ὄγκος) attached to or forming the upper part of the mask, and shoes or buskins (κόθορνοι) having very thick

---

[51] Pollux, ıv, 127.

[52] Hissing, *e.g.*, Demosth., xviii, 265 ; the actor hissed off the stage was said ἐκπίπτειν, *ibid.* ; stamping, as a mark of disapproval, to drive an actor off the stage (ἐκβάλλειν), Pollux, iv, 122. For the number of actors, see Haigh, p. 221 *sqq.*

[53] Haigh, *Theatre*, p. 234 *sqq.*

soles. Their apparent height being thus increased by something like a foot or more, they were also padded, so as not to seem disproportionately thin.[54] The effect of this was to prevent their seeming too small from the point of view of the spectators, most of whom, even in the front seats, were further from the stage than those in the ' gods ' of our theatres are. Euripides made some attempt to introduce more realistic costumes, and is ridiculed by Aristophanes [55] for dressing his heroes and heroines in rags. The chorus, having to dance, was naturally not arrayed in such heavy dresses, but was costumed, often splendidly, though apparently not masked.

The plays were never, at least while drama flourished at Athens, produced merely for entertainment, but formed a definite part of a religious festival in honour of Dionysos. The principal occasion for the production of new tragedies was the Great Dionysia, in the month Elaphebolion, which was, speaking very roughly, about equivalent to our March.[56]. At this feast, perhaps three days were devoted to performances in the theatre. After choral songs by men and boys, about which we know but little, came the tragedies ; it is usually supposed that on each day four plays, all by the same author, were staged, and followed by a comedy. Thus three tragedians and three comedians competed at each festival. Nothing definite is known as to how they applied to be admitted to the competition, or who had the task of selecting the three to compete, if there happened, as may very often have been the case, to be more than that number of applicants. The four plays of each contestant are known collectively as a tetralogy, and the three tragedies which this group included, as a trilogy ; neither word has any better authority, in this sense, than grammarians and other writers very much later than the poets now under discussion, but they are convenient terms and in general use. The fourth play was normally a satyr-drama. It was often, but not always or necessarily, the case that the trilogy dealt with different parts of the same story, forming as it were the three acts of a long play (on an average, about as long as *Hamlet*). Thus, Aeschylus competed with the *Agamemnon*, *Choephoroe* and *Eumenides*, which tell the legend of the murder of Agamemnon, Orestes' revenge and his final justification by the Areiopagos ; but on another occasion, the plays he presented were the *Phineus*, *Persians* and *Glaukos*, none of which had any

---

[54] Haigh, *Theatre*, p. 238 *sqq.*   [55] Especially *Acharn.*, 414 *sqq.*
[56] The calendar being soli-lunar, no exact equivalent is possible ; any given Attic date shifts in different years about as much as our Easter, relatively to the Julian calendar. See Addenda, p. 422.

discoverable connexion with the others. The fourth play might, if the poet saw fit, deal in a semi-burlesque fashion with some detail of the legend handled by the three tragedies ; for example, the *Oresteia* ended with the *Proteus*, dealing with a minor adventure of one of the House of Atreus, that described in Odyssey iv (see p. 24), into which comic touches might easily be introduced. Here again, there need be no connexion between the satyr-play and the trilogy, and Euripides at least did not always write one ; the *Alcestis* is not a satyr-play but a tragedy with a happy ending and one mildly amusing scene, or rather one slightly comic speech in a scene otherwise serious, but we know that it was the fourth play of a tetralogy.[57] As already indicated, the very large proportion of satyr-plays among the works of Pratinas is inconsistent, if the tradition is correct, with the later arrangement, unless indeed, as has been suggested, he wrote satyr-plays to complete the tetralogies of other poets.[58]

The cost of these performances was borne by the State ; not, however, by a direct subsidy, but indirectly. All well-to-do citizens were liable to a form of capital tax known as λητουργίαι or public services ; *i.e.*, they were chosen, in more or less regular order and with fairly efficient precautions against victimization, to perform at their own expense certain public works, such as furnishing and paying the crew of a warship for a year (τριηραρχία); and among these was reckoned the furnishing of a chorus for one of the competing dramatists (χορηγία), which would include meeting other necessary expenses of the performance, such as the παραχορηγήματα already spoken of (see p. 144). Although the person thus called upon was known as the *choregos* or chorus-leader, he did not, as such, take any part in the actual singing

[57] See the second of the ancient arguments to the play. For the whole question of tetralogies, see Haigh, *op. cit.*, p. 10 *sqq.* There is some evidence that strictly speaking a trilogy (tetralogy) is a group of three (four) plays connected in subject ; but it is convenient to use the words of any group of the requisite number put on by one poet at one time. Later, such evidence as we have strongly suggests that the practice was abandoned and each tragedian might compete with one or two plays. Whether tetralogies were ever the rule at other festivals than the Great Dionysia we do not know, nor, considering their lesser importance, does it seem very probable.

[58] The suggestion is due to Capps, and is commented upon by Pickard-Cambridge, *Dithyramb*, p. 93 and n. 3. Quite possible also are the suggestions of Haigh, *Drama*, p. 42, n. 3, that the numbers given by Suidas are merely those of the known works of Pratinas, many others having been lost, or that in his day the system of tetralogies was not yet in vogue (it is quite unknown when it began) and poets might put on what plays they chose.

and dancing, but, at most, conducted the chorus to its place in the orchestra.[59] The leader of it, in the sense of the chief singer or speaker, was known as the κορυφαῖος or ' head man '. The chorus regularly numbered, in tragedy, either twelve or fifteen persons,[60] and was formed up, not in a circle, but in ranks ; hence it is at times spoken of as a ' square ' chorus, in contradistinction to the ' circular ' chorus of dithyramb.

It is clear that this form of encouragement to dramatic art might well have resulted in the production, year by year, of a number of clever and efficiently constructed prize poems. It is very probable that this, and no more, was what it produced in the fourth century. But the history of literature, like all history, is primarily an account of what certain notable men did with the materials that their surroundings furnished them, and it so happened that in the fifth century there existed in Athens a little group of first-rate poets, whereof two must be reckoned among the very foremost of the whole world, while the other, if a little less great than they, would alone be sufficient to make any literature famous. We have now to sketch their careers.

AESCHYLUS, or more properly AISCHYLOS (Αἰσχύλος), son of Euphorion, of a good family resident in Eleusis, was born in or about the year 525 B.C. In accordance with the usual ancient habit, though by no means confined to antiquity, of decorating the lives of poets with miracles, it is said that Dionysos in person appeared to him while still a boy and bade him write tragedies , it is also said that he was a Pythagorean, which is probably due to the later tendency to connect Pythagoras somehow with every philosopher or theologian. That he was an initiate of the Eleusinian mysteries has been repeatedly asserted, and whether we believe it or not depends on our interpretation of an ambiguous remark of Aristotle. The known facts of his career are that he fought very bravely at Marathon and, ten years later, at the chief battles of Athens and her allies against Xerxes ; that he exhibited tragedies for the first time in the seventieth Olympiad (500–497 B.C.) and won his first prize in 484, thereafter being

[59] See Haigh, *op. cit.*, pp. 53–6. That the choregos did sometimes lead in the chorus we see from Demosthenes, xxi, 74 ; this however was a dithyrambic and not a tragic chorus, and the incident he describes occurred in his own days. In Aristophanes' time the poet was formally bidden, by a herald or some official, to ' lead in his chorus ', see *Acharn.*, 11.

[60] Originally twelve, but increased to fifteen by Sophokles, according to the tradition, *Vita Sophoclis*, 4. See Haigh, *op. cit.*, p. 288 *sqq.* ; the conjecture which he mentions that a tragic chorus was originally as nearly as possible one-fourth that of a dithyramb depends on the Aristotelian theory of the origin of Tragedy, discussed above, p. 129.

for some time the most popular poet in Athens ; that he accepted
an invitation from Hieron to go to Syracuse, sometime between
472 and 468 ; that he returned to Athens and left the city again
after 458, never to return ; that he died near Gela in Sicily in
456/5. We also know that he won the first prize thirteen times
in all. Why he died in a sort of voluntary exile is not known ;
certainly it was not for want of appreciation in Athens, for his
last victory was shortly before his departure, but political events
may have had something to do with it, since his plays show no
love for extreme democracy and considerable admiration for the
older Athenian constitutional forms. Or it may have been some
private reason of which we know nothing.[61]

More important than the events of his life are his plays. Of
these he wrote about ninety,[62] whereof there survive seven.

[61] See Christ-Schmid, i, pp. 284–7 ; Haigh, *Drama*, p. 45 *sqq.* ; Norwood, *Tragedy*, pp. 10–12. The ancient sources are a life (Βίος Αἰσχύλου)
contained in the Codex Mediceus of his plays and printed in most modern
editions, a notice in Suidas and a number of passages scattered through
various authors. For his alleged Pythagoreanism, see Cicero, *Tusc.*, ii,
23, written long after the legends of Pythagoras and his early followers
had formed ; the vision of Dionysos is in Pausanias, i, 21, 2. For his
initiation, see especially Aristotle, *Eth. Nic.*, 1111[a] 9 *sqq.* ; Aeschylus was
accused of having revealed the Mysteries in one of his plays and defended
himself by saying that he did not know that the matter spoken of or acted
was secret. This might mean that he had never been initiated and had
accidentally hit upon something which resembled a piece of Eleusinian
ritual, and from this interpretation of the story may come the statement
of Clement of Alexandria, *strom.*, ii, 60 (p. 461 Pott.) that he defended
himself by proving that he had never been initiated. Or it might be
supposed that Aeschylus was an initiate, but had not quite grasped the
distinction between the secret and the open parts of the ritual (ἀπόρρητα,
φανερῶς δρώμενα). More details of the story, some highly improbable,
are given by Eustratios, *comment. in Eth. Nic.*, p. 145, 49 *sqq.* Heylbut,
who cites as his authority Herakleides Pontikos ; Aelian, *uar. hist.*, v, 19 ;
and in the *Life*. As to his dates, the Marmor Parium gives (59) 456/5
as the year of his death and his age then as 68, which makes his birth-year
524/3 ; the *Life* says he was born Olymp. 63, which is 528–525 B.C.
Suidas gives the date of his first contest, the Marmor Parium that of his
first victory. The first visit to Sicily must have been after the presentation
of the *Persians* in Athens (see p. 149), for he produced it again in Sicily,
according to the *Life* (line 90 Dindorf), and before the *Seven*, for he must
have been in Athens to produce that.

[62] Suidas says ninety ; a list, preserved in the Cod. Mediceus, gives
72 titles, to which we can add half a dozen or so from other sources.
Probably the copyist of the list has omitted a column of some 18 titles
from his original, or copied from an earlier list already so mutilated.
The *Life*, line 66 Dind., says 70, including 5 satyric, which is plainly
corrupt ; possibly, as Dind. suggests, the sense of the original passage
was ' 70, of which . . . are satyric, and also 5 whose authenticity is
disputed '.

These, however, are not a random but a fairly careful and intelligent selection, including some of his most famous works and one complete trilogy. Of fragments we have not many, and the reconstruction of the lost plays is very hazardous. The surviving pieces are the following.

(1) The *Suppliants* ('Ικέτιδες), past all question the earliest specimen of Tragedy now surviving.[63] It appears to have been neglected in antiquity ; certainly it was ill-copied and has come down to us with many passages mutilated or hopelessly corrupt. The chief characters are the chorus, and there is but one scene requiring a second actor. The plot is as follows. Danaos, with his daughters and their attendants, who compose the chorus, arrives in Argos, and the women take refuge at the statues of the local gods. Presently the king of Argos arrives and asks their business. They claim his protection against the sons of Aigyptos as descendants of the Argive Io. After consultation with the popular assembly he grants their request. Meanwhile the sons of Aigyptos have reached the coast and their herald tries to make the daughters of Danaos come away ; the timely return of the king, however, frustrates him and Danaos and his daughters leave for the city.

Manifestly, this is but the first act of the play. There were two more tragedies continuing the story, the *Egyptians* (Αἰγύπτιοι) and *Daughters of Danaos* (Δαναΐδες ; it may have been also called the *Attendants of the Bride-Chamber*, Θαλαμοποιοί), which probably told between them of the decision to settle the quarrel by marrying Danaos' daughters, despite their unwillingness, to Aigyptos' sons, the murder of the latter on the bridal night and the trial of Hypermestra for sparing her husband Lynkeus.[64] Aphrodite took part in the last play, perhaps as Hypermestra's advocate, with a most eloquent plea which stressed the all-pervading power of love.

Next in order of time comes the *Persians* (spring of 472), one of a tetralogy whose subjects seem to have been in no way con-

[63] For all the following plays, see Haigh, *Drama*, p. 61 *sqq.* ; Wilamowitz, *Interp.*, *passim* ; Norwood, *Tragedy*, chap. iii. The date of the *Suppliants* is uncertain ; its simplicity makes it obvious that it must be old, and possibly the laudatory mentions of Argos and the absence of any allusion to disaster befalling that State may be taken to signify a year earlier than the annihilation of the Argive army by Kleomenes (see p. 111) and the unpopularity caused by Argos' inactivity in face of the Persian menace, *i.e.*, somewhere in the nineties of the century. For further discussion, see the introductions to the various modern editions of the play, as Tucker, Vürtheim, Mazon. See p. 422.

[64] For the legend, see Rose, *Mythol.*, p. 272. I follow the reconstruction of Welcker, rejecting other views of the end of the trilogy, for which see Vürtheim, *Aischylos' Schutzflehende*, p. 72.

nected, since the other plays were the *Phineus*, dealing with an incident of the Argonautic saga, the *Glaukos*, which treated either of Glaukos of the Sea, the fisherman who was turned into a merman, or Glaukos of Potniai, who was torn to pieces by his own horses, and finally a *Prometheus*, a satyr-play.[65] These are lost ; but the *Persians* survives as perhaps the noblest expression of triumphant thanksgiving for a great national deliverance that has yet been written. Its tone is that of the States General's *flauit* יהוה *et dissipati sunt*. The scene is laid in the Persian court, and the chorus composed of elders forming the royal council. After an opening passage in which they express their anxiety for the long-absent army of Xerxes, they are joined by the Queen-Dowager, Atossa, who tells them of a disquieting dream that seems to presage ill success to her son. When, by their advice, she is about to go and fetch materials for a sacrifice to the powers of the under-world, a messenger enters with news of the utter destruction of the fleet at Salamis and the annihilation of most of the army in the retreat. The Queen, hearing that Xerxes himself is safe, goes out and, after a long lament from the chorus, returns. She and they together now evoke the ghost of Dareios, who appears to them, hears the news and expounds the cause of the disaster ; it was an old doom which he had hoped would not be fulfilled for many years yet, but the rash and impious presumption of Xerxes has hastened it ; ' for when one is eager of himself, Heaven lends a hand '. After bidding the elders make the most of the little time they have left on earth, he disappears. The queen having gone back to the palace, Xerxes enters, alone and in rags, and is escorted to the palace by the elders. Throughout, though the Persians are shown grieving and almost in despair, there is not a shadow of blatant exultation over them, nor are they represented as in any way undignified or unworthy.

The next surviving play is the *Seven against Thebes* (467), this time one of a continuous trilogy recounting the story of the Theban royal house. The first play, *Laios*, seems to have dealt with that king's sin against his host Pelops ; the next, *Oidipus*, continued the tale of the curse which his wickedness and disobedience brought upon his line, down to the death or blinding of Oidipus and the death of Iokaste ; the *Seven* takes up the story on the morning of the final attack by Polyneikes and his allies upon the city.[66] The central character is Eteokles, who is

[65] The argument to the *Persians* calls this play simply Προμηθεύς. A Π. Πυρφόρος is mentioned several times ; this may have been it, or the Π. Πυρκαεύς, if that was not the same ; see p. 153.

[66] See, for the story, Rose, *Mythol.*, p. 190 *sqq.*

shown as a man heavily burdened by the double load of his public responsibility for the welfare of the State and his own consciousness that doom is approaching and will be fulfilled. There is little action ; after an opening scene in which he addresses the citizens,[67] the chorus enters, in wild panic ; it is composed of Theban girls, expecting every moment to find themselves at the mercy of the Argive army. The king re-enters, rebukes and tries to calm them, and goes out again. After a choral ode, he and a scout come in from opposite sides of the stage ; there follows a long scene rather epic than dramatic, in which he is told of the preparations of the seven chieftains, each of whom is to attack one gate, and names seven Thebans to oppose them. The last of these is himself, and the champion whom he is to face is his own brother Polyneikes. The chorus vainly try to dissuade him ; the doom of Apollo is on his house and he will not try to avert it. He leaves the stage, and shortly after a messenger relates the defeat of the attacking army and the death of Eteokles and Polyneikes by each other's hands. The bodies are brought in and the play closes with the lamentations of the chorus over them.

So the play ended as written by Aeschylus ; but as given in our MSS., there is a spurious last scene, founded on the *Antigone* of Sophokles. Antigone and Ismene enter to join in the wailing ; a herald informs them that it is forbidden to bury Polyneikes ; Antigone defies him and part of the chorus support her. Whoever wrote this scene was a passable versifier and imitated the style of Aeschylus tolerably well ; that the poet himself should thus have ended his trilogy just at the beginning of a new episode is past belief. Probably the alteration was made for a fourth-century revival of the play, before an audience which knew its Sophokles.[68]

The date of the *Prometheus Bound* is uncertain, though it possibly was written not long after the great eruption of Aetna in 479/8 ; [69] it is a not improbable hypothesis that the·allusion to this which the play contains [70] arises from its having been composed, or revised, while the author was in Sicily. If he wrote it during his stay with Hieron, this would further explain why the

[67] Represented possibly by a stage crowd ' ; more likely Eteokles simply addressed the audience in their seats.

[68] See Wilamowitz, *Interp.*, pp. 88–95 ; I can but agree with his remark that any one who still thinks this scene genuine is past teaching (*unbelehrbar*).

[69] The date is given by the Marmor Parium (52). Thucydides, iii, 116, 2, says that the eruption which took place in the sixth year of the Peloponnesian War (426/5) was fifty years later than this one, but is probably speaking in round numbers.

[70] *Prom.*, 367 *sqq.* See Christ-Schmid, i, 297.

existing argument of the tragedy gives no date ; for the *didaskaliai*, or brief introductions, which we have, date by the Athenian archons, and if the *Prometheus* was not acted in Athens originally, it might well be that no record of the official Athenian date survived for the Alexandrian scholars to use.　Further, if we suppose that Aeschylus did not write for his fellow-countrymen, it is easier to understand the remarkable experiments in stage technique which the drama contains.[71]　It does not appear that the chorus, which is composed of sea-nymphs, ever enters the orchestra at all, and its part is unusually short and the lyrics much less interesting than one expects from Aeschylus.　There is a great deal to be said for Wilamowitz' supposition [72] that the seamaidens remain grouped about the huge figure of Prometheus throughout, on a comparatively small platform, which, at the end of the play, is lowered out of sight, carrying him and them with it.

The play opens with the fastening of Prometheus to a lonely crag, somewhere at the ends of the earth in ' the land of the Scythians, a desert where no man treads '.　The Titan is manifestly represented by a wooden or other artificial figure, from behind which an actor spoke the part ; for, under the directions of Strength and Might (Κράτος and Βία), the Hesiodic attendants of Zeus,[73] Hephaistos not only attaches him with fetters, or rather strong iron bands, which make it impossible to move hand or foot, but drives a heavy spike through his chest into the rock beyond.　However unrealistically this might be done, no actor could maintain so rigid a position throughout the play without most acute discomfort, such as would very seriously interfere with his delivery of the long speeches involved.　Moreover, it is plain that Hephaistos has to clamber up and down to reach the arms and legs of Prometheus, a mere absurdity if the Titan is represented by an actor of human proportions, whom the tragic costume might make, at most, seven or eight feet tall.　During the fettering, Prometheus is silent (*i.e.*, his part was spoken by the actor who had played Hephaistos, and then went behind the scenes and climbed to his place back of the great image).　He now bursts out into an indignant soliloquy, setting forth the

[71] Wilamowitz, *Interp.*, p. 114 *sqq.*, has an excellent discussion of the question.　I do not waste paper in discussing a fantastic theory that the play is spurious ; those who wish to follow this aberration may consult Schmid-Stählin I, ii, 193 and references there, to be supplemented from the recent reviews of work on Greek literature in Bursian's *Jahresberichte*. For the moral problem of the play, see especially Farnell in *J.H.S.*, liii (1933), pp. 40–50.

[72] *Op. cit.*, p. 117.　*See* Addenda, p. 422.　[73] Hesiod, *Theog.*, 385 *sqq.*

injustice of his treatment at the hands of Zeus. To him enter the chorus, and to them he tells the story of his alliance with Zeus against his fellow-Titans, and the gross perfidy with which Zeus has turned against him. Okeanos, the father of the nymphs, now enters ; as his daughters had already done, he comes in a winged car. His professions of sympathy and counsels of moderation are treated with coldness by Prometheus. After he is gone, and the chorus have sung a short ode, Prometheus again speaks, and tells of his services to man, for whose sake he is now tortured, because he prevented Zeus from destroying them. Then enters Io, on her maddened wanderings, the victim of Zeus' love as Prometheus is of his hate. He tells her of her own and her offspring's destinies, including the fact that his own deliverer (Herakles) is the thirteenth in descent from her. When she is gone, he tells the chorus plainly that Zeus will be overthrown by a marriage against which only Prometheus can warn him. Now Hermes enters, demanding on behalf of Zeus to know the secret ; Prometheus defies and mocks him, and the play ends amid thunder and earthquake, in which Prometheus and the chorus, who refuse to leave him, are swallowed up.

That a play representing Zeus as a harsh and unjust tyrant presents no small difficulty in a poet like Aeschylus is plain. For him, Zeus is normally the all-wise and all-good lord of the universe (see p. 159). The story as we have it is indeed incomplete, and whatever may have been the third play, the next in order was plainly the *Prometheus Unbound*. But in this, so far as we can judge of it from the fragments, little light was thrown on the riddle of its predecessor. It showed Prometheus again restored to the light of day after long imprisonment underground, but afflicted with a new torment, an eagle which came every other day and tore his liver. A chorus of Titans, set free apparently by Zeus from their bonds, entered to sympathize with him. After some conversation and possibly other episodes, Herakles came, received from Prometheus directions concerning the journey on which he was bound, to fetch the cattle of Geryon, and in return shot the eagle and was hailed by Prometheus as ' beloved son of a hated sire '. It does not therefore appear that any reconciliation had been reached by that time, and we do not know what other plays the trilogy consisted of (the assignment of the *Prometheus Πυρφόρος* and *Prometheus Πυρκαεύς* to this tetralogy or that containing the *Persians* is a moot point, as is the question whether they were two plays, or one with a slight variation of title ; in any case they were satyr-dramas) and therefore cannot point with any degree of certainty to a third tragedy which might have cleared the matter up. Indeed, if Aeschylus was writing for a Sicilian audience, what right have we to suppose that he put on a tetralogy at all, or that the rules framed for competitions at the Great Dionysia applied to what may well have been a ' command performance ' for Hieron and his court ?   The only supposition at all resembling a solution of the difficulty, that Aeschylus represented Zeus as having learned wisdom and gentleness with experience of rule, is completely devoid of positive evidence on its behalf, though in itself not at all impossible.

Passing from this puzzle, we come to the last and greatest Aeschylean work, the *Oresteia*,[74] consisting of three plays, the one trilogy that survives.   They are as follows :

Agamemnon.   Scene, the royal palace at Mycenae, or Argos, on a winter night in the last year of the Trojan War.[75]   A watchman on the palace roof sees a beacon-fire, the signal that Troy has fallen, and shouts the news to Klytaimestra.   Enter now the chorus, old men forming the royal council.   Klytaimestra is seen for a moment bustling about with preparations for sacrifices of thanksgiving.   When at length she is at leisure, they question her, and receive a detailed and brilliant description of the chain of beacons between Argos and Troy, by which the news has been telegraphed.   They fall into reflections on the sin which began the war and the misery that it has caused.   During the singing of their ode, some months are supposed to elapse.   A herald now enters to announce the arrival of Agamemnon, also the dispersal of the Greek fleet by a storm.   Their further reflections are interrupted by the coming of Agamemnon himself, attended by a few guards and followed by Kassandra, who drives behind him in a carriage.   After a long dialogue with Klytaimestra, the king is induced to enter the palace in the most conspicuously invidious way, walking upon tapestries laid down to carpet the ground.   Kassandra remains stonily silent, and Klytaimestra, getting no answer from her, leaves the stage angrily.   Kassandra now breaks out into a prophetic frenzy, in which she tells, or rather hints at, the horrors of the Thyestean banquet, and then goes on to warn the chorus, who utterly fail to understand her, that Agamemnon is in imminent danger of being murdered by his wife.   At last, tearing off her prophetic insignia, she goes into the palace, and a moment later the king's death-cries are heard. The chorus hurriedly debate what is best to do, when the door of the palace is flung open (*i.e.*, the *ekkyklema* rolls out) and Klytaimestra is seen standing over the bodies of Agamemnon and Kassandra.   She proclaims and exults in her deed, declaring it

[74] The title is given by Aristophanes, *Frogs*, 1124.
[75] Troy falls ἀμφὶ Πλειάδων δύσιν, *Agam.*, 826.   The herald arrives δεκάτῳ φέγγει ἔτους, 504, which it is natural to interpret as ' on the tenth light (= day) of the year ' (so Farnell), *i.e.*, by Attic reckoning, about July.

to be an act of justice for the murder of Iphigeneia, and further that it is the curse of the house, not she, who is really responsible. The debate between her and the chorus is ended by the appearance of Aigisthos, who swaggeringly justifies his part in the murder, by recalling the wrong done to his father Thyestes by Atreus ; he and the chorus quarrel, and are about to come to blows when Klytaimestra stops them and takes Aigisthos within.

The *Choephoroe* or *Libation-bearers* also has its scene in front of the palace. Orestes, who in the *Agamemnon* is mentioned as being a child, sent to Phokis out of harm's way, is now a young man and returns home, attended by his friend Pylades. Here he meets and after a little time is recognized by his sister Elektra, who has been sent by Klytaimestra, along with a number of slave-women, to pour libations at the tomb of Agamemnon, shown on the stage. These women form the chorus from which the play takes its title, according to the usual custom of naming a tragedy either from the principal actor or from the chorus. Brother and sister proceed to utter a long invocation to their dead father ; when this is finished, the two young men go off, disguise themselves as wayfarers from Phokis,[76] and return to the palace, asking for a night's lodging. Meeting Klytaimestra, they tell her Orestes is dead. She sends a servant, Orestes' old nurse, to bid Aigisthos come ; the chorus ask her to change the message a little ; the strangers have very private information for him, and he is to come unattended. On entering the palace, he is at once killed ; Klytaimestra, running out at the news, is confronted with his body (shown by the *ekkyklema*) and by her son. She pleads stoutly for life, but Pylades reminds Orestes that Apollo commands her to be slain, and she is taken within and dispatched. Orestes now shows the bodies, but as he justifies himself is seized with a disturbance of spirit, in which he sees the Erinyes haunting him. The chorus advise him to go to Delphoi, and he leaves the stage.

In this fine but difficult play, rendered more difficult by grave corruption of the text at many points, the chorus has played a comparatively subordinate part, though it has several majestic odes to sing between the episodes of the drama.[77] In the last of the trilogy the chorus is a principal actor.

The *Eumenides* opens before the temple at Delphoi, and a priestess enters, telling the legend of the shrine. She goes into

---

[76] They say (563) that they will speak the Phokian dialect, but the audience are left to imagine this, for Orestes uses pure Attic throughout.

[77] Episode (ἐπεισόδιον) means what we should call an act of the play ; the *entractes* of the chorus are called στάσιμα.

the temple, and comes stumbling out again, terrified by the sight of the Erinyes. The temple is disclosed : Orestes is sitting at the sacred *omphalos* with the sleeping Erinyes around him : Apollo promises him help and bids him go to Athens, there to be freed from his tormentors ; Hermes is to attend him on the way. As soon as he is gone, the ghost of Klytaimestra appears and rouses the Erinyes, who, after a debate with Apollo, leave the temple in pursuit of Orestes. The scene now changes to Athens, where Athena summons the Areios Pagos to judge the matter.[78] The Erinyes press the charge against Orestes ; Apollo bears testimony in his favour, and raises the curious plea that son and mother are not really akin, the father being the only true parent. The votes of the court are equally divided, and Athena gives the casting-vote in Orestes' favour. She then calms the rage of the baffled chorus and induces them to remain in Athens as beneficent powers, henceforth to be called Eumenides (Kindly goddesses), not Erinyes. The trilogy ends with a solemn procession escorting them to the shrine which was theirs in historical times.

The fragments of Aeschylus' other plays are often so scanty that reconstruction of the plot is extremely hazardous. Some have already been mentioned ; the others are as follows, so far as they are known, in their Greek alphabetical order : *Athamas* ;[79] *Aitnaiai*, of which the title shows that its chorus was connected with the new city of Aitna, founded by Hieron, while one fragment (6 Nauck) mentions the native Sicilian cult of the Palikoi : *Alkmene*, whose very existence is doubtful ;[80] *Amymone*, dealing with the story of Poseidon and Amymone daughter of Danaos ; it may have been the satyr-play of the tetralogy to which the *Suppliants* belonged ; *Argeioi* (*The Argives* ; possibly a copyist's mistake for the name of Argeia, daughter of Adrastos), dealing with some part of the Theban saga ; *Argo*, also called Κωπευστής (*The Oarsman* ; perhaps the name should be in the plural and referred to the members of the chorus) ; *Atalante*, of which we know nothing but the name ; two plays dealing with some part of the Dionysiac mythology, *Bakchai* and *Bassarai* ; *Glaukos Pontios* and *Glaukos Potnieus* ; *Diktyulkoi*, i.e., the *Drawers of Nets*, namely the Seriphian fisherman who found Danae and her child ;[80a] Διονύσου τροφοί, *The Nurses of Dionysos*, of quite unknown content ; the *Eleusinians*, which handled the same story as the *Suppliants* of Euripides, with the difference that Theseus did not force, but persuaded the Thebans

---

[78] There is probably a political allusion here ; Aeschylus praises this ancient senate, whose powers were being attacked by the democratic party. For Apollo, cf. Winnington-Ingram in *C.R.*, xlvii, pp. 97–104.

[79] See Rose, *Mythol.*, p. 151, for his legend.

[80] It rests on a citation of one word (ἀποστάς) from it in a gloss of Hesychios, whose text is notoriously full of corruptions. [80a] See p. 422.

to give burial to the dead Seven ; [81] the *Epigonoi*, handling the next portion of the Theban saga ; the *Edonians* ('Ηδωνοί), which with the *Bassarai* or *Bassarides*, already mentioned, Νεανίσκοι or *Young Men* and a satyr-play, the *Lykurgos*, formed a tetralogy, known as the *Lykurgeia*, dealing obviously with the story how Lykurgos, king of the Thracians, opposed Dionysos and was worsted after an apparent success, as is related by several poets from Homer on ; [82] the 'Ηλιάδες or *Daughters of the Sun*, which treated of Phaethon's fall ; the *Herakleidai*, concerning which the title tells us that it handled some part of the story of Herakles' descendants and their adventures, while a fragment shows that the chorus told something at least of the tale of the Labours ; the Θεωροί otherwise called the 'Ισθμιασται, a satyr-play ; [82a] the Θρῆσσαι named from its chorus of captive Thracian women, dealing with the death of Aias ; [83] the 'Ιέρειαι, or *Priestesses*, concerning which we may conjecture that it had something to do with a temple of Artemis, for it speaks of certain ' bee-keepers ', who are going to open Artemis' shrine, and we know that her priestesses, at Ephesos and elsewhere, were called ' bees ' ; the *Ixion* and the *Iphigeneia*, clearly dealing with some portions of these well-known legends, but with what portions is not known ; the *Kabeiroi*, again a play dealing with the Argonauts, for all we know of its plot is that in one scene Jason and his companions appeared drunk ; it may have dealt with the halt at Samothrace, where they were initiated,[84] and conceivably was a satyr-play ; the *Kallisto*, of which again we do not know how it handled the legend ; the *Karians* or *Europê*, of which a fragment survives to show that Europê told the story of her union with Zeus ; the *Kerkyon*, the Κήρυκες, or *Heralds*, and the *Kirke*, all satyr-plays ; the Κρῆσσαι, or *Women of Crete*, again of unknown content ; there may have been a *Kyknos*, for Kyknos son of Ares had something to do in one of the plays ; [85] a satyr-play known as Λέων, whether ' *The Lion* ' or some person called Leon we do not know ; the *Lemnians*, whereof we have nothing at all but the title ; the *Memnon*, *Myrmidones* and *Mysians*, with plots taken from the Troy-saga (the last dealt with Telephos) ; the *Nemea*, which, possibly together with the *Hypsipyle*, may have dealt with the founding of the Nemean games, and certainly mentioned that event ; the *Nereids*, possibly Thetis' companions, with some

---

[81] For the legend, see Rose, *Mythol.*, pp. 192–3. We owe this bit of information about the play to Plutarch, *Theseus*, 29.

[82] Iliad, vi, 130 *sqq.*, and then in a number of authors down to Nonnos, *Dionys.*, xx, 149 *sqq.* [82a] See p. 423.

[83] The information about this play comes from the scholiast on the *Aiax* of Sophokles ; references in Nauck.

[84] This incident is told briefly by Apollonios Rhodios, *Arg.*, i, 915–21, followed by Valerius Flaccus, *Arg.*, ii, 431–40 and ' Orpheus ', *Arg.*, 466–70. Whether they owe anything to Aeschylus is not known.

[85] The evidence is simply Ar., *Frogs*, 963, where Euripides says he did not try to frighten his audience, as Aeschylus did, Κύκνους ποιῶν καὶ Μέμνονας. As there was a *Memnon*, there may have been a *Kyknos*, but this is pure conjecture.

reference to their visit to Achilles or their mourning for his death ; [86]
the *Niobe*, of which play we would gladly know more, if only for the
almost blasphemous outburst of an unidentified speaker, that ' God
plants guilt in men when he wishes utterly to ruin a house ' ; [86a] the
Xantriai, which dealt with the story of Pentheus ; the *"Οπλων κρίσις*,
or *Judgement of the Armour*, on the story of how Aias and Odysseus
both claimed the arms of Achilles—this may have been of the same
trilogy as the *Θρῆσσαι*, and a possible third play is the *Salaminiai*,
which might have dealt with the return of Teukros or his founding of
Salamis in Cyprus ; the *'Οστολόγοι*, the title of which seems to refer
to the ' gathering of the bones ' from a funeral pyre, for burial, while
two fragments tell of riotous feasting in which a certain Eurymachos
takes part ; as he was one of the wooers of Penelope, a satyr-drama
forming part of the story of Odysseus seems possible ; the *Palamedes*,
possibly with the same plot as Euripides' play (see p. 206) ; the *Pentheus* ; the *Perrhaibians*, of which nothing is certainly known ; the
Penelope, of which we can see that the plot dealt with an incident in
the Odyssey, the meeting of Odysseus, presumably in his disguise as
a beggar, with his wife, so that this and the *'Οστολόγοι* may have
been parts of the same tetralogy ; [87] the *Polydeukes* and *Προπομποί*,
mere names to us ; the *Proteus*, the satyr-play of the *Oresteia* ; the
Σαλαμίνιαι, already mentioned ; the *Semele* or *Water-carriers* (*'Υδροφόροι*)
which treated of the mother of Dionysos ; another satyr-play, as
it probably was, the *Sisyphos* (*Σίσυφος δραπέτης* or *πετροκυλιστής*),
telling of the trickster's attempt to cheat Death ; yet another, the
Sphinx, belonging to the same tetralogy as the *Seven* ; the *Telephos*,
whether or not telling the same story as the Euripidean play of that
name ; the *Τοξοτίδες*, or *Female Archers*, perhaps Artemis' attendants,
for Aktaion had a part in the action, or at least was mentioned ; the
Hypsipyle, concerning which we are quite in the dark as to what part
of her story it dealt with ; the *Philoktetes*, of which more will be said
when dealing with Sophokles' play of the same title ; the *Phineus*,
again on an Argonautic subject ; the *Phorkides*, or *Daughters of Phorkys*,
which is known to have been satyric ; the *Phrygians* or *Ransom of
Hektor*, whose title is sufficient indication of its plot ; a doubtful
title, *Φρύγιοι*, may refer to the same play ; the *Ψυχαγωγοί*, *i.e.*, *Necro-
mancers*, apparently dealing with Odysseus' visit to Hades ; the
Ψυχοστασία, or *Weighing of Souls*, *in* which Zeus, in the presence of
Eos and Thetis, weighed the souls of Memnon and Achilles against
each other, to show which was fated to fall by the other's hand ;
finally the *Oreithyia*.   Of some others we do not even know the titles,

[86] The plot, that is, was very likely taken from Iliad xviii, or else
from the last book of the Odyssey ; see above, pp. 21, 30.

[86a] A fragment of 21 lines has been published from a papyrus by Norsa
and Vitelli in *Bull. Soc. arch. Alex.*, no. xxviii (1932) : cf. Cazzaniga in
Rendiconti d. R. Istituto lombardo, Ser. ii. vol. lxvi (1933/XI), pp. 843-52.
See Addenda, p. 422.

[87] Cf. frag. 187, *ἐγὼ γένος μέν εἰμι Κρὴς ἀρχέστατον*, with Od. xix,
172 *sqq*.

and a few fragments remain which have not been assigned to any particular play.

One point which must not be passed over in discussing Aeschylus is his theology, for he was one of those poets who are also prophets. A reasoned and philosophical system one does not look for in a dramatist, especially as he must often voice the opinions of his characters and not his own ; but so great a master of lyric poetry had abundant opportunities, in the odes sung by his chorus, to set forth his visions concerning God and man. Aeschylus begins early to do so, in the lofty praises of Zeus which form one of the striking features of the *Suppliants* ; [88] the chief theme of the *Persians* and of the trilogy to which the *Seven* belonged may be said to be the judgements of God on the sinful and presumptuous ; the riddle of the *Prometheus* has already been touched upon. But the poet's most developed and original thought is contained in the *Oresteia*. Practically, Aeschylus was a monotheist, not that he denied the existence of other deities, for we may gather that quite apart from mythology he was ready enough to admit the reality of such beings as Athena or Apollo, but that he subordinates all else to Zeus, including the gods who were before him, Uranos and Kronos. He had no dogma of the immutability of deity, but seems rather to suppose a sort of divine evolution, or more accurately, to interpret the myths of the *Theogony* and other traditional sources as recording a series of catastrophic changes in the government of the universe. But now at all events the power is in the hands of Zeus, ' whoever he be, if it please him to be invoked by that name '.[89] This supreme deity is perfectly wise, beneficent and just ; that his ways are past finding out is insisted upon in the earliest surviving work ; ' how can I look into the mind of Zeus, that abyss where sight is lost ? ' ask the Danaids.[90] Concerning his justice, Aeschylus will not believe that prosperity stirs him to jealousy ; wealth will bring no ruin in its train if it is properly used, but men's own folly may move them to insolent frowardness ($\H{v}\beta\varrho\iota\varsigma$), and that meets with deserved punishment, extending beyond the transgressor's own life.[91] But in the divine severity, which extends not only to those who sin against man but even to such offenders as the wanton plunderers of a bird's nest,[92] there is mercy hidden ; the rule of Zeus is that men shall not only ' have done to them according as they have done ' ($\delta\varrho\acute{a}\sigma\alpha\nu\tau\iota\ \pi\alpha\theta\varepsilon\tilde{\iota}\nu$) but also ' learn

[88] Notably 86–101 ; 524–6, and the whole of that stasimon.
[89] *Agam.*, 160.   [90] *Suppl.*, 1057–8.
[91] *Agam.*, 750 *sqq.* ; cf. Aeschylus' handling of the Theban saga.
[92] *Ibid.*, 55 *sqq.*

by what they undergo' (πάθει μάθος).[93] Nor is the justice that punishes them any mere formal code, taking no account of intention or mitigating circumstances ; this seems to be the moral of the defeat of the Erinyes, who regard only the deed itself, before a court representing a higher and more enlightened law.

Such a theology as this, set forth in Aeschylus' ruggedly grand style, and accompanied, especially in his mature work, by powers of depicting character which even Euripides never surpassed, make him worthy of the reverence his contemporaries and, generally speaking, posterity gave him. He was, however, not unjustly considered a difficult author, both by reason of his style and from the occasional obscurity of his thought ; hence he seems never to have been popular in the sense that the other two tragedians were. This explains the scantiness of our fragments, to which Egypt has added little of any importance.

While very great as a poet, he left much for his successors to do in the technique of the drama. As we have seen, some of his works, notably the *Seven*, tell their story rather after the fashion of epic than of any sort of play ; or, like the *Suppliants*, are of the nature of lyrical narrative interspersed with a little dialogue. Very considerable advance is shown in the plays of the trilogy, but even here we do not always find that close connexion between scene and scene which is one of the merits of Sophokles, and for that matter of all great playwrights. In this as in several other respects there is a real resemblance between Aeschylus and Marlowe, although the Englishman was the lesser poet.

The best of the old piety towards the gods is to be seen in Aeschylus and Pindar ; a few years more, and the questioning of their justice and interest in human affairs which Aeschylus deprecates [94] was becoming general, though not yet triumphant, and there was room for a poet whose chief interest, like that of Homer, was once more in man. Such a one was SOPHOKLES, perhaps the most characteristic embodiment of the fifth century at its best. Decorously pious, yet plainly interested in what was, to the Athens of his day, the new learning ; a lover of pleasure, without being debauched or mastered by it ; of a remarkably sweet and happy temperament, but neither weak nor blind to the sadness of life ; artistic and refined to an extraordinary degree, but not a recluse nor shunning, on occasion, public service ; he was of a type which his fellow-countrymen could not but appreciate and love. Moreover, he was not only a poet who would have made his mark in any form of composition, but one of the most admirable playwrights ever born. His pieces have

[93] *Agam.*, 176.   [94] Notably *Agam.*, 369 *sqq.*

the simplicity and at the same time the perfect and harmonious construction of the masterworks of contemporary art ; his language is neither affected nor designedly obscure, but has that subtlety which comes from absolute mastery by a great artist of his native tongue. To us, he is often difficult, for we are obliged to resort to observation and analogy to decide, if we can, what departures might be made from the ordinary usage of Attic ; to those of his own day, and especially to the more cultured among them, the difficulties which confront us would not exist, but appear as what they were, delicate innovations, making a marvellously accurate and flexible speech express itself with even more precision and beauty than it ordinarily did.

He was born sometime between 497 and 494 B.C.,[95] at Kolonos Hippios, a deme of the tribe Aigeïs, situated just outside Athens. His family appears to have been of some importance socially, and was certainly not poor, for his father owned a manufactory of swords or metal-work of some kind, a profitable industry in a century whose history consists largely of wars.[96] Sophokles would appear to have had some ambition to become an actor, and appeared at least twice, in the parts of Thamyris and Nausikaa, in his own plays. His personal beauty and grace of movement gained applause, but his voice was not powerful enough for the demands made on it by Tragedy ; hence he turned his attention wholly to composition, and produced in all upwards of 125 plays, whereof but seven survive complete ;[97] he is said to have won 20 victories, or perhaps more exactly 24, 18 at the Great Dionysia and the remainder, presumably, at the Lenaia. The first of these was won against Aeschylus, in 469/8.[98] Of his public career we know that he was *strategos* once, if not twice.[99] Less

[95] The Marmor Parium (64) says that he was 92 when he died in 406/5, *i.e.*, that he was born in 497/6 ; the *Life* (good critical ed. in Pearson's text of Sophokles, in *Bib. Class. Ox.*) says (2) that he was born Olymp. lxxi, 2 = 495/4 B.C.

[96] So most ancient authorities, as the *Life*, 1. That he was *principe loco genitus* (Pliny, *N.H.*, xxxvii, 40) seems rather an exaggeration.

[97] Acts the part of Thamyris, *Life*, 5 ; of Nausikaa, Athenaios, 21 f. Most authorities say that he took part in a chorus in celebration of the victory at Salamis. Plays number 130, including 17 considered spurious, Aristophanes of Byzantion in the *Life*, 18 ; 123 ' but according to some, considerably more', Suidas *s.u. Σοφοκλῆς Σοφίλου*.

[98] 20 victories, *Life*, 8, adding that he was often second but never third. Date of first victory, Marmor Parium 56 ; opponent Aeschylus, Plut., *Cimon*, 8. 24, Suidas ; 18, Diod. Sic., xiii, 103, 4, explained by *I.G.*, ii, 977 A [*Σοφ*]*οκλῆς ΔΠΙΙΙ* ; it is a list of victors at the Great Dionysia, and Diodoros must have drawn upon a similar document.

[99] Strategos in 438, *Life*, 9, but the figure is probably corrupt, for he was at Samos in 440, see Jebb's ed. of the *Antigone, Introd.*, p. xliii *sqq.* ;

important information, and much more doubtful, is comprised in the statements, perfectly possible in themselves, that Lampros taught him music and Aeschylus tragedy, and that he was chosen after the battle of Salamis to lead a chorus of boys who sang a hymn in honour of the victory. The usual crop of anecdotes grew up around him, and need not be considered in any detail.[100] He was about 90 years old when he died, as the result, it is said, of a trifling accident or exertion, and thus outlived his younger rival Euripides. Of his alleged improvements in the setting of the plays something is said in notes 49 and 60. More important is the skill with which he wrote them, abandoning entirely the quasi-epic manner of Aeschylus' earlier work and reaching a most happy compromise between the primitive form of Tragedy, in which the chorus was the principal feature, and the modern type of play (which, as we shall see, is of ancient origin) in which there is no chorus at all. His chorus has a most valuable function, for it puts before the audience the reaction to the deeds and experiences of the chief characters of a reasonable and sympathetic spectator. But that this spectator should never be in the way but always seem naturally present demands high skill ; even so good a poet as Euripides often felt his chorus a handicap, as we shall see later. Sophokles is as absolute master of his as of the language and metres he employs.

By an annoying accident, most of the plays have come down to us without *didaskaliai*, or notes of their date, and we are therefore reduced to conjecture regarding the order in which they were composed. However, the internal evidence is sufficient to arrange them pretty well, with some slight differences of opinion here and there.[101]

The earliest is probably the *Aiax* (Αἴας μαστιγοφόρος, or simply Αἴας ; the adjective ' scourge-bearing ' was added by some

on some undated occasion when he was a colleague of Nikias, Plut., *Nic.*, 15. Some confusion as to his political career has been caused by failing to distinguish him from SOPHOKLES the orator, see Cope on Arist., *Rhet.*, i, 14, 3, iii, 18, 6.

[100] Some will be found in the *Life*. The most famous, that he was indicted by his son Iophon in his old age for dementia and defended himself by reading part of the *Oedipus Coloneus*, is so manifestly taken from a comedy that it is strange it should have found credence with some in both ancient and modern times. Those who cannot see this fact for themselves from *Life*, 13, are referred to Jebb, p. xxxix of his ed. of the *O.C.*

[101] For the date and other matters concerning the plays, the most convenient source of information is Jebb's edition, which has very full and excellent introductions. More references in Schmid-Stählin, I, ii, p. 325 *sqq.*

unknown ancient to differentiate this from other tragedies dealing
with Aias, and alludes to the fact that at his first appearance the
hero carries a whip),for it very seldom divides a line between
two or more speakers (ἀντιλαβή), and it alone marches the chorus
on to an anapaestic passage, which is the usual Aeschylean practice. The subject is the madness and death of Aias son of Telamon. In the prologue,[102] Odysseus is seen outside the tent of
Aias ; Athena speaks to him, probably from the *theologeion*,
telling him that Aias, in a rage at the adjudication of Achilles'
arms to Odysseus, has gone forth in the night to take vengeance,
but she has brought a madness upon him, so that he took the
sheep for his enemies, and has slaughtered many of them. Others
he has brought back with him in bonds and is now torturing,
supposing them human. A series of scenes now display Aias'
recovery, remorse and suicide. As his friends begin to make
preparations for his burial, Menelaos appears and forbids it ;
the body, by command of the whole host, is to be left unburied,
as that of a traitor. Teukros, his half-brother, flatly refuses
obedience, and the funeral preparations go on. The wailing of
the chorus over the body is stopped by the entry of Agamemnon,
whose furious orders, seasoned with taunts at Teukros' parentage,[103] are met with plain defiance and counter-taunts. When the
situation is at its most tense, Odysseus enters, succeeds in calming
both disputants, and secures the burial, with due honour, of his
dead rival.

Some moderns have alleged that the play begins to lose interest
after the death of Aias. It might be suggested to such that they
imagine a drama, written by a fervent Catholic for an audience
of like beliefs, in which the hero, a man of otherwise noble character but guilty of one of the deadly sins, is not dead but dying,
and an implacable enemy tries by every means to prevent a
priest coming to shrive him and administer extreme unction.
Given sufficient ability in the playwright, such a piece would by
no means lack interest, nor does the second half of the *Aiax*
lack it, to any reader who can take the Greek point of view. To
be flung out unburied was the last penalty, reserved for traitors [104]

[102] The prologue (πρόλογος) is that part of the play which precedes
the entry of the chorus, see Arist., *Poet.*, 1452ᵇ 19.

[103] He was the son of Hesione, daughter of Laomedon king of Troy
and slave-concubine of Telamon.

[104] That the insult proposed to the body of Aias would be tantamount
to declaring him a traitor is well brought out by A. C. Pearson, *C.Q.*, xvi
(1922), p. 104 *sqq.* Thus Aias' enemies would deprive him of the only
kind of immortality the normal Greek hoped for, the remembrance of his
worth in time to come.

and other desperate and abandoned criminals. Aias, by his death, has nobly escaped from his hopeless position ; as the gods of this world, and its human inhabitants also, have turned against him, he makes a dignified departure to the realm of Hades. Now, just as all his debts are paid,[105] comes the interference of Menelaos and his brother, who would leave Aias a homeless ghost, outcast from both worlds. Furthermore, the moral interest of the second part is high, for it represents the triumph of reason and humanity over hate. Those who cannot see the beauty and force of the great concluding scenes are advised to have no more to do with Greek thought, for their minds are barbarian in the worst sense.

The *Antigone*, the second play, by general consent, which we have left from Sophokles, was composed about 442 B.C., as follows from these facts : there is an absurd story that Sophokles was elected *strategos* on account of the favour which he won by this play.[106] Such a tale would hardly have got about if the play had not come shortly before the election ; since he was *strategos* in 440 (see note 99), 441 or 442 seems a reasonable date for the *Antigone*. But in 441, Euripides won first prize (see p. 179), therefore 442 is on the whole more likely. The play is one of the finest we have, being a magnificent setting forth of a moral problem permanently interesting, the conflict between private and public duty. Kreon, king of Thebes after the defeat of the Seven, forbids the burial of Polyneikes, as having been an enemy to his country. Antigone, Polyneikes' sister, refuses obedience and contrives to give the body formal interment. Kreon condemns her to be shut up alive in a vault. Rebuked by Teiresias,[107] he yields after much hesitation and goes to set her free, but is too late ; she has hanged herself, Kreon's son Haimon, who was betrothed to her, kills himself, and his queen Eurydike does likewise on hearing what has happened. Kreon, after a lament over the bodies, leaves the stage utterly broken.

The interest of the play is chiefly in the contrast between the

---

[105] οὗ κάτοισθ' ἐγὼ θεοῖς/ὡς οὐδὲν ἀρκεῖν εἰμ' ὀφειλέτης ἔτι, he says to Tekmessa, 589–90. In other words, he is as good as dead already, cf. Vergil's *nil iam caelestibus ullis debentem*, *Aen.*, xi, 51, of a dead man.

[106] Argument to *Antigone*.

[107] He had been doubly impious, first in violating the rights of the gods below (refusing burial, *i.e.*, formal entrance into their realm, to the dead and putting a living woman into a tomb), secondly in taking into his own hands the punishment of a woman betrothed to and therefore under the guardianship of his son ; on the latter point see Roussel in *Rev. ét. grecques*, 1922, p. 63 *sqq.*, and cf. Rose in *Class. Quart.*, xix (1925), p. 147 *sqq.*

two types of stubbornness. Kreon is not a mere melodramatic tyrant, for his cruelty springs from a narrow and unintelligent adherence to principles respectable enough in themselves. Antigone again Sophokles has not made especially amiable; she is noble, but has something of the ferocity that might be expected of her father's daughter,[108] and is too wrapped up in her own self-sought martyrdom to spare more than one passing word for the grief of Haimon, while her attitude towards her weak but amiable sister Ismene is needlessly harsh. Of the minor characters, one, a soldier, is half-comic, with more than one touch of humour in what he says and does.

It is a curious fact that the most famous and perfect example of a Greek tragedy, the *Oedipus Tyrannus*, should be of quite uncertain date, when we know the year of production of many less important works. That it was written when Sophokles was at the height of his powers we may reasonably conclude, and it lacks certain small features of his later style. Perhaps, then, we are justified in saying that it is later than the *Aiax*, the *Antigone* and, it may be, the *Electra* also, earlier than the *Trachiniae* and *Philoctetes*. The plot is handled in a manner which would seem to be original with Sophokles,[109] though naturally, here as elsewhere, the main outlines of the legend are untouched. The play opens some years after the marriage of Oidipus and Iokaste, when four children have been born to them. A plague has fallen upon the city, and Oidipus is informed from Delphoi that the city is polluted by the presence in it of the slayer or slayers of King Laios. He formally calls upon all and sundry to inform him if they have any knowledge of the matter. If the killer will make himself known, he shall be sent unharmed into banishment; but against him and also any who shelter him the king pronounces a solemn curse. Teiresias the seer, on being consulted, declares that Oidipus lies under his own curse, and that the slayer is a Theban who is called a stranger; and further, that he is the brother of his own children. Kreon, hearing that Oidipus has been speaking against him, enters and defends himself against any suspicion of disloyalty.[110] Oidipus abuses him violently, and Iokaste, hearing the noise, comes out and tries to bring both men to a calmer frame of mind. For the oracle, there is nothing

---

[108] δηλοῖ τὸ γέννημ' ὠμὸν ἐξ ὠμοῦ πατρός, the chorus say of her (471). Her single reference to Haimon is 572.

[109] For the fullest discussion of the legend in its various forms, literary and other, see Robert's *Oidipus*.

[110] In this play, Kreon is portrayed as a moderate and reasonable man, a foil to Oidipus' headstrong self-confidence.

in it to trouble any one, as she can testify. Laios was assured that his own son would be his death ; therefore, when Iokaste's child was born, Laios exposed him, and was himself killed long afterwards by brigands at a certain place where three roads meet. Far from being reassured, Oidipus is much troubled by this detail. He himself, he tells the queen, was the son of Polybos of Corinth. Being taunted with being a suppositious child, he went to Delphoi to inquire if this were so, and got the answer that he was destined to kill his father and marry his mother. He therefore turned his back for ever on Corinth, and on his way to Thebes met and quarrelled with a stranger whom he killed in a scuffle. He now fears that this may have been Laios. Iokaste sends for a servant of Laios who had been with him at the time of his death and shall now tell all he knows of the matter.[111] Now enters a messenger from Corinth, to say that Polybos is dead and the people wish Oidipus to return and be their king. Oidipus hesitates to do so, because his mother is still alive and possibly Polybos died of grief at his absence ; so the oracle may yet be fulfilled. The messenger reassures him by revealing the secret of how he found him, a new-born babe, in the hands of one of Laios' servants on Mount Kithairon, and gave him to the childless king, who reared him as his own son. Iokaste now guesses the truth, and begs Oidipus to inquire no further. He imagines that she fears lest he be low-born, and proudly declares that he is the child of Fortune. The servant of Laios, much against his will, is forced to tell the whole truth, that Oidipus is both the son and husband of Iokaste, son and slayer of Laios. He rushes wildly from the stage ; after a lamentation from the chorus, a messenger enters to say he has blinded himself and that Iokaste is dead by her own hand. Oidipus now re-enters ; after a lyrical scene between him and the chorus, Kreon appears and gently bids him leave the country, in accordance with his own decree. He takes leave of his two little daughters and departs.[112]

[111] It has been noticed by many generations of critics from Aristotle (*Poet.*, 1460ᵃ 30) on that Sophokles falls into an improbability in making Oidipus ignorant of the circumstances of Laios' death. That he himself should not have seen this is most unlikely ; it would rather appear that he deliberately allowed his plot to have this small fault in order to increase the interest of the play by making Oidipus find out both secrets together, that of his parentage and of his patricide.

[112] He ends the play, in our texts, with some sententious lines which recur, almost verbatim, at the end of the *Phoenissae*. As the chorus usually has the last word, it seems very probable that these verses come from an acting version, a late revival in which the chorus was omitted or its part much cut down.

The *Electra* is again of uncertain date, and there is no cogent reason for putting it before or after the *Oedipus Tyrannus*. The plot is that of the *Choephoroe*, with differences of detail and a wide difference in tone. Sophokles' Orestes moves in a Homeric atmosphere ; his deed, if painful, is just and necessary ; [113] no Erinyes haunt him, and he receives nothing but commendation. He gains admittance to the palace by sending an old servant to say that he has been killed in an accident at the Pythian Games. Elektra now tries vainly to induce her sister Chrysothemis [114] to join in a desperate attempt to kill Aigisthos. Orestes now comes in, bearing an urn supposed to contain his own ashes. He so pities Elektra's hopeless grief that he takes the grave risk of making himself known to her. He and the servant between them quiet her outbursts of joy, and he enters the palace, whence Klytaimestra's final appeals and death-cries are heard. Now Aigisthos comes in, and is easily disposed of. All these scenes are interspersed in the usual way with comments from the chorus, but the odes nowhere reach such heights of poetry as some in the *Oedipus Tyrannus*.

The *Trachiniae* (*Maidens of Trachis*) is again of unknown date, but certainly not early. The heroine, Deianeira, begins the play almost in Euripides' manner by explaining who she is ; the chorus has little to do beyond listening to her and the other actors and singing some of the loveliest odes in all Sophokles ; the play ends with a solo from an actor. The central figure throughout is Deianeira, and the interest of the play lies in her character, that of a woman conventionally good by the standards of the day, in whose goodness lies the germ of the tragedy.[115] She is Herakles' wife, and he has been absent from her a whole year. According to a certain oracle which he had disclosed to her, the end of that time will bring his death or his release from all toils. News now comes of his capture of Oichalia, and his servant Lichas brings with him captive Oichalian women, including Iole, whose beauty and noble air attract Deianeira at once. But he lets out the truth, that Iole is Herakles' new consort, and Deianeira feels that she, who has hitherto been as patient as Greek tradition demanded of her husband's infidelities, is now asked for too much ; in one house there can be but one wife, whatever Herakles may

[113] See Rose, *Mythol.*, p. 86.
[114] The name is Homeric, Il. ix, 145, 287 ; Stesichoros was apparently the first to call one of Agamemnon's daughters Elektra.
[115] For the legend, see Rose, *Mythol.*, pp. 218–19 ; I have discussed the play in *Aberystwyth Studies*, viii (1926), pp. 1–9. See also Norwood, *Tragedy*, pp. 155–60.

do away from home. She will not harm Iole, for she recognizes that love is all-powerful ; but it is lawful to win Herakles' lasting affection back again by a spell, and that she has, the blood of the centaur Nessos, who assured her in dying that it would be most potent for such a purpose. She therefore secretly puts it on a new garment, which she sends to her husband by Lichas. Herakles, having put on the robe, is horribly attacked by the poison (Nessos' blood being infected with the venom of the Hydra from Herakles' arrow). Deianeira, cursed by her son Hyllos as his father's murderer, goes silently out, and her old nurse appears shortly after to say that she has killed herself. Herakles is now brought in by attendants, accompanied by Hyllos ; he is asleep, but presently wakes, in horrible pain. Growing calmer as the worst of his agony subsides, he listens to Hyllos, who has now heard the truth about his mother, and proceeds to give directions for his own pyre on Mount Oite. Hyllos reluctantly assents to his orders, and leaves the stage with him.

The *Philoctetes* can be exactly dated, for we have, at the end of the ancient argument, a note that it was performed in the archonship of Glaukippos, which is 409/8 B.C. It shows, more than the *Trachiniae*, the influence of Euripides, and has for its central feature a moral problem, the conflict between patriotism and humanity. Philoktetes has been abandoned on Lemnos, which for the purposes of this play is a desert island ; at least, the part in which the hero lives is deserted. He suffers from a disease at once painful and loathsome,[116] and long solitude has turned his naturally noble temper into bitter, almost monomaniacal hatred for Agamemnon and his chiefs, who have callously abandoned him. Now the army before Troy learn that without the bow of Herakles, which Philoktetes owns, the city cannot be taken : they have therefore sent Odysseus and Neoptolemos to fetch him, by fair means or foul. Neoptolemos is a true son of Achilles, an honest and high-minded young soldier, somewhat in awe of his experienced companion but slow to consent to the crooked ways which Odysseus in the Tragic tradition generally follows. However, he is persuaded to join in a stratagem to induce Philoktetes to come away with them, and succeeds by it in getting possession of the bow. But Philoktetes' despair moves

[116] The disease is an imaginary one, caused by the bite of a serpent. As Sophokles conceives it, Philoktetes has a sort of sore or ulcer on his foot which will not heal and at times becomes violently and unendurably painful. This condition has lasted for ten years without growing either worse or better. That no serpent's bite would have such an effect is obvious now, but was not so then. *See* Addenda, p. 422.

Neoptolemos to give it him again, despite Odysseus' protests, and even to consent to take him home. At this point the glorified spirit of Herakles appears and commands Philoktetes to sail for Troy, where Asklepios himself shall heal him and the bow fulfil its destiny and be instrumental in taking the city a second time. The play thus ends, in true Euripidean fashion, with a reconciliation brought about by divine intervention.

Thanks to an essay of Dion of Prusa (see p. 406), which compares the three plays, we know how Aeschylus and Euripides handled the same theme.[117] The former made Odysseus the chief character, and represented him as ' sharp and crafty, for a man of those days, but far removed from the subtleties of modern villainy '. He did not trouble to avoid certain improbabilities, but simply assumed that Philoktetes would not recognize his enemy, and brought in a chorus of Lemnians without concerning himself with the question how the hero came to be so long neglected, on an inhabited island. Euripides was much more elaborate ; Odysseus was again the central figure, and opened the play with a monologue on his own rashness in running continual risks for the benefit of other people. But Athena had commanded him to fetch the bow of Herakles, and protected him by changing his shape and voice. He was therefore able to pass himself off as an obscure Achaian, a personal enemy of Odysseus, and so to secure Philoktetes' good will. The chorus was again composed of Lemnians, who awkwardly apologized for not having visited the hero sooner, and one Lemnian, a certain Aktor, had helped him and took some part in the action of the play. The plot was complicated by an embassy of Trojans, headed by Paris, to persuade Philoktetes to join them and not the Greeks, and a debate between them and the disguised Odysseus (or less probably, Diomedes, who accompanied him) probably formed the central scene of the play. Difficult though it is to judge of lost works of art, it seems as if Dion was right in saying that Sophokles' handling of the plot is the ' best and most plausible ' of the three ; in particular, his introduction of Neoptolemos, not the traditional Diomedes,[118] as Odysseus' companion enables him to present a most effective contrast not only of temperament but of ages.

The last surviving play of Sophokles, and probably the last that he ever wrote, is also one of his finest, the *Oedipus Coloneus*. The plot is simple enough, although lengthened and diversified

---

[117] Orat., lii (35), which compares the three plays, and lix (42), which paraphrases the opening scene of Euripides' drama. The remarks concerning Odysseus and the handling of the plot by Sophokles are respectively from lii, 5 and 15.

[118] Euripides introduces Diomedes ὁμηρικῶς, *i.e.*, in accordance with Epic tradition, says Dion, lii, 14. See the introduction to Jebb's ed. of the *Phil.*, p. xiv.

with episodes skilfully introduced. Oidipus, blind, old and in beggary and exile, wanders, attended by Antigone, to Kolonos, Sophokles' own birthplace, just outside Athens.   Here he unwittingly trespasses upon the precinct of the Venerable Goddesses (Σεμναὶ θεαί), ancient earth-deities identified with the Eumenides. On learning where he is, he recognizes that this is the spot where Apollo had assured him he should meet his death.   He therefore sends for Theseus, king of Athens, for he knows that the land where his bones lie shall be blessed by the possession of them. After telling his story to the chorus of elders of Kolonos (who are so horrified that they bid him leave the country, but are won to consent to his staying by the entreaty of Antigone), he is visited by Ismene.   She tells him that Thebes is on the verge of war with Argos, which espouses the cause of Polyneikes, and that Kreon is anxious to fetch Oidipus back, because he has heard that the safety of the country depends on him.   While Ismene is off the stage, performing certain necessary rites to secure the favour of the Semnai for her father, Oidipus justifies himself to the chorus, pointing out that his deeds with regard to Laios and Iokaste were involuntary.[119]   Theseus now enters and accepts Oidipus as an inhabitant of Attica.   On his departure, and after the singing by the chorus of the ode in praise of Kolonos, one of the most beautiful utterances of Greek lyric poetry, Kreon enters, and after vainly trying to induce Oidipus to come with him and live just outside the borders of Thebes,[120] he and his attendants seize Antigone and Ismene and carry them off.   Theseus is at once informed, pursues and captures Kreon, rescues the two girls and sends the Thebans home.   Now word is brought that Polyneikes begs to see his father.   Oidipus consents, but reluctantly, at Theseus' and Antigone's request ; he listens to a long plea from his son for his help,[121] answers it with a formal and solemn curse, and Polyneikes departs after a touching scene in which Antigone tries to persuade him to abandon his enterprise.   After he leaves the stage, a violent clap of thunder warns Oidipus that his end is at hand ; he sends once more, in great haste, for Theseus, and takes him with him to a retired place ; presently, after a song by the chorus invoking the grace of the nether powers on Oidipus, a messenger enters and tells them that he has vanished mys-

[119] This is Sophokles' modernization of the legend ; like Aeschylus in the *Eumenides*, he upholds the ethical principle of the all-importance of motive for evaluating conduct.

[120] He may not live in Thebes, cf. the *O.T.* ; Kreon wants possession of his body when he dies.

[121] Whichever side Oidipus favours will be victorious (1332), hence Polyneikes' eagerness.

teriously. Only Theseus knows the exact manner of his passing and the place where honours may be paid to his ghost.

Such is the marvellous play, one of the most moving in any language, that the imagination of a great poet has made out of an obscure local legend to the effect that the body of Oidipus lay somewhere in Attic soil at a spot known only to successive kings and presumably also to those annual magistrates who bore the name and performed some few of the functions of royalty under the democracy.[122] The exact date of its composition is not known, but the fact that it needs a fourth actor fits very well with the tradition (see note 100) that it is the work of Sophokles' old age.

We have no other complete tragedies, but there has been discovered in recent times a large fragment of a satyr-play, the *Trackers* ('Ἰχνευταί), which, but for the *Cyclops* of Euripides (see p. 199), is the only specimen of this *genre* left to us.[123] It was apparently short and simple, written with the light-hearted verve which is appropriate to such a composition, handled by such a poet. The theme is the birth and first adventure of Hermes, as related in the 'Homeric' hymn (see p. 54). A band of satyrs, who of course form the chorus, and with them Seilenos, are the slaves of some one, perhaps Apollo. At all events, Apollo promises them freedom if they will find his lost cattle for him. They set out, but are soon checked and frightened by a strange sound. The nymph Kyllene appears to them, bids them be quiet, tells them of the birth of a son to Zeus, and explains the sound as the voice of a dead beast ; after some verbal fencing, she expounds her riddle ; it is the lyre of Hermes, which has a tortoise's shell for its sounding-board. The chorus at once conclude that so clever a god as Hermes must be the thief of Apollo's cattle. Despite Kyllene's protests, they inform Apollo, and presumably, for here the papyrus fails completely, the two deities meet and are finally reconciled, as in the hymn.

Of the other plays of Sophokles we know the following facts. He seems to have written two dramas dealing with Athamas, whereof very little survives.[124] Almost equally obscure are the *Aias the*

[122] The reference is to the official called βασιλεύς (the modern ' archon basileus ' is without ancient authority).

[123] *Oxyrh. Pap.*, 1174 ; included in Hunt's *F.T.P.* and Jebb-Pearson (see Bibliography). Cf. Pickard-Cambridge in Powell 3, pp. 87–95.

[124] The fullest discussion of the fragments is that of Jebb-Pearson (see Bibliography). A few more details will be found in Pickard-Cambridge in Powell 3, p. 68 *sqq.* To the former the reader is referred in general for information regarding the sources of the fragments, conjectural restoration of plots and so forth.

Lokrian (Αἴας Λοκρός), Aigeus, Aigisthos and Ethiopians (Αἰθίοπες).
What the plot was of the Αἰχμαλωτίδες, or Captive Women, we do
not know and have no grounds for even a reasonable guess ; it might
conceivably have resembled the Troades of Euripides (see p. 187).
We are no less in the dark as to the Akrisios, if it was not the same
as the Danae. The Aleadai dealt with Auge, daughter of Aleos, and
her son by Herakles, Telephos.[125] The Alexandros told the story of
Alexandros (Paris) making himself known to his parents and brothers
by his prowess.[126] The Aletes, it would seem, dealt with the son of
Aigisthos and Klytaimestra and his feud with Orestes. The Alkmeon
no doubt had something to do with the tragic history of Alkmeon
or Alkmaion son of Amphiaraos, but precisely what part of the story
it told we cannot now say. The Amykos was a satyr-play and treated
no doubt of the king of the Bebrykes (see p. 324). That the Amphiareos
was also a satyr-play we know, on the authority of Athenaios,[127] but
what part of that woful tale Sophokles managed to burlesque we
cannot say. The Andromeda dramatized a very well-known legend ;
the Antenoridai or Sons of Antenor is supposed to have handled the
taking of Troy and the sparing of Antenor and his house by the
victorious Greeks in return for his friendly attitude towards them.
What part of the legend of the Pelopidai was treated in the Atreus
or Women of Mycenae is not exactly known. Of the Ἀχαιῶν σύλλογος
we have a score of lines on a papyrus,[128] but do not know the plot ;
it may have resembled that of Euripides' Telephos (p. 207). The
Ἀχιλλέως ἐρασταί was a satyr-play ; very likely the chorus of
satyrs were comically attracted by the young hero's beauty. Of the
Daidalos we know nothing ; the Danae can hardly have dealt with
anything else than the birth of Perseus or some part of his mother's
adventures afterwards. The Dionysiskos was again a satyr-play, and
to judge by the diminutive form of the title it treated of the god's
infancy. While the title and fragments of the Dolopes tell us nothing
of the subject, the Rape of Helen (Ἑλένης ἁρπαγή) if it is not a mere
blunder of the one authority that mentions it [129] is self-explanatory,
as is that of a play known certainly to have existed, the Reclaiming
of Helen (Ἑλένης ἀπαίτησις). The Marriage of Helen (Ἑλένης γάμος)
was a satyr-play ; which of her marriages it dealt with is not
clear. The Epigonoi, founded on a part of the Theban saga, was
famous in antiquity. The Eris most likely treated of the famous

[125] For this legend, see Rose, Mythol., pp. 275, 285, n. 68.

[126] See ibid., pp. 233-4.

[127] Athen., 454 f, who says also that the poet ' introduced some
one dancing the letters of the alphabet ', i.e., imitating their shapes
by his gestures ; certainly not an incident appropriate to a serious
play.

[128] Berliner Klassikertexte, v, 2, p. 64 sqq.

[129] The unknown author of the argument to the Aiax says that among
plays (he means plays of Sophokles, for the other titles he cites are known
to be his) dealing with Troy was this one. There is no other mention
of it, and it may be the same as the Reclaiming.

tale of the Apple of Discord.[130] The *Hermione* had much the same
subject as Euripides' *Andromache* (see p. 184). The *Eumelos* is a
mere name to us ; the *Euryalos* probably handled an incident in the
posthomeric story of Odysseus, while the *Eurypylos*, whereof a
papyrus has restored some very battered lines to us,[131] told one of
the later incidents of the Trojan War. The *Eurysakes* plainly had
something to do with Aias' son ; the legend of Herakles furnished
materials for two plays, it would seem, one a satyr-drama, known
simply as *Herakles* or as *The Satyrs at Tainaron* and dealing with his
descent into Hades, while the other, *Herakleiskos* (*The Infant Herakles*),
probably handled the legend of Hera's attempt to destroy him in his
cradle by sending serpents to attack him. The *Erigone* is obscure,
since we do not know whether it told of Ikarios' or Aigisthos'
daughter.[132] It may be supposed that the *Thamyras* told the story
of how Thamyris the minstrel was blinded for trying to rival the
Muses, a tale as old as Homer (Iliad, ii, 594 *sqq.*). There was also a
play, perhaps two plays, dealing with Thyestes ; it or one of them
seems to have been called *Thyestes at Sekyon* and may have treated
of the horrible story of his incest with his own daughter. The title
of the *Iberians* tells us little (it might deal with Geryon) and there
are no fragments. The *Inachos* handled the legend of Io ; of the
Ixion and the *Iobates* we know that there were such plays ; the latter
no doubt dealt with the adventures of Bellerophon (the Lykian king
to whom Bellerophon is sent is called Iobates in the later authors,
though not in Homer), while the former may not have been by
Sophokles at all, since the evidence for it is merely a statement that
'Sophokles in the *Ixion*' used the word δίψιον in a peculiar sense,
and it is quite possible that the name should be Aeschylus (see p. 157).
The *Hipponus* dealt with an obscure legend ; Hipponoos, king of
Olenos in Achaia, had a daughter Periboia. Discovering that she
was with child (as to the child's father our authorities differ) he sent
her to Oineus of Kalydon, with secret directions to put her to death ;
but Oineus spared and married her, his wife Althaia being dead, and
she bore the famous hero Tydeus. The *Iphigeneia* dealt with the
incident at Aulis, and was not unlike Euripides' play in plot (see p.
194). The *Ἰχνευταί* has already been discussed (p. 171). The *Ion*
seems to have been another title for the *Kreusa* and both to have
dealt with the same subject as Euripides' *Ion* (p. 189). The *Kamikoi*
treated of the death of Minos in Sicily.[133] The *Kedalion* was a satyr-
play, dealing with an incident of the story of Orion ; Kedalion was
a servant of Hephaistos who guided Orion, when blinded, to meet the
Sun, who gave him his sight again.[134] The *Kolchides* (*Women of
Kolchis*) told of Jason's winning of the Fleece by the help of Medeia.
The *Κρίσις* (*Judgement*, sc. of Paris) was again a satyr-play ; what
the satyrs had to do with the goddesses and Paris we cannot tell

[130] See Rose, *Mythol.*, p. 106. [131] *Oxyrh. Pap.*, 1175.
[132] See Rose, *op. cit.*, pp. 154-5 ; add Hyginus, *fabulae*, 122.
[133] See Rose *Mythol.*, p. 269. [134] *Ibid.*, p. 115.

from the insignificant fragments. The Κωφοί (*Dumb Men*) is a puzzle ;
it was a satyr-play, but we do not know who were dumb, nor why.
The *Lakainai* and the *Laokoon* had plots from the Troy-saga ; probably
the first told of the entry of Odysseus into Troy disguised as a beggar,
while the second certainly had the death of Laokoon for its subject,
a theme which, for us, survives in the second book of the *Aeneid* and
the famous group in the Vatican. In the *Larisaioi* or *Men of Larisa*
the subject was the accidental killing of Akrisios by Perseus.[135] The
Lemniai dealt with the stay of the Argonauts at Lemnos, or else with
the killing by the women of that island of all their men. The Μάντεις,
or *Diviners*, also called the *Polyidos*, told a legend of Crete. Minos
had lost his son Glaukos, who had fallen into a large jar of honey
and been drowned ; an oracle directed him how to find the most
accomplished soothsayer, and further informed him that that soothsayer could restore him his son. The test pointed to Polyidos, who
proceeded by divination to find the boy's body. Being further ordered
to bring him to life, he declared that he could not, and was entombed
with him ; whereon, discovering by chance a certain magic herb, he
restored the child with it. Of the *Meleagros* it is to be supposed that
it told the same story as that made familiar by Swinburne's *Atalanta*.
The *Minos* may have been the same play as the *Kamikoi*. Of the
Muses we know nothing ; the *Mysians* probably dealt with some part
of the legend of Telephos. The *Momos* no doubt had something to
do with the spirit of fault-finding ; it was a satyr-play. Concerning
Nauplios, father of Palamedes, who wrecked the Greek fleet on its
way back from Troy to avenge the death of his son, Sophokles wrote
certainly one play, perhaps two ; we have the titles Ναύπλιος
καταπλέων and Ναύπλιος πυρκαεύς, whereof the latter refers to the
false beacons by which he accomplished his end, while the former
indicates that he arrived by sea, whence and whither is not known.
The *Nausikaa*, otherwise known as the *Washerwomen* (Πλύντριαι),
had a plot taken from the Odyssey (see p. 25). The *Niobe* is tantalizing ; a papyrus has yielded several lines, but in so bad a condition
that next to nothing can be made of them.[136] Equally tantalizing
is the statement of a scholiast [137] that there was a play called
Ξοανηφόροι (*The Image-bearers*), which showed the gods leaving Troy
and carrying away their own cult-statues. It would be interesting
to know how Sophokles handled this, or if it really was a leading
incident of a separate play, not a mere passing reference in one of
the other dramas dealing with Troy. Two more plays dealt with
Odysseus ; one, distinguished by the epithet ἀκανθοπλήξ,[138] treated

[135] See Rose, *Mythol.*, p. 273.

[136] Brit. Mus. pap. DCXC, in Grenfell-Hunt, *Greek Papyri*, ser. 2
(Oxford, 1897), p. 14.

[137] On Aeschylus, *Seven*, 291.

[138] Telegonos killed him with a spear barbed with fish-bone, hence
the name. That the play was also called Νίπτρα, or *The Foot-washing*,
I do not believe, although there is some evidence for it, see Jebb-Pearson,

of the catastrophe of the *Telegonia* (see p. 51), and the other, μαινόμενος, with a much earlier incident of his life, when he feigned insanity to avoid having to go to Troy. Whether there was a play called *Oikles* and, if so, what it was about are highly dubious points. The *Oineus*, the *Oinomaos* and the *Palamedes* all had very well-known figures for their chief characters ; very little is left of any of them. The *Pandora*, no doubt, got its plot from Hesiod ; it was a satyr-play with the subtitle σφυροκόποι, probably meaning ' hammerers '. As satyrs in satyr-plays were often slaves, to judge by the little we know of such dramas, perhaps the chorus had been pressed into service by Hephaistos to help him in his work-shop.[138a] The *Peleus* dealt with the old age of that hero, probably recounting how his grandson Neoptolemos avenged him of the wrong done him by Akastos, or Akastos' sons, who expelled him from his kingdom after Achilles was dead.[139] The *Shepherds* (Ποιμένες) probably told of early episodes in the War of Troy, the death of Protesilaos and the slaying of Kyknos by Achilles ; the ' shepherds ' may well have been Trojan or Phrygian rustics forming the chorus. The *Polyxene* covered part of the same ground as Euripides' *Hecuba* (p. 184). Two famous names, *Priam* and *Prokris*, belonged to plays of which we know nothing at all. The *Root-gatherers* (Ῥιζοτόμοι) treated of Medeia's magic. We do not know how the subject of the *Salmoneus* was handled so as to make it a satyr-play ; nor how near the *Sinon* agreed with the character which Vergil afterwards gave Sinon in the second book of the *Aeneid*. Like Aeschylus (p. 158), Sophokles wrote a *Sisyphos*, but one fragment consisting of two words is all that survives. The *Scythians* (Σκύθαι) was another Argonautic play. The *Skyrians* had reference to the island where Achilles was hidden for a while by his mother, and his son Neoptolemos spent his early years ; it probably dealt with the departure of one or other of them for Troy, and more likely the latter.[138a] The *Guests at the Banquet* (Σύνδειπνοι) would appear to have handled an incident very obscure to us, but better known to those who had the *Kypria* before them (see p. 48) ; there was a quarrel between Achilles and Agamemnon at Tenedos before the army reached Troy, arising out of a slight to the former in connexion with a feast. The *Tantalos* had something to do with the disasters that followed on that king's abused prosperity ; so much we may gather from two quotations and a score of badly mutilated verses in a papyrus.[140] The *Teukros* doubtless concerned the return of Aias' half-brother to Salamis and his banishment by his father, but very little survives of it , the *Telephos* is represented by one word. A good deal survives from the *Tereus*, but not enough to show at all

ii, p. 105 *sqq.*, since that is the traditional title of the incident in the Odyssey of the washing of Odysseus' feet (see p. 28), and seems very unlikely to be applied to anything else.

[138a] See further Addenda, p. 422.

[139] Such a legend was known to Euripides, *Troad.*, 1126 *sqq.*, as explained by the scholiast there.

[140] *Oxyrh. Pap.*, 213.

clearly how the ' tragic tale of Philomel ' was handled. The *Triptolemos* plainly had to do with the legend of how Demeter sent Triptolemos from Eleusis all over the world with her new gift of corn. The *Troilos* had something to do with the piteous death of Priam's young and valiant son at the hands of Achilles. Of the Τυμπανισταί we know that it mentioned the legend of Phineus, but who the ' drummers ' or ' timbrel-players ' of the title were is obscure. What incidents in the history of *Tyndareos* made the plot of the play which bore his name, or how *Tyro*'s adventures were spread over two plays are matters on which we are at liberty to conjecture as freely as we like from scanty material. Greek tragedies always are named from persons or incidents, usually the former ; therefore when we hear of one called Ὕβρις, we may safely conjecture that it did not tell of ' frowardness ' in the abstract, but of Hybris, the ' froward ' or ' wanton ' nymph who, in an obscure legend, was mother of Pan. If this is so, it was probably a satyr-play. We do not know for whom the *Water-carriers* (Ὑδροφόροι) carried water, nor what was the plot of the *Phaiakes*, though the name suggests the Odyssey (see p. 25). That the *Phaidra* must have resembled Euripides' *Hippolytus* (see p. 182) in subject, however it differed in treatment, is plain, but we lack detailed knowledge. Of the *Phthiotides* (*Women of Phthia*) we know still less. Its chief merit was its character-drawing, in Aristotle's opinion.[141] The *Philoktetes at Troy* doubtless continued the story of the *Philoctetes* which we have (p. 168). The two plays called *Phineus* seem to have narrated respectively his sin and his punishment.[142] There were also a *Phoinix* (dealing with Achilles' old attendant, not the fabulous bird), a *Phrixos* and a *Phrygians*, but it is rather unprofitable to guess at their contents. Last in the alphabetical order comes the Χρύσης ; there is a tale in Hyginus to the effect that Chryseis had a son by Agamemnon called after her father (see p. 16), who when he grew up took some part in the adventures of his half-brother Orestes. Whether this story owes anything to Sophokles is unknown.[143]

[141] *Poet.*, 1456ᵇ 1.   [142] See Rose, *Mythol.*, p. 201.
[143] Hyginus, *fab.*, 121. For more information as to the fragments of Sophokles, *see* D. L. Page, *Greek Literary Papyri I* (Loeb Library, No. 360).

ADDITIONAL NOTE

Some lyric verses in Favorinus' essay *On Exile* (below, p. 406, note 34) may be from the *Tereus*, see I. Cazzaniga in *Rendiconti R. Istit. lombardo*, lxvii, 293 *sqq.*

CHAPTER VII

EURIPIDES AND THE MINOR TRAGEDIANS

WITH Sophokles Greek Tragedy reaches its culmination. EURIPIDES, great poet though he was, represents the first symptom of the inevitable decline, for in him we can recognize a certain impatience with the form he found ready to his hand ; and when a first-rate writer feels this, it is time to look for a new mode of expression.

He was born, according to tradition, on the day of Salamis, in the summer of 480 ; or in 485/4, the year of Aeschylus' first victory.[1] Neither account need be taken too literally, for

[1] The latter date is that of the Marmor Parium, corrected (at this point, all its dates are a year too early) ; the former is given in the ancient Life of him which is preserved in different forms by Suidas and in several MSS., and reproduced in most of the principal modern editions of his works and in Dindorf's and Schwartz' editions of the scholia on his plays. Of late much light has been thrown on the sources of the Life by the lucky discovery of a biography, cast in the form of a dialogue, by Satyros (see p. 357), first published in the *Oxyrhynchus Papyri*, No. 1176. Much of it is clearly the original work of which the Life formerly known is an epitome, though it is not the only source used by the later biographer. The quality alike of Satyros' work and of the later one is poor and uncritical. Euripides was a favourite butt of the comedians, especially of Aristophanes, and consequently numerous anecdotes concerning him were afloat in later days, many in all probability pure fiction. For example, Satyros (frag. 39, col. x) seems to take seriously Aristophanes' wild farce, the *Thesmophoriazusae* (see p. 236). We need not therefore spend much time over such tales of him as that his wife was unfaithful to him, her lover being a young man called Kephisophon, who was a member of his household and apparently acted as his secretary or in some way helped him in writing his plays ; that some of his work was really by Sokrates (this is nothing but a comic way of saying that he was interested in philosophy and his plays showed it), and so forth. Suidas preserves a probably true statement of Philochoros that his family was of high social standing ; his mother is called a herb-woman in several passages, for instance Ar., *Thesm.*, 387. The tone of many passages in the plays suggests a man of high birth (insistence on the disadvantages of being low-born is frequent) but ready to recognize merit anywhere, even in the

obviously there would be a great temptation to connect so notable a poet with a notable event in history, and hardly less to join the first and the last of the three classical tragedians ; but we may suppose them approximately right, *i.e.*, put his birth not earlier than the middle of the second decade of the century. His family was of good social position ; why the comedians represented his mother as a greengrocer (λαχανοπωλήτρια) we do not know, and it is unprofitable to attempt to re-discover the point of a joke 2,500 years old. He received a good education [1] and retained throughout his life an absorbing interest in matters intellectual which at times almost obscured his poetical and dramatic ability. His quick brain and reflective habits, reinforced by considerable scientific and philosophical study, showed him very clearly that all was not right with the times he lived in or the opinions currently held ; he was not of the small number of intellectual giants who can make important and positive contributions to the betterment of human life and thought, but he could and did study both, critically and sympathetically. He evidently felt more intensely than Sophokles for the sufferings and follies of mankind—not that the elder poet was lacking in tenderness, but that the younger was hyper-sensitive—and his plays set forth what he thought and felt. Hence he has been excessively abused by those who quarrel with a classical author if he does not embody their ideal of classicism, and excessively praised by others whose well-founded dislike of a cold and bloodless writer drives them to the extreme of valuing restlessness and discontent. It is to the credit of our own age that Euripides has been studied with discrimination, so that it is possible to see, for example, that he was neither the woman-hater Aristophanes made him out nor the feminist that some moderns have imagined him to be. The truth is that the emotions interested him intensely, and rather as an object to analyse and at the same time pity than as a theme for admiration or facile idealizing ; hence he was greatly interested in women, whether good or bad, and particularly in those whom strange circumstances or a morbid temperament arouse to an unusually vivid emotional life. He

---

socially lowest (virtuous slaves and artisans are not uncommon characters). He is said to have married twice, and the names of his children are given as Mnesilochos, Mnesarchides and Euripides.

[1] The biographies say he was for a while an athlete—probable enough, for most young men of respectable family were—and name several well-known philosophers (Anaxagoras, Sokrates, the great sophists Prodikos and Protagoras) as having been his friends or teachers. This need be no more than a conclusion from the various allusions to philosophic doctrines in his plays, but there is nothing in the least impossible in it.

could tell a story well, and comment on it in exquisite lyrical verse, coupled, to judge by what contemporaries say of him,[3] with music of the latest and most original form. But his chief interest was always and everywhere the feelings and motives of his heroes and heroines, who must be human at whatever sacrifice of greatness. Once the occasion for the display of strong emotion has reached its climax, his interest wanes, and often the tale is huddled to an end by the arbitrary interference of a god, as though he would say, ' we are told that these persons survived to do this and that ; how, I do not know ; suppose then if you will that a power greater than themselves took a hand and shaped their destinies for them '.

Hence it is that the action is on occasion interrupted, in a way stranger to us than to the Athenians, by long scenes in which the pros and cons of some one's actions are debated at full length, with speeches reminiscent of forensic eloquence ; or by equally long expressions of feeling, sometimes in the shape of lyric solos from the stage. Had he lived to-day, Euripides would probably have been a psychological novelist of the first rank ; as a dramatist, and committed to a form of art which above all demands action, he is erratic, some of his works being hardly dramas at all. Nor has he any one style, but varies from problem-plays to poetical romances, with occasional pieces which for construction and fitness for acting could hardly have been bettered even by Sophokles. But he is always eminently readable.

For reasons partly good, such as his occasional glaring faults as a playwright, partly bad, namely popular prejudice against the unorthodox views which his characters often express, he was seldom successful, winning in all but five first prizes in his whole career.[4] But a strong minority, especially of the younger generation, always favoured him, and no poet was more widely read in later ages. Hence we have more of him than of the other two put together, seventeen [5] tragedies and a satyr-play complete, a large part of another tragedy, and a multitude of fragments from which the plot and something of the treatment of several more works can be restored with some degree of certainty.

[3] For instance, Ar., *Frogs*, 1301 *sqq.*

[4] So the *Life* (Suidas), adding that the fifth was won after his death, when his nephew Euripides (? the same person who is elsewhere called his son) brought out a play of his (? the *Iphigenia in Aulide*). The first was in 441, see *Mar. Par.*, ep. 61. See further Haigh, *Drama*, Chapter iv ; Norwood, *Tragedy*, Chapter v ; Christ-Schmid, i, pp. 346—88.

[5] The *Rhesos* not being counted ; see p. 212.

His first appearance before the public was in 455,[6] but the earliest surviving work is the *Alcestis*, acted in 438 as the fourth play of a tetralogy, instead of a satyr-drama.[7] It is one of a group of plays dealing with women as affected by various strong emotions ; in this case, profound and self-sacrificing love for a somewhat unworthy husband. The subject, which had already been handled by Phrynichos, was an old folktale, widely spread in both ancient and modern times. A certain man was doomed to die at a particular time, but the powers which rule human destiny were persuaded to let him live if the lifetime of some one else were transferred to him. His father and mother refused to give him their remaining years, but his wife consented and died in his stead. She had her reward, for either the gods below, touched by such nobility, let her come back to earth, or a mighty hero did battle with Death for her and forced him to set her free. In the story as Euripides knew it, the husband and wife were Admetos, king of Pherai in Thessaly, and Alkestis, daughter of Pelias ; he used the version in which force, not pity, secured Alkestis' release, and employed, probably in accordance with an existing tradition, Herakles to perform the miracle.[8] Euripides, when he wrote this play, had already found his formula ; assume that the ancient legends are substantially true, and ask to what manner of men and women such things might have happened. The folktale, engrossed with the moral that a good wife is her husband's best friend, had not noticed that a husband who accepted such a sacrifice would be a very poor creature. Euripides gives his Admetos all the conventional virtues, thus throwing his baseness into higher relief, and makes him finally realize and repent of his own vileness, when Alkestis is dead.[8]

[6] So the *Life*, lines 33 and 137 of the ed. in Dindorf's *Poetae scenici*.[6]

[7] So the surviving didaskalia of the play. That the plot is taken from a folktale, whatever Euripides' immediate source may have been, ought always to have been obvious, but the craze which recently prevailed for finding ' faded gods ' in the characters of saga has led to some wild nonsense of a learned kind being written about Admetos and his wife. For those who can understand cogent evidence, there are the works of A. Lesky, *Alkestis, der Mythus und das Drama*, Sitz.-Ber. d. Wien. Akad., Phil.-Hist. Klasse, vol. cciii (1925) Abh. 2, and of G. Megas in *Archiv für Religionswissenschaft*, xxx (1933), p. 1 *sqq.*, containing valuable supplements and corrections of Lesky.

[8] It is necessary to mention here the notorious theory of Verrall, put forward in his book *Euripides the Rationalist*, pp. 1–128. According to this, Alkestis never dies at all, but swoons from emotional exhaustion ; Herakles, rambling half-drunk to her tomb, finds her just reviving and brings her home. This and similar theories of his, which the curious may find in the work cited and in his *Four Plays of Euripides* (Cambridge

His Herakles is a good simple fellow, on whom such moral subtleties are quite lost. Admetos, in his view, is a man of extraordinary virtue, who has entertained him in the midst of his
own grief, keeping the death of his wife secret. Such exemplary
hospitality must be rewarded, and he duly brings Alkestis back
and hands her over to her husband, leaving the pair, with his
blessing, to readjust themselves as best they may.

This play, says the author of one of the ancient arguments
to it, is almost comic in its dénouement.[9] No such criticism
could be levelled at the next play, the *Medea*, 431. The heroine,
Jason's wife, is a woman of strong character and high intelligence,
capable of as devoted affection as Alkestis herself, but demanding
in return fidelity and recognition of her rights. To benefit
Jason, she has left her father, murdered her brother, robbed her
family of its treasure, the Golden Fleece, and treacherously
contrived the death of Pelias. To crown all, she has been a
faithful wife to him and has borne him two sons. Now he wrongs
her past all excuse, by proposing to put her away and marry
the daughter of Kreon, king of Corinth. After a long outburst
of sheer despair, she induces Kreon to let her stay in Corinth
till the next morning ; Jason, who tries to prove to her that he
has acted for the best and wisely provided for the future of their
children, retires somewhat discomfited before her withering in-
vectives and refusal of the help and support he offers her if she
will go away quietly. A chance meeting with Aigeus, king of
Athens, enables her to provide a refuge for herself ; she now
proceeds quite deliberately to destroy Jason and all who are
connected with him. Her children, because they are also his,
must die too, after being made the instruments of her vengeance.
The plot succeeds ; Kreon's daughter is destroyed by strong
poisons, and Kreon with her.[10] Medeia herself, in one of the most
heart-rending scenes of Tragedy, kills the children. The pathos
and horror of it are the more emphasized by her saying little ;

Univ. Press, 1905) all involve a somewhat gross confusion between the
true proposition that Euripides did not accept as historical all the details
of the traditional stories, and especially the supernatural elements, and
the false one that he would not assume their truth for literary purposes,
as every dealer in poetry and fiction has always done. The truth which
interested Euripides was psychological, not historical ; supposing that
the remarkable things in the myths and sagas did happen, how would
the characters feel and act ?

[9] κωμικωτέραν ἔχει τὴν καταστροφήν.

[10] Here and in the *Trachiniae* (see p. 168) the author imagines some
kind of powerful corrosive, like a very strong acid. On what, if anything,
this is founded is not known.

to realize the heights to which Euripides rises here it is perhaps necessary to see the play well acted.[11]   Jason now rushes in, vowing vengeance ; as he tries to force the doors of the house, Medeia suddenly appears above, a daimonic figure, borne on a fiery car sent by her grandfather the Sun-god.   Her revenge is complete ; she will not allow Jason even to touch the bodies of the children, but will herself bury them in the precinct of Hera, where they shall receive worship in time to come.[12]   The car moves out of sight and he is left vainly protesting against her cruelty.

The *Medea* shows a woman turned into a bloodthirsty fiend by an unbearable injustice ; the next play, the *Hippolytus* (428 B.C.), again has for its central figure a woman subjected to an intolerable strain, but this time purely psychological.   Phaidra, wife of Theseus, is a woman chaste and modest,[13] but, to use the modern catch-word, over-sexed.   Euripides expresses it mythically by making her and her stepson Hippolytos the victims of Aphrodite's anger, and it is hardly exaggeration to say that Aphrodite and Artemis, who appear respectively in the prologue and the concluding scene of this drama, are abstractions, Passion and Asceticism, provided with traditional names.   Hippolytos is at the opposite extreme from Phaidra ; though in other respects healthy and normal, a lover of hunting and of manly sport generally, he has an instinctive repugnance towards sexual passion, a ' virgin's soul ', as he himself puts it.[14]   Consequently, he not only does not return the violent love which Phaidra, after a long

[11] To see, for example, Dame Sibyl Thorndyke's performance of G.G.A. Murray's version is enough to make the spectator realize that a first-rate play can overcome not merely the passage of time but the transference to another language and other stage-conventions, if only translator and players have intelligence and sympathy.

[12] Here, as very often, Euripides touches on the facts of cult, which seem to have interested him, whatever his private beliefs may have been. There was at Corinth a cult of the children of Medeia, who were locally said to have been killed by the Corinthians themselves, not by their mother.   Euripides' account of their death may be his own invention ; see Rose, *Mythol.*, p. 204.

[13] It would appear that Euripides made two studies of Phaidra, one in this play, the other in a second *Hippolytos*, called by the ancient grammarians Ἱππόλυτος καλυπτόμενος (veiled, probably because he had a covering over his face in the death-scene), the surviving play being distinguished as Ἱππόλυτος στεφανίας, from a scene at the beginning in which Hippolytos offers a garland to a statue of Artemis.   In the lost play, to judge from what is said of it by two or three ancient authorities (see Nauck *, p. 491), Phaidra was not the modest character she is in the surviving drama.

[14] παρθένον ψυχὴν ἔχων, 1006.

resistance which almost kills her, finally is forced to confess, through the agency of her nurse,[15] but repulses her with horrified brutality. She kills herself, but by way of revenge leaves behind a letter in which she accuses him of violating her. Theseus returns from a long absence just in time to find her body and read the letter; he meets Hippolytos, refuses to listen to his perfectly true protestations of innocence (he will not defend himself by accusing the dead woman, of whose passion he had been told under pledge of secrecy),[16] and banishes him, invoking at the same time a curse on him. Here Euripides again uses a theme from folktale. Poseidon, Theseus' father, has given him three wishes, and the curse, being one of them, is straightway fulfilled; Poseidon sends a sea-monster to frighten the horses of Hippolytos' chariot, which bolt, smash the chariot and drag him to death. He lives just long enough to be reconciled to his father, whose eyes are opened by Artemis in person, grieved and angered at the death of Hippolytos, her true worshipper and companion, but unable, by the ancient laws of the gods, to oppose the act of another deity. Thus, and Euripides is fully alive to the pity of the situation, two virtuous people die largely because of their virtue, Phaidra because she is not a wanton, but exquisitely sensitive to shame and intensely aware of the illicit nature of the desire she cannot check, Hippolytos because he is chaste and honourable, and will neither wrong his father nor break his word. At the same time, their tragedy is due to abnormalities in their nature (again to use more modern language than what was modern when the play was written), for he cannot understand what it is to be deeply in love, and she is more liable than a normal woman to what, in Euripides' opinion and that of many of his time, was a kind of madness or disease.

Love and jealousy are strong passions enough, but maternal affection has depths no less profound, and three years after the *Hippolytus* Euripides studied, in a magnificent but singularly

[15] The Nurse or duenna is an admirable foil to her mistress; a good-natured and quite non-moral creature, totally puzzled alike by Phaidra's scruples and Hippolytos' repugnances.

[16] In the first anger at hearing Phaidra's message, he had threatened to inform Theseus, or so the Nurse understood him (608 *sqq.*); on being reminded that he was sworn to secrecy, he had replied in the much-quoted line ἡ γλῶσσ' ὀμώμοχ', ἡ δὲ φρὴν ἀνώμοτος, 'My lips have sworn it, but my heart is free'. Having had time for reflection when he meets his father, he preserves the secret, not out of chivalry towards Phaidra (this is rather a modern sentiment), but simply because, although he feels that his oath was got from him by a trick, he is nevertheless sworn, and will not be even formally perjured.

painful play, the *Hecuba*, the transformation of a rather pathetic
old lady into a vengeful devil.   Hekabe, Priam's queen, is sorely
broken by her sorrows after the fall of Troy, and further stricken
by the sacrifice of her daughter Polyxene to the ghost of Achilles,
an episode made all the more moving by the vain pleas of the
mother and the quiet courage of the young girl.   Now she discovers that her last son, Polydoros, has been treacherously
murdered by the Thracian king Polymestor to whom he had been
entrusted.   A desperate appeal to Agamemnon, who after much
hesitation consents to sacrifice his Thracian ally to the mother
of his concubine Kassandra, leaves her free to entice Polymestor
into her quarters.   There she and her women kill his two sons
before his eyes and blind him.   Agamemnon, enraged by some
unpalatable prophecies which he utters, further orders him to
be marooned on a desert island ; and the play ends with the
grim old queen departing to bury her dead, while the other women
make ready to follow their new masters on board ship.

The exact date of the play is not known.   The interest in and
knowledge of Thracian matters suggests a date not very far distant
from that of Aristophanes' *Acharnians* (see p. 232) and the metre
leans rather towards the peculiarities of the earlier than the later
Euripidean usage.[17]   Some time about 425 B.C. would fit these
indications well enough.

Another play dealing principally with the psychology of
women, this time two contrasted types, with both of whom one
can feel some sympathy, is the *Andromache*.   This was classed
by the ancient critics among those which have a ' happy ending ',[18]
but it is hardly a cheerful piece.   Andromache, widow of Hektor,
has passed into the possession of Neoptolemos after the fall of
Troy and has become by him the mother of a child, Molossos.
Neoptolemos has since married Hermione, daughter of Menelaos
and Helen, whose father, an embodiment of all that is most
odious in the scheming and remorseless Spartan character, as

---

[17] In the iambic trimeter (see p. 82) a foot of three syllables, known
technically as a resolved foot, can be substituted, with certain restrictions,
for the iambus.   The older tragedians make but sparing use of this
licence (about once in twenty lines on an average).   Euripides began by
following their practice in the three plays anterior to the *Hecuba* ; in the
Hec. itself, the average rises to one resolved foot in ten lines, and in all
the other plays it is higher, the *Andromache* being nearest to the *Hecuba*
(109 resolved feet per 1000 lines).   See A. Church in *Class. Rev.*, xiv
(1900), p. 433.

[18] τὸ δὲ δρᾶμα τῶν δευτέρων, Arg. ii ; *i.e.*, it belongs to Aristotle's
class of second-best plays, *Poet.*, 1453ª 30, with a double action resulting
in prosperity to the good characters and adversity to the bad.

seen through Athenian eyes amid the fog of war, has preferred him, as a sane man with an assured position, to the half-mad and discredited Orestes, to whom she had been betrothed. Menelaos now is of opinion that Andromache and her child are no longer desirable members of his daughter's household, and proposes to kill them both in cold blood. Andromache, who is an unsympathetic portrait of the conventionally good Greek woman, contrives nearly to madden Hermione, a high-strung and proud young wife, sensitive about her own childlessness and furiously jealous of her rival, by a long sermon on conjugal duty. She therefore does nothing to oppose her father's plans, but the opportune arrival of old Peleus saves mother and son. Menelaos now swaggers off the stage ; but Hermione, realizing that she has ruined herself in the eyes alike of Pyrrhos and of his unforgiving old grandfather, thinks at first of suicide. Orestes arriving at this moment (a weak point in the play is the number of opportune arrivals), she consents to go with him, on being assured that her husband is in no position to interfere. This is explained in the next scene, when word is brought of his murder at Delphoi, by Orestes' contrivance and with the approval of Apollo.[19] Peleus' lamentations are interrupted by the entrance of Thetis, who bids him bury his grandson at Delphoi, to its perpetual reproach, while as for himself, he shall never die but join his son Achilles, who has also been made immortal, on the island of Leuke.[20]

Again the date is unknown ; the play was not produced at Athens (schol. on 445), and therefore must have appeared at one of the ' rural ' Dionysia. The freshness and vigour of the anti-Spartan feeling, shown especially in the hateful and treacherous character of Menelaos, suggests a date not long after the beginning of the Peloponnesian War, perhaps not far from 425. With this the metre, which is nearer that of the *Hecuba* than of any other play (cf. note 17), agrees.

Two plays may fairly be described as war-time propaganda ; their literary merit suffers from this fact. Much the poorer is the *Children of Herakles* (Ἡρακλεῖδαι). Herakles' children, accompanied by his aged mother Alkmene and his old comrade and nephew Iolaos, take refuge at Marathon from Eurystheus' hostility. He demands that they be handed over to him ;

---

[19] Euripides, who has little regard for any of the traditional gods, is positively venomous against Apollo, whose oracle was notoriously pro-Spartan, see especially Thucydides, i, 118, 3.

[20] An island near the mouth of the Danube, where there was a cult of Achilles ; legends of his appearances there were common, see Farnell, *Greek Hero-Cults* (Oxford, Clar. Press, 1921), pp. 285–7.

Demophon, king of Athens, refuses, and Eurystheus declares war. An oracle having said that the Athenians cannot win unless a virgin is sacrificed, Makaria, daughter of Herakles, offers herself as victim. Much of her part, including the description of her death, has apparently been lost,[21] but at best she seems to have been but a pale reflection of Polyxene in the *Hecuba*. However, her heroism is rewarded ; Eurystheus is defeated, captured by Iolaos, whose strength has been miraculously restored for one day, and is brought to Alkmene. She, despite the protests of the chorus, insists on his execution ; before his death he promises that if the Athenians give him honourable burial, he will be their friend when the ungrateful descendants of the Herakleidai (*i.e.*, the Dorians, and in particular the Spartans) invade the country.

There is no very clear indication of date ; the metre has fewer resolved feet than the *Hecuba*, about 84 per 1,000 lines. ' Early in the Peloponnesian War ' is perhaps as near as we can come to placing the drama.[22]

The *Suppliants* ('Ικέτιδες) has nothing but the title in common with Aeschylus' play (see p. 149). It is better than the *Children of Herakles*, but by no means one of Euripides' best. The mothers of the Seven, after the failure of the expedition against Thebes, take sanctuary at Eleusis, and Theseus, at the prayer of his mother Aithra, champions them, defeats the Thebans on their own ground and brings back the bodies for honourable burial. The rest of the play consists of the funeral, the suicide of Euadne, wife of Kapaneus, on her husband's pyre, some politenesses between Theseus and Adrastos, and finally a gratuitous epiphany of Athena, who engages Adrastos to swear that he will never invade Attica, but hinder any who try to do so.

The pointed allusion to the future relations of Athens with Adrastos' city of Argos suggests that the play was acted about 420, when an alliance between the two states was negotiated by Alkibiades.[23]

As the war progressed, Euripides seems to have grown heartily sick of it, and increasingly uncertain that Athens was the champion of righteousness. About December 416 or January 415 occurred the capture and destruction by the Athenians of Melos, a small Dorian island community whose only offence was trying to remain neutral. It is commonly held that indignation at this deed, the one completely unjustifiable action of Athens throughout the

---

[21] So most recent editors suppose, I think rightly.
[22] So Christ-Schmid, i, p. 362.   [23] Thucyd., v, 46, 5 *sqq.*

war, roused Euripides to write his *Trojan Women* (*Τρῳάδες*), though if so he must have composed and staged the play very rapidly, since it appeared at the Great Dionysia of 415, *i.e.*, about March.[24]

However this may be, the work is rather a pageant of the miseries of war, more especially of defeat, than a tragedy. After a prologue between Athena and Poseidon (the latter appearing, against all tradition, as the friend of Troy) in which they decide to wreck the returning Greek fleet in punishment for the sin of Aias the Lokrian against Kassandra,[25] there follows a series of scenes, portraying the misery of Hekabe, the apportionment of her daughters, herself and her daughter-in-law Andromache among the victors (Polyxene, as in the *Hecuba*, is sacrificed at the tomb of Achillés, but this is less emphasized than in the latter play), the mad exultation of Kassandra, who has a prophetic foreknowledge of the misfortunes of the Greeks, the putting to death of Astyanax, son of Andromache and Hektor, the meeting of Menelaos with Helen (whom Hekabe accuses so eloquently that Menelaos, again contrary to tradition, decides to execute her when they return), and finally the burning of Troy and the departure of the captives.

One magnificent play, arranged in a most effective scheme of crescendo and diminuendo of its hero's greatness, deals neither with war nor with women, but with an extraordinary man, Herakles himself, after whom the tragedy is named.[26] The first half shows his triumphant return from his most terrible adventure, the descent into Hades, just in time to rescue his wife and children, who, together with his reputed father Amphitryon, are about to be murdered by Lykos, tyrant of Thebes. The death of Lykos calls forth a song of rejoicing from the chorus, which is composed of Theban elders ; but this is cut short by the appearance of Iris, guiding the spirit of madness (*Λύσσα*) into the house to incite him to murder those whom he has just saved. The very fiend is ashamed of her task, imposed on her by the senseless hostility of Hera to Herakles. The resentment of the poet against the brute malignity which nature seems sometimes to show, especially when it results in unmerited suffering, could hardly find more picturesque expression. Herakles is not actually shown on the stage raving and murdering—the play is Tragedy, not Grand

[24] For the date, see Aelian, *uar. hist.*, ii, 8, presumably from some lost didaskalia. He gives Olympiad 91, doubtless meaning the first year of it, 416–15. I have to thank Mr. W. L. Lorimer for pointing out the chronological difficulties.

[25] See Rose, *Mythol.*, p. 143.

[26] It is called simply *Ἡρακλῆς* in antiquity ; its modern title, *Ἡρακλῆς μαινόμενος*, *Hercules furens*, dates only from the Aldine edition.

Guignol—but a servant runs out from the house to tell the tale
of it. Then the *ekkyklema* reveals him, bound by the survivors
of his mania to a pillar as he lies in a heavy sleep. Awakening,
he is seen to be sane enough, and old Amphitryon breaks the news
to him. In contrast to the serene and cheerful confidence of his
first appearance, he now falls into the blackest of despair, pro-
claiming himself unfit to live. He is rescued from suicide by the
entry of one who seems to represent the honest and thoughtful
normal man, Theseus. Herakles had saved him from Hades ;
he now brings such comfort as is possible, showing his friend that
for this bitter misfortune no least blame rests on him and offering
him an asylum at Athens. Herakles submissively accepts, and
leaves the stage hand in hand with Theseus.

The date of the play is unknown ; the famous ode on the miseries
of old age which the chorus sing (637 *sqq.*), suggests that the poet
is there voicing his own feelings, and consequently that he was past
middle life when he wrote. With this the indications of metre agree,
for there is a resolved foot to every five iambic lines on an average,
or twice as many as in the *Hecuba*. It is hardly possible to come
nearer to an exact date than Wilamowitz does in his well-known
edition of the play, namely to put it somewhere between 420 and
410 B.C.

For a while, Euripides seems to have sought relief from the
unwelcome happenings around him by writing romantic plays,
whose plots took him into a poetical or imaginative world. The
earliest of these, perhaps, is the *Iphigenia in Tauris*. The plot
turns on one of the few happy episodes in the history of the
Atreidai. Iphigeneia (cf. p. 194), rescued from Aulis by Artemis,
was conveyed by her to the land of the Taurians, a barbarous
folk who worshipped the goddess with human sacrifices. Here
she became Artemis' priestess, and thus was given her own
brother Orestes and his friend Pylades to prepare for the altar.
Discovering by chance who they are, she plots to rescue them.
They have come at the bidding of Apollo, who promises Orestes
relief from his madness [27] if he can bring the image of Artemis
from the Taurian land to Greece. The chorus of Greek slave
women, whose functions are to sing very lovely odes and get
horribly in the way of the actors when they want to conspire,
are taken into her confidence, and she tells Thoas, the Taurian
king, that she must take image and victims down to the sea-

[27] To Euripides, Orestes was not driven mad by the horror of the
Erinyes who pursued him ; he was mad already at his own matricide,
and the Erinyes are the phantoms of his imagination.

shore, to purify them from the taint of homicide which one of the strangers has brought. He readily agrees that she must have every facility for performing such a rite, and makes arrangements for her to be left undisturbed. Here one would expect that the three Greeks, with the image, would slip quietly aboard their vessel and make off ; but the chorus is once more in the way. Obviously, Thoas will not be too gentle in his treatment of Iphigeneia's Greek attendants when he finds out the truth, indeed on learning it he says as much. Therefore the departure is supernaturally delayed by great waves which wash the ship back to the land, and Athena appears in person to assure Thoas that all is as the gods decree ; the image is to go to Attica,[28] Iphigeneia to continue to be a priestess there, and receive worship herself when she dies ; the chorus are to be sent home. The worthy barbarian agrees to everything, and Athena is heard commanding the winds to carry the ship to Greece.

Since the iambics have nearly as many resolved feet as those of the *Herakles* (186 per 1000) and there are a few other indications inconsistent with early style, we may suppose that this work also was composed in the ' 'teens ' of the century ; nearer than that we can hardly come. One of the interesting things about the play, which has been deservedly popular ever since it was written, is that it has distinct comic features ; everything turns on the cleverness with which Iphigeneia outwits the duller-brained Thoas. Athena's part is little more than a stage device for getting the chorus away unmurdered and an opportunity for displaying the author's learning. For a lay figure, the goddess has dignity, and even beauty of a stiff kind.

Another romantic drama, which to judge by the metre, our only test, is rather later than the *Iphigenia in Tauris*, is the *Ion*, essentially a sentimental but very fine specimen of New Comedy, complete with long-lost child and virtuous but sadly wronged heroine. Some flavour of Tragedy is imparted by making gods appear and two characters be in temporary danger of their lives ; neither of these features is essential. Kreusa, daughter of Erechtheus king of Athens, has been violated by Apollo, borne a child and exposed him. The god has conveyed the baby to Delphoi, where by the time the play begins he is living, a pious and happy temple-servant. Meanwhile his mother has married a foreigner, Xuthos, her father's ally. They have no children,

[28] This, as so often in Euripides, connects his play with a local cult. At Halai in Attica and at Brauron near by there were ancient cults of Artemis, involving a pretence of human sacrifice, an old image, and the titles Tauropolos and Iphigeneia given to the goddess ; see Farnell, *C.G.S.*, ii, p. 435 *sqq.* Hence the legend.

and so come to Delphoi, he to ask how he may have offspring, she to inquire secretly what has become of her child.　Her inquiries are repulsed by the boy, who declares that Apollo would not answer a question so little to his credit—one of the many places in which Euripides' own opinions intrude unseasonably on his dramatic situation.　But Xuthos is told that the first person he meets when going (*ἰὼν*) from the temple is his son.　He meets the young temple-servant, accepts him, supposing that he is the fruit of a casual affair of his own at a festival in Delphoi, and calls him Ion (*Ἴων*).　Kreusa, wild with jealousy, tries to kill Ion ; the plot fails, and Ion is about to kill her when the priestess of Apollo, who had reared him, enters and in the very manner of New Comedy produces the clothes and ornaments he had worn when she received him.　Kreusa recognizes these, and Athena appears, tells mother and son all that has happened, and foretells the glorious future of Ion, the destined ancestor of the Ionians (*Ἴωνες*).　Xuthos apparently is not to be undeceived.　Thus the play ends happily, Apollo preserving some shreds of credit.

The *Helena*, spoken of as a new play in 411, and therefor reasonably dated 412,[29] is not unlike the *Iphigenia in Tauris* ; it also has its virtuous heroine who tricks and escapes from a barbarian king.　Following Stesichoros (see p. 109), Euripides makes the real Helen go go Egypt, while a phantom of her goes to Troy.　The good king Proteus who had sheltered her is dead when the play begins, and she has taken refuge at his tomb against the advances of his son Theoklymenos.　Now Menelaos, with the phantom, is wrecked on the coast of Egypt, and on coming to the palace is startled to discover that the king puts all Greeks to death and utterly amazed to be told that Helen, daughter of Zeus, is living there.　The arrival of one of his men with news of the phantom's disappearance solves the mystery, and he and the real Helen plot to escape.　After consultation with Theonoe, Theoklymenos' sister, who is a prophetess and knows the will of the gods in the matter, Helen informs the king that she has certain news of her husband's death and will accept his offer of marriage after she has paid the due rites to Menelaos' spirit, which involve the use of a ship.　With some reluctance he consents to lend her one ; Menelaos and his men overpower the Egyptian crew, and an appearance of Helen's deified brothers, Kastor and Polydeukes, stops pursuit.

While this is by no means a bad play, we should probably gain if we could exchange it for another that was produced at the same

[29] Aristophanes, *Thesm.*, 850 ; see p. 236.

time, the lost *Andromeda*.[30]   The plot of this was the familiar legend of the rescue of Kepheus' daughter from the sea-monster by Perseus, and the fragments are sufficiently plentiful for us to know that it included a novel effect, a solo by Andromeda in which her laments were repeated by an echo.   There was also a dialogue between the hero and heroine, including it would seem warm protestations of his love, and an apostrophe to the Love-god, greatly admired in antiquity. Indeed the whole play was apparently a favourite, and it is hard to tell what chance has deprived us of it, when several inferior pieces have survived.

In or about 413 [31] Euripides composed a play which perhaps brings his good and bad qualities into as strong relief as any of his works, the *Electra*.   That it is powerful and acts well cannot be denied ; its construction is far better than that of many of his plays, for he could, when he chose, construct a drama admirably, but was apt to be careless and merely write a sequence of scenes, like the *Troades*, or interrupt the action for long periods to give an actor opportunity to sing or recite, a fault which is very con-spicuous in the *Ion*.   But it is unrelievedly painful, a study of warped and perverted minds, and it shows an utter lack of his-torical imagination.   The revenge of Orestes could have occurred only in a stage of society which recognized blood-feud as a holy duty, *i.e.*, one in which the modern ideas of homicide and its treatment by the law did not exist.   Euripides stages the whole action practically in his own day, although he keeps the tradi-tional names and places.   Therefore he makes Orestes and Elektra the only kind of persons who under modern conditions could be guilty of matricide in cold blood, namely fanatical monomaniacs, driven mad, not so much by injustice as by their own brooding over it.   The only novel incident he introduces is the marriage of Elektra to a peasant-farmer, the one thoroughly honest man in the play.   He knows that she has been given to him solely to prevent her bearing children of high enough social standing to concern themselves with the quarrels of a princely house, and therefore he has never treated her as his wife.   So far as she is capable of affection and gratitude, she feels them for him ; but she ostentatiously parades her grievances, dressing in rags and engaging in the daily toil of a peasant-woman.   Orestes and Pylades arrive, pretending to be strangers who can give Elektra

[30] Cf. Rose, *Myth.*, p. 273.

[31] Line 1347 seems to allude to the great expedition to Sicily, which sailed from Athens in the summer of 415, a reinforcement following in 413 and the whole force being annihilated before the autumn of the latter year.

news of Orestes. She sends her husband to fetch an old servant of Agamemnon and ask him to bring materials for the entertainment of her guests. The old man has seen Orestes' footprints by Agamemnon's tomb and a lock of his hair lying on it ; Elektra rejects these proofs of her brother's return [32] rather contemptuously, but he recognizes Orestes by the mark of a scar on his forehead. Brother and sister plot the destruction of Aigisthos and Klytaimestra, Elektra, who is the stronger spirit of the two, taking upon herself quite calmly the murder of her mother. The two young men find means to approach Aigisthos as he is sacrificing, and kill him with the sacrificial knife. Elektra meanwhile has sent word to Klytaimestra that she has just had a child and wants to see her. The queen drives up in her carriage, attended by Trojan slave-women. She is far from being the Aeschylean Klytaimestra, but rather resembles the Queen in *Hamlet*, with a slight strain of cruelty added and even that weakened by her natural affection for her daughter and interest in the supposed grandchild. When verbally attacked by Elektra for her conduct in the past, she defends herself moderately and without venom ; finally she goes indoors, after dismissing her attendants. Her death-screams are heard, and Orestes and Elektra re-enter. Their strained minds have now changed from hysterical ruthlessness to hysterical remorse ; but their wailings are checked by the appearance of Kastor and Polydeukes. These direct Orestes to go to Athens ; Elektra is to marry Pylades and her nominal husband to be well rewarded. The matricide is Apollo's fault. That a stage god should so frankly criticize a god, even a pro-Spartan one, gives an idea of the width of Athenian tolerance.

The *Phoenissae* is some two or three years later. [33] The chorus give the play its name, but have little to do with the action ; they are Phoenician slave-women on their way to Delphoi, detained by the war of the Seven at Thebes, with which city they feel sympathy because the 'Phoenician' Kadmos founded it.

---

[32] This is a hit at Aeschylus. In the *Choephoroe* (see p. 155), Elektra sees the footmarks and hair, and argues from the shape of the one and colour of the other that they belong to a member of her own family, and therefore to Orestes. Aeschylus' reasoning is really sound enough, as Verrall pointed out in his edition of that play (*Introd.*, p. xliv *sqq.*). The family were traditionally foreigners and might well be supposed to have visible physical differences from the native Peloponnesians.

[33] In the archonship of Nausikrates, says the Argument, but no such archon is known at any reasonably likely date. Internal evidence suggests 410 approximately, see J. U. Powell in his edition of the play (London, Constable, 1911), p. 34 *sqq.*

The play as we have it is unwieldily long, although the individual scenes are good, and represent Euripides' best-known handling of the Theban saga. Spurious additions are generally supposed to exist ; possibly some parts were incorporated from the poet's own rough draft, which his own judgement would have rejected. It shows us successively, after a prologue by Iokaste, Antigone looking from the walls at the Argive army, Polyneikes, who comes under safe-conduct to a last and futile interview with his brother, at the instance of Iokaste, a council of war between Eteokles and Kreon which incidentally criticizes Aeschylus by implication,[34] and then an episode in which Teiresias announces that the city can be saved only by the sacrifice of Menoikeus, Kreon's son. Kreon tries to prevent this, but the young man slays himself on the walls without his father's knowledge.[35] Then comes word that the Thebans are victorious, but Eteokles and Polyneikes just about to fight each other. Iokaste rushes out to part them ; another messenger announces that she has been too late and has killed herself over their bodies. Now Antigone enters with a long aria on the woes of her family ; Oidipus comes out of his retirement and, after a quarrel between Antigone and Kreon about the disposal of Polyneikes' body, father and daughter leave the stage, in a scene containing a patent allusion to the *Oedipus Coloneus*, and therefore probably spurious, since the latter play (see p. 169) was almost certainly not written till some years later.

In 408,[36] Euripides produced the *Orestes*, an exciting melo-drama in which the hero's morbid character forms the central interest. The writer of one of the ancient arguments says that it is ' one of the successes of the stage, but its characters are vile, the only decent person being Pylades '. He might have added Hermione, but Orestes is not only mad but a cold-blooded prig between his fits of mania, Menelaos is a time-server, Helen an almost comically vain woman, Elektra a fanatic whose only redeeming quality is unselfish devotion to her brother. The play begins with a long sick-room scene, Elektra acting as Orestes' nurse and hushing the chorus (friendly Argive women, come to inquire after the patient) as they enter. During Orestes' alternating fits of raving and dozing, Helen sends Hermione out with offerings to Klytaimestra's tomb, since she herself dare not go and Elektra refuses. Menelaos entering, Orestes, sane for the

---

[34] 751, Eteokles says it would be waste of time to name the men entrusted with the defence, an evident hit at the *Seven*, see p. 151.

[35] Tennyson's *Tiresias* rehandles this story.

[36] In the archonship of Diokles (409–8), schol. on 371.

time being, explains that he is to be tried for his life before the
Argive assembly ; this anachronism [37] is followed by a worse
one, for old Tyndareos comes to upbraid him for killing his mother
instead of indicting her in proper legal form. Orestes' reply
that he has taught erring wives a wholesome lesson wins neither
the approval of the old man nor the support of Menelaos, on
which he had counted, and shortly afterwards, Pylades escorts
him to his trial. Condemned, with his sister, to death, but given
the privilege of suicide, he and she plot to kill Helen, who mysteriously disappears when Pylades and Orestes look for her, and
seize Hermione as a hostage to force Menelaos to intervene. On
his return, Menelaos finds Orestes with his knife at Hermione's
throat, while Elektra and Pylades are setting the palace on fire.
Now, since the logical sequel of murder, suicide and arson was
not available to the author, who must follow the main outlines
of the legend, Apollo appears, explains that he has done all for
the best and that he is even now escorting Helen to heaven,
promises to reconcile Orestes to the Argives, whose king he is
to be, and decrees that Hermione shall marry him and Menelaos
return to Sparta. Orestes starts at once for Athens, to be rid
there of his Erinyes, and Apollo, in whom any of the audience
who choose clearly have Euripides' permission to believe, departs
for the green-room to take off his mask and robes. As Aristophanes the grammarian well says in his Argument to the play,
it is rather like a comic ending. [38]

About this time Euripides may have begun the *Iphigenia in
Aulide*, which he never finished. As it was produced after his
death, [39] some one must have supplied the missing parts, but his
supplement, perhaps because it was known not to be Euripides'
own, is lost, and we have only the wretched work of some late
scribbler who knew enough mythology to get the ending right,
but nothing of classical metre. As it stands, omitting two arias
by the heroine and the odes (beautiful, but dramatically negligible)
sung by the chorus of tourists from Chalkis, the plot runs thus.
Agamemnon, a man of utterly irresolute character and sorely
afraid of the army he is supposed to command, has bidden
Klytaimestra fetch Iphigeneia to Aulis, under pretence of marry-

[37] A duty of blood-revenge and courts competent to try homicide
could not co-exist in the same nation. A somewhat similar, but less
glaring anachronism is the characteristically modern scruples felt by
Shakespeare's Hamlet ; the Hamlet of the original legend had none.

[38] κωμικωτέραν ἔχει τὴν καταστροφήν, cf. note 9.

[39] See schol. on Aristophanes, *Frogs*, 67. It was revived in 342, *I.G.*,
ii, 973. Murray, who gives the facts at the beginning of the play in his
edition of Euripides, interprets them somewhat differently.

ing her to Achilles, really to sacrifice her to appease the wrath of Artemis. He tries to send a letter countermanding his orders,[40] but Menelaos intercepts it and heaps reproaches on his brother. On the arrival of the women, Agamemnon's distress is so pitiable that Menelaos suggests abandoning the whole expedition ; it is now Agamemnon who insists on going forward with the sacrifice, as the army will never allow themselves to be baulked. He tries feebly to get Klytaimestra out of the camp, but without success, and she learns, partly from her husband's serving-man and partly from Achilles, who is very indignant at the misuse that has been made of his name, the whole truth. Appealed to for help, Achilles answers with pedantic morality, but it is honourable pedantry. If persuasion fails, he will defend Iphigeneia by force. An appeal to Agamemnon's natural feelings proving quite impotent to overcome his panic at his war-mad [41] army, Achilles in turn fails ; entering with a few armed followers, he explains that the rest of the host has turned against him. Iphigeneia now volunteers to die, as a patriotic duty. Achilles, for the first time taking some personal interest in her, promises still to defend her sword in hand if she should change her mind, and so departs. Our text stops with a messenger bringing an account of the sacrifice ; neglecting the worthless supplement, we may suppose from a fragment that is left of the older conclusion, Euripides' or another's, that Artemis appeared to Klytaimestra and explained that Iphigeneia had been saved by her.[42]

Euripides left for Macedonia some time between the spring of 408 and the summer of the following year, invited by King Archelaos, who sought to bring representatives of Hellenic culture to his court.[43] He held the poet in high honour, and a lost play, the *Archelaos*, whose fragments do not enable us to reconstruct the plot from them, may reasonably be supposed to have treated the legend of the king's namesake, founder of the Macedonian dynasty ; for, as he was, according to the story, a Greek of one

[40] This is shown in the prologue of the play, which is in anapaests ; a second prologue, in iambics, I take to be a feeble imitation of Euripides at his worst by some later writer. See p. 423.

[41] The original is stronger yet : μέμηνε δ᾽ Ἀφροδίτη τις Ἑλλήνων στρατῷ, 1264.

[42] Three lines are cited by Aelian, *de nat. anim.*, vii, 39, as by Euripides in the *Iphigeneia '*.

[43] Presumably after the *Orestes*, see note 36, and some few months at least before his death in 407/6 (Parian Chronicle, 63). It may be mentioned here that the Letters of Euripides, professing to date from about this time, are notoriously a late forgery ; see Bentley, *Epistles of Themistocles etc.*, p. 114 *sqq.* (p. 554 *sqq.*, Wagner).

of the ancient heroic families,[44] he would be an acceptable fore-bear to kings who were putting forward their claim to be considered Greeks and not barbarians. But the poet found something better to do. In Macedonia, the cult of Dionysos seems not to have been the tamed and civilized affair it had become in Greece. Euripides had opportunities to see something of it in its half-savage vigour, and thus, probably for the first time in his life, met with people capable of genuine religious enthusiasm, the power of which, for good or evil, a much less intelligent man than he could have recognized. The result was that he wrote his greatest play, the *Bacchae*, reverting in it to a technique which he had not used for years, in that he gave the chorus an important part in the action, as well as songs of extraordinary power and beauty. The plot was taken from a Theban legend, how Pentheus, grandson of Kadmos, resisted the coming of Dionysos, to his own ruin. The god in person speaks the prologue. He has returned from his triumphant progress through Asia to his own native city. His mother's sisters, including Pentheus' mother Agaue, at first denied his divinity, but were overcome with the Bacchic frenzy, and they, with most or all the women of Thebes, are now on Mount Kithairon, where he goes to join them. His departure is followed by the entry of the chorus, Asiatic women who are the companions of his wanderings. Their long and ecstatic hymn being ended, two half-comic old men enter, Kadmos, who is a zealous believer in the new god, and Teiresias, the prophet, who lacks his enthusiasm but judges it politic not to oppose anything like a supernatural power. Pentheus tries to stop them going out, as they intend, to join the votaries on the hill-side ; the chorus exclaim at his impiety, Teiresias gives him a sermon on the nature and functions of the new god, and Kadmos warns him to beware of a fate like Aktaion's, who was devoured by his own hounds for presuming to rival Artemis as a hunter. He replies angrily, and they leave him, while the chorus sings a hauntingly beautiful ode on Holiness. A servant of Pentheus now enters with a prisoner, the only one he and his fellows have taken, for the women whom they seized upon have escaped, their bonds falling off them by miracle. The captive is quite unperturbed at Pentheus' examination of him and equally unmoved by his threats. Pentheus finally orders him to be imprisoned in the stables of the palace.

Who the stranger is, is the chief problem of the play. He is traditionally called Dionysos, but no one in the tragedy itself

[44] The Temenidai. The legend, which may or may not be derived from this play, is in Hyginus, *fabulae*, 219.

gives him that or any other name. I prefer, with Professor Norwood,[45] to believe that his account of himself to Pentheus is meant to be true ; he is a young Oriental, a votary and prophet of the god. At all events, once imprisoned, he escapes easily enough, being apparently possessed by the power of Dionysos himself. He and the chorus see the palace crash as with an earthquake, while fire blazes from the shrine of Semele which forms part of the building. Having emerged from his prison, he comforts the chorus and replies calmly when Pentheus arrives in pursuit of him and threatens further violence. A messenger now brings a long tale of the miracles attending the revels of the women on the mountain ; the stranger easily persuades the king to disguise himself as a Bacchante and go to spy on them. Soon after his departure, news is brought that the women have caught him and torn him in pieces, Agaue leading them. She enters, carrying Pentheus' head, which in her madness she supposes to be that of a lion. Kadmos succeeds in bringing her to her senses, and their laments are cut short by the appearance of Dionysos in person, who apparently (for a great part of his speech has been lost) foretold the future destinies of Kadmos and his family and justified his own vengeance on those who had disbelieved in him.

To call the play an attack on or a defence of religion in general or any form of it in particular is quite to miss the meaning. It is a study, by a poet who was deeply interested in all religious phenomena, of one of the most notable of them, the wild and fanatical enthusiasm of which the worship of Dionysos, in its northern forms, furnished a conspicuous example. As he neither attacks nor defends sexual passion in the *Hippolytus*, but studies it sympathetically and with profound pity for its victims, so here he deals with an equally potent force, which he shows exalting some of those affected by it to the raptures of the chorus, and ruining others, like Pentheus and Agaue. If he has a lesson to teach, it is one typically Greek, the duty of moderation, and the dangers, on the one hand, of lack of self-control, on the other, of what it is now the fashion to call ' repressions '.

[45] He argues for this at length in *The Riddle of the Bacchae*. This much of his theory, and of Verrall's adaptation of it, in *The Bacchants of Euripides*, but only this much, I accept. See *Aberystwyth Studies*, iv (1922), pp. 24–8. The destruction of the palace I believe to be wholly subjective, a fancy of the prophet and the chorus, for no one else even mentions it. It should be remembered that a follower of Dionysos, when filled with the god's influence, was Dionysos himself (Βάκχος can be used of either) for the time being.

In all the tragedies, Euripides' chief concern is to make his characters human ; he is, of all Greek authors, perhaps the most obviously interested in psychology. Almost equally prominent is his interest in religion in all forms ; it is the interest of a student, not of a pious believer, but all the more vigorous on that account. Myths, legends of the foundations of particular worships, tales of wonder of all sorts, clearly held a fascination for him, not lessened by his own somewhat drily rationalistic theories, at which he hints constantly, often to the detriment of his plot (it is, for example, awkward in the extreme to insert into a speech of Herakles, son of Zeus and Alkmene, philosophic doubts as to the possibility of a god having children by an irregular union) [46] and of course to the scandal of the more conservatively pious among his hearers in antiquity. This rationalism was but one side of his nature, for he was an exceptionally good writer of lyric and of romantic, fanciful poetry, witness such plays as the *Helen* and, to judge from what we know of it, the *Andromeda*, and many of the songs of his choruses. Such passages as the hymn which Ion sings in the play that bears his name, the great ode to Love in the *Hippolytus*, and above all the extraordinary songs of the *Bacchae*, [47] fuller perhaps than any other surviving passages in classical Greek of delight in and sympathy with wild Nature, form a remarkable contrast to the tone of much of the dialogue, which often carries realism so far as to be prosy and commonplace. Something a little like this is to be found in Ibsen, if one compares the fantastic beauty of parts of *Peer Gynt* with the dialogue of, say, *The Doll's House*, or that again with the gloomy symbolism of *Rosmersholm*, or the last scene of *The Master-Builder*. Broadly speaking, we may say that Euripides kept his poetry for the chorus, his psychological analysis for the actors, to whose share fell also the brilliant rhetoric, forensic in tone, which is a constant feature of the plays, often retarding the action more than a modern audience would wish ; but the Greek love of argument made a debate (ἀγών) a welcome ornament to a dramatic performance.

It thus comes about that there is almost always a certain lack of unity, even in those plays which are well constructed as regards the organic relation of each scene to the rest. After an episode in which heroes and heroines use language rather human than heroic, we frequently get a *stasimon* which reflects in the language of exalted poetic fancy on their doings ; then will come another scene of prosaic thought couched in loose, though always har-

[46] *Herc. Fur.*, 1341–2.
[47] *Ion.*, 82 *sqq.* ; *Hipp.*, 525 *sqq.* ; *Bacch.*, 862 *sqq.*, and elsewhere.

monious verse, and so throughout. Many plays could be divided into two independent parts, the episodes in one and the *stasima* in another, each having much merit but neither being necessary to the other. As we have seen, the chorus is frequently no more than an intruder ; Euripides plainly foreshadows the technique of New Comedy, which will be discussed in the next chapter.

As a thinker, Euripides deserves a place alongside Aeschylus, despite the immense differences between them. The older poet was a theologian and a prophet ; the younger was the apostle of a new school, which made man the centre of its interest, and ethics, not theology, the all-important study. Euripides' gods may be roughly divided into two classes. Some are embodied criticisms of the still prevalent popular views, the poet's unbelief in them and the actions imputed to them showing itself in every line they utter. The figure oftenest set in this light is Apollo. Others are rather personifications of natural or, more often, of psychological forces, Passion, Asceticism, Madness, Fanaticism. Here there is real belief, however much Euripides may doubt that any superhuman persons actually embodied such powers. For the old themes of divine vengeance and divine justice are generally substituted the newer ones of right and wrong in general, great laws to which any being, god or man, must conform or stand condemned. The particular applications of these laws are doubtful, however, few actions being so clearly evil or good that a case cannot be made out for or against them. Hence the doubts, misunderstandings and aberrations which make tragic happenings. But at almost any moment the poet in Euripides may take control, bidding philosophic questionings rest for a while, and we have such romances as the *Iphigenia in Tauris*, with a deity who is hardly more than a good fairy coming to the rescue of the distressed.

Euripides plainly disliked satyr-plays as a rule, and it is therefore rather remarkable that the one specimen we have from him of this kind of drama is by no means without merit. It is the *Cyclops*, and borrows its plot from the Odyssey (see p. 26). The cast is very simple, consisting of three speaking parts only, Odysseus, Polyphemos and Seilenos ; the chorus of satyrs have been enslaved by the giant, and the action passes substantially as in Homer, but with the ridiculous additions which the *genre* demands, Seilenos being very active when Odysseus produces his wine-skin and stealing a good share of its contents, after having tried to sell his master's sheep in exchange for the precious drink. Polyphemos himself is a huge figure of fun, whose cannibalism it is hard to take very seriously,[48] and the whole play goes with an undeniable swing and vigorous, rough humour.

Euripides' plays are said to have numbered 92, of which 77, or 78, were preserved when the documents to which the existing Lives go back were written.[49] We have far more fragments of him than of Aeschylus and Sophokles put together, owing to his great popularity, both as poet and moralist, in the centuries following his death. Papyrus finds have considerably increased the number, and even supplied us with so large a part of one play, the *Hypsipyle*, as to enable us to restore the plot with confidence, and reconstruct many of the scenes. Another, the *Phaethon*, has been very ingeniously put together from fragments great and small by Wilamowitz-Möllendorff. Concerning the rest we know much less.

The *Hypsipyle* takes its plot from the Theban cycle, combined with elements from the story of the Argonauts. Hypsipyle, daughter of Thoas king of Lemnos, was the only woman in the island who did not join in the massacre of the men,[50] but rescued her father and got him secretly away. Later, when the Argonauts came, she was united to Jason, and bore him twin sons, Thoas and Euneos. After the Argonauts had gone, she was banished by the other women for her mercy to her father, and, falling probably into the hands of pirates, was made a slave and sold to Lykurgos, priest of Zeus at Nemea. When the play opened, she apparently was seen with his child, Opheltes, in her arms ; a novel effect was introduced by making her sing to the baby with a rattle by way, apparently, of accompaniment. A lyrical duet with the chorus followed ; these would appear to have been young women of the neighbourhood who knew her story and sympathized with her. Now appeared Amphiaraos, asking to be shown running water which he could use for sacrificial purposes ; the details of the action are obscure, owing to the fragmentary nature of what we have, but clearly she went with him, leaving the child somewhere. Then followed the killing of Opheltes by the dragon which guarded the spring ; Hypsipyle was seized by her mistress, Eurydike, the child's mother, Lykurgos being absent. The timely return of Amphiaraos saved her from being put to death ; Eurydike was consoled by the assurance that her baby's tomb should be a famous place and the centre of the Nemean Games, and Hypsipyle was pardoned. Now came her reunion with her sons, who, unknown

[48] Naturally the killing and devouring of Odysseus' men takes place behind the scenes, the hero himself coming out from the cave (which, to the detriment of the story, is not closed by a huge rock as in Homer) to tell the tale to the chorus.

[49] The *Life*, as given in the Codex Ambrosianus, says 92 and 78 ; the Vaticanus, 98 and 67 + 3 doubtful + 8 satyr-plays ; Suidas, 75 or 92 and 77 (*sic*).

[50] See Rose, *Myth.*, pp. 191, 199. The papyrus is *Ox. Pap.* 852 ; a convenient text is that in Hunt, *F.T.P.* (see Bibliography). The latest discussion is Pickard-Cambridge in Powell, 3, p. 120 *sqq.*

to her, had been present all along. Some business having brought them to Nemea, she had herself admitted them to the house, remarking on their beauty as she did so ; they now re-entered, were made known to her, probably by means of Amphiaraos' powers as a seer, and exchanged stories of their adventures since they parted from her. The play thus ended happily for the heroine.

The title of the *Phaethon* is alone enough to make it clear that the play dealt with the tale of the Sungod's child who tried, disastrously, to drive his father's chariot.[51] But there is a long fragment, contained in the Codex Claremontanus, now at Paris, which throws much light on the handling of the plot. This begins with the concluding words of a dialogue between Phaethon and his mother Klymene, in which he has evidently learned of his parentage and, encouraged by her, is setting out to reach the abode of the Sun. Then follows a chorus, lovely even for Euripides, in which the singers announce that it is Phaethon's wedding-day. A later passage makes it clear that his bride is a goddess, possibly Aphrodite herself. At all events, a most striking dramatic effect was produced by the climax of the play, which is preserved to us in the same MS. Word is brought to Klymene of the death of her son ; as she goes to tend the body and bring it into the palace of her husband, Merops king of Ethiopia, Merops himself arrives leading the bridal procession. A servant meets him and warns him that the treasury of the palace has caught fire. He hurries to attend to it, and shortly afterwards is heard lamenting ; evidently the burning body of Phaethon is in the building, and the smoke and flames the servant has seen proceed from it. Precisely how the play ended we do not know.

The *Antiope*, one of Euripides' most popular plays, can also be largely reconstructed, owing to the many quotations from it in ancient authors, to which we can add some fragments of a close imitation in Latin by Pacuvius and an important papyrus fragment.[52] The general outlines of the plot are familiar from several late authors who tell the story, though probably none of them draws directly upon the play.[53] Nykteus, king of Thebes, or rather of the Kadmeia, the little town which, according to tradition, occupied part of the site, had a fair daughter Antiope, and discovered that she was with child. Not believing her story that her lover was Zeus, he threatened her, and she fled to Sekyon. Shortly afterwards, Nykteus died, leaving as a last charge to his brother Lykos to punish Antiope. This he did, killing the king of Sekyon who protected her and bringing her back

[51] For the story, see Rose, *Mythol.*, 261. The fragments are in Nauck, p. 599 *sqq.*, which also gives references to the most important modern articles on the play ; add Pickard-Cambridge in Powell 3, p. 143 *sqq.* ; H. Volmer, *De Euripidis fabula quae Φαέθων inscribitur restituenda*, Münster, Aschendorff, 1930.

[52] Brit. Mus. Pap. 485. See, for the latest discussion, Pickard-Cambridge, *ibid.*, p. 105 *sqq.*

[53] Pseudo-Apollodoros (see p. 392), iii, 42 *sqq.* ; scholiast on Apollonios Rhodios, iv. 1090 ; Hyginus, *fabulae*, 7 and 8.

to captivity. On the way, she bore twins, whom she left by the wayside. A shepherd adopted them, not knowing, at least till later, whose children they were. At the beginning of the play Antiope is the ill-treated slave of Lykos' wife Dirke, and her sons are grown to manhood. One of them, Zethos, is the man of action, his brother Amphion a musician, and, as such, the representative of the life of art and philosophy. A long debate between them seems to have formed one of the early scenes of the play. Then followed an appeal from Antiope, who had escaped from her prison, to her sons to shelter her. Amphion was moved and Zethos repelled by her plight ; presently she was followed by Dirke, who had left her house to join in a Dionysiac revel ; her fellow-bacchantes seem to have formed a second chorus, the principal one consisting apparently of men. Finding Antiope, she seized upon her to put her to death ; but Amphion and Zethos, who had in the meantime learned who their parents were, came to the rescue and bound Dirke to the horns of a wild bull, which dragged her to death, the end, probably, which she had designed for Antiope. Lykos was then captured by a ruse, and a novel scene followed, for while his cries were heard off the stage, he presently re-entered with the two young men, and an appearance of Hermes reconciled them ; Lykos yielded up his kingship to them, and their different temperaments were satisfied by different tasks, Zethos being entrusted with the defence of the state in war, while Amphion by his magical music was to cause the stones to come together to make its walls.

As with the other dramatists, the remaining plays will now be discussed in their Greek alphabetical order. The *Aigeus* dealt with the same story as that handled by Bakchylides in his fourth dithyramb (see pp. 125, 129). The *Aiolos* had for its plot the incestuous love of Makareus, son of Aiolos, for his sister Kanake, but it is not known in any detail how the story was told. The *Alexandros* dealt with the same story as Sophokles' play of that name (see p. 172). It was acted along with the *Troades* (see p. 187), the other plays of the tetralogy being the *Palamedes* and *Sisyphos*.[54] The story of Alkmeon furnished material for two plays, *Alkmeon in Psophis* and *Alkmeon at Corinth*. The former dealt with his wanderings after the slaying of his mother, and his marriage with Arsinoe, daughter of king Phegeus. The latter had a romantic plot, very suggestive of New Comedy. Alkmeon during his mad wanderings met with Manto, daughter of Teiresias the Theban seer, and had by her a son and a daughter. The children were entrusted to the king of Corinth to nurture, but the daughter grew into so beautiful a woman that the queen became jealous and sold her as a slave. The purchaser was none other than Alkmeon himself, who somehow recognized her as his daughter, and was thus re-united to her and her brother.[55] The

[54] Aelian, passage cited in note 26.

[55] For Alkmeon, see Rose, *Myth.*, p. 194. The date of the second play is given by schol. Ar., *Frogs*, 67 ; the plot, by [Apollodoros], iii, 94–5.

date of the two plays was widely different, for the former was acted with the *Alcestis*, the latter with the *Bacchae*. The *Alope* we see from its title to have dealt with one of the amours of Poseidon, with Alope daughter of Kerkyon (hence the play was also called *Kerkyon*), who bore him a son Hippothoos and after suffering much from her father's anger was rescued by Theseus, or at least, for the plot is quite uncertain, her son's rights were maintained by that hero. The *Andromeda* has already been discussed (see p. 191). The *Antigone* followed a quite different version of the legend from that used by Sophokles ; in both cases, it is far from certain that the plot was not invented, wholly or in large measure, by the dramatist. Euripides made Kreon hand Antigone over to Haimon for execution ; Haimon saved her, hid her among country folk, and visited her secretly. This had happened some time before the play began, and it would seem that its plot turned upon the adventures of their son. He appeared in Thebes and was recognized by the spear-shaped birth-mark characteristic of all the family (the Spartoi) to which his father belonged. Kreon would seem then to have ordered the execution of the parents and son, but these were saved by a divine intervention, probably of Dionysos.[56] Of the *Archelaos* something has already been said (p. 195). The *Auge* dealt with the beginning of the legend of Telephos, how Herakles loved Auge, daughter of the Arkadian prince Aleos ; how she bore a child and exposed it on Mount Parthenion, and, very possibly, how Herakles himself rescued the infant, which had been nursed by a hind, from death. But we cannot reconstruct the play from the little that is left of it, or say exactly how much of this story Euripides told. The *Bellerophontes* and the *Stheneboia* between them dealt with the chief incidents in the legend of Bellerophon, the former including the hero's impious attempt to fly up to heaven on the back of Pegasos, the latter his revenge on Stheneboia.[57] The *Busiris* was a satyr-play ; just how it dealt with the attempt of the legendary king of Egypt to sacrifice Herakles to his gods and the rout and destruction of the Egyptians by their intended victim is not known.[58] Of the *Danae*, the plot of which cannot have differed much from that of Sophokles' play of the same title (see p. 172), we have a good many genuine fragments and one long spurious one, the attempt of some Byzantine to forge the prologue and a little of the first *stasimon* of a Euripidean drama ; but we cannot restore the details of the action. The *Diktys*, which was acted at the same time as the *Medea*, presumably continued the story of Danae and her son, for Diktys was the name of the fisherman, or prince, who found her when she drifted ashore on Seriphos. Of the *Epeios* we have the title and no more ; as Epeios was the builder of the Wooden Horse we can guess at the subject. The *Erechtheus* is much better known ;

[56] See Robert, *Oidipus*, p. 382 ; Rose, *Modern Methods*, p. 42.
[57] The *Stheneboia* has recently become rather better known, see Pickard-Cambridge, *op. cit.*, p. 131 *sqq.*
[58] For the story, see Rose, *Mythol.*, p. 217.

it hardly needs any explanation to an English reader, for Swinburne treats the same story, in a not un-Euripidean way, in his play of the same title. The *Eurystheus* was a satyr-play ; some of the fragments indicate, what indeed we might judge from the title, that the Labours of Herakles came somehow into the action. Of the Θερισταί or *Reapers* we know that it was the satyr-play of the tetralogy to which the *Medea* belonged. The *Theseus* seems to have dealt with the slaying of the Minotaur ; one curious episode was that the hero, arriving somewhere, wrote his name in a conspicuous place, and an unlettered man saw the writing and described the characters whose meaning he did not know. The *Thyestes*, whatever part of the story it may have treated, showed its hero in rags, a favourite device of the poet, for which Aristophanes made unmerciful fun of him (see p. 232). The *Ino* we know something about, for Hyginus professes to give its plot,[59] though not much dependence can be placed on his statements. But we may believe him thus far, that it had to do with the rivalry between Ino, the former wife of Athamas, and her successor Themisto, which resulted in the latter being misled into killing her own children by mistake for Ino's. This would fit well enough the tone of some of the fragments, which speak of the unhappy lot of women generally, of the advisability of having more wives than one, and of jealousy or envy (φθόνος). The *Ixion* treated of the punishment of its central character, but how much else of the legend it told we do not know.[60] Of the lost *Hippolytos* something has been said in discussing the surviving one (p. 182). The *Kadmos* is for us a title and two fragments, one highly uncertain as to text and authenticity, the other doubtfully from this play.[61] The *Kerkyon* is but another name for the *Alope* ; the *Kresphontes* had the same plot as was utilized by Matthew Arnold in his *Merope*. Two plays had titles differing only in gender, the Κρῆσσαι and the Κρῆτες, respectively the *Women of Crete* and the *Men of Crete*. Concerning the former we know next to nothing, except that it concerned Aerope, daughter of Katreus the Cretan ; according to a scholiast on Sophokles she had

[59] *Fabulae*, iv. Hyginus draws on a lost Greek manual of mythology, which in turn drew, not directly on the tragedians, but on mythographers who had borrowed from them as well as from other sources. See Rose, *Modern Methods*, p. 36 *sqq.* ; and for details, *Hygini fabulae*, Leiden, Sijthoff, 1933.

[60] The most positive statement about it is in Plutarch, *de audiendis poetis*, 19 e ; Euripides, on being abused for the impious character of Ixion, answered that he got him fairly fastened to his wheel before his final exit.

[61] One is preserved in the so-called Probus, on Vergil, *Ecl.*, vi, 31, and having passed through the hands of Latin scribes is extremely corrupt. The other, found in Hermogenes (*Rhetores Graeci*, vol. iii, p. 180 Walz), is said by him to be from Euripides and would fit the transformation of Kadmos into a serpent, but it is so utterly absurd that I incline to think it the parody of some comedian ; it runs, οἴμοι, δράκων μοι γίγνεται τό γ' (γ' add. Barnes) ἥμισυ·/τέκνον, περιπλάκηθι τῷ λοιπῷ πατρί.

had an intrigue with a serving-man and was condemned by her father to be cast into the sea, but was rescued by the agent charged with this task and married to Pleisthenes, a vague figure who in this form of the story replaces Atreus as father of Agamemnon and Menelaos.[62] The Cretan women in question presumably formed the chorus. The latter play, as we now know more definitely from a recent discovery of a papyrus fragment,[63] handled the tale of Pasiphae and the bull. We have part of her elaborate defence of her conduct, on the ground that it was so utterly unnatural as to be an involuntary act, the result of a·madness sent by divine power. Another notable fragment is part of a chorus, the members of which introduce themselves (apparently at their first entrance, for it is in the anapaestic metre commonly used to bring the chorus into the orchestra) as votaries of a mystic cult, that of Zeus of Ida, to describe which Euripides seems to have used, among other materials, elements from Orphism. To what extent he has given a picture of any cult really existing in Crete is doubtful. That he wrote a play called *Lamia* is stated by one or two late authors, and seems very doubtful, for the title, being the name of a nursery bogey, hardly suggests a tragedy. The *Likymnios* seems to have been lost very early, and nothing definite is known of it.[64] Concerning the two plays dealing with Melanippe, we are far better informed. One of these was called in antiquity *Melanippe the Wise*, the other *Melanippe in Bonds* (Μελανίππη ἡ σοφή, M. δεσμῶτις). The plot of the former is pretty well known from two synopses of it ;[65] Melanippe, daughter of Aiolos the son of Hellen, had twin children by Poseidon, and exposed them in a cattle-kraal. Her father, when the infants were discovered, imagined that they were portentous births of a cow, and intended to burn them ; Melanippe (hence the title of the play) seems to have pled for them in a long argument proving that such births were an impossibility and the

[62] See schol. Soph., *Ai.*, 1297. Pleisthenes (Very Strong One, *i.e.*, Mighty Prince) is a stopgap name, of a kind not infrequent in genealogies. For his various appearances in that of the house of Tantalos, see Roscher's Lexikon, *s.u.*

[63] The fragment was first published in *Berliner Klassikertexte*, ii, p. 73 ; it will be found in Hunt, *T.F.P.* An amusing instance of the dangers of restoring lost plays from insufficient data is provided by Verrall's confident assertion, *Class. Rev.*, xv (1901), p. 365, that Euripides followed the rationalizing form of the story according to which Pasiphae loved a man called Tauros and not a literal bull. The whole point of her defence is now seen to be that, since her passion was not for anything human, she cannot be called an adulteress, but only pitied for her insanity.

[64] Kallimachos *ap.* schol. Ar., *Birds*, 1242, says no mention of it was to be found in the records, or, for the text of the scholiast is uncertain and corrupt, some one else said that Kallimachos' *Didaskaliai* (see p. 318) did not mention it.

[65] Gregory of Corinth in *Rhetores Graeci*, vol. vii, p. 1313 Walz ; [Dion. Hal.], *ars rhetorica*, viii, 10 (vol. ii, pp. 308–9 Usener-Radermacher). A little more has come to light recently ; see Hunt, *T.F.P.*, and Pickard-Cambridge, *op. cit.*, p. 113 *sqq.*

children must have a human mother. In the other play, we are reduced to reconstructing the plot as well as we can from the slippery evidence of Hyginus and one long fragment. The former says that the children of Melanippe, Aiolos and Boiotos, were found by herdsmen after they had been exposed, and soon after given to the childless queen Theano, wife of Metapontos, who passed them off for her own. Later, however, she herself had two sons, and, telling them her secret, directed them to murder the suppositious children while out hunting. They attempted to do so, but were themselves killed. Poseidon now revealed to Boiotos and Aiolos whose children they were ; they rescued their mother, who had been blinded and imprisoned by her father, and Poseidon restored her sight ; Metapontos married her, for Theano had committed suicide on the death of her sons, and adopted Boiotos and Aiolos.[66] Now a fragment, 494 in Nauck's collection, contains a messenger's speech, describing just such an encounter as that between the children of Melanippe and of Theano ; it may be therefore that Hyginus' tale is substantially Euripides' plot. Over the *Meleagros* we need not linger, for the plot will have been much the same as that of Swinburne's *Atalanta* (the English poet going for the story to several later classical authors who in turn owed more or less to Euripides), and we do not know in detail how it was handled. As regards the *Oidipus*, one of the surviving fragments (541 Nauck [2]) shows that the hero was blinded, not by himself but by others ; apart from this we cannot tell exactly how it differed from Sophokles' treatment of the story. The *Oineus* showed its chief character in rags,[67] according to Aristophanes, and his scholiast explains that the subject of the play was Oineus' ejection from his kingdom in old age by the children of his brother Agrios, and his restoration by Diomedes. The *Oinomaos* was acted along with the *Phoenissae*, but nothing has come down to us that will serve to reconstruct it. The *Palamedes*, acted along with the *Troades*, was a famous play in its time ; it dealt with the treachery of Odysseus towards Palamedes, whom he hated and contrived to destroy by a plausible accusation, strengthened by manufactured evidence.[68] Two curious things are known concerning it, apart from the general plot. One is that Palamedes in one scene wrote messages, apparently on wooden tablets and to his brother Oiax, and set them afloat in hopes of reaching him [69] ; the other is the mention of him not only as ' the all-wise ' but as ' the Muses' nightingale, who harmed none ', strongly suggesting that, since the Palamedes of the legend is not a poet, his figure hinted at some contemporary (Euripides himself ?) who was. Of the *Peirithoos* the ancients were not certain

[66] Hyginus, *fab.*, 186 ; Pickard-Cambridge, *loc. cit.*
[67] Ar., *Acharn.*, 418–20 and schol. there.
[68] See Rose, *Mythol.*, p. 238.
[69] This is alluded to in Aristophanes' parody, *Thesmoph.*, 769 *sqq.*, which makes it tolerably clear that the messages were written on wooden tablets and thrown somewhere, probably into the sea ; the schol. there says absurdly they were written on the ships.

whether it was by Euripides or by Kritias (see p. 211) ; it dealt with the adventure of Theseus and Peirithoos in Hades and their rescue by Herakles.[70] The *Peliades* or *Daughters of Pelias* was one of the plays of Euripides' first public appearance ; its theme was the deceit by which Medeia contrived that Pelias should be killed by his own daughters in hopes of restoring him to youth by her arts. Concerning the *Pleisthenes* we have no ground for reasonable conjectures, for that phantasmal figure (see p. 205) occurs in several different places in the legend of the Tantalids. The *Polyidos* we can restore in outline, at least ; it told how Glaukos, son of Minos of Crete, was accidentally killed, and how Polyidos the seer first discovered by his art where the body was and then hit upon a magic herb which would bring the child to life again. The story of the *Protesilaos* is familiar enough, for it is the legend handled in Wordsworth's *Laodamia*. The *Rhadamanthys* was considered spurious by ancient critics, we do not know on what grounds, nor what the play was about. The *Stheneboia* has already been discussed (p. 203) The *Sisyphos* and the *Skiron* were both satyr-plays. The *Skyrians* [70a] (Σκύριοι, less likely Σκύριαι), for the plot of which see p. 175, seems to have dwelt upon the love of Deidameia, daughter of king Lykomedes, for Achilles, since a surviving fragment (682) introduces some one telling the king that the girl is ill, probably meaning that she is love-lorn. The *Syleus* was another satyr-play ; Syleus was a temporary master of Herakles, who got little profit out of the huge and unmanageable strength of his new servant. The *Tennes* was again a spurious play. The *Telephos* was one of Euripides' most popular works. As he seems to have told the story, Telephos, son of Herakles and Auge, having become king of Mysia, found his country invaded by the Greeks on their way to Troy. He resisted them stoutly, and in the fighting, received an incurable wound from Achilles' spear. Inquiring of Apollo how he might be healed, he was answered, ' the giver of the wound shall also cure it '. He then disguised himself as a beggar, entered Agamemnon's camp at Aulis, got possession of the infant Orestes, and by threatening to kill him if he were not allowed to plead his cause, got a hearing. His eloquent speech now won the Greeks to consent to cure him, which was done by putting the rust of the spear on his wound ; in return, he guided the host to Troy. Of the *Temenidai* and the *Temenos* we can say only that they must have dealt with some of the legends of the Peloponnesian Dorians. The *Hypsipyle* has been already discussed, also the *Phaethon* and *Philoktetes* (pp. 200, 201, 169). In the *Phoinix*, Euripides followed, or invented, a more elaborate story than that which Homer puts into the hero's mouth in Il. ix. There he says that he left home because of a quarrel with his father ; urged on by his mother, he had possessed his father's slave-concubine, and was cursed by the old man with childlessness. In Euripides, the vengeance of Amyntor, as both call the father, took a different form, for he blinded his son ; Phoinix

---

[70] See further Pickard-Cambridge, *op. cit.*, p. 148 *sqq.*
[70a] See Addenda, p. 422.

also was the innocent victim of slander, and was in the end healed by Cheiron.[71] The *Phrixos* seems to have been revised and brought out a second time ; at all events, the scholiast on Aristophanes identifies a quotation from it as belonging to the second version.[72] The evidence as to what portion of the adventures of Phrixos it treated is somewhat uncertain.[73] The *Chrysippos* dealt with the same subject as Aeschylus' *Laios* (see p. 150).

Here, quite suddenly, the history of Tragedy as an important literary *genre* ends. With Sophokles and Euripides dead, Aristophanes makes Dionysos complain, some of the poets are gone and the rest worthless.[74] The new impetus Euripides had given to drama lived and presently proved that it was active ; but it found an outlet in another sphere, that of Comedy, as the next chapter will show.

The only other name of real importance, so far as can be judged, is that of AGATHON, whose person is well known to us from Aristophanes and Plato. The former makes broad fun of his somewhat effeminate beauty and his dandified ways, but gives no indication that his poetry was contemptible ; indeed, he says, with a pun on his name, that he was a good (ἀγαθός) writer.[75] The latter puts the scene of the *Symposium* (see p. 266) at his house, and treats him with affectionate humour throughout. We learn from Aristotle that he used the chorus very loosely, merely to provide a sort of incidental music between the episodes ; also, that in one play at least, the *Antheus*, he invented the whole plot. We know from another source what the plot was ; a romantic tale, of the same type as that of Joseph and Potiphar's wife, ending in the death of the young man, Antheus, by the woman's contrivance.[76] The few fragments that survive of him show a pretty, polished style, rather too full of the rhetorical devices of Gorgias and his school (see p. 279), which is exactly how Plato represents him as speaking when he delivers a formal oration. It would seem therefore that he developed along the lines Euripides had laid down and went somewhat further. He

[71] This version of the story is in the so-called Apollodóros, iii, 175 ; that it is Euripidean is indicated by several allusions to it elsewhere, for which see Nauck, p. 621.

[72] Schol. Ar., *Frogs*, 1225.

[73] Hyginus, *fab.* 4, claims to be giving the story as Euripides tells it, but for his evidential value see note 59, and in any case the play he mentions is, if any, the *Ino*.

[74] *Frogs*, 71–2.   [75] Ar., *Thesm.*, 33 *sqq.* ; *Frogs*, 83–4.

[76] Arist., *Poet.*, 1456ᵃ 29 ; 1451ᵇ 20, where he uses the *Antheus* to prove that it is not necessary to use traditional stories to compose a successful tragedy ; Parthenios. ἐρωτ. παθ. 14, not directly from Agathon but citing ' Aristotle and the writers of the Milesian Tales '. But see p. 213.

was an Athenian by birth, and his first victory was in 416, at the Lenaia ; [77] in 407 he, like Euripides, accepted an invitation from Archelaos to Macedonia, and in that country he would seem to have ended his days.[78]

Of the rest, we know a number of names and little else ; for example, THEOGNIS is represented for us by three contemptuous references in Aristophanes and one quotation of two words.[79] The art of Tragedy seems to have been to some extent hereditary, a natural thing enough if we remember that only a man of some means could make a name as a tragedian, since the composition of any considerable number of plays must have needed much time and could bring no reward in anything but reputation. Aeschylus was the ancestor of a whole line of poets. One son, BION or EUAION, is said to have composed tragedies, but we know nothing of him ; the other, EUPHORION, according to Suidas won four victories with unpublished works of his father (it seems more likely that they were revivals) and also wrote plays of his own ; he was victorious over Sophokles and Euripides in 431.[80] Aeschylus' sister had a son PHILOKLES, whose works can hardly have been worthless, for he won the prize over Sophokles' *Oedipus Tyrannus*.[81] His son was called MORSIMOS, and essayed Tragedy also, though Aristophanes speaks of him with utter contempt.[82] Morsimos became the father of yet another tragic poet, ASTYDAMAS by name, and Astydamas of a second ASTYDAMAS and another PHILOKLES, thus carrying on the line well into the fourth century. Sophokles also had a son, called IOPHON, who won the second prize when Euripides' *Hippolytus* was awarded the first ; Aristophanes expresses doubt of his ability to do much without the help of his father,[83] and from what we can hear of him, we have no reason to suppose that he was a very great poet, or to believe the strange statement that the *Antigone* was his work.[84] But we have only four lines and a half left of him. Sophokles had also an illegitimate son, by name ARISTON, who may have been a tragedian and certainly became the father of one, SOPHOKLES THE YOUNGER.[85] As already mentioned, Euripides had a son, and also a nephew, of the same name as himself, if indeed the two are not really one ; at all

[77] Athenaios, 217 a, ὁ μὲν γὰρ (sc. ᾿Αγάθων) ἐπὶ ἄρχοντος Εὐφήμου (417–16) στεφανοῦται Ληναίοις.

[78] Schol. on Ar., *Frogs*, 85.　　[79] Ar., *Acharn.*, 11, 140 ; *Thesm.*, 170.

[80] Suidas *s.uu.* Αἰσχύλος, Εὐφορίων, Φιλοκλῆς ; arg. Eurip. *Med.*

[81] Argum. Soph. *Oed. Tyr.* ; see Jebb's *Introduction* to his edition, p. xxii.

[82] Ar., *Knights*, 401 ; *Peace*, 801 ; *Frogs*, 151.

[83] Arg. Eur. *Hipp.* ; Ar., *Frogs*, 73–9 ; Suid., *s.u.* ᾿Ιοφῶν.

[84] This seems to be the meaning of a corrupt passage in Cramer's *Anecdota Oxoniensia*, iv, p. 315, 22.

[85] Suid., *s.u.* ᾿Ιοφῶν, mentions Ariston, and Diog. Laert., vii, 164, says that there was a tragic poet of that name, but not that he was Sophokles' son. For the younger Sophokles, see Suid., *s.u.* Σοφοκλῆς ἐξ ᾿Αρίστωνος.

events, a younger EURIPIDES produced the posthumous work of the elder and wrote a few plays himself.[86]

Rather more important than these was ION OF CHIOS, a man of considerable ability and varied talent ; as a playwright, we gather from the so-called Longinus (see p. 123) he was to Sophokles what Bakchylides was to Pindar. He also wrote a book of memoirs, from which sundry anecdotes concerning celebrated men of that day still survive in the works of later writers ; a historical work on the foundation of Chios ; a philosophical treatise, the Τριαγμοί or Τριαγμός ; besides trying his hand at elegies and dithyrambs.[87] He was born early enough in the century to be acquainted with Kimon and Aeschylus, produced his first plays in the eighty-second Olympiad (452–49) and was dead when Aristophanes wrote his *Peace* (see p. 234).[88] Another foreigner of some repute was ACHAIOS OF ERETRIA, born in the seventy-fourth Olympiad (484–1), and therefore somewhat younger than Sophokles. His satyr-plays were well thought of, with how much justice we cannot tell from the little that is left.[89] But a whole family of poets had, or came to have, foreign connexions. The father, KARKINOS, was *strategos* in 431. His son, XENOKLES, of whom Aristophanes has not a good word to say, contrived to defeat Euripides in 415 (cf. Aelian, cited p. 187, n. 24) ; Xenokles in turn became the father of a second KARKINOS, who enjoyed the favour of Dionysios the Younger of Syracuse and was apparently a very prolific writer ;[90] his son was another XENOKLES and likewise wrote tragedies. It is rather more remarkable that so backward a district as Arkadia produced a tragedian, ARISTARCHOS OF TEGEA, a contemporary of Euripides. His *Achilles* was famous enough in later times to be translated or imitated in Latin by Ennius.[91]

[86] For Euripides' family, see note 1.

[87] References to ancient and modern literature concerning him in Schmid-Stählin I, ii, 514–20. His prose fragments are in *F.H.G.*, ii, pp. 44–51 ; for his elegies, see Athen., 436 f ; dithyrambs, arg. Soph. *Ant.* ; philosophical work, in Diels, i, p. 220.

[88] *Peace*, 835, indicates clearly that Ion was dead at that time.

[89] So one gathers from the fact that nearly all the extant quotations are taken from them. For his date, see Suidas *s.u.* Ἀχαιός.

[90] The chief sources of information are the relevant articles in Suidas, which draw largely on commentaries upon Aristophanes, and the scholia on Aristophanes themselves. That one of the family lived at Akragas we know from Suidas, but he does not specify which one ; that Karkinos the elder was strategos in 431 is known from Thucyd., ii, 23, 2.

[91] Suidas says he and Euripides were contemporaries (*s.u.* Ἀρίσταρχος Τεγεάτης), and adds the curious information that he ' gave plays their present length '. What is meant by ' present ' (νῦν) we do not know, since his source cannot be named, but probably it is a Hellenistic writer, who meant that Aristarchos' plays were rather short ; cf. the *Rhesos* (p. 212), which has but 996 lines, while the average play of Sophokles has about 1470. Eusebios' Chronicle makes him ' known ' as early as 453, possibly the date of his first victory. For Ennius' rendering of him, see Ribbeck, *Tragicorum Romanorum fragmenta*.

With the passing of the fifth century Tragedy enters upon a new phase, tending towards closet-drama ; we hear indeed of plays composed primarily for reading, not acting (Aristotle speaks of their composers as ἀναγνωστικοί, reading-authors).[92] We may perhaps name KRITIAS, the philosophical politician who has the honourable distinction of having been a friend of Sokrates and the less honourable one of being a member of the notorious Thirty who governed Athens for a short time after the Peloponnesian War, as marking a transition to this style. There survives a long passage from his *Sisyphos* which is simply popular philosophy put into indifferent verse, and contains an exposition of the doctrine that religion began as a device of government for the overawing of the unruly. That some of his plays, however, had dramatic value is clear enough from the fact already mentioned that some considered the *Peirithoos* to be his composition. A rather mysterious name is that of NEOPHRON. We are informed that some considered Euripides to have plagiarized the *Medea* from a work of his with the same title ; but if we examine the fragments surviving, the suspicious circumstance comes to light that one embodies a formal improvement, remedying a defect pointed out by Aristotle.[93] If there ever was any such person as this Neophron (the very name is a little dubious ; is it more than ' The New Idea ' ?), he probably came well after Euripides, not before him, and tried his hand at improving a play already on its way to be classical. That his *Medea* was ever acted we have no evidence. THEODEKTES, to judge by what Aristotle says of him and the fragments that survive, was at least a very respectable rhetorician and could devise a plausible argument.[94] CHAIREMON was something of a poet ; there are two very pretty fragments of him, suggestive of good Alexandrian love-poetry, describing the beauty of women. A notable, if unsuccessful amateur of the fourth century was DIONYSIOS THE YOUNGER, tyrant of Syracuse. An interesting testimony to the purely literary nature which Tragedy was assuming is furnished by the fact that two notable philosophers, both Cynics, DIOGENES OF SINOPE and KRATES, occasionally wrote it. We catch an echo of this sort of composition in the Latin tragedies of Seneca the younger, a curious mixture of rhetoric, sensationalism and popularized Stoic philosophy.

More important to us than these writers and a number of

[92] Arist., *Rhet.*, 1413[b] 12 *sqq.*, instancing Chairemon.

[93] Arist., *Poet.*, 1461[b] 19 says it is blameworthy for a poet to introduce an unnecessary irrational element, ' as Euripides does in his Aigeus ' ; the reference seems to be to the fact that Aigeus in the *Medea* arrives at Corinth for no particular reason except that Euripides needs him for his plot. In Neophron, frag. I, preserved in the scholiast on the *Medea*, 666, he is given a good reason for coming ; he wishes to submit a riddling oracle to her known wisdom for solution.

[94] Aristotle, who quotes him several times, uses him, *Rhet.* 1401[a] 35, to furnish an example of how two correct statements may be put together into a plausible, but not necessarily true or just argument.

others of whom we have a few lines or a reference in Aristophanes, Aristotle or some later author is the chief anonymous survival from the fourth century, the *Rhesus*. It is quite unknown who wrote it ; it came to be ascribed to Euripides and has been pre-served under his name, but formal and aesthetic grounds alike forbid us to suppose it his. Formally, it is a mixture, for it opens with an anapaestic passage, a dialogue between the sen-tinels of the Trojan camp and Hektor, reminiscent of the manner in which the *Iphigenia in Aulide* begins, but its trimeters have not the loose rhythm of the later Euripidean work.[95] The language also is more like Euripides than any other author, but every here and there departs from his manner and vocabulary. Aesthetically, while not a bad melodrama and quite actable, it is not good enough for Euripides, especially in the important matter of character-drawing ; Hektor and the other heroes bluster at each other in a thrasonic style totally unworthy of a master of his standing. The plot is taken from the tenth book of the Iliad (see p. 19). Hektor, after some discussion with Aineias, resolves to send a scout to discover if the Greeks are really sailing away, as he supposes ; Dolon volunteers, and after his departure a messenger announces the approach of Rhesos with a strong force of Thracians. Hektor receives him ungra-ciously, saying that he should have come long ago, before the fighting was so nearly over ; he retorts by undertaking to end the war in one day. After a little more discussion between them, and the passage across the orchestra of the two halves of the chorus, representing two patrols, Odysseus and Diomedes enter, having caught Dolon and got the password from him. They are about to leave the camp when Athena appears and guides them to Rhesos' lines ; there follows a very lively scene, in which Paris raises the alarm, but is quieted by Athena, pretending to be Aphrodite, and after his departure the guards nearly catch Odys-seus, who bluffs his way out of their hands. Rhesos' charioteer now enters with the news that his master is killed, and furious recriminations from all concerned, in which Hektor takes a noisy part, are stopped by the entry of Rhesos' mother, one of the

---

[95] About 7 per cent. of the lines contain resolved feet ; of these, approximately half are accounted for by proper names and the unavoid-able word πολέμιος. But for these, the play would have about the rhythm of the *Medea* (3·7 per cent.). The only real argument I have ever seen in favour of the genuineness of the play is the statement of the ὑπόθεσις that ἐν ταῖς διδασκαλίαις ὡς γνήσιον ἀναγέγραπται ; from which I would conclude, not that Euripides really wrote a *Rhesos*, which was lost early and this play somehow mistaken for it, but simply that the Didask-aliai were wrong on this point. See Haigh, *Drama*, p. 284.

Muses, who wails over and carries off the body of her son, promising him a sort of immortality in a cave on Mount Pangaion.

With this curious piece we may take leave of Tragedy. It never appeared again as a living species of literature ; but something of it survives, not so much in the neo-classic drama which imagined that it reproduced its form, as in those plays, by authors as different from one another as Shakespere and Ibsen, which in their own varying manners have re-interpreted its spirit.

ADDITIONAL NOTE (see Note 76)

S. M. Pitcher, in *Amer. Journ. Phil.*, lx (1939), p. 145 *sqq.*, would connect Agathon's play rather with the story of Anthos, for which see Antoninus Liberalis, 7.

For further information on tragic fragments, see D. L. Page, *Greek Literary Papyri I* (Loeb Library, No. 360).

CHAPTER VIII

COMEDY

THE origins of Comedy, the last of the great species of poetry given by Greece to the world, are fully as obscure as those of Tragedy. We know the following facts, which are plainly insufficient to tell us, in the absence of documents covering the sixth century, how Comedy reached the form known to us from Aristophanes, but enable us to make a fairly reasonable guess at what may have happened.[1]

Both literary and archaeological evidence show that it was a custom in early times at Athens and the smaller towns and villages of Attica to engage in a performance known as a *komos*, or band of revelling dancers and singers, who often wore grotesque disguises, including masks, &c., representing beasts or birds. This was not mere merry-making, at least not regularly or normally so ; rather was it a religious ceremony of a joyous type. The mummers, if we may call them so, were honouring deities of fertility, and especially, it would seem, the greatest and most popular of such divinities, Dionysos himself. It was the opinion of Aristotle that Comedy originated from the leaders of these processions or dances, which he calls *phallika*, because they regularly carried large images of the male organ of reproduction, the phallos.[2] That such people had anything like dialogue or dramatic representation of any kind as part of their performance, in Attica, we are not told, though it is not an unlikely thing in itself that they had.

In Sparta there were certain mummers called *deikelistai*, who dressed in costumes including comic clay masks, some of which have been found during excavations there, and acted little farces dealing with everyday life, *e.g.*, a thief robbing an orchard,

---

[1] The references for these statements are so completely and conveniently given in Pickard-Cambridge, *Dithyramb*, Chap. iii, that I give only a few of the most important in these notes.

[2] Arist., *Poet.*, 1449ᵃ 11.

or a foreign doctor talking an absurd jargon.[3] In Magna Graecia similar things existed, notably at Taras (Tarentum), where the actors in such little pieces were called *phlyakes*. There can be little doubt that the mime (see pp. 252, 339) developed out of this sort of performance, and it may very well be that Epicharmos (see p. 250) was but giving literary form to their Syracusan equivalent. Other Dorian cities seem to have had a similar custom, and in particular, the Megarians claimed to have had a sort of Comedy long before any such thing was known, or at all events before it had public recognition, in Athens. It is noteworthy that the few alleged fragments of Megarian pieces [4] are in iambics, the usual metre of Attic dramatic dialogue, tragic or comic. Thebes again had some such mummings, the actors in them being called simply volunteers or amateurs (ἐθελονταί), but we know nothing of the date at which these began.[5]

At Sekyon there was a somewhat different custom. A *komos*, to use the familiar Attic word, known simply as phallos-bearers, used to enter the theatre, or, before regular theatres were built, some other convenient place of assembly, and make a little speech (the text as we have it is in iambics) in honour of Dionysos, after which they ran forward towards the spectators and made jokes at them.[6] This is distinctly suggestive of the *parabasis* of Attic Comedy, to be presently described. Other performances of a somewhat similar kind are reported elsewhere in Greece.

It is thus clear that there may have been in Attica a native custom of acting a sort of little play, interspersed with plenty of personalities and with songs and hymns, at country festivals in honour of agricultural deities.[7] Or, if this was not so, at least there was the custom of guising, to use the English term, in other words of 'dressing up' and performing traditional absurdities, which were liked by the common people, partly because they were good fun and partly, in all probability, because they were also good ritual, likely to promote the beneficent activities of the powers from whom came the food supply. In addition, there were the plays of the Theban 'volunteers' and their

[3] Sosibios (*c.* 300 B.C.), *ap.* Athen., 621 d, e.

[4] See Kock, i, p. 3 *sq.* As the lines we have are in Attic, not Megarian Doric, it is clear that they are at best an imitation of the Megarian style, if not simply forgeries of comparatively late date.

[5] Athenaios, *ibid.*, f.

[6] Semos of Delos (? about 200 B.C.), *ap.* Athen., 622 c, d.

[7] I have attempted to reconstruct the outlines of these hypothetical plays, on a basis of the elements regularly found in existing comedies and therefore likely to be traditional, *Jubilee Congress of the Folk-Lore Society* (London, Glaisher, 1928), pp. 113-21.

Megarian equivalents, just over the border either way, and it would need much less sharp wits than those in Attica to think of combining the native merry-making with some imported fun, and thus getting a combination of *komos*-song (κωμῳδία, Comedy) with rather formless drama. Sooner or later an artist was sure to arise who should give this something like a plot and some sort of unity, by making one absurd idea run through the whole piece from beginning to end, however many digressions he might allow or his audience call for.

If we ask the name of this artist, tradition seems to say that he was called SUSARION and that he was a Megarian. The Parian Chronicle, in a battered but fairly intelligible passage, says [8] that the people of Ikaria, one of the country districts (*demoi*) of Attica, were the first to have a comic chorus, that is to say a regular performance of Comedy, that Susarion was the inventor, and that the prize offered was a basket of dried figs and a *metretes* (39.39 litres) of wine. How much truth there is in this we do not know ; the date, which has disappeared on the marble, must have been somewhere between 582 and 560 B.C. After this time, supposing the Chronicle to be reliable, comes a period of which we know nothing, but may suppose that Comedy was growing in popularity and taking more literary shape ; we hear of it as a regular and established entertainment, admitted like Tragedy to compete at (presumably) the Great Dionysia, in 488/7, when the prize was awarded to a certain CHIONIDES,[9] a misty figure enough, of whom we have the titles of four plays and a few small fragments, already showing the unmistakable flavour of Attic wit. Then come a few more names, preserved for us for the most part in a famous passage of Aristophanes,[10] in which he reviews his predecessors in Comedy and blames the public for the shabby treatment they had met with when their day of popularity was over. MAGNES, says Aristophanes, won more victories at Comedy than any one else had ever done ; we know little of them, but later scholarship had records of eleven, with the titles of some nine plays by this author.[11] His most notable characteristic seems to have been a fertile and fantastic variety of costuming ; ' he twanged his harps and he flapped his

[8] Mar. Par. 39.

[9] Suidas, *s.u. Χιωνίδης*, says that he was the πρωταγωνιστής (no doubt, as Wilamowitz and Pickard-Cambridge have seen, a mistake for πρῶτος ἀγωνιστής, first competitor) in Comedy and that he put on a play ' eight years before the Persian Wars '.

[10] *Knights*, 520 *sqq.*

[11] Eleven victories, the record of comic poets in *I.G.*, ii, 977 ; Suidas, *s.u. Μάγνης*, says two, and mentions the nine plays.

wings, he played the Lydian and he played the gall-fly and he
dyed himself frog-green '.   A scholiast on the passage explains
that Magnes wrote plays called *Harp-Players* (Βαρβιτισταί), *Birds*,
Gall-Flies (Ψῆνες), *Frogs* and *Lydians*, doubtless referring in all
cases to the costume of the chorus ; we shall find two of these
titles again in Aristophanes. ◦That he was a native of Ikaria,
which as we have seen was an early home of Comedy, and that
he was a younger contemporary of Epicharmos we also learn
from Suidas ; the scholiast as we have him has lost this bit of
information.   Another extract, manifestly from the same source,
tells us that the *Lydians* survived for a while in a revised form,
perhaps intended for some revival of the play in the fourth century or later ; [12] while Athenaios speaks of plays ' attributed to
Magnes '.[13]   It would seem therefore that only an occasional
stage-copy of what he wrote came into the hands of the Alexandrians, and even these were few and doubtful.   As to his date,
Aristophanes in 425 remembered him as an old man, which fits
well with his having won a victory in 472.[14]

A mistier figure still is that ' very ancient writer ' EKPHANTIDES,
of whom scarcely anything is left.   He won four victories at the Great
Dionysia, and he seems to have been alive and writing in the last
third of the century.   Everything else is conjecture.[15]

Far more important is KRATINOS, the next in Aristophanes'
list, who seems to have been piqued by that poet's inclusion of
him among the writers of the past.   At all events, he produced,
the next year, a play which defeated Aristophanes' *Clouds*, this
being one of a total of nine victories, six at the Great Dionysia
and three at the Lenaia, which he won during his career as a
playwright.   He was old enough to have supported Kimon and
attacked Perikles ; hence he was active about the middle of the
century, for the latter of these statesmen put forward and carried,
in 456, a motion to recall the former from exile.   This agrees
very well with the date, 453, which Eusebios' chronicle gives for
his first appearance in the theatre.   His views, so far as we can
reconstruct them from our inadequate knowledge, were so like

[12] Hesychios *s.u.* λυδίζων.   Photios *s.u.* λυδιάζων (*sic*) seems to have
a mutilated excerpt from the same source.

[13] Athen., 646 a, Μάγνης ἤ ὁ ποιήσας τὰς εἰς αὐτὸν ἀναφερομένας κωμῳδίας.

[14] *I.G.*, ii, 971, col. 3, 2 ; the inscription gives a list of victors at the
Great Dionysia, in chronological order.

[15] παλαιότατος, schol. on Arist., *Eth. Nic.*, *Comment in Arist. Graec.*,
vol. xx, p. 186, 17 (Heylbut) ; victories, inscr. cited in note 11 ; date,
he attacked the demagogue Androkles, who was also attacked by
Aristophanes and contemporaries of his, schol. Ar. *Wasps* 1187.

those of Aristophanes himself that they need not be stated here.
In private life, one leading characteristic of him was his fondness
for wine.   Ill fortune and the arbitrary selection by late antiquity
of one comedian only to read and study have robbed us of every
play he wrote.   These, according to Suidas, numbered twenty-
one ; [16] we know twenty-six titles of works attributed to him,
without being in a position to decide whether Suidas drew upon
an incomplete list (those entered for the Great Dionysia, for
instance) or some of the plays we hear of were spurious.   That
he was an excellent comedian we may well believe, on the strength
of Aristophanes' commendation of him, [17] supported by such
fragments as we have.   By his day, that form of Comedy which,
following the ancient critics, we class as Old had taken definite
shape, and we know exactly from Aristophanes what that shape
was.   In the first part of the play, something happens which
produces a grotesque situation, the more topsy-turvy the better.
This done, the chorus turns to the audience (the movement is
technically known as a *parabasis*) and addresses them.   The
parabasis has a regular form, and it has been noted that the same
form is to be found in many scenes of Comedy. [18]   First comes a
' tag ' (κομμάτιον) of anapaests, to get the characters off the
stage and leave the theatre to the chorus.   Now follows the
parabasis proper, often called ' the anapaests ', because it is,
more often than not, in that metre. [19]   This, if in anapaests,
regularly ends with a bit of patter, delivered at full speed and
appropriately called the πνῖγος (choker).   Now follows the Ode,
a more or less serious, and often beautiful, hymn to some deity.
Then comes the *epirrheme*, another address to the audience,
often, indeed characteristically, in trochaic tetrameters.   An
antode, the antistrophe of which the ode is the strophe, [20] succeeds,
and is followed by the *antepirrheme*, which is of the same length
and in the same metre as the *epirrheme*.   Sometimes one or more
of these members is omitted, but the above is the full form.
The *parabasis* being over, there commonly follows a string of
farcical scenes, showing the results of the comic revolution brought
about in the first half of the play ; these sometimes form, however, a kind of second act, following upon one another with some

---

[16] Suid., *s.u.* Κρατῖνος.   *See* p. 423.   [17] Ar., *Frogs*, 357.

[18] By Zielinski, *Gliederung der altattischen Komödie*.   Such a complex
is technically called an epirrhematic syzygy. See Pickard-Cambridge,
Dithyramb, App. A ;   Norwood, *Comedy*, p. 6, n. 2.

[19] The comedians, and especially Aristophanes, commonly use a long
line, having precisely the rhythm of the air (not the words) of the *Vicar
of Bray*.   This is often employed for dialogue also

[20] See p. 110.

regularity and developing, not merely illustrating and commenting upon, the situation. Regularly, though not always, these
scenes lead up to a feast, marriage procession, or other form of
merry-making.

The farcical situation may be brought about in two ways. It
may arise out of burlesque mythology, not unlike a satyr-play
but apparently with this difference, that in a satyr-drama the
heroic characters preserve a certain dignity, ' Tragedy behaves
like a lady obliged to join in holiday jiggings ', says Horace ; [21]
while in Comedy of this type, all alike might play the fool heartily.
We have no such play left entire, but possess an abstract of one
by Kratınos, the *Dionysalexandros*.[22] In this farce, which must
have been extremely amusing, Alexandros son of Priam, better
known as Paris, was called upon to judge between the three
goddesses. Thus far orthodox mythology ; but it would appear
that Kratinos' Alexandros took fright and fairly ran before the
celestial beauties ; then, after an interlude, presumably a *parabasis*, in which a chorus of satyrs addressed the audience, Dionysos
appeared, took the form and the duties of Paris, gave his verdict
in favour of Aphrodite, and sailed off to Greece to get his reward,
in the shape of Helen.[23] Returning with her, he was appalled
by the news that the Greek army was in the country. Hastily
turning himself into a ram and Helen into a goose,[24] he hid her
in a basket. Now the real Paris entered, penetrated the disguises, and after some parley kept Helen for himself, but handed
over Dionysos and the whole chorus with him to the mercies of
the Greeks.

The author of the epitome adds the information that Perikles
was attacked very convincingly in this play, though only by
innuendo. The absence of direct attack would not be due to any
considerations of chronology, which a Greek minded even less
than the average Elizabethan in works of the imagination, but
to Perikles' immense personal influence and the fact that the
Peloponnesian War had begun. One point that strikes a modern
as extraordinary is the utter lack of respect shown, here and
elsewhere, to the gods. It should be remembered that this does
not signify any lack of belief in them, or even of reverence for

[21] Horace, *ars poet.*, 232, *ut festis matrona moueri iussa diebus.*
[22] *Oxyr. Pap.*, 663 = Demiańczuk, pp. 31–3.
[23] The modern unities of Time and Place troubled tragedians little
and comedians less.
[24] Or merely pretending that she was a goose ; the Greek has ὦσπ
. . . κρύψας, and —ερ χῆνα is the ingenious supplement of Koerte for
the lost letters ; the divine swan's daughter might well become a goose
in burlesque.

them. To throw off, at stated times, some or all customary restraints is a wholesome usage, psychologically quite justified, which has come down from primitive times and was in full force in the best ages of antiquity.[25] The Dionysiac festivals were such occasions, and to make all manner of ribald fun of the very god in whose honour the plays were produced was but to honour him the more by entering into the spirit of the rite.

Another equally popular form of Comedy had no mythological content at all, however travestied, but took for its central figure either a typical imaginary Athenian or some well-known man of the day. The ridiculous complications were quite as certain to follow either way, but what they were depended wholly on the poet's powers of imagination ; there were apparently no stock patterns for him to follow, so long as he was sufficiently absurd. Hence it is that to reconstruct a lost comedy from its fragments is generally impossible, unless we have something to guide us as to the general drift of the plot. Even then it is much harder than in the case of a tragedy, for there the title will often furnish a synopsis in itself ; a *Philoktetes* for example will almost certainly deal with the happenings on Lemnos, or the incidents which preceded or followed them.[26]

Whatever the precise form of the play, political satire was commonly present in one shape or another, and might include the most outrageous attacks on prominent men. The importance of these has often been exaggerated in modern times, and indeed also in later antiquity, just as the burlesqued gods have been taken to imply a blasphemous spirit in the comedians and their audience.[27] To some extent they also imply a ceremonial release from restraint ; at the same time they may be taken to have fulfilled much the same function as the modern caricature ; they were, that is to say, a ready and welcome means of ' sniping ' at political opponents. Now and then a politician would lose his

[25] For an admirable exposition of this, see R. R. Marett, *Sacraments of Simple Folk* (Oxford. Clar. Press, 1933), p. 184 *sqq.*

[26] Hence the humorous contention of Antiphanes, frag. 191 Kock, that Comedy is much harder to write than Tragedy, since the latter starts with a ready-made set of characters, while the former has to invent everything, without a *deus ex machina* to help at a difficulty.

[27] For an ancient example of the latter misunderstanding, see Aspasios' commentary on Arist., *Eth. Nic.* (second century A.D.), p. 125, 20 Heylbut ; the older comedians, out of sheer βωμολοχία (vulgar, unrestrained jesting) made fun even of the gods ; for the former, the story known and denounced as fictitious by Cicero, *ad Att.*, vi, 1, 18, on the authority of Eratosthenes, that Alkibiades drowned Eupolis for satirizing him in the *Baptai*. The tale is still repeated, for instance, by Platonios, Dübner, p. xiii, 24–26.

temper and strike back; thus Kleon, in annoyance at Aristophanes' lampoons against him, brought suit against the comedian, probably on the stock charge of being of foreign origin,[28] and there is some evidence that for a short time a law against attacking any one by name in Comedy (μὴ κωμῳδεῖν ὀνομαστί) was in force; it lasted, if it ever existed, but two years.[29] In general, little offence was taken, and we may be fairly sure that in many cases none was meant. It was a mean creature who would try to take revenge on the comedians because he had been 'made sport of in the ancestral rites of Dionysos', says Aristophanes.[30]

The butts of the jokes were not always politicians by any means. We have Aristophanes' admirable *Clouds* directed against Sokrates as the sophist *par excellence*;[31] there is reason to suppose that Kratinos' *Panoptai* was an attack on Hippon of Rhegion, in the same capacity.[32] Literature also came in for its share; again to illustrate from Kratinos, the *Archilochoi* seems to have brought back that formidable satirist (see p. 89) from the dead and either to have multiplied him to, or have provided him with, a chorus of attendants like-minded with himself. The object of his outspoken criticism was perhaps epic poetry, in part at least, for some of the surviving fragments are in hexameters and one mentions a 'swarm of sophists', which we happen to know meant poets here.[33] Aristophanes therefore had plenty of good precedent for the *Thesmophoriazusae* and the *Frogs*.

The theatre in which these plays were performed was the same as that used for Tragedy, and it would appear that the machinery for having a play approved for performance was the same also. Comedy had nothing corresponding to the tetralogy, however, each poet of the three admitted to compete entering one play, which was acted in the evening, after one of the tragedians had put on his contribution. The actors naturally did not wear the tragic costume, but there is a very fair amount of evidence that they used one of their own, grotesquely padded to give a mis-

[28] See note 74.
[29] Schol. Ar., *Acharn.*, 67 says that such a law was passed in the archonship of Morychides, 440/39 B.C., was in force the next two years and was repealed under Euthymenes (438/7). For other alleged laws of the same type, see Norwood, *Comedy*, p. 26 *sqq*.
[30] *Frogs*, 366–7.
[31] He is still Σωκράτης ὁ σοφιστής in Aischines, i, 173, the best part of a century later.
[32] See Kratinos, frag. 155 Kock.
[33] Krat., frag. 2 Kock, quoted and explained by Clement of Alexandria, *Strom.*, i, 24 (p. 329 Pott.).

shapen figure, with huge belly or rump, or both, and generally decorated in front with a great leather phallos.[34] As we have already seen, the costume of the chorus varied with the author's fancy, and no doubt also with the amount the choregos could be induced to spend. Its number is commonly said to have been twenty-four ; but Aristophanes, in a well-known passage in which he enumerates his chorus and mentions the dress of each member (the plumage of a different species of bird) brings them to a total of twenty-eight.[35] I would conclude, since his evidence outweighs all other in such a case, that the comic chorus was regularly double the number of the tragic, i.e., twenty-four or thirty, presumably at different dates. As in the case of Tragedy, its importance declined as time went on, till from being the all-important *komos* to which everything else was accessory, it became, by Menander's day, a mere band of dancers, who may have sung but had no words written for them by the poet and nothing to do with the plot. The beginning of this is already to be seen in Aristophanes' later work.[36]

What we can learn of Kratinos' work from the surviving fragments is briefly this. He wrote, besides the *Archilochoi* already mentioned, the *Βουκόλοι* (*Herdsmen*) of which we know nothing ; the *Busiris*, no doubt dealing with Herakles' Egyptian adventure (cf. p. 203) ; the *Women of Delos* (*Δηλιάδες*), of unknown plot ; the *Didaskaliai* (was this an anticipation of *The Rehearsal* ?) ; the *Dionysalexandros*, already discussed ; the *Runaways* (*Δραπέτιδες* ; the form of the word shows that they were women, but what the play was about is a matter of doubtful conjecture) ; the *Ἐμπιμπράμενοι*, otherwise called the *Ἰδαῖοι* ; who were ' set on fire ' or why, what they were doing on either the Cretan or the Trojan Ida and even whether the play existed at all are matters beyond our knowledge.[37] Of the *Euneidai* we know a little more ; it presumably had a mythological content, for the Euneidai are the descendants of Euneos son of Jason and

[34] The evidence, literary and archaeological, is collected by Haigh, *Theatre*, pp. 257 *sqq.*, 290 *sqq.* ; Pickard-Cambridge, *Dithyramb*, Chap. iii.

[35] Ar., *Birds*, 268 *sqq.* ; the schol. on 297 supposes that only 24 of the persons enumerated belonged to the chorus, the rest being presumably *παραχορηγήματα*. This is the merest special pleading. Besides this note, the schol. on *Acharn.*, 219, supported by Pollux, iv, 109 and other passages (see Haigh, *op. cit.*, p. 289, n. 5) all give 24.

[36] *Eccl.* and *Plut.*, besides a few choral songs, have several times merely the direction *χοροῦ*, i.e., ' (performance) of the chorus '. This is not uncommon in Menander.

[37] Schol. Ar., *Thesm.*, 215 and Clement of Alexandria, *Strom.*, vi, 26 (pp. 751–2 Pott.) say vaguely that Aristophanes borrowed from this play. We know nothing about it and can only conjecture where these late writers got their information.

Hypsipyle ; Aristophanes mentions two songs, *Our Lady Bribery shod
with fig* (Δωροῖ συκοπέδιλε, a parody of the Homeric phrase "Ηρη
χρυσοπέδιλος) and *Craftsmen of chants so deftly wrought* (τέκτονες
εὐπαλάμων ὕμνων) as having been extremely popular,[38] and his scholiast
explains that they came from this play. The Θρᾷτται (*Thracian
Women*, probably meaning Thracian slave-girls) contained one famous
passage which described Perikles as ' the squill-headed Zeus ' and
credited him with wearing the Odeion (as we might say, the Albert
Hall ; it was a large domed building intended for musical performances)
on his head, an allusion to his immense influence and at the same
time to the peculiar shape of his skull, which he disguised by commonly
wearing a helmet.[39] The *Kleobulinai* seems to have had a literary
subject, for the Kleobulina in question (Plutarch says her real name
was Eumetis) had a reputation for her skill in composing riddles.[40]
There may have been a play called *Lakones* ; [41] there certainly was
one entitled Μαλθακοί, *i.e.*, *The Softies*. The *Nemesis* was again
mythological in content ; the title does not mean Retribution, but is
the name of a local deity of Rhamnus in Attica, who being visited
by Zeus in bird-form laid the divine egg from which Helen was
produced. One fragment shows the egg being handed over to Leda,
with explicit directions to sit on it like a hen until it hatches. In
the *Laws* (Νόμοι) there may have been a chorus of personified statutes,
shown as old men ; certainly one scene brought forward certain
venerable persons leaning on staffs. The *Odysses* (plural of Odysseus ;
here as with the similar titles *Archilochoi* and *Kleobulinai* the plural
may mean ' O. and his companions ') dealt with the same subject
as Euripides' *Cyclops* (see p. 199). The *Panoptai* (*See-alls*) has already
been mentioned ; perhaps there was a chorus of philosophers. The
Plutoi (these ' Wealths ' are the ' wealth-giving daimones' of Hesiodic tradition, see *W.D.*, 121) is one of many plays which told of
a blissful Land of Cocaigne, where all manner of good food was to
be had ready-cooked for the taking ; but in this case it was not a
country but a time, the Golden Age. The *Pylaia* must have had
something to do with the meeting of the Amphiktyonic League at
Thermopylai. The Πυτίνη (*Wicker bottle*), the comedy which defeated
the *Clouds* and was probably the last play its author ever wrote, told
of the domestic sorrows of Kratinos, who had deserted his true wife

---

[38] Ar., *Knights*, 529–20 and the schol. there. The ' fig-tree shoes ',
like most mentions of figs in Comedy, are an allusion to that ever-present
plague in litigious Athens, the sycophant or informer.

[39] Frag. 71, quoted by Plut., *Perikles* 13, see *ibid.*, 5.

[40] Plut., *sept. sap. conuiuium*, 148 d ; she was said to be the daughter
of Kleobulos of Lindos, one of the Seven Sages, Diog. Laert., i, 89.

[41] Clement of Alexandria says, *Strom.*, vi, 5, p. 738 Pott., Κρατῖνος
δὲ ἐν τοῖς Λάκωσι φοβερὸν ἀνθρώποις τόδ᾿ αὖ, κταμένοις ἐπ᾿ αἰζηοῖσι καυχᾶσθαι
μέγα. It depends on how we punctuate this whether it will mean ' Kratinos says in *The Lakonians*, '' It is a fearful thing '' &c.' or ' Kratinos
says (in some unnamed play), '' It is a fearful thing among the Lakonians ''
&c.'

Comedy for the too strong attractions of tippling, and how the pair were at last reconciled. The *Satyrs* we know only by name ; it came second to Aristophanes' *Knights* in 425.[42] The *Seriphians* seems to have dealt with the legend of Perseus ; Seriphos is the island on which he was brought up, and one fragment contains directions for a journey, leading to the city of that strange tribe the Rascal Profiteers (νεοπλουτοπόνηροι) and other places not usually to be found in an atlas. This would fit a comic description of the hero's wanderings in search of the Gorgon. The *Trophonios* either dealt with a visit of some one to the oracle of that hero near Lebadeia in Boiotia (Comedy liked to parody oracular style) or else was again mythological, for a story was told of Trophonios' doings while in life which made him out an amusing rascal, the Master Thief of folktale.[43] The χειμαζόμενοι (*Caught in a Storm*) came second to Aristophanes' *Acharnians* ; we know nothing else about it. The *Cheirones* apparently pluralized the wise Centaur who brought up Achilles and made him into a chorus ; the *Maxims of Cheiron* were alluded to, and in one passage there had been a successful hunt, the game consisting of notable rascals of contemporary Athens.[44] Of the 'Ωραι (Seasons) we know neither plot nor date.

Another poet, the last on Aristophanes' list,[45] was KRATES, said to have been an actor who turned writer apparently under the influence of Kratinos. Aristophanes credits him with a subtle and delicate wit, plays which were light and not showy, but good, and a fair amount of success. Aristotle adds that he was the first to write general plots, not personal lampoons.[46] The inscription already several times cited (see notes 11, 15) gives him three victories at the Great Dionysia, but either he had none at the Lenaia or the mention of them is lost from that badly battered stone.

Of his plays we have fifteen titles, some doubtfully his and none telling us much of the content. One, the *Beasts* (Θηρία), was full of wonders : it may have been set in the good old days when the beasts could talk. At all events, it contained a reformer who would put an end to the servant problem for ever by introducing household gear which came when it was called, utensils which kneaded bread, washed themselves, waited at table and were generally useful, fish which explained that they could not serve themselves up yet because they were fried on one side only, and hot water which called ' Turn off the tap ' when the bath was full. Some one else seems to have been preaching vegetarianism, apparently one of the beasts, who had not un-

[42] Argum. Ar., *Knights*, 4.   [43] See Rose, *Mythol.*, p. 301.
[44] See frags. 233, 235 Kock ; for the Maxims of Cheiron see above, p. 66.
[45] Ar., *Knights*, 537 *sqq.*   [46] Arist., *Poet.*, 1449ᵇ 7.

natural objections to being eaten. These tastes of his style make one wish that more of him had survived, for clearly Aristophanes was quite right and he had a pretty wit.

Of PHEREKRATES we have the interesting notice that ' he gave up personal abuse and enjoyed a great reputation for novelties, being clever at inventing plots '. The same authority says that he was a rival of Krates, whether as actor or as author is not stated.[47] The fragments of the fourteen, or eighteen, plays he wrote do him scant justice though some of the titles are interesting. His first victory was in 437 probably, another in 420.[48]

The most notable play of Pherekrates, or at all events the one of whose contents we are least ignorant, was the Ἄγριοι (Savages). It appears that the ' noble savage ', or some similar piece of foolish speculation, had been heard of in Athens ; the play represented certain persons who, like the heroes of Aristophanes' Birds (see p. 235), had had enough of civilized life and were looking for something simpler. It would seem also that they were comically disillusioned and glad to meet even the familiar rascals of Athens again.[49] The other titles we have of him are as follows : Ἀγαθοί (this may have meant The Conservatives or simply The Worthies), which some attributed to the less-known STRATTIS ; one character, possibly Herakles, was to be heard explaining that he had but a poor appetite and could barely manage some six bushels of corn a day. Of the Αὐτόμολοι (Deserters) and Γρᾶες (Old Women) we know far too little for a reconstruction. The Δουλοδιδάσκαλος (School for Slaves) seems to have been satirical, perhaps dealing with the lack of discipline among Athenian servants. The Ἐπιλήσμων (Forgetful Man) was also called Thalatta, the latter title not meaning The Sea but being the name of a notorious courtesan ; she therefore had some part to play in it. Of the Ἰπνός (we do not know whether the name meant Oven or Kitchen ; it was also called Παννυχίς, or The Vigil) there is nothing to be said except that women seem to have played prominent parts in it.[50] The Korianno again bore the name of a courtesan, and had much to say about hard drinking, to judge from the fragments. The Κραπάταλος had as its

[47] Anonymus de comoedia, p. xv, 38 sqq., Dübner. The text is a little uncertain : Φερεκράτης Ἀθηναῖος νικᾷ ἐπὶ θεάτρου (ἐπὶ Θεοδώρου, i.e., 438/7 B.C., Dobrée), γενόμενος δ' ὑπόπικρος (so Dindorf, for γινόμενος ὁ δ' ὑποκριτὴς) ἐζήλωκε Κράτητα, κτέ.

[48] Athenaios, 218 d.

[49] This we know, not so much from the fragments, but from a reference in Plato, Protagoras, 327 d.

[50] Frag. 64 Kock explains that women know their place far better than men do theirs. As it is in a metre used only for choric passages, we may conjecture that the chorus was composed of women. It is to be remembered that the female parts, at least the speaking parts, in Comedy as in Tragedy, were taken by men.

title the name of a worthless sort of fish, and seems to have had
something to say about the lower world, where money is of no value
and one of these fish will buy—something, the corrupt state of the
text prevents us from knowing what.[51] It also bade the judges judge
the play fairly, ' or Pherekrates will grow much more abusive than
this '. The Λῆροι (Gew-gaws) we know little or nothing about. The
Μεταλλῆς (Miners) has left us a long fragment concerning the Land
of Cocaigne (cf. p. 223). The Μέτοικοι (Resident Aliens), which may
or may not have been by Pherekrates, is represented by a single word.
The Μυρμηκάνθρωποι (Ant-Men) may have had something to do with
the legend of how Aigina was unpeopled by a plague till Zeus in pity
for good king Aiakos turned the whole contents of an ant-hill into
men.[52] Of the Persians the ancients did not know who had written
it, and we do not know what it was about, save that yet another Land
of Cocaigne was described. The Petale again we know nothing about ;
the Tyranny described a banquet in which the women got all the
wine for themselves. The Cheiron is more interesting ; one of the
characters was Music, who had a long complaint about the wrongs
done her by modern composers. Whether Pherekrates, NIKOMACHOS
or Platon wrote it was a disputed point.[53] The Pseudo-Herakles has
left us one fragment of three lines.

About the same time there were some comedians, not without
note in their own day, who to us are hardly more than names.
TELEKLEIDES must have had some merit, for he won the prize five
times at the Lenaia and (probably ; the name is mutilated) three
times at the Great Dionysia.[54] We know little of him, partly because
no surviving play of Aristophanes mentions him and therefore we
have none of the useful information which his scholia and the late
lexicographers who draw upon them often give us on literary matters.
Enough fragments survive for us to know five titles, one being doubtful
(Amphiktyones, 'Αψευδεῖς, i.e., No Lies, Hesiods, Πρυτάνεις, i.e.,
Chairmen or Presiding Magistrates, Στερροί, perhaps Obstinate Fellows ;
the second of these plays was regarded as of doubtful authenticity).
We know that he attacked Perikles (frags. 42-44) ; he had something
to say (frag. 41) of a sycophant who was doing a lively trade in
blackmail, Nikias, the famous general to whose doddering incompetence
the failure of the great Syracusan expedition was mostly due, being a
large contributor ; he was eloquent concerning the Golden Age
(frag. 1). HERMIPPOS was of some prominence. He was a one-eyed
man who is said to have written forty plays, winning, the inscription
already often quoted tells us, four victories at the Lenaia and some,
the number is lost, at the Great Dionysia.[55] He accused Aspasia,

[51] It seems to have been a current joke that everything was very
cheap in Hades. See Kallimachos, epigr. 15 (Anth. Pal. vii, 524) with
Mair's note.
[52] See Rose, Myth., p. 260.   [53] Athen., 364 a.
[54] See the inscription cited in note 11.
[55] Besides the inscription, see Suidas s.u. Ἕρμιππος (a).

Perikles' mistress, of impiety, not in a comedy but seriously in a
court of law ; on the stage he attacked Hyperbolos, Kleon's successor
as the leading democratic politician, with enough vigour to attract
Aristophanes' attention.[56]   We have the following titles of his plays :
The Birth of Athena ('Aθηνᾶς γοναί), *Bread-Sellers* ('Aρτοπώλιδες ;
this was the play which attacked Hyperbolos, and it must therefore
have been written before Aristophanes' *Clouds*), Δημόται (*Fellow-
townsmen*), *Europê, Gods, Kerkopes, Fates, Soldiers, Burden-bearers*
(Φορμοφόροι ;   this contained a catalogue of imports, couched in
mock-epic hexameters, and varied in typically comic style, for it
included ' groats and ribs of beef from Italy, the itch from Sitalkas,
[a Thracian kinglet] consigned to the Spartans, several shiploads of
lies from Perdikkas, hogs and cheese from Syracuse ', frag. 63 Kock),
and some non-dramatic works in verse.   Whether his *Agamemnon*
(frag. 1 Demiańczuk) was a play or not is uncertain.   Of MYRTILOS,
ALKIMENES and PHILONIDES we know that there were such persons,
and hardly more than that.

Much more important is EUPOLIS, whom later ages ranked
with Kratinos and Aristophanes.[57]   Though his works are lost,
we have a considerable number of his fragments, and these,
together with what others say of him, enable us to form some
idea of his merits.   His literary activities coincided largely with
the time of the Peloponnesian War, in which he fell, about 411.
His especial aversion seems to have been Hyperbolos [58] and the
extreme democrats generally ;   Perikles was by this time dead,
and besides, had been by comparison moderate, therefore he is
mentioned with respect.   He was the best speaker that ever
lived, says one famous passage (frag. 94 Kock), leaving the others
ten foot behind ;   not only that, but Persuasion sat on his lips
and his words had a sting like a bee's which they left in the
hearer's ears.   As a final compliment, he is classed with Miltiades,
though only the latter is addressed as ' Lord ' (ἄναξ), as one might
say ' saint ' (frag. 100).   The *Flatterers* is the earliest ancestor we
know of a long and brilliant line, for it contained (frag. 159)
the first description of the flatterer (κόλαξ) ;   we may perhaps say
the professional diner-out, destined to be prominent, under that
name and the later designation of parasite, in New Comedy and
in its Latin and modern imitations.   He was fond of quaint

[56] Plutarch, *Perikles*, 32 ; Ar., *Clouds*, 557.

[57] *Eupolis atque Cratinus Aristophanesque poetae*, Horace, *Sat.*, i, 4, 1 ;
iratum Eupolidem praegrandi cum sene, Persius i, 124 (the ' grand old
man ' is of course Aristophanes) ;   the *Baptai* is alluded to by Juvenal,
ii, 92.   Satire regarded Old Comedy as its great archetype, see especially
the first of these passages.

[58] Ar., *Clouds*, 553 ;   but he had something to say of Kleon also,
frags. 290, 308 Kock.

misuses of words, such as absurd divisions of them between lines, against the ordinary rules of metre ; some persons, probably Alkibiades and his friends,

> Are now engaged ; they have a weighty de-
> Cree of the Senate, State affairs, on hand.[59]

Again, he would coin some new and unheard of inflection. An aging lover sighs,

> He has a wife, a mighty handsome lady,
> She loved me once, while yet I juvenized.[60]

But such trifles were no important part of his stock in trade ; even the battered remains show us an author comparable to Aristophanes himself, full of vigour and fertile in expression, and a great master of metre (Aristophanes learned a new line from him, which is still called the Eupolidean).

We learn that he first exhibited when but seventeen years old, in 430/29 ; he therefore was born about 447, and thus was Aristophanes' contemporary. The relations between the two masters seem not always to have been quite smooth ; Eupolis alleges that he helped to write the *Knights* ' and made a present of it to Bald-Head ', while Aristophanes retorts that the *Marikas* is nothing but a wretched travesty of the *Knights*.[61] Eupolis is said to have won seven victories, whereof we know, from the inscription, that three were at the Lenaia, and to have put on seventeen or fourteen plays.[62]

If these figures are correct, and he can hardly have composed many more dramas in his short life, we know the titles at least of about as many plays as the ancient scholars had. In the *Αἶγες* (*Goats*) the chorus seem to have been dressed as goats and gave a long list of the herbs they fed on ; the plot is unknown. The *Ἀστράτευτοι*, otherwise *Ἀνδρογύναι* (respectively *Shirkers of Service* and *Men-Women*) is also of unknown plot. The *Autolykos* was first put on in 420, and later a revised edition was brought out. Its hero was one of the most handsome men of the day ; the action of the play seems to have been largely concerned with the unspeakable habits of certain people, perhaps Autolykos himself and his father

---

[59] Frag. 73 Kock : ἀλλ᾽ οὐχὶ δυνατόν ἐστιν, οὐ γὰρ ἀλλὰ προ-/βούλευμα βαστάζουσι τῆς πόλεως πέρι.

[60] *Ibid.*, 109 Kock : γυναῖκ᾽ ἔχοντα μάλα καλήν τε κἀγαθήν/αὕτη νεανικοῦντος ἐπεθύμησέ μου. For better treatment of language than this, see, *e.g.*, frags. 95 and 100 Kock.

[61] Eupolis, frag. 78 Kock ; Ar., *Clouds*, 553-4.

[62] Suidas *s.u. Εὔπολις* ; anon. *de com.*, p. xv, 46 Dübner.

and mother. The Βάπται (Dippers ; the word seems to refer to some rite of lustration) we know abused Alkibiades heartily and dealt with the worship of the Thracian goddess Kotytto. Probably he and his friends were represented as worshipping her in some immoral and effeminate fashion, hence the feminine form of the title. The Δῆμοι (Districts ; Attica was divided into a number of these demes) was political ; the fragments, augmented by finds in Egypt,[63] not a common happening in the case of Old Comedy, show us that the great men of the past, Miltiades, Solon, Aristeides and others, appeared on earth in it, doubtless for the sake of unflattering comparisons of the contemporary politicians to them. The existence of the Diaiton and the Dias is very doubtful ; they are mentioned once each by Pollux, whose text is none of the best. The authorship of the Helots was disputed in antiquity, we do not know with what justice, for the fragments are scanty and tell us very little. One very doubtful passage seems to mention a play called Κλοπαί, i.e., Thefts, but probably the title is nothing but Εἵλωτες miswritten. The Flatterers has already been mentioned ; a central figure was apparently the great sophist Protagoras. Whether the Lakones is the title of a play, another name for the Helots or a mere blunder we do not know. The Marikas brought in Hyperbolos under that name, which has none too polite a meaning, and represented his mother as a drunken old trot dancing the kordax, a performance more vigorous than dignified. The Νουμηνίαι or Days of New Moon, which came third when the Acharnians won the prize, has left us no fragments at all. The Πόλεις (Cities) seems to have had a chorus each member of which represented one of the dependent states of the Athenian empire ; the theme therefore was political. Of the Prospaltians not much can be said ; perhaps, as the people of Prospalta, one of the Attic demes, were said to be litigious, it was a satire on Athenian law-courts. The Ταξίαρχοι (Captains) apparently introduced Dionysos in person going to look for a good commander and finding one in the other world. What the 'Υβριστοδίκαι was about we cannot tell, for nothing of it has survived ; the word is said to mean persons who refuse to enter suit. The Friends (Φίλοι) is also obscure, save for more or less probable conjectures. The Golden Race (Χρυσοῦν Γένος) seems from frag. 276 Kock to have had a chorus of maimed, halt, blind and ragged ; the title probably was ironical.

PHRYNICHOS, whom the inscription names as having won two victories at the Lenaia and some (the number is missing) at the Great Dionysia, never reached such celebrity as Eupolis, but what we know of him suggests that he was a passable comedian. Tradition concerning him is confused by his often being taken for his namesake the tragedian (see p. 136) ; but it would appear that he first came before the public in 429 or a little earlier,

---

⁶³ Frags. 7-12 Demiańczuk.

and outlived Sophokles, at all events by a short time.[44] Ten plays by him are mentioned in Suidas, and we have some few fragments.

The *Ephialtes* (*Nightmare* ?) contained one rather puzzling passage, warning all and sundry against certain persons, ' the fair flower of youth, but no friends of mankind ' (μισάνθρωπον ἄνθος ἥβης) who are very pleasant in public, but when they get together by themselves, apparently in the theatre, tear in pieces those whom they recently flattered and laugh over it. These seem to be young and irresponsible critics, but without the context we cannot tell. The *Konnos* dealt with a musician of that name, a favourite butt, for some reason, of comedians. We know nothing of the *Kronos*, assuming that it is not *Konnos* miswritten. The Κωμασταί has not left us enough to judge it by ; the title, *Revellers*, tells us but little. The *Solitary* (Μονότροπος) introduced an eccentric who, as he explained, presumably in a prologue, chose to live like Timon (the famous misanthrope), ' with no wife and no slave, a bad temper, no society, no laughing, no conversation, and a way of my own ' (frag. 18). The *Muses*, which may have been not unlike the *Frogs* in plot, contained a tribute to Sophokles which showed that even a second-rate comedian need not always be commonplace. The *Mystics* we know nothing about. The Ποάστριαι (*Weeders*) is equally obscure. The *Tragedians*, otherwise known as the *Freedmen*, doubtless had a literary theme.

But all these names pale before that of ARISTOPHANES. Whether, if we had the work of Kratinos and Eupolis, he would appear as great as he does now is an open question ; great he certainly is. To find another such, we must come down to modern times and compare him to Rabelais. The Frenchman was indeed the deeper and more original thinker ; but they have in common fantastic imagination, apparent ribaldry with an underlying moral purpose, strange mixtures of beauty and ugliness and mastery of all known earlier literature.

Like most, probably all, masters of Old Comedy, Aristophanes was a supporter of what we may loosely call the Conservative party in Athens. This means that he was opposed, not only to the extremer forms of democracy, but to the Peloponnesian War ; not indeed to the point of advocating peace at any price, but strongly enough to make him the staunch upholder of all reasonable means of putting an end to it and renewing the friendship

[44] Suidas says his *début* was in Olymp. 86, which is 435–432 B.C. ; but the anon. *de com.*, p. xv, 44 Dübner, says he and Eupolis began at the same time. Since the *Muses* mentioned Sophokles' death and was put on at the same time as the *Frogs*, Phrynichos cannot have died sooner than about 404.

with Sparta which had been the ideal, now and then realized to some extent and for a short time, of the older politicians such as Kimon. One reason for this attitude is probably that the backbone of the Athenian, as of all other, Conservatives was the land-holding class, who had little to gain from Imperial expansion and consequent increase of overseas trade, much to lose from the invasion of the country. The democrats, on the other hand, or at least those of them who were the most regular attendants at the Assembly and the courts of law, were principally artisans and tradesmen, large and small, led by such men as Kleon the ' tanner ' (*i.e.*, proprietor of a tannery). To them, war meant extra employment rather than the lack of it, for the fleet needed rowers, thus absorbing many of the poorer labourers at good rates of wages, together with the usual chances of profiteering on what we should call army contracts and the like and the decided possibility of ousting commercial rivals by force of arms and thus opening up new markets. Hence what we might name the left wing of the Athenian Labour party was warlike and Imperialist, while the Right and Centre parties were, if not pacifist, at least anxious for peace and unenthusiastic about the overseas commitments of the State, whether in the form of alliances with Thracian and Macedonian princes or interferences with the internal affairs of Sicily. If it be asked why Comedy, always a popular performance, sided so regularly with this party and not with its political opponents, a possible answer seems to be that it was originally a country amusement, and so came traditionally to express the views of what was and continued to be a country party. We shall see that later on it, like most art, became wholly a thing of the town.

But the greatness of Aristophanes is not dependent upon the traditions of the medium in which he worked. He was, besides being a great poet and a man of inexhaustible wit, a humanitarian in the broadest sense of that term. His hero is regularly the average natural man as he saw him ; and his message is, if it can be summed up in a sentence, the fundamental wholesomeness and good sense to be found, amid all the absurdities due to lust and ignorance, prejudice and bad reasoning, in such a man. Of all surviving Greek authors he is one of the most moral and sympathetic, while remaining, in many places, superficially one of the most indecent.

Of his considerable output of comedies [65] there remain eleven complete, which were well edited in antiquity and much studied for the sake of their language and antiquarian interest,

[65] 44 (Suidas), including 4 spurious (anon. *de com.*, p. 8, 47, Kaibel).

though often by men totally incapable of appreciating their finer qualities. Hence we have also a mass of scholia, containing a great deal of excellent Alexandrian scholarship, both linguistic and historical, which throw light on many passages that would otherwise be unintelligible to us. In brief outline, the plots are as follows.

The *Acharnians* is the earliest surviving play, having been produced at the Lenaia of 425. The poet had already made his reputation with two earlier productions, the *Banqueters* (Δαιταλῆς) and *Babylonians*, now lost and of uncertain content. In the *Acharnians*, the hero is one Dikaiopolis, who, disgusted at the behaviour of the Assembly and the magistrates in relation to the conduct of the war, and especially with their hostility to all proposals for an early peace on reasonable terms, contrives to negotiate a separate truce for himself and his household. For this he is violently attacked by the chorus, consisting of charcoal-burners from the populous district of Acharnai. He gains a hearing, visits Euripides, enlists his sympathy, borrows from him Telephos' beggar's rags, and delivers an oration proving that the Spartans were not wholly to blame for the war. The chorus are persuaded, and watch his further proceedings with approval. There now comes, after the parabasis, a series of delightfully funny scenes, in which Dikaiopolis is visited by comic foreigners anxious to trade with him on terms highly profitable to himself, by Athenians who want to share in his good things, and finally by a messenger inviting him to a feast. Meanwhile he is watched very sourly by one of the best-known officers of the time, Lamachos, who finds himself obliged to hurry forth to guard the frontiers and catch a hostile raiding-party just as Dikaiopolis goes out to the banquet. The two return together, Lamachos with a hurt leg, lamenting in para-tragic style, Dikaiopolis very drunk, leaning on two flute-girls and making love to both at once. He leaves the stage in triumph, supported by the admiring chorus.

The next play, the *Knights* ('Ιππῆς, Lenaia, 424) is an attack on the most prominent leader of the democratic party, Kleon. Demos (The Public) is an old man of uncertain temper, apparently stupid and easily led, but with much more shrewdness than he is generally credited with possessing. He has given his household into the care of a rascally Paphlagonian slave (*i.e.*, Kleon ; as usual, it is implied that he was no true-born Athenian, but there is a pun on the verb παφλάζειν, to splutter), who makes life a burden for the rest. Two, generally and not without reason identified with the well-known generals Nikias and Demosthenes, conspire against him. Stealing his private collection of oracles

(a hit at the craze then prevalent for such things) they discover
that he is destined to be succeeded by a fellow yet viler than
himself, and such a man they discover in Agorakritos, a seller of
allantes, a sort of black-pudding or haggis.   Encouraged to meet
and outfront the Paphlagonian, this man, whose only hindrance
to political success is that he can read and write a little, shows
himself more than a match for his older opponent, whom he
outdoes at every turn in shamelessness, vote-catching motions,
and base flattery of the secretly amused Demos.   Finally the
Paphlagonian is deposed and Agorakritos appointed to his post.
Now, by a quite unexpected turn, he proves himself the best
possible manager of the old man's affairs, for he boils him and
makes him young again, presenting him to the audience no longer
the shabby figure he was at the beginning of the play, but an
Athenian gentleman of the good old times, and he leaves the stage
merrily wooing certain ladies who personify the Conservative
aspiration for a lasting peace with Sparta.

Next year came the *Clouds* (Νεφέλαι), which won but third
place at the Dionysia ; the revised version which Aristophanes
planned to put on later, but apparently never actually produced,
is the one we have.   Why it should have been a failure is a mystery, even supposing Kratinos' comedy (see p. 223) to have been
one of extraordinary merit, for Aristophanes justly regarded it
as the best play [66] he had written.   It is not political, but consists of a most humorous attack upon sophistry and sophists,
embodied in the conspicuous person of Sokrates.   To what extent
actual characteristics of that great man are shown in the play
is one of the controversial points ; it is a sensible remark of
Christ-Schmid that the very different portraits which Plato and
Xenophon give of him show him as he was twenty years later.[67]
Strepsiades, a simple old countryman, has married an aristocratic
town-bred wife, whose son takes after his mother and ruins his
father with the fashionable extravagance of horse-racing.   Unable
to pay his debts, Strepsiades decides to send his son, Pheidippides, to learn from Sokrates the art of sophistic rhetoric, and
in particular, to master the ' worse case ' (ἥττων λόγος), whereby
to confute the creditors when they bring suit.   Pheidippides
refuses, and the old man goes himself, is initiated into the mysteries of the Phrontisterion ('Reflectory'), Sokrates' college,
under the auspices of the chorus of clouds, and studies for a while,
till Sokrates expels him for his stupidity.   He now contrives to
persuade Pheidippides to go.   The young man listens to a debate
between the Just and the Unjust Case (or Reason, λόγος), and

⁶⁶ *Clouds*, 522.   ⁶⁷ i, p. 423, n. 6.

in a short time has so completely learned the ways of the latter that his father has no more fear of the claims of any creditor. But his son now applies the new learning to reviling his father's old-fashioned tastes, and finally gives the old man a sound beating, and justifies himself for so doing. Strepsiades can stand this no longer, and the play ends with the burning of the Phrontisterion by him and his slaves.

·   In the next year, 422, Aristophanes took the second prize at the Lenaia with the *Wasps* (Σφῆκες), a good play, from which Racine was to get the idea of *Les Plaideurs*, but inferior to the *Clouds*. It is a satire on the jury-system of Athens, under which citizens were given a small fee, three obols a day, or about half the wage of a skilled artisan, to act as jurymen. In this capacity they had not only the functions of the modern jury but most of those exercised by our judges, and a majority was sufficient to decide the case. Since all trials in which the state was concerned were held before such courts, their political importance was great, and it was a standing grievance of the allies that Athens was the only legal venue for many matters which chiefly concerned them. Old Philokleon (the name may be freely rendered Bless-Kleon) is a zealous and indefatigable juryman. His son, Bdelykleon (Blast-Kleon), tries by all means to cure his father of his insane love of this unprofitable pursuit, and finally imprisons him in the house and defeats an attempt by the wasps, *i.e.*, his fellow-jurors, who form the chorus, to get him out. In a formal debate he convinces his father and the chorus that the jurymen are the tools of unscrupulous politicians, who put most of the revenues into their own pockets (another stock charge, not to be taken too seriously ; we have no real evidence that Kleon was other than personally honest). Bless-Kleon consents to a compromise ; he will stay at home and hold a private court there. Now follows the trial of the dog Labes (Grab) for stealing a Sicilian cheese. There is an obvious allusion to the politician Laches, who had recently been in bad odour for alleged misconduct in Sicily. By mistake, Bless-Kleon acquits the defendant, a thing he had never done in his life before, and faints from shock. To raise his spirits, Blast-Kleon introduces him into fashionable society, and he comes home in the last scene, very drunk and dancing wildly, with the assistance of the three sons of Karkinos the tragedian.

At the Dionysia of 421 preparations for the Peace of Nikias were well advanced, Kleon and his great Spartan opponent Brasidas were dead, and Aristophanes won another second prize with the *Peace* (Εἰρήνη). Trygaios, an honest countryman (the name means Vintager), breeds a huge dung-beetle, because in

Aesop's fables it is said that this creature once flew up to heaven. Arriving there on the beetle's back, he meets Hermes, all the other gods except War having gone away, out of hearing of the complaints from earth. Hermes is persuaded to tell him where Peace is buried. Before returning to earth, he collects honest men from all quarters and after much difficulty they (*i.e.*, the chorus) dig up the lost goddess, thus defeating the intentions of War to pound all Greece up in his mortar. He now climbs down, using the huge figure of Peace as his ladder, and there follow amusing scenes in which war-profiteers and other villains are discomfited, while honest and peaceful men rejoice. Finally Trygaios goes off the stage in a wedding procession, to marry Opora (Fruit), one of the attendants of Peace.

Another play which, surprisingly enough, won only a second prize, was the *Birds* (Ὄρνιθες), produced at the Great Dionysia of 414, during the Sicilian Expedition, to which it somewhat guardedly alludes, in the form of a fantastic satire on all far-reaching projects such as that was. Two Athenians, Peisetairos (we may render his name by Plausible) [68] and his faithful companion Euelpides (Hopeful) are tired of life in Athens and go to look for a more satisfactory residence, where there are no interfering officials and pleasure is the main business. They manage to discover the home of the Hoopoe, who having been a man himself and the husband of an Athenian lady will have a fellow-feeling for them. After some parley, and a furious attack upon the intruders by the chorus of birds, they obtain a hearing for a brilliant new plan. The birds, who should by rights be lords of the world, are to leave their vagrant ways of life and found a great new city, Nephelokokkygia (Cloud-Cuckoo-Town), in mid-air, half-way between earth and heaven. The plan succeeds admirably. The new settlement commands the trade-route by which the fumes of sacrifice ascend to the gods ; Zeus is obliged to treat with the new power, and sends an embassy composed of Poseidon, Herakles and a foreign god, a Triballian from Thrace, who cannot speak intelligible Greek. Warned by Prometheus, Plausible insists on Zeus handing over the sceptre of the universe and agreeing to his marriage with the celestial housekeeper, Basileia (Princess). Poseidon is unwilling (this aristocratic god is usually treated with respect even by the boldest comedians), but Herakles is easily won over by the scent of a good dinner which Plausible is cooking, and Herakles' fists are a cogent

[68] His name has the impossible form Peisthetairos in the MSS. ; the choice lies between Peisetairos (Persuade-comrade) and Pisthetairos (Faithful-comrade), and the former suits his character infinitely better.

argument to the Triballian. So the treaty is concluded, and the play, like the *Peace*, ends with a marriage hymn. This is good fooling ; but in addition, the comedy has most exquisite bird-lyrics, a glorious mock-serious parabasis dealing with cosmology as the birds conceive it, and a series of irresistibly funny scenes in which a number of strange persons apply for citizenship in Cloud-Cuckoo-Town.

In 411 Aristophanes brought out two plays. The former, which appeared at the Lenaia, is one of his very best works, the *Lysistrata* (Madam Demobilizer). The plot is simple, but riotously funny, with a true Aristophanic undercurrent of seriousness. The women of Greece have become tired of the long war, and under the leadership of Lysistrate, an Athenian matron, they form a conspiracy to have nothing to do with the men, whether as husbands or lovers, until peace is made. Lysistrate and her immediate associates seize the Akropolis, and with it the state treasure, and hold it valiantly against a party of fire-eating old men, who try to dislodge them. One of them, Myrrhine, is proof also against the pitiful plaint of her husband, Kinesias (a real person, in all probability in the theatre looking on), who is amorously inclined, and of her baby, who, Kinesias protests, has not been washed or fed these five days. Soon a distressed-looking ambassador arrives from Sparta, demanding in the broadest Doric to see the Athenian authorities at once. Pleni-potentiaries come not long after, and with the assistance of Lysistrate a truce is soon agreed upon. The play ends with a feast in honour of the ambassadors, and songs in Attic and Lakonian sung by hosts and guests.

By the time of the Great Dionysia the revolution of the Four Hundred was in progress, and political topics were probably not too safe. Aristophanes at all events produced a play mostly literary in its subject, the *Thesmophoriazusae*. The women, assembled as they were every year for the ancient ceremony of the Thesmophoria, conducted by them alone, take the opportunity to plot against Euripides, who has been abusing them in his plays. This in itself is interesting, as an early example of the false idea that the tragedian was a woman-hater. Euripides gets wind of the plot and tries to induce Agathon (see p. 208) to pass himself off as a woman, go among them and defend him. Agathon flatly refuses to do anything of the kind, and Euripides then proceeds to dress up his kinsman Mnesilochos as a grotesque parody of a woman. Thus attired, Mnesilochos gains admission to the Thesmophoreion, or place where the rite was held. He is successful at first, but arouses anger and suspicion by a speech in which he declares that women are really far worse than Euripides makes out. He is examined, his sex discovered, and he is then handed over to the police authorities, who shackle him to a plank, a form of crucifixion used in the case of particularly vile criminals. Euripides now tries a number of devices, taken from his own tragedies, to set him free, and after several comic failures succeeds in getting the Scythian policeman on guard to go off with a courtesan. He then lets Mnesilochos loose, with the connivance of the chorus of women, with whom he has come to terms ; both make off, and the unfortunate Scythian, returning to find his charge gone, ends the play amusingly by running this way and that in search and bawling in very broken Greek.

In the last stages of the war Aristophanes won the first prize with one of the finest plays, the *Frogs* (Βάτραχοι), produced at the Lenaia in 405. Dionysos, now that Sophokles and Euripides are both dead, finds himself without a good tragedian, and so starts off for Hades to fetch Euripides back. He gets advice from Herakles concerning the way thither, and has disguised himself with a lion's skin in order to pass for that hero. With him goes a comic slave, Xanthias. They make their way to the Styx, where Charon takes Dionysos over (Xanthias, being a slave, is not admitted to the boat and has to go around by land), to the music of a chorus of frogs who give the play its name. On the other side they meet the main chorus, composed of the initiated in the Eleusinian Mysteries, and are directed by them to Pluton's palace. Dionysos now gets into many ridiculous and painful situations, due partly to his own extreme cowardice, partly to being mistaken for the real Herakles, whose bullying ways, dog-stealing and huge appetite have made him unpopular in the lower world. But at last he is welcomed by Pluton. Euripides has been making trouble. Aeschylus occupies the seat of honour reserved for the best tragedian, and now the new-comer claims it, backed by all the rascality of the place. Pluton is no expert in such matters, and Dionysos is chosen to adjudicate between the rivals. Now follows a delightful scene of mingled farce and good criticism, in which the two poets attack each other's style unmercifully. After long hesitation Dionysos, upon whom the subtler parts of their debate have been quite lost, decides that after all he prefers Aeschylus, and takes him back to earth with him.

The ruin of Athens in the Peloponnesian War brought with it the ruin of Old Comedy, and the rest of Aristophanes' work belongs to what it has been the fashion, since Hellenistic times, to call Middle Comedy.[69] In 392, or 389,[70] he brought out the *Women in Parliament* ('Ἐκκλησιάζουσαι*), a play almost without personal satire and with a sadly diminished choral part. The plot is interesting, both in itself and for a grotesque resemblance it bears to the views on women set forth in Plato's *Republic* [71] (see p. 265). The women of Athens plan to seize the government of the state for themselves. Rising very early in the morning, they steal their husbands' clothes, pack a meeting of the Assembly, and rush through a bill giving them the whole power, chiefly on the grounds that they are the only steady-going and reliably conservative element. They now introduce a Communistic state, and the rest of the play is a grotesque series of scenes illustrating life under the new régime and ending with an invitation to a communal dinner, the chief dish in which has a name some seven lines long. It is not bad fun, but falls much behind the verve and varied interest and charm of Old Comedy proper.

The last play of Aristophanes that survives to us, and the last he ever produced under his own name, is the *Plutus*, 388. As we have it, it is a revised edition, the first draft having appeared in 408. Chremylos, an honest poor man, with his slave Karion, has gone to Delphoi to ask the oracle whether he should bring up his son as a respectable man or a rascal. Apollo bids him persuade the first person he meets on leaving the temple to come home with him. This proves to be a blind and wretched-looking individual, who is, however, the god of Wealth (Plutos). After much persuasion, he consents to accept Chremylos' hospitality, and despite the skepticism of the latter's neighbour Blepsidemos and the protests of Poverty herself that but for her all the world would be idle, he is taken to the temple of Asklepios, where the god restores his sight. He is now able to distinguish honest men from rogues, and the rest of the play shows the joy of Chremylos and his friends, the woes of all the dishonest, who find themselves

[69] The terms ἀρχαία, μέση, νέα κωμῳδία, current among the later grammarians, are rather artificial. The first and last perhaps go back to Aristotle's distinction, *Eth. Nic.*, 1128ᵃ 22, between παλαιαί and καιναί κωμῳδίαι, whereof the former used broad and unrestrained jesting, βωμολοχία, the latter innuendo. The earliest known writer to speak of Middle Comedy was ANTIOCHOS of Alexandria, who wrote under Hadrian, but did not originate the term.

[70] Philochoros, cited by the schol. on 193, gives the earlier date. It has been suggested, see Christ-Schmid, i, p. 431, n. 4, that the lost didaskalia gave the date as the archonship of Demostratos ; now there were two archons of this name, one in 392 and the other in 389.

[71] The two authors are independent of one another, but the coincidence shows that communism and the equality of the sexes were views currently discussed in the early fourth century.

suddenly poor, and the arrival of Hermes, full of threats from Zeus because no one pays any attention now to the old gods, only to take service under the new master of wealth, as an assistant to Karion. The play has a chorus, which does little save take part in some of the dialogue ; often its appearance is indicated, not by any written words, but by the marginal direction χοροῦ, *i.e.*, (performance) of the chorus, a note found also occasionally in the *Ecclesiazusae* and in the plays of Menander.

Of the poet's life but little is known.[72] He was the son of a certain Philippos. As he himself suggests that he had lived in Aigina, it is probable that the family owned property there ; [73] but there seems to have been some doubt of his being of pure Athenian stock. Otherwise it is hard to understand what the charge was which Kleon brought against him, why he says that he was for a while unable to produce comedies under his own name,[74] and why he continued at various times to bring his plays out in the same manner. Of the date of his birth there is no record, but it must have been about the middle of the fifth century, as his first play was produced in 427,[75] his last two, brought out by his son Araros, after the *Plutus*, and there is no indication that he lived to be very old. Of his lost plays the following facts are known.

The *Aiolosikon* was one of the two produced under the name of Araros. We are told that it had no choric parts, *i.e.*, the poet had written nothing for them to sing, and they merely danced, or performed in some way, in the pauses of the action. The same statement, this time quite incredible, is made concerning the *Odysses* of Kratinos (see p. 223). It parodied the story of Aiolos (probably the son of Hellen, not the wind-god) ; the second half of its name refers to a professional cook or caterer, by name Sikon, whose occupation was a favourite subject for Middle Comedy. It was revised and produced a second time. The *Amphiareos* was not mythological in subject ; it dealt with a visit to the prophetic shrine of that hero at Oropos in Boiotia, and a cure of some one by Asklepios also occurred. It was

[72] Our information is derived firstly from the plays themselves, secondly from ancient lives, preserved in Suidas, in the MSS. of the plays and briefly in the anon. *de com.*, p. 8, 41–48 Kaibel.

[73] Acharn., 652 *sqq.*, where see scholia.

[74] Something hindered him for a while ; ' I was a maid and might not have a child ', he makes the chorus say (*Clouds*, 530), ' so another girl took up my bantling and you gave it a good rearing ', *i.e.*, the *Daitales* was brought out by some one else. That this means Aristophanes was too young to be allowed to compete is an idea wholly lacking evidence ; nothing proves that there was any kind of age-limit, and we have seen (p. 228) that Eupolis began his career at 17.

[75] Anon. *de com.*, p. xv, 50 Dübner, 8, 43 Kaibel.

produced at the Lenaia, the same year as the *Birds*. The *Anagyros* bore the name of the local hero of one of the Attic demes, but its plot is quite uncertain. The *Babylonians* ' ridiculed the elected magistrates and those chosen by lot, also Kleon, before strangers ', *i.e.*, at the Great Dionysia, in 426 ; [76] it won him Kleon's hatred, but again the plot is not certainly known. The Γεωργοί (*Farmers*) contained praises of the blessings of peace and an allusion to the pitiful and cowardly shufflings of Nikias in the affair of Pylos, 424 ; probably therefore it was produced about that time, when the victory of Demosthenes and Kleon over the Spartans gave hopes of an early truce. The Γῆρας (*Old Age*) is of uncertain date ; the old age may be that of the chorus, and from the tone of certain fragments they seem to have cast it off. The *Gerytades* dealt with a visit to Hades, and so perhaps resembled the *Frogs*. The *Daidalos* would seem to have treated of a mythological theme ; one fragment refers, not to Daidalos, but to the egg which Leda, or Nemesis, laid (cf. p. 223). The *Daitales* (Banqueters) was Aristophanes' first play. It included a scene in which two persons, apparently father and son, mock each other's tricks of speech and notions of what constitutes education (the old man knows no terms of law, the young one cannot construe Homer and is full of oratorical catch-phrases). We know from Aristophanes himself that two of the characters were a respectable young man and a rake, possibly his brother.[77] All else is conjecture. The *Danaides* must have had a mythological plot, doubtless parody. A play called *Twice Shipwrecked* (Δὶς ναυαγός) was by some ascribed to Aristophanes ; the title sounds very unlikely for Old Comedy, but we know nothing of the piece. Very puzzling is the title *Dramata*, which normally means simply ' plays ', given to two comedies, whose sub-titles were respectively *The Centaur* and *Niobos*, presumably ' the male Niobe '. The latter play was doubtfully authentic. Unless personified tragedies and comedies appeared among the characters, it is not easy to see why they were so named. The former made much play with Herakles' huge appetite, and was earlier in date than the *Wasps* ; [78] the latter contained the famous story of Sophokles' trial for dementia (see chap. vi, n. 100), if we accept Hermann's almost certain interpretation of the passage in the Life of Sophokles referring to it (Δράμασιν for δράμασιν). Some quotations are referred simply to *Dramata* without distinction of title ; that this was yet a third play is simply incredible. Of the second editions of the *Peace* and the *Thesmophoriazusae* we have a few fragments : the plot of the *Heroes* is unknown. The *Kokalos*, one of the two plays which Araros brought out, had, we are told,[79] the stock episodes of New Comedy, a rape, a subsequent recognition, and ' all the other features which Menander imitated '. The *Lemnians* was again a piece of burlesque mythology. The Νῆσοι (*Islands*) was thought by some to be the

---

[76] Schol. on *Acharn.*, 378.   [77] *Clouds*, 529.
[78] Schol., *Wasps*, 60, reading ἐν τοῖς πρὸ τούτου δεδιδαγμένοις Δράμασιν.
[79] *Life*, p. xxviii, 69 Dübner.

work of ARCHIPPOS ; certainly the few fragments do not much suggest Aristophanes' style. The Ὁλκάδες (Merchant-ships) we know to have been a protest against the war.[80] Of the Πελαργοί (Storks) we have neither the plot nor the date. The Ποίησις (Poetry), if it was by him and not by Antiphanes, is equally obscure, as is the Proagon (Rehearsal). Whether Aristophanes or Platon (see below) wrote the Σκευαί is not known [81] and was uncertain in antiquity ; the title may mean something like Costumes. The title of the Σκηνὰς καταλαμβάνουσαι signifies women taking possession of tents or booth's of some kind, presumably for a festival and possibly for the Thesmophoria. The fairly numerous fragments of the Ταγηνισταί tell us only that it had a good deal to say of eating, and the title suits this, for it means something like The Frying-Pan Club. The Telemesses may very probably have made fun of diviners and divining ; its title is the name of a Karian people celebrated for their seercraft. Of the Triphales nothing certain is known ; the name signifies exceedingly lustful persons. The Phoinissai, which there is some reason to suppose a late play, not much earlier than the Frogs, may have burlesqued Euripides (cf. p. 192). The Ὧραι (Seasons) contained a scene in which some one, perhaps one of the Horai, or goddesses of the seasons, promised summer fruit all the year round, except for Athens, which has that blessing already thanks to its mild climate.

A somewhat younger contemporary of Aristophanes, apparently a comedian of merit, was PLATON : it is convenient to keep the Greek form of his name to distinguish him from the philosopher, but he is often styled Plato Comicus. We judge of his performance rather from the numerous mentions of him in antiquity and the fact, mentioned above, that one play was attributed sometimes to him and sometimes to Aristophanes than by what the somewhat insignificant fragments tell us. His dates are not exactly known, but his first appearance was between 428 and 425, the latest allusion contained in what we have of him can be dated 390.[82] Of his titles, certain and doubtful, we have altogether some thirty ; it is clear that his subjects included politics (Kleophon, Hyperbolos, Ambassadors, Alliance), mock-mythology (Adonis, Amphiareos, Europê, Laios) and the scandal about Sappho and Phaon (Phaon ; cf. chap. iv, note 39). It is said that he was poor, and earned money by writing plays for others to exhibit under their own names.[83]

[80] So Argument I (Hall-Geldart) to the Peace. Very possibly the chorus consisted of personified merchant-ships.

[81] Chamaileon cited by Athen., 628 e, leaves the question open, but most authorities quote the play as by Platon, with no mention of Aristophanes.

[82] First appearance, Cyril, aduers. Iul., i, 13b Spannheim ; latest dateable allusion, to the demagogue Agyrrhios, frag. 185 Kock.

[83] See Suidas, s.u. Ἀρκάδας μιμούμενοι and Πλάτων (a)

Passing over a number of obscurer writers, we come to what is generally called MIDDLE COMEDY, a somewhat dreary period whereof not much is known. Of poets' names we have no lack ; fragments are tolerably plentiful ; but there is no evidence enabling us to reconstruct even a single comedy with certainty, and what we have in the way of quotations never suggests that any great store of wit or dramatic power has been lost to us in the disappearance of the hundreds of plays produced, often with much applause, during this time, roughly the first two-thirds of the fourth century. Without doing any injustice, we may imagine the poets of this time of transition writing works somewhat resembling Aristophanes' *Ecclesiazusae* and *Plutus*, but with less wit and a diminishing use of the chorus ; or again, since the whole distinction of Middle and New is so largely artificial, producing something, now and again, which would suggest Menander, but hardly his best work. ' The poets ', says the Anonymus *de Comoedia*, ' did not meddle with poetic inventions, but used the common everyday speech, and their excellences are those of prose, so that it is rare to find in their work any poetical flavour. They all pay much attention to plots. There are fifty-seven poets of Middle Comedy, and of their plays 607 survive.' [84] All the fifty-seven are shadowy figures to us, and no such formidable mass of plays has come down, even in fragments.

In trying to judge of these writers, we must remember that our fragments are largely due to Athenaios, who was looking mostly for facts concerning eating and drinking, Pollux, whose interest was lexicographical, and Stobaios,[85] who was on the watch for moral sayings. No ancient who has come down to us ever made a selection of passages to illustrate the wit or the dramatic capabilities of the ' Middle ' comedians. With this proviso, we may note that they seem to have dealt largely in stock characters, much like those of New Comedy, among whom the caterer (μάγειρος ; it is misleading to render this by ' cook ', which is rather ὀψοποιός) was prominent, and raised a laugh by disquisitions, often wearisomely long to our taste, on his skill. There were also favourite butts, occasionally historical persons (Plato comes in for his share of raillery, much less pointed than that of Old Comedy), often whole classes ; fishmongers are

---

[84] Anon. *de com.*, p. xiv, 56 *sqq.* Dübner, 8, 49 *sqq.* Kaibel. The number of plays is uncertain ; Athenaios, 336 d, or some one on whom he draws, claims to have read over 800.

[85] Ioannes Stobaeus, John of Stobi, who in the sixth century A.D. made a large anthology of scientific and philosophical dicta from all manner of writers.

much abused, notably by Antiphanes, though Xenarchos has
the best joke against them.[86] The ' Flatterer ' continues to play
a prominent part, and during this period gets his name of παράσιτος,
properly ' guest ', originally a perfectly respectable word, having
associations especially with one of the local cults of Herakles.[87]
Parodies of tragedy, and burlesques of mythological subjects,
are very common, most of EUBULOS' titles being of this kind.
Gradually we can see the coming of the Menandrean play ; thus
Anaxandrides, of whom Suidas wrongly says that he was the
inventor of plots involving ' love and wronged maidens ', has a
passage quite suggestive of a situation in New Comedy, in which
a wife is thinking of leaving her husband.[88]

A few of the less obscure names, with the approximate dates, are
the following. ALEXIS must have lived through a good part of the
century, for he used a chorus sometimes (fr. 237 is in Eupolideans),
yet he perhaps mentions Antigonos and Demetrios Poliorketes (fr.
III, doubtfully genuine) and certainly Ptolemy I (fr. 244), calling
him king, which he was not till 305. We must allow him at least one
good comic passage, for fr. 257 describes that supposedly modern
plague, the gate-crasher, in lively style. He was not an Athenian
but a Thurian by birth, if we may believe Suidas, and was Menander's
uncle. The same authority credits him with the huge total of 245
plays. AMPHIS, who must have been contemporary with Plato's
activities as a philosophic teacher, to judge by his references to him
(frs. 6, 13), gives us incidentally a bit of interesting linguistic information. Slovenly speakers (the fishmongers, it seems, were guilty of
this together with other offences) were beginning to drop unaccented
syllables, saying 'κτὼ 'βολῶν for ὀκτὼ ὀβολῶν and the like (fr. 30).
ANAXANDRIDES, said to be either a Rhodian or a Kolophonian, and
to have written 55 plays and won ten victories (so Suidas), was active
fairly early in the century ; two of his plays, Herakles and Theseus,
were represented in 382/1 and 374/3 respectively. To him belongs
one of the most famous parodies of Euripides [89] and an early appearance of a famous name of Comedy, ἀλαζών, the braggart or false
pretender (fr. 49). ANTIPHANES, another foreigner, of whose native
country different accounts were given, had a long career ; he seems
to have been born between 407 and 404 and his age when he died is

[86] Fr. 7 Kock : they were not allowed to sprinkle their fish with water,
so they would stage a fight ; one of them would fall senseless across his
stall, and the rest would water him, and the fish, generously, to revive
him.
[87] Diodoros of Sinope, fr. 3 Kock, mentions this fact, which is confirmed
from other sources.
[88] Fr. 56 Kock. It runs, χαλεπή, λέγω σοι, καὶ προσάντης, ὦ τέκνον, |ὁδός
ἐστιν ὡς τὸν πατέρ' ἀπελθεῖν οἴκαδε |παρὰ τἀνδρός, ἥτις ἐστὶ κοσμία γυνή· | ὁ γὰρ
δίαυλός ἐστιν αἰσχύνην ἔχων.
[89] ἡ πόλις (Eur. said φύσις) ἐβούλεθ', ᾗ νόμων οὐδὲν μέλει, fr. 67.

given as 74. His plays were numerous, but many fragments show a feeble wordiness of style, unworthy of the best traditions of Attica, together·with a tendency to overwork certain jokes. Here and there we find a self-conscious insistence on the correct Attic way of expressing something (frs. 97, 182). One long-lived jest makes perhaps its first appearance in him (fr. 221). ' " He's married." " What's that you say ? Is he really married ? Why, he was alive and going about his business when I left him." ' The three sons of Aristophanes, ARAROS, NIKOSTRATOS and PHILETAIROS, have all left us a few fragments, but nothing to show that they inherited much of their great father's wit. Indeed, Alexis commends a well by saying that its water is ' colder than Araros ' (ψυχρότερον 'Αραρότος ; ψυχρὸς in Greek criticism means artificial and affected). DIODOROS OF SINOPE has already been mentioned ; he was active in the middle of the century, two of his plays appearing in 359. EUHIPPOS, whose allusions range from Alexandros of Pherai, in the first third of the century, to Demosthenes and Plato, has left us a neat sample of his wit. A spendthrift son wishes his father to go and buy him fish ' of age and experience, not babies, please ', whereat the old man says reprovingly ' Don't you know that money is worth its weight in silver ? (τάργύριόν ἐστ' ἰσάργυρον ; fr. 21 Kock, who, being constitutionally incapable of seeing a joke, wished to emend this one away). EPIKRATES must have been his contemporary. He assured himself a certain notoriety, if no more, by writing an *Antilaïs*, ' counter-blast to Laïs ', the most famous courtesan of the day. Apparently she was past her prime when he attacked her, and as she was born in 422, the ungallant comedy may have been written about 375. It is just worth while to mention the insignificant KRATINOS THE YOUNGER, for the sake of the great name he bore ; some of the numerous attacks on Plato are his. MNESIMACHOS, contemporary with Philip of Macedon, has left us one of the most intolerably long-winded of all the passages dealing with food (fr. 4, a host sends his slave to recite the whole menu to tardy guests) and one very pretty line, ' Sleep is the Lesser Mysteries of Death ' (fr. 11, alluding to the Lesser Mysteries at Agrai, initiation into which must precede initiation at Eleusis). The obscure THEOPHILOS, TIMOKLES and XENARCHOS are each memorable for one passage of interest, besides that quoted already from the third of them. Theophilos presents (fr. 1) us with the resolve of·a slave not to fail his master in some difficulty, because ' through him I learned the ways of Greece, was taught to read and became an initiate into the mysteries of the gods ' ; there is reason to suppose this true to life, for the Athenians were considerate, as a rule, to their dependants. Timokles has a long and interesting passage on Tragedy as a consoler for our ills ; if one is bereaved, blind, lame, &c., there is always a tragic figure who suffered yet more sorely (fr. 6). Xenarchos deduces, from the fact that only the male cicala can chirp, the conclusion that they must be happy, ' since their wives have no voices at all ' (fr. 14).

But the chief interest of Middle Comedy is that it leads up to New, and New, for us, means MENANDER and the Latin imitators of him and his rivals. Till a few years ago, Menander (properly MENANDROS, but like Alexander the Great, he has become naturalized in English under the Latin form of his name) was no more than a reputation and a collection of fragments to us ; but Egypt has given us back much that he wrote, and in particular, the famous Cairo papyrus [90] has restored us three plays nearly enough complete to show the plot and characters with some approach to certainty, with a considerable fragment of another. We are thus able to read him for ourselves, instead of accepting the judgements of ancient critics, or the imitations of Terence ; for the more original genius of Plautus, one of the best comic writers of the world, did not allow him to follow so different an author as Menander, or indeed any Greek, with sufficient closeness for us to criticize the original on the basis of his adaptation. We can now see that Menander and the school of which, by common consent of antiquity, he was the best representative, originated the modern play, and more especially the modern Comedy of Manners. In his work, those features which strike us as most unlike our own drama in Aristophanes or Sophokles have wholly disappeared, or at most have left but faint traces to remind us that they once were there. The chorus has dwindled to a little band of performers who dance, and presumably sing, in the pauses of the action. These probably came often enough to give the division, traditional by the time of Horace, into five *epeisodia* or acts.[91] The characters are no longer individuals with known names, but imaginary persons, drawn from real life in contemporary Athens, and therefore generally differ not at all from modern stage-figures. The plots are neither fantastic nor mythical, but consist of events such as might quite possibly take place under ordinary circumstances. Indeed, only two stock incidents differ from what a playwright, drawing life as he saw it in London or New York to-day, might offer his audience. We have no slaves, and so the freeing in the last scene of a faithful or wily servitor, or threats of violence

[90] First published in 1907, by G. Lefebvre. For this and other papyrus evidence, up to 1921, see the convenient summary of Allinson (Loeb ed.), p. xxiii *sqq.* Modern editions, before and after the discovery, *ibid.*, xxviii. In so short a treatment as mine, a certain amount that is controversial must be taken for granted with regard to text and interpretation alike. For some recent discoveries of New Comedy, see Platnauer in Powell 3, p. 167 *sqq.*

[91] Horace, *ars poet.*, 189, neue minor neu sit quinto productior actu fabula.

towards him earlier in the play, have disappeared from our theatres. Neither law nor public opinion now permits an unwanted baby to be exposed (*i.e.*, abandoned alone, to die or be picked up as might happen), and therefore, if a modern author needs a foundling, or a long-lost relative, he must contrive the event in some other way. On the other hand, the hardest worked of our theatrical situations, the ' eternal triangle ', does not seem to have formed part of the Menandrean stock-in-trade. A Greek woman of respectable position met very few men indeed ; hence if two lovers are to quarrel over one woman, she is generally a courtesan, and therefore cannot be the wife of either.

Not much is known of Menander's life, which apparently was quiet and uneventful, save for his literary activity. His dates, certain to within a year, are 343/2–292/1.[92] His parents were Diopeithes of Kephisia and his wife Hegesistrate ; his uncle, as already mentioned (p. 243), was Alexis the comedian. He never saw Athens in her greatness, for the battle of Chaironeia came when he was about five years old ; his Athens was hardly more than a large provincial town, respected and to some extent indulged by the powers of the day for her glorious past and her literary importance. Of the 105 (or 108, or 109) plays which he is said to have written, the earliest was produced in 324/3 ; his first victory (he gained but eight altogether) was in 316/15. Whether the stories told of his amorous nature and especially of his relations to the courtesan Glykera [93] have any truth in them matters very little ; true or false, they were inevitable, since he wrote much of love and lovers. It may fairly be gathered from his plays that he was a man of gentle character, sympathetic, not expecting heroism or wisdom from the average man or woman, but far from a misanthrope. It may be mentioned, for on this point he has been misunderstood, that he was not and did not try to be a particularly funny writer. He wished rather to draw pictures of ordinary human nature, acting under not too violent stress, and in this he succeeded. To compare him to the greatest dramatists is absurd ; if we compare him even to the greatest modern of his own class, Molière, the advantage is certainly not with the Athenian. Rather, he was a good second-rate author, who partly by his real merit, partly owing to circumstances existing long after his death, exercised an enormous influence, mostly indirect, the effects of which are still clearly to be seen.

[92] Allinson, p. xii *sqq.*, and the authors cited by him, give the chronological details. See also Christ-Schmid, ii. pp. 38–46.

[93] *E.g.*, Suidas *s.u. Μένανδρος*, and Athenaios 594 d.

A sketch of that play which has survived most nearly complete, the 'Επιτρέποντες (*The Arbitration*), will give an idea of his manner. An Athenian, Charisios (Charming), has married Pamphile (Miss Lovely), daughter of Smikrines (Mr. Smallways). Not long (some five months) after the marriage, he learns, apparently from his slave Onesimos (Profitable : Philemon, St. Paul's correspondent, perhaps named his runaway slave out of Menander), that she has given birth to a child. In great distress, for he loves her, he ceases to live with her and tries vainly to find consolation with a harp-girl, Habrotonon (a flower-name, love-in-idleness, of a sort common among such women), a good-natured, non-moral creature. Now two country fellows refer a case to Smikrines' decision, rather than take it into court (hence the name of the play). One of them has found an exposed child with some trinkets about it, and given it to the other to rear ; ought he to retain the trinkets ? Smikrines decides that they are the child's property and must be handed over with it. Onesimos happens to see one of them, a ring, and recognizes it as his master's. Largely through the good offices of Habrotonon, it comes to light that the child is Pamphile's, and the father Charisios himself, who had violated her some time before the marriage at a nocturnal festival, neither knowing who the other was. The plot is typical of New Comedy (it is, for instance, practically that of the *Hecyra* of Terence) ; it ends with a general reconciliation, and the merit of the play, which is not small, lies in the good character-drawing (Smikrines is peppery, Onesimos impudent and prone to utter tags of philosophy, Habrotonon a lifelike mixture of kindliness and self-seeking, Pamphile a pathetic little figure, less wooden than most heroines of artificial comedy, Charisios fairly credible and the two rustics excellent sketches). The language is Attic of the day, in easy, harmonious verse, chiefly iambic trimeters, with some of the livelier scenes in trochees. The most manifest literary influence is not that of any earlier form of Comedy, but of Euripidean tragedy. Not only do the characters quote Euripides at one another, and philosophize after his manner on occasion ; not only is the plot reminiscent of the *Ion* (p. 189) ; but there is direct imitation of one of the lost tragedies, the *Alope*, especially in the scene of the arbitration itself.

The evidence is as follows. Hyginus tells us (*fab.* 187) that Alope exposed her child by Poseidon, which was then picked up by a shepherd and given by him to another shepherd, but without the clothing it wore. The new foster-father claimed the clothing, as being the only evidence that the infant was freeborn ; the two could not agree, and they asked Kerkyon, Alope's father, to decide between them. The legendary divine and royal personages have been replaced, in Menander, by middle-class Athenians, but otherwise the situation is the same, and one of the rustics themselves (l. 108) says it is like a tragedy, although he instances Tyro's twins, not Alope's child. That the *Alope* has, by different routes, furnished Hyginus' unknown Greek authority with the legend and Menander with the idea for his scene is extremely likely.

Two other plays of Menander can be fairly well restored. The *Samia* (*Girl from Samos*) dealt with a lovers' intrigue and its consequences. Chrysis, a freeborn woman from Samos, who gives the play its title, is the concubine of an Athenian, Demeas by name. Demeas has an adopted son, Moschion, who loves and is loved by Plangon (Dolly), daughter of Demeas' next-door neighbour Nikeratos,[94] a poor, and apparently superstitious and credulous man. Plangon bears a child, which apparently (the papyrus is very defective) Chrysis undertakes, out of kindness towards the girl, to bring up, pretending it is a foundling. Demeas, returning from an absence, accidentally discovers that Moschion is the baby's father ; he jumps at the conclusion that Chrysis is the mother, and further, that she is a wanton and designing hussy who has seduced his idolized adopted son. He drives her out of the house ; she takes refuge with Nikeratos ; he somehow discovers that Plangon is the child's mother and is beside himself with rage, although Demeas tries to make him believe that the real father must be some god. Finally, though the details are obscure, after various complications all is settled, Chrysis is restored to favour (possibly discovered to be no Samian but an Athenian, and so a fitting wife for Demeas), and Moschion, after some delay caused by his own wounded vanity, married to Plangon.

The Περικειρομένη (*Shaven and Shorn*) was famous in antiquity ;[95] it is a comedy of misunderstandings. Glykera (Dulcie) has another Moschion for her twin brother. By the usual machinery of exposure, finding and adoption they have been separated since infancy. She, having been brought up by a poor woman, has become the deeply-loved mistress of a sentimental and hot-tempered soldier, Polemon (Warrior), Moschion having been adopted by a well-to-do lady, who has married a man of some means, Pataikos. Glykera knows that Moschion is her brother, but he has not yet been told the secret. He is a handsome young ass who fancies every woman in love with him, and manages to steal a kiss from Glykera, who does not repulse him, but grieves that their disparity in fortune hinders her from making herself known. At this moment Polemon arrives, imagines Moschion to be Glykera's lover, and in anger cuts off her hair. She

[94] If New Comedy introduces two families, it generally shows both houses on the stage ; hence some rather unlikely juxtapositions of poor and rich, respectable and disreputable houses. The action takes place on the street or at the house-doors ; the ekkyklema is not used.

[95] See, *e.g.*, *Anth. Pal.*, v, 218 ; xii, 233.

is mortally offended, and takes refuge with Moschion's adopted mother. Polemon induces Pataikos to try to win her to forgive him, and in the course of negotiations the latter discovers that she is his own daughter, exposed years before when he had become suddenly poor and lost his wife. She forgives Polemon, marries him with a substantial dowry from her new-found father, and Moschion is provided also with a wife.

A fourth play, the *Hero*, we know in outline, for an ancient argument has survived, together with the first scene, in the Cairo papyrus. The title cannot be certainly explained, but probably a hero (quasi-deified dead man) appeared at some point to explain the plot to the audience, after the fashion of a Euripidean prologue ; an abstraction, Agnoia (Ignorance, Misunderstanding), does the same in the *Περικειρομένη*. Myrrhine, wife of Laches, years ago had two illegitimate children, of whom Laches himself was the father. They passed into the keeping of a poor man, since dead, a debtor of Laches, and are now in the latter's household, working off their foster-father's indebtedness, without having any idea of their real birth. One of the children is a girl, another Plangon, who is seduced by a neighbour's son. A slave of Laches loves her, pretends to have been her seducer, and wishes to marry her. Myrrhine, who probably feels responsible for Plangon, is very angry, and some complications seem to have followed, the end being that the relationship was discovered, Plangon respectably married to her seducer, her brother received as Laches' son, and presumably her slave-admirer rewarded in some way. See p. 423.

Of Menander's successful rival, PHILEMON, we know about as much as we did concerning Menander himself before the recent discoveries. His fragments are numerous, and if we could suppose that Plautus' *Mercator* and *Trinummus* are close imitations of his *Ἔμπορος* and *Θησαυρός*, we could say with confidence that he was a very good playwright. The *Mostellaria* also is supposed to be an adaptation of his *Phasma*, and there were several other Latin imitations of him. As it is, we can only acquiesce in the ancient verdict that he was inferior only to Menander. His dates are 361–263 B.C., his native place was Syracuse, and his plays [96] numbered 101, or 97.

Less famous and popular, but clearly a good comedian, or he would not have had so much influence on the Latin stage,[97] was DIPHILOS of Sinope, one of several foreigners whose success in the Attic theatre at once shows how wide was the influence of Athenian literature and explains some little peculiarities of diction (there seems

---

[96] Marmor Parium, p. 194 Jacoby ; Quintilian, x, 1, 72 ; anon. *de com.*, p. xv, 74 Dübner, 9, 66 Kaibel ; Suidas *s.u. Φιλήμων*.

[97] Plautus took the *Casina, Rudens, Vidularia* and the lost *Commorientes* from Diphilos ; Terence, one of the main episodes of the *Adelphi*.

to be no departure from normal Attic grammar, but the vocabulary contains strange elements) to be found in the fragments of New Comedy. He wrote 100 plays, according to the Anonymus *de comoedia* (p. xv, 83 Dübner, 10, 75 Kaibel), who also says that he died in Smyrna. His birth-date is unknown, but he outlived Menander by at least two or three years.[98]

Of the long list of lesser names which have come down to us, together with some few fragments of their works, two deserve mention. APOLLODOROS OF KARYSTOS provided Terence with the models for two plays, the *Phormio* (the original was called 'Επιδικαζόμενος) and the *Hecyra* ; his other four were all founded on Menander. PHILIPPIDES may or may not have possessed much merit as a playwright ; very little of him remains ; but his is the one voice which we know to have been raised, in tones not utterly unworthy of Old Comedy, in protest against Demetrios Poliorketes and the sickening flattery with which Athens surrounded him.[99]

Of this important branch of literature, which spread far beyond Athens even before it began to influence Rome, and lasted, as an active force, for well over a century, it may be said that its language was generally sedulously decent. It must be added that its morality was far below that of Old Comedy. A series of plays in which good-nature and liberality in money matters, the virtues in fact of a Charles Surface, are always considered as more than atoning for vices much worse than his and including rape and seduction ; in which none of the intellectual virtues seem ever to come in for commendation, and the one enterprising and adventurous life left in an over-sophisticated world, that of a soldier of fortune under Alexander or one of his successors, is represented as fit only for a bully or an utterly desperate man ; in which there is no trace of a great, or even of a consistently upright character ; these make but a poor showing, morally, in any literature, and particularly in that of Greece. The culture of Athens had as a matter of fact grown tired, and political insignificance was bringing ethical degeneracy in its train.

While Old Comedy was developing in Athens, Sicily brought to a brief perfection a very different form, which apparently used no chorus and never indulged in personal lampoon or satire to any noticeable extent. The one great name here is that of EPICHARMOS, of whom we know that he lived in Syracuse, though he is said to have been born in Kos, that his date was near the beginning of the fifth century (roughly 550–460 would account for most

---

[98] For his dates, see Kaibel in Pauly-Wissowa, v. 1153, 21 *sqq.*
[99] Frag. 25, preserved in Plutarch, *Demetr.*, 26 and 12.

of the facts stated concerning him),[100] that he wrote a number of plays in Doric, his native speech,[101] and that he was an excellent dramatist, especially distinguished for his liveliness.[102] This last we are obliged to take on trust, for no play, or even scene, has come down to us. The scanty fragments show grace and ease of language, mastery of metre (usually trochees) and a considerable interest in the philosophy of the day. Indeed, Epicharmos came to be regarded as a moralist and philosopher, and a great proportion of what we have under his name is not, apparently, from his plays, but from a moralizing and philosophic poem, seemingly of early date,[103] put forth by an unknown author as his, and written in his dialect and his favourite trochaic tetrameters. The titles of the comedies indicate that some of them were mythological (as *Amykos, Busirides*—we do not know why the name of Busiris was in the plural, but the one considerable fragment, 21 Kaibel, describes the gluttony of Herakles—*The Marriage of Hera*, the *Muses*, and one of which we can guess the plot ; it was called *The Revellers* or *Hephaistos, Κωμασταὶ ἢ Ἄφαιστος*, and seems to have told how Hephaistos, in anger at his mother Hera, bound her fast in a magic chair, where she sat helpless until Dionysos made Hephaistos genially drunk and so persuaded him to be reconciled and set her free).[104] Others, but apparently not so many, had titles suggestive of Attic Comedy, as *The Festival* (Ἑορτά), *The Islands* (Νᾶσοι), while a few suggest the *contentiones* which were so popular in later times, as *Earth and Sea* (the two apparently were disputing which was the richer). *Master and Mistress Argument* (Λόγος καὶ Λογίνα).

More obscure is PHORMIS, mentioned along with Epicharmos by some glossator of Aristotle [105] and a few later writers as his contemporary and a fellow-poet of the same school. We have nothing left of him. Of DEINOLOCHOS we are told that he was the son or

[100] We have a life of him in Suidas, a short notice in Diogenes Laertios, viii, 3, another in the Anonymus *de com.*, p. xiv, 19 Dübner, 7, 16 Kaibel, a date in the Marmor Parium (71 ; it is 472/1), and a number of references in various authors. These are collected in Kaibel, pp. 88–90.

[101] The number is variously stated at from 35 to 52.

[102] It was the correct thing in Horace's day (*epp.*, ii, 1, 58) to say of Plautus that his rapid and lively movement reminded one of Epicharmos, *ad exemplar Siculi properasse Epicharmi*. If there is any truth in this (Horace implies that it is too high praise for the Latin comedian), it may give us some idea of the Sicilian's merits.

[103] There is some reason to suppose that Euripides had read it, see Kaibel, p. 134.

[104] Boethos *ap.* Photios and Suidas *s.u.* Ἥρας δὲ δεσμούς ; cf. Hyginus *fab.* 166.

[105] *Poet.*, 1449ᵇ 6 ; cf. Suidas *s.u.* Ἐπίχαρμος, Φόρμος (so he calls him).

pupil of Epicharmos.[106] He may of course have been either or both, but the notice means no more than that he was a comedian and somewhat younger. We have no fragments of any consequence.

Another tantalizing name is that of SOPHRON of Syracuse. He wrote mimes, μῖμοι, that is to say short dramatic pieces with subjects taken from common life. He, or his ancient editors, divided these into 'women's mimes' (γυναῖκεῖοι) and 'men's mimes' (ἀνδρεῖοι), according to the sex of all or most of the characters. One of the former, having the rather clumsy title of *The women who say they will drive out the goddess* (Hekate ?), *Ταὶ γυναῖκες αἱ τὰν θεόν φαντι ἐξελᾶν*, has left us the only considerable fragment we have ; it is a scene of popular magic, apparently an attempt to drive away the supernatural power supposed to possess some one. Theokritos is alleged to have drawn upon it for Idyll ii (see p. 333). Another was *Women watching the Isthmian Games* (*Ταὶ θάμεναι τὰ "Ισθμια*), another *The Bridesmaid* (*Νυμφοπόνος*), a fourth *The Mother-in-Law* (*Πενθέρα*). The dialect in all was Doric, the medium highly rhythmical prose or very irregular metre, probably the former.[107] The best testimony to their literary merit is their imitation, not only by Theokritos, but by Plato[108] and Herodas (see pp. 339, 424).

From Italy we have some few scraps of comic plays developing out of the *phlyakes* (see p. 215). The best-known name in this connexion is that of RHINTHON of Taras (Tarentum), or Syracuse, who is said to have written burlesque tragedies.[109]. Four other writers, SKIRAS of Taras, the much later BLAESUS of Capreae, SOPATROS of Paphos and possibly an otherwise unknown HERAKLEIDES,[110] are names to us and no more.

[106] Suidas *s.u. Δεινόλοχος* ; Aelian, *de nat. anim.*, vi, 51, calls him a rival of Epicharmos.

[107] See, in general, Kaibel, pp. 152-53 ; the fragment is in *Studi italiani di Filol. class.*, *n.s.*, x (1933), p. 119 *sqq.* (Norsa and Vitelli) ; see also Gow in *Class. Rev.*, xlvii, pp. 113-15 ; Latte in *Philologus*, lxxxviii, p. 259 *sqq.* ; Eitrem in *Symbolae Osloenses*, fasc. xii, p. 10 *sqq.* Sophron was 'contemporary with Xerxes and Euripides' (*Suid., s.u.*), *i.e.*, lived in the fifth century.

[108] See Diog. Laert., iii, 18.

[109] Kaibel, p. 185 *sqq.* He was a contemporary of Ptolemy I.

[110] Athenaios, 71 a, calls Sopatros a Knidian and says he was contemporary with Alexander the Great. Elsewhere, as 86 a, he says he was a φλυακογράφος, elsewhere again, as 158 d, a parodist. No other author mentions him. For Herakleides, see Diog. Laert., v, 93, reading, with Wilamowitz, φλύακας for the MS. φλυαρίας.

ADDITIONAL NOTE

For comic fragments, *see* also D. L. Page, *op. cit.* (above, p. 213).

CHAPTER IX

CLASSICAL PROSE

THE Greeks, like every other nation, developed poetry long before prose, as a literary medium, was thought of. Thus we have seen Hesiod using the hexameter for essentially prosaic matter, political pamphlets written in elegiacs, and, it may be added, those parts of Comedy which seem most to call for prose still following the convention of verse, which only the Alexandrian music-halls were to throw off (see p. 346).[1] This curious fact is probably to be explained by the consideration that early literature seeks, in its beginnings, a medium strikingly different from ordinary speech and easy to remember, while the many subtle differences between literary prose and everyday language require a highly evolved literary consciousness for even their possibility to be recognized.

I.   Among the earliest writers to cultivate anything like a literary prose style were the philosophers.   Since the first Ionians, such as Thales, and, in the west, Pythagoras, wrote nothing, or at least nothing that has come down to us,[2] we must begin with HERAKLEITOS of Ephesos, not unjustly termed the Obscure.   It seems to have been his considered opinion that philosophy should not be easy, since only the highest minds can grasp it in any case.[3]   His style is literally oracular : ' our Lord whose oracle is

---

[1] For the general question of verse and prose, see Quiller-Couch, *Art of Writing*, pp. 70–92.

[2] The letters attributed to many of these early philosophers are notorious forgeries.   Those who, like Xenophanes and Parmenides, wrote in verse have already been dealt with.   The chief authority for their lives is Diogenes Laertios, a writer of date somewhere between the third and fifth centuries A.D., whose work, in ten books, is a compilation from various authors and rises or falls in value with the worth of the source

[3] Frag. 2 Bywater, 1 Diels.   For the doctrines of these philosophers, see in general Zeller's *History of Greek Philosophy* (*Geschichte der griechischen Philosophie*) and Burnet, *Greek Philosophy from Thales to Plato*. Their fragments, unless otherwise stated, are from Diels (see Bibliography).

at Delphoi ', he says, ' neither speaks out nor keeps aught hidden, but signifies it ',[4] and this describes his own manner.   In general his clauses are short, tending to fall into antithetical pairs ; the vocabulary, as in several early prose writers, contains poetical elements ; the tone of haughty wisdom and the real profundity of thought make him impressive, even in the battered remains we have of his work *Concerning Nature* (Περὶ φύσιος).   His dialect is his native Ionic, and his dates about 540–480 B.C.[5]

Much less important was MELISSOS of Samos, about the middle of the fifth century.[6] He too wrote Ionic, using short sentences, to judge by what is left of his book *On Nature or Reality*.   But they were the short sentences of a man reasoning clearly and accurately to prove his points in detail.   The famous ANAXAGORAS of Klazomenai, whose probable dates are about 500–428, thus touches both Herakleitos and Melissos.[7] He would appear rather to have lacked clearness and ease, although there was no designed obscurity, and to have been given, at times, to a tone as dogmatic as the great Ephesian's.   On occasion he could use a sentence of some length, though of simple construction, a mere accumulation of clauses ; this and his somewhat rudimentary terminology alike show that philosophic prose was as yet far from complete.   His contemporary, DIOGENES of Apollonia, held the very sound opinion (frag. 1) that ' every discussion should start from an unexceptionable proposition, and its style should be simple but dignified '.   The fairly extensive fragments seem all to belong to one work, *On Nature*, which was divided, at least in later times, into two books.   His Ionic has in it something of the manner of an Attic writer, especially the ability to manage a long complex sentence without departing from his own ideal of lucidity.   Sometimes his anxiety to be perfectly clear makes him a little wordy.

Of a philosopher perhaps the greatest of all who wrote in Ionic, DEMOKRITOS of Abdera, not much can be said here.   His fragments are numerous, but generally short, extending but to a line or two apiece.   Many consist of some pithy turn of phrase attributed to him, such as ' Neither excellence of speech can hide an evil act, nor a good act be harmed by abuse in words ',[8] or ' Pleasures out of season bring forth unpleasantnesses '.[9]   Only here and

---

[4] Frag. 11 (93).
[5] He flourished Olymp. 69 (504–501 B.C.), Diog. Laert., ix, 1 ; *i.e.*, he was then about 40.   He died at the age of 60, *ibid.*, 3.
[6] See, for his life, Diog. Laert., ix, 24, Suidas *s.u.* Μέλισσος.   He served against Athens in Olymp. 81 (444–441).
[7] By what seem the most probable readings in Diog. Laert., ii, 7, Apollodoros (see p. 392) put his birth in Olymp. 70 (500–497), his death at Olymp. 88, 1 (428).
[8] Fr. 177.   [9] *Ibid.*, 71.

there, for example in fr. 191, have we a long enough extract to see that his style was that of a practised and experienced writer, capable of expounding his views with fullness and even eloquence, and not of a mere coiner of epigrams.

It is a very regrettable gap in our knowledge of the history of philosophy that we have lost the works of this notable man, the father of the atomic theory. Even of his life we are but ill informed, his great age having been doubtless exaggerated [10] and his dates therefore uncertain ; he was some thirty or forty years younger than the fifth century and lived well into the fourth. More than the usual number of anecdotes were told of him and need not be considered save in a work on folklore.

In addition to the anecdotes, a most portentous literature of forgeries grew up around him. He was a wise man, therefore he had travelled and met Eastern sages and Egyptian priests, the fountain-heads of knowledge and wisdom ; therefore there were works dealing with his travels and the wonders he had seen. So later ages seem to have reasoned, and the works were soon forthcoming. A certain Bolos, early enough for Vitruvius, in the time of Augustus, to take him for genuine Demokritos, wrote a work dealing with sympathies and antipathies, whereof a good many fragments remain, and this was fathered on the sane and scientifically minded philosopher, by those who had not read him.[11] Later still, his name was attached to alchemical writings.

About contemporary with Demokritos was the great HIPPO-KRATES, concerning whom we have enough knowledge to see how absurd it is to style him the Father of Medicine. That art was past its first beginnings in Homer's day, and a great school flourished in Italy and Sicily about the beginning of the fifth century. Hippokrates, however, may be named as the first scientific physician of whom we have definite and detailed record. He is said to have been born in 460,[12] a date suspiciously near the birth-date of Demokritos, with whom the anecdotes connect him, as friend or pupil. It is perfectly possible that they knew and influenced one another, but the facts that they were both interested in medicine, wrote in Ionic, and lived in the same period would be enough to set the stories going regardless of

[10] That he was old when he died may very well be true, but the age of 109 given by Hipparchos *ap.* Diog. Laert., ix, 43, is hardly credible. Apollodoros reckoned the year of his birth as Olymp. 80 (460–457), Thrasyllos as Olymp. 77, 3 (470), *ibid.*, 41.

[11] See Diels, ii, p. 207 *sqq.*

[12] So Istomachos, cited in the *Life of Hipp.*, taken largely from Soranos (see p. 385), which survives.

truth. There has come down to us, besides some amusing letters, obviously not genuine but perhaps as old as the time of Nero.[13] a collection of fifty-three works on medicine, mostly Hippokratic in the sense that they are the writings[13a], technical with a few popular, of members of and sympathizers with the school to which he belonged, the Asklepiadai of Kos.[14] That they are all in Ionic is interesting, since Hippokrates himself was no Ionian, being perhaps of Thessalian descent and living on an island whose language was Doric. The explanation is the supremacy, at his date, of Ionic as the language of prose, although no longer of poetry. It was doubted in ancient times which of the treatises he himself had written, and the question is still far from being settled ; but the following are almost certainly his : *Prognostics* (Προγνωστικά) ; the first book of the work *On Diet in acute Illnesses* (περὶ διαίτης ὀξέων), Books i and iii of the Ἐπιδημίαι (*Epidemics*, a great collection of cases observed and described) ; *On Head-wounds* (περὶ τῶν ἐν κεφαλῇ τρωμάτων). Less generally acknowledged as his, but certainly good early works, are those *On ancient Medicine* (περὶ ἀρχαίης ἰητρικῆς), *On Fractures* (περὶ ἀγμῶν), *Concerning Humours* (περὶ χυμῶν), *On Airs, Waters and Places* (περὶ ἀέρων ὑδάτων τόπων, a most interesting treatise in three books dealing with the characteristics of healthy and unhealthy localities and speculating on the causes of endemic diseases), *On Epilepsy* (περὶ ἱερῆς νούσου, literally ' on the sacred illness ', a magnificent protest, in the name of science and of sound theology, against those magician-quacks who claimed that epilepsy, or any other disease, was supernatural), *On the Replacement of Dislocations* (περὶ ἄρθρων ἐμβολῆς). The work *On the Human Organism* (περὶ φύσιος ἀνθρώπου) is cited by Aristotle as being by POLYBOS, Hippokrates' son-in-law,[15] and some other parts of the collection may be as old as the great physician himself.

All the books are interesting rather for their content than their style, which is generally plain to the point of dullness, necessarily full of technical words and phrases, making it obscure to the layman, and seldom seeks any higher merit than that of saying accurately what has to be said. The two or three works which affect eloquence are later. However, there are passages here and there in which the need to support sound against

---

[13] Seneca, *epp.*, lxxix, 14, knows a story of Hippokrates and Demokritos, which may have come to him from the letters. Plutarch certainly knew them. [13a] *See* p. 423.

[14] A gild, like the Homeridai, not an actual clan ; I doubt all statements that H.'s own family claimed the god as its ancestor.

[15] Arist., *hist. anim.*, 512[b] 12.

unsound views of medicine rouses the writer to something like oratorical vigour. The question of authorship is complicated by the nature of the writings, for since they are scientific treatises, they were nearly as liable as such books are now to be revised, by the author or another, in accordance with the advance of knowledge.

The activities of the Pythagoreans in Sicily and Italy seem for a while to have made it probable that Doric, in some of its western forms, would come forward as a serious rival to Ionic. We are not, however, in a position to judge to what extent, if any, the capabilities of the dialect or the skill of those who wrote it made it deserve so high a place, for we have hardly anything left of what was written. There are some fragments of PHILOLAOS, whose date is approximately fixed by the statement, credible enough, of a number of writers that Plato bought some Pythagorean books from him. They are somewhat obscure, partly from the nature of their subject, the transcendental arithmetic of their author's school. ARCHYTAS, the mathematician, his contemporary, has also left us a little. His subject being for the most part mathematical technicalities, it is not to be expected that his purely literary interest should be high ; one quaint passage essaying to prove that calculation alone is able to breed confidence among men and prevent strife (fr. 3) indicates that he was able to express himself, on occasion, well enough by other means than figures and diagrams. Apart from these two men we have almost no Doric prose, late forgeries excluded,[16] except the wretched lucubrations of an unknown sophist, some of whose pupils apparently thought it worth while to record his shallow arguments for and against the propositions that honourable and shameful, just and unjust, etc., are indistinguishable from one another in all but name.[17] Since he mentions the Peloponnesian War as a recent event, it would seem that he lived about the end of the fifth century.

But we have once more to turn to Athens, which again shows influences from both east and west. Ionian philosophy had found a footing there (Anaxagoras was Perikles' friend and was known certainly through his works, perhaps also personally, to Euripides), and of the great sophists who taught there in the fifth century, Gorgias, of whom we shall have more to say in discussing rhetoric, was one, while Pythagoreanism had some influence, at the very latest during Plato's lifetime, quite possibly

[16] The Neo-Pythagorean movement, from about the last century B.C. on, produced a great demand for Pythagorean writings, which was duly supplied. Some of the resulting works were in what was intended for Doric.

[17] Diels, ii, p. 405 sqq.; the war is mentioned in i, 8. A certain similarity of subject has caused these much earlier writings to be preserved in the MSS. of Sextus Empiricus.

through Sokrates also. But of philosophic writing dating from the fifth century and expressed in Attic we have almost nothing. The brilliant series of Athenian philosophic authors begins, for us, very modestly indeed with an unknown man, called for convenience the ANONYMVS IAMBLICHI, because what we have left of him is embedded in the *Protreptikos* of Iamblichos the Neo-Platonist.[18] He seems to have produced a not ill-written work, containing sound, if not very deep, arguments in favour of justice and virtue in the individual, and especially of obedience to the laws. We shall find Isokrates writing not dissimilar commonplaces later, but this man seems still to be under the influence of the earlier rhetoric, using somewhat poetical language at times and being rather too free with his neat antitheses. To put him, as Blass does, about the time of the Peloponnesian War is reasonable enough.

Another glimpse of what was taught to the philosophically inclined in the years when Sokrates was reforming philosophy is furnished by Xenophon, who puts into his own words, but a style more ornate and rhetorical than he usually writes, the famous discourse of PRODIKOS the sophist on the *Choice of Herakles*.[19] It is a neat fable enough ; Herakles, when just coming to manhood, was met by two women, Virtue and Vice (who, however, called herself Joy), and was invited by one to a life of pleasure, by the other to one of unselfish activity. The interest lay in the speeches delivered by these two allegorical figures, and the whole contained more brilliant rhetoric than solid philosophical argument.

But the foundations of all that was most characteristic in Attic philosophical works were laid by one who never wrote anything himself [20] nor claimed to be a teacher. SOKRATES (469–399) seems always to have used the method of question and answer for those never-ending searches after accurate conceptions, to form a reasoned basis for ethics, to which his whole life was devoted. For this reason, if for no other, those of his

---

[18] The discovery was first made by Blass, Kieler Programm, Jan. 27, 1889 and is generally accepted ; the text of the Anonymus is in Diels, ii, p. 400 *sqq.*

[19] Xenophon, *Memor.*, ii, 1, 21–33. As examples of the (Gorgian) rhetoric which belongs rather to Prodikos than to Xenophon himself may be instanced the riming and balancing clauses in 28, τὰς πολεμικὰς τέχνας αὐτάς τε παρὰ τῶν ἐπισταμένων μαθητέον | καὶ ὅπως αὐταῖς δεῖ χρῆσθαι ἀσκητέον, and 30, πρὶν μὲν πεινῆν ἐσθίουσα, | πρὶν δὲ διψῆν πίνουσα.

[20] Unless we count his attempts at poetry ᛫ while in prison, Plato, *Phaedo*, 60 C *sqq.* We have four indifferent verses attributed to him, Diehl, i, p. 85.

pupils who, after his judicial murder, sought to carry on his traditions, threw much of their own work into dialogue form. To what extent this was purely and simply an effort to reproduce in writing the effect of Sokrates' speech, or how much the literary precedent of the mimes of Sophron (p. 252), influenced them is rather an idle question now ; certain it is that the dialogue form began to be commonly used very early in the fourth century, and by Athenian writers. By that time, as will be seen from the discussion of oratory, later in this chapter, rhetoric was well advanced, and in particular, what the Greeks called *ethos*, the adaptation of the language, as in a play, rather to the character and mannerisms of the supposed speaker than to the writer's own ideas of style, had already a great exponent in Lysias.

We have unfortunately lost the works of one celebrated author who used this form, AISCHINES (often called ' the Sokratic ', to distinguish him from the orator of that name), of the deme Sphettos, whose dialogues were said to be a particularly accurate picture of Sokrates' manner.[21] For us, he is represented by a few titles and fragments.

Of other philosophers of that time we know the views, at least in outline, for they are preserved by sundry later writers ; but their works are lost or represented by scanty fragments. EUKLEIDES or Megara was said in antiquity to have written six dialogues, but their authenticity was doubtful.[22] His pupil BRYSON is one of those whom Plato was said to have plagiarized,[23] but is hardly more than a name to us. STILPON, about 380–300 B.C., head of the Megarian school of philosophy, also wrote dialogues,[24] as did PHAIDON of Elis, the narrator, in Plato's *Phaedo*, of Sokrates' last day. ANTISTHENES, to whom the Cynics traced their origin, was an Athenian, pupil first of Gorgias and then of Sokrates, and a vigorous opponent of Plato ; his philosophical works are gone, and he is represented by two short declamations, the *Aias* and *Odysseus*, in which the two heroes set forth their respective claims to the arms of Achilles, while Dion of Prusa (see p. 406) may have used his *Archelaos* for his own thirteenth speech.[25] Diogenes Laertios gives a list of dialogues supposed to be the work of ARISTIPPOS the founder of the Cyrenaic school ; if they really were his, he wrote sometimes in Attic and sometimes in his

[21] See Diog. Laert., ii, 61 ; K. F. Hermann, *de Aeschinis Socratici reliquiis*, Göttingen 1850. The frags. are edited by Krauss, Teubner 1911.

[22] Diog. Laert., ii, 64.

[23] Along with Aristippos and Antisthenes, Theopompos of Chios *ap.* Athen., 508 c. Plato, like most writers of the first rank, was venomously traduced after his death by a number of small men, and a great amount of their muck-raking has found its way into Athenaios.

[24] Diog. Laert., ii, 120

[25] See Christ-Schmid, i, p. 655, n. 7.

native Doric.[26] XENOPHON will be dealt with in connexion with historiography.

We come therefore to PLATO, one of the greatest names, not only in philosophy but in literature, an unexampled combination of immense and original powers of thought with stylistic ability which would have made a second-rate thinker famous, or won him high rank as a dramatist or orator if he had not been a philosopher.[27] We are not very well informed concerning his life ; he lived to be old (his dates are 427–348/7) and was becoming a legendary figure to his own younger contemporaries ; hence, although our lives of him go back ultimately to his nephew Speusippos, his pupil Philip of Opus and other writers of the same or not much later date, these men seem already to have let their imaginations work ; Speusippos in particular has a tale to the effect that he was the son of Apollo and not of a mortal father.[28] His parents were an Athenian of ancient family, Ariston, and his wife Periktione ; he had two brothers, Glaukon and Adeimantos, known to us chiefly from their appearance in the *Republic*, and one sister, Potone, afterwards Speusippos' mother. It is said that his own name was originally Aristokles, after his grandfather, and that he came to be called Plato (Πλάτων) because he was of sturdy build and unusually broad (πλατύς) across the shoulders. From both parents he inherited naturally aristocratic sympathies, for his mother was a kinswoman of Kritias, the dilettante philosopher and man of letters who was one of the Thirty. The excesses of that body, however, thoroughly sickened him of oligarchy as practised in Athens, and although far too sound a political thinker ever to countenance democracy in any form,[29] he took no further part in their intrigues, but lived peacefully enough under the restored popular government of Thrasybulos and his colleagues and successors. It is said, however, that he and some others of Sokrates' followers withdrew for a while after the martyrdom of their master, Plato going to

[26] Diog. Laert., ii, 84 *sq.*

[27] We have a life of him in Diog. Laert., iii, shorter accounts in Olympiodoros' commentary on *Alcib.* i, printed in Hermann's (Teubner) ed. of Plato, vi, p. 190 *sqq.*, and by Apuleius, *de Platone*, i, 1 *sqq.*, besides numerous references in other writers. The most authentic material, so far as it goes, is his own letters, especially the seventh.

[28] Speus. *ap.* Diog. Laert., iii, 2.

[29] By the time of Plato's maturity, the utter failure of democracy in its most brilliant and promising embodiment, the Athenian republic, was so evident that henceforth no serious philosopher could do other than condemn it. Plato's own political ideals were manifestly influenced by the Dorian governments, notably that of Sparta.

Eukleides at Megara. More important were his visits to Sicily. His interest in politics lasted all his life, and he apparently despaired of doing any good at Athens, save as a teacher and theoretician ; but abroad there might be more hope. Hence he accepted an invitation from Dionysios I, tyrant of Syracuse, somewhere about the year 388, to visit his court. Plato could make no impression on the tyrant [30] and was disgusted with the luxurious life of the Sicilian Greeks in general, but he found one most devoted follower, Dion, cousin of Dionysios, who persuaded him, after he had returned to Greece, to come again and endeavour to make a philosopher-king of Dionysios II, by this time come to the throne. Plato accepted, feeling rightly that this was a challenge to philosophy. Dionysios, however, banished Dion some three months after Plato's arrival, and while professing great admiration for the philosopher, would neither take his lofty and idealistic advice nor let him go. When at length he contrived to leave Sicily, he was again invited by Dionysios to visit him, and consented to do so, with no better results and some danger to himself. The only positive outcome of these courageous missionary journeys was friendly association with the Pythagoreans who survived in the West and a consequent influence of their views upon his which, although grossly exaggerated in later times, was real and considerable. He made a last attempt to intervene in Sicilian affairs by letter (the seventh and eighth epistles), but without success, for Dion was by that time dead and the surviving members of his party could or would do nothing effective. For the rest of his life Plato was purely a teacher and an inspirer of action, as well as thought, in others.

Precisely when he began to write the Dialogues which we have is not known, though the likely assumption is usually made that it was not before Sokrates' death. They do not represent his lectures, save in so far as these may have followed the Sokratic model and made great use of question and answer, but are rather essays on particular points of methodology, ethics, or metaphysics in which his thought has crystallized out into unsurpassable form. We are in the unusually fortunate position of having everything he wrote, with the addition of a few short pieces which are not by him but imitations, more or less clever and

---

[30] That he handed Plato over to the Spartan envoy, who sold him as a slave, to be bought in Aigina by Annikeris of Kyrene and set free, is stated on respectable authority, see Christ-Schmid, i, p. 661, n. 2, but not mentioned by Plato himself, who tells the story of his Sicilian experiences *ep.* vii, 326 B *sqq.*

all apparently early, of his manner; [31] the text is generally good, although numerous small difficulties are present, as indeed they are bound to be in an author so widely read and so many times copied. The task of the modern is to appreciate and interpret.

No chronological arrangement has come down from antiquity, save for one or two notes of the date of a particular dialogue, the most important fact recorded being that the *Laws* was his last work. After many futile, because subjective, attempts to arrange them chronologically, the proper method was set forth by the late Professor Lewis Campbell of St. Andrews, in the preface to his edition of the *Sophist* and *Politicus*, Oxford, 1867, and has since been developed by many writers, notably Lutoslawski (*Origin and Growth of Plato's Logic*, London, 1897); several of these will be found in Christ-Schmid, i, p. 670, n. 7. It consists in collecting as many peculiarities of style and grammar as possible from those works, particularly the *Laws*, which are known or for good reasons supposed to belong to the author's latest period, and observing the frequency with which these occur in other dialogues. If then it is found, *e.g.*, that one dialogue uses commonly 100 of these, another but 60, it is reasonable to suppose the former to be nearer in time to the *Laws*, *i.e.*, later. Confidence in the soundness of this method is increased by the fact that the dialogues, arranged according to it, show an intelligible and self-consistent development of the doctrines expressed. The best-known ancient arrangement is the very bad one due to Thrasyllos, court astrologer to the Emperor Tiberius, by tetralogies according to subject, which results in several tetralogies consisting of works of very different lengths and dates, and occasionally in the inclusion of a spurious or doubtful dialogue to make up the four.

When arranged approximately in the order in which they probably were written, the dialogues are seen to fall into four groups.

I. *The Sokratic group*, consisting of short works in which Sokrates is always the principal figure. With one exception, the *Apology*, which is not a dialogue but, apparently, an idealized version of Sokrates' defence at his trial, these are eristic in tone, seeking rather to upset the contentions of Sokrates' opponents in debate than to establish anything positive. Thus, in the *Euthyphro*, successive attempts to define holiness or piety (τὸ ὅσιον) are overthrown by arguments sometimes sound, sometimes merely *ad hominem* or otherwise sophistical. To this group belong

[31] Besides the prose writings, there exist a number of little poems said to be of his composition. After subtracting several which are most obviously later, there remain some which may well be the work of a fourth-century Athenian. The reason for hesitating to ascribe them to Plato is simply the absence of any cogent evidence, external or internal, that he wrote them. They are collected in Diehl, i, p. 87 *sqq.*

Apology, Crito, Charmides, Laches, Euthyphro, Hippias Minor,
and, if it is by Plato at all, *Hippias Maior,*[32] *Ion* (the title has
nothing to do with Euripides' play ; Ion is a rhapsode whose
pretensions to wisdom, founded on his knowledge of Homer,
Sokrates disposes of in most humorous fashion), *Lysis.* Apart
from their philosophic interest—dialectic developing and becoming gradually more accurate in the analysis of ethical themes—
all these little works are distinguished by their vividness of style
and character-drawing ; thus the modest and charming boy
Lysis, in the dialogue named after him, his more self-confident
friend Menexenos and his shy admirer Hippothales are all brought
to life with a few words of description and a few short speeches
from them, while Sokrates' attitude towards the boys is delightful,
and pedagogically perfect.

II. *The First and Second Platonic Groups* need not, for purely
literary purposes, be sharply distinguished. They have two outstanding characteristics which differentiate them from the Sokratic.
Sokrates, while still prominent and the chief speaker, is become
more a mouthpiece either for Plato's original views or for ideas
which the pupil considered to have been latent in the master's own
teaching and now develops at greater length. The first group
was almost entirely what the ancient critics called Σωκρατικοὶ
λόγοι, sketches of Sokrates, and probably, allowing for a little
natural idealization, are very like what he really did and said.
Now come a number of positive doctrines, some of them very
likely the fruits, not so much of Sokrates' direct influence, though
this is a doubtful point,[33] as of Plato's own reflections on what

---

[32] The terms *maior* and *minor*, μείζων and ἐλάττων, refer simply to
the length of the two dialogues, respectively 9 and about 4½ pages in
Stallbaum's one-volume edition of Plato. My objection to accepting
the *H. maior* as authentic, despite its undoubted resemblance to Plato's
language, is the clumsiness with which the sophist Hippias is caricatured.
He is made to reason, not merely like an uncritical man, but like a fool.

[33] It is, for instance, Taylor's opinion that a large amount of Pythagorean influence and metaphysical doctrine reached Plato through
Sokrates himself. Against this perhaps the most pertinent objection is,
that if Sokrates had taught anything like the immortality of the soul,
or the Theory of Forms, we should expect to hear something of these
doctrines in the earliest work of Plato, whereas they seem to develop
gradually as we reach the later periods. See the good, though brief
criticisms of Ross in *Proc. Class. Ass.*, 1933, p. 7 *sqq.* On the other hand,
dogmatically to deny that Sokrates can have had any such interests is
to go beyond the evidence. One may hold, for example, that the elaborate
arguments for immortality in the *Phaedo* are Plato's own without com-
mitting oneself to the position that Sokrates held no discussion with his
friends on his last day, or never speculated with them whether or not
he might hope to live on after his body died.

he had learned from his Pythagorean friends and the writings of their school. Prominent among these are the insistence on the immortality of the soul and the famous Theory of Forms, or Ideas (εἴδη, ἰδέαι), according to which there exist, beyond time and space, realities corresponding to our abstract concepts, and some kind of connexion (never very clearly analysed or defined) with these gives the particular objects in the material world such reality as they can claim ; a white object, for instance, is not a mere phantom, because it somehow participates in the Form of Whiteness. Having so much positively to teach, although negative conclusions and brilliant, often sophistical, eristic argument are by no means at an end, these works give proportionately more space to philosophical discussion, less to dramatic description and the other incidentals which make the shorter pieces so delightfully vivid. On the other hand, several of this group have a new and most fascinating feature, the myth.[34] A great part of Plato's eschatology is expressed, not in fully reasoned statements, but in prose poems, represented as revelations of sages or other venerable and inspired teachings, which claim no higher degree of truth than accordance with what can be known or guessed concerning those transcendental realities which are beyond our comprehension. Allegory naturally plays a large part in these, Orphic-Pythagorean doctrines are certainly laid under contribution, and the tone rises, not only above the delicate simplicities of ordinary Platonic narrative, but above all ordinary limits of prose, so that it was held by some that the author had gone too far in this direction, and trespassed upon the territory of the dithyramb.[35]

Early in this group, apparently, come several dialogues directed against sophists and sophistry, the general thesis being that these men, despite their renown as teachers, had no really sound and critical views, positive or negative, to offer and were themselves at the mercy of cleverer dialecticians, including Sokrates, should he choose to chop logic with them. In the *Gorgias*, the great rhetorician is treated with some consideration ; but his disciples Polos and Kallikles, who push his opportunism to lengths beyond what he would himself sanction, are utterly routed. In the *Protagoras*, the respectable and moral sophist is overthrown by an argument which he cannot fathom. The *Euthydemus* is broad farce, a pair of minor sophists being led through a most

---

[34] The most interesting book (though debatable at some points) on this subject, at all events in English, is still J. E. Stewart, *Myths of Plato*, London, Macmillan, 1905.

[35] See Dion. Hal., *de Demosth.*, 7 (p. 142, 2 *sqq.*, Usener-Radermacher).

amusing maze of fallacies. The *Cratylus* is interesting in many ways ; it is our first surviving treatise on etymology, for Kratylos, after whom it is named, introduces the theory that the ' right ' words have a natural affinity with the things they signify, and Sokrates elaborates this for a while in a series of most marvellous derivations ; its conclusion, moreover, leads up to the Theory of Forms by insisting on the existence of certain realities behind the words, which alone are the true objects of knowledge. The *Phaedo* is not polemic, save in so far as it is a defence and glorification of Sokrates. It unites with an account of his last day, which is one of the masterpieces of the pathetic in any literature, a description of the debate he held with a few friends concerning immortality, ending with the great eschatological myth of the True Surface of the Earth. A longer work, Plato's literary masterpiece and in many respects his most important contribution to philosophy as well, belongs to this group. The *Republic* falls into ten books, which divide into three groups, probably composed at different times. In Book I, Sokrates, visiting the aged Kephalos at the Peiraieus, falls into a discussion, first with him, then with his son Polemarchos (brother of the orator Lysias), finally with the famous sophist Thrasymachos of Chalkedon (see p. 279) on the nature of justice. The conclusions are negative, Thrasymachos being defeated when he defines justice as the advantage of the stronger. In the next three books, Sokrates tries himself to define justice, at the instance of Glaukon and Adeimantos, Plato's brothers. In order to do so, he constructs a model state, as being larger and easier to interpret than the individual. It is a sort of philosophic communism, with a highly trained ruling class, the Guardians, who have no private property at all. In this, justice is found to consist in the performance by every class of citizens of its own proper functions and no other (τὰ ἑαυτοῦ πράττειν), whence it is concluded that the same applies to the individual, the three parts of whose soul will, if he is just, perform each its own function, the higher ruling and the lower obeying. The remaining books consist of very elaborate discussions of sundry difficulties, such as the position of women in the model state, the nature of marriage among the Guardians and the details of their education, and the causes which might bring such a state into being and in time overthrow it. Finally, the great Myth of Er contains a vision of the lot of the just and the unjust in the after-life.

Less important members of this group are, first, the *Meno*, a discussion, named after Menon the Thessalian, who is Sokrates' interlocutor, of whether virtue or excellence (ἀρετή) can be taught ;

one point of interest is the introduction of the theory that all learning is reminiscence (ἀνάμνησις) of the perfect knowledge gained by the disembodied soul from contemplation of the verities of nature.[36] Next, the first *Alcibiades*, (if genuine ; the second is certainly spurious and of no importance), dealing with the necessity of real knowledge to the statesman. On the outskirts of the group, probably early, and placed by a quite anachronistic allusion somewhere about the end of the Corinthian War,[37] is the puzzling *Menexenus*, consisting largely of a funeral oration supposedly written by Aspasia (the ' morganatic ' wife of Perikles) and usually considered a satire on the commonplaces and falsified history characteristic of such speeches.

Two of the most important dialogues are the *Phaedrus* and the *Symposium*, in which, more especially in the last, is elaborated the doctrine of Platonic love. This, in the true sense, not in the jargon of some inferior moderns, is a passion which, excited in the first instance by the sight of a beautiful body, rises to less and less material objects, finally becoming an intense desire for Beauty itself, a supersensuous reality, one of the Forms, and perceptible only to the mind. The former dialogue, a conversation between Sokrates and a young admirer of Lysias, Phaidros by name, runs off into an interesting criticism of the orators of the day ; the latter describes a banquet (hence the title) held at the house of Agathon, and after all the principal guests have spoken in praise of love, Sokrates of course setting forth the Platonic doctrine, introduces Alkibiades, whose speech is a glorification of Sokrates as the perfect lover. Both dialogues are distinguished further by their extraordinarily magnificent and beautiful myths.

As this group draws towards its end, a new interest arises. The *Theaetetus* deals with epistemology, and is the best refutation yet written of the theory now known as Pragmatism, in the form of Protagoras' dictum that man is the measure of all things. The *Parmenides* is a work which many students of Plato have, not unnaturally, found puzzling. Sokrates, represented as a young man, is introduced in discussion with Zenon and Parmenides the Eleatic philosophers. He defends the Theory of Forms and is utterly defeated in debate, and advised to make a more careful study of dialectic in order to develop his own great powers to the full. A brilliant dialectical exhibition then follows.

---

[36] *Meno*, 82 B *sqq.* ; the theory is illustrated by a lesson in geometry which is the earliest instance we have of the application of the Hebartian method (ancient, like most ' modern ' educational developments).

[37] *Menex.*, 244 D. See p. 424.

I personally believe this to be serious, Sokrates to represent Plato's own earlier views, now abandoned, and the dialogue to signify a complete change of attitude, extraordinary in a man who must then have been some 60 years old. Certain it is that the Theory of Forms is no longer seriously used in the remaining works.

III. These comprise the *Third Platonic Group*, and are few, but important. In form, all are very simple, none having the elaborate setting of some of the earlier works.[38] Sokrates is prominent in but one, absent from some ; the mystical tone to be found in more than one work of the First and Second Platonic Groups is almost entirely lacking : there are few myths, and these generally unimportant. Two, *Sophist* and *Politicus*, have, besides the material suggested by their titles, a further interest in their method of approaching the subject, great use being made of dichotomy. One, the *Timaeus*, is a cosmology, which returns again to the Theory of Forms, but in a significant context ; Timaios, into whose mouth it is put, claims nothing more than reasonable probability for his or any human theories on such a matter.[39] Following on this is the *Critias*, which was never finished. What there is of it continues from the *Timaeus* the famous tale of Atlantis, the island which once existed in the Atlantic. Its origin is Plato's imagination, working upon travellers' tales of some of the islands which really lie beyond the Straits of Gibraltar ; he is not to blame for the wild work which cranks of various dates have made of it. There was to have been another dialogue, *Hermokrates*,[40] making, with the *Republic*, *Timaeus* and *Critias*, a tetralogy dealing with the universe, man and human government ; but it was never written.

Sokrates makes his last appearance as leader of the discussion on pleasure in the *Philebus*, in which also something like the old liveliness of dialogue is seen here and there ; most of this group tend to degenerate into lectures from one speaker, with occasional

[38] A Platonic dialogue may be (1) purely dramatic, the speakers' names being set at the head of their speeches as in a play, with no introduction or explanation ; (2) wholly narrative, as the *Republic*, in which Sokrates gives an account of the conversation in which he took part ; (3) reported narrative, as the *Symposium* ; Apollodoros repeats the account he had heard from Aristodemos ; (4) a dialogue read ; this is the form of the *Theaetetus*, in which Eukleides' slave reads to his master and Terpsion a report, made by the former in consultation with Sokrates, of a discussion. (2)–(4) all may have introductions, and in (1) the conversation may run for a while on other than the main topic. The dialogues of the Third Platonic group are all of form (1).

[39] *Tim.*, 28 D.   [40] See *Crit.*, 108 A.

remarks and questions from the rest. He is entirely absent from the *Laws*, Plato's last work. In this an Athenian stranger, who if he is not Plato himself certainly embodies his views, expounds to a Cretan and a Spartan how he would have a new colony governed which it is proposed to found. Very roughly and inadequately, this long and difficult work [41] may be described as a modification of the *Republic* in the direction of practicability. That it should represent a philosopher as consulted regarding a constitution is in accordance, not only with Plato's abiding interest in the science of politics, but with fact ; several philosophers actually drew up constitutions for Greek states at about that period.

The *Epistles*, as we have them, number thirteen, whereof all but the first profess to be from Plato to various persons. Opinions have differed very widely as to their genuineness,[42] but that Plato wrote the most important, the seventh, is stylistically and with regard to the content so likely that it may be regarded as practically certain. The other long letters, the eighth, which like the seventh is to Dion's relations and friends, some at least of those to Dionysios (Nos. 2, 3, 13), the sixth, to Hermeias, Erastos and Koriskos, possibly the fourth, to Dion, may well be genuine : the ninth, tenth and twelfth, to Archytas and Aristodoros, are obvious pieces of rhetorician's trifling, and in any case they, like the fifth (to Perdikkas) and the eleventh (to Laodamas), are of no importance. The tone of the longer epistles is throughout rather that of manifestoes than of familiar correspondence.

In addition, a number of short works in some sense Platonic have come down to us. Perhaps the most likely to be his is the *Epinomis*, or *Supplement to the Laws*, stated by Diogenes Laertios (iii, 37) to be the work of Philip of Opus. Briefly speaking, it may be urged in favour of its being Plato's own that the style is very like his ; against it, that the doctrine contained in it, including an elaborate system of demonology, is not to be exactly paralleled from the undoubted works.[43] The *Hippias maior* has already been mentioned ; if spurious, it is an early and good imitation. The same may be said, so far as style goes, of the *Minos*, which reveals itself as by an imitator largely by taking seriously an absurd piece of rationalism at which the

---

[41] It is divided into twelve books and is roughly 20 per cent. longer than the next largest work, the *Republic*. Certain difficulties of language give colour to the statement of Diog. Laert., iii, 37, that Plato did not live to revise it finally.

[42] See, for review of the question, J. Harward, *The Platonic Epistles*, Cambridge, Univ. Press, 1932. Much relevant matter in F. Novotný, *Platonis epistulae commentariis illustratae*, Brno, 1930.

[43] For a recent discussion, see Taylor in *Proc. Brit. Acad.*, xv.

real Plato would have laughed.[44]   The *Timaeus Locrus* is in Doric, and does not profess to be by Plato, but by the philosopher, Timaios of Lokris in Italy, who is the chief speaker in the *Timaeus*.   This it is not, but a forgery, put together from Plato's work by some unknown hand, not later than about' the first century A.D., for it is cited as genuine in the second.[45]   The *Axiochus* introduces Sokrates comforting a sick man, after whom the work is named, with some interesting but quite un-Platonic eschatology.   The *Clitophon* is a criticism of Sokrates, to the effect that he proves excellently the necessity for curing the ills of the soul, but' gives no practical directions how to do it.   The *Amatores, de iusto, de uirtute, Demodocus, Eryxias, Sisyphus*, and *Theages* are all unimportant essays on popular philosophy, with many obvious imitations of Platonic dialogues.   The *Definitions* are no doubt the product of his school, the Academy,[46] but not of himself.

Although the Academy continued for many generations and produced more than one respectable philosopher, it never again had a leader comparable to its founder, and of the numerous writings it turned out, almost nothing is left ; in any case, there is no evidence that their literary importance was considerable.   It is highly probable that many of the little works just enumerated are Academic, some of them early.

We therefore pass at once to ARISTOTLE ('Ἀριστοτέλης), Plato's greatest pupil, his one serious rival in antiquity for the throne of philosophy, and to all time one of the foremost names in the history of thought, perhaps the most influential of all who have ever written, both for good, when his endless thirst for systema- tized knowledge and boundless industry have found worthy followers, and for evil, when a superstitious reverence for his authority has led to accepting his tentative conclusions and suggestions as final and absolute truth, needing only to be com- mented upon and explained.[47]   In literature, however, he is less important than his master.   He wrote a number of popular and semi-popular works in a style which gained the praise of so excel- lent a judge as Cicero.[48]   These we have lost, though a good deal

[44] *Minos*, 320 C, Talos (Rose, *Myth.*, p. 204) was fabled to be a man of bronze because he was Minos' justiciar, and carried about copies of his laws on bronze tablets !   [45] By Nikomachos, *harmon.*, xi, 6.

[46] So called because Plato originally taught and lectured in the 'Ἀκαδήμεια, or precinct of the hero Akademos or Hekademos.   His teaching developed into a regular curriculum, it would appear, and his group of disciples into a kind of college.   Being a man of not incon- siderable private means, he would take no fees.

[47] As throughout the Middle Ages.   Much the same is true of Hippo- krates and Galen.

[48] Cicero, *Acad.*, ii, 119.   It has been remarked (see Madvig's ed. of the *de finibus*, Exc. vii) that Cicero, who often uses Aristotle, shows no knowledge of his principal works.

of information survives regarding their contents. His more important and technical writings were bequeathed by him to Theophrastos (see p. 351), from whom they passed to Neleus of Skepsis, his pupil. Neleus' heirs were ignorant boors, and shut their precious legacy up in a cellar, lest it be discovered by Attalos, king of Pergamos, who was then forming his library, a rival to that of Alexandria. At last the books passed into the possession of Apellikon of Teos, a man of literary tastes, who published them after a fashion. But they had been damaged by vermin and damp, and he lacked the specialist's knowledge necessary to correct and supplement them. Fortunately, Sulla, while in Athens, got possession of Apellikon's library, containing the original manuscripts, carried them to Rome, and there deposited them in a safe place. They now received the competent attention of two good scholars, Tyrannion the *grammaticus* and Andronikos of Rhodes, and intelligent attempts were made by them at critical editions, although their efforts were hampered by the greed and haste of publishers, who put hurriedly and badly made copies on the market.[49] Hence our texts, when they go back to Tyrannion or Andronikos, must every here and there lie open to the suspicion that they give us what these men conjectured about the beginning of the Christian era, not what Aristotle himself wrote in the fourth century. Fortunately, the philosopher often repeats himself, and therefore careful and intelligent supplements, such as they would make, no doubt are often right in sense and not infrequently in wording.

Concerning Aristotle's life, the following facts are reported.[50] He was born in 384, the son of a physician of Stageiros in the Thracian Chalkidide, by name Nikomachos, and his wife Phaistias. His parents dying, he was brought up by a certain Proxenos of Atarneus, who seems to have treated him with much kindness and taken great pains to have him well educated. Coming to Athens in 367, he became Plato's pupil, and remained for twenty years a member of the Academy. Plato dying, Aristotle left for Mysia, where he spent the next period of his life with Hermeias, tyrant of Atarneus, a friend and correspondent of Plato.[51] Hermeias treated him as a friend and an equal and married him to Pythias, his own niece and adopted daughter. In 342/1,

[49] Strabo, xiii, 1, 54 ; Plutarch, *Sulla*, 26.

[50] We have, besides isolated bits of information, a life in Diog. Laert., v, 1 *sqq.*, in which the dates are from Apollodoros ; another by Ammonios, of much less account ; and a brief and good outline in Dion. Hal., *ad Ammaeum*, 5.

[51] He is one of the addressees of the sixth Platonic epistle.

Hermeias was killed, and Aristotle, whose father had been court physician to Amyntas, king of Macedon, went to the court of Philip II, where he became tutor to the young prince, afterwards Alexander the Great, who was then 15 years old.[52] In 335/4 he returned to Athens. Xenokrates was by this time head of the Academy ; Aristotle founded a new and similar association, the Lykeion (Latinized into Lyceum), named from its meeting-place, a precinct of Apollo Lykeios not far from Athens. The next eighteen years were actively spent in teaching and writing ; after the death of Alexander, the anti-Macedonian party came temporarily to power, and Aristotle left the city for Chalkis, where he died in the summer of 322.

Aristotle's prodigious activity extended to most branches of the higher learning, except mathematics and music. How much he wrote was a disputed point in antiquity ; two estimates which have come down to us give respectively 400 and 1,000 book-rolls. Doubtless the larger and it may be the smaller include some spurious works ; we have forty-seven treatises, large and small, genuine and spurious, which bear his name, besides many fragments of others and some verses said to be of his composition.

Of his popular works, to which no doubt Cicero's estimate of his style was meant to apply, we have none complete. We know, however, that they included an essay of a kind destined to become popular, a *Protreptikos*, or exhortation to the study of philosophy. There were also a number of dialogues, dealing with very diverse themes (philosophy in general, including the history of the subject, wealth, love, education, friendship, drunkenness, the difficulties in Homer). In all of these, the tendency to be found in some of the Platonic dialogues for the discussion to pass into a long disquisition by one speaker was modified in the direction of having two or more such speakers, who each stated his case at length ; an arrangement which was familiar to the sophists and re-appears, for us, who have lost the intervening works of this kind, in the philosophical writings of Cicero, for instance the *de diuinatione*.[53]

Aristotle's regular method, in handling any subject, was to

---

[52] Hence much picturesque fable about the famous teacher and pupil, as that Aristotle taught the infant Alexander his letters, and many forged writings supposed to be communications from one to the other.

[53] These works seem identical with what were known as his exoteric or 'University extension' teaching, meant for the cultivated public in general ; the more specialized and technical writings and lectures were called, at least by some later writers, esoteric. The word conveys no idea of secrecy or mystery-mongering ; an ἐσωτερικὸς λόγος is a discourse meant for those inside, *i.e.*, belonging to, a given body, in this case the Lykeion.

begin with an assemblage of facts, as large and complete as possible, then to write a series of works each carrying the analysis of the material to a higher point of abstraction. Of this system we have a complete example in his biological treatises. There is first the *Enquiry concerning Animals* (περὶ τὰ ζῷα ἱστορίαι, *Historia animalium*), which, as we have it, is in ten books ; of these, however, the ninth certainly, the seventh probably, are not Aristotle's, and the tenth, in the form now existing, does not seem to be ancient at all.[54] It contains a great array of facts, showing a surprising amount of accurate knowledge and observation. Three other treatises, *On the Members of Animals*, in four books, *On the Reproduction of Animals*, in five, and *On the Locomotion of Animals*, in one,[55] handle selected parts of the material from the standpoint of physiology rather than of descriptive zoology. Crowning the series is the important work, in three books, *On the Soul* (περὶ ψυχῆς, *de anima* ; the title might equally well be rendered *On the Vital Principle*), while a number of small treatises, collectively known by their mediaeval title of the *Parua naturalia*,[56] discuss particular problems.

There are numerous treatises dealing with natural history in one way or another which have come down to us under Aristotle's name, but either have no connexion with him or represent ideas of his expressed by others, now and then making use of some of his lost works. The little treatise *On Plants* is a production of the Revival of Letters, a retranslation into Greek of a Latin version of an Arabic version of a lost Greek book not by Aristotle himself, although he probably did write a work on botany. The curious little treatise, or sermon, generally known as the *de mundo*, is late, perhaps of about the beginning of the Imperial period ; it deals with the order and government of the universe, and was immensely popular.[57] The

---

[54] See Christ-Schmid, i, p. 734, n. 4. The idea has often been expressed that Aristotle got his fondness for biology from his father ; but supposing that Nikomachos lived long enough to influence his son's tastes, he, being a physician, would rather be interested in medical botany than in zoology.

[55] Περὶ ζῴων μορίων, περὶ ζῴων γενέσεως, περὶ ζῴων πορείας. There is also a spurious work, περὶ ζῴων κινήσεως.

[56] *On Perception and Perceptibles* (περὶ αἰσθήσεως καὶ αἰσθητῶν) ; *On Memory and Recollection* (περὶ μνήμης καὶ ἀναμνήσεως) ; *On Sleep and Waking* (περὶ ὕπνου καὶ ἐγρηγόρσεως) ; *On Divination from Dreams* (περὶ ἐνυπνίων καὶ τῆς καθ᾽ ὕπνον μαντικῆς) ; *On Length and Shortness of Life* (περὶ μακροβιότητος καὶ βραχυβιότητος) ; *On Youth and Old Age* (περὶ νεότητος καὶ γήρως) ; *On Life and Death* (περὶ ζωῆς καὶ θανάτου) ; *On Respiration* (περὶ ἀναπνοῆς).

[57] It has been adequately edited, and something like order brought into the chaos of its MSS. and translations, by W. L. Lorimer, Paris, Les Belles Lettres, 1933.

Problems are a long and by no means unimportant work, in the form of questions and attempted answers, on all manner of scientific and a few literary topics ; their very heterogeneous material owes a good deal to Aristotle himself and his immediate successors, besides later sources. The *Mechanica* deals with problems of mechanics, and, whoever may actually have written it, is fairly early ; it passed for Aristotle's own, which it is not, when the lists we have of his works were composed. Two works, the *Physiognomica* and the περὶ θαυμασίων ἀκουσμάτων, the former on the bodily peculiarities which accompany different characters, the latter, as its title implies, on ' marvellous reports ', *i.e.*, extraordinary phenomena alleged to exist in various countries, may contain Aristotelian material, but seem to date from about the time of Hadrian. The others of this class are mere trifles.[58]

No other group is so complete. Thus for literature and many sciences we have lost the long series of works dealing with the history of the subjects which Aristotle began and his pupils and successors continued. These included the *Didaskaliai*, or list of plays successful at the Dionysia and Lenaia, the source probably of all that we now have concerning the date of tragedies and comedies, also lists of victors in the Olympian and Pythian Games ; while only fragments and references are left to us of the great collections on rhetoric (συναγωγὴ τεχνῶν, *i.e.*, *Collection of Treatises on the Art*, sc., of speech), on arithmetic, mathematics and astronomy (these three were by Eudemos of Rhodes), and Theophrastos' eighteen books on *Opinions of the Physical Philosophers* (δόξαι φυσικῶν ; a scrap of an epitome of it is left and deals with objects of sense). Of the huge collection of *Constitutions* (πολιτεῖαι), describing the government of every state the college could hear of, we have a large part of one volume, the damaged, but valuable, work on *The Constitution of Athens*.[59]

There survive, however, Aristotle's own chief theoretical works on philosophy, science and literature. First is the so-called *Organon (Instrument, Tool)*, easily the most important group of writings on logic that has survived from antiquity, and the most influential of its kind in the world. As usually arranged, it begins with the *Categories*, mainly a discussion of the famous ten classes into which all predicables may be divided. Following on this is the Περὶ ἑρμηνείας, commonly known by its absurd Latin

---

[58] *On Breath, On (natural) Colouring, On the Rising of the Nile*—this was a genuine work, but we have only a Latin version of an epitome of it—*Positions and Names of the Winds*.

[59] First published, from a papyrus found in Egypt, by (Sir) F. G. Kenyon, London, 1891 ; since then often re-edited and commented upon, notably by Blass, Wilamowitz-Moellendorff, Sandys and Kenyon himself.

title *de interpretatione*. It is more nearly *On Predication*, and not only formal logic but grammatical analysis owe much to it, short though it is. The eight books of the *Topica* [60] treat of the manner in which a proposition may be satisfactorily analysed and discussed ; the treatise on fallacies known as the Σοφιστικοὶ ἔλεγχοι (refutations in the manner of the sophists, *i.e.*, logically unsound and made simply to score in debate), forms a supplement to it. The great works of this series are the two *Analytics*, *Prior* and *Posterior*, each in two books. The former deals with formal logic, the latter is concerned rather with epistemology. Of all the Aristotelian corpus, this series and the *Metaphysics* perhaps show most clearly what is more or less characteristic of everything we have from this author, the style of a lecture-room, indeed of the lecturer's own notes, or perhaps in some cases the note-book of a student. Their Greek, for the most part, not only is crabbed, devoid of ornament, and often highly elliptical, but is crammed with phrases of an allusive kind, often hard to interpret, generally quite impossible to translate literally. One of the commonest and most famous is τὸ τί ἦν εἶναι , literally ' the what was it (for something) to be (what it is) ', *i.e.*, the essential nature of the thing in question, as it would be expressed by a good definition. Such tricks of speech, and also the habit of alluding in three or four words to an illustrative anecdote, are perfectly intelligible if we are dealing with notes, which might be expanded and explained orally as need arose ; one can hardly imagine any one indulging in them in works intended for publication. The same impression is produced when, for example, in the *Nikomachean Ethics*, we find so weighty and difficult a matter as the criticism of the Platonic Theory of Forms set out in a highly compressed outline, while sundry sections quite easy to understand and of much less importance are written out in full.[61] Probably Aristotle found it easier to state a metaphysical problem which interested him deeply than to set forth ethical details in a fluent and attractive style, and so trusted to his memory and the inspiration of the moment much more in the former than in the latter case.

The title *Physics* for one of Aristotle's principal works is misleading to a modern ; as a matter of fact the ancient name for it

[60] The genuineness of the concluding part of the *Categories*, the whole of the *de interp*. and the fifth book of the *Topics*, has been doubted in ancient and modern times. That they are of the school of Aristotle is certain ; the question is merely whether he actually composed them all himself.

[61] See *Eth. Nic.*, i, ch. 6 ; contrast, *e.g.*, practically the whole of Bk. iv.

is φυσικὴ ἀκρόασις, *i.e.*, *Lectures* (literally ' hearing ') *on Nature*.
It discusses, not such laws as are generally studied by a modern
physicist, but rather the fundamental ideas of matter, motion and
so forth, leading up to the famous conception of God as the
unmoved first mover of the whole.   Hence it is that it is traditionally followed (since Andronikos' edition) by a work, or rather
a somewhat loose congeries of works, on what Aristotle himself
called primary philosophy (πρώτη φιλοσοφία) or theology, but has
carried into modern times the nickname of ' what comes after
the *Physics* ', τὰ μετὰ τὰ Φυσικά.   The *Metaphysics*, then, deals
with the ultimate questions of being, essence, potentiality and
activity, unity and so forth.   There are, in the usual arrangement,
fourteen books, usually denoted by the first thirteen letters of
the Greek alphabet, the insignificant little book which stands
second being called a ἔλαττον, in contradistinction to the important first (A).   Belonging to this series, but much more closely
connected with the *Physics* than the *Metaphysics*, are three works
of some importance, *On the Heavens* (περὶ οὐρανοῦ, *de caelo* ;
not to be confused with the spurious *de mundo*), in four books,
giving a reasoned statement of the geocentric theory of the
universe, followed by a discussion of the elements and of what
we should now call gravitation ; [62] *On Becoming and Passing*
(περὶ γενέσεως καὶ φθορᾶς, *de generatione et corruptione*), in two
books, and *Meteorologica* (mostly on atmospheric phenomena,
but dealing to some extent with what were not yet clearly distinguished from them, viz., comets and meteors, and also with
the nature of the sea), in four. [63]

Of more lasting importance than the physical treatises are
the ethical and political writings.   The chief of the former is the
so-called *Nikomachean Ethics*, already incidentally mentioned,
which is perhaps the greatest and most famous of all works on
morals. certainly the most notable exposition of Greek ethics.
The title is derived from the name of Aristotle's son Nikomachos,
called after his grandfather.   It falls into ten books, and its

[62] Aristotle, like most of the ancient physicists, was perfectly aware
that a falling body is simply one moving towards the centre of the earth,
which he imagined to be also the centre of the universe, and that there
is no such thing as an absolute up or down.   The defects of his doctrine
are the idea that some bodies have a tendency to fall away from the
centre, *i.e.*, have negative weight, and the absence of any means of esti-
mating the gravitational pull quantitatively.

[63] The *Metaphysics* have been admirably edited and commented by
H. Bonitz, Bonn, 1848-9 (2 vols.) and more recently by W. D. Ross, Oxford,
1924 ; the *de gen. et corr.* by H. H. Joachim, Oxford, 1922 ; the *Meteor.*
by F. H. Fobes, Harvard Univ. Press, 1918 (text and app. crit. only).

fundamental principle is the doctrine of the Mean, according to which every virtue is a proper blend of two opposed and non-moral tendencies (as courage, of fear and daring), and lies between two vices, resulting from the exaggeration of one tendency or the other.   The shorter *Eudemian Ethics* (seven books) is certainly closely connected with the *Nikomachean*, having large sections in common, even to verbal identity ; but the relations between it and the longer work, and also its connexion with Aristotle's scholar Eudemos, are matters still unsettled.[64]   The shortest treatise on ethics, despite its title, is the so-called *Magna Moralia*, in two books, usually considered a Peripatetic work of later date (about third or second century B.C.) based on Aristotle.[65]   The little list of definitions generally called *de uirtutibus et uitiis* is manifestly not Aristotle's.

Closely allied to ethics, for Aristotle as for all Greeks, is Politics, and the treatise bearing that name is one of his best-known and most widely read, in both ancient and modern times. That its eight books either stand in the order in which he would have them studied or were all composed at one time, or from one point of view, are assertions which no critical scholar would make.[66]   Indeed, it would be strange if the work were complete and rounded off ; for to Aristotle, politics were the very crown of philosophical study, as indeed they are, and the ultimate end of the State to provide an environment in which those capable of the highest mental and moral development might attain thereto.   Hence his researches on the subject began early and never ended, embracing the historical,[67] theoretical and practical aspects.   The important sections of this great work are the sketch of the ideal state, Books vii and viii and the end of iii, the account of the various forms of government in Books iv–vi ; shorter, but weighty, the discussions of sovranty and responsibility (iii, chap. x *sqq.*) and of kingship (iii, xiv, *sqq.*).   It is typical of the vast influence which the idealist Plato had over his realist pupil that Aristotle, living under Philip and Alexander, still has a belief in the possibility of an improved city-state on traditional Greek lines as an independent power and does not realize that the day of empires and great kingdoms is definitely come.

[64] See Christ-Schmid, i, p. 743.

[65] See W. Jäger, *Aristoteles* (Weidmann, 1923), p. 237 ; W. D. Ross, *Aristotle* (Methuen, 1923), p. 15.

[66] For a fuller sketch of the *Politics*, see Christ-Schmid, i, p. 746 *sqq.* ; for details, see the works referred to *ibid.*, note 57, and the larger editions of the work itself, as Susemihl-Hicks.

[67] Besides the Πολιτεῖαι, there was a work *On barbarian customs* (νόμιμα βαρβαρικά) and a collection of statutes (δικαιώματα).

Who wrote the little work, in two books, known as *Oeconomica* is uncertain, but the first book probably, the second certainly, is not Aristotle's. The former deals with economy in the strict etymological sense, *i.e.*, with the proper management of a household and private estate, and has little or nothing to do with our science of Economics, of which the Greeks had barely the first beginnings. The second is a collection of examples, often very amusing, of the ways in which individuals and states have contrived to raise funds in emergencies. Its author was very likely a Peripatetic,[68] though not the master himself.

Of Aristotle's studies in literature two great examples have survived, though very much has been lost. The *Poetics* is the first work we have which is devoted solely and professedly to literary criticism. In its original shape, it consisted of a treatment of three great forms, Epic, Tragedy and Comedy ; but the part dealing with Comedy is wholly lost,[69] that on Epic is much mutilated ; the work, therefore, as we have it is mostly a discussion of Tragedy. As such, within its self-imposed limits, it is admirable,[70] and has exercised an enormous influence, largely through translations and amid a fog of misunderstandings. Thus, of the famous Three Unities it teaches but one, that of Action. Concerning Time, it states the plain fact [71] that Tragedy does usually confine the events described to a period not much exceeding twenty-four hours (' one revolution of the sun '). Of Unity of Place there is not a hint, and no such restriction is known to any Greek dramatist, although the scene does not often change, as a rule, especially in Comedy. To the *Poetics* also we owe the famous and much-discussed definition of Tragedy as ' an imitation of a serious and complete matter of considerable extent . . . which by means of pity and fear brings about a purification [72] of the corresponding passions '.

[68] The name Peripatetics (*Περιπατητικοί*) commonly given to Aristotle's followers arises from the circumstance that his lectures were conducted in the walks or avenues (*περίπατοι*) of the Lykeion.

[69] An unsuccessful attempt to reconstruct it, mostly on the basis of the Tractatus Coislinianus (see p. 400), has been made by Lane Cooper, *Aristotle's Theory of Comedy*.

[70] It does not treat either of the psychological condition of the poet himself, in other words of ' inspiration ', or of the relation of poetry to morals.

[71] *Poet.*, 1449^b 12. What he there says is true of the later works especially, including most of Euripides' plays, and also of New Comedy, which had no choric odes to cover the passage of time between episodes. See Rose in *Aberystwyth Studies*, vol. vi, pp. 1–22.

[72] *Ibid.*, 1449^b 24–28. By ' imitation ' (*μίμησις*) Aristotle, here and elsewhere, does not mean photographically accurate reproduction of the

The *Rhetoric* is not a handbook of the subject, but rather an analysis of the means by which argument is persuasive when not logically cogent. The chief matters discussed are the subjects of oratory, the forms of reasoning, or semi-reasoning, and of appeals to the emotions, and the types of emotion which the speaker may expect to find or excite. It is thus a work largely psychological in its interest. But the third book [73] approaches more nearly to the common manuals which in later times drew upon and displaced it, for it deals with style, arrangement and, in an interesting section to which later writings on grammar were to owe much, with language.

There is another work on rhetoric in the Aristotelian corpus, the so-called *Rhetorica ad Alexandrum*. This is far inferior, being hardly more than a book of practical advice how to befool an audience by the usual oratorical tricks. Its author is certainly not Aristotle ; it is generally supposed to have been written by ANAXIMENES of Lampsakos (see p. 310).[74]

II. *Oratory*, that is oratory which was thought of sufficient importance to commit to writing and preserve, is in some sense an offshoot of philosophy. The Greeks indeed practised and valued persuasive speech from very early times, as is clearly proved, if it needs proof, by Homer's many references to it. But oratory as a conscious art begins, so far as we know, in Sicily, and its great age is roughly from Gorgias to Aristotle.

The earliest names we hear of, themselves become almost legendary, are those of KORAX and TEISIAS, two Sicilians, the former being called the teacher of the latter. At all events, both wrote handbooks of rhetoric (τέχναι), which have not survived, but were known to Aristotle.[75] Their approximate date can be

subject, which is not art at all, but its re-expression in terms of the material, in this case words, of the art in question. Whether ' purification ' (κάθαρσις) is a harmless discharge of the feelings of fear and pity, leaving the spectator ' with calm of mind, all passion spent ' or the ridding of these feelings of their impure and harmful elements, changing, *e.g.*, that pity for an individual which is largely dread of the misfortunes he suffers befalling oneself into sympathy for the sorrows of humanity at large or of some class of human beings, and whether, in the one or the other case, the theory is psychologically sound, are all disputed points.

[73] An attempt has been made to prove the third book not Aristotle's, see F. Marx in *Berichte der sächs. Ges.*, lii (1900), pp. 314–28.

[74] See Christ-Schmid, i, p. 534.

[75] See *Rhet.*, 1402ᵃ 17, where he characterizes the work of Korax as consisting of quibbles about ' probability ' (τὸ εἰκός) ; Cic., *Brut.*, 46, where he is quoted as mentioning both and giving their approximate date (*sublatis in Sicilia tyrannis*).

determined by the political circumstances; after the downfall of the great tyrants, especially those of Syracuse, and the establishment of democracies in the island, there was an urgent demand for the art which claimed to ' manufacture persuasion ' (πειθοῦς δημιουργὸς was Korax' description of rhetoric), and thus to sway assemblies and law-courts. A great figure soon arose, in the person of GORGIAS of Leontinoi, the famous sophist who lived through most of the fifth century. In accordance with his own despair of positive knowledge,[76] he naturally devoted much attention to that substitute for it which might be practically useful, and began regularly to study and apply the means by which prose may be made impressive and interesting, while retaining its own character. His chief contribution was the so-called Gorgian figures (σχήματα), in other words an elaborate arrangement of thought and language alike in a series of effective antitheses, elaborately worked out to give a rhythmical effect by the pairing of clauses (often riming) [77] of the same length (parisosis).

A short example, imitated from his funeral oration delivered, or professing to be delivered, over the Athenian dead (fr. 6 Diels) will give some idea of his manner. ' Servants of the undeservedly unfortunate, punishers of the undeservedly fortunate ; advantageously of bold intent, in fit season ready to relent ; by the minds' prudence overcoming valour's rudeness ; froward against the froward, gentle to the gentle, fearless against the fearless, dread in the hour of dread.' This would very soon pall either on a modern or on Greeks of the time of Demosthenes ; but when Gorgias used it, it had the charm of novelty.

THRASYMACHOS of Chalkedon, who was teaching in Athens during the Peloponnesian War, introduced both by precept and example (he wrote a manual and a number of model speeches) the use of the period, or complex, rounded sentence which is characteristic of the best oratory, both Greek and Latin, and with it a sort of natural punctuation, by the employment of a definite rhythm, the paean (one long and three short syllables) to mark the beginning and end. That he also used the Gorgian figures need hardly be said ; what we have of him suggests that he used them rather more moderately.

With these two men, leaving minor teachers aside, there was,

[76] He taught (fr. 3 Diels) that nothing exists ; or if it exists, it cannot be comprehended ; or if it exists and can be comprehended, it cannot be communicated.

[77] Rime is rare in verse, characteristic of prose in antiquity. For a discussion of the figures, see Norden, i, p. 15 sqq.

toward the end of the fifth century, a highly developed art of rhetoric to add ornateness and technical brilliancy to the existing eloquence. Of the great statesmen of the time, such as Perikles, we have no authentic monuments, and therefore must begin with the Alexandrian canon of the orators (see p. 390).

Here the earliest name is that of ANTIPHON of Rhamnus in Attica, who was put to death for his share in the abortive revolution of the Four Hundred, in 411 B.C. There survive three speeches attributed to him, and a most interesting set of rhetorical exercises, known as the *Tetralogies*, which also bears his name. Of the genuineness of the speeches there is no very serious doubt, though in antiquity a number of spurious orations circulated as his.[78] All three are written for cases of homicide, the first for the prosecution, the others for the defence ; for Antiphon was apparently a poor man, son of a school-teacher and largely self-trained, who supported himself by giving instruction in rhetoric (Thucydides is said to have been one of his pupils) and by the profession of a λογογράφος, or speech-writer. Attic law did not allow counsel to plead for either party to a suit, but required litigants to state their own cases ; hence a brisk demand for speeches written to their instructions for them to deliver. The language of the orations is somewhat old-fashioned, as might be expected from their date, and has at times a slightly poetical flavour ; Gorgias' and Thrasymachos' devices are used, sometimes rather crudely, especially in the first speech ; but the general effect is earnest and impressive. Antiphon's most famous speech, his own defence on the charge of treason for which he was executed, is lost, and we can say only that it won the admiration of such excellent judges as Thucydides and Agathon.[79]

The authorship of the *Tetralogies* has been doubted, on grounds chiefly of style,[80] and cannot be called certain, though perhaps the balance of probability is in their favour. At all events, they are among the earliest rhetorical exercises we possess.

[78] Besides the *Vitae X oratorum*, falsely ascribed to Plutarch, we have a short life (γένος) of Antiphon preserved in his MSS., but of no independent authority, and notices, of equally little value, in Suidas and other lexicographers. ' Plutarch ' quotes from Caecilius (p. 400) the statement that there were twenty-five spurious speeches out of a total of sixty ascribed to him. Cf. in general, for all the orators, F. Blass, *Die attische Beredsamkeit*[2], Berlin, 1887–98 (3 vols.).

[79] Thucyd., viii, 68, 2 ; the whole passage praises A. highly. For Agathon, see Arist., *Eth. Eud.*, 1232[b] 6–9. Some few scraps of the speech, from a papyrus, are published as fr. 1 in Thalheim's edition (Teubner, 1914).

[80] See Christ-Schmid, i, p. 552, n. 2. See p. 424.

There are three groups of four speeches each (hence the name), two for the prosecution and two for the defence, after the usual Athenian procedure. Again all are cases of homicide ; in one, a man has been murdered together with his personal slave, who before dying accuses an enemy of his master ; the latter is now put on trial. In another, a boy practising javelin-throwing has caused the death of another who ran across the range ; the dead boy's father seeks the extreme penalty. In the third, a violent quarrel has resulted in a killing, and the slayer raises the plea of self-defence.

It is convenient to notice here one or two other minor or nameless works of early Attic oratory. There is a treatise falsely ascribed to Xenophon, dealing with the Constitution of Athens (it is usually cited under its Latin title, *de re publica Atheniensium*, the Aristotelian work of like title, see p. 273, being commonly cited in Greek). It is an informal speech, probably intended to be circulated as what we should call a pamphlet, and its theme is that the Athenian constitution, while utterly wrong in principle, is at least self-consistent in its administration. The tone is bitter in the extreme, and the author clearly no friend of the democracy and, from his style and allusions, earlier than Xenophon's literary activity, perhaps about 425 B.C. Being wholly unknown, he is not infrequently referred to as ' the Old Oligarch '.

A contemporary of Antiphon the orator, often confused with him, was ANTIPHON THE SOPHIST, of whom no complete work survives. Fragments (collected in Diels) show that he wrote a discourse *On Concord* (περὶ ὁμονοίας) and works dealing with mathematics, physics and other philosophic and scientific subjects.[81]

Less important than Antiphon, but interesting, is ANDOKIDES, a member of an ancient Eleusinian family, the Kerykes [82] or Heralds. His life was one long series of adventures and disgraces. Born not many years before the Peloponnesian War began (his exact dates are uncertain), he was implicated with Alkibiades and many others in the double scandal of the mutila-

[81] His approximate date is clear from Xenophon's introduction of him (*Memor.*, i, 6) as an acquaintance of Sokrates with whom he disputed on several occasions. His mathematical attempts included an early and crude method of ' squaring the circle ' thus : inscribe in any given circle a rectilinear figure ; to each side of this apply an isosceles triangle whose vertex touches the circumference of the circle , continue this process until the sides of the triangles are so small that they coincide with the arcs they subtend (which of course they could never exactly do) ; draw a square equal to the resulting polygon and it will also be equal to the circle. See fr. 13 Diels.

[82] The ' Plutarchean ' life is derived mostly from the speeches themselves, but gives some further facts.

tion of the Hermai and the profanation of the Mysteries, on the eve of the Sicilian expedition. He saved his life by turning State's evidence, but was sentenced to loss of civic rights (ἀτιμία) and left Athens. In 411 and again after the fall of the Four Hundred, he made unsuccessful attempts to persuade the people to restore him to full citizenship. Later, after the war was over and the democracy restored under Thrasybulos, he took advantage of the Act of Oblivion passed by the new government, returned, triumphantly defended himself against a charge of impiety raked up out of the fifteen-year-old scandal of the Mysteries [83] and became fairly prominent in public life, being one of the plenipotentiaries sent to negotiate peace with Sparta during the Corinthian War. Out of this employment, however, grew a sentence of banishment, and he left Athens once more.

All his surviving orations relate to his own affairs, for it does not appear that he ever composed speeches for others. The first is by far the most interesting, for it is his defence on the charge of impiety and gives a long account of the whole business of the Hermai. The second and third are respectively an abortive attempt to secure his restoration (407) and a recommendation of the terms of peace offered by the Spartans (392/1).[84] There is a fourth speech generally thought spurious, a supposed indictment of Alkibiades.[84a] His style is that of a man naturally fluent and eloquent, not of a practised rhetorician ; the very absence of studied effects gives it a certain freshness and vigour.

A much greater orator, indeed unsurpassed in his own manner, is LYSIAS.[85] His father was Kephalos, a native of Syracuse,

[83] The date of the trial was 399 ; the sixth oration of those attributed to Lysias, whose genuineness is anything but certain, professes to be for the prosecution in the same case, but not the speech of the chief accuser, Kephisios, see sect. 42. Since political actions in the past could not be made matter of accusation owing to the amnesty, other excuses were sought, and impiety (ἀσέβεια) was more than once found convenient : the impeachment of Sokrates was of the same kind.

[84] The date is fixed by Philochoros *ap*. Didymos, *in Demosth. Phil. x*, col. 7, 19 *sqq.*   [84a] See Addenda, p. 424.

[85] Our best authorities for his life, so far as they go, are his own orat. xii and Dion. Hal. *de Lysia* ; pseudo-Plutarch and some notices in the lexicographers give a certain amount of help. His dates are not exactly known. Dionysios supposes (p. 8, Usener-Radermacher) that he was born 459 B.C., but this seems to rest on the following combination : he went as a colonist to Thurioi (a fact of which there seems to be no doubt) ; he was then 15 years old (source of this unknown, possibly one of his own speeches) ; Thurioi was founded 444. But he need not have been one of the first settlers, therefore the reasoning is not cogent. Kephalos came to Athens at Perikles' invitation (Lys., xii, 4), therefore not before 459 ; he lived there thirty years (*ibid.*), therefore he died not earlier than

who lived in the Peiraieus as a metic, or resident alien (μέτοικος), in very comfortable circumstances, and is best known from the sympathetic portrait of him in the first book of Plato's *Republic*. Of Kephalos' two sons, one, Polemarchos, was put to death by the Thirty ; Lysias escaped with the loss of most of his patrimony, and not unnaturally became a strong supporter of Thrasybulos and the democratic faction. After their triumph, he enjoyed citizenship for a little while, under a decree of Thrasybulos which granted it to resident aliens, and in 403 impeached Eratosthenes, one of the Thirty, in an attempt to take vengeance for the death of Polymarchos. The speech he delivered, the twelfth of our collection, does not seem to have achieved its end, and the decree under which he had gained civic rights was shortly afterwards revoked. Lysias thus became once more a metic, and supported himself by writing speeches, an occupation in which he was remarkably successful, owing partly no doubt to the supreme knowledge of every rhetorical trick which he disguised under a style apparently simple and invested with that charm noticed by Dionysios [86] and not entirely lost even on a modern, but still more to his remarkable power of identifying himself with his client and making the audience feel that it is not a paid λογογράφος whose production they are hearing, but the very words of the litigant, no orator, but an honest man stung to eloquence by his grievous wrongs, or to ironical wit by the sheer absurdity of the villains who attack him. To take a few speeches in the order which our editions give, No. 1, which is incomplete, is the defence of a man accused of homicide, who is telling the jury, plainly and even garrulously, exactly what happened—how he discovered that the dead man was his wife's lover, caught him in the act, and used the privilege the law gave him of avenging his own honour then and there. No. 3 seems to bear the very stamp of truth, although we have no means of knowing how much of it is fact and how much fiction : the speaker shamefacedly admits that his unruly desires and those of his accuser have led to a breach of the peace, but maintains that he has been guilty of no more than a little human frailty, while the other party is a violent and insolent rascal, and a great liar to boot. In the tenth, a man who has been grossly libelled produces witnesses formally to

429 ; it was possibly then that his sons emigrated. That Lysias studied rhetoric in Italy or Sicily is stated by our authorities and is likely enough in itself ; he and Polemarchos, who had accompanied him, returned to Athens in 412, when the anti-Athenian faction got the upper hand in Thurioi, after the failure of the Sicilian expedition.

[86] See Chap. i, note 31.

prove the offence, and then discusses some interesting verbal quibbles raised by the defence over the antique phraseology of the relevant statute. In the sixteenth, a dignified citizen, undergoing the statutory inquiry (δοκιμασία) at his entry upon some office, improves the occasion and forestalls certain persons who mean to raise objections to his conduct, by reviewing his whole career. In No. 24, a humorous old fellow, clearly a well-known ' character ', in receipt of a dole from the public funds in respect of his poverty and bodily infirmities, defends himself against a charge of wrongfully claiming it. Thus the tone changes from speech to speech, but the language is always the purest and most natural Attic, the words arranged with an air of careless ease, the product of the most consummate skill. Majesty and the power to move the passions of an audience strongly are lacking ; Lysias is not a representative of what ancient critics called the grand, but of the simple style, and the best exponent of that style who has come down to us. It is all the more to be regretted that we have but thirty-five speeches, genuine, spurious and doubtful, under his name, together with a few fragments ; in antiquity there were 425, whereof 233 were supposed to be his.[87]

About contemporary with Lysias was a man to whom subsequent European prose owes, directly or indirectly, perhaps more than to any one other stylist, ISOKRATES son of Theodoros, of the deme Erchia.[88] His dates are 436–338, thus covering practically the whole period of the best Attic prose ; we have thirty works attributed to him, mostly in the form of speeches, but including nine letters. Nearly all of these are genuine,[89] and form the bulk of what he wrote ; the ancients knew of sixty orations attributed to him, whereof the best opinion considered twenty-five, or at most twenty-eight, to be really his.[90] Isokrates' life was quiet and on the whole successful. He failed utterly as a speaker, his own explanation [91] being that he lacked audacity and a strong voice. As a λογογράφος he had better success, and

[87] These figures are given by ' Plutarch ', who cites Dionysios and Caecilius as his authorities, *uit. X orat.*, 836 a.

[88] The authorities for his life are practically the same as those for Lysias, see n. 87. The statements in this paragraph are due to them, or to the writings of Isokrates himself.

[89] No. 1 (*ad Demonicum*) is pretty certainly not his ; *ep.* 3 (to Philip, after Chaironeia) is disputed, see for the latest discussion P. Treves in *Rendiconti del R. Istituto lombardo di scienze e lettere*, vol. lxvi, p. 308 *sqq.*

[90] Dion. Hal. gives the lower, Caecilius the higher number ; see [Plut.], 838 d.

[91] *Orat.*, xii, 10.

several of his earlier surviving works were composed by him in that capacity. But he made his mark as a teacher and a pamphleteer. From 388 on, he was the head of a school which taught what he was pleased to call philosophy (he had a most unphilosophic mind and no turn for speculation either ethical or metaphysical), together with rhetoric in its highest form ; he wrote no text-book and had no cut-and-dried system,[92] although certain rules of euphony and vocabulary were insisted upon, but rather sought to develop the latent possibilities of each pupil to their highest and correct his besetting faults. His own idea of style was that the words should be those in everyday use, but carefully chosen and so arranged as to give the maximum of easy smoothness ; the period should be freely used, and the whole composition perfectly clear, even at some cost to conciseness and force. Hence he is always pleasant reading, but never very impressive ; his is the ' middle ' or ' florid ' style, the classical form of dignified and leisurely narrative or non-technical argument, such as the popular treatise or lecture. His pupils and his pupils' pupils between them included the bulk of the noteworthy writers of later Greece ; through them and their tradition Cicero was profoundly influenced, and through him and his imitators, all subsequent literature.

Besides the surviving forensic speeches which he wrote for clients [93] (they are by no means his best work) his writings may be divided into three classes. There are a few purely epideiktic, or model speeches, superior rhetorical exercises, such as the tenth and eleventh orations (respectively *Helen* and *Busiris* ; but each has a prologue, dealing with controversial matter). There are controversial treatises, setting forth his own views on education and attacking those of others ; one of the best examples of this

---

[92] A handbook of rhetoric was attributed to him in antiquity (frs. in Benseler-Blass' ed., ii, p. 275), and what is left of it shows that it was put together from dicta of Isokrates himself (see Christ-Schmid, i, p. 567, n. 7 and p. 569). He himself strongly deprecated all over-formal methods, see orat., xiii, 12–13. His most characteristic features, as seen alike by ancient and modern critics, were strict avoidance of hiatus, free use of the Gorgian figures, and attention to rhythm, this last a subject too technical and too imperfectly studied to be discussed in a book of this kind. There survives an attack on Isokrates, in good Isokratean style, by a contemporary, as he seems to be, for Isokr., iv, 11, probably alludes to him, ALKIDAMAS. This is the speech, or pamphlet, *Concerning those who write out their speeches*, or more briefly, *Concerning sophists* (περὶ σοφιστῶν), which advocates giving most attention to extempore speech. The declamation, *Odysseus*, which also goes under Alkidamas' name, is not by him, nor in fourth-century Attic at all, but by some Atticist

[93] Nos. 16–21 of the orations.

is the thirteenth speech (*Against the Sophists*) and perhaps the most elaborate is the fifteenth (the *Antidosis*). There are moreover several pamphlets in the form of addresses or open letters, some dealing with ethical matters (the ninth oration, *Euagoras*, while it has the form of an encomium on Euagoras king of Cyprus, sent to his son Nikokles, is really an essay on the duties of a king), others on political topics, as the fourth, the famous *Panegyric*,[94] the seventh (*Areopagiticus*) and the twelfth (*Panathenaicus*) ; these are all more or less in an idealizing vein, but others, as the fifth (*Philip*) and the open letters addressed to Philip, Alexander, and other prominent men of the time, are in closer touch with actual events. The tone is reasonable and moderate, and the suggestions made, while distinctly those of a student and not a man of action, are generally unexceptionable ; the recurrent theme is the necessity for the Greeks to leave their suicidal quarrels and unite against the common enemy, Persia, if not under Athens, then under Philip.

Of very much less importance to the history of literature, but still a good orator, is Isaios,[95] a foreigner (he was born at Chalkis in Euboia and never gained Athenian citizenship) who lived and wrote about the first half of the fourth century. By profession he was a λογογράφος and apparently a teacher of rhetoric also, for he is said to have taught Demosthenes, and indeed there is a slight resemblance in their styles. In general, he may be described as a more obviously rhetorical Lysias, without Lysias' extraordinary faculty of identifying himself with his client. In one notable point, avoidance of hiatus, he resembles Isokrates, whose pupil he is said to have been,[96] a statement which need mean no more than that Isokrates influenced him, as he did most writers of the day, including Plato himself. Of his works there seems to have survived one volume, and that not complete ; we have ten speeches and part of another, the end being lost, all dealing with cases of succession. Such a subject gives no room

---

[94] λόγος πανηγυρικός, speech intended to be delivered at a festival, viz., Olympia, in 380 B.C. Our meaning of ' panegyric ' is secondary and not classical. *See* p. 423.

[95] The sources are of the same kind as those for the lives of Lysias and Isokrates ; see note 87. He is to be distinguished from the much later Isaios the rhetorician, for whom see Juvenal, iii, 74, and commentators *ad loc.*

[96] For his relations to Dem. and Is., see Dion. Hal., *de Isaeo*, 1 and 3, and [Plut.] *uit. X orat.* 849 f. Dion. makes the epigrammatic remark (*op. cit.*, 4) that Isaios and Demosthenes with a good case sound suspicious from their very cleverness, whereas Lysias and Isokrates keep an air of honest simplicity even if they have a bad one.

for very exalted eloquence, but the speeches are interesting,[97] both for the light they throw on Athenian laws of inheritance and on family relations generally, and for the illustration they furnish of the tolerance of ancient courts for ingenious discussions based on probabilities and general considerations, not only in default of but actually in opposition to documents of uncontested genuineness. It is to be remembered that in Athens there was no judge in our sense of the word, *i.e.*, no presiding and authoritative official whose business it was to understand the relevant law and expound it impartially, when needed, to the jury. A large part of a twelfth speech is preserved by Dionysios ; in this, a certain Euphiletos of Erchia, one of the Attic demes, has been struck from the burgess-roll, and his brother sues before the Athenian courts to have his name restored, on the ground that it was unjustly removed.

But by far the greatest name in Greek oratory is, by common consent, that of DEMOSTHENES, son of Demosthenes, of the deme Paiania. His father was a sword-maker, that is to say the owner of a factory, large as ancient factories went, which turned out swords and other cutlery. He was left an orphan when 7 years old, and the greater part of his father's considerable estate had been filched by Aphobos, Demophon and Therippos, his guardians, by the time he came of age. The worthy trio probably were much pained when the stuttering and inexperienced boy they had robbed proceeded to sue them, finally recovering a part of his own and his sister's property by some sort of composition.[98] Isaios' teaching perhaps, his own diligence and genius certainly, had already made him a finished master of rhetoric, and no mean lawyer, at 20 years old, *i.e.*, in 364, his probable birth-date being 384. He now turned λογογράφος, and we have a number of his

<hr />

[97] There is a good edition with an excellent full commentary by W. Wyse, Cambridge 1904.

[98] The sources for his life are practically the same as those in note 78, together with Libanios' proem to his synopses of the orations, his own speeches and those of his opponents. His birth-date was 481/80 according to Apollodoros ; the chief passages for fixing it are *orat.* xxx, 15 and xxi, 154 ; see Christ-Schmid, i, p. 582. He was a Scythian according to Deinarchos, *adu. Dem.*, 15 ; *i.e.*, his mother was said to have northern blood of some kind, Aischines, iii, 172. It is the usual charge, made *pro forma* against every one. That he stuttered is stated, *e.g.*, by Libanios, 6, who adds various tales of his efforts to control his physical defects. The relevant speeches for the affair of his guardians and the further litigation arising out of it are xxvii, xxviii, xxx and xxxi. Aischines, iii, 173, says he was ' ridiculously choused out of ' his estate, and it is agreed that he did not recover by any means all of it. Probably a good deal had been squandered.

speeches written for various clients. They lack the suppleness and character-drawing of Lysias, for Demosthenes, at his best in the ' grand ' style, is less happy where he has no opportunity to thunder ; but vigour and persuasiveness they always have, together with a tone of moral earnestness, which never quite left him, even when, as happened at least once, he was retained by both sides at different stages of the same proceedings.[99] He seems to have been ambitious from the very beginning to be a great servant of a great state, and therefore readily undertook public charges which were really beyond his means, was probably often very short of money, and naturally was accused of taking bribes.[100] Throughout his life, a certain noble blindness prevented him seeing that the slack and weary Athens of his day was no longer, and never could be again, the Athens of Perikles. His political career must be left to historians to sketch ; the upshot of it was that, without wealth, personal influence, or even any very remarkable abilities as a statesman, by sheer dynamic personality and the lash of his terrible eloquence, he roused a people of defeatists, many of whom were either pacifists or avowed pro-Macedonians, first into offering not altogether ineffective resistance to Philip, the greatest soldier and incomparably the ablest politician of the day, then into forming a confederacy, out of the unpromising materials to hand, which made his success doubtful for a while, finally into continuing some kind of opposition even to Alexander.

Practically all the speeches which he himself delivered are somehow connected with his politics. We have attributed to him sixty-one orations, six letters and a book of fifty-four proems. The last contains some which are also found at the beginnings of actual speeches,[101] and therefore must be genuine ; from which it does not follow that Demosthenes wrote the rest, or made the collection. The authenticity of the letters also is uncertain.[102]

Setting aside these two minor matters, and taking the actual orations, the following are at least doubtful. No. 7 (here as for all the orators the numbering of the orations found in Blass's and later

[99] Viz., *orat.*, xxxvi, for Phormion the banker, against Apollodoros, son of his former master Pasion ; xlv, against Stephanos, one of Phormion's witnesses, for perjury.

[100] See Aisch., iii, 173 ; Dein., *in Demos.*, 13.

[101] Thus, proem 4 = orat. i, 1 ; proem 1, 1 = orat. iv, 1 ; proem 27 = orat. xv, 1, 2. One possibility is that these and other genuinely Demosthenic exordia were used as models and had imitations, adaptations, and other rhetorical products gradually added to them.

[102] For some of the varying opinions concerning them, see Christ-Schmid, i, p. 601, note 1.

editions is followed) was supposed in antiquity [103] to be the work of HEGESIPPOS, a political ally and colleague of Demosthenes ; it certainly is not worthy of Demosthenes' own powers. No. 10, the Fourth Philippic, is considered by some, but not all, modern scholars to be spurious ; in any case it is unimportant.[104] The eleventh and twelfth items of our collection are from the *Philippika* of Anaximenes the historian (see p. 310) ; [105] they profess to be respectively a speech of Demosthenes to the assembly in answer to a letter of Philip, complaining of Athenian intervention on behalf of Byzantion and Perinthos during the Peace of Philokrates, and the text of the letter itself. The historian's imitation was good enough to deceive many readers until positive evidence of the authorship of these two pieces came to hand ; he had used genuine Demosthenic speeches as his model, and may well have had knowledge of what Demosthenes really said and Philip really wrote. No. 13 is of somewhat doubtful authenticity ; the sentiments, however, are Demosthenic enough and the style at any rate a good imitation of his.[106] No. 17 has from ancient times been considered the work of some one other than Demosthenes ; Hypereides was suggested as the real author.[107] Nos. 25 and 26, the two accusations of the demagogue Aristogeiton, were pronounced spurious by Dionysios, and after him, by most moderns.[108] All these are of the class of public orations, either actual addresses to the assembly or, in the last case, belonging to the trial of a man politically important. The remaining speeches are nearly all short private orations, *i.e.*, with the exception of those delivered against his fraudulent guardians they were written by Demosthenes for his clients. Such speeches presumably passed into the possession of the clients concerned, who might or might not ever think it worth while to let further copies be made, and were by no means always men of literary interests who would publish anything like a critical edition of the material in their desks. Hence when anything was published, it might very well be that it was simply the papers of an individual litigant, by all manner of authors. This seems to have been the case with Apollodoros, the opponent of Phormion the banker in a long series of suits. Eight speeches of the Demosthenic corpus (xxxvi, xlv, xlvi, xlix, l, lii, liii, lix) have to do with this complicated business. Of this group, xxxvi and xlv are in all probability by Demosthenes ; the best modern opinion supposes the rest to be the work of one author, unknown, who is not he. Of the other private speeches, the following are with more or less reason suspect : xxxiii,

---

[103] See Libanios' argument to the speech, and Photios *s.u.* Ἡγήσιππος.

[104] Christ-Schmid, i, p. 591, n. 5.

[105] See Didymos, *in Demosth.*, col. 11, 10, which states that the speech is in Anaximenes' *Philippika*, Bk. vii, ' almost letter for letter '.

[106] Christ-Schmid, i, p. 588 and note 2.

[107] See Libanios' argument to the speech.

[108] Dion. Hal., *de Demosth.*, 57. The religious sentiments in xxv, 11 and 52–3, are unlike anything in the undoubted works of D.

xxxiv, xxxv, xl (the second speech against a certain Boiotos ; the first, xxxix, is genuine), xlii, xliii, xliv, xlvii, xlviii—I should personally be inclined to add li, which contains, sect. 12, a forced conceit such as I doubt if Demosthenes would indulge in—lvi and lix. By some blunder, there has been included among the private speeches one, lviii, the indictment of Theokrines, which has nothing to do with any private suit and, so far from being the work of Demosthenes, violently attacks him (42-4). Libanios says in his argument that it was commonly supposed to be by Deinarchos. Finally, at the end of our collection of orations, there are two which seem to be rhetorical exercises by unknown hands. No. lx professes to be the funeral oration which Demosthenes delivered over those who fell at Chaironeia. If it is, it is unworthy of him ; if an imitation, it is a fairly good one. No. lxi is a lover's address to a real or imaginary boy called Epikrates, and is as unlike the orator's style as can well be imagined.

We have then at most thirty-seven and at fewest thirty-four speeches actually by the great orator. Of these, five, Nos. xxvii–xxxi, belong to his earliest appearance, the suit against his guardians. Not long after, he began to feel his way towards a political career, by writing speeches for suits, his own or another's, which had some relation to public affairs. If No. li is his, it is the first of this kind ; its date is 459 and its subject a claim by a trierarch for a garland (the usual ancient form of decoration, corresponding to our orders and medals) in recognition of his efficient service. The subject gave opportunity for some remarks on naval matters. In 355/4 Diodoros impeached Androtion on the common charge of unconstitutional proposals (a γραφὴ παρανόμων), and Demosthenes wrote the speech for him (No. xxii). Again the subject concerned the fleet ; Androtion had proposed to ' garland ' the retiring Senate of the year just concluded, and Diodoros' objection was that it had done nothing for the navy.[109] In the same year Demosthenes appeared in person, though not as the chief accuser, but as a supporter (συνήγορος) of the prosecutor, against a certain Leptines, who had introduced a piece of panic legislation, depriving the State (in low water financially, then as always) of its power to grant exemption from taxation to benefactors. His speech on this occasion is No. xx. The next year saw his first address to the assembly, a speech (No. xiv) advocating a sound policy which, fourteen years later, he managed to carry. A war scare was filling Athens with rumours and anti-Persian rhetoric ; Demosthenes advised that she should avoid all provocative acts, and meanwhile put her navy in order by revising the

[109] He had impeached Kephisodotos, also in connexion with his conduct of naval affairs, in 459, to judge from Aischines, iii, 51-2 ; this speech is lost.

methods by which the expenses of fitting it out were met. The next year produced the sixteenth oration, which favours supporting the weaker Megalopolitans against the stronger Lakedaimonians with a view to gaining a grateful ally and enfeebling a possible enemy. About the same time, in No. xv (*On the Freedom of the Rhodians*) he advised supporting the democrats of that island (recently the enemy of Athens) against the designs of Maussollos of Karia, their former ally, who had contrived to over-throw their republican constitution. If No. xiii is his, it must have been delivered about 350.

Now begins a more interesting and characteristic period of his activity. Philip II had been king of Macedon since 359, and by 351 the boldness and vastness of his designs were becoming obvious to so penetrating a mind as the orator's, if not to the general public. The series of speeches known by the general title of the *Philippics* [110] is one long warning against the growing Macedonian power, coupled with practical advice for countering it. No. iv (the First Philippic) was delivered in 351 ; the three Olynthiacs (i–iii) fall between that date and 348. In 346, when the unsatisfactory Peace of Philokrates brought about a pause in the long and inefficiently conducted war, Demosthenes delivered No. v (*On the Peace*) in favour of keeping the recently signed pact.

Demosthenes and his party now turned upon the pro-Mace-donians of Athens, and not least upon Aischines. Timarchos and Demosthenes tried to impeach him, in 345, for wilfully neglecting the interests of Athens while a member of the embassy which had negotiated the peace (παραπρεσβεία). He parried cleverly by impeaching Timarchos for grossly immoral conduct (ἑταιρεία ; the speech is No. i of Aischines' orations), convicting him and securing deprivation of civic rights (ἀτιμία), which effectively debarred him from further proceedings. Demosthenes made another attempt to press the charge, in 343 ; he was unsuccessful, but published, as a pamphlet, what appears to be a combination of the speech he actually delivered then and the one he had prepared for the earlier attack (No. xix). [111] In the meantime

---

[110] *I.e.*, Φιλιππικοὶ λόγοι, speeches dealing with Philip. Cicero's borrowing of the title for his speeches against Antony is a literary allusion ; he, like Demosthenes, is warning his state against a formidable and unscrupulous enemy. The modern connotation of ' philippic ' arises from the vigorous attacks made by both orators on the characters of their respective enemies.

[111] The reason for supposing this is that Aischines' defence (the second of his speeches) is preserved, and clearly is not an answer to the existing speech of D., but to one differing from it at several points.

the Second Philippic (No. vi) had been delivered, arising out of the negotiations and counter-negotiations for Peloponnesian support ; in 341, events in the north provoked the comments embodied in Nos. viii and ix. The peace came to an end in 340, and the Battle of Chaironeia, in August 338, ended all effective resistance to Philip.

Demosthenes had still one great oratorical effort to make. In 336, a minor member of his party, Ktesiphon, proposed to garland him in recognition of his services to the State. Aischines set on foot a formal accusation of Ktesiphon for a legal irregularity in the proposal ; this was of course in effect an attack on Demosthenes' whole policy. Six years later (the reason for the delay is unknown) the trial took place. Aischines pushed the accusation with all his eloquence ; Demosthenes replied in the masterpiece of ancient oratory, the eighteenth speech, commonly known in modern times as the *de corona*. It is partly a formal rebuttal of the charge against Ktesiphon, but this is the weakest part of it, for technically Aischines had the law on his side. Substantially, it is a magnificent defence of the principles guiding the anti-Macedonian party, justifying them in face of failure. Less to modern taste is its bitter personal attack on Aischines, who however had not spared Demosthenes in his own speech. This great work is the latest in date of the surviving speeches, though the orator's life was prolonged for another eight years.

Of the remaining orations, several are connected with suits having a political colour. No. xxi, the accusation of Meidias, is of this type. Meidias, a political opponent of the orator and a man of violent character, had assaulted him during a festival in the theatre ; the dispute was settled out of court, apparently in 347, and the speech seems never to have been finished ; when and by whom it was published is unknown. Our twenty-third speech, that against Aristokrates, was delivered in 352, by Euthykles ; it is another charge of unconstitutional proposals, arising out of some incidents in the Thracian Chersonese. To the same year belongs No. xxiv, in which Diodoros, the prosecutor of Androtion, takes proceedings, apparently without success, against Timokrates, regarding a motion introduced by the latter to relieve public debtors. The remaining genuine speeches (xxxii, xxxvi, xxxvii, xxxviii, xxxix, xli, xlv, liv, lv, lvii) have no political significance, and were written for various clients to deliver in private suits.[111a]

A less important man in every way, yet not without his influence on the history of oratory, was AISCHINES, (389—about 314), all of whose surviving speeches have already been mentioned

[111a] *See* p. 423.

in discussing Demosthenes.[112] He was the son of poor parents,[113] who before he entered a political career supported himself by a small governmental post (he was a ὑπογραμματεύς, a sort of clerk of the court) and as a professional actor, for which his fine voice and handsome presence fitted him.[114] What is not known is how and where he acquired his good style and experience as an orator, for we hear of no genuine speech of his save the three that we still have,[115] which can by no possibility be the works of a man without previous training in the art. While lacking the terrific vigour of his great opponent, he always writes persuasively and with force, and with his good delivery, must have been very effective. The failure of his impeachment of Ktesiphon (see p. 292) led to loss of civic rights, for he did not obtain the necessary minimum of one-fifth of the votes cast. He left Athens, and is said to have gone to Rhodes and taught rhetoric there.[116] If this is true, it marks the beginnings of Rhodian interest in the subject ; if not, it is a sort of reflection of the reputation which the Rhodian school of oratory enjoyed in later times.

There are preserved twelve letters ascribed to him, manifestly forgeries, but not very late nor without merit.

One of the most respectable and able members of the anti-Macedonian party was LYKURGOS, whose activities were chiefly those of a statesman, not an orator, for he was not a ready speaker,[117] though a most diligent student and a pupil of Iso-krates. He was older than Demosthenes,[118] born perhaps about 390, and seems to have died before him, not later than 325 or so.[119] He would seem to have been a lover of literature, for he

[112] Besides pseudo-Plut. and Suidas, we have two lives of Aischines, one by an otherwise unknown Apollonios, the other anonymous, and a section (i, 18) in Philostratos' *Lives of the Sophists*. The facts are much confused by the charges and counter-charges of the two orators. He was in his forty-fifth year in 345, *orat.* i, 49, hence born in 389 ; the date of his death is uncertain.

[113] Demosthenes will have it (xviii, 129, 259) that they were also disreputable, an ex-slave married to a harlot and hedge-priestess ; Aischines, ii, 78, that they were highly connected.

[114] Demosthenes of course says he was a very bad actor, xviii, 265, 267.

[115] Apollonios mentions and rejects a fourth, supposed to have been delivered at Delos, for the sound reason that Aischines never represented Athens there, being replaced in that office by Hypereides.

[116] The earliest authority for this is Philostratos, *loc. cit.*

[117] Our only life of him is in pseudo-Plut., which however can be supplemented by a number of references in historians and others.

[118] *Arg.* [Dem.] *orat.*, xxv, 7.

[119] Dem., *ep.* iii, 6, if genuine, mentions him as dead.

was the author of the decree by which official copies of the three great tragedians were made and kept in the archives. He certainly was a religious man, as became a member of his ancient priestly family, the Eteobutadai, and also of deep moral earnestness. With two exceptions, all his orations were indictments, directed against persons who in one way or another had failed in the higher duties of a citizen. Of a total of fifteen speeches known in antiquity under his name, we have but one, the accusation of a certain Leokrates for treason, in that he had taken refuge at Rhodes after Chaironeia. The precise legal grounds of the proceedings are somewhat obscure, but they were very nearly successful, for the votes of the jury were equally divided [120] (this, by Athenian law, amounted to acquittal). The speech is what we might expect from its author, a dignified, slightly monotonous insistence on the duties of a patriot, with copious illustrations from mythology and numerous poetical quotations.

HYPEREIDES was a fellow-partisan of Demosthenes and Lykurgos, but quite unlike them in character. Had any such thing as the more scandalous kind of ‘ society ’ paper existed then, allusions to him would have been frequent in it, but as it did not, the comedians seized on him and his doings eagerly, and a considerable deposit of their jokes has come down to us in Athenaios ; [121] if we may put any faith in them, his two principal affections were for fish and women. In style, he was more like Lysias than any other author, and ancient critics variously characterize him as a pentathlete, *i.e.*, an all-round second-best, and as a blend of Lysias and Demosthenes. [122] Until the middle of the last century, we were obliged to take his reputation at second hand ; since then, various considerable discoveries have been made which give us battered papyrus copies of six of his speeches. These include his accusation of Atherogenes, which was much valued in antiquity, but not his most notorious speech, the defence of the courtesan Phryne. [123] He seems to have been born in 389, and he met his end at the same time as Demosthenes,

---

[120] This is gathered from Aisch., iii, 252. For the proceedings, see Rehdantz' ed. of the speech (Leipzig, Teubner, 1876), p. 13 *sqq.*

[121] Pp. 341 f *sqq.*, 590 c *sqq.* Athenaios' immediate source may well be one of his favourite scandal-mongers, IDOMENEUS of Lampsakos, who wrote a book *On Demagogues.* There are lives of H. in [Plut.] and Suidas.

[122] Pseudo-Longinus, *de sublim.*, 34, 2.

[123] Since she was a woman and a foreigner, she could not plead in person. It was in this speech that H. was said to have influenced a somewhat hostile jury by suddenly stripping his client, who had a beautiful body but a much less attractive face, and bidding them spare ‘ Aphrodite’s prophetess and sacristan ’ ; Athen., 590 e.

in 322,[124] being handed over to the cruelty of Antipatros when he took refuge in Aigina after the Lamian War. His total output of speeches was considerable ; 77 were attributed to him, of which the ancient critics supposed 52 to be genuine.[125]

Demosthenes and Hypereides being dead, there still remained one orator of some note, who was not, however, a native Athenian. DEINARCHOS of Corinth, whom some called the ' barley Demosthenes ', meaning that he was to him as a coarse barley scone to wheaten bread,[126] came to Athens about 342, being then a young man, and consequently must have been born about 360. A protégé of Demetrios of Phaleron, he was exiled in 307, spent fifteen years in Chalkis, returned, through the good offices of Theophrastos, whose pupil he had been, and others of his friends, and apparently gained citizenship in addition, for there survived in antiquity a speech delivered by him in person after his return, in a private suit against a certain Proxenos, whom he alleged to have brought about the loss of some money of his by negligence. He was then old, but it is not known how much longer he survived. Of his numerous speeches (160 circulated under his name, whereof 100 were supposed spurious) we have left only three, which were written by him for the use of prosecutors at the time of the Harpalos scandal. Of these the first, a furious indictment of Demosthenes for his share in the alleged wholesale·acceptance of bribes, was judged spurious by Demetrios of Magnesia.[127] The other two, against Aristogeiton and Philokles, are not so much accusations as screams of real or simulated rage. Style of his own he has none, but imitations of the earlier and better orators and free use of all manner of rhetorical figures are everywhere to be found.

DEMADES, who from being a hanger-on of Philip turned anti-Macedonian after Alexander's death and was executed by Krateros, had a great reputation as a wit and an extempore speaker. He left no written orations, but some unknown rhetorician amused himself by forging one, which will be found, so far as it survives, at the end of Blass' edition of Deinarchos. Of numerous other orators of that

---

[124] The birth-date is calculated by Th. Reinach, *Rev. ét. gr.*, v (1892) p. 250.

[125] See [Plut.], 849 d.

[126] These facts are taken from four sources, the lives of Deinarchos in Dion. Hal., [Plut.] and Suidas, and the short critique of him in Hermogenes, περὶ ἰδεῶν B, p. 384 Walz. All are conveniently assembled in the preface to Blass' Teubner edition of Dein. ; the epigram is from Herm., Dion. giving it in the weaker form ' rustic (ἀγροικος) Demosthenes '.

[127] Dion. Hal., *de Dinarch.*, 1.

troubled time we have no remains, unless some of the spurious speeches attributed to the better-known men be theirs ; cf. above, note 103.

III. The very name of *History* takes us to Ionia, for ίστορίη is the Ionic for inquiry or research ; we still speak of ' natural history ', *historia naturalis*, inquiry into Nature. That some kind of local records or chronicles were kept from very early times is highly likely, although we have none of them left ; they would be composed in the local dialects and in an artless sort of prose. But it was not until the sixth century, so far as we are aware, that anything like books of history in an attempt at a literary dialect began ; their home was Ionia, and the earliest names surviving are those of the Milesian KADMOS, son of Pandion,[128] who ' composed a work on the colonization of Miletos and of Ionia in general, in four books ', and PHEREKYDES, son of Babys, of Syra, or Syros, a little island not far from Delos, who ' was contemporary with the Seven Sages and is placed about the forty-fifth Olympiad ', *i.e.*, near the beginning of the sixth century. He wrote, according to the confused accounts we have, ' the *Five* (*Seven*, Suidas) *Recesses*, or the *Blending of the Gods*, which is a mythological work in ten books, containing the origin and succession of the deities '.[129] Here, assuredly, was a spiritual child of Hesiod and the Orphics— he may indeed have been an Orphic himself—combining some sort of mythological form with quasi-scientific speculation, for his five recesses would seem to correspond to aether, fire, air, water and earth. Somewhat later than these forgotten worthies, but still early, come the first of a class of writers whom it has been customary since Creuzer's time to call *logographi*.[130] They were mostly Ionians ; we have the substance of much that they said preserved for us by later authors, but few verbatim quotations, for they were read in later times, when they were read at all, as repositories of information, not models of style ; they probably were plain to dryness. They represent a first endeavour, praise-worthy though as yet uncritical, to bring order into the scattered mythological and other traditions of the race. Here they continued, and beyond doubt utilized, the later epics, discussed in

---

[128] Suidas, *s.u. Κάδμος* (b).

[129] Suid., *s.u. Φερεκύδης* (b), corrected from Eudemos, p. 170 Spengel. These men have later namesakes, KADMOS son of Archelaos, also a Milesian and author of a history of Attica, and the Pherekydes discussed below, p. 298.

[130] In allusion, apparently, to Thucyd., i, 21, 1, which contrasts scientific history with the work of poets and of λογογράφοι (writers of prose ? fictionists ?) who care more for attractiveness than truth. λόγιος is a prose writer as early as Pindar, *Pyth.*, i, 94.

Chapter III. All alike employed the genealogical method of dating, for it is hard to see what other generally applicable form of reckoning chronology there was available, though here and there existing lists of winners at games, or priests or priestesses of some famous temple, might furnish a sort of check. The temptation to combine, modify, even forge genealogical links was of course present and probably often yielded to ; yet in a country with so many noble families, proud of their pedigrees, at least the more recent parts of the chronological schemes thus formed were not worthless, and have sometimes been treated with too little respect by modern historians.[131]

Most of these logographi are to us names, vague dates, and a collection of statements about persons and events of a remote past. Among the less obscure names is that of SKYLAX of Karyanda ; a comparison of a mention in Herodotos,[132] a confused notice in Suidas, and the fourth-century work which falsely bears his name, indicates that he was employed by Dareios to make geographical researches, perhaps embodied them in a περίπλους, or record of a coastal voyage, of Arabia, and wrote a monograph concerning Herakleides of Mylasa, a king who was for some reason made the subject of good stories regarding his cunning. AKUSILAOS of Argos frankly called his work *Genealogies*, and combined local with panhellenic legends. CHARON of Lampsakos wrote a chronicle (ὧροι) of his own city and a work on Persia (Περσικά) ; his date is the early and middle fifth century. Histories of one sort or another were composed by EUGEON of Samos, DIONYSIOS of Miletos, DEIOCHOS of Prokonnesos, EUDEMOS of Paros, DEMOKLES and AMELESAGORAS of Chalkedon. HEKATAIOS of Miletos is a better-known figure, partly because of his real importance, partly because Herodotos uses him frequently and often takes exception to his statements. He lived early enough to take a prominent part in the Ionian revolt,[133] so cannot have been born later than about 525 B.C., and probably was older than that, since to Herakleitos he was a well-known writer with an undeserved reputation for wisdom.[134] Two works were attributed to him, the *Genealogies* and the Περίοδος γῆς, or *Voyage around the World*, whereof the latter was illustrated by a map, the second known to have been made.[135] His style was pure Ionic,[136] which probably means that it was less literary and conventional than that of Herodotos.

[131] Fragments and ancient notices, with commentary, in Müller and, more recently, in Jacoby (see Bibliography).
[132] iv, 44, 1–2. [133] Herodotos, v, 36, 2 ; 125.
[134] Herakl., fr. 16 Bywater, 40 Diels.
[135] Anaximandros made the first, according to Eratosthenes *ap*. Strabo, i, 1, 11. Aristagoras of Miletos had one (Hdt., v, 49, 1), but who its author was is unknown.
[136] Hermogenes περὶ ἰδεῶν, p. 423, 25 Spengel, 399, 6 Walz.

The above writers may be roughly grouped as the earlier logographi ; a later group, after the Persian Wars and coming down to the end of the fifth century, consists of the following. XANTHOS the Lydian is reputed to have been the first barbarian author to use Greek ; he appears to have lived and written between the sixties and twenties of the fifth century,[137] and he composed a history of his own country (Λυδιακά). Concerning PHEREKYDES we are not certain whether he was one writer or two ; Pherekydes of Athens is said to have ' flourished ' in 454/3, wrote in Ionic and dealt with the history of the great families, Attic and other, from the days of the gods. Pherekydes of Leros may or may not be the same man.[138] Less important was his rather obscure contemporary, BION of Prokonnesos. Later in the century comes a notable chronologist, HELLANIKOS of Mytilene, who wrote two treatises very useful for purposes of dating, a list of the priestesses of Hera at Argos and another of the victors in the Karneia at Sparta. Athenaios quotes the latter, which he or his authority had seen in a versified form, doubtless of later date, as well as in the original prose version,[139] for the date of Terpandros ; clearly such a compilation was of use for other things than the history of athletics, for the Karneia included a musical competition. He also wrote a number of monographs on the history of various parts of Greece (as Atthis, dealing with Attica, Phoronis, with Argos, Asopis, with Boiotia), on Persian history and on the Trojan War. Of other names belonging to this epoch may be mentioned HERODOROS of Herakleia in the Pontos, who wrote a rationalizing work on Herakles and a long treatise on the Argonauts,[140] and the great sophist HIPPIAS of Elis, who was the author, among other things, of a list of the Olympic victors ('Ολυμπιονίκων ἀναγραφή).

There were similar writers in the west. HIPPYS of Rhegion [141] wrote on matters concerning Italy and Sicily for the most part, but used Ionic, not Doric ; his date was about the time of the Persian Wars. His fellow-countryman THEAGENES, a contemporary of Kambyses if we may believe Tatian,[142] wrote concerning Homer, and thus ranked as the first grammarian ; another, GLAUKOS by name, wrote a book On ancient Poets and Musicians, which survived' long

---

[137] Suidas, s.u. Ξάνθος, says he lived at the time of the capture of Sardis, 546 B.C., but he himself (fr. 3 Müller) mentions Artaxerxes (king of Persia 465–424). Probably his history ended with the capture and the extinction of Lydian independence.

[138] The date is from Eusebios ; Suid., in two very muddled articles, distinguishes the Athenian from the Lerian. The principal work of Ph. is variously called 'Ιστορίαι, Γενεαλογίαι, and Αὐτόχθονες.

[139] Athen., 635 e ; this explains why Suid. says he wrote both prose and verse. Dion. Hal., antiquit., i, 72, mentions a list of the priestesses which included the events contemporary with each of them, but names no author.

[140] Numerous quotations from the latter work in the scholiast on Apollonios Rhodios.

[141] Suidas s.u. 　　　　　　[142] Tatian, aduers. Graec., 31.

enough to become one of the sources of the Plutarchean *de musica* (see p. 104). ANTIOCHOS of Syracuse, author of a *History of Sicily* and a *Colonisation of Italy*, both in Ionic, is considered to have been one of the sources of Thucydides.[143]

But the first great name is that of HERODOTOS of Halikarnassos, not ineptly called the Father of History ; [144] for although, as we have seen, many before him wrote concerning events of the past and made praiseworthy attempts to systematize available knowledge, it is with him that a genuinely critical handling and an attempt to make the subject truly philosophic by correlating causes and effects instead of merely setting down, more or less accurately, what had taken place, may be said to commence. Of his life we know very little.[145] His parents were called Lyxes and Dryo ; he is said to have left his native city when Lygdamis became tyrant, *i.e.*, not long before the middle of the fifth century. He travelled much ; for a great while he lived in Athens or on Athenian territory, being one of the original colonists to Thurioi, in 444, and so possibly having acquired citizenship. He was the friend of Sophokles.[146] Born a decade or so after the century began, he died some time after the Peloponnesian War had started,[147] perhaps in Thurioi.[148]

Much more important is his character as a thinker and writer. He combined with a keen and critical Ionian brain [149] a some-

[143] References for this conveniently assembled in Classen-Steup's Thucydides, appendix to Bk. vi.

[144] First by Cicero, *de legg.*, i, 5.

[145] There is no ancient biography of him save a short notice in Suidas ; the rest is made up from mentions in various authors (notably Plut., *de malign*. *Herod.*) and what he tells us himself. See the preface to How-Wells, *Commentary on H.*

[146] Plut., *an seni*, 785 b, mentions the friendship ; it is reflected in numerous passages in which S. imitates H., among them the famous echo of Hdt. iii, 119 in *Antig.*, 905 *sqq.*, a passage whose rejection by many critics of the last century is a quaint episode in the history of scholarship.

[147] He mentions the Spartan invasions of Attica, ix, 73, 3, but no event of the later parts of the war. He may have died about 425. As to his birth, we have no sure evidence. Pamphila *ap.* Aulus Gellius, xv, 23, 2, gives 484, but this is merely the date of the founding of Thurioi, assumed to be H.'s ' prime ' and therefore his fortieth year, plus 40. Dion. Hal., *de Thuc.*, 5, (p. 331, 18 Usener-Radermacher), says ' before the Persian Wars ', which might mean either 490+ or 480+.

[148] Suidas mentions two traditions, one that he was buried there, cf. Stephanos of Byzantion, *s.u.* Θούριοι, who cites the inscription alleged to have been engraved on his tomb, the other that he died in Pella, a piece of Macedonian philhellenism.

[149] Strictly speaking, his city was Dorian, but it had become Ionian in speech, as its inscriptions show, and certainly in spirit.

what old-fashioned piety, quite free from fanaticism, a warm-hearted reverence for noble conduct in man or woman, an insatiable curiosity for facts and theories of all sorts, and a love of a good story equalled only by Plutarch. Hence it is that we never find him deliberately misleading, and mistaken far less often than might be expected, considering that he knew no language but Greek and had few documents to help him for recent events ; but at the same time, when he reports what he has heard without vouching for its truth, he is a treasure-house of marvels. ' It is my business ', he says,[150] ' to tell what was told me, but not necessarily to believe it '. Where he does give anything as definitely true, it is safe to assume, not of course that he is infallible, but that there are solid facts of some sort underlying the statements.[151] No historian is freer from the guilt of deception, or from concealment of his own ignorance or uncertainty.

His language is literary Ionic, that is to say not the dialect of any part of Ionia, as comparison with inscriptions shows, but one having the general features common to all or most of them. It is a kind of prose successor of the Epic dialect, and indeed epic poetry was cultivated in his family, Panyassis (see p. 315) being his first cousin. His style is for the most part simple in structure and phraseology, having a charming air of *naiveté*, without periods or complicated structure of any kind, the ' strung-together style ' (λέξις εἰρομένη) of ancient criticism. Yet here and there we have a reminder that Gorgias was his contemporary, as in the speech of the Corinthian deputy Sosikles to the Spartans : [152] ' Verily, heaven will be below the earth, and the earth on high above the heavens ; men will have their dwelling in the sea and fish where men once dwelt ; when you, Lakedaimonians, go about to overthrow equal rights and bring tyrannies into states.'

The scope of his work, as he himself explains, [153] is ' to save that which has occurred from passing out of men's memory by

---

[150] vii, 152, 3.

[151] To take some of his most contested statements, his account of Egyptian history in Bk. ii, while very far from the facts as shown to us by the monuments, is considered by competent modern Egyptologists to be an excellent reproduction of what the average Egyptian of that time supposed to be the history of his country ; his battles, while they leave much to be desired from the point of view of strategy, give everywhere the impression of telling us what the men in the ranks thought of them. Scarcely an archaeological discovery has failed to show the fundamental truth of some apparently guileless tale in him.

[152] v, 92 a. [153] i, prologue.

lapse of time, and from oblivion the great and marvellous deeds of Greeks and barbarians alike, and especially the reason for their going to war with one another '. His subject, in other words, is the Persian Wars and the events leading up to and connected with them. The breadth of the theme is epic, the treatment no less so. The actual campaigns of the Greeks against Xerxes occupy but the last three books of the nine into which the work is conventionally divided ; the rest is taken up with other matters, chiefly the history of Greece and Anatolia from the beginning of the rise of the Persian Empire, but also with excursuses of all kinds, largely geographical and ethnological, as the account of Egypt in the second book, Scythia in the fourth, and many shorter passages ; nor is very strict chronological order observed, since, for example, in the midst of the events of 490 he stops [154] to sketch the early history of the Alkmeonidai, containing the famous tale of how Hippokleides danced away his marriage. This is the more interesting because it is an Oriental story, the Jataka of the Dancing Peacock.[155] Where Herodotos got it is not known, possibly from some guide during his travels in the Near East.

Such retrogressions, episodes and enlivening incidents make the work curiously fascinating reading. It has a sort of loose unity, partly from its always returning to the main theme of the struggle between East and West, partly from the divine machinery, again an epic trait, which is not crudely obtruded into the story, but always present in the background, showing itself in an occasional miracle or oracular response,[156] or in references to the old doctrine of the ' envy of the gods ' which causes them to put down the mighty and lower the haughtiness of the proud and overweening.[157] Whether it was finished by its author is a moot point. As we have it, it ends suddenly, with no formal conclusion, unless we count as such the moral tale of Cyrus and the Persians which forms the last chapter of Book ix. In favour of supposing the work complete it may be urged that it has come down to the capture of Sestos in 478, which marks the riddance of Europe from the Persian menace, and that the apologue, which represents Cyrus as bidding the Persians remain in their mountains, lest they should degenerate in a milder and more fruitful region, forms a sort of commentary on their loss of power. Against it, we must set occasional references to parts of the

---

[154] v, 125 sqq.

[155] vi, 129 ; see Warren in *Hermes*, xxix (1894), p. 476 sqq., and Macan *ad loc*.

[156] As viii, 65 ; vii, 141. [157] First expounded by Hdt. in i, 32. See p. 424.

history which do not exist,[158] together with the fact that other
stopping-places at least as appropriate could be found. The
writer's own impression is that Herodotos himself found the
subject so endlessly fascinating that he never made up his mind
where he was to end, and would have gone on adding to and
re-writing his book if he had not been prevented by death, or
possibly by the distractions of the war in which his adopted
country was engaged.

It is significant for the trend of prose literature away from
Ionia to Athens that this great writer left no successors and had
no imitators until Imperial times. History from that time on
was written in Attic, or in the ' common dialect ' which took its
place in the Hellenistic age. The next name is that of THUCY-
DIDES (Θουκυδίδης), son of Oloros, perhaps the greatest historian
who has yet lived, incontestably the greatest in antiquity. Not
a quarter of a century separates him from Herodotos, indeed the
younger man may well have been collecting materials for his
work while the older was still writing his, and their deaths lie
perhaps thirty years apart, Thucydides' dates being about
460–400. But in tone they seem to be of different ages. Herodotos has something about him of the freshness of the dawn ; he
had seen a new era come, full of promise, with the dispelling of
the Persian menace and the rise of Periklean Athens. Enthusiastic for his adopted country, he retains a belief in its democratic
institutions, a generous delusion which, while it lasts, seems in
all ages to breed a lovable and optimistic philanthropy. Thucydides had seen every ideal of the fifth century laid in the dust,
Athens ruined, democracy, to use his own words,[159] shown a
confessed folly, Persia once more powerful, and become a possible
ally to bargain with, not a national enemy to excite the zeal of
crusaders. For him, the main interest is not the uncertain
events of the past,[160] but the grim present, which must be
impartially analysed and accurately described, for the permanent
instruction of mankind.[161]

The main facts of his life are well enough known.[162] He was

---

[158] In i, 184, he promises to give an account of the kings of Babylon
' in the section on Assyria ' ; vii, 213, 3, he will explain ' later ' how and
why the traitor Ephialtes was put to death.

[159] Thuc., vi, 89, 6.   [160] See *ibid.*, i, 1, 3 ; 20, 1 ; 21, 1.

[161] *Ibid.*, i, 22, 4.

[162] We have a life of him by a certain Marcellinus (fifth century A.D.),
another anonymous biography, and a notice in Suidas, besides what he
tells us of himself and sundry mentions in authors such as Plutarch.
None of them give trustworthy information as to his dates ; but he was
old enough to take an intelligent interest in public affairs when the war

of a rich and noble Athenian family, descended on the distaff side from Miltiades and his Thracian wife Hegesipyle, daughter of the petty king Oloros, after whom the historian's father was named. He either inherited, or had with his wife, who came from Skapte Hyle on the Thracian coast,[163] a considerable interest in the rich mines of that district. In 424 he was entrusted with the command of an Athenian force operating in Thrace ; but by ill-luck he found himself opposed to Brasidas, the most able and enterprising of the Spartan commanders, and met with poor success against him, for either by Thucydides' negligence or his opponent's superior dash and vigour, the important city of Amphipolis fell to the Spartans. Knowing that, rightly or wrongly, he would be blamed for this, Thucydides did not return to Athens, but retired to Thrace, was banished in his absence, and spent the rest of the war largely in contact with the Spartan allies, from whom he learned their point of view. He apparently retained his possessions and was left unmolested, travelling about to various places, which would seem to have included Sicily.[164] Returning after the war, he died and was buried at Athens.[165]

His history, after a preface sketching the principal events up to the declaration of the Peloponnesian War, tells with minute and scientific accuracy the story of that conflict down to 411. The method is annalistic, the events of each summer and each winter being related in order. This has the advantage of great clarity, but the disadvantage that the narrative of some important matter has often to stop half-way in order to mention quite trivial incidents which happened to occur at the same time in some other part of the theatre of war. At suitable intervals, speeches are inserted. By Thucydides' own account,[166] these give the substance of what he supposes the real speakers likely to have said ; but they furnish him with an admirable method of commenting, not only on the actual situations as they occur,

began (v, 26, 5), *i.e.*, he was probably a grown man in 431 ; he was in exile twenty years after the affair of Amphipolis (*ibid.*, 5), so must have returned to Athens in or about 404, whether by virtue of the general amnesty after the war or as a result of a special decree (so Pausanias, i, 23, 9). How much longer he lived is unknown, but the unfinished condition of the history suggests that it was not very long. For conjectures, see Christ-Schmid, i, pp. 481–2.

[163] Plut., *Cim.*, 4, is ambiguous, Marcell., 19, says it was his wife's property.

[164] Timaios *ap*. Marcell., 25 and 33, supported in some measure by Th.'s intimate and accurate knowledge of the topography of Syracuse.

[165] So Marcell., 32–3, rejecting stories that he died in Thrace or Italy ; but cf. Classen's introd. (vol. i, p. xxxi of his 3rd ed.).

[166] Thuc. i. 22, 1.

but on the hopes and ideals of both parties. Thus the great Funeral Oration of Perikles (ii, 35–46) over the fallen in the first year of the war may very possibly follow the general lines of what he really said, and certainly agrees in form with the other compositions of this sort that have come down to us ; but its chief merit is that it states the ideals of democratic Athens as entertained by her best and most intelligent citizens at that time. In like manner, the various addresses put into the mouths of generals before important battles give summaries of the strategic and tactical situation at the time. This device, therefore, is never a mere indulgence in rhetoric but takes the place of much comment that a modern historian would make in his own person, whether in the text or in footnotes and appendices. Herein it differs from the speeches in Herodotos, which are fewer and far less important, forming merely a natural part of the narrative, save in a few cases. The tone of the whole work is extraordinarily impartial, practically nothing of national or personal animus appearing anywhere save perhaps in handling the character and actions of Kleon.

The style is unique. In narrative it is straightforward enough, though always compact, rapid and succinct. But in passages of a reflective nature, and especially in many of the speeches, Thucydides strains the language to breaking-point in his anxiety to crowd the maximum of thought into the minimum of words. Ancient critics noted [167] his neglect of all the lesser elegances, his curious word-order, often harsh to the ear as well as difficult to the understanding, his fondness for extreme brevity and other peculiarities. No translation can give an idea of his manner, any more than of Pindar's. Sometimes there is a certain resemblance to Antiphon, who perhaps for this reason was asserted to have been his teacher,[168] and the Gorgian figures are used, but in Thucydides' own extraordinary way. The dialect is not quite the spoken Attic of his day, but a more archaic form, somewhat resembling that of Tragedy and influenced by Ionic here and there.

The work is divided in our MSS. into eight books ; this, says Marcellinus, was the usual arrangement and approved by Asklepiades, but some divided it into thirteen and others in other ways. For this statement there is support from other authors.[169]

---

[167] See Dion. Hal., *de Thuc.*, 24 *sqq.* ; Marcell., 50.

[168] As by Marcell., 22, who also says that Anaxagoras taught him philosophy ; [Plut.] *uit. X orat.*, 832 e, where it is specifically given as a conjecture of Caecilius.

[169] Marcell., 58 ; Diod. Sic., xii, 37, 2, xiii, 42, 5, and several passages in the scholia on Thuc.

Thucydides' work was admired and studied apparently almost from the moment it was published ; [170] among its readers may be named practically every prose writer of importance during the rest of the century. Of direct imitation of so individual a style there was little, however, and few or none were found to imitate the scientific impartiality of his method. As great historians, he and Herodotos [171] stand alone until the Hellenistic age.

For ' great ' is not the word to use of XENOPHON. In him, a mind which it would be flattery to call second-rate and a character hide-bound with convention attain somehow to very respectable literary expression and are presented with at least two subjects on which it is nearly impossible to be wholly dull. Born about 430 (the exact date is unknown) [172] in Erchia, he seems to have had the ordinary education of a young man of respectable and well-to-do family. But towards the end of the century he made the acquaintance of Sokrates, and while utterly incapable of appreciating his philosophy, was charmed with his moral precepts, admired him personally, and so became an enthusiastic hanger-on of the outer Sokratic circles. A Boiotian friend of his family, Proxenos, [173] in 401 was recruiting for Cyrus the Younger's famous expedition against his brother Artaxerxes II ; Xenophon accepted his invitation to join the Greek corps then forming for this hazardous service, and after Cyrus' death found an opportunity to exercise his two great and undoubted virtues, personal courage in danger and an extraordinary power of managing a half-disciplined body of men in a series of critical situations. Thanks chiefly to having elected him as their leader when all the senior officers had been captured or murdered, the Greeks made their way back through hostile country to the coast, and many of them, including Xenophon, passed into the service of Agesilaos, king of Sparta, in his Asiatic campaigns. Always an admirer of everything Spartan, he so far identified himself with his new allegiance as to fight against the Boiotian allies of Athens at Koroneia, in 394 ; being banished for this disloyalty,

[170] The time and manner of its publication are unknown, though it must have been after the death of Thucydides.

[171] Thucydides had a certain antagonism to Herodotos. This may be seen, *e.g.*, from his somewhat slighting reference to the Persian Wars, i, 23, 1, and from certain passages in which he tacitly corrects him, as vi, 57, 1, cf. Hdt., v, 56, 2, but still more from the whole tone of the work. It is the quarrel of realist and romanticist.

[172] Materials ; his own references to himself, a life in Diogenes Laertios (ii, 48–59), a notice (unimportant) in Suidas and a few passages elsewhere. None give trustworthy dates.

[173] Xen., *Anab.*, iii, 1, 4 *sqq.*

he comforted himself with an estate at Skillus in Elis, where under Spartan protection he lived for some time the life of a country gentleman, on the proceeds of his war-booty. Here it presumably was that he wrote his chief works, though he may very well have made notes and memoranda for them earlier. In 370, Skillus was taken by the Eleans and Xenophon escaped to Corinth, was probably recalled from banishment and spent the rest of his life in Athens.[174] His two sons served in the Athenian cavalry and one, Gryllos, fell at the battle of Mantineia in 362. Xenophon lived at least until after 359 ; [175] the date of his death is not exactly known.

He was a voluminous writer, with a simple and lucid style, his language being Attic somewhat corrupted by his long residence abroad. In the higher virtues of a stylist, especially sense of proportion and power of arranging the matter effectively, he is notably lacking ; [176] hence he is incomparably at his best when the subject carries its own arrangement with it and is interesting in itself. Consequently, the *Anabasis*, or history of Cyrus' expedition and the subsequent retreat of the Greeks, is his master-piece and has always been deservedly admired. In this, he had but to set down plainly and, so far as can be judged, truthfully [177] the thrilling events of that campaign, from the beginning of the quarrel between Cyrus and his brother to the moment when the Greek contingent, or such as were left of it, was incorporated in the Spartan force under Thibron. The work, besides being excellent reading, is a store of information concerning the

[174] Xen., *Anab.*, v, 3, 7 *sqq.* ; Diog. Laert., ii, 56 says he died in Corinth, in 352.

[175] He mentions the death of Alexandros of Pherai, *Hell.*, vi, 4, 36 ; this took place in 359.

[176] A larger and a smaller example of this may be given. In *Hell.*, vii, 2, he devotes the whole chapter to the happenings at Phlius, giving as his reason that the notable deeds of so small a city may otherwise be forgotten. The story is without doubt interesting, but not of such importance as to deserve inclusion at the cost of much that had far greater effects on the course of events. In *Anab.*, i, 8, 29, he has the moving tale to tell of how Artapates, a faithful retainer of Cyrus, died on his master's body, and breaks it off to explain that the sword with which Artapates killed himself was of gold.

[177] It may be that he somewhat overstresses his own services, but the distinction with which the Spartan high command treated him suggests that they considered the preservation of so useful a force as the Ten Thousand very largely due to him. There are of course literary devices in the work ; the speeches which are interspersed throughout need not be taken as literal reproductions of what was said, and the authorship was concealed for a while under a mystification ; Xenophon himself cites it, *Hell.*, iii, 1, 2, as by Themistogenes of Syracuse.

geography and ethnology of Asia Minor at that date ; it is not a little unfortunate that it is spoiled for many by being the first Greek they read, and therefore associated with tedious construings and painful thumbing of dictionaries and grammars.

His other important historical work, the *Hellenica* or *History of Greece*, begins well as a continuation of Thucydides, and in the first two of its seven books something of the spirit of the greater historian still breathes here and there. Nor are the descriptions of Agesilaos' campaigns in the following books by any means devoid of merit or interest. But as he comes to the Corinthian War, Xenophon begins to lose grip of the subject ; for example, the Lakedaimonian defeat at Knidos, which put an end to their naval supremacy, is not even mentioned, and the utterly disgraceful Peace of Antalkidas is hurried over without comment. The latter part of the history, containing the rise of Thebes and the downfall of Sparta, begins with a piece of orthodox piety which would not be surprising in Herodotos, but sounds very archaic in the middle of the fourth century ; the one reason suggested for the decline of Spartan power is the anger of heaven at their breach of their sworn word.[178] It ends at an appropriate moment, the death of Epameinondas and the beginning of the general confusion which followed ; but between these two points the author gives us rather scattered notes for a history of the times than the history itself, and has continually to be supplemented from such other sources as are available.

A sort of pendant to the *Hellenica* is the *Agesilaus*, a laudation of Agesilaos king of Sparta, published after his death in 361/60. It consists to a considerable extent of extracts from the *Hellenica*, a little modified to fit their new context. Although Athenian by birth, Xenophon had obviously been reared in the Dorizing traditions of part of the Athenian gentry, and being himself a man of action, idolized the two most efficient leaders of men he had met, Cyrus and Agesilaos. Hence it was that, by a sort of accident, his highly conventional and old-fashionedly respectable mind was in one respect abreast of the most advanced thought of his day ; he was a pronounced monarchist.

Unfortunately, he felt impelled to embody his ideals of royalty in a work of the imagination, a sort of composition for which he was singularly unfitted. The *Cyropaedia* (Κύρου παιδεία, *Education of Cyrus*) has the distinction of being the first historical novel and the first moral romance that has come down to us. It is further distinguished by being one of the dullest writings in any tongue. In eight books, it traces the career of Cyrus the

[178] *Hell.*, v, 4, 1.

Great from his childhood to his edifying death, diversifying the story with a number of episodes, some less intolerable than the main plot, and abundance of speeches, highly moral in tone. One of these episodes is a love-story, concerning a certain Pantheia and her husband Abradatas ; it is quite the best thing in the work, and in a way anticipates some of the themes of the next age.   An extraordinary fact is the popularity of the *Cyropaedia* among men otherwise of good taste, notably Scipio Africanus the Younger and Cicero,[179] both of whom, it is true, were moving towards monarchist conceptions themselves.

The *Cyropaedia* is, at least in intention, a quasi-philosophic work ;   there is a group which is definitely Sokratic.   The *Memoirs of Sokrates* (ἀπομνημονεύματα Σωκράτους, usually called the *Memorabilia*) is a defence of Sokrates against those who represented him as a bad influence.   A series of scenes shows the philosopher conversing with all manner of people, mostly well known, always giving them good advice and refuting immoral views if they put them forward.   Although here and there we seem to catch the authentic tone of Sokratic disputation, and there is much valuable information contained in the work,[180] it is surprising how little is made of its fascinating subject.   The founder of dialectic and reformer of ethics too often appears as a mere sermonizer with a certain turn for debate, and the reader is very apt to find the four books much too long.   A shorter treatise on the same theme is the *Apology of Sokrates*, which unlike Plato's work with the same title does not profess to be the speech he delivered at his trial, but sets forth his conduct and utterances before, during and after the proceedings.   The *Symposium*, one of Xenophon's most readable works, shows Sokrates in a lighter mood, at a dinner in the house of Kallias. The *Oeconomicus* (Οἰκονομικὸς λόγος, *Discourse on Household Management*) introduces him as the reporter of a long description, by one Ischomachos, of how the latter trained his young wife to be a good housekeeper.   Ischomachos is a prig of the first water, but the details of Greek private life give the work a factitious interest.   In form, it is another section of the *Memorabilia*. Last of this philosophical group is the *Hieron*, which introduces that monarch discoursing with Simonides on the troubles of a tyrant (cf. p. 115).

[179] See Cicero, *ad Q. frat.*, i, 1, 23 ; *ad famil.*, ix, 25, 1 ; *de senect.*, 79 *sqq*.

[180] Where Xenophon got his information, how correct it is, and whether he or Plato is rather to be believed when their portraits of S. differ, are all points hotly disputed but outside the scope of this book.

There remains a group of essays on various subjects, some of them doubtfully Xenophontic. Two of the best probably date from the time when his sons were in the Athenian cavalry, for the first of them alludes to Boiotians as enemies and apparently to Spartans as allies,[181] which suits the situation before Mantineia very well, and the second cites it.[182] They are the *Hipparchicus* and the *de re equestri*, respectively giving advice to the commander of cavalry and the trooper. A sort of companion piece, the tractate *On Hunting* (Κυνηγετικός) is also full of interest and written by some one who knew his subject ; but the style is totally different from Xenophon's and its author is unknown.[183] On the other hand, he probably is the author of the *Constitution of Sparta* (Λακεδαιμονίων πολιτεία) and the essay *On Revenues* (Πόροι ἤ περὶ προσόδων), the former well-informed but idealizing, the latter containing here and there excellent suggestions for the encouragement of trade.

That the *Constitution of Athens* is not his is noted on p. 281 ; his alleged letters are notoriously spurious.[184]

The fourth century produced a number of other historians, some not without merit, whose works are unfortunately lost. Artaxerxes II had a court physician, by name KTESIAS, who wrote a work, in fourteen books, on Assyrian and Persian history, in the Ionic dialect. We have an epitome of an epitome, and to judge by this, he was an amusing liar when discussing anything outside his own immediate knowledge.[185] He seems to have used Xanthos, Hellanikos and Herodotos, and set himself to correct the errors of the last-named. He wrote also one book on India, then quite an unknown land to Greeks, giving abundant scope for tales of wonder, and a geography (περίπλους or περιήγησις).[186] More serious writers were THEO-POMPOS and KRATIPPOS, whom a recent accidental discovery has associated, unlike to one another as they were. The latter seems, from his undoubted fragments and references to him,[187] to have written

---

[181] *Hipp.*, 7, 3 ; 9, 4.   [182] *De re equ.*, 12, 14.
[183] So Wilamowitz, *S.S.*, p. 125 ; Christ-Schmid, i, p. 516 ; the author entirely agrees.
[184] First formally proved to be so by Bentley, *Discourse upon the Epistles of Socrates*, pp. 110–12.
[185] Pamphila, a learned lady of the time of Nero, epitomized him, and Photios read her epitome and excerpted it. We have also some fragments. These are collected at the end of the Didot Herodotos ; see also Christ-Schmid, i, p. 523, n. 6.
[186] The last is known by some citations in Stephanos of Byzantion. There was another Ionian historian, apparently of about this time, AGATHOKLES of Kyzikos, who wrote a history of his native country, but his date is far from certain ; frags. in Müller, *F.H.G.*, iv, 288 *sqq.*
[187] See *F.H.G.*, ii, 75 *sqq.* ; Jacoby, ii, p. 13 *sqq.* ; cf. next note.

a plain, straightforward, unrhetorical supplement to Thucydides, carrying the story down to the rebuilding of the Long Walls by Konon. A large papyrus from Oxyrhynchos [188] contains part of just such a continuation, well-informed and superior to Xenophon as a historical document. Kratippos has naturally been suggested as its author, the more so as it seems to have been written by a man contemporary with the Corinthian War. On the other hand, the style, though plain, has one Isokratean feature, avoidance of hiatus, and this suggests that pupil of Isokrates who is known to have handled the same period, namely Theopompos. This man was a Chian, who for political reasons spent a good part of his life in Athens and ended his days in Egypt, where he was put to death by Ptolemy I ; he was born in 376. Besides much that was purely rhetorical, in the shape of epideiktic speeches, he wrote two considerable historical works, *Hellenika* in twelve books, taking the narrative from where Thucydides left it to the Battle of Knidos in 394, and *Philippika* in fifty-eight, a history, full of digressions on all manner of topics, of events to the death of Philip II.[189] A somewhat older writer, also a pupil of Isokrates, was EPHOROS, of Kyme in Asia Minor, whose scope was more ambitious, for his subject was the entire history of Greece, down to within a short time of his own death (he was born between 408 and 405 and died while Alexander was in Asia ; presumably he would, had he lived, have continued the story to the final conquest of Persia). He was much read in later times ; the total loss of his own books is to some extent compensated for us by the fact that Diodoros (see p. 412) copies out long passages from him almost word for word.[190] ANAXIMENES of Lampsakos (about 380–320) has already been mentioned (pp. 278, 289). He, like Theopompos, wrote *Hellenika* and *Philippika*, adding later a *History of Alexander* (τὰ περὶ Ἀλέξανδρον).[191] Lesser men, about contemporary with him, were KEPHISODOROS of Thebes, HERAKLEIDES of Kyme, THEOKRITOS of Chios, DAÏMACHOS of Plataiai and ARISTAGORAS of Kyme. Their works dealt mostly with the history of the chief oriental countries, especially Persia, and with Greece.

[188] *Ox. Pap.* 842 (vol. v, p. 142 *sqq.*), with commentary by the editors ; see also Grenfell-Hunt, *Hellenica Oxyrhynchia cum Theopompi et Cratippi fragmentis*, Oxford, 1909 ; Jacoby, ii, p. 17 *sqq.* Select literature on the controversy regarding authorship down to 1911, Christ-Schmid, i, p. 522, n. 4 ; Jacoby doubtfully identifies the author with Daïmachos, see his commentary.

[189] For his frags., cf. last note, and add *F.H.G.*, i, 278 *sqq.* ; Jacoby, ii, p. 526 *sqq.*

[190] This had been long suspected, and is now proved beyond doubt by the considerable fragment of Ephoros (*Ox. Pap.* 1610 = fr. 191 Jacoby) which shows close and constant resemblance to the corresponding passages of Diodoros. For his frags.. see *F.H.G.*, i, 234 *sqq.* ; Jacoby, ii, p. 37 *sqq.*

[191] His frags. are at the end of the Didot Arrian, and in Jacoby, ii, p. 112 *sqq.*

All the writers enumerated in the last paragraph, save Ktesias, who is a belated representative of Ionia, and Kratippos, belong to what may be called the Isokratean school of history. From their master, for they were mostly his pupils and all influenced by him, they took over three things : regard for a seemly style, rhetorical without being too showy, and pleasant and dignified to read or hear ; interest in a respectable, but by no means original doctrine, or group of doctrines, both ethical and political ; and a didactic attitude. For such men, history was not a science, as it is to the best of the moderns ; they took the facts where they could get them, using little research and a good deal of shallow reasoning on *a priori* rationalistic lines, and were often capable of distorting them to get a better and more edifying story, though lip-service was paid to the difference between the historian and the panegyrist. Their business was to supplant the poets as popular teachers ; [192] the chief figures in their works were bright examples of what kings, generals and statesmen should be, or awful warnings of the effects of wickedness in high places. History had thus become an important branch of rhetoric, and was destined to keep that position for many centuries, which included the whole of classical Roman historiography and the bulk of the moderns down to the middle of the nineteenth century.

One historian of about this period was not a rhetorician but a statesman. PHILISTOS or PHILISKOS of Syracuse seems to have been born about the thirties of the fifth century, for he was not a child when the Athenian expedition came. He wrote the history of his own country, a first part, in seven books, dealing with Sicily down to the accession of Dionysios I, while a second, in six, gave the story of the two Dionysioi, whose minister he was in the intervals of disgrace and banishment. He is said (we have but insignificant fragments of him) to have imitated Thucydides even to plagiarism and to have flattered Dionysios I vilely.[193]

The sister science of geography is represented by one great, but long unappreciated name, PYTHEAS of Massilia, who about the time of Alexander's expeditions made his way through the Straits of Gibraltar up the west coast of Europe to the British Isles, penetrating to the Orkneys and Shetlands and perhaps farther. The information he brought back from these hitherto unknown regions was so opposed

[192] See, for statements of this principle, Isokr., ii, 48 and ix, 6.
[193] There are very confused notices of him in Suidas, *s.uu. Φιλίσκος* and *Φίλιστος*. He was *paene pusillus Thucydides*, Cicero, *ad Q. frat.*, ii, 11, 4 ; imitated all his model's worst points, Dion. Hal., *ad Pomp.*, 5, which also accuses him of flattery ; took his account of the Sicilian expedition almost verbatim from Thuc., Theon, *progymnast.*, p. 63, 25 Spengel. Fragments, etc., *F.H.G.*, i, 185, iv, 369.

to the preconceived ideas of those and later days that we have now to reconstruct it from the writings of men, chiefly Strabo (see p. 383) who cite him to show what a romancer he was. In point of fact, he was remarkably correct, clearly a very good observer and a bold explorer.[194] A real romancer who professed to have information from the same regions was the notorious ANTIPHANES of Bergê (hence the verb βεργιάζειν, to lie unblushingly), who wrote a book appropriately called *Incredibilities* (Ἄπιστα), and seems to be of earlier date than Pytheas.[195] Finally, somewhere about this time must come the translation into Greek, by an unknown hand, of the *Voyage around Africa* of HANNO the Carthaginian, the first surviving work to mention the gorilla.[196]

[194] Besides Strabo, we have Avienus (fourth century A.D.), whose *ora maritima* used a later work which had in turn used Pytheas. Literature in Christ-Schmid, i, pp. 540–1 and notes; Heiberg, pp. 84, 85. Good popular account by J. Malye in *Bull. Ass. G. Budé*, 41 (Oct., 1933), pp. 34–47.

[195] See W. Schmid in Pauly-Wissowa, i, 2521 *sq.*; Wilamowitz in *Hermes*, xl (1905), p. 149; *contra*, Knaack in *Rhein. Mus.*, lxi (1906), p. 135 *sqq.*, who supposes that he was later than Polybios and parodied Pytheas.

[196] Text in Müller, *Geographi Graeci minores*, i, p.135*sqq.*The date is approximately fixed by pseudo-Arist. *de mirab. aus.*, 37 (35), which goes back to Theophrastos.

CHAPTER X

HELLENISTIC POETRY

BETWEEN the decline of Epic and the full development of Prose one characteristic has been common to all the writings discussed ; they have been the native expression of but part, sometimes a small part, of the Greek world, and the best of them, Attic literature, the product of a single city. It is indeed true that great movements like Lyric spread beyond their original bounds, and that foreigners are fairly numerous among at least the minor Attic authors ; nevertheless, as a rule we may say that every writer was addressing himself to fellow-countrymen, by birth or by adoption, and could count on their understanding his presuppositions and taking an interest in the themes which interested him. Further, he wrote for them, if not in the dialect locally spoken, at least in a conventional speech locally produced, addressing Athenians, for instance, in slightly archaic Attic, or singing to Dorians in Doric modified a little by borrowings from Homer.

With the coming of the great Hellenistic monarchies which followed the conquests of Alexander, all this changed. Wealth and political power alike were now to be found in Anatolia and Egypt, and the relative and absolute importance of Greece declined rapidly. Boiotia, Attica, the Peloponnesos, whatever their nominal status, were in effect provinces, usually of Macedonia, or at best maintained some sort of independence in a belated attempt at federation ; while the West had, from about 250 B.C. on, the choice of subjection to Carthage or to Rome, generally, in the latter case especially, under some decent pretence of alliance. The natural result was that learning and talent drifted towards the new capitals, Alexandria and Pergamos, where Greek was the official language and Greek culture was valued, until, after some two centuries, Rome became largely Hellenized and also the capital of the civilized world, and the current set away from the east to Italy. Hence we begin a new epoch of literature, which may conveniently be divided into two periods, the Alexandrian or Hellenistic, from about 325 to the downfall of the Ptolemaic dynasty in Egypt, and the Roman, from the Battle of Actium in 31 B.C. onwards.

The new capitals, and not least Alexandria, were no longer Greek city-states, though they might and did mimic something of the forms of them, but the seats of great imperial governments. Their population was not wholly or principally Greek, but included a Greek-speaking class, the superiors in culture and privilege, composed mostly of Hellenes, pure-blooded or otherwise, but in some small part of Macedonian officials, Greek in speech, for their own tongue remained barbarous, and largely Greek in habits also.[1] In such a population it was inevitable that a new and simplified form of Greek should grow up, the so-called Common Dialect (κοινὴ διάλεκτος, or simply κοινή), whose relation to Attic, on which it was principally founded, was very like that of American to standard English. That is to say, it was less subtle and more monotonous in its syntax, its inflections were more uniform, and its vocabulary, while large, was less expressive because less accurate. Within the limits of this speech, which soon drove the local dialects out of use, save for artificial revivals, there was room for differences of style as wide as that existing between the worst American journals and the novels of Henry James ; and in addition, scholars and writers (the two classes were generally one) were of course capable of composing in the old literary dialects more or less accurately, much as to-day there are some who can express themselves in very passable imitations of Ciceronian Latin or Chaucerian English.

It is very plain that such an environment as this was not favourable to poetry. The fundamental human emotions with which a great poet deals are indeed much the same at all times and places ; but their expression varies so widely that unless there is considerable homogeneity of thought and culture between the poet and his audience, he is hampered at every turn and will either remain unintelligible (witness the difficulty with which Shakespere has won appreciation in France and Racine in England) or let his inspiration evaporate while he tries to explain. The cultural and emotional antecedents of the various classes in the great Hellenistic cities differed as widely as those of Parisians of the seventeenth century, Victorian Londoners and New Yorkers of to-day ; and in addition, poetry had for some time been declining into a secondary place, while prose, under the influence of men like Isokrates, took the lead as the chief medium of both instruction and entertainment.

[1] See page 424.

We have seen that Middle and New Comedy had nothing poetical in them save their use of verse ; in other words, the only popular poems still flourishing were grown prosaic. But attempts to write poetry on the old models or a modification of them had never ceased. PEISANDROS of Rhodes wrote a *Herakleia* or *Exploits of Herakles*, in two books, some time in the sixth century,[1] which seems, from the favourable judgement of one or two ancient critics,[2] to have been a poem of some merit ; Herodotos' cousin PANYASSIS tried his hand at the same theme in a much lengthier work of fourteen books, and also wrote *Ionika*, a work in elegiacs dealing with the settlement of Ionia by the Greeks.[3] A younger man was CHOIRILOS of Samos, said to have been a favourite of Herodotos, whom he certainly used ; complaining, in really graceful verses, that all the land of the Muses is now divided up and no new chariot is available to any who will enter their race,[4] he tried to find something new and turned recent history into hexameters ; the *Perseis*, *Medika*, *Barbarika*, or *Persika* which he wrote dealt among other things with the defeat of Xerxes. He lived long enough to win favour with Lysandros towards the end of the Peloponnesian War. There existed therefore a tradition of learned epic, and Elegy was not dead. As a kind of logical consequence of this there arose a poet, ANTIMACHOS of Kolophon, who, though heartily abused by many of the Alexandrians, was in some sense their forerunner.[5] Two poems of importance were written by him, a *Thebais*, of whose portentous length stories were told in later days,[6] and two books of elegiacs called, in memory of his dead wife, *Lyde*. Not much is left of these performances, but the little we have shows that, whereas Peisandros and Panyassis had merely written in a form no longer popular (we may compare Beddoes' attempt, under Victoria, to revive Elizabethan poetical drama), Antimachos' writings could hardly have been understood except by scholars, being full of recondite learning and strange words, partly archaic, partly invented.

---

[1] This seems a reasonable date, to judge from the frags. (Kinkel, pp. 248-53), see Wilamowitz, *Herakles*, i, 309 ; Suidas gives several dates from 'older than Hesiod' to Olymp. 33 (648-645 B.C.).

[2] *E.g.*, Quintil., x, 1, 56.   [3] Suid., *s.u.*

[4] Frag. 1 (*Choerili Samii quae supersunt coll.* F. Naeke, Leipzig 1817). See Suid., *s.u.* ; Powell, *C.A.*, p. 250.

[5] *E.g.*, Kallim., frag. 398 Pfeiffer (Epigr. fr. 5 Mair), Λύδη καὶ παχὺ γράμμα καὶ οὐ τορόν, and Catullus, xcv, 10, *at populus tumido gaudeat Antimacho*. His elegiac frags. are in Diehl and Bergk ; epic in Kinkel, p. 273 *sqq.*

[6] See Cicero, *Brutus*, 191 ; for the *Lyde*, see [Plut.]. *consol. ad Apoll.*, 106 b. His frags. have been edited by B. Wyss (Berlin, Weidmann, 1936).

To avoid confusion, it may be mentioned that there was another PEISANDROS, a versifier of the time of Alexander Severus ; Panyassis is a not uncommon name in Ionia, but the other bearers of it were not men of letters ; a certain CHOIRILOS of Iasos in Karia wrote very bad verses on Alexander the Great, about a century after the time of the Samian poet, and it is to him that Horace refers, *epp.*, ii, 1, 232–4 ; A.P., 357–8 ; cf. Curtius Rufus, viii, 5, 8 ; Ausonius, *ep.* 12 (vol. ii, p. 34 Loeb ed.) ; Naecke, *op. cit.*, p. 37 *sqq.*

While Epic and Elegy were thus reviving, at least in the study, Lyric was in a parlous condition. Its chief form was the dithyramb, and this, under MELANIPPIDES of Melos, KINESIAS of Athens, one of Aristophanes' favourite butts, PHILOXENOS of Kythera [7] and others, seems to have become a very loose composition, abounding in variety of metres, extraordinary epithets, quaint phraseology and new, elaborate forms of music. The most popular composer of the fifth and fourth centuries was TIMOTHEOS of Miletos, who chiefly prided himself on his music [8] and was a conscious and deliberate innovator. We have enough of him to know that, whatever his merits in this sphere may have been, he was a most degenerate poet. His *Persians*, of which we have the greater part,[9] is in outward form a *nomos*, the old Terpandrean type of lyric (see p. 112), which had never gone out of use. Here its resemblance to ancient models ends, for its language exhibits every possible type of bad taste, including wanton obscurity, and its metre is restless and undignified, suggesting the modern horrors of ' jazz '. His dates are, at the earliest, 455–365, at latest, 447–357.[10]

Since, then, the new cosmopolitan cities could furnish no audience comparable to that which listened to Sophokles, or even Korinna ; since popular taste even in Greece itself was at so low an ebb, and since the fashion of writing poetry for the connoisseur rather than the ordinary man had already begun, it was not surprising that there arose, notably at Alexandria

[7] Frags. of all these in Diehl and Bergk. For Melanippides' innovations, see Pherekrates *ap.* Plut. (?) *de musica*, 1141 d. He died in Macedonia, in 413. Philoxenos is the hero of a well-known anecdote (Diod. Sic.. xv, 6, 3–4). He was sent to the quarries at Syracuse for criticizing Dionysios I's verses. Being released, and hearing more specimens of the royal compositions, he begged to be taken back to the quarries.

[8] Timoth., frags. 6, 224 *sqq.*, and 7 Diehl.

[9] Edited from a Berlin papyrus by Wilam., *Timotheos, Die Perser*, Leipzig 1903 ; it is fr. 6 of Tim. in Diehl, *q.u.* (ii, p. 138) for literature. The subject is the Battle of Salamis.

[10] Marmor Parium, 76 ; see Jacoby, p. 189.

itself but also in other centres, that kind of poetry which we call Alexandrian. This, so far from seeking popularity, deliberately avoided it, and wrote solely for the learned and discriminating few. Whether, under such circumstances, the greatest poetry could arise may be doubted ; certain it is that no poet of the first rank came forward to grace the Hellenistic world. But there were several whose natural powers were by no means contemptible, their taste fine and their technical skill great.

All the Alexandrians had in common one characteristic, showing itself in a variety of forms, namely avoidance of the trite and commonplace. Hence all alike sought restlessly for subjects either new or capable of being treated from some new angle ; and all used language which, while retaining the flavour of antiquity, showed at every turn some novelty of formation, shade of meaning, or collocation. All alike were rather for polished and elegant simplicity in the matter of metre than for complications ; stanzas were rarely used when lyrical compositions were attempted, but rather those verses of solo Lyric which were capable of being repeated indefinitely (κατὰ στίχον, to use the technical phrase), while the hexameter and the elegiac couplet, both of them still further refined after the refinements of the older poets had been taken over, were not seldom used, notably by Kallimachos [11] for passages of lyrical flavour. But beyond these common features their agreement did not extend, and from the first they divided into two schools, which we may perhaps call the Kallimacheian and the Apollonian. Of these, the former held that the day of poetical works on a grand scale was over, and the future lay wholly with the shorter, more exquisitely finished performance : one might almost say, with the cameo, not the full-size statue or frieze. The latter was still hopeful, not, perhaps, of another Iliad or Oresteia, but of the possibility of epic not too restricted in volume. It could cite respectable authorities of recent date, such as Panyassis and Antimachos, for its views ; but the Kallimacheians were more original in their development.

KALLIMACHOS himself, one of the most important writers of later antiquity, is a man of whose life very little is known. Ancient, in no case very ancient, authorities [12] give us the follow-

---

[11] See Cahen, *Callimaque*, p. 297.

[12] An article in Suidas, scrappy, confused and no doubt corrupt : the so-called *scholium Plautinum* (found in a MS. of Plautus in 1819, published by Ritschel in 1838, often reprinted, *e.g.*, in Dübner, p. xxii) : a similar notice in Cramer's *Anecdota Graeca*, i, p. 3 *sqq.* ; the *Prolegomena* to Aristophanes of John Tzetzes, who is also perhaps the author of the last two notices. The gist of these is in Mair, p. 1 *sqq.* ; very full discussion in Cahen, *op. cit.*, p. 11 *sqq.*

ing information, got from uncertain sources. He was a Kyrenian, son of Battos and Mesatma (the latter name is doubtful). He lived in the days of Ptolemy II, Philadelphos, 285–247 B.C., and survived to the reign of Ptolemy III, Euergetes. He was librarian of the royal library at Alexandria, and in that capacity wrote the *pinakes* or catalogue of the books, apparently no mere list of titles and authors but a *catalogue raisonné*, containing much information on literary history. He was the author likewise of a number of literary and antiquarian treatises, and of poetry in different metres : some 800 volumes in all were ascribed to him. It is hardly too much to say that every one of these statements has been contested and very variously interpreted, save the matter of his birth and his father's name, which come direct from his own works. But this much we may claim to know. He must have been born somewhere about 310, to make him of a competent age for the datable events of his life. He was poor— perhaps the unquiet state of politics in Kyrene had ruined his family—and for a while was a schoolmaster in Eleusis, a suburb of Alexandria ; but there he seems to have formed literary acquaintances and laid the foundations of a poetical reputation : the *Hymn to Zeus*, evidently written early in the reign of Ptolemy Philadelphos, sounds like a serious attempt to put forward his claims to royal recognition. It cannot have been very long after that that he obtained some kind of an official post, and the status of a librarian ; whether he was ever chief librarian is doubtful, and of no great importance. By 270, when the great Queen Arsinoe died, he clearly was a leading figure, for his poem on her death, of which we have a part, savours much of the performance of a kind of poet laureate. In the forties of the century, he was still ready to write court poetry, and to that period belongs the *Lock of Berenike*. Precisely when he died is not known.

The character of his poetry can hardly be better given than in his own words, from the recently discovered prologue to the *Aitia*, composed in his old age.[13] Apollo tells him that a poet should offer as fat a victim as he can, but keep his verse slender ; he also advises him to ' walk on the path where the carriages do not journey, not to drive his car in the tracks of others, nor travel the broad way, but on a road of his own, though it be a strait one.' ' I obeyed him ', says the poet, ' for I sing among those that love the cicala's slender piping, not the asses' bray.' Delicacy, high finish, very moderate length, and of course, for he

[13] Frag. 1 Pfeiffer : for K.'s age, see line 6 ; the passage given above is 22–30.

wrote for the learned only, a wealth of literary and mythological allusion, are his characteristics : it is the poetry of a man of talent and, usually, of good taste, who writes because he chooses to do so, not because his nature compels him to. Perhaps a modern reader will come most quickly to an understanding of what he accomplished if he compares his poetry to that of Edgar Allan Poe, omitting, however, the flashes of morbid genius which illuminate everything the American wrote but are not to be found in the consistently sane work of the poet of Kyrene. Despite all differences, the *Aitia* and *The Raven* have in common the important characteristic that they are the exposition in an actual work of theories of aesthetics and metre.

Since he says that Apollo gave him these commands when he first began to write, *i.e.*, he formed these theories early in his career and never departed from them, the chronological order of his works, which is obscure, matters but little. It is extremely unfortunate that we have lost most of what he wrote, only the Hymns and some epigrams being preserved entire. The former, while by no means his most characteristic or best work, are interesting nevertheless.[14] They number six : the first to Zeus, telling the story of his birth and upbringing in a subtle imitation of the manner of the Homeric hymns and passing on to a parallel, clear enough but not crudely insisted upon, between the might of Zeus and the might of Ptolemy. The second is to Apollo, and pretends (it is highly unlikely that this and similar pretences in the Hymns are to be taken seriously) to be sung at the ancient Dorian festival of the Karneia, in Kyrene. It deals, professedly, mostly with the glory of the god ; there are allusions to contemporary politics decorously loyal in tone, but rather obscure for us owing to our imperfect knowledge, and one famous one, to be treated later, to the quarrel with Apollonios of Rhodes. The third is to Artemis, and is a curious and not always happy blend of a humorous sketch of the little-girl goddess with a mass of learning about her titles and functions. The fourth, to Delos, re-tells the story of Apollo's birth with a wealth of mythology and a compliment to Ptolemy for his successful campaigns against the Gauls. No. V breaks away from the tone of the earlier hymns. Written in elegiacs, it tells the story of the Bath of Pallas, *i.e.*, of how Teiresias, like Aktaion, unwittingly saw her bathing, and was struck blind in consequence. The last hymn, to Demeter, is again in hexameters, dealing with the goddess' wanderings in search of Kore and with one of her miracles, the

[14] The latest commentary is that of Cahen (see Bibliography), which gives some account of the earlier commentators.

punishment of Erysichthon, for his impiety towards her sacred grove, with insatiable hunger. In language, the first four hymns are in more or less epic dialect, with all manner of subtle variations from the actual phraseology of the older works and also many innovations in vocabulary, largely by borrowings from Tragedy and other post-Epic forms of composition, but also by what may be called euphuism, *i.e.*, the usage of words in a sense justified by their etymology, but not by their history or former meanings.[15] The last two hymns, however, are in Doric—conventionalized literary Doric, not of any particular time or place, although it is probable that a Doric dialect was what the poet, in his own home, habitually spoke.[16]

A far more important work, unhappily represented for us by fragments only, is the *Aitia*, four books in elegiacs, dealing, at least in part,[17] with the αἴτια, legendary causes or origins, of various places, rites and so forth. One interesting fragment, the No. 178 in Pfeiffer's edition, shows us how this was managed ; Kallimachos meets an agreeable stranger from Ikos and asks him why the inhabitants of that island pay such reverence to Peleus. No doubt he went on to tell how the stranger courteously enlightened him. In this, and doubtless in a score of other ways, he was enabled to bring in all manner of stories. Some of these were amatory, as the most famous of all, that concerning Akontios and Kydippe,[18] which we have practically in full. This is symptomatic ; the love-story, not much regarded by earlier writers, was one of the favourite themes of Alexandrians, and most of the famous tales of that kind go back to them, either directly or through some intermediary who has perhaps altered the names and a few of the minor circumstances a little.

It is clear that by writing on the plan of the *Aitia*, Kallimachos

[15] As Shakespeare makes Don Armado (*L.L.L.*, v, 1) use excrement' to mean 'mustachio' (as *growing from* the lip), so Kallimachos, for instance, uses ἄβροχος, which in all Greek before his time means 'rainless', to signify 'waterless', 'having no rivers' ; ἐλατήρ, properly a charioteer, of one driving defeated enemies before him, and so on.

[16] Kyrene has abundance of Doric inscriptions ; attempts to make K. out as having written in his local dialect are not satisfactory ; he rather imitated, if anything, those forms of Doric which had a literature, *i.e.*, principally Sicilian.

[17] The title of an ancient book may refer simply to the subject of its first part ; *e.g.*, Cato's *Origines* began with the origins of Italian cities but went on to deal with their later history ; Theokritos' *Pastorals* was apparently a collection beginning with pastoral poems. So we often name a whole book of short stories after the first one in the collection.

[18] For the story, see Rose, *Myth.*, pp. 276–7.

was able to reconcile his passion for brevity with a fairly large
total output, the whole having a sort of loose unity, even a framework, for there was an episode, perhaps prefaratory to the whole,
in which Kallimachos dreamed he was on Helikon, talking with
the Muses. An equally famous poem, the *Hekale*, achieved a
similar result by a different route. In form it was not exactly
an epic, but an episode of epic, such as we now generally call
an *epyllion*.[19] Theseus, on his way to hunt the Marathonian Bull,
is entertained by a poor but hospitable old woman, whose name
gives the piece its title. This seems to have given an excuse for
all manner of excursuses, ranging from the names of the salads she
served him for his supper to legends and fables quite unconnected
with the plot, which, we may conjecture, she told him for his
amusement. Here again we have a most characteristic Alexandrian composition. In such pieces, the story which forms the
ostensible subject is assumed as known, or told only in the briefest
outline, but some picturesque detail, or one giving excuse for
elaborate description or other ornament, is related very fully,
perhaps for three or four hundred lines. We shall find such poems
in Theokritos also, and the *genre* survives, little changed, into
modern work.[20]

Other, minor works of Kallimachos included the *Lock of
Berenike*, which we know, not so much from the score of lines
surviving, as from the fairly literal translation of Catullus.[21]
It is a pretty bit of courtly astronomy ; Konon the astronomer
had identified a small group of stars near Leo as a new constellation, the Lock of Hair. and declared it must be a lock dedicated
by the queen which had mysteriously disappeared from its place
in the temple ; Kallimachos gives the very words of the glorified
tress, which greets its royal mistress and would fain be back on
her beloved head. There was also an adaptation in elegiacs of the
Pindaric *epinikion*, in honour of Sosibios, a prominent member of
the Ptolemaic court. It probably was composed about the same
time as the *Lock*.[21a]

Of two other poems, the *Galateia*, perhaps an epyllion on the same
subject as Theokritos' *Cyclops*, and the *Grapheion* (stilus ?) of unknown

[19] 'Επύλλιον is passable Greek for ' little epic ', but does not seem
to have been used in this technical sense by any ancient.
[20] Shakespeare's *Lucrece* is an overgrown epyllion, Tennyson's *Oenone*
quite a good specimen of this sort of composition.
[21] Catullus, 66 : frag. 110 Pfeiffer, who supposes it the last episode of
the *Aitia*.
[21a] See frags. 384, 384a Pfeiffer, and Cahen, *Callimaque*, pp. 20–3,
318–19, 637–41.

subject, we have not quite six lines. The former was in hexameters, the latter in elegiacs.

The *Iambi* were in a different vein altogether, for they revived, no doubt with the usual amount of variation and originality of treatment, something of the manner of the early Ionian iambic poets ; a part was in scazons and was put (we have a long fragment of it) into the mouth of Hipponax (see p. 92), risen from the dead. But he clearly had lost much of his scurrility in the other world, and what we have is rather humorous and mildly satirical, making use of fables and apologues, very much as we find Horace doing later.

Suidas and one or two others preserve for us a few more titles, to which no fragment can be fitted with any approach to certainty and of whose contents we have no clear knowledge. Some of them may be sub-titles of parts of the *Aitia*.[22]

Kallimachos is several times spoken of by later writers [23] as a notable erotic poet. In the general wreck of Alexandrian love-elegies, his have vanished, if indeed (for even this is uncertain) he ever wrote any on a scale comparable to Ovid's *Amores*, for example. What he could do in this respect, however, is made clear to us, not by the episode of Akontios and Kydippe, which tells the story in a quiet and unemotional way, with no attempt to interpret the feelings of either actor, but by certain of the justly admired Epigrams. Of these a not inconsiderable collection seems to have existed in antiquity, though we do not know who made it ; [24] what we have presumably consists of selections from this, made by the anthologists, with something of the usual admixture of spurious work. With Kallimachos the epigram manifestly and unmistakably emerges as a literary type, set free from the association with inscriptions which it once had. No doubt purely literary epigrams, never intended to be carved on any monument, had been composed before his day ; but he is the acknowledged master of this, as Simonides (see p. 115) had been of the earlier, inscriptional kind. Many of the little pieces we have from him (they number rather more than sixty) still keep something of the old form. There are, for instance, epitaphs on real or imaginary people, distinguished from real ones by the

[22] Such are the *Arrival of Io* (presumably in Egypt), *Semele*, *Arkadia*. For the *Ibis*, see below.

[23] As Propertius, iii, 1, 1.

[24] This is proved by half a dozen quotations said to be from his epigrams, but corresponding to nothing in any epigram of his we have.

absence of the particulars concerning name, parentage and so
forth which a real tomb would need. Others have these particulars, but show by some turn of the thought that they are not
meant actually to be inscribed.[25] Some may be real.[26] Other
epigrams again are amatory, and these contain some of Kallimachos' most pleasant and ingenious work, being generally lightly-
sketched pictures of lovers' woes ; some are in form dedicatory
inscriptions. But a few make no shadow of pretence to being
anything but short expressions of personal feeling. Thus, one [27]
is a favourable criticism of Aratos ; another,[28] a gentle bit of
ridicule of one of the cyclic poems, the *Capture of Oichalia* (see
p. 52) ; another, one of the most perfect small works of all
literature, is the lament for his friend Herakleitos of Halikarnassos ;[29] while one is a short literary manifesto with a sudden
turn at the end that makes it into an attack on a faithless love.[30]
Certainly, an author who can give such adequate and formally
perfect expression to a wide range of emotions in so restricted a
form would be capable of writing a good elegy in the style, say,
of those which Propertius was one day to compose, setting forth
love, jealousy, or other suitable themes.

But it is unfortunately true that of the whole mass of Alexandrian erotic poetry very little survives, and we judge of its size
and importance chiefly by the admiring references of Latin poets
and their supposed imitations of it. What is left will be dealt
with in this chapter under the names of the various authors.
Of epigram, on the other hand, we have a good deal from this
age, written by practically every poet of any importance, and on
the whole of excellent quality.

We are better able to estimate Kallimachos' enemy, APOL-
LONIOS of Rhodes. According to the ancient biography of this
poet, he was really an Alexandrian, afterwards given Rhodian
citizenship during his stay in that island. He was a pupil of
Kallimachos ; he wrote the first draft of his surviving work, the
Argonautica, in Alexandria, but it was so complete a failure that
he left the city for Rhodes, where he revised his poem into the
form we have. Returning, he was much more successful in
obtaining recognition, became librarian after Kallimachos and
was buried with him.

This needs a good deal of correcting. Kallimachos probably

---

[25] For instance, Nos. 13 (11) and 15 (13).
[26] As 11 (9) and 61 (60).   [27] 29 (27).
[28] 7 (6).   [29] 2.
[30] 30 ; the sense is ' I hate all common things, poems, roads, light-o'-
loves, fountains ; and therefore, Lysanias, I hate you.'

was never librarian, if by that is meant librarian-in-chief ; a valuable document which we now possess [31] shows Apollonios' name second on the list of librarians, Zenodotos having been the first. Coming so early as this, he can hardly have been young enough for Kallimachos to have taught him ; this is a piece of grammarian's chronology, in an attempt to associate the two well-known names. Nor does there seem to be much time left for a long stay in Rhodes, though he may have visited the place fairly early in his career. Probably he and Kallimachos were of about the same age, and all the better fitted to be literary opponents on that account.

Much more important is Apollonios' work, which has come down to us in its revised form. [32] It is a deliberate challenge of Kallimachos' fundamental principle that poems should be short, for it fills four lengthy books with its 5,835 lines. The poem moreover has a kind of unity, for it has but one nominal subject, the journey of the Argonauts to Kolchis and their return via the great rivers of Europe (partly fabulous), the mainland of Northern Africa and the Mediterranean. Actually, however, it proves Kallimachos' contention up to the hilt, for it badly lacks all real unity. It is rather a book of excellent stories told in good verse than a regular and unified epic poem, and its merit lies in its episodes, notably in the admirable telling of the loves of Jason and Medeia which fills the third book and part of the fourth. [33] Other passages, however, such as the fight between Polydeukes and the churlish giant Amykos, king of the Bebrykes, the loss of Hylas and the meeting with the Hesperides are far from worthless. [34] The poem is tedious only if an attempt be made to read it as one would the Iliad or Paradise Lost ; read discontinuously, it is pleasant and not too pedantically learned. The language is founded on Homer, with careful avoidance of exactly repeating any phrase of his, [35] and often a tacit explanation of some difficult

[31] *Oxyrh. Pap.*, 1241 ; see for a recent discussion Cahen, *Callimaque*, p. 53. The ancient Life is found in Suidas, *s.u.* 'Aπoλλώνιος, and in two different versions in the Laurentian MS. of the *Argonautica* and scholia. For a sketch of the quarrel with some references to recent literature, see Gillies, *The Argonautica, Book III* (Camb., 1928), p. xliii *sqq.*, and for a recent critique of Apollonios, Wilam., *Hell. Dicht.*, ii, p. 165 *sqq.*

[32] Several lines from the earlier version are quoted in the scholia. See Mooney's edition, p. 403 *sqq.* ; Powell, *C.A.*, p. 4 *sqq.*

[33] iii and iv, 1–182.   [34] ii, 1 *sqq.* ; i, 1172 *sqq.* ; iv, 1393 *sqq.*

[35] *E.g.*, Homer has the phrase κλέα ἀνδρῶν or ' glorious deeds of heroes ', forming the subject of the songs which Achilles sings, Il. ix, 189. Apollonios' first line proposes the same subject for his own poem ; but he alters it into κλέα φωτῶν.

and disputed word in him, conveyed by placing it in such a context that its meaning cannot be mistaken.[36]

Apollonios clearly had a following, although Kallimachos remained the leader of orthodox literary opinion, and the two poets did not spare each other. Kallimachos was the subtler in his attacks, so subtle in fact that the point of that one which is most certainly directed against Apollonios in person was not perceived until a short while ago. He makes Envy say to Apollo [37] ' I cannot admire that bard who sings not even as much as Pontos '. This at first sight would seem to mean ' as much as the sea ', which is pure nonsense, the sea being proverbially noisy and ' not even ' therefore meaningless. It acquires a meaning, however, when we recollect that Pontos is, by one account, the father of the spiteful Telchines, and that Telchines was Kallimachos' name for his literary opponents in general.[38] Apollonios for his part produced a terse epigram, purporting to be two entries from a dictionary, as follows : ' *Kallimachos* ; synonyms, *Rubbish, Fribble, Blockhead. Αἴτιος* (he puns on the meanings " originator " and " criminal ") ; one who writes Kallimachos' *Aitia.*' [39] Doubtless there was much more of this caustic wit current in Alexandria ; we shall see later that Theokritos took sides in the contest.

It was during this contest, the most famous literary quarrel in antiquity, that Kallimachos wrote his *Ibis*, a poem now completely lost, but described for us by Ovid and Suidas.[40] It was an attack on Apollonios, who seems to have been called Ibis throughout, whether because he, like the bird of that name, was a native, in some sense, of Egypt, or, which is perhaps more likely, because the ibis was credited by the ancients with very disgusting habits. It was, moreover, a riddle-poem, of a kind to be described later ; the ' Ibis ' was cursed with all the plagues of the obscurer unfortunates of mythology, who were not so much named as alluded to.

[36] Thus, it seems to have been disputed whether ἔνδιος in Homer meant ' noon ' or ' evening '. Apollonios' opinion was that it could mean either ; for iv, 1312 he speaks of i. as the time when the sun is hottest, in i, 603 as the time when a ship finishes her day's run. See the preface to Keil's ed. of the *Argon.*, pp. xxxvii *sqq.* and clxviii *sqq.*

[37] Kall., *hymn.*, ii, 106.

[38] As in the opening verse of the newly found prologue to the *Aitia*, frag. 1, 1 Pfeiffer. I owe this explanation to Mr. E. A. Barber, who has briefly mentioned it, *Class. Rev.*, xlvi (1932), p. 163.

[39] *Anth. Pal.*, xi. 275. It runs. Καλλίμαχος· τὸ κάθαρμα· τὸ παίγνιον· ὁ ξύλινος νοῦς. αἴτιος· ὁ γράψας Αἴτια Καλλιμάχου. The author of this, the only punctuation which gives the epigram point and wit, seems to be A. Croiset, *La lit. grecque*, V, p. 211, n. 5.

[40] Ovid, *Ibis*, 55–60, well commented on by R. Ellis, pp. xxxi–xxxix of the Prolegomena to his edition of the poem ; Suidas, *s.u.* Καλλίμαχος. Conjectures are rife, see for instance Wilam. and Cahen, *opp. citt.*, i, p. 207 and p. 68 *sqq.* respectively ; I can find little but ingenuity to praise in them.

Apollonios is credited with several works besides the *Argonautica* ; a collection of epigrams passed under his name, with how much justice we cannot tell, for only the one quoted above has survived. Besides these, he seems to have written a poem, or group of poems rather, for the metre was not the same throughout, called *Foundations* (*Κτίσεις*), dealing with the foundation-legends of a number of cities, including Alexandria itself. This might well be taken to be a deliberate poaching on Kallimachos' own preserves, if the foundations of cities and islands ' attributed to the latter were all in verse.[41] He also wrote philological works in prose, which included an *Address to Zenodotos* (cf. p. 388), on the text of Homer, and his opinions on Hesiod are cited occasionally,[42] but these may have been *obiter dicta* in his Homeric treatise. A not dissimilar uncertainty attaches to mentions of his works *On Archilochos*, *On the Egyptians*, the *Trierikos* (description of a trireme, *i.e.*, probably a sort of dictionary of technical terms relating to that form of ship), and the citations of him by the scholiast on Aristophanes. The works mentioned may be chapters or alternative titles of his other writings in some cases, while not all are definitely said to be by this Apollonios ; the name is common enough.[43]

A slightly older contemporary of Kallimachos, his friend and apparently his fellow-student, was ARATOS of Soloi in Kilikia,[44] a man whose immense fame in later antiquity is hard for a modern to appreciate, for judged objectively, he did no more than to put into smooth and pleasant verses a short handbook of astronomy by Eudoxos of Rhodes (see p. 378).[45] If he had let an exuberant fancy work on the star-myths which were by that time fairly common in Greece, or even if he had brought to his task the fervent rhetoric and profound astrological conviction which the Latin Manilius was to display some three and a half centuries later, it would be easier to see why he was popular ; but his poem, although the language is poetical throughout, avoiding

[41] Suid., *loc. cit.* Fragments in Powell, *C.A.*, p. 4 *sqq*.

[42] Schol. on Hes., *Theog.*, 26 (p. 383 Gaisford) ; Proclus on *W.D.* 824 (826), p. 368 Gaisford ; arg. No. 1 to *Shield*.

[43] See Athen., 451 d, 191 f, 97 d ; Mooney, pp. 49–52.

[44] We have an ancient life of him, preserved in Suidas, *s.u.* Ἄρατος and in various MSS. of his poem, giving five versions in all, collected in Westermann, *Biographoi* (Brunswick, 1859), p. 52 *sqq.* and before him in Buhle's ed. of Aratos, i, 3–4 and ii, 429–46. He was born probably about 315 ; the facts are briefly collected and discussed in the Loeb edition (G. R. Mair) of the *Phaenomena*, p. 359 *sqq*.

[45] This is shown in detail by the great astronomer Hipparchos (see p. 379) in his surviving *Commentary on Aratos and Eudoxos* (best ed., by C. Manitius, Teubner, 1894), i, 2, 1 *sqq.*, who points out numerous errors of Eudoxos which Aratos had followed, and some blunders of Aratos' own arising from misunderstanding his authority.

both prosy turns of style and turgid periphrases and, as Kalli-machos said of it, skimming the cream of Hesiod,[46] does no more than express quite briefly the facts, or rather, for Aratos was himself no astronomer, the poet's notion of Eudoxos' account of the facts, concerning the heavens as observable from the latitude of Rhodes or thereabouts. One episode (98–136) is all that breaks the smooth monotony of his description, which passes in regular order from one constellation to another, beginning at the north, and then gives a list of those groups of stars which rise and set together. A second part, which it used to be the fashion to write or print as a separate poem, gives an account of weather-signs, and is probably based on the essay on the same subject which we have from Theophrastos (see p. 353).[47]

That such a writer should be esteemed as a good maker of verses is intelligible ; but his reputation, from his own times onwards, was so enormous as to place his amongst the great names of this period. There were already several commentaries on him extant when Hipparchos wrote his in the middle of the second century B.C.,[48] i.e., within a hundred years or so of the poet's death, and he never ceased to be studied, commented upon and imitated. The Latins especially admired him, for besides the obvious influence of his poem upon Vergil, to name no others, we have three translations of him, one fragmentary, made by Cicero in his youth, one by Germanicus (probably the younger Germanicus, son of Nero Claudius Drusus Germanicus and father by the elder Agrippina of the emperor Caligula) and one by Sextus Rufus Avienus, in the fourth century A.D. As a reason for this it may be perhaps suggested that the Alexandrian age was wistfully anxious to produce a great poet ; that literary taste and criticism were enlightened enough to be aware that the subject of great poetry must be truth in one form or another ; and that, not having sufficient genius to produce that highest and timeless truth which belongs to the creations of a writer of Homer's or Sophokles' calibre, they fell back on the truth of scientific fact, hoping to find poetical inspiration in material which by its nature can inspire only to intellectual activity and the zeal of a researcher. In Aratos' own case, the selection of

---

[46] Or literally, ' wiping off the most honied part ', τὸ μελιχρότατον ἀπεμάξατο, epigr., 29 (27).

[47] See Mair, p. 378.

[48] Hipparchos, op. cit., i, 1, 3 ; he prefers that by Attalos ; another was by Boethos the Stoic, Geminus, Isag., 17, 48. To some one of these, or to a later commentary put together from them, the biography to which the existing Lives seem to go back may be due.

a subject may have been influenced by the growing importance of astral religion, which later was to swamp popular Greek ideas of deity under a veritable flood of astrology and sun-worship in various forms, derived mostly from the East. For his stately prologue, an invocation of Zeus which is far from being the worst of Greek religious poetry, suggests that he was a pious man, to whom the stars were not simply interesting and curious objects, about which he might utter clever conceits in metre and language skilfully adapted from the ancients, as Kallimachos did about myths, but appeared somewhat as they did to the psalmist, ' the heavens, the work of Thy fingers ', and none the less impressive because he had some idea of the laws governing their apparent movements.

The poem as a whole is usually called the *Phaenomena* (Φαινόμενα), with a separate title in some ancient authorities, Συνανατολαί, for verses 559–732, on the risings and settings,[49] and another, Διοσημίαι, for the long section on weather-signs, 733–1154.

Like Kallimachos and Apollonios, Aratos was a scholar, indeed none but a scholar could have written in his style and metre ; a modern equivalent would be a poem which followed the *Canterbury Tales* fairly closely in these respects. The surviving Lives ascribe to him, with varying degrees of probability, a critical edition (διόρθωσις) of the Ödyssey and a dissertation *On Homer and the Iliad*, another didactic poem, *Iatrika*, Ἰατρικαὶ δυνάμεις (medicinal virtues, presumably those of herbs or minerals), from which Pollux has preserved a few lines treating of the sutures of the skull,[50] a collection of epigrams and another of miscellaneous short poems (κατὰ λεπτόν, a title afterwards borrowed by Vergil or the editors of the little pieces ascribed to him), and several other poems on various topics, together with a few works of which we do not know if they were in prose or verse, or even whether they were more than alternative titles for those already mentioned, or sections of them. A collection of letters once existed under his name, but was of doubtful authenticity.[51]

Being so prominent a figure in the cultural life of his time, Aratos did not want patrons, for already the prominence of Alexandria in respect of literature was exciting emulation and jealousy in other Hellenistic kingdoms. Therefore it is not surprising to learn from the Lives that he was at the court of

[49] As Hipparchos, *op. cit.*, i, 1, 1, where see Manitius' commentary.
[50] Pollux, *Onom.*, ii, 38. Two or three other works on medical subjects are ascribed to him, and serve to account for the impression which some authorities, rightly or wrongly, held that he was a physician.
[51] See Bentley, *Epist. of Themistocles, etc.*, pp. 115, 133 (554, 568, Wagner).

Macedonia, in the time of Antigonos Gonatas, who is said to have suggested the subject of the *Phaenomena* to him, and also, presumably before the stay with Antigonos, at that of Antiochos I (Soter),[52] king of Syria.

Aratos having set the example, several others tried their hands at didactic poems on scientific or quasi-scientific subjects. Most of these have vanished (see next paragraph), but one survives, NIKANDROS of Kolophon,[53] who was contemporary with Attalos III, the last king of Pergamon (138–133 B.C.). This man seems to have had considerable medical knowledge, at least theoretical, and with it a passion for unusual modes of expression, for his surviving poems are full of curious words and word-forms, often found in no other author and not seldom doubtfully correct. Besides a poem *On Farming* (*Georgika* ; Vergil was afterwards to borrow the title), which Cicero praises for its style,[54] another *On Shape-changings* ('Ετεροιούμενα ; the subject, though not the title, resembled that of Ovid's *Metamorphoses*, and the Latin poet was acquainted with it), in five books, and some others, attributed to him by our authorities,[55] he composed two works of considerable length, if indeed they are not rather to be regarded as the two books of one poem, the *Theriaca* (Θηριακά, *i.e.*, treatise on noxious beasts, viz., serpents) and the *Alexipharmaca*, on the virtues of herbs. Save for a few efforts to enliven these works by

[52] Antiochos became king in 280. It has been supposed by some (see, *e.g.*, Mair, p. 363 of the Loeb Aratos) that the poet was in Macedonia from the beginning of Antigonos' reign (276) till the invasion of Pyrrhos (about 273), then visited Antiochos, then returned to Antigonos when Pyrrhos had been driven out ; but the Lives say nothing of these journeys back and forth, only that he was in Macedonia when he died. See, for some sensible remarks, Wilam., *Hell. Dicht.*, ii, pp. 274–6. The facts and conjectures are collected handily by Knaack, art. ARATOS, in Pauly-Wissowa.

[53] We have a short life of him prefixed to the considerable body of scholia on his poems, also an article in Suidas. He calls himself a Klarian, *Ther.*, 958, and the Life says he was an Aitolian, which may be true, for in the Hellenistic age migration was common enough. His own statement, if not a mere poetical flourish (a poet is Apollo's servant and Apollo's temple at Klaros, not far from Kolophon, was famous) may mean that he held some position among the priesthood there.

[54] *De orat.*, i, 69 ; to prove that it suffices for an orator to prepare sufficient learning for the subject in hand, in other words to get up his brief, without being a real expert, he instances the facts that Aratos knew no astronomy and Nikandros was a town mouse (*ab agro remotissimus*), yet both wrote excellently on subjects of which they were ignorant.

[55] See the authorities cited in note 53. There was another NIKANDROS, also a poet, who lived in the third century and is mentioned in a Delphic inscription, Dittenberger 452 ; he, or some third writer, may well have been confused with the Kolophonian by whoever compiled the list.

occasional episodes, mythological and other, the author has contented himself with an enumeration of the characteristics of various snakes, real and imaginary, and the best methods of treating their bites, while the second poem discusses the symptoms of different poisons, each being followed by an account of the approved antidotes. For the historian of medicine, or occasionally for the folklorist, he has a good deal of incidental interest ; in antiquity we sometimes find him quoted as a respectable authority on his subject. But from the point of view of poetry, he ranks with a man who should amuse himself by turning some pages of the *British Pharmacopoeia* into English verses in the style of Spenser, with additional false archaisms of his own.

Between Nikandros and Aratos we know the names of several poets who were the authors of didactic works. Aratos himself had several imitators of no great account, according to the Lives ; we cannot judge of their merits, for their poems are lost. One NUMENIOS, who must have lived about the middle of the third century, wrote a work called *The Banquet*, dealing with cookery, a poem on fishing (*Halieutika*) and another with the same title and apparently much the same subject as Nikandros' *Theriaca*.[56] A pupil of Kallimachos, PHILOSTEPHANOS, produced a work in elegiacs, *On extraordinary Rivers*, a symptom of the taste of that age, which was growing fond of lists of odd phenomena, real or supposed, a fashion which later on replaced serious scientific investigation and led up later still to such mediaeval compilations as the *Physiologus*.[57] Earlier than either of these was ARCHESTRATOS, a Geloan or Syracusan, who wrote a poem on foods of various kinds, where to buy and how to prepare them. To judge by his fragments, nearly all from Athenaios, he treated his subject with a certain humorous solemnity and a vast deal of curious knowledge ; like most didactic poets, he wrote in hexameters, and his date would seem to be the fourth century.[58]

Returning now to the contemporaries of Kallimachos, we have

[56] Banquet (δεῖπνον), Athen., 5a ; it is not known whether this was prose or verse. *Halieutika*, Athen., 282a and many other passages, with quotations. *Theriaka*, schol. Nikand., *Ther.*, 637. His fragments are collected in the Didot *Poetae bucolici et didactici*.

[57] The one surviving fragment, preserved in Tzetzes, *Chiliad.*, vii, 670 *sqq.*, is given in Diehl, ii, p. 283.

[58] The facts are given by Wellmann in Pauly-Wissowa, art. ARCHESTRATOS. Athenaios seems to have had all his fragments from Pamphilos, a pupil of Aristarchos. That Archestratos was about contemporary with Alexander is clear from Athen., 163f. His work seems to have been called 'Ηδυπάθεια, though other titles are mentioned. The fragments are collected in *Corpusculum poes. epic. Graec. ludib.* (Teubner series), and in the Didot volume cited in note 56.

next to mention that one who has the best right to be considered a poet of high, though not the highest order. This is THEOKRITOS of Syracuse, the reviver of the mime (see p. 252) in a new form and the father of bucolic or pastoral poetry. He seems to have been of undistinguished origin,[59] and to have embarked on the career of professional poet fairly early in life. At first he wrote in his native city, producing a laudatory poem (xvi of the conventional numbering)[60] addressed to Hieron II (king or tyrant of Syracuse 270–216), but seems to have got little encouragement from that monarch, who had his hands full with a difficult political and military situation. Doubtless some of the excellent epigrams we have from him are also of this period, for they include one written for the pedestal of a statue of Epicharmos (cf. p. 250). However, he tired of his unprofitable home and migrated to the eastern Mediterranean, where he seems to have lived for some time on the island of Kos, the scene of the Seventh Idyll. Alexandria, which he visited about the seventies[61] of the century, proved apparently a much more profitable place, and it would seem that the younger poet established himself in the good graces of Kallimachos, in whose support he wrote two telling works. Apollonios had included the loss of Hylas and the fight with Amykos in his *Argonautica* (see p. 324). Theokritos rehandled the same material by way of an object-lesson, making each episode the subject of a short poem or epyllion by itself, Nos. xiii and xxii, the latter in form a hymn of Homeric type. It was

[59] The epigram prefixed to one of the ancient editions of his poems (*Anth. Pal.* ix, 434, and in the MSS. of his scholia) calls him εἷς ἀπὸ τῶν πολλῶν Συρακοσίων.

[60] This numbering has little to recommend it save familiarity and therefore convenience for citation ; it is neither chronological nor in accordance with the ancient editions. What their exact order was, however, is not known ; an ingenious attempt at reconstructing it by Wilam., *Textgesch. Bukol.*, is shown to be inaccurate by the arrangement in the important papyrus (Pap. Oxyrh. 2064 ; see Hunt-Johnson, *Two Theocritus Papyri*, London, Oxford Univ. Press, 1930, p. 3) which has thrown much new light on the text of his poems.

[61] The chronology of his life and works is very obscure. His address to Hieron implies that the latter is not yet king ; Wilamowitz, *op. cit.*, p. 156, would date the poem 276/5. Addressing Ptolemy II he implies that he is married to his sister (xvii, 130), *i.e.*, Arsinoe II ; the marriage was not earlier than 275, see Macurdy, *Hellenistic Queens* (Baltimore and London, 1932), p. 117 ; also (123) that Ptolemy I and Berenike have been deified (275 at latest). Of course he need not have been in Syracuse or Alexandria when either work was written, but it seems highly probable that he went to the latter city to seek his fortune. A convenient and ingenious discussion in English of the facts will be found in the introduction to Cholmeley's edition.

effective criticism, for he produced decidedly better work than Apollonios had done.

In Kos, he made a number of pleasant acquaintances, some of them men of literary distinction. Several of these are introduced into the Seventh Idyll, but mostly under fanciful names ; thus, Theokritos himself is Simichidas ; he converses with Lykidas, who is possibly Dosiadas (see p. 336).[62] They mention a certain Sikelidas, who may perhaps be Asklepiades [63] (see p. 349) ; Philitas (see p. 341) is spoken of by name ; others are as yet unidentified, Tityros, Ageanax, Aratos (not the poet, whom we have no reason to suppose to have visited Kos and whose name has a long A in the first syllable, while this man's has a short one), Aristis, and finally two unnamed ' shepherds ', one from Acharnai and the other from Lykope in Aitolia. In this poem Theokritos speaks of himself, despite some conventional modesty, as a poet of high repute and one whose songs have attracted the attention of ' Zeus ', meaning no doubt Ptolemy. It is thus unlikely that the poem was written very early in his career.

Theokritos wrote also two or three more epyllia, an *Epithalamium of Helen* (No. xviii), an *Infant Herakles* (Ἡρακλίσκος, No. xxiv), while another poem, dealing with the adventure of Herakles with the Nemean lion (No. xxv) is doubtfully his and seems to be unfinished. But his fame rests chiefly on his Idylls, as they are generally called, mimes in hexameter verse and the Doric dialect, which, when allowance is made for the inevitable epic forms and idioms, seems, so far as our scanty knowledge will let us judge, to differ not very widely from his native Syracusan speech and be far less conventional than the language of most Alexandrians. It seems also to grow somewhat more or less broad according as a character of lower or higher rank speaks. All these little works are highly dramatic, lifelike and full of admirable touches in character ; masquerades like that in No. vii are quite exceptional, and even there the actors, though not really shepherds, are really in the country and speak of places Theokritos knew. In our conventional order of the poems, No. i is the friendly encounter of two shepherds, of whom one sings the other an exquisite song on the death of Daphnis, how he had

---

[62] Wilamowitz, *Hell. Dicht.*, ii, 138, but doubtfully. Legrand (*Rev. ét. grecques*, vii, p. 192 ; *Étude sur Théocrite*, p. 45) suggests Leonidas of Tarentum (Wolfson for Lionson, by a sort of pun), but he was in Epeiros during the seventies of the third century, Wilam., *op. cit.*, i, p. 139, not in or near Kos, and the poem probably dates from that period.

[63] So the schol. on vii, 40, giving as the reason that his father's name was Sikelos.

defied Aphrodite and died in the end of the struggle against a
love to which he would not yield. It is an old Sicilian folktale,
and, allowing for the difference which a literary handling makes,
probably the sort of legend which a real Sicilian shepherd might
sing. No. ii is not rustic at all. A girl has been deserted by her
lover ; she tries to recall him by an elaborate charm and, when
that does not bring him, sends her maid to try one more spell
and meanwhile confesses her whole unhappy story to the Moon.
No. iii is a rustic serenade to an unresponsive Amaryllis ; No. iv
simply the chat of two herdsmen on a summer's day. No. v
brings in two lads, a shepherd and a goatherd, who first quarrel
and then sing against each other with a wood-cutter for umpire.
It is no conventional scene, but exactly the sort of rustic contest
in song which did take place. No. vi is a slighter piece, two young
herdsmen meeting and each singing something to please the other.
Nos. viii and ix are not by Theokritos ; No. x is a dialogue of
reapers, one of whom chaffs the other for being in love. No. xi
is the admirable *Cyclops* ; Polyphemos, a much less formidable
monster than in Homer, is in love with a sea-nymph, Galateia,
and pleads his cause in a song full of delightful humour at the
singer's expense, finally giving it up as hopeless. No. xiii is the
Hylas, already mentioned ; No. xiv has its scene laid in a town,
like No. ii ; a young man has quarrelled with his mistress and is
going to emigrate to Egypt and take service under Ptolemy.
No. xv, the *Women at the Adonia* ('Αδωνιάζουσαι), is a little
masterpiece. A good housewife, Gorgo, calls on her friend
Praxinoa, who lives in a suburb of Alexandria. After some
gossip, they go to the palace, thrown open to the public on the
occasion of the festival of Adonis, still commenting volubly on
everything and everyone. On their chatter breaks the exquisite
hymn of a singer, praising Adonis and Aphrodite, and they start
for home with a word of praise for the soloist and the god.

He also composed some trifles—an address (No. xii) to a real
or imaginary boy, written in Ionic ; three more pieces of the same
tone, but composed in Aiolic (Nos. xxix and xxx, with another
represented by the beginnings of a few lines in the Antinoe
papyrus),[64] and in lyric metres of a simple kind, the bulk of his
work being in hexameters ; another Aiolic lyric, the *Distaff*
(No. xxviii), a delightfully graceful and humorous poetical letter
to the wife of his friend Nikias, accompanying the present of an
ivory distaff. We know of but one other work, a poem called
Berenike, presumably in honour of the deified consort of Ptolemy
I, from which Athenaios has preserved a few lines because they

[64] See Hunt-Johnson, pp. 24, 59 of the work cited in note 60.

mention a sort of fish.[65] Thus his output was distinguished by its poetical value, not its bulk ; it would fill, clearly printed, about sixty pages of this book, but it is worth nearly all else that we have from the Alexandrians.

It was inevitable that Theokritos should have imitators. Some of their poems have been preserved by ancient editors [66] under the impression that they were his own ; to this class belongs No. viii, a contest of song between two boys, a shepherd and a neat-herd, containing some lines of which no poet need have been ashamed, but resembling Theokritos only as Watteau's pastoral scenes resemble Murillo's peasant-lads. No. ix is a slight affair, a little interchange of songs, faintly pretty, which has imposed on some critics as genuine Theokritos, at least in part. No. xix is a trifle of eight lines, Eros stung by a bee ; the author of the 25th pseudo-Anakreontic poem (see p. 102) has imitated it. No. xx, the complaint of a rejected lover, has imitations of Theokritos and suggestions also of Bion about it. No. xxi, of quite unknown date and authorship, describes two fishermen who wake in the night and discuss a dream one of them has had. No. xxiii has been supposed Theokritean, but although it has merit, it is not in his manner. It is a piteous tale of a rejected lover's suicide. No. xxvi is a curious performance. After telling, with no great distinction of language, the story of Pentheus' death (see p. 196), it makes the cryptic remark that the woes of an enemy of Dionysos deserve no pity, though it be a child of nine or ten that suffers. As Pentheus was a grown man, this suggests that a recent incident involving the murder of a child is alluded to, but what and when it was we have no means of telling. No. xxvii, the beginning of which is lost, is a scene of rustic courtship, not without a certain freshness and realism.

Less shadowy figures than these nameless authors are MOSCHOS and BION. The former, according to a notice in Suidas, was a Syracusan and an acquaintance of Aristarchos, presumably the great Homeric critic. If so, he must have flourished about 150 B.C. The poems attributed to him do not rise above prettiness at best. There is an epyllion, *Europa*, the central incident being the carrying off of Europê by Zeus disguised as a bull. Another, but rather poorer performance in the same vein is a dialogue between Megara and Alkmene, the wife and mother of Herakles, on the sorrows they and he have endured and a boding dream which seems to portend evil

---

[65] Athen., 284 a.

[66] The fullest and best discussion of ancient editions is that in Wilam., *Textgesch. Buk.*, summed up briefly in the preface to his ed. of the Bucolici (O.C.T.). One was an edition, without commentary, of all the bucolic poets, by Artemidoros (time of Sulla) ; one, of Theokritos only, with notes, by Artemidoros' son Theon. Suidas, *s.u.* Θεόκριτος, names several other pieces which were ascribed to him, but all trace of these has disappeared.

to him and his brother Iphikles. There are also some short poems, some of them mere fragments preserved to us by Stobaios, on various subjects. Bion seems to have been later, since Suidas says that Moschos was the next after Theokritos to write pastorals. He also is mostly represented by fragments from Stobaios, but we have a complete poem, a pretty lament for Adonis, and a considerable fragment of a pastoral in Doric, in which one shepherd at the other's request sings of the love of Achilles for Deidameia. But nothing of Bion's which has survived (the most part of his work is lost) [67] is nearly so good as the lament for him, after his death by poison, which some unnamed pupil and friend composed ; it is a poem comparable to Milton's *Lycidas*, which imitates it, for sweetness, though by no means for power. A sort of pendant to Bion's work is formed by a kind of free paraphrase of his Adonis-song in Anacreontics, by some unknown hand.

About contemporary with Kallimachos was LYKOPHRON of Chalkis, one of the group of tragic poets known as the Pleias, from their number, seven. The works of the others cannot be criticized, for they are lost ; a few lines from a satyr-play of Lykophron, preserved by Athenaios, suggest that when he chose he could be plain and vigorous in style ; [68] it was called *Ménedemos*, apparently from some good-natured raillery of his old friend, the eccentric Eretrian philosopher of whose sayings and doings (for he wrote nothing) we have an account in Diogenes Laertios. [69] Another fragment, from the *Pelopidai*, one of a score of tragedies whose titles have been preserved by Suidas, [70] sets forth in perfectly clear language a commonplace about men's attitude towards death. But Lykophron's chief title to fame is the extreme and designed obscurity of his one complete work that has come down to us. The Alexandrians one and all liked a style full of learned allusions, and some of them playfully exaggerated this in clever little poems definitely meant to be riddles and no doubt composed largely for circulation among the authors' friends.

[67] The *Lament* ('Επιτάφιος Βίωνος) gives, 80–4, a list of his subjects, all pastoral or amatory.

[68] Athenaios, 55c, says he wrote it to mock Menedemos ; Diog. Laert., ii, 140, not having Ath.'s prejudice against philosophers, gives the more likely account that he praised him.

[69] Diog. Laert., ii, 125 *sqq.*

[70] Suid., *s.u. Λυκόφρων.* Most of the subjects were clearly mythological, but one, the Κασσανδρεῖς or Men of Kassandreia, is generally taken to have dealt with an event in recent history, the treacherous murder by Ptolemy Keraunos of the children of Arsinoe II, afterwards Ptolemy Philadelphos' second wife, at that place in 280, see Justin, xxiv, 3, 1–9.

We have a small number of poetical jokes, some of them riddles and all figure-poems (*i.e.*, with the lengths of their lines so arranged that when written out they form a shape, axe, pair of wings, altar, etc.). One of the best is the *Pan-Pipe* of Theokritos(?). The lines dwindle from 16 to 3 syllables to express the diminishing lengths of the reeds ; they are supposed to be written on the instrument itself, dedicated by Theokritos to Pan. The dedicator is called Paris, by a play on words ; *Theokritos* means ' god-chosen ', but could be taken to signify ' judger of deities ' with a shift of accent. The god himself is said to be the son of ' No-Man's couchmate, the mother of Makroptolemos ', *i.e.*, Penelope (because Odysseus told Polyphemos that his name was Nobody ; Makroptolemos is a paraphrase of Telemachos, *i.e.*, Fighting far away) and ' driver of the nurse of the rock-replaced ' (Pan was the herdsman of the goat Amaltheia, on whose milk Zeus was fed after Kronos had been deceived into swallowing a stone instead of him). Other such trifles are the *Axe* and *Egg* of Simias, the *Altar* of DOSIADAS, and another poem of the same name by an obscure writer, BESANTINOS. They are most conveniently accessible at the end of Wilamowitz-Moellendorff's *Bucolici Graeci*, and are generally called τεχνοπαίγνια.

These riddle-poems were passable enough as academic jokes, but Lykophron in a perverse mood applied his very considerable powers to outdoing them all, and composed a monstrous riddle, the *Alexandra*, 1,474 lines long. In form it is the speech of a messenger, a servant of Priam, obviously gifted with a superhuman memory, coming to tell his master that Kassandra (= Alexandra) has just delivered a mysterious oracle, which he recites verbatim. A tragedy proportionate to such a speech would be about the size of Swinburne's Mary Stuart trilogy. The prophecy concerns the whole history of Troy, the Trojans and their descendants, together with the fates of the Greeks for many generations to come, and from beginning to end it calls nothing and no one by any well-known name, personal or geographical. For instance, Herakles is ' the Lion of the triple evening ' (the night when he was begotten was thrice the normal length), line 33 ; Dardanos, ancestor of the Trojan kings, is ' Atlas' daughter's diving son ', 72–3 (his mother was Elektra the Pleiad, daughter of Atlas, and he swam to the Troad during the Flood) ; Egypt is ' the shore furrowed by the outflow of Triton ' (*i.e.*, the Nile), 118–19 ; Helen is ' the five times wedded madwoman, of Pleuron's line ' (Pleuron was the great-grandfather of her mother Leda, and various stories made her the wife or mistress of Theseus, Menelaos, Paris, Deiphobos and Achilles), 143 ; instead of Phthia, or Thessaly, ' the crag of Tymphrestos ' is mentioned, 420 ; Baiae in Italy is a little more intelligibly named as ' the tomb of Baios the helmsman ', 694 ;

Harpe (762) is Corcyra, because the *harpe* or curved sword with which Zeus mutilated Kronos in one obscure form of the myth was supposed to be buried there ; and so on to the end of the poem. The amount of learning and ingenuity which has gone to this extraordinary composition must have been immense, and every here and there a gleam of real poetical feeling shines through the obscure allusions and the equally obscure phraseology.[71] Where Lykophron got his wide knowledge we may easily guess ; he was one of the officials of the Alexandrian Library, charged especially with the arrangement of the comedians, on whom he wrote a prose work in several books, now lost, but appearing from numerous quotations in later authors (notably Athenaios and the scholiast on Aristophanes) to have had a great deal to say about vocabulary.[72] It is therefore fairly obvious that he was in Alexandria with the resources of the Library at hand when he wrote. An upper limit to the date of the work may also be set. Lykophron shows great interest in the West, including Rome. Timaios the historian (see p. 369) is probably the source of much of his information,[73] but the remarkable fact is that he appreciates something of the growing importance of the Roman power. Kassandra foretells that a kinsman of hers (Aineias) shall leave behind him a pair of lion-whelps (apparently Romulus and Remus), ' a breed excelling in strength ' ($\dot{\varrho}\acute{\omega}\mu\eta$, a favourite pun on the name of the city), and that this race shall have ' the sceptre and sole empery of land and sea '.[74] Later, in a very obscure passage even for Lykophron, she says that a certain ' tawny one ' (lion ? the allusion may be to Alexander the Great) shall put an end to the long strife between Europe and Asia, and that six generations from that event, a ' wrestler ' shall ' battle valiantly by land and sea and make a treaty ' by reason of which he shall be hailed as ' chief among friends ' and take the first-fruits of the spoils. This fits so well with the Macedonian Wars, although the six generations are a difficulty (for Macedonia became a Roman dependency much less than six generations, or 200 years, after Alexander, to say nothing of Pyrrhos, another claimant for

---

[71] Bayle (Dictionary, art. LYCOPHRON) does justice to his talent, which has been unfairly depreciated. For his vocabulary, see Christ-Schmid, ii, p. 177, n. 2 ; some 50 per cent. of his words are rare, over 10 per cent. not found elsewhere.

[72] Post in library, anon. *de comoed.*, p. xix, 16 Dübner, and many other passages. The highest-numbered book of his treatise cited is xi.

[73] For the principal authors upholding this theory, see C. v. Holzinger, *Lykophron's Alexandra*, Leipzig, Teubner, 1895, p. 3 ; the whole introduction contains a detailed study of the poet's life and works.

[74] *Alex.*, 1229.

identification with the ' tawny one '),[75] that it has been repeatedly suggested that the lines must be a prophecy after the event, written by some unknown person in the second century, not by Lykophron in the third. But I think, with Wilamowitz,[76] that all such speculations are on a wrong track. Lykophron we may suppose to have seen and been impressed by the Roman embassy to Ptolemy in reply to his embassy to them in 273, and generally to have remarked that the king was paying no little attention to the new power. The ' empery ' attributed to them need not be taken too literally ; it probably was meant to be over the land and sea of their own part of the world. The six generations are but another literary allusion ; a verse ascribed to Orpheus [77] named the sixth generation as a stopping-point, and probably Lykophron means no more than that, at some distant time, a distinguished Roman will make common cause with a successor of Ptolemy and help him to bring a war to an issue satisfactory to both. It was his good fortune that, long after his death, something did happen which could be twisted into fitting his purposely obscure and ambiguous language.

Of the other six members of the Pleiad we know very little, not even being certain who they were. Besides Lykophron, the scholiast on Hephaistion, *Enchiridion*, p. 53 Gaisford, names ALEXANDROS of Aitolia, HOMEROS (of Byzantion, son of a certain Andromachos and MYRO or MOIRO, a minor poetess), SOSITHEOS (of Alexandria in the Troad ; he seems to have written satyr-plays containing personal attacks on contemporaries),[78] PHILIKOS (of Corcyra ; his name is often written PHILISKOS ; 42 tragedies were attributed to him, and he held the office of priest of Dionysos),[79] DIONYSIADES (of Tarsos, or Mallos in Kilikia ; he is said to have written a work of literary criticism or anecdote called Χαρακτῆρες ἢ φιλοκώμῳδοι, ' in which he

---

[75] See, for Pyrrhos, Holzinger's note on 1439, the line in question. αἴθων might mean, among other things, an eagle, cf. Hyginus, *fab.*, xxxi, 5, and my note there ; but this gets us no nearer determining what man the metaphorical creature represents.

[76] *Hell. Dicht.*, ii, p. 146.

[77] Quoted by Plato, *Phileb.*, 66 C, ἕκτῃ δ' ἐν γενεῇ καταπαύσατε κόσμον (?, οἶμον Kroll, θυμὸν Plutarch, *de E ap. Delph.*, 391 d) ἀοιδῆς. It is a curious fact that Perseus, the last king of Macedon, was actually the sixth in descent from a contemporary of Philip II and Alexander, but it is probably a mere accidental coincidence.

[78] Suid., *s.u.* Σωσίθεος (here and elsewhere he gives Olymp. 124 (284–1) as the *floruit* of these poets) ; Dioskorides in *Anth. Palat.*, vii, 707 ; Diog. Laert., vii, 173.

[79] Suid., *s.u.* Φίλισκος Κερκυραῖος. Presumably he was employed in connexion with Ptolemy II's great Dionysiac festival, for which see Athen., 196 a *sqq*.

describes the characteristics of the poets ') [80] and the obscure
AIANTIADES. Another scholiast on the same passage (p. 185 Gaisf.)
omits Dionysiades and substitutes SOSIPHANES (of Syracuse, born
306/5) ; and there are one or two more candidates for the seventh
place, adduced by late and obscure authors. The fact is that the
whole group was part of a well-meant endeavour of Ptolemy II to
transfer to his own city the glory of the Athenian Dionysiac festivals ;
he was able to give the god plenty of outward splendour, but for some
reason Tragedy would not flourish outside of its native country.
Their works were soon forgotten, and we can but conjecture that
some of the late and romantic forms of myths may owe something
to them.[81] See p. 424.

Alexandria, however, did produce one poet who wrote semi-
dramatic works of a remarkable kind, the mime-writer HERODAS
(less correctly HERONDAS).[82] Till recently we knew next to nothing
about him, but in 1891 a papyrus came to light in Egypt, was published by Kenyon and promptly became the object of a great deal of
critical interest and sagacity. It contained the text of seven mimes
fairly complete, large portions of an eighth, battered remnants
of a ninth and a scrap of a prologue in which the author proclaims
that his model is Hipponax. This is true so far as metre and
language go ; the poems are written in Ionic, or a learned attempt
to reconstruct that dialect, and in scazons (see p. 92) ; but the
spirit is rather that of Sophron, and Herodas may claim originality
at all events for uniting the style of one with the matter of the
other. His date is not far removed from that of the other poets
we have discussed ; such allusions as are found in him (we have
no ancient life and can go only by his own works) suggest the
reign of Ptolemy II or at latest that of his successor Ptolemy III,
Euergetes.[83] His subjects are of much the same kind as those of
Theokritos' No. xv, but, in keeping with his Ionian and probably
also his Sicilian model, he has a coarseness of tone which the
Syracusan avoids. The contents are as follows. In No. i, the
Match-Maker (Προκυκλὶς ἢ μάστροπος), a young wife, Metriche,

---

[80] Suid., *s.u. Διονυσιάδης*.　　[81] So for example Rohde, *Gr. Rom.*, p. 37 *sqq*.

[82] The great store-house of information about Herodas is the edition
of Headlam-Knox, Cambridge, 1922. The few ancient mentions of him
vary between Herodas and Herondas ; the difference is merely the
presence or absence, in both Greek and Latin writing, of a stroke over
the o, and the objection to the latter form is simply that it is typically
Boiotian, and he seems to have been a Koan.

[83] He alludes to the cult of Ptolemy II and Arsinoe II, i, 30 ; this was
established after her death in 370 ; iv, 72 *sqq*. speaks of Apelles the painter
as if he were dead (he died in the seventies of the century) ; No. vi
imitates Theokritos xv, and so may be of any date from Ptolemy II on.
Nothing seems to point to a time much later than Ptolemy II.

is visited by an old acquaintance, Gyllis, who tries in vain to persuade her that her husband, now in Egypt (the scene of the mime is probably Kos, which is also that of the others, so far as it is definable at all ; it was most likely the poet's native place), has quite forgotten her and she cannot do better than oblige a promising young athlete who is wildly in love with her. No. ii, the *Brothel-Keeper* (*Πορνοβοσκός*), is a sort of parody of Attic forensic eloquence ; an old rascal, Battaros, appears in court to claim, with all the tricks of rhetoric, damages against a young man who has carried off an inmate of his disreputable establishment. No. iii, the *Schoolmaster* (*Διδάσκαλος*), introduces a very worthy pedagogue who obliges the mother of one of his pupils by giving her son the thrashing which she has not the muscle to inflict and the boy, by her account, most thoroughly deserves. No. iv, *The Women visit Asklepios* (*Ἀσκληπίῳ ἀνατιθεῖσαι καὶ θυσιάζουσαι*), is sufficiently explained by its title, but it is little more than an excuse for a discussion, put into the mouths of the visitors, of certain works of art contained in the temple. No. v, *A Jealous Woman* (*Ζηλότυπος*), is an unpleasant scene with a slave-gigolo. No. vi, *A Private Conversation* (*Φιλιάζουσαι ἢ ἰδιάζουσαι*), is the chat of two women, one of whom has come to visit the other ; they are as lively as Gorgo and Praxinoa, but less clean-mouthed. After a while one of them strongly recommends a shoemaker and leather-worker (*σκυτεύς*) to the other, thus leading up to the next mime, *The Shoemaker*, in which the same pair visit the shop of a certain Kerdon, obviously a very fashionable artist in his own line, to judge by the enormous prices he asks for his wares, and enterprising, since he promises one of them a pair of slippers as commission for introducing the new customer. The eighth mime, *The Dream* (*Ἐνύπνιον*), is too battered for certain restoration ; a woman rouses her slave-girls to tell them what she has dreamt, but her story is mostly lost beyond recovery. Of No. ix, *The Breakfast Party* (*Ἀπονηστιζόμεναι*), only the opening lines, in which a woman welcomes her guests, are left to us. It is not improbable that Herodas, like Sophron, had divided his mimes into ' female ' and ' male ', and that if we had all his works we should find other pieces in which men were the principal or only characters.

Hitherto we have been dealing with writers of whom some works at least survive complete. It is a symptom of the general neglect into which Alexandrian literature fell as a result of the classicizing movement (see p. 396) that several important authors are represented only by scanty fragments. The principal ones are as follows.

ERINNA, of the little island of Telos, near Knidos, lived probably in the fourth century, about the middle of it, and so is pre-Alexandrian in date. In spirit, however, she has one characteristic of their best poets, the expression, by other media than lyric, of intimate personal feeling.[84] She seems to have been the daughter of cultured people, and it is a likely conjecture that she got hold of a copy of Sappho's poems, or of some of them, and was thereby led to compose on her own account. This at all events would explain why she mixes her native Doric with Aiolic. Her short life—she died, unmarried, at nineteen—had one great interest, her affection for a certain Baukis, her friend from early childhood, and her consequent grief at the separation caused by Baukis' marriage and, shortly afterwards, her death. This Erinna recorded in a poem of 300 lines, the *Distaff* ('Αλακάτα ; the title alludes to the two girls working together), her one considerable work. She also wrote the epitaphs for her friend's tomb. How her poem came to be published is not known, but it would appear that Asklepiades (see p. 349) got to know of it and wrote a graceful epigram, still surviving, as a preface to it, likely enough on the occasion of it being given to the public.[85] We have a sadly damaged, but early copy of about one-fifth of it, and a few stray quotations ; even these remnants are enough to show that it was exquisite, perfectly simple and yet artistic, despite its mongrel dialect, and its authoress a poet of high promise.

In PHILITAS (less correctly PHILETAS) [86] of Kos we have lost a poet of reputation second only to Kallimachos ; [87] there remain of him some fifty lines, cited by various authors from his different works. He was born in the reign of Philip II of Macedon (killed 336) and lived long enough to be tutor to Ptolemy II in the

---

[84] Suid., *s.u.* "Ηριννα, who also gives Teos, Lesbos (absurd ; arises from an idea, which he also mentions, that she was Sappho's contemporary) and Rhodes as her native country, on what authority we do not know. Handiest account of her in English, Bowra in Powell 3, pp. 180–5. Older frags. and epigrams in Diehl, i, pp. 486–8 ; for the important new discoveries, see Bowra. Date, Olymp. 106–7 according to Eusebios ; I follow this as the only reasonable one in any ancient.

[85] See *Anth. Pal.*, vii, 11, absurdly included among epitaphs because it mentions her death. If Erinna really lived, as Sir C. M. Bowra thinks, in the third century, Asklepiades may have known her, or her family, and perhaps have been, to use modern terminology, her literary executor ; but all this is pure conjecture.

[86] Φιλήτας, Φιλητᾶς, Φιλτᾶς, *Philetas* in various authorities ; the occurrence of the form Φιλτᾶς on Koan inscriptions seems to settle the point, see Powell, *C. A.*, p. 90, where the fragments are gathered and annotated.

[87] See Propertius, iii (iv), 1, 1 ; Quintilian, x, 1, 58.

latter's youth, and to know Theokritos.[88] He, like Kallimachos, was a writer of amatory poems, including elegies ; a branch of Alexandrian literature of which so little is now known that it cannot even be determined with certainty [89] whether the Latin elegiac poets are imitating or originating. Philitas addressed Bitis, who perhaps was his wife.[90] We have left none of these poems, and but little of the others ; besides some prose works on philological subjects, he wrote an epyllion, *Hermes*, dealing with the love of Odysseus for a daughter of Aiolos ; an elegiac poem concerning Demeter ; another, of unknown content, called *Telephos* (whether the legendary king of Mysia or the poet's own father, who bore that name, is disputed, and in any case nothing survives of the work), and some shorter pieces.

HERMESIANAX of Kolophon was, we are informed, Philitas' friend, and wrote a work called *Persika*, presumably an epic, if the information is correct, and a poem to Leontion his mistress.[91] Of this we have a long fragment in Athenaios, besides numerous references to it as an authority on mythology. It gave a long list of the loves of famous writers from Orpheus down, and included some quaint literary history, as that Hesiod was enamoured of some one called Ehoie and commemorated her in the title of the Ehoiai (see p. 64), and that Homer knew and loved Penelope.[92] It was composed in very respectable elegiacs.

Perhaps later was PHANOKLES, who may have got from Hermesianax the idea for his own poem *Loves, or Fair Lads* (Ἔρωτες ἢ Καλοί), which, to judge from a long fragment, dealt with the affection of Orpheus, Dionysos, Tantalos and others for beautiful boys. We know little or nothing about him.[93]

SIMIAS [94] of Rhodes was the author of other poems than his ' egg ' and ' wings ' (see p. 336). He too was a scholar,[95] but also a skilful metrician and composer of two pieces of epic, or epyllia, the *Apollo*, which among other things dealt with the Hyperboreans,

[88] Theokr., vii, 40 ; Suid., *s.u. Φιλητᾶς*. That Theokritos was his pupil, as one or two very late authors (the *Life of Theokritos* prefixed to the scholia, and Choiroboskos the grammarian) tell us, need mean no more than that Philitas was the elder.

[89] See Christ-Schmid, ii, p. 118.

[90] If she was, it gives more point to Ovid, *Tristia*, i, 6, 2, who couples her with Lyde (see p. 315) and with his own wife.

[91] Scholiast on Nikandros, *Ther.*, 3.

[92] The fragment is in Athen., 597 b *sqq.* ; Powell, *op. cit.*, p. 98 *sqq.*

[93] Powell, p. 106 ; the source is Stobaios, lxiv, 14.

[94] Not Simmias ; the name means Snub-nose (σιμός).

[95] Suid., *s.u. Σιμίας*, who says that he wrote a work on γλῶσσαι (rare words) ; cf. Strabo, xiv, 2, 13.

and the *Gorgo*, with a plot taken from the saga of Troy, apparently.[96] There are, moreover, a few epigrams, not among the
best that we have.

ALEXANDROS of Pleuron in Aitolia, already mentioned (p. 338)
as one of the Pleiad, wrote poems of various kinds. We have surviving a few scraps of epic poems, probably short ; an episode from
a work called *Apollo*, in which the god seems to have foretold a
series of amatory adventures, set forth in elegiacs ; one or two
fragments from another elegiac poem, *The Muses* ; and a few
stray lines from other works. He seems to have had the careful
elegance one would expect from a contemporary, and probably
an imitator, of Kallimachos ; more we cannot say.[97]

A little later than these men, imitators of Kallimachos'
manner were still fairly common. ERATOSTHENES, the great
scholar and scientist (see pp. 382, 392) who was born about 275,
was blessed with a number of nicknames, all indicating that he
was second-best at everything.[98] One of these things was poetry,
and we have evidence that he was fairly active in verse-making.
One work of his, the *Erigone*, is usually considered the chief
source of the pretty legend of Erigone and Ikarios as we have it
from later writers ; [99] another, the *Hermes*, seems to have combined the mythology of that god with an episode in which the
heavens were described somewhat after the manner of Aratos ;
this was in hexameters. A few more fragments belong to poems
on various themes.

EUPHORION of Chalkis was not without reputation, and
imitators of him in later times included Gallus, the oldest of the
great Latin elegiac poets.[100] He was born about the same time
as Eratosthenes, found favour, presumably on account of his
learning, with Antiochos the Great of Syria (224–187) and ended
his days as his librarian. What is left of his work suggests that
he wrote poems obscurely learned, on various mythological
themes, in good hexameters and a style which did not add to

[96] See Powell, *op. cit.*, p. 109 *sqq.*
[97] Short notice of him in Suidas *s.u.* ’Aλέξανδρος (b) ; frags. in Powell,
op. cit., p. 121 *sqq.* ; see Christ-Schmid, ii, p. 173 *sq.*
[98] Suid., *s.u.* ’Ερατοσθένης, gives among other names Beta (*i.e.*, No. 2)
and Pentathlete (pentathletes were from the nature of the event fairly
good all round men). Frags. in Powell, pp. 58–68.
[99] See for example M. P. Nilsson in *Eranos*, xv, p. 187 *sqq.* ; Rose,
Myth., p. 154. That Eratosthenes is the only source of the later writers
is anything but certain.
[100] See for instance Vergil, Ecl. x, 50, with the note of Servius ; vi,
64 *sqq.*, with the note of Servius on 72, which proves that Gallus translated
or imitated in Latin an epyllion of Euphorion on the foundation of the
cult of Apollo at Grynion in Mysia, cf. frag. 78 Powell.

the obscurity by any great peculiarities of vocabulary or structure. The titles and number of these works are doubtful,[101]
owing to the frequency with which a section of a poem is cited
by our authorities under a title of its own (as if we were to
call the third book of Paradise Lost, *Satan in Eden*, or the
like).

All these we may roughly call Kallimacheians ; Apollonios
of Rhodes was apparently not without a following. RHIANOS of
Crete (contemporary with Eratosthenes) was the author of
several epic poems of considerable length. We hear of his
Herakleia, apparently four books long, *Achaïka, Eliaka, Thessalika*
(at least sixteen books) and *Messeniaka*, of not less than six books.
Some of these may have been versified collections of local legends,
but the last named was certainly a historical epic, for Pausanias [102]
preserves the plot of at least part of it, a highly coloured account
of the Second Messenian War. Aristomenes, the half-legendary
leader of the Messenians in their struggle with Sparta, was the
hero, and the fighting was diversified with some romantic
incidents. What Rhianos' merits as a poet may have been
is hard to say, for very little of his verse is left to us ; he
seems at least to have been able to put an interesting story
together.

So far we have dealt with learned poetry ; there was also a
considerable amount of verse which had something of a popular
appeal, since it dealt in satire, moralizing of a not too profound
sort, and other themes which do not need a learned reader. At
that time philosophy, represented by no first-rate intellect
after the death of Aristotle and, outside the Stoic school, not
attempting much original work, was passing into mere ethics,
often of a dogmatic kind, and produced a goodly number of
popular preachers, or lecturers, among whom the Cynics were
prominent. Corresponding to the harangues of these men, in
lecture-rooms or in the public streets, were poems such as those
produced by the obscure KERKIDAS. His date is anything but
certain ; it seems likely, however, that he flourished about

---

[101] We may be sure of two or three separate poems, as that on Apollo
Gryneios, mentioned in the last note ; a humorous piece called *The
Curses, or the Cupstealer* ('Aραὶ ἢ ποτηριοκλέπτης), somewhat after the
manner of Kallimachos' *Ibis*, so far as we can judge (frag. 9, Powell ;
the fragments of Euphorion are on pp. 28–58 of his collection) ; and
(unless this is the whole of which the *Curses* are a part) a poem in five
books, the *Chiliades* or thousands (perhaps so named from the number
of verses in each book) setting forth the punishment awaiting some persons
who had cheated him.

[102] iv, 1, 6 *sqq.* ; Suidas, *s.u.* ʿΡιανός ; Powell, pp. 9–21.

250.[103] A good deal of what he wrote has come to light recently, though in a damaged form, as is usually the case with papyri. He wrote in lyric metres of a simple kind, and so apparently meant his works to be sung. The dialect is Doric ; there are also, however, some fragments plausibly attributed to him which are in Ionic and whose metre is the scazon. The subject is regularly ethics of a popular and even chatty kind, with emphasis on the folly of high-flown speculations and elaborate ways of satisfying natural desire. Several parallels from Horace can be found, and the tone is at times Horatian, though less urbane, as becomes a professed Cynic.[104] There is no doubt that we have here a fragment of the literature out of which Roman satire grew.[105]

PHOINIX of Kolophon, of whom we have not much left, included similar subjects in his *Iamboi* ; our chief remains of him are a passage (frag. 1 Powell) on Ninos,[106] the mythical founder of Nineveh, concerning the vanity of all mortal glory and the need to make the most of one's brief life, and another (frag. 2) paraphrasing a traditional song sung by what would in England be called guisers, *koronistai*, who went about at certain seasons carrying a crow (κορώνη) or a figure of one, collecting contributions of food and the like ; a custom not uncommon in either ancient or modern Europe.[107] One is again reminded of the miscellaneous contents which gave Roman satire its name.

We have likewise, from about this age, some moral verses falsely attributed to Epicharmos, recognized in antiquity to be

[103] He mentions, as of a former generation, Diogenes the Cynic (fr. 1, Powell, *q.u.*, p. 201 *sqq.*) ; Zeno (died about 260) is apparently his contemporary, fr. 4, 5. He can hardly therefore be that Kerkidas who was Demosthenes' contemporary, Dem. xviii, 295.

[104] He is described as ' Kerkidas the Cynic ' at the end of the papyrus (Ox. Pap., 1082) containing the principal surviving fragments.

[105] When Quintilian (x, 1, 93) says *satura quidem tota nostra est*, he either shows strange ignorance of literary history, if he means that none but Romans had written it, or, more likely, he means that in that field the Romans had so outdistanced the Greeks as to have the subject practically to themselves (see Rennie in *Class. Rev.*, xxvi, 1922, p. 21).

[106] The sentiment ascribed to Ninos, that in death he has only what he enjoyed, is usually attributed to Sardanapallos (Ashur-bani-pal) and said to have been expressed on his epitaph, see for instance Athen., 336 a ; Cicero, *Tusc.*, v, 101 and *de fin.*, ii, 106, which prove that the story was in some lost work of Aristotle. The form ' what I spent, I had ; what I gave, I have ; what I saved, I lost ' is a Christian modification.

[107] The frag. is from Athen., 359 e *sqq.*, who goes on to cite a similar song, this time genuinely popular, with a swallow instead of a crow, 360 c *sqq.* ; cf. the ' Homeric ' Eiresione, *supra*, p. 56.

the work of a certain AXIOPISTOS (about 300 B.C.) and of one CHRYSOGONOS.[108] There are also some edifying precepts attributed, of all unlikely authors, to Sotades (see below).

A less pleasing class of writers is the so-called *kinaidologoi*, or specialists in indecency. One of these only need be mentioned, SOTADES of Maroneia in Crete. His date is fixed approximately by the fact that he wrote a lampoon on Ptolemy II, for which he is said to have been put to death by one of the king's subordinates. He was remembered chiefly for a peculiar metre, called after him Sotadean, and for his extreme foulness of language.[109] His writings included *The Descent into Hades*, *The Amazon*, and some other pieces, of which little is known, for very few of his verses survive, also a kind of travesty of the Iliad in Sotadeans and a poem called *Priapos*.

This would seem to be connected with a class of light verse which begins about this epoch but is known to us mostly by Latin specimens. Priapos, a god of fertility, represented by a grotesque and not over-decent human figure, was originally worshipped at Lampsakos on the Hellespont, but became widely popular all over the ancient world in the Hellenistic age. It was apparently a common custom to inscribe jocular little poems alluding to his functions, especially in the gardens where his statue stood as patron deity and scarecrow combined. Of these a fairly large number survive, though we have no Greek collection of them, as we have for Latin. Their character naturally varies widely, from delicately witty to merely obscene.[110]

Alongside this semi-popular poetry, we have evidence that the people, at least of Alexandria itself, were not voiceless, for a few fragments have come down to us which appear to be from what we may not too inaccurately name the music-halls of that city. The most celebrated is the so-called *Alexandrian erotic fragment*, a kind of ballad, in which a girl laments the faithlessness of her lover.[111] It is not learned, in style or contents ; the language has but a few forms alien to the ordinary use of about the second century B.C., or perhaps a little earlier ; it probably could be readily followed, when sung, by any Greek-speaking member of the audience. There remain also a few similar scraps of verse, and, what is distinctly interesting, part of a little farce

---

[108] The remains are in Powell, p. 219 *sqq*.

[109] For the facts concerning him, our principal sources are Athen., 620f *sqq*., and Suidas *s.u.* The frags. are in Powell, p. 238 *sqq*.

[110] The best work on Priapos is H. Herter, *De Priapo*, Giessen, Töpelmann, 1932. He gives an account of the poems, p. 15 *sqq*.

[111] See, for this work and the literature on it, Powell, p. 177 *sqq*.

in prose.[112]   The situation is a kind of parody on the *Iphigenia in Tauris* ; a Greek girl is living among Indians, and her friends manage to carry her off, after complications in which the Indian king and his retinue take a prominent part, while a clown continually breaks into the action with remarks and inarticulate sounds, not always of the most refined.

The great defect of the age was that the scholarly poetry remained scholarly only, and lost contact with popular speech and thought alike, while the popular performances were thus deprived of the very influence which might have raised them into real literature of a new kind.   As it was, the only good literature which seems to owe anything to these not unpromising beginnings is not Greek at all ; Plautus may have got the idea for the many lyrics in his plays from popular Alexandrian models, whether produced in Alexandria itself or not.[113]

So far as we are concerned, one of the principal features of Alexandrian poetical activity is its large contribution to the collection of epigrams which we know as the *Palatine Anthology*. Collections of epigrams were made as early as the fourth century,[114] to say nothing of individual poems which had been copied from monuments by earlier writers, such as Herodotos. What we have is a MS. once belonging to the library of the Elector Palatine, at Heidelberg (hence the name), and containing fifteen books of epigrams collected by Konstantinos Kephalas, a Byzantine official, about A.D. 900.   Books iv–vii and ix–xi are taken over from three older collections, of which the later supplemented the earlier ; one, made about 100 B.C. by MELEAGROS of Gadara, himself a very tolerable poet, who included a good deal of his own work and furnished his collection, entitled by him the *Garland* (στέφανος), with a preface in verse, full of pretty conceits, in which each of the forty-one poets he names is compared to a flower or plant ; a second, by a certain PHILIPPOS, who lived and made his *Garland* (for he copied Meleagros' title and feebly imitated his proem) under Caligula ; and the third by Agathias, a Byzantine of the sixth century A.D.[115]   Kephalas added three books of epigrams by Christian authors, the first, second and eighth ; a group of nineteen inscriptions which had stood under

[112] Oxyrh. Pap., 413 ; Powell-Barber 1, p. 121, Powell 3, p. 215 *sqq*. The Indians speak something which is at least intended for an Indian language ; Kanarese has been suggested, but apparently on insufficient grounds.

[113] See for example W. M. Lindsay, *The Captiui of Plautus* (London, Methuen, 1900), p. 56 *sqq*.

[114] Theognis as we have him may represent a collection earlier still.

[115] The proems of the three editors form Book iv of the *Anthology*.

works of art in a temple at Kyzikos (Book iii) ; a collection of verses addressed to real or imaginary boys, which forms the twelfth book, and was originally compiled by a certain STRATON of Sardis ; another, of epigrams in a variety of metres, which fills the thirteenth book; both these collections date from the third century B.C. ; and two more books, the fourteenth and fifteenth, whereof the former is a collection of puzzles (arithmetical problems in verse) and riddles, the latter of miscellaneous contents. In addition to this, a collection was made in the year 1301 by Maximos Planudes, whose autograph copy survives. He was a learned man after the uncritical fashion of his day, and although Kephalas was his chief source, he included some epigrams which are not in the latter's Anthology, besides copying others from a better MS. than that which we have. These additional pieces it is now usual to print as a kind of sixteenth book of the *Palatine Anthology*, and they are generally known as the *Appendix Planudea*. Further, we have a certain quantity of epigrams preserved in surviving Greek authors, but not included in the Palatine and Planudean collections, and a growing number found inscribed on stone and other permanent records, epigrams in the true etymological sense.[116]

Many of the poets included in the *Anthology* lie outside the scope of this book altogether, being Byzantines and not always writing in classical metres. Those who fall within its limits are so numerous, and often so little known,[117] that it is impossible to do more than mention a few of the most prominent. Besides the greater authors already spoken of as having written epigrams, there are poems by PHALAIKOS, of unknown but apparently

---

[116] See Christ-Schmid, ii, p. 158 *sqq*. Besides older editions, the *Anthology* has been edited by Jacobs, Leipzig, 1794–1814, with Latin notes, a smaller edition appearing, also at Leipzig, in 1813–17 ; by Dübner, in the Didot series, Paris, 1864 and 1872 ; by Städtmüller, in the Teubner series, 1894–1906, still incomplete, the editor having died ; by Paton, in the Loeb series ; while publications of selected epigrams, often with translations in various modern languages, are too numerous to be given here. The epigrams not in the *Anthology* have been collected by several editors, the best known being Kaibel (*Epigrammata Graeca ex lapidibus collecta*, Berlin, 1878) and Cougny (the third vol. of the Didot ed., Paris, 1890). There is an edition of the *Anthology* partly completed in the Budé series.

[117] Articles on those of whom anything definite can be said will be found in Pauly-Wissowa ; the indices of the Loeb edition and the list of authors prefixed to Liddell and Scott, ninth ed., give the dates, when known, of a number. There is room for a new commentary on the whole *Anthology* with a copious index, or introduction, giving an account of all the authors.

early date (fourth century ?),[118] after whom the Phalaecian verse
is named ; ANYTE of Tegea, about 300 B.C. ; [119] another poetess,
NOSSIS of Lokris in Italy, probably of the third century, who,
like Erinna, seems to have found inspiration in a study of
Sappho ; [120] Theokritos' friend ASKLEPIADES (see p. 332), chief,
it would appear, of a whole school of writers of light verse whose
headquarters were in Samos ; [121] he also has a metre named after
him, the Asclepiadic, familiar to readers of Horace's *Odes*. An
influential poet in his way, well-known to later writers, was
LEONIDAS of Taras (Tarentum), a poor man whose search for a
living took him afield ; [122] since one of his temporary patrons
seems to have been Pyrrhos of Epeiros, he wrote fairly early in
the third century. A not unpleasing characteristic of him is
that he sympathized with other poor men, and some of his
prettiest epigrams profess to be their dedications. These and
several others for the most part have that clear simplicity of style
which marks not only the early epigrammatists but also the best
Alexandrians ; Leonidas now and then is somewhat florid.
The later writers are by no means all Greeks by birth ; Meleagros, despite his name, would appear to have been a Syrian,
ANTIPATROS of Sidon also ; both have a certain tendency to
pile up clever phrases more elaborately and ostentatiously than
a true Greek of a good period would do. Among them are several
Romans, including no less a person than GERMANICUS CAESAR, the
translator of Aratos (see p. 327), from whom we have two or three

[118] See Wilam., *Hell. Dicht.*, i, p. 134.
[119] She had her statue carved by Euthykrates and Kephisodotos,
Tatian *adu. Graec.*, 33 ; both these sculptors flourished Olymp. 121, *i.e.*,
about 296, Pliny, *N.H.*, xxxiv, 51.
[120] *Anth. Pal.*, vii, 718, sometimes misinterpreted, by a false reading,
as a claim to be equal to Sappho. Nossis, perhaps in a preface to a book
of poems, rather shyly asks the reader, if he should go to Lesbos, to say
that there was a poetess in Lokris, and her name was Nossis. The ghost
of Sappho, she implies, perhaps would like to know that another woman
appreciates and tries to imitate her. The poem is formally an epitaph,
a literary device common in the *Anthology* and not to be taken too
seriously.
[121] So we may gather from an epigram of HEDYLOS, another of this
school, preserved in Ath., 473 a, which speaks of him, by his Theokritean
name of Sikelidas, as the standard of good poetry of this kind.
[122] The evidence is gathered from his own works, notably vii, 715.
There is a collected edition of his poems by E. Bevan, Oxford, Univ.
Press, 1931. He must not be confused with LEONIDAS OF ALEXANDRIA,
a mathematician and astrologer of Nero's time, who has left us some
trifles, including ἰσόψηφα, *i.e.*, epigrams so arranged that the numerical
value of the letters in one line or couplet equals that of those in the next
(all Greek letters being used as numerals also).

trifles, while later still the emperor HADRIAN makes his appearance as a minor poet. There are in addition a good many Roman names of Greeks or other easterners who had been granted citizenship.

All these writers use elegiacs for the most part, occasionally writing in other metres. A general tendency is to write little descriptive pieces, generally rustic, which make a faint pretence of being dedicatory or funereal inscriptions ; a good example is one of the best compositions of Leonidas (vii, 657), in which a dead shepherd begs the survivors to do their work near his tomb, that he may listen to the familiar country sounds. There are numerous epigrams which drop all pretence and are frankly occasional pieces, often comic or satirical descriptions of the ways of sundry people, mostly imaginary. Another noteworthy thing is the frequency with which the epigrammatists echo and imitate, not only the greater poets, but each other. This the ancient editors recognized, and it is common to find little groups of epigrams, arranged more or less in chronological order, each imitating a predecessor. Thus, vi, 302, by Leonidas, is followed immediately by an imitation, the work of an obscure versifier called ARISTON.[123] In vi, 131, Leonidas says of certain spoils taken from the enemy that they wistfully desire the men and horses of the army to which they once belonged. The next epigram is by Nossis. Her countrymen had dedicated shields dropped by a routed enemy ; in patent allusion to Leonidas she says, in her inscription upon them, that they have no desire for the arms of the cowards who let them fall. So in vii, 163 and 164, the first is again by Leonidas, the second a very close imitation by Antipatros of Sidon ; sometimes the editors, or the copyists, have mistaken the imitation for a second poem by the original author, as vi, 262 and 263 ; vii, 448 and 449—one of the many causes for examining carefully the claims of each epigram to be really by the poet whose name stands at its head in our texts. Sometimes a whole fashion can be followed through the *Anthology* ; for instance, epitaphs on pets, which were not rare in the Hellenistic age. One variety, epitaphs on cicalas (kept in little cages because their chirping was liked), was set going by Anyte and followed by several others.[124]

[123] There were several writers called Ariston, though none of great importance ; none of them can be clearly identified with the Ariston of the *Anthology*, whose epigrams number but two or three in all.

[124] On this subject, see G. Herrlinger, *Totenklage um Tiere in der antiken Dichtung*, Stuttgart, Kohlhammer, 1930.

CHAPTER XI

PHILOSOPHY, RHETORIC AND HISTORY

WHILE Alexandria was hopefully experimenting with new poetical fashions, Athens was still an important centre of the higher learning. Her schools of philosophy remained the principal centres of that subject, in all its branches,[1] and the activity of their members, mostly by this time non-Athenians, was great. It is unfortunate that we have very little left ; for although no works comparable to the masterpieces of Plato or the gigantic researches of Aristotle were produced, the loss of what the philosophers wrote during the next century or two after Aristotle's death has deprived us of much that was worth reading.

The first name chronologically, and perhaps the greatest also, is that of THEOPHRASTOS of Eresos, the successor of Aristotle.[2] He lived about 372–287, was head of the Peripatetic school from 322 to his death and the founder of the buildings in which the lectures were given thenceforth, and showed himself, in what he taught and in his methods of work, a true follower of his great master. It is perhaps not unfair to say that he was rather a teacher of philosophy than an original philosopher ; his chief interest would appear to have been scientific, and this is characteristic of his age. For philosophy tended to become more and more a practical guide to life, not a form of original speculation having a practical side,[3] and therefore to degenerate into sermons, satire or mere rhetoric ;[4] but this was the great age of Greek

---

[1] It is to be remembered that philosophy to begin with included the sciences.

[2] Life, in Diogenes Laertios, v, 36 *sqq*. The dates there given are by olympiads only, not years ; Theophrastos died Olymp. 123 (288–5), v, 58, being then 85 years old, v, 40.

[3] See for one example out of many of the Hellenistic (and Roman) conception of philosophy, Cicero, *Tusc.*, ii, 11.

[4] Cicero, who cannot be accused of undervaluing rhetoric, complains that two of Theophrastos' successors, Lykon and Ariston, have an excellent style but lack matter and weight ; *de finib.*, v, 13.

science in all branches, until the deadening influence of the Romans, of all great peoples the most completely lacking in intellectual curiosity, began to make itself felt here as elsewhere. We have the titles and some few fragments of an immense number of Theophrastos' works, mostly covering much the same ground as Aristotle's, so far as can be judged, and very likely amounting, in many cases, to no more than his lecture notes, for he was a most successful teacher and is said to have had 2,000 pupils.[5] But there survive only two works which we can be sure are complete, and both deal with botany. The *Enquiry into Plants* (*Historia Plantarum*, περὶ φυτῶν ἱστορία) is divided into nine books ; the first eight deal with (i) classification—the first attempt which survives at solving this fundamental problem of botany and all other descriptive sciences, (ii) propagation (it need hardly be said that such things as the sexual anatomy of plants were still undiscovered), (iii) wild trees, (iv) botanical geography (here it is obvious that Theophrastos made good use of the abundant sources of information available by reason of Alexander's campaigns, and probable that he employed his pupils to make inquiries in various regions), (v) timber and its uses, (vi–viii) plants smaller than trees, both wild and cultivated, with some remarks on methods of cultivation, relations between wild and cultivated species and so forth. Book ix treats of the products, other than timber, of plants of all sorts, with their medical uses and some notes on the popular beliefs concerning the right way to gather them, alleged magical properties, and other matters not strictly scientific.[6] The other work is concerned with physiology and bears the title αἰτίαι φυτικαί, which may be freely rendered *How Plants Grow* ; it is usually cited as *de causis plantarum*.   It falls into six books ; the first five treat of the manner of propagation of various plants, great attention being devoted to vines ; the sixth deals with their various juices and saps.   To some extent, therefore, the two works cover the same ground.   The style is clear, plain and rather pleasant to read, the language different a little, but not conspicuously, from classical Attic, *i.e.*, from the speech of a generation earlier ; in short, it is what the style of a scientific work should be.

There also survives a little essay known as the *Metaphysics*, a discussion of the first cause of the universe and its relation to

---

[5] Not incredible ; he was head of the Lyceum some thirty-five years, and this means an annual entry of between fifty and sixty new students.

[6] The handiest edition for English readers is that of Sir Arthur Hort in the Loeb series.

the particulars, written in almost as crabbed and technical a style as Aristotle's.[7]

But for most moderns, the fame of Theophrastos rests upon the *Characters* (Χαρακτῆρες, properly ' distinguishing marks '), the ancestor of a long line of similar works, whereof La Bruyère's *Caractères* is the most famous. How he came to write it, and whether it is an independent work or not are disputed points : it is mentioned by Diogenes Laertios, who draws his information probably from Andronikos (see p. 270), under its own title, but that it consists of extracts from some longer work, for instance the treatise *On Ethics* which Theophrastos is known to have written, or possibly those *On the Laughable* and *On Comedy* (περὶ γελοίων, περὶ κωμῳδίας) has been often suggested [8] and has nothing impossible in it. At all events, omitting the prologue, which is from some writer considerably later, the book contains thirty little sketches of persons distinguished by some ridiculous failing, such as officiousness or garrulity, or one of the lesser vices, as timidity or mean avarice. In a somewhat dry and donnish manner which masks quick observation and keen, satirical wit, each of these failings is defined and illustrated ; it has been remarked a hundred times that the persons described are very like characters in Comedy of Manners, and it must not be forgotten that Menander is said to have been one of Theophrastos' pupils.[9] But the characters were not drawn from Menander's or any one else's plays, but from Athenian streets and houses. They are generalized and simplified, but never unreal.

The rest of Theophrastos is, for us, a mass of fragments great and small. There survive extracts dealing with weather-signs, which Aratos used for the last part of his poem, with odours, the winds, water, fatigue, dizziness and sweating, clearly taken from larger works. A considerable part of a treatise *On Piety* has been reconstructed by Bernays from Porphyry's curious essay *On abstinence from flesh food* (*De esu carnium*).[10] That his many works on literary subjects were drawn upon by later critics who survive to us, such as the so-called Demetrios (p. 399) and Latin writers is reasonably certain. A long list of his titles in Diogenes Laertios testifies to his immense industry.

That his real name was Tyrtamos and Theophrastos an honorific nickname given him by Aristotle because of his excellent style is

---

[7] This work has recently been edited, with good text, translation and commentary, by Ross and Fobes, Oxford, Clar. Press, 1929.

[8] Some of the theories are discussed in the preface to Jebb-Sandys' edition, Macmillan, 1909 ; see also Christ-Schmid, ii, p. 65.

[9] Diog. Laert., v, 36.

[10] J. Bernays, *Theophrastos' Schrift über Frommigkeit*, Berlin, 1866.

asserted by several ancients.[11] The facts may be right ; the reason suggested is wrong, for Theophrastos does not mean ' divine speaker ' but rather ' marked or noted by a god '.

Contemporary with Theophrastos and said to have been his rival for the headship of the Peripatetics was ARISTOXENOS of Taras (Tarentum).[12] A very voluminous writer, said to have produced 453 book-rolls, he has left us nothing complete save three books (not a continuous treatise) on Music, generally called the *Harmonics*, although the exact title varies in our authorities. They are our fundamental document for the study of Greek music. Save for the information he provides, there is nothing very attractive about Aristoxenos. Macran says, not unfairly :

' The faults of his style are so glaring—his endless repetitions, his pompous reiterations of '' Alone I did it '', his petty parade of logical thoroughness, his triumphant vindication of the obvious by chains of syllogisms—that we are apt to overlook the services which such an irritating writer rendered to the cause of musical science. And yet these services were of great importance.' [13]

Besides his merits as a musical theoretician, he wrote to good effect on metre ; of his work on this subject, however ('Ρυθμικὰ στοιχεῖα, *Elements of Rhythm*), not even a single book has survived complete, though we have a large fragment from the second and a number of shorter fragments or passages in later writers which have drawn on it.[14]

His other claim to remembrance is that he wrote a series of biographies, none of which has survived but which are often used by later authors. The general title seems to have been *Lives of (famous) Men* (Βίοι ἀνδρῶν).[15] This is the beginning of a long list of lives, notably those of writers and philosophers, by various members of the Peripatetic school.

A writer whose loss there is good reason to regret is HERA-

[11] Diog. Laert., v, 38 ; Cicero, *orator*, 62 ; Strabo, xiii, 2, 4 ; Quintilian, x, 1, 83.

[12] See Suid., *s.u.* 'Αριστόξενος : Christ-Schmid, ii, p. 68 *sqq.* ; Macran (see next note), p. 86 *sqq.*, and the literature there cited.

[13] H. S. Macran, *The Harmonics of Aristoxenus* (Oxford, Clar. Press, 1902, the most convenient ed. for English readers ; the fundamental one is that of Marquardt, Berlin, 1868), p. 87.

[14] Most of what survives from this work is in the first vol. of R. Westphal's *Metrik*, Leipzig, 1861.

[15] Plutarch, *non posse suauiter*, 1093 c ; the form of the title suggests that Aristoxenos wrote or planned a series of lives of women also. Jerome, *de uiris illustr.*, *prolog. ad Dextrum* (vol. ii, p. 807, Vallarsius) says he was *longe doctissimus* of the Peripatetic biographers ; Gellius, iv, 11, 4, had already called him *litterarum ueterum diligentissimus*.

KLEIDES of Herakleia on the Pontos Euxeinos (Black Sea ; hence he is known as Heraclides Ponticus). He was a student under Speusippos, Plato's successor- (who seems also to have taken his place during one of his absences), Plato himself and Aristotle, besides having some connexion with the surviving Pythagoreans.[16] Besides a number of other works on literary and philological subjects, he wrote dialogues of the Aristotelian form (see p. 271) into which he seems to have introduced historical personages as speakers, and to have diversified the matter, generally philosophical, with curious and marvellous tales. His interests included science, and he was perhaps the first to suggest that the sun and not the earth was the centre of what we now call the solar system.[17] His exact dates are not known, but we may suppose him born about 385.

Falsely attributed to him are a trifling work *On Constitutions*, excerpted from the Aristotelian Constitutions (see p. 273), which has come down to us in a very scrappy form and was probably compiled by a later HERAKLEIDES, surnamed KALLITIANOS and nicknamed LEMBOS, contemporary with Ptolemy VI, and a curious treatise on *Homeric Allegories*, now rightly ascribed to a certain HERAKLEITOS, of about the first century A.D., which is one of our chief sources of information for the allegorical method of interpreting that poet, by reading into him whatever philosophical doctrines the commentator held to be true.[18]

Another author of considerable importance who is represented for us by fragments was DIKAIARCHOS of Messene in Sicily. His works included a treatise on *Life in Greece* (Βίος Ἑλλάδος), in three books, a number of essays dealing with particular points of antiquarian or cultural interest, and several works on philosophy, including one which taught the mortality of the soul.[19]

[16] See Diog. Laert., v, 86. The following sections give some account of his life and works.

[17] The fragments of his works are collected by Voss, *de Heraclidis Pontici uita et scriptis*, Rostock, 1896. For the doubtful evidence of his heliocentric theory, see Christ-Schmid, ii, p. 73, n. 3 ; Heiberg, p. 52. He is often quoted for marvellous stories, with which he seems to have ornamented his dialogues ; Cicero, *de nat. deor.*, i, 34, makes the Epicurean Velleius complain of his ' childish fables ' ; Plutarch, *Camill.*, 22, says he is μυθώδης καὶ πλασματίας.

[18] For the *Constitutions*, see *F.H.G.*, ii, p. 197 *sqq.* The *Homeric Allegories*, or Ὁμηρικὰ προβλήματα, are well edited in the Teubner series (1910).

[19] See Cicero, *Tusc. disp.*, i, 21, 77 ; the latter passage calls D. one of his favourite authors, *deliciae meae*. The philosophical frags. are in *F.H.G.*, ii, p. 265 *sqq.*, at the end of the historical and geographical remains.

He was also a great geographer, being mentioned as a leading authority, comparable to Eratosthenes.[20] His *Circuit of the Earth* (*Γῆς περίοδος*) is lost, like his other works ; but there is a little uncertain evidence for supposing him the author of an interesting series of descriptions of the Greek cities and their inhabitants which has come down to us. The probabilities, however, are against this.

These excerpts, as they seem to be, are taken from the work of some man of good information and quick intelligence ; but it reflects little credit on some of the older modern scholars that for a while Dikaiarchos was supposed, on the authority of a subscription in the MS., to have written a copy of pitiful iambic trimeters containing part of a versified description of Greece. It was left to Karl Lehrs (1802–78) to point out that the first 23 lines of this rubbish are an acrostic of the name of their obscure author, one DIONYSIOS, son of Kalliphon.[21]

DEMETRIOS of Phaleron, born about 350, besides being a statesman of some note and in favour with the first Ptolemy, was a stylist[22] and a philosopher, the friend and pupil of Theophrastos.[23] He lived most of his life in Athens, was driven out by Demetrios Poliorketes in 307, went to Egypt, fell out of favour when Ptolemy II succeeded, and was put to death in or about 283. We cannot judge of his speeches, his paeans in honour of Sarapis, or his miscellaneous philosophical writings ;[24] he was interested in literary criticism, for he wrote several works on Homer, and he is the first writer we know who produced a book of Aesopic fables.[25]

[20] For instance, by Strabo, ii, 4, 1, and repeatedly by Pliny. The fragments of the work on the Greek cities (probably from a *περιήγησις* of Greece) are in *F.H.G.*, *loc. cit.*, p. 254 *sqq.*, *G.G.M.*, i, p. 97 *sqq.*, which see for a discussion of authorship.

[21] See *G.G.M.*, i, p. 238 *sqq.* The MS. writes the verses as prose and joins them to the work mentioned in the preceding note ; at the end is written *Δικαιάρχου ἀναγραφὴ τῆς Ἑλλάδος*. The work being dedicated to an unknown Theophrastos, it is to be supposed that some reader took this to be Aristotle's successor and so supplied the name of the geographer nearest him in time.

[22] Style, see Cicero, *Brutus*, 38 ; *orator*, 92 ; Quintilian, x, 1, 33 and 80 ; he had a soft, pleasant style, not well fitted for practical oratory, and used many words in metaphorical senses. Life in Diog. Laert., v, 75 *sqq.*, on whom Suid., *s.u. Δημήτριος* (c), depends.

[23] Paeans, Diog. Laert., *ibid.*, 76 ; Artemidoros, p. 148, 23 Hercher, says he wrote three books (of paeans ?), on the dreams and cures sent by the god. His writings are listed in Diog., *ibid.*, 80 *sqq.*

[24] Diog., *l.c.*

[25] Diog., *ibid.*, 80. The earlier mentions of such fables are fairly numerous, but none imply a written collection. Cf. Chap. iv, n. 25.

He certainly is not the author of the work *On Style* dealt with on p. 399 ; another spurious book is the collection of *Model Letters* (τύποι ἐπιστολικοί) which bears his name ; it is of unknown, but later, date and authorship.[26]

Several other Peripatetics, mostly writers of biography, are known to us by name and by fragments, sometimes tolerably abundant, of their works.[27] Such are PHAINIAS, or PHANIAS, of Eresos in Lesbos, a pupil of Aristotle ; KLEARCHOS of Soloi in Cyprus, who, however, did not write biography in the proper sense, but περὶ βίων, or concerning ways of life (in different cities or among different types of men ; he devoted a special work to flatterers and called it Gergithios, after a hanger-on of Alexander), and also was the author of a book *On Skeletons*, the first known osteological treatise, besides other works, showing a distinct fondness for gossip and scandal ; CHAMAILEON, Herakleides' fellow-countryman, notable for his quite uncritical anecdotes and personal touches, suggestive of a type of journalistic biography now popular ; HIERONYMOS of Rhodes, a little later, who has the same fault, indeed a tendency to include mere gossip runs through all Hellenistic biography and passes thence into Roman works, notably Suetonius and the *Augustan History* ; SATYROS, who flourished about 200, and whose *Life of Euripides* has already been mentioned ; HERMIPPOS of Smyrna, his contemporary ; ANTISTHENES of Rhodes, one of whose works was *The Successions* (Διαδοχαί ; viz., to the headship of the philosophical schools), and some minor figures.

The other schools wrote far less, and of what they did write, comparatively little has survived. The most original, from the literary point of view, were the CYNICS, to whom is due the development of the diatribe (διατριβή, familiar conversation or address ; the connotation of abusiveness has been imported into it in modern times), also certain forms of parody and satiric verse, or at least the beginnings thereof. Kerkidas, already mentioned (p. 344), belongs to this movement. BION the Borysthenite is credited with founding it ; he was ' the first to clothe philosophy in motley ',[28] by composing miscellaneous pieces of this kind, in a very varied style. His date is determined roughly

[26] Text in Hercher, *Epistolographi Graeci*, pp. 1–6.

[27] For their frags., see *F.H.G.*, ii, p. 293 *sqq.*, 302 *sqq.*, iii, 35, 159, 182 , more particulars in Christ-Schmid, ii, p. 80 *sqq.*

[28] His life is in Diog. Laert., iv, 46 *sqq.* The saying translated in the text is that of Eratosthenes, cited *ibid.*, 52, πρῶτος Βίων τὴν φιλοσοφίαν ἀνθινὰ ἐνέδυσεν. The word means properly gaudily embroidered garments, such as courtesans wore. His frags. are in Mullach, ii, p. 419 *sqq.*, but a few additions are to be made from papyri, see Christ-Schmid, ii, p. 87, n. 4. He exercised a certain amount of influence, how much it is hardly possible to judge owing to the loss of his works, on Latin writers, see *ibid.*, n. 7.

by the fact that Antigonas Gonatas, who died 240, was his protector for a time. Little survives of what he wrote ; rather more of good sayings attributed to him. A better-known writer, to us, is TELES, who was about contemporary with him, for Stobaios cites a number of passages from his works.[29] MENIPPOS' works are likewise lost ; but they exercised a considerable influence on Varro, who wrote *saturae Menippeae* in Latin, and on Lucian (see p. 419). From these and one or two other imitators, rather than from the very little that is left of him, we gather that he criticized every one and everything, gave his works on occasion fantastic settings (such as a *Descent into Hades*, or Νέκυια, one of the numerous offspring of Odyssey xi), and mixed verse, original or quoted, with his prose.[30]

The SKEPTICS produced at least one rather notable writer, who may conveniently be mentioned here, although he seems to have written chiefly in verse. This was TIMON of Phleius (not the misanthrope), whose best-known work bore the general title of Σίλλοι, literally ' squint-eyed ' pieces, or more freely, ' mockeries '. So far as it can be reconstructed [31] from scanty fragments and ancient mentions of its contents, it consisted of three books : one, after a prologue, described a mock-heroic battle in which the combatants were well-known philosophers, living and dead, followed by an episode in which, apparently, an old woman was fishing, her quarry being shoals of philosophers, one of them led by Plato (frag. 30 Diels). The second book was a descent into Hades, where Timon met the shades of the philosophers. The third seems to have continued this story, ending with an epilogue to the whole poem. The metre was mock-Homeric hexameters, and the chief matter, within the fantastic framework, raillery of all and sundry, save Pyrrhon and one or two others,

---

[29] The remains are collected by O. Hense, *Teletis reliquiae*, ed. 2, Leipzig, 1909. Allusions to Antigonos Gonatas and other persons and events of the middle of the third century fix his approximate date.

[30] He was a pupil of Metrokles, who was a pupil of Theophrastos, Diog. Laert., vi, 95, who also gives a short life of him, *ibid.*, 99–101. He therefore is of the early third century. His native place was Gadara in the Syrian dodekapolis, see Christ-Schmid, ii, p. 88, n. 12, and he began life as a slave, apparently.

[31] The materials for forming a judgement of him (chiefly his life in Diog. Laert., ix, 109–115 and a long extract, in Eusebios' *praepar. euang.*, xiv, 18, from the work of ARISTOKLES the Peripatetic περὶ φιλοσοφίας) and his fragments, also largely from Diog., are in Diels, *Poetarum philosophorum fragmenta*, Berlin, Weidmann, 1901, pp. 173–206. He was a pupil of Pyrrhon, the founder of Skepticism, and a contemporary of Ptolemy II and Antigonos Gonatas, Diog., *loc. cit.*, 110 ; hence his date is the middle of the third century.

including Xenophanes (see p. 77), who were represented as coming somewhere near his spirit of universal skepticism.

Timon also wrote a work in elegiacs, called 'Ινδαλμοί (*Appearances, Opinions*), tragedies and satyr-plays, doubtless intended for the closet and not the stage, and a few prose works, apparently of popular philosophy. He is said also (Diog. Laert., ix, 110) to have written κίναιδοι, or poems of deliberate indecency, like those of Sotades (p. 346).

KRATES the Cynic also wrote verses, which went by the general title of Παίγνια (trifles). The surviving fragments show that they included mock-heroics, like Timon's *Silloi*, whereof one was called *The Wallet* (Πήρα, the beggar's 'wallet which Cynics carried), elegiacs, which included a parody of Solon (frag. 10 Diels, parodying Solon frag. 1 Diehl), plays, full of Cynic maxims, and one or two others.[32]

This was the period in which STOICISM arose and produced its most famous writers. If this were a history of philosophy, much space would necessarily be devoted to these men, for their importance from that point of view was very considerable. But not much need be said here, partly because all their works are lost, save for very numerous fragments and references,[33] partly also because none of them seems to have been distinguished as a stylist or originated any new literary form. It therefore suffices to mention the names, dates and principal classes of works of the leading Stoics.

ZENON, the founder of the school, was perhaps not a native Greek, for he was born at Kition in Cyprus, a town partly Phoenician in population.[34] His dates are not exactly known, but he seems to have lived through about the last third of the fourth century and the first third of the next. He was the first to divide philosophy into what soon became its recognized and traditional three parts, physical, ethical and logical,[35] and his writings covered all these fields, as was but natural in a philosopher who was a great and subtle reasoner, the founder of a new moral doctrine, that only virtue and vice can be called good or bad, and the author of a theory of the universe adapted from Herakleitos with considerable alterations and developments. He was, moreover, not without literary interests, for he wrote

[32] Life in Diog. Laert., vi, 85 *sqq.*; frags. in Diels, *op. cit.*, pp. 216–23. The epistles attributed to him are all spurious. His *floruit* was Olymp. 113, Diog. *loc. cit.*, 87, *i.e.*, 328–5.

[33] Best collected by J. von Arnim, *Stoicorum ueterum fragmenta*. Teubner, 1905–24 (4 vols.).

[34] Life, Diog. Laert., vii, 1 *sqq.*

[35] Diog. Laert., *op. cit.*, 39. 'Logical' (λογικόν) includes rhetoric and grammar.

commentaries on Hesiod and Homer, although these seem to have dealt more with contents than style ; the Stoics as a school were zealous allegorizers, intent to find their own doctrines hinted at in those writers who were most esteemed for wisdom and antiquity.

His immediate disciples, ARISTON of Chios, APOLLOPHANES, HERILLOS of Carthage, DIONYSIOS of Herakleia, known as Μεταθέμενος, or Turn-Coat, because he began as Stoic and ended as a Cyrenaic, PERSAIOS of Kition, KLEANTHES of Assos and SPHAIROS of Bosporos, all seem to have been fairly voluminous writers and active in developing their teacher's ideas ; but the one work of theirs which is of any considerable literary interest is not in prose but in hexameters. Kleanthes wrote a famous and really noble hymn to Zeus,[36] not the traditional god of mythology but the supreme ruler of an orderly universe, ' without whom nothing is done save only that which the wicked perform in their folly '. But the nobility of the poem arises from its exalted thought rather than from any beauty of language ; it is popularized Stoicism hitched into passable verse.

The second founder of the school, however, was CHRYSIPPOS, Kleanthes' pupil, who died in the 143rd Olympiad (208–205) aged 73.[37] His activity was enormous ; he is said to have written 705 rolls.[38] These dealt with every possible aspect of philosophy, including logic (some of the famous logical puzzles are attributed to him), law (the discussions of natural law in his ethical writings greatly interested the Roman lawyers), divination (in which the Stoics were vigorous believers) and much else, but all in a style which was bad in the extreme, harsh, long-winded and obscure. Hence he was less widely read than referred to, and though we are tolerably well informed concerning his opinions, they have come down to us rather in the words of later writers than in his own.

Of the pupils and successors of Chrysippos not much need be said for the moment, but they included some who must be mentioned

---

[36] Preserved by Stobaios, eclog. phys., i, 1, 12 ; vol. i, frag. 537 Arnim, and edited in many other collections.

[37] For his life, see Diog. Laert., vii, 179 sqq. ; the dates are given 184, from Apollodoros. It was commonly said of him εἰ μὴ γὰρ ἦν Χρύσιππος, οὐκ ἂν ἦν Στοά, ibid. 183. His frags. fill the 348 pages of von Arnim's second volume and nearly 200 of his third.

[38] Diog. Laert., loc. cit., 180. The number, though very large, is not incredible. Supposing each roll to have contained as much matter as a book of Plato's Republic, the total works out at the equivalent of between 28,000 and 29,000 Teubner pages. For a brief account of his writings, see Christ-Schmid, ii, pp. 104–07.

later, such as KRATES of Mallos the grammarian and APOLLODOROS the chronologist. Others, less known, were ZENON of Tarsos, DIOGENES of Babylonia, one of the embassy of philosophers who visited Rome from Athens in 155 B.C. (his colleagues were KARNEADES the Academician and KRITOLAOS the Peripatetic) [39] and his pupil [40] ANTIPATROS.

Antipatros, however, had a pupil whose name was known far outside the circle of professed philosophers, POSEIDONIOS of Apameia, a pupil also of PANAITIOS. The latter, although an obscurer man, had the double distinction of founding what was known as the Middle Stoa, a school which made several compromises with the Stoics' formidable critics of the Academy, and of introducing philosophy into Rome. Poseidonios not only was, like his teacher, a friend of Roman *litterati*, but also one of the most influential of Hellenistic writers. [41] He was an eclectic philosopher, nominally a Stoic, but a most unorthodox one, for he combined the doctrines of his own school with those of practically all the rest save the Epicureans and Skeptics, and thus produced a blend of good practical ethics combined with comforting eschatological doctrine, a leaning towards mysticism and a quasi-scientific justification of wonders of all sorts. Of his learning and many-sided industry there can be no doubt ; besides treatises on epistemology ($\pi\epsilon\rho\grave{\iota}$ $\varkappa\rho\iota\tau\eta\rho\acute{\iota}o\upsilon$), on ethics, the nature of the soul and of the universe, astronomy, fate, divination, and the nature of the gods, he was the author of books on literary criticism and rhetoric, and finally of a long historical work in fifty-five books, beginning where Polybios (see p. 370) had ended, and of dissertations on meteorology and on geographical subjects. It is therefore no wonder that he was drawn upon by writers on all these topics, the more so as his style seems to have been pleasant and lively and much of what he wrote, at all events on geography and ethnology, the fruit of his own travels and first-hand observations. It is a pardonable exaggeration to trace to him almost everything in Roman and later Greek writers which deals with any of his subjects and cannot be definitely assigned

[39] For the date, see Cicero, *Acad. prior.*, ii, 137 ; the event is mentioned in a number of writers, among them Plutarch. *Cat. maior*, 22, Aulus Gellius, vi, 14, 8–9.

[40] [Galen], *hist. philos.*, vol. xix, p. 227 of Kühn's Galen.

[41] The latest full-length discussion of him is K. Reinhardt, *Poseidonios*, Munich, Beck, 1921, with its pendant, *Kosmos und Sympathie* (same author and publisher), 1925. A sketch will be found in Christ-Schmid, ii, pp. 347–55. The only collection of his fragments aiming at completeness is that of Bake, Leiden, 1810, which is badly out of date. The historical frags. are in *F.H.G.*, iii, pp. 245–96, with a collection of data concerning his life.

to another source ; but it is an exaggeration nevertheless, and criticism is beginning to correct the too exuberant assumptions of enthusiasts for this highly important, but unfortunately lost writer.   He probably was born about 135, or at most some eight or nine years sooner ; he lived in Rhodes for some time from about 97 onwards, till Panaitios died ; after that he set out on his travels, which included the western countries (Gaul and Spain) then almost unknown to Greeks.   He died somewhere between 60 and 50 B.C.

Compared with the Stoics, the EPICUREANS make a very poor showing.   EPICURUS ('Επίκουρος) himself despised eloquence and thought that the one necessary quality of style was ready intelligibility.[42]   His surviving works [43] indicate that he himself attained, at best, but this modest standard.   They consist, besides some considerable fragments from the writings of Philodemos (p. 410) and the long inscription, containing a summary of Epicureanism, which DIOGENES of Oinoanda caused to be set up,[44] for the benefit of the public, of three long letters, addressed to his friends Herodotos, Pythokles and Menoikeus, and a number of the ' Select tenets ' (κύριαι δόξαι) which were regarded by him as containing the marrow of his doctrine.   From all these it is very evident that it was not by eloquence or subtlety of logic that the philosopher won followers, but rather by a certain mild dogmatism, combined with a curiously lovable personality, which seemed to offer a harbour of gentle and rational refuge from a troubled age.   For Epicurean eloquence we must go to Latin authors.

Passing now to the rhetoricians of the Hellenistic period, we are confronted with a difficulty.   We know that a new style, Asianism, arose and was immensely influential ; but the Attic reaction, discussed in a later chapter, worked havoc with the monuments of this style, and we have little, at least in Greek, on which to base any judgement of it.   To Atticizing critics, it was all that is abominable.   Dionysios of Halikarnassos rejoices that the harlot Asianism is giving place at last to the true wife ; [45] elsewhere he denounces, in sufficiently vigorous terms, the ' affected, degenerate, emasculate way of arranging words ' of ' Hegesias, the high-priest of this kind of nonsense '.[46]   Cicero,

---

[42] Diog. Laert., x, 13 ; the account of Epicurus fills this entire book.

[43] Principal collections, Usener, *Epicurea*, Leipzig, 1887 (anastatic reprint 1908) ; C. Bailey, *Epicurus*, Oxford, Clar. Press, 1926.   There is no complete edition of all known material.

[44] Edited by I. William, Teubner, 1907, among others.

[45] Dion. Hal., *de ant. orat.*, 1–2.

[46] *De compos. uerb.*, 4 (p. 19, 10, Usener-Radermacher) ; the translation is that of Rhys Roberts, p. 91 of his edition.

who himself owed not a little to Asianism, although his good taste kept him from imitating its excesses, is more moderate, but severe enough : the same Hegesias is prone to use jerky, short clauses ; the Asians generally are too fond of ending with one particular rhythm, the dichoreus or double trochee ($- \smile - \smile$) ; they will, to get a desired effect, include in the sentence words which have no meaning.[47] Under all this vituperation, Asianism in time wholly disappeared from Greek practice, although Latin kept it up, notably in the style of the younger Seneca, during periods of anti-Ciceronian reaction. With it disappeared its exemplars, no longer read or treasured as models ; and to criticize them we are reduced to scanty fragments, often quoted for no other purpose than to show how execrably their authors wrote.

Of the arch-corrupter of style HEGESIAS we know that he was a native of Magnesia near Mount Sipylos ; his date is probably not far on in the third century, and one at least of his principal subjects was the history of Alexander. To what is left of him we may add a long inscription, set up by King ANTIOCHOS of Kommagene in the first century B.C., and discovered in 1890 amid the ruins of the monument to which it belonged, on Nemrud-Dagh.[48] Both alike, despite the difference in age and authorship, are typical Asianic ; Norden assigns Hegesias to Cicero's first class of Asianism (see note 47), Antiochos to the second. The result of an examination is to justify what the ancient critics say. Neither author has anything remarkable to set forth ; both return to the worst faults of Gorgian style (see p. 279), neglecting the improvements of the intervening centuries, and adding thereto a rhythm so marked that the reader hardly knows whether he has before him prose compositions or somewhat irregular lyrics. The dithyrambs of Timotheos and this sort of prose are not far apart. In Hegesias especially the word-order is strained and extraordinary, everything else being sacrificed to sound ; Antiochos offends less in this respect, but, precisely as Cicero says, fills up his clauses with unnecessary words to get the rhythmical effect he desires, or merely in an effort at novelty. Thus Mount Tauros becomes ' the heights of Taureian crests ', ' the heroes ' is ' the holy graces of heroic nature ', ' setting out

---

[47] Cicero, *orator*, 226, cf. *ad Att.*, xii, 6, 1 ; *orator*, 212–13 ; 231. He adds that there were two kinds of Asianism, one marked especially by frequency of neat and pretty epigrammatic phrases, lacking in weight, the other by the rush of words (*Brutus*, 325).

[48] See Norden, *Kunstprosa*, p. 140 *sqq.*, for text and criticism ; the preceding pages deal with Hegesias.

full bowls of wine ' becomes ' filling press-fed mixing-bowls with bounteous mixture ', and so forth, in what should be a plain and simple set of directions for a festival which the king wishes to have celebrated in perpetuity. It does not surprise us to learn that reciters of this sort of prose rather sang than spoke.[49] That it was intended to give sensuous pleasure of a not very elevating kind and wholly unsuited for close reasoning, vigorous discussion, or virile narrative is obvious. Its one contribution to the literature of the world is, that under the better taste of the first century B.C. it contributed to the adorning of Cicero's style, which has a similarly elaborate system of rhythm, but more varied and used with far greater skill.

After Demetrios of Phaleron this age produced no oratory which was thought worthy of remembrance ; indeed with the disappearance of democratic governments having more than municipal importance, it had no longer much justification for existence. History remained as a field for those rhetorically inclined, as among the fourth-century writers discussed in the last chapter. Others had enough taste to reject Asianism, but not sufficient talent to form a fitting style of their own ; and so, if we may believe Dionysios, there were produced numerous writings which no one could have the patience to read through.[50] We have lost them all but one, to our great damage, for however poor these authors may have been as stylists, they wrote on interesting subjects concerning which our information is far from complete.

The exploits of Alexander the Great produced not one work of literary importance in this period. Besides certain official records kept by Alexander's own orders, PTOLEMY I, after becoming king of Egypt, published a book of memoirs of the campaigns which he had shared with his former leader ;[51] Alexander's admiral NEARCHOS and another of his naval officers, ANDROSTHENES, described the new countries they had seen ;[52] MARSYAS of Pella wrote a history of Macedon and an account of Alex-

---

[49] Cicero, *orator*, 27 (*cum uero inclinata ululantique uoce more Asiatico cancre coepisset*).

[50] Dion. Hal., *de comp. uerb.*, 4, p. 21, 1, Usener-Radermacher, 94, 4 Roberts. The list includes Polybios !

[51] These historians of Alexander are conveniently gathered in Jacoby, ii, p. 618 *sqq.* ; an older collection of their fragments is that by Müller at the end of the Didot Arrian. Ptolemy, whom Arrian (praef. 2) prefers for the delightful reason that he was a king and it would be beneath his dignity to lie, will be found on p. 752 *sqq.* of Jacoby.

[52] Nearchos, Jacoby, p. 677 *sqq.* ; Androsthenes is to appear in his fifth part.

ander,[53] and ARISTOBULOS of Kassandreia, in his old age, wrote a history of the events through which he had lived.[54] KALLISTHENES of Olynthos was fairly prolific ; he wrote *Hellenika* (ten books, covering the period 387–357), a work on the Sacred War and another called *The Deeds of Alexander* (Πράξεις 'Αλεξάνδρου), whose follower he was and who ultimately put him to death for too plain speaking.[55] His style was apparently rhetorical, ' not sublime but highflown ', ' almost like a declamation ', say two good critics ; [56] but KLEITARCHOS, Hegesias' fellow-sinner in the opinion of later writers, was worse on the same subject.[57]

Under Kallisthenes' name some much later writer, of uncertain date and unknown personality, put forth one of the earlier versions of the Alexander romance, destined to bulk largely in mediaeval literature, European and other. This important department of folk-lore falls, chronologically and to some extent by virtue of its subject and style, outside our scope.[58]

The history of Alexander's successors also found many writers, but none of great merit. One of Dionysios' list of unreadables was HIERONYMOS of Kardia, who served with distinction under four kings, Eumenes, Antigonos, Demetrios Poliorketes and Antigonos Gonatas. Of his history of the events from Alexander's death to the time of Pyrrhos of Epeiros (323–about 265), not a word survives, but it is often referred to as an authority.[59] DURIS of Samos, another of Dionysios' list, wrote an account in at least twenty-two books of events from the Battle of Leuktra to

[53] Marsyas, Jacoby, p. 737 *sqq.*, together with his namesake, MARSYAS of Philippoi ; it is not always certain to which of them a given fragment belongs.

[54] Most conflicting accounts are given of Aristobulos, see the *testimonia* assembled by Jacoby, p. 769. His history was reliable (Arrian, *loc. cit.*) ; he flattered Alexander grossly (Lucian, *quomodo hist.*, 12, anon. *epit. rhetor.*, iii, p. 610, 18 Walz) ; he accompanied Alexander and wrote part of the history at least while with him (Luc., *loc. cit.*) ; he began to write after Alexander was dead, when he himself was in his 84th year (Arrian, *loc. cit.*, pseudo-Lucian, Μακρόβιοι, 22). Perhaps the truth is that A. was in Alexander's suite and so had good opportunities for knowing the facts, making his history reliable enough if allowance was made for his subservience to the king, and that he revised and published it towards the end of his long life, adding the preface from which pseudo-Lucian takes the statement about his age.

[55] Life in Suidas, *s.u.* Καλλισθένης ; frags., Jacoby, p. 631 *sqq.*

[56] Pseudo-Longinus, *de sublim.*, 3, 2 ; Cicero, *de orat.*, ii, 58.

[57] Pseudo-Long., *ibid.* ; his frags. in Jacoby, p. 741 *sqq.*

[58] See Schmid-Stählin, ii, p. 813 *sqq.* ; pseudo-Kallisthenes has been edited by W. Kroll, Berlin, Weidmann, 1926.

[59] These references are collected by Jacoby, ii, pp. 829–35.

about 100 years later, a history of Samos and a number of smaller works. DIYLLOS of Athens continued Kallisthenes' *Hellenika*, PSAON, towards 200 B.C., continued Diyllos ; NYMPHIS of Herakleia, whose known dates are 280 and 240 (how much earlier and later he lived is unknown), brought his history down to 246 ; PHYLARCHOS of Athens (his native country is rather uncertain) continued Hieronymos and Duris, MENODOTOS of Perinthos perhaps continued him. Writers of memoirs (the most notable was the statesman ARATOS of Sekyon, 271–213), biographies and the like are past counting ; the collections of historical fragments contain their names, dates, and what else is known of them.[60] We need do no more than mention that several writers busied themselves with the antiquities of Attica, their works being known generically as *Atthides*, *i.e.*, Attic researches or histories ('Ατθίδες, sc. ἰστορίαι) and themselves as Atthidographoi. The most notable of these was PHILOCHOROS, who was put to death by Antigonos Gonatas about 263, or a little later.[61] But there can hardly have been a town or district in Greece so obscure as not to have had its historian in this period.

Others, taking advantage of the new knowledge won by Alexander's conquests, interested themselves in the barbarian lands. XENOPHILOS, of whom very little is known, wrote a history of Lydia, MENEKRATES of Xanthos, one of Lykia ; LYKOS of Rhegion wrote on Libya, *i.e.*, North Africa, a district which interested one or two other writers also ; ERATOSTHENES, not the geographer and poet (see pp. 343, 382, 392), produced a history of Galatia ; while HEKATAIOS of Teos or Abdera, not to be confused with his namesake of Miletos (p. 297), besides one or two works which were frankly romance,[62] produced a long dissertation on Egypt which passed for sober history ; what it was like we may judge from the first book of Diodoros of Sicily, who seems to have gone to it for his account of how that country, under wise kings such as Osiris, originated civilization and passed it on to the rest of the world. More important is the fact that a native Egyptian tried his hand at writing the history of his own country in Greek. This was MANETHO of Sebennytos, who, like Hekataios, lived at the beginning of the Ptolemaic period and took part in Ptolemy I's

---

[60] Jacoby, ii, p. 136 *sqq.* (Duris), 130–2 (Diyllos), 158–9 (Psaon), 161 *sqq.* (Phylarchos), 189 (Menodotos), 974 *sqq.* (Aratos) ; Nymphis appears in his Pt. iii B, p. 328 *sqq.*, and in Müller, iii, p. 12 *sqq.*

[61] *See* F. Jacoby, *Atthis*, Oxford 1949.

[62] Xenophilos, Müller, iv, p. 530 ; Menekrates, ii, 343 ; Lykos, ii, 370–74 ; Eratosthenes, in the Didot Herodotos, p. 182 of the appendix ; Hekataios, Müller, ii, p. 384 *sqq.*

introduction of the new Graeco-Egyptian cult of Sarapis.[63] Beginning with the mythical age, he brought his history down to what we still call, using his enumeration, the 31st dynasty, *i.e.*, to Alexander the Great. His information was not always very accurate, for the Egyptians were far from being great historians ; but they did possess extensive records, as we now know, and Manetho could read them. Hence what he wrote, true or false, was at least Egyptian, and the little that is left of him (a passably complete list of the kings) is of great use to our Egyptologists. It is therefore extraordinary that his work remained without influence, apparently unread, until Christian antiquaries, looking for material to make a Biblical chronology, came across it at some period between the time of Vespasian and the end of the second century A.D. Our fragments are painfully gathered from Julius Africanus, the Christian chronologer, himself fragmentary, Eusebios the ecclesiastical historian and one or two others. His contemporaries preferred the lies of Hekataios.

BEROSSOS, priest of Marduk at Babylon, also wrote in Greek, and dealt with the history, or mythology, of his own land. His work consisted of three books, the first covering 432,000 years and coming down to the Flood, the second a mere thirty-odd thousand, to 747 B.C., while the third ended with the death of Alexander. The historian himself lived under Antiochos I (281–261) ; the first nameable author to use him was Alexandros Polyhistor (p. 405), on whom the later writers, mostly Christians, drew.[64]

It is convenient to mention here, though he is much later in date, another celebrated interpreter of Oriental ideas. PHILON of Byblos (Gebal, the modern Jebail), born probably A.D. 64, wrote several historical or quasi-historical works, whereof some fragments remain (*F.H.G.*, iii, p. 560 *sqq.*). By far his most famous production, however, was his translation, or adaptation, of SANCHUNIATHON (Σαγχουνιάθων, Σαγχωνιάθων, *i.e.*, Sankun- or Sakkun-yaton, ' Sakkun has given '). This Phoenician author was stated by Philon to have written a Phoenician history, apparently from the creation to his own date, about the time of the Trojan War. Philon's rendering, of which a good deal is preserved, principally by Eusebios, seems to have been a strange mixture of genuine Semitic tradition and legend with Greek Euhemerism, and the question of how much he really derived from a Phoenician original and what additions of his own he made to it can hardly be said to be decided. The most accessible account of the

[63] Müller, ii, p. 511 *sqq.* Cf. Waddell's edition (Loeb Library).
[64] *Ibid.*, p. 495 *sqq.* ; later and better is P. Schnabel, *Berossos und die babylonisch-hellenistische Literatur*, Teubner, 1923 (contains fragments).

matter is perhaps that given in Hastings, *Encyclopaedia of Religion and Ethics*, arts. PHILO BYBLIUS, SANCHUNIATHON.

MEGASTHENES, an Ionian who between 302 and 291 was several times sent on embassies to the great Indian king Chandragupta (Sandrokottos in Greek), had good opportunities for learning something of India, and was the author of a work in four books on the country, *Indika*. Unfortunately, he mixed correct information with sheer fable (Dionysos' conquest of India, the mythical parallel which the imagination of the age produced to the real invasion by Alexander, becomes an Indian tradition under his pen), and consequently gave the Greek world a far less dependable account of a country with which it had manifold relations, commercial and political, than the importance of the subject called for. Of other writers on the East (DAÏMACHOS of Plataiai and PATROKLES ; the former was an ambassador to Chandragupta's successor and the latter held an official post near the Caspian Sea, which he was the first Greek to describe with any accuracy) we know less.[65] Minor writers of the time were MENANDROS of Ephesos, who wrote on Phoenicia, and DEMETRIOS, a Jew, who wrote a work *On the Jewish Kings* towards the end of the third century.[66] To this period also belongs the Parian Chronicle, already many times quoted in the notes to this book (it reckons all dates backwards from 264/3 B.C.), also the chronicle of the temple of Athena at Lindos.[67]

Important for its consequences, which were wholly bad, is the foolish production of EUHEMEROS of Messene, who was in the service of Kassandros (311–298) and put his absurdities concerning mythology into the form of a spurious history. He professed to have journeyed to a distant land, the island of Panchaia in the Indian Ocean, and there to have found an inscription recording the deeds of the mythological gods, Zeus and the rest, when they were kings on earth This framework enclosed a shallow rationalizing theory to the effect that, apart from certain natural objects such as the sun, the Greek gods were human princes and other notable people who had been deified after their death, out of admiration or flattery. The legends concerning them he transmuted into exceedingly stupid tales from which the supernatural element was excluded. This dreary trash, which the Greeks were on the whole too acute to take seriously, imposed

[65] Müller, ii, p. 397 *sqq.* (Megasthenes), 440 (Daïmachos), 442 (Patrokles).

[66] *Ibid.*, iii, pp. 214, 224 (frags. 8 and 16 of Alexandros Polyhistor).

[67] See *Die lindische Tempelchronik*, Chr. Blinkenberg, Bonn, 1915. It is contained in an inscription of 99 B.C.

upon the Romans, to whom it was made known through Ennius' Latin version, and later on was cited *ad nauseam* by Christian apologists. Its title was *The Sacred Record* ('Ιερὰ ἀναγραφή).[68] A similar piece of rationalism, equally stupid, was the work of a certain PALAIPHATOS, of dubious date, but perhaps a pupil of Aristotle,[69] *On Incredible Tales* (Περὶ ἀπίστων), whereof an epitome survives. It explains the Centaurs as mounted men who came from a village called Nephele (Cloud), Kallisto as a girl who was eaten by bears while out hunting and so was said to have turned into a bear, and so forth, in a way suggestive of an ill-natured parody on Max Müller's ' disease of language '.

It may also be mentioned that this age produced a mass of popular books semi-historical in character. The ' writers of things unexpected ' (παραδοξογράφοι), as they are called, to whom belonged the author of the treatise on marvels falsely attributed to Aristotle (p. 273), are represented by ANTIGONOS of Karystos, author of certain biographies of philosophers after the Peripatetic fashion (see p. 357), who wrote, in the neighbourhood of 240 B.C., a little treatise very like the pseudo-Aristotle's in content, which still survives.[70] A less innocent kind of popular literature is represented by a work of MACHON, a minor writer of New Comedy, who put forth a sort of *chronique scandaleuse* in iambic verse, concerning the doings and sayings of the most celebrated Athenian courtesans. This he called χρεῖαι, *i.e.*, *bons mots*.[71] Delicacy was not its most remarkable feature, but certain references indicate that there were other authors of Hellenistic date whose calculated obscenities gained them the name of ἀναισχυντοσυγγράφοι or shameless writers.

Most of the above historians and quasi-historians were never considered by any one to be of first-rate importance. But there are two great names which must now be dealt with, one considered the more important in antiquity, the other by moderns. TIMAIOS of Tauromenion (the new town which his father Andro-

---

[68] His fragments are collected by G. Nemethý, *Euhemeri reliquiae*, Budapest, 1889. The chief account of his work is in Eusebios, *praepar. euang.*, ii, pp. 59 c–61 a Vigerius, 129–33 Gaisford, from the lost sixth book of Diodorus Siculus. See p. 424.

[69] The epitome is in pt. iii, 2, of *Mythographi Graeci* (Teubner, 1902), edited by N Festa. There were four writers called Palaiphatos (Suidas, *s.u.*), and it is not certain which is the author in question.

[70] It is included in Westermann's *Paradoxographi Graeci* (Brunswick and London, 1839), pp 61–102. For the identity of its author, a matter of some doubt, see Christ-Schmid, ii, p. 236.

[71] Our knowledge of this work is derived from long excerpts in Athenaios, mostly in Bk. xiii.

machos had founded and governed to replace the older Naxos, destroyed earlier in the century) was born about 346 and is said to have lived ninety-six years.[72] Driven from his native country by the tyranny of Agathokles of Syracuse (usurped power 317), he spent the next half-century in Athens, learned rhetoric from Philiskos (see p. 311) and, like him, turned to writing history, taking for his subject the events, real or legendary, in Sicily and the adjacent countries from mythical times down to his own. We are reduced to judging of his style from criticisms, mostly unfriendly, passed by Polybios, pseudo-Longinus and others, and from a very few verbatim quotations. Even allowing for this refracting medium (Polybios hated and despised him), we cannot rate it highly ; he seems to have been one of the rhetorical historians of the Isokratean school, and to have been especially fond of puerilities and commonplaces, expressed at great length, with poetical quotations and other adornments in doubtful taste. As to the matter, he certainly was learned ; he had read diligently all that earlier writers could teach him concerning the West, and was not sparing of criticism, even of Ephoros, whose reputation stood high and survived his attacks. Practical knowledge of war or statesmanship he had none, and his topographical accuracy seems not to have been above suspicion. Save in the last five books of his long work, where his venomous hatred of Agathokles found vent in every kind of slander of him, no one but Polybios charges him with deliberate falsehood ;[73] but even in the earlier books, his irritable, cranky nature (Aristotle seems to have been his pet aversion, and concerning him he would believe any scandal) and his lack of real critical sense made him unreliable, though a storehouse of curious information and good stories. He remained the chief authority for the times and places of which he treated, and our knowledge of him comes from a mass of quotations and references in such men as Diodoros, who goes to him for historical fact, and Athenaios, who picks out bits of gossip, literary history and the like.

POLYBIOS was a very different writer, and is the last Greek

---

[72] So [Lucian], *Μακρόβιοι* 22. ISTROS, one of Kallimachos' followers, called him Epitimaios or Fault-finder, Athen., 272 b. Frags. in Müller, i, pp. 193–233.

[73] *ἑκούσιος ψευδογραφία*, Polyb. xii, 25[k] (vol. iii, p. 219, 28 Büttner-Wobst). But Polybios could be as bitter as Timaios himself, and was not always just. Thus, in iii, 20, 5, he gives the reader to understand that SOSYLOS of Sparta, the friend of Hannibal, was little better than a gossip-writer ; yet a fragment of his memoirs (Pt. ii, p. 903 *sqq.*, Jacoby) indicates rather a sober historian, full of interesting information in a not contemptible style.

historian who may claim high rank. Even so, he is far below Thucydides ; but he presents so refreshing a contrast to rhetoricians like Timaios that a certain dullness and heaviness of style and a fondness for proving the obvious may easily be forgiven one whose arrangement is good, his knowledge, both theoretical and practical, extensive and his desire to arrive at the truth always sincere and not often frustrated. After a career of some distinction in the service of the Achaian League, he was taken as a hostage by the Romans in 167, being then about 35 years old. Himself a soldier and a statesman, and never a definite enemy of Rome, he made the acquaintance of some of the leading public men, and notably of the young Scipio Aemilianus, who became his close friend. He studied the language, customs and history of the Romans, conceived a warm admiration for them, and had the excellent idea of writing a history which, while remaining strictly within the limits of truth (he himself called his work a ' pragmatic inquiry ', πραγματικὴ ἱστορία, meaning a systematic treatment of matters of fact [74]) should have for its unifying principle the stages by which Rome achieved her destined and deserved supremacy over the civilized world. His first two books sketched the relations of Rome and Carthage from 266 to 221 ; the remaining thirty-eight detailed the events of 221–120, many of which Polybios had himself witnessed, while for much more he could supplement his written sources (these included Roman archives)with the reminiscences of men who had taken a prominent part in them. He rightly conceived that the historian must also be a geographer, and this science formed the material of one entire book, the thirty-fourth. The end of history, as all professed and Polybios really believed, was to discover truth ; its benefit was to provide the statesman of the future with a clear explanation of how, subject always to the somewhat capricious intervention of chance (Τύχη, the one superhuman power in which he had a genuine faith),[75] a state might rise to greatness.

For us, Polybios is represented by five complete books (i–v),

---

[74] Polyb., i, 2, 8. What we know of P. is very largely from his own work, supplemented by a short account of him in Suidas. [Lucian], Μακρόβιοι, 22 says he died, as the result of a fall from his horse, at 82. The best edition of him is that by Büttner-Wobst, in the Teubner series.

[75] See Polyb., xxix, 21, where he quotes with full approval some remarks of Demetrios of Phaleron on the subject. Concerning the conventional religions of the day, he held the not uncommon theory that they were a useful device for keeping in order that large section of any community which is too stupid and passionate to be reasoned with, vi, 56, 11–12.

large extracts from the next eleven, and smaller excerpts and fragments of the others, with the exception of xvii, xix, xxxviii and xl.[76]

He wrote two smaller works, now lost, before he set about his *History*, a Life, in three books, of Philopoimen the famous Achaian statesman and general,[77] and a treatise on tactics.[78] Cicero (*ad familiares*, v, 12, 2) mentions a third, an account of the Numantian War, which he says was a separate work ; but it seems possible that it was a sort of appendix to the *History*.

[76] Büttner-Wobst gives a short account of our sources for reconstituting Polybios in his preface, vol. i, p. iii *sqq.*
[77] Cited by Plutarch, *Philopoem.*, 16, who doubtless made direct or indirect use of it for the facts of Philopoimen's career.
[78] Polyb., ix, 20, 4. Geminos of Rhodes (see p. 379) says, *Isag.*, 16, 32, that he wrote a book entitled *On the habitable district at the equator*, but this may have been only a large excerpt from Book 34 of the *History*.

CHAPTER XII

SCIENCE, SCHOLARSHIP, CRITICISM

WE have already met, in the last chapter, certain writers who were rather scientists than philosophers. Hippokrates was credited with having been the first to disjoin his art from philosophy, that is, to make it a separate discipline and not part of a larger subject which could be studied as a whole ; [1] his example was followed, with varying degrees of consciousness and thoroughness, by many students, both of medicine and of other subjects, and the result was a decided advance in specialist knowledge during the Hellenistic period, despite the weakening of both philosophy and literature in general.

To begin with the most fundamental discipline of all, and one which in the nature of the case must receive only cursory treatment in a manual of literature, [2] MATHEMATICS made enormous progress between the death of Alexander and the establishment of Roman supremacy. The Pythagoreans had devoted great attention to it, and some of them, notably Archytas (see p. 257), were a long way past the rudiments of the subject. Plato had regarded it as one of the most important branches of the training of a philosopher, and was himself a good mathematician, keenly interested in the development of the study, though only on its theoretical side. [3] Many of his scholars followed their master in this respect, and some of them, notably EUDOXOS, attained eminence ; Eudoxos' pupil MENAICHMOS is regarded as the founder of the theory of conic sections, [4] which was continued by ARISTAIOS, in the third century. Outside these schools, DEMO-

---

[1] Celsus, *Medic.*, i, p. 2, 14, Daremberg : *Hippocrates . . . ab studio sapientiae disciplinam hanc separauit.*

[2] Short account in Turnbull, chaps. i–iv ; in Heiberg, p. 1 *sqq.* ; full treatment of important parts of the subject in the various works of Sir Thos. Heath (see Heiberg's and Turnbull's bibliographies).

[3] See especially *Repub.*, 522 c *sqq.*

[4] See Heiberg, pp. 10, 13. Most of our knowledge of these men is derived from Pappos' Συναγωγή (see p. 377).

KRITOS (see p. 254) had done more than a little to advance mathematics,[5] apparently attaining at least a rudimentary idea of infinitesimals and more than a rudimentary idea of projection.

There was thus a considerable body of knowledge from which further advances might start, and of it the Alexandrians made excellent use, for enough of their work remains for us to judge with some exactness how much they knew.[6] The most famous name is that of EUCLID (*Εὐκλείδης*, not to be confused with the Megarian philosopher of that name, see p. 259). Of his life we know nothing, but as he used Eudoxos, and Archimedes (see below) used him, probably his activities lie towards the beginning of the third century B.C. His great work, familiar till recently in our schools, is the *Elements* (*Στοιχεῖα*), the mathematical handbook for the rest of antiquity (even the totally unmathematical Romans heard of it), and for most later ages. It is preserved entire ; of its thirteen books, the first six deal with plane geometry, the next three with arithmetic, Book X, the longest of all, with irrational quantities, and the remainder with solid geometry. A sort of appendix, not by Euclid, is conventionally labelled Books XIV and XV.[7] One other work of his on pure mathematics survives, the *Data* (*Δεδομένα*) ; but in addition we have notices of several more, the treatise *On Divisions* (of plane figures), whereof part is preserved in an Arabic version, that on *Conic Sections* (*Κωνικά*), the *Porismata* (*Πορίσματα*, problems on the determination, from certain data, of some part of a figure; the simplest example was ' given a circle, to find its centre '), that on *Mathematical Fallacies* (*Ψευδάρια* ; one is reminded of De Morgan's *Bundle of Paradoxes*). The *Optics* is preserved in a later compilation, *Ὁ μικρὸς ἀστρονομούμενος* (we may render this freely, *Outlines of Astronomical Mathematics* ; the epithet ' little ' implies a contrast with Ptolemy's Almagest, see p. 380), dating from the third century A.D. or thereabouts, and with it the *Phaenomena*, an elementary astronomical treatise. Of the *Τόποι πρὸς ἐπιφανείᾳ* we know [8] that it dealt with conic

---

[5] His titles included *Ἐκπέτασματα*, Diog. Laert., ix, 47 ; for infinitesimals, see fr. 155 Diels.

[6] The Arabs, who could make but little of Greek literature, studied Greek science, including mathematics, with zeal and intelligence, and translated into their own tongue a large number of treatises. They thus fill some of the gaps in our tradition.

[7] The former of these books is by HYPSIKLES, about 170 B.C., the latter dates from the sixth century A.D. Both are in Heiberg's critical ed. of Euclid (Teubner), vol. v.

[8] Pappos, *Συναγωγή*, p. 636, 23, Hultsch. The fragments of the lost works are in the Teubner Euclid, vol. viii, p. 227 *sqq*.

sections, and consisted of two books. A little work on music also survives, entitled *The Division of the Monochord* (Κατατομὴ κανόνος), *i.e.*, the arithmetical relations between the notes of the diatonic scale.[9]

Falsely ascribed to him are the *Catoptrics* and the *Introduction to Musical Theory* (Εἰσαγωγὴ ἁρμονική).

Euclid seems to have been not so much an original discoverer as an organizer of mathematical knowledge. Of other members of the Alexandrian school we know the names of KONON the astronomer (see p. 321), who was the friend and correspondent of Archimedes, ERATOSTHENES the geographer (see p. 382), who invented a mathematical instrument, the μεσόλαβος, for finding the two mean proportionals necessary for the duplicature of a cube,[10] and, about a century after Euclid, APOLLONIOS of Perge, author of a work on conic sections (Κωνικά), which survives partly in the original, partly in an Arabic version, a treatise on harmonic section (Περὶ λόγου ἀποτομῆς), whereof an Arabic translation only has come down to us, and several other works now lost. This man was trained and lived partly in Pergamon, which in science as in literature was the rival of Alexandria.[11]

A greater mathematician than any of the above was ARCHIMEDES of Syracuse, who also was trained in Alexandria, though he owed most to his own genius. His dates are 287–212.[12] Mathematical ability was perhaps a family characteristic, for his father Pheidias was an astronomer.[13] The young Archimedes began with applied mathematics, his earliest known work, *On Mechanical Theorems* (Περὶ τῶν μηχανικῶν θεωρημάτων), being dedicated to Eratosthenes. But he soon passed on to more abstract problems, some of which were discussed in his treatise *On Sphere and Cylinder* (Περὶ σφαίρας καὶ κυλίνδρου). This he had meant to dedicate to Konon, but as the latter died before the work was ready, he dedicated it to his pupil Dositheos. There followed a more

---

[9] Published in Jan's *Scriptores musici Graeci* (Teubner), i, p. 148 *sqq.* and in the Teubner Euclid, vol. viii, p. 158 *sqq.*

[10] See his own epigram on it, Powell, p. 66, who discusses the question whether it is genuine. The machine is sharply criticized by Nikomachos, *Arithmet.*, i, 13.

[11] See Heiberg, p. 29 *sqq.* The Greek part of Apollonios is edited by him (Teubner, 1891).

[12] Death, at capture of Syracuse in 212, Livy xxv, 31, 9 and several later authors; Tzetzes, *Chilad.*, ii, 105, says he was 75 years old. A life of him by a certain Herakleides existed in antiquity, see Heiberg, p. 23.

[13] Archim., Ψαμμίτης, i, 9.

important work, *On conoidal and spheroidal figures* (Περὶ κωνοειδέων καὶ σφαιροειδέων), which among other things discussed the problem, already famous, of 'squaring the circle'. A little work which has not come down to us in its original form attacked the same problem from another angle, and evaluated π within fairly close limits ; yet another, now lost, calculated it still more closely.[14] This and other questions which interested him involved finding a better system of numeration than that generally in use among Greeks ; [15] from this sprung a popular essay, addressed to Gelon, son of Hieron II of Syracuse, known as *The Sand-reckoner* (Ψαμμίτης), showing that it was perfectly possible to reckon the number of grains of sand required to fill the whole universe, by employing an ingenious system of his own for expressing high figures, and therefore that the common proverb ' numberless as the sands ' was wrong.[16] For Archimedes was capable of joking, provided the joke was mathematical ; he seems to have liked puzzles, since there survive fragments of a work on the theory of the *stomachion* (' teaser '), a sort of tangram, whose fourteen pieces can be put together into a square and also into figures of various sorts ; [17] he is also alleged to be the author of an epigram inviting the reader to calculate the number of the cattle of the Sun (cf. p. 27) from data the working out of which involves handling numbers which run into many millions.[18] In more serious mood he wrote a work *On Spirals* (Περὶ ἑλίκων), another on equilibrium (Περὶ ἰσορροπιῶν), in other words on statics, yet another, preserved complete in a Latin translation of 1543 from a MS. now lost, partly in a palimpsest discovered by Heiberg, on hydrostatics (Περὶ ὀχουμένων, literally *On things carried*, sc., on water or other fluid, *i.e.*, floating). Other works are preserved in fragments, or not at all.

[14] For particulars, see Heiberg, p. 26.
[15] There is no name in ordinary Greek usage for a larger number than 10,000, and figures were expressed by letters of the alphabet in a manner far less convenient than our Arabic numerals.
[16] The difference between infinity and a very large finite number is by no means clear to the non-mathematical ; Horace (*Odes*, i, 38, 1) makes Archytas ' measure the unnumbered sands ', perhaps confusing him with Archimedes, and Apollo expresses his own omniscience by declaring that he knows ' the number of the sands and the measures of the sea ', Herodotos, i, 47, 3. Cf. Pindar, *Ol.* ii, 98.
[17] Good account, with diagram, by R. D. Oldham in *Nature*, 1926, p. 337. Text in vol. ii, pp. 416–24, of Heiberg's ed. of Archimedes, (Teubner). Cf. Ausonius, *Cento nuptialis*, in the prefatory letter (vol. i, p. 374 of the Loeb ed., where correct the corrupt *ostomachium* of MSS. and editors).
[18] Vol. ii, p. 528 *sqq.*, Heiberg. It is called πρόβλημα βοεικόν.

After the great age, mathematics continued to be studied, even to make advances here and there, for several centuries. ZENODOROS is of uncertain date ; we have a work of his *On Figures of equal Perimeter* (Περὶ ἰσοπεριμέτρων σχημάτων). Out of several works dealing with spherical trigonometry we have an Arabic version of one, the *Sphaerica* of MENELAOS of Alexandria, who lived in the first century A.D. The discovery of a MS. at Constantinople [19] has given us a writing of HERON, *On Mensuration* (Μετρικά) ; he also commented on Euclid's *Elements*. NIKOMACHOS, a Neo-Pythagorean of about the second century A.D., wrote an *Introduction to Arithmetic* ('Αριθμητική εἰσαγωγή) which we still have, and a work on *Arithmetical Theology* ('Αριθμητικὰ θεολογούμενα), *i.e.*, on the mystic meanings given by Pythagoreanism to the first ten numbers, of which we have an abstract and some fragments. A better author, though later (third century A.D.), is DIOPHANTOS of Alexandria, of whose thirteen books on arithmetic ('Αριθμητικά) six survive ; their contents include a good deal of what we now call algebra. PAPPOS, also of the third century, was a very respectable mathematician, widely read in the classical works of Archimedes and the rest ; hence his *Collection* (Συναγωγή) of comments on and supplements to their writings, with historical notes and other welcome information, is of much use to students of the history of the subject, besides presenting a picture of what mathematical studies were like at that date. After Pappos comes a long line of commentators, reaching to the Revival of Letters and leading up to the modern renaissance and progress of the subject.

Mathematical knowledge was required, then as now, for any serious work on ASTRONOMY. This was ardently studied at Alexandria, and great progress made, which might have been greater if ARISTARCHOS of Samos had succeeded in convincing the world that the sun and not the earth is the centre of our system. [20] Unhappily for the progress of science, his theory was rejected, partly on theological grounds ; his works are lost, save for a little treatise *On the sizes and distances of the Sun and Moon* (Περὶ μεγεθῶν καὶ ἀποστημάτων ἡλίου καὶ σελήνης), and his only known follower was the rather obscure Seleukos, about 150 B.C., that is to say some 130 years later. [21] But most of the astro-

[19] First published in 1903 by H. Schöne, *Heronis opera*, iii (Teubner).
[20] Archimedes, Ψαμμίτης, i, 4 *sqq.* ; Plutarch, *de facie in orbe lunae*, 923 a ; Kleanthes the Stoic (see p. 360), declared, presumably in his work *Against Aristarchos*, Diog. Laert., vii, 174, that he ought to be prosecuted for impiety in ' disturbing the hearth of the universe ', *i.e.*, the earth ; Sextus Empiricus Πρὸς δογματικούς, iv, 174. Copernicus, when framing his hypothesis, was much comforted to find he had an ancient authority to support him.
[21] Plutarch, *Platon. quaest.*, 1006 c, who says S. gave a proof of the theory.

nomical works which are known to us are observational rather than theoretical, and their increasing accuracy fills a modern student with respect for the powers of their authors, unassisted as they were by any but the rudest instruments. EUDOXOS, already mentioned (p. 373), had published a handbook describing the relative positions and apparent movements of the stars (*Phainomena*), which contained a good many misstatements, as might be expected of an early attempt (his dates are 408–355). He also interested himself in calendar reform ; like METON of Athens before, KALLIPPOS of Knidos and HIPPARCHOS of Nikaia after him, he proposed a cycle of lunar years which should, by carefully arranged intercalations, amount to the same total number of days as the same number of solar years.[22] Our earliest surviving work, however, is by a later writer, AUTOLYKOS of Pitane, who lived towards the end of the fourth century and wrote, so far as we know, two little treatises, one *On the Moving Sphere* (Περὶ κινουμένης σφαίρας), the other *On Risings and Settings* (sc., of the fixed stars).[23] HYPSIKLES, already mentioned (p. 374, n. 7), is the first surviving author to mention, in an essay called Ἀναφορικός,[24] what he clearly did not invent or introduce, the division of a circle into 360 degrees. As 60 is a common Babylonian factor (*e.g.*, the talent, which is of Babylonian origin, is divided into 60 minae), it is fairly certain that we have here Babylonian influence, be it direct or otherwise. Hence it is not surprising that the very obscure KLEOSTRATOS,[25] said to have been the first Greek to mention the signs of the zodiac, owes something—how much is a point as disputable as his date, which is variously computed at the sixth century or the fourth—to the Babylonians also. At all events, their observations were, at least in some measure, accessible to Greek astronomers after Alexander. Hence the constellations, especially those of the zodiac, become familiar subjects at this epoch, though scattered mentions of them are to be found from Homer onwards, and the differences between the Greek and the non-Greek picture of the heavens a

---

[22] See any work on ancient chronology. The extremely vexed question of the authorship of these cycles cannot be gone into here. Strictly speaking, the problem is insoluble, for the solar and lunar years are practically incommensurable.

[23] These are edited by F. Hultsch in the Teubner series, 1885.

[24] *I.e.*, ἀναφορικὸς λόγος, ' discourse on rising ' (of heavenly bodies).

[25] For a discussion of Kleostratos, see especially J. K. Fotheringham in *Journ. Hell. Stud.*, xxxix (1919), p. 164 *sqq.* ; xl (1920), p. 208 *sq.* ; E. J. Webb, *ibid.*, xli (1921), p. 70 *sqq.* Nothing survives of him but two lines from a poem on astronomy, apparently something like that of Aratos in content.

matter for comment.[26] With constellations came star-myths,
very rare things in pre-Alexandrian times, apart from fanciful
interpretations by moderns. That KONON furnished Kallimachos
with material for a new one has already been mentioned (p. 321).
ERATOSTHENES was therefore quite in accordance with the taste
of his day when he wrote a work on catasterisms (καταστερισμοί),
i.e., miraculous transformations of mythological persons into
constellations, Kallisto into the Great Bear and so forth, whereof
an epitome by some unknown hand survives.[27]

It is very significant of the relative importance of literature
and science for the succeeding generations that what we have
left of Alexandrian astronomy concerns itself largely with Aratos'
poem. HIPPARCHOS of Nikaia was a very notable astronomer
and mathematician, making careful use of Babylonian records
of eclipses and of his own amazingly exact observations for such
weighty matters as determining the exact length of the solar
year, drawing up a catalogue of the fixed stars, settling the
exact time of the apparent risings and settings of the heavenly
bodies, and other things well worth the interest of a genuine
scientist ; yet all we have left of him, apart from mentions in
later authors, is one little work, in which he corrects the errors
in Eudoxos, and consequently in Aratos, for the benefit of a
friend interested in astronomical studies.[28] His date is fixed by
certain observations which he is known to have made at the
second century B.C. GEMINOS of Rhodes is later, about the
seventies of the first century B.C. He would appear to have
written a commentary on the astronomical work of Poseidonios
(see p. 361), and is the author of a short handbook, the *Introduction to Astronomy* (Εἰσαγωγὴ εἰς τὰ φαινόμενα), which still survives.[29] POSEIDONIOS' own astronomical studies were probably
the result of his interest in philosophy in general rather than
this science in particular, but there seems little doubt that he
wrote a considerable work, the Περὶ μετεώρων or Μετεωρολογικὴ

[26] Nigidius Figulus (contemporary with Cicero) called them respectively
sphaera Graecanica and *sphaera barbarica* ; see Varro *ap.* Servius on Vergil,
Georg., i, 19 and 43. He doubtless used Greek sources for his researches
n them.
[27] Latest ed., by Olivieri, in the Teubner series (1897). Eratosthenes
is a principal source for Hyginus' *Poetica Astronomica*, Bk. ii. The
fundamental modern work on the subject is F. Boll, *Sphaera* (Leipzig,
1903).
[28] Best ed., by C. Manitius (Teubner, 1894), with German trans. and
commentary ; for the life of Hipparchos, see p. 282 *sqq.*
[29] Best ed., by C. Manitius (Teubner, 1898) ; on p. 237 *sqq.* the date,
&c., of Geminos are discussed.

στοιχείωσις, besides some smaller essays ; of the former we have perhaps a sort of synopsis in the compendium of astronomy by KLEOMEDES, a writer otherwise unknown. THEON of Smyrna was frankly writing for non-specialists when he produced a monograph whose title may be rendered *Mathematics for Students of Plato* (Τὰ κατὰ τὸ μαθηματικὸν χρήσιμα εἰς τὴν Πλάτωνος ἀνάγνωσιν).[30]

But the most famous name in this connexion is that of PTOLEMY (CLAUDIUS PTOLEMAEUS), a contemporary of Theon, whose works, through the fault chiefly of readers and not of himself, kept astronomy at a standstill for more than a millennium after his death. He lived in the second century A.D., about 100–178,[31] and was evidently a man of great learning and capable of at least routine observational work. His most important writing is familiar to later ages under its Arabic title of *Almagest* (*Tabrir al magesthi*) ; he himself called it the *System of Mathematics* (Μαθηματικὴ σύνταξις). It is a textbook of astronomy, with tables and diagrams suggestive of a modern author, although in some respects its contents were already antiquated when he wrote ; especially, his firm upholding of the geocentric theory of the universe has caused that view to be called Ptolemaic in modern times. Its thirteen books cover 1254 Teubner pages in all, and contain, in its author's opinion, 'practically everything that should be studied in such a system, in the light of contemporary knowledge'.[32] Hence it served as the manual of all serious students down to the great developments associated with the names of Copernicus and Galileo. Besides some minor writings, Ptolemy also composed an astrological treatise in four books, hence known as the *Tetrabiblos*;[32a] for astrology was flourishing in his day, and had done so since about the third century B.C.

A mass of astrological works have come down, but remain largely unpublished ; a full list of all known MSS. containing them, with extracts from those not yet printed, exists under the general title of *Catalogus codicum astrologorum Graecorum*,[33] and we have two considerable treatises in verse, one by a certain MAXIMUS, perhaps about contemporary with Geminus, another by several hands and of very different dates, all thrown together by some late copyist or editor under the name of MANETHO. There exist also fragments of a more

[30] See Heiberg, p. 58.
[31] His own observations help to fix his date. The Arabic title of his book implies a Greek title μεγίστη (σύνταξις) ; our sources give μεγάλη, or simply σύνταξις.
[32] Σύνταξις, last paragraph. [32a] Convenient edition by F. E. Robbins in the Loeb Library. [33] Brussels, 1898–1924.

famous poet of this kind, DOROTHEOS, who is supposed to have lived about the same time as Ptolemy.[34] Numerous other writers in prose and verse are known to us by their (real or assumed) names and citations from their works. The interest of all these writers is non-literary ; there is room for a full treatise on this curious aberration, but it would fall wholly outside the scope of a book like this.[35] The one poet of any merit astrology produced was the Latin Manilius.

Another development of mathematics was MECHANICS, a department of knowledge concerning which the Greeks seem to have written comparatively little. ARCHIMEDES, however, gave considerable attention to it. Besides his writings (see p. 375) he was on occasion active as an engineer, and even those who knew nothing of his science remembered, and probably exaggerated, the efficiency and ingenuity of the machines with which he defended Syracuse.[36] The most renowned of Alexandrian authorities on this subject, KTESIBIOS, who may have lived in the third century B.C., has not come down to us directly, but later writers make use of him. Among these are PHILON of Byzantion, of whom we have a certain amount left, partly in the original and partly in Arabic and Latin versions,[37] and HERON (about 50 B.C. ?), who was concerned less with mechanical theory than with practical, and often very ingenious, methods of constructing machines great and small, from war engines to toys of various sorts, including puppet-theatres and one or two rudimentary applications of the power of steam.[38]

Not unconnected with mathematics is MUSIC, and it may be mentioned here that Ptolemy wrote three books of *Harmonics* ('Αρμονικά, *i.e.*, musical theory, not what our musicians call harmony, for that did not exist in Greek music), which still survive, and another writer, perhaps of the third century A.D., ARISTEIDES QUINTILIANUS, also produced three books, *On Music*. Of other writers, notably AELIUS DIONYSIOS,[39] we know something from references to them, but have no complete works.

Clearly, none of the above subjects give much scope for purely literary treatment ; it may be said generally that these technical writers have plain, straightforward styles, free from misplaced attempts at eloquence. They write in the Greek of

---

[34] All these are published at the end of the Didot Aratos.
[35] Bouché-Leclercq, *L'Astrologie grecque*, Paris, 1899, is now both out of print and out of date.
[36] See Polybios, viii, 3 *sqq.* for a sober account.
[37] See Heiberg, p. 70.   [38] *Ibid.*, p. 71.
[39] Aristeides is edited by A. Jahn, Berlin, 1882 ; for Aelius, see Schmidt-Stählin, ii, p. 870 *sq.*

their own day, that is in the ' common dialect ' (κοινή), for the most part ; Archimedes uses his native Sicilian Doric for several works (in the case of some which are in the common dialect, it may be suspected that they were originally in Doric also). The worst, stylistically, is perhaps Ptolemy, who is prone to heavy, over-long sentences and a certain pretentious pedantry.

More nearly literary is GEOGRAPHY, which by this time was definitely a science, concerning itself with mathematical theories of the shape and size of the earth, the climates of different zones and so forth, and tolerably expert in calculating latitude and longitude ; while at the same time such departments as ethnography were fairly well advanced. Hence it is to be regretted that we have not the three books on this subject written by the many-sided ERATOSTHENES (cf. pp. 343, 392), nor the more popular work of POSEIDONIOS (p. 361).[40] There remain, however, two considerable writings, capable of teaching us much that is interesting, the more so as their authors were rather compilers than original researchers, and so tell us something of the older geographers as well.

STRABO (Στράβων) of Amiseia in the Roman province of Pontos, was born about 63 B.C., and seems to have lived till about A.D. 19.[41] He was of a good family, originally Cretan, and was thoroughly educated under some of the most distinguished teachers of the day. He became a Stoic of the same moderate sort as Panaitios and Poseidonios, lived for some time in Rome (about 29–24 B.C., and again a few years later) and travelled over a great part of the known world. Evidently Polybios influenced him ; for not only did he, like most scientists of the time, keep clear of the craze for Atticism which began in his day (see next chapter) but his work was modelled to a great extent on that of the earlier writer. He composed a long history (43 books) leading up to Polybios and then continuing him, evidently in considerable detail, down to his own day.[42] This is unfortunately lost ; but we have the greater part of the seventeen books on geography which earned him the title of ' The Geographer ' in the Middle Ages, as Homer was ' The Poet '.[43] This is a description on a generous scale of the then known world, starting in the

[40] See Heiberg, p. 84 *sqq.*, for more particulars. Eratosthenes is quoted in Strabo and other authors often enough for us to form a tolerably clear idea of his work.

[41] There is no ancient biography of him save a rubbishy notice in Suidas, but a good deal can be gathered concerning his life from his own references.

[42] Fragments in *F H.G.*, iii, pp. 490–4 ; Jacoby, ii, pp. 430–6.

[43] Book vii is partly missing.

west and continuing to the farthest east with which Graeco-Roman civilization had any acquaintance. It is such a treatise as one would expect from an admirer of Polybios who was not, like his model, a man of action and practical experience. History and geography, the former taken from his own work, go hand in hand ; there is little interest shown in the purely scientific aspects, much in such things as may furnish useful moral lessons. The sources, despite Strabo's first-hand knowledge of several countries, are usually books, and these of various dates and degrees of trustworthiness, not always critically handled or their discrepancies noticed and accounted for. Probably some part of this failing is due to the work not having received its final revision when its author died ; [44] but his critical abilities were not great, and therefore he was somewhat prone to treat his authorities from the standpoint of his own, or his school's, notions of probability, making little, if any, original inquiry. Thus he greatly undervalues Pytheas, for instance (see p. 312), although he has the good sense to recognize Megasthenes' fables (p. 368) as such. [45]

Before and after Strabo a number of writers produced works on geography, mostly in prose but occasionally in verse : their remains are to be found in Müller's *Geographi Graeci minores*. Of these, several had no literary pretensions at all, but wrote lists of the towns and other conspicuous features to which a traveller along a given coast would come, with notices of the distances between them. A good example of this type of guide-book is the anonymous *Voyage around the Red Sea* (Περίπλους τῆς Ἐρυθραίας θαλάσσης ; the name includes more than our ' Red Sea ', for the regions described extend to India), written by some unknown Graeco-Egyptian merchant of about the first century A.D., a practical man who set down plainly what he knew about routes, the character of the inhabitants, the goods to be had (they include sugar, μέλι τὸ καλάμινον τὸ λεγόμενον σάκχαρι) and other such matters. The MS. of this treatise absurdly names ARRIAN (see p. 412) as its author ; the real Arrian wrote a description of India (Ἰνδική) and a *Periplus* of the Euxine, the former derived from older authors, the latter from observations of his own. There is a work, apparently much interpolated by those who used it as a school-book, falsely attributed to SKYLAX of Karyanda (p. 297), but really composed about the thirties of the fourth century B.C., the Περίπλους τῆς θαλάσσης τῆς οἰκουμένης, which takes the reader around the shores of the entire civilized world as known to

[44] This is a very plausible conjecture of A. Meineke, *Vindiciae Strabonianae* (Berlin, 1852), p. 81 ; there is, however, no direct evidence that the work is unfinished.
[45] See Strabo ii, 14, 1 (drawing on Polybios), xv, 1, 7 *sqq.*

the author, diversifying the list of names by notes on ethnology, local myths and the like. Of more pretentious writings, rather literary than either scientific or practical in intention, the considerable remains of AGATHARCHIDES' works may serve as a specimen. He was a Peripatetic, apparently a man of upright character as well as considerable learning, and a determined opponent of the Asianists (see p. 362). A native of Knidos, he spent a great part of his life in Alexandria, where he was tutor to the young Ptolemy VIII. His best-known work, preserved for us in extracts and an epitome by Photios,[46] is the treatise *On the Red Sea*, originally in five books. It contained much that was interesting, including a famous description of the inhuman treatment of convicts in the gold-mines at the southern extremity of Egypt, but it was by no means confined to geographical facts, much less to the advancement of the theory of that science, but digressed on all manner of topics, mythological, stylistic and moral. Of the verse writers, two deserve mention ; one used iambic trimeters, explaining in a sort of preface why he did so ; they are the metre of Comedy, which has the great virtue of putting things clearly, briefly and at the same time pleasantly. Who he was is not known. For some time he was called SKYMNOS of Chios ; but Skymnos, as we now know from inscriptional evidence, was living 185/4 B.C., while this man dedicates his work to Nikomedes II of Bithynia, 147–95.[47] The real Skymnos wrote a description of Europe, Asia and Africa, whereof some fragments are preserved in the scholia on Apollonios Rhodios, but it was in prose. The other versifying geographer is DIONYSIOS, sometimes called the Periegete to distinguish him from the numerous other persons of the same name ; much ink was spilt over the question of his age and country, until G. Leue [48] had the perspicacity to notice that the poem is signed and dated ; lines 113–134 (Müller) and 522–532 are acrostics, informing us respectively that the work is Διονυσίου τῶν ἐντὸς Φάρου, 'by Dionysios, one of those inside Pharos', *i.e.*, in Alexandria, and ἐπὶ 'Αδριανοῦ, 'of the time of Hadrian'. The Byzantine schools seized upon this work—its 1187 hexameters are not an impossible amount to learn by heart—and consequently we have a mass of scholia, also a commentary of portentous length by Eustathios, bishop of Thessalonike (Saloniki) ; but that it was popular in the West also is indicated by the fact that Avienus, in the fourth century, turned it into Latin verse.

More important than any of these is the geography, or rather gazetteer, of PTOLEMY (cf. p. 380), in eight books, under the

---

[46] Photios, who excerpts from but two books, can be supplemented from other authors, especially Diod. Sic. See Müller, i, pp. liv *sqq.* (life, &c., of Agatharchides), 111 *sqq.* (fragments).

[47] See Dittenberger, *Sylloge* [3], 585, 86. There is some doubt whether the dedication is to Nikomedes II or III, see Christ-Schmid, ii, p. 171, n. 2.

[48] Leue in *Philologos* xlii (1884), p. 175 *sqq.*

general title of Γεωγραφικὴ ὑφήγησις. Book I is introductory, Book VIII gives full directions for drawing a map of the then known world, the intervening books consist of lists of place-names, 8,000 or so in all, arranged by provinces of the Roman Empire, and with the latitude and longitude of each carefully set down. The absence of literary merit, and therefore of interest to the non-specialist, the immense amount of work involved in sifting the MSS. tradition—this is extensive and includes maps, whose exact relation to Ptolemy himself is anything but certain—and the recurrent problems of identifying doubtful names and deciding whether a given mistake is due to the author or a copyist have combined to prevent a full critical edition being published hitherto.[49]

In no department is the loss of Alexandrian literature more deplorable than in MEDICINE. We know, from many references and some direct quotations in later writers, such as Celsus and Galen, that Alexandria produced great physicians and surgeons during the third century B.C. HEROPHILOS, under the early Ptole-mies, had opportunity not only to study anatomy on the dead subject, as our learners do, but actually to perform vivisection on criminals condemned to death ; yet his treatise on anatomy ('Ανατομικά), which contained among other matters the discovery of the nervous system,[50] is lost to us, together with the works of ERASISTRATOS of Antioch, whose researches continued his and included the distinction of sensory and motor nerves. Of later writers we have a little here and there, for instance, Latin translations of SORANOS' treatises on the diseases of women and on acute and chronic ailments ; a Byzantine epitome of the former survives. We thus know something of the state of medicine in his time, the second century A.D., and can add the surviving works of a somewhat later man, ARETAIOS of Kappadokia, whose eight books, dealing in order with *The Symptoms* and *The Treatment of Acute and Chronic Illnesses*, have come down, and contain a considerable amount of material from an earlier (first century) author, ARCHIGENES of Apameia.

But the greatest name, and not undeservedly so, is that of GALEN (GALENOS), A.D. 129–199. Born at Pergamon, he came to Rome in 161, and there spent most of his remaining years. In

---

[49] There is still no complete ed. but Müller-Fischer, Didot 1883–1901. His chief MSS. have now been critically studied, however, by Dr. Fischer, and published in facsimile (No. xix of *Codices e Vaticanis selecti, series maior*, Brill, Leiden, and Harrassowitz, Leipzig).

[50] Hence the modern meaning of neuro- in neurology, neurasthenia, &c. ; before Herophilos, νεῦρον means only a sinew. For his and Erasistratos' vivisections, see Celsus, *de med.*, i, p. 4, 37 Daremberg.

character he was not wholly admirable ; one is not prejudiced in favour of a man who complacently records that he learned much, not only from the virtues of his father, but from the shrewishness of his mother ; it was not in the best traditions of his profession hurriedly to quit Rome when a pestilence broke out, to find an excuse for not accompanying the Emperor Marcus Aurelius on his German campaign, or to be so careful to record his own successes as a practitioner.[51] Nor is his style of the most attractive, being ponderous, long-winded and pedantic. Nevertheless, priggishness and a certain lack of physical courage may well be pardoned in a man so sincerely desirous as he was of knowing and applying the art of healing, and withal so colossally industrious. Besides his extensive practice, he found time to write a mass of literature the remains of which [52] fill twenty volumes of Kühn's edition. It covers anatomy,[53] pathology,[54] therapeutics,[55] pharmacology,[56] physiology,[57] psychology,[58] diagnostics,[59] and the history, controversies and even lexicography of his art ; [60] it includes also, not merely popular treatises recommending the study of medicine,[61] but works on non-medical

---

[51] What we know of Galen is mostly from his own works. He is often called Claudius Galenus by moderns, but the former name has no ancient authority, Mewaldt, col. 578, 22. The references are to περὶ ψυχῆς παθῶν 8 (v, p. 41 Kühn) ; περὶ τῶν ἰδίων βιβλίων, 1 (xix, p. 15), ibid., 2 (p. 19). For the dates, see ii, 215 K ; as an example of his self-advertisement, xiv, 605 sqq. All relevant passages regarding his life are collected in Pauly-Wissowa, art. GALENOS (Mewaldt).

[52] A great deal was destroyed by a fire in his own lifetime, περὶ τῶν ἰδίων βιβλίων, p. 19 ; this book contains our longest ancient list of his works.

[53] Chief work, de usu partium (Περὶ χρείας τῶν μορίων).

[54] As the six books de locis affectis (Περὶ τῶν πεπονθότων τόπων).

[55] The principal work is the Θεραπευτικὴ μέθοδος.

[56] Περὶ κράσεως καὶ δυνάμεως τῶν ἁπλῶν φαρμάκων, and many others.

[57] Including the work On the Natural Faculties, the only one which has yet appeared in the Loeb series.

[58] For instance, the interesting treatises Περὶ ψυχῆς παθῶν, Περὶ ψ. ἁμαρτημάτων (its second book) and Ὅτι ταῖς τοῦ σώματος κράσεσιν αἱ τῆς ψυχῆς δυνάμεις ἕπονται.

[59] Including four books on the pulse, Περὶ διαφορᾶς σφυγμῶν.

[60] He wrote commentaries on Hippokrates, a glossary to his works (τῶν τοῦ Ἱπποκράτους γλωσσῶν ἐξήγησις) ; for a sample of his controversies, see Περὶ τῶν ἰδίων βιβλίων, p. 14.

[61] As the Προτρεπτικός, which appropriately begins the series of his works in Kühn ; he argues, sometimes with real eloquence, for he felt intensely on the subject, that professional studies of some kind are the only fit occupation for a young man with something better in him than the mind of a beast, and that of these the finest is Medicine ; also the Περὶ αἱρέσεων τοῖς εἰσαγομένοις (Student's Guide to the Medical Sects), hinting to the beginner to be, like himself, eclectic, and neither Dogmatist, Empiric nor Methodist.

subjects, both philological [61] and philosophic,[62] for he was strongly of opinion that a physician ought to acquire a sound general education before he began to specialize on medical matters.[64]

Along with this last great writer on medicine in antiquity we may mention the first of the herbalists. DIOSKURIDES (less correctly DIOSCORIDES) was a Roman army doctor, or at all events had seen service of some kind in the army.[65] About A.D. 65 (his work is dedicated to Areios of Tarsos, who was a friend of C. Laecanius Bassus, consul A.D. 64) he published a description, in five books, of some 600 plants, with their names in several tongues, under the title of *Materia medica* (Περὶ ὕλης ἰατρικῆς). Drawing himself upon KRATEUAS (first century B.C.) and SEXTIUS NIGER, besides his own observations, he became in turn the source of innumerable herbals in various languages and of dates extending down to the great revival of medicine in modern times and the coming of botany as we now understand it.[66]

But the best-known achievements of Hellenistic learning, at least to students of literature, are philological. Although Alexandrian literature was not, and did not consider itself valueless, it was during this age that the conviction grew that the ancients were unapproachable. The conception of a classical literature, consisting of the great writers from Homer to Menander, took shape, and on this literature study was concentrated, besides such imitation as in time led to the Atticizing movement to be described in the next chapter. Two periods may be distinguished, rather more clearly than in the case of the sciences. In the former, which we may call Alexandrian, the chief business of philology was textual criticism, together with such discussion of difficulties, appraisement of relative literary merits and so forth as was suitable for readers studying their native language, or at least the only literary language known to them. In the later, or Roman period the nature of the demand had altered somewhat. A large number of the students for whom experts wrote were

---

[61] These are lost, but we have a list of them, Περὶ τῶν ἰδίων βιβλίων, 17 (p. 48 Kühn).

[62] For example, the little handbook of elementary logic, Εἰσαγωγὴ διαλεκτική, discovered on Mount Athos and first published in 1844 by Menas, but more critically by Kalbfleisch (Teubner, 1896).

[64] See especially *On the Natural Faculties*, iii, p. 179 Kühn (p. 278 of the Loeb ed.).

[65] He himself says merely, ' you know I have lived a soldier's life ' (στρατιωτικὸν τὸν βίον), *praef.* 4.

[66] For the relation of Dioskurides to the earlier and later herbalists, see especially Singer in *J.H.S.*, xlvii (1927), p. 1 *sqq.*

Romans, to whom Greek, though often very well known, was a foreign language, and who therefore welcomed running commentaries of moderate length, rather than the bulky discussions on particular points which seem to have been the favourite form of earlier treatises. As antiquity drew near its close, such commentaries shortened and appeared more and more as marginal notes, or scholia ; it is these which have survived and give us a tolerably clear idea of the nature and value of the earlier work.

Something has already been said of the studies of those Alexandrians who were themselves poets ; it remains to discuss the rest, beginning with the Homeric scholars.

By the third century, not only innumerable MSS. of Homer existed but also, it would appear, several recensions, differing sometimes widely from one another, especially in the number of verses,[67] The Alexandrian scholars were not slow to accept the challenge of such a text.

The first great name is that of ZENODOTOS, who was also the first librarian of Alexandria.[68] That he edited Homer, using MS. evidence but suggesting a great number of excisions and alterations, mostly on subjective grounds, such as the impropriety of the traditional reading,[69] seems certain ; it is the harder to judge of him because we hear of him from a hostile source, the scholia which reproduce the opinions of Aristarchos. After

[67] These πολύστιχα (ἀντίγραφα) have left traces here and there on later MSS., as will be seen on consulting the apparatus criticus of any good edition of Homer. Among the editions were some κατὰ πόλεις, representing traditions (however arrived at) peculiar to particular cities, as Massilia.

[68] See chapter X, note 31. In general, the evidence for the activities of all these men, except a few of the later ones, whose works have survived, has had to be painfully collected from late authors, often ill-informed, and from the scholia on Homer (which are mostly very ill-edited and worse indexed), supplemented by the medieval commentary of Eustathios, of which there is no critical edition. Hence the monographs dealing with them are highly technical. I have therefore thought it enough, for the most part, to refer to Sandys and Christ-Schmid or Schmid-Stählin. See also Cessi, p. 572 sqq.

[69] Propriety (τὸ πρέπον) was the great canon of subjective criticism, as indeed it must be ; the word does not signify decency of conduct or speech, but the attribution to each character of words and actions suitable to him ; thus, Zenodotos wished to correct Il. iii, 424, where Aphrodite sets a chair for Helen, because it is unsuitable (ἀπρεπές) to her divine rank to wait upon any mortal ; some one, perhaps Aristarchos, replied that Aphrodite is here pretending to be an old serving-woman ; see scholia on the passage. The criterion is good ; the weakness is the narrow way in which it is applied ; Alexandrian etiquette is not to be looked for in Homer, nor philosophic ideas of the divine nature, dating from long after him. The age was beginning to lose historical sense.

him, RHIANOS the poet (see p. 344) put forth an edition, of which little is known ; more important was that of ARISTOPHANES of Byzantion, librarian about 195. This man, who is credited on doubtful grounds with introducing the accents, marks of punctuation and signs of quantity which we still use with little alteration in writing Greek,[70] also provided his text with a number of critical signs, which sometimes survive in the MSS. we have and continued in use for critical editions of various authors.[71]

They were, the obelos (–) already used by Zenodotos, marking a spurious line ; the *keraunion* (thunderbolt), like a large T, to indicate that a whole passage was spurious ; the asterisk (having the form ※) signifying incomplete sense, or, in editions of lyric poets, the end of a colon, or metrical phrase ; and the *antisigma*, like a C turned left instead of right, to mark a tautology ; Aristarchos used it later to signify that the lines were in wrong order. Aristarchos also added two signs, the *diplê*, $>$ and dotted *diplê*, $\dot{>}$ meaning respectively that something in the text called for remark and that his reading differed from Zenodotos', together with the simple dot (.), which meant, if no other sign was present, that a textual corruption was suspected, and in conjunction with the *antisigma*, that the line or lines so marked should come immediately after that by which the latter sign stood.

Under Ptolemy Philometor, 181–146, lived the greatest of all Alexandrian scholars, ARISTARCHOS of Samothrace, who produced a text of Homer to which it is perhaps not unjust to say our editions go back. This does not mean that our MSS. commonly contain the readings that he favoured, for his practice seems to have been to put in his actual text that reading which the MSS. at his disposal, or the best of them, contained, setting his critical signs in the margin and explaining in one or another of his bulky writings (they are said to have amounted to 800 volumes) his opinions as to what ought to be read and how it should be interpreted. Hence we very commonly find in our MSS., and usually print, readings of which he personally disapproved. The same applies to the other scholars ; no large proportion of readings favoured by them but not in the common tradition of their day seems to have affected the copyists ; their texts rather excluded eccentric readings, found in few or inferior copies, than introduced what was to be found in none at all. Herein they differed from a modern critical edition, which, having its *apparatus* at the foot

[70] See Sandys, p. 126. The difference between Aristophanes' punctuation-marks and ours is merely that his hyphen was a curved stroke under the word ; this we still use to indicate the running together of two vowels into one syllable.

[71] *Ibid*, pp. 127, 132.

of the page, or in some other part of the same volume, need not hesitate to insert in the text conjectures made or adopted by the editor.[72]

DIDYMOS, surnamed Chalkenteros or Bronze-guts, because of his gigantic capacity for work, closes the series of notable Homeric critics. By his time, about 65 B.C.–A.D. 10, the editions of Aristarchos seem to have been lost ; he restored them as best he could from copies and from other writings of Aristarchos, and added the opinions of Zenodotos, Aristophanes and himself to make up a very full commentary. This was later epitomized by some unknown hand ; from the epitome two series of extracts, one more numerous but shorter, the other fuller but fewer, were made ; and these in turn, surviving especially in the famous Codex Venetus of Homer, are our chief source of information concerning Alexandrian Homeric studies.[73]

All these men studied other matters also. Zenodotos edited the *Theogony* of Hesiod, besides a glossary to Homer ; Aristophanes edited Hesiod, Alkaios, Anakreon and Pindar, of whom he seems to have produced the collected edition whereof our Pindar is part ; he wrote on Euripides and the comedian Aristophanes, whether he edited them or not, and produced a lexicographical work, the *Lexeis*, lost save for a fragment but not without influence on later writers. It would seem that he began the lists (κανόνες, canons) of classical authors of various kinds, epic, lyric and so forth, the exact authorship and date of which are uncertain.[74] Aristarchos edited, or at all events commented on, the same lyric poets as Aristophanes, edited Archilochos and

---

[72] See Sandys, pp. 134–5, but the best proof of this is the critical notes of a good modern Homer. For Aristarchos see Sandys, p. 131 *sqq.*

[73] See A. Ludwich, *Aristarchs homerische Textkritik,* p. 102.

[74] See Sandys, p. 131. The authors listed are : *Epic,* Homer, Hesiod, Peisandros, Panyassis, Antimachos. *Iambic,* Semonides, Archilochos, Hipponax. *Tragic,* Aeschylus, Sophokles, Euripides, Ion, Achaios. *Comic* : *Old Comedy,* Epicharmos, Kratinos, Eupolis, Aristophanes, Pherekrates, Krates, Platon ; *Middle,* Antiphanes, Alexis ; *New,* Menander, Philippides, Diphilos, Philemon, Apollodoros. *Elegiac,* Kallinos, Mimnermos, Philitas, Kallimachos. *Lyric,* see p. 123. *Orators,* those discussed in chapter ix. *Historians,* Herodotos, Thucydides, Xenophon, Philistos, Theopompos, Ephoros, Anaximenes, Kallisthenes, Hellanikos, Polybios, the last clearly a later addition. The whole subject is rather doubtful. That ' canonical ' lists of the best writers existed from fairly early days is plain from Quintilian, x, 1, 54, who mentions only poets ; Caecilius was certainly interested in the historians, see Dion. Hal., *ad Pompeium,* 3, p. 240, 14 Usener-Radermacher, and some one had drawn up a list of the best orators, for both Dionysios and pseudo-Plutarch indicate that there were exactly ten, while allusions to some sort of lists generally agreed upon are quite common. See Christ-Schmid, ii, pp. 28–9.

Hesiod, and wrote largely on grammar, the names of the eight parts of speech being his, while his pupil, DIONYSIOS THRAX, wrote a grammar still extant, the core (it fills but sixteen printed pages) of many grammars which succeeded it. This study, and those allied to it, were continued by Dionysios' pupil, TYRANNION, already mentioned (p. 270) in connexion with Aristotle, by the indefatigable Didymos (who also edited or commented on Hesiod, Pindar, Bakchylides, the three great tragedians, several of the orators, and Thucydides),[75] and, much later, by APOLLONIOS DYSKOLOS (' the crabbed ', whether in style or temper) and his son HERODIAN ('Ηρωδιανός), contemporaries respectively of Hadrian and Marcus Aurelius.[76] By the age of Tiberius, the earlier Alexandrian poets were themselves becoming classics, and THEON, son of ARTEMIDOROS, who has already been mentioned (p. 334, n. 66), followed his father's example in studying the bucolic poets.[77] His activities extended also to Kallimachos, Apollonios of Rhodes, Lykophon and Nikandros.

To the labours of these scholars, together with others of less note and mostly later, we owe the really learned commentaries which underlie the scholia (themselves often very corrupt, full of Byzantine rubbish and confused) on Homer, Pindar, Aristophanes, Euripides (those on the other two tragedians have less good ancient material left in them), Apollonios, Theokritos, Nikandros and some others ; also the good information in the Byzantine lexica (Suidas for instance in many cases has simply copied out a scholion, and Hesychios draws upon dictionaries which themselves drew upon glosses to particular passages in ancient writers), and in such repositories of muddled learning as Tzetzes.

While Alexandria thus flourished, neither Athens nor the rival centre to Alexandria, Pergamon, was idle. At the former place the Stoic activity in grammar originated,[78] much of the terminology we still use being traceable to that school. Not less important was the revival by them of a method of interpretation which had earlier been current and flourished henceforth, that of finding allegories in those myths and poetical fictions which on the one hand were too venerable to be treated with mere neglect, on the other too inconsistent with a highly developed ethical system to pass unchallenged.[79] An early champion of this method

[75] Sandys, p. 142.   [76] Ibid., pp. 319, 321.   [77] Ibid., p. 144.
[78] For these scholars and their activities, see Sandys, chap. ix. A good short account of the early history of grammar is given by P. B. R. Forbes in C.R., xlvii (1933), p. 105 sqq.
[79] For allegorical interpretations and their history, see J. Tate in C.R., xli (1927), pp. 214–15 ; C.Q., xxiii (1929), p. 142 sqq., xxiv (1930), p. 1 sqq., xxvii (1933), p. 74 sqq.

was KLEANTHES (see p. 360), the first known writer to use the word
ἀλληγορικῶς. At Pergamon, several celebrated scholars worked,
taking a different line from their Alexandrian colleagues, for they
seem to have paid but little attention to textual criticism, much
to antiquarian study. DEMETRIOS of Skepsis (in the Troad) is
known to us chiefly through Strabo.. His principal work was a
commentary on the catalogue of the Trojan allies in Iliad ii ;
on its sixty lines he wrote thirty books, going in vast detail into
questions of topography, history and so forth, and showing, it
would appear, not wordiness but real and extensive learning. His
date is the second century B.C. ; about the same time, KRATES of
Mallos continued the tradition of allegorical interpretation, set
forth his views on grammar (he was an anomalist, *i.e.*, opposed
to the analogical school which tried to rid the language of its
apparent irregularities) and commented largely on Homer.

Another department of activity in Alexandria, at once
philological and historical, was CHRONOLOGY. The first notable
name is once more ERATOSTHENES ; of his chronicle but few
fragments remain, but it is spoken of with respect and cited as an
authority by several judicious writers.[80] More famous, though
there is no reason to suppose that his work was better, was
APOLLODOROS of Athens, a many-sided scholar of the second
century B.C.,[81] who also wrote twenty-four books *On the Gods*,[82]
a dissertation, in twelve books, on the Homeric Catalogue of the
Ships, and several other works. His *Chronicle* (Χρονικὴ σύνταξις),
the contents of which can be largely reconstructed from the very
numerous appeals to it, covered the period from the fall of Troy
to his own day ; originally it seems to have come down to the
reign of Attalos II, Philadelphos, of Pergamon (159–138) to whom
it was dedicated, and then to have been continued to about
120. It is known from pseudo-Skymnos (see p. 384) that he
wrote it in iambic trimeters of the form used in comedy.[83] He
perhaps got the idea from Machon (see p. 369), but there were
practical reasons for such a medium ; verse is easier to remember
than prose, and the work was of necessity crammed with names
and numerals, both very subject to corruption by a scribe ;

[80] Frags. in Jacoby, ii, p. 1010 *sqq.*

[81] Life in Pauly-Wissowa, *s.u.* ; see also Christ-Schmid, ii, p. 394 *sqq.*,
Sandys, p. 137.

[82] This has nothing to do with the *Bibliotheca*, a handbook of mythology
by an unknown but well-informed author, which still survives. He may
have borne the very common name of Apollodoros, or have intended to
pass off his work as that of the celebrated author of the περὶ θεῶν ; his
date is quite uncertain.

[83] Pseudo-Skymnos, 16 *sqq.*

miswriting would often, by spoiling the metre, draw the reader's attention to itself and at least prevent him from accepting nonsense or false arithmetic as being what the author meant. It seems to have been a weakness of Apollodoros, when definite biographical dates were not to be had, to set down a datable event of importance as the prime (ἀκμή) of the person or persons concerned in it, and then to, suppose that a man in his prime is 40 years old and consequently to reckon the birth of the person in question forty years earlier than the event recorded. The resulting uncertainty as to the real dates of many notable Greeks leaves its mark on this and every other modern work on their history or literature.

Strabo quotes as by Apollodoros [84] a compendium of geography, *Concerning the Earth* (Περὶ γῆς), also in iambics ; its genuineness is doubted by some moderns, including Jacoby, but in any case it is lost.

A less known chronicler was KASTOR of Rhodes,[85] perhaps the son-in-law of Cicero's client, king Deiotarus, certainly his contemporary ; his six books started in mythical times and ended at 60 B.C. Considerable fragments survive. Several minor names, of all manner of dates to the end of antiquity, are known, partly from the use the Christian chronologers, Eusebios and the rest, make of them ; and occasional papyrus fragments, none as yet certainly identified with the work of any known author, indicate that such things were popular, as indeed similar works are now, from their obvious utility.

We may conclude this chapter with an interesting little group of technical writers, the Tacticians. Of these, besides fragments, five of some note have come down to us. The earliest, although his date is uncertain, is probably AINEIAS (AENEAS TACTICUS), perhaps of the fourth, or early third, century B.C.[86] He has left us a little work, divided by the editors into forty chapters, on the tactics to be employed in offence or defence ; the general title is πῶς χρὴ πολιορκούμενον ἀντέχειν, ' how to hold out when

---

[84] Strabo, xiv, 5, 22.
[85] For his fragments and those of the rest, see Jacoby, ii, p. 1128 *sqq.*
[86] The only sound argument is that none of his examples seem later than about the middle of the fourth century. That he mentions, as still in being, the Lokrian maiden-tribute to Athena of Ilion (xxxi, 24 ; cf. Farnell, *Hero-Cults*, p. 293 *sqq.*) proves merely that he is older than Plutarch. The statement cited from Timaios *ap.* Tzetzes on Lykophron, 1144, that the custom ceased in 346, is simply untrue, see Farnell, *loc. cit.*, and the inscription (first published in the *Jahresheft d. österr. arch. Inst.*, xiv, 1911, pp. 168–9) which has been supposed to refer to the same event has no such reference. Hence the positive arguments of the latest editors (the Illinois Greek Club and L. W. Hunter) fall to the ground.

besieged ', but the advice given covers somewhat wider ground than that. A certain freshness and zest about the examples adduced, and the rather uncouth style, combine to suggest that the author was a man of action rather than letters. ASKLEPIO-DOTOS the Philosopher, as the MS. of his work calls him, is quite likely to be an Asklepiodotos known to have been one of Posei-donios' pupils. His τέχνη τακτική, then, dates from about the first century B.C., and reveals itself as the work of an antiquarian by its contents, a sort of drill-book for the phalanx, by then an obsolescent, if not quite obsolete formation.[87] As such, however, it is interesting, and gives an idea of how a Hellenistic army manœuvred, at least on the parade ground. ONOSANDROS, or ONASANDROS,[88] dates himself approximately by his opening sentence, which addresses Quintus Veranius, consul A.D. 49, died 59. His subject is the qualities which a general should have, hence his title Στρατηγικὸς (sc. λόγος, Discourse concerning commanders, rather than On Strategy). It is well-written and shows not a little insight, whether the author's own or borrowed from another, into military psychology and the requirements of leadership. The fourth writer, AELIANUS (not the Aelian discussed below, p. 404), dedicated to Trajan a tolerably impudent plagiarism from Asklepiodotos ; ARRIAN (see p. 412), who also used Asklepiodotos, had something of his own to say, as may be seen from his two little works, one bearing the same title as Asklepiodotos' book, the other, known as Battle order against the Alani ("Εκταξις κατ' 'Αλανῶν), seeming to be an actual report to Hadrian on the dispositions to be made in face of a real and concrete enemy, though doubtless he may have revised it for publication.

With these we may mention an entertaining though trifling work, the collection of ruses, mostly military, in eight books, under the general title Strategemata, which POLYAINOS, a rhe-torician and advocate, dedicated to the emperors Marcus Aurelius and Verus, in A.D. 162 ; it survives almost complete.[89]

[87] For a brief discussion, see p. 230 sqq. of the Loeb edition.
[88] Ibid., p. 343 sqq.
[89] His other works, for which see Suidas s.u., Schmid-Stählin, ii, p. 754, have not survived.

CHAPTER XIII

GREEK LITERATURE IN THE EMPIRE

NOTHING, perhaps, testifies more strongly to the vitality of Greek thought than the persistence of the literature for centuries after all political importance had vanished from the nation. After Actium, not only the old centres such as Athens, but the later ones, Alexandria and Pergamon, were in a state of political dependence, ranking, at best, as provincial centres of some importance, and having as much self-government as the lords of the world chose to leave them. Moreover, Rome had by this time a literature of her own, daily growing in importance and indeed excelling the contemporary Greek output. Nevertheless, the Greeks not only continued to write but, when the Augustan age was over, wrote distinctly better than their masters and at one time nearly ousted Latin from the position of a literary language.[1] Furthermore, during the Roman period they produced a new philosophy and a new literary *genre*. It should, indeed, be noted that many of that epoch who were culturally Greeks were ethnologically nothing of the kind ; yet the number of writers who were of the ancient Hellenic stock, more or less pure, remains astonishingly large.

Poetry at this time was of very little importance. There were no doubt many who could and did write verse, including not a few who possessed great technical skill, like that of Cicero's client Archias ;[2] but the only living movements concerned prose. Besides those authors incidentally treated in the last chapter, only three need be named here, all belonging to the period of the Antonines. The two Oppians dedicated their didactic poems to the emperor Caracalla. Of these writers, one, sometimes called

---

[1] The third century produced scarcely any literary works in Latin except Christian treatises, but a number in Greek, some of them by Romans.

[2] Cicero, *pro Archia poeta*, 18 ; Archias had a remarkable facility in extemporizing verses.

OPPIANOS OF KILIKIA,[3] wrote five books in hexameters on fish and fishing, *Halieutica*, far from uninteresting in content, and in style at all events much less intolerable than Nikandros (see p. 329), while the technique of the verses is good. The other Oppian, who is often confused with him, wrote four books on hunting (*Cynegetica*) ; that the two works have not the same author is clear, both from the difference in style (the second Oppian has less skill in metre than the first), and from the fact that the author of the *Cynegetica* also mentions his native land [4] and makes it clear enough that he was of Apameia in Syria. Another work, said to be by Oppian of Kilikia, on fowling [5] (*Ixeutika*), is lost.

A similar performance was the poem on birds (*Ornithiaka*) said to be by DIONYSIOS the Periegete (see p. 384), of which there survives a prose paraphrase.

Somewhat more original than these didactic poets was BABRIOS, the first surviving Greek fabulist. The name is thought to be Etruscan ; of the man himself nothing certain is known. The fables, as we have them,[6] are in alphabetical order of their first letters ; they are addressed to a certain Branchos, son of ' King Alexandros ', who has never been identified with any certainty.[7] They are well told, with the light touch appropriate to such trifles ; the metre is scazons, but showing the influence of the accent (especially in the fact that the last syllable but one of the line is always accented) [8] in a way impossible to a classical author and very possibly due in part to the fact that the author was not Greek-born and was influenced by Latin metre. The date is perhaps about the second century A.D. See p. 424.

Turning now to prose, we begin by noticing a curious classicizing movement, known as Atticism. By about the first century B.C. a strong revulsion against the absurdities of Asianism (see p. 362) had set in, and the Attic authors were zealously studied. In so far as this meant a return to their good taste, sanity and

---

[3] So called by Athenaios, 13b (Ὀππιανὸν τὸν Κίλικα), which agrees with his own testimony as to his native country, *Hal.*, iii, 206 *sqq.*

[4] *Cyneg.*, ii, 115 *sqq.*

[5] Mentioned by Suidas, *s.u.* Ὀππιανός, and in the Life of the two Oppians (conflated into one) prefixed to the scholia on the poems.

[6] Mostly from a MS. found on Mount Athos in 1840 by Menas (Mynas), others from one in the Vatican, a few from other sources ; see Rutherford's preface to his ed., Macmillan 1883.

[7] See Schmid-Stählin, ii, pp. 682, 1493, for this and other relevant matters. A good many fables in scazons, whether Babrios' or not, can be approximately restored from prose paraphrases.

[8] *I.e.*, a line may end, *e.g.*, ἀνθρώπων, but not ἄνθρωποι nor ἀνδρῶν.

absence of false ornament, it was wholly laudable ; but unfortunately, it brought with it a craze for writing in their dialect
also, *i.e.*, in a form of Greek which had long ceased to be any
one's mother-tongue.   To make matters worse, most of the would-
be Atticists did not understand Attic thoroughly, and made
mistakes which not only would have been at once apparent to a
contemporary of Thucydides or Demosthenes, could he have read
their works, but to any modern who has a tolerable knowledge of
the older authors.   The chief marks of their archaizing style are,
firstly, the revival of a number of words common in Attic authors
but since disused ; these often are poetical, so far as our evidence
goes, and no part of the genuine spoken Attic of the days of
Plato and the orators ; secondly, a deliberate breaking of Isokrates' rule that hiatus should be avoided, a precept which the
more careful prose authors of the Hellenistic age had followed ;
thirdly, a studied carelessness of syntax, in feeble emulation of
the liberties which the older masters had taken with their own
tongue.[9]   The effect of all this upon the more sensible writers
was not bad, amounting to little more than a slight archaism in
vocabulary, permissible enough in literary language ; generally
those who had most to say [10] were freest from such affectations.
One incidental result, for modern students, was that many of the
grammarians of the Empire devoted attention to Attic usage and
published lexicons and other such works, founded on a more
extensive knowledge of the literature than we can now have,
when so much has been lost.   Thus we have considerable extracts
from the work of PHRYNICHOS, *The Atticist, or Concerning Attic
Words* ('Αττικιστὴς ἢ περὶ 'Αττικῶν ὀνομάτων),[11] dedicated to
Cornelianus, a civil servant under Marcus Antoninus and Verus ;

---

[9] As examples, the following may serve.   The word ἀγάλλομαι,
' exult ', is good Attic, the Hellenistic equivalent being ἀγαλλιάομαι ;
Polemon (see below) uses the former.   He also has the poetical word
λῆμα, ' spirit, courage ', familiar enough to Attic tragedy, not to their
prose.   He admits hiatus, ἀρετὴ ἦγεν (p. 8, 4 Hinck), τροπαιούχου ἄνωθεν
(14, 20), though far less commonly than several other Atticists.   As to
construction, besides cases of sheer involuntary bad grammar, Bentley
long ago pointed out (*Ep. of Phalaris*, p. 319 [331 Wagner]) that Philostratos and Aelian are especially fond of starting a sentence with a nomina-
tive and then changing to another construction, as οἱ δὲ 'Ωρεῖται,
χαλκαῖ μὲν αὐτοῖς αἱ πέτραι, χαλκῆ δὲ ἡ ψάμμος, Phil., *Apollon.*, iii, 54.
[10] For example, such scientific works as fall within this period (see
last chapter) are in Hellenistic, with perhaps a tinge of Atticism here
and there.
[11] Edited, in 1820, by C. M. Lobeck (*Phrynichi Eclogae nominum*,
&c., Leipzig, Weidmann), and in 1881, by W. G. Rutherford (*The new
Phrynichus*, London, Macmillan), both with valuable commentaries.

the *Lexicon to the Ten Orators* (Λέξεις τῶν δέκα ῥητόρων) of HARPOKRATION, dating from about the same time [12] and containing much that is interesting concerning Attic law ; while IULIUS POLYDEUKES (POLLUX), who was professor of rhetoric at Athens under Commodus, has left us a compendium of Attic words, drawn probably from the lexicographical writings of the Alexandrians and containing a great deal of very interesting information ; it goes under the title of *Onomastikon*.

More important, from the purely literary standpoint, are some good works of criticism written under the early Empire. First in date is DIONYSIOS of Halikarnassos, already several times referred to. This man came to Rome about 30 B.C. [13] and there spent at least twenty-two years, probably longer. He occupied himself in teaching rhetoric, made a number of friends of high social standing, learned Latin passably well, and wrote a *History of Rome*, also several works of literary criticism, whereof we have a considerable part. They are, the treatise *On the Arrangement of Words* (Περὶ συνθέσεως ὀνομάτων, *de compositione uerborum*) ; three ' literary letters ', as Rhys Roberts calls them, one *To Ammaeus*, refuting an absurd suggestion that Demosthenes owed his eloquence to the study of Aristotle's *Rhetoric*, another, *To Pompeius Geminus*, on the style of Plato and of the principal historians, a third, again addressed to Ammaeus, *On the Peculiarities of Thucydides* (Περὶ τῶν Θουκυδίδου ἰδιωμάτων) ; a treatise *On the Ancient Orators* (Περὶ τῶν ἀρχαίων ῥητόρων), whereof there survive the sections on Lysias, Isokrates, Isaios and Demosthenes, the long discussion of whose style has often been treated by moderns as a separate work and given the title *de admirabili ui dicendi in Demosthene* ; a separate essay *On Deinarchos*, and further detailed studies, discussing the genuineness of the speeches attributed to several, possibly all, of them ; of this only fragments are left. Finally, a work *On Imitation* has left us fragments and extracts, and a handbook of rhetoric has come down under his name, but is not his, being a compilation of precepts, largely on the composition of epideiktic speeches, apparently by several hands.

In the genuine works, Dionysios shows himself an excellent critic, though not quite of the first rank. His taste is good, his comments usually both just and subtle, his knowledge of classical literature very wide. His limitations are, that he cannot appre-

---

[12] A Harpokration was one of Verus' teachers, *Historia Augusta*, v, 2, 5, and this may well be the same man.

[13] *Antiquit. Roman.*, i, 7, 2 ; see Roberts, L.L. (cf. Bibliography), pp. 1–3.

ciate that very lofty type of prose which trespasses on the domain of lyric poetry [14] and that he does not realize that a book of no stylistic pretensions may yet be valuable and readable if the matter is good.[15]

In his History (ʿΡωμαϊκὴ ʾΑρχαιολογία, *Antiquitates Romanae*) Dionysios is seen to less advantage than in his critical works. He writes, as might be expected, in the rhetorical tradition, and as a result his book is nearly worthless as history, devoting much space to elaborate retelling of the late and artificial mythology of Rome. For this very reason, however, it is of some service to students of Roman antiquities, for it preserves a good many interesting facts concerning the earliest civil and religious institutions. We have eleven books left, with excerpts from nine more, carrying the narrative down to 271 B.C.

An unknown, but good writer of about this epoch is called DEMETRIOS by several late, Demetrios of Phaleron by a few medieval authorities.[16] This is an impossible identification, as the style of his treatise shows ; his name may really have been Demetrios and confusion with the best-known prose author so styled would then be easy. His exact date cannot be determined, and might be anything from about 100 B.C. to A.D. 100, the later being perhaps rather the more probable. At all events, his work, *On Style* (Περὶ ἑρμηνείας, *de elocutione*), is a sort of half-way house between general literary criticism and a rhetorical handbook ; if it is definitely of any school, it is in the tradition of the Peripatetics. He begins by discussing the period and its subdivisions, the colon and comma, and then gives the familiar division of styles into grand or elevated (μεγαλοπρεπής), elegant (γλαφυρός), and plain (ἰσχνός), adding a fourth, the striking or forceful (δεινός). These are analysed, with well-chosen examples from poetry and prose, together with the vices corresponding to the first three, frigidity, affectation and aridity.

We have lost several other writers on literary criticism, of this and earlier periods. NEOPTOLEMOS of Parion probably lived about 300 B.C. ; his views are well known, at least in general outline, for we are credibly informed that Horace used him for the *Ars Poetica*, to analyse which would take us outside of the limits imposed on this

---

[14] See *de admir. ui dic.*, 5–7, *ad Pomp. Gem.*, 2. See J. W. Atkins, *Literary Criticism in Antiquity* (Cambridge, University Press, 1934), vol. i, ch. vi, for more detail concerning Dionysios and the other Greek critics.

[15] See the passage cited in chapter xi, note 50.

[16] See Roberts, *Demetrius*, p. 49 *sqq.* ; for D. of Phaleron, see above p. 356.

work by the artificial habit of studying Greek and Latin literature separately.[17]   A scrap of what seems Peripatetic teaching has come down to us in the so-called *Tractatus Coislinianus* ; [18] it defines Comedy as a form of dramatic ' imitation ' (μίμησις) which ' by means of pleasure and laughter effects the purification of the corresponding passions ', and goes on to analyse the sources and forms of laughter and wit.   The resemblance to the Aristotelian definition of Tragedy is patent, but what work, or by what author, lies behind this very brief epitome is unknown.   A friend of Dionysios was CAECILIUS of Kale Akte in Sicily, a freedman of Jewish origin, who, among several other works on rhetoric and criticism, wrote a treatise against Asianism and another on the characteristics of the ten orators.[19]

Undoubtedly the greatest critic of this period was the man conventionally called LONGINUS.   This cannot be Cassius Longinus, the minister of queen Zenobia, in the third century A.D., for our author mentions no one later than the first, and speaks of Caecilius, Dionysios' contemporary, in a way strongly suggesting that his work is quite recent.   Indeed, it is anything but certain that his name is Longinus at all, or even that it was considered to be so by the Byzantines.[20]   But his treatise (Περὶ ὕψους, *de sublimitate*), which unfortunately has several gaps, is in a different class from Dionysios or Demetrios. They had written well on style, and certainly were aware of the commonplace that training alone, without natural genius, will not make a great author ; but Longinus, to give him the traditional name, analyses ideas and the psychology of writing with a depth of which they seem incapable, abundantly supplying the defect he had found in Caecilius' treatment of the subject, who had ' somehow omitted as unnecessary the means by which we may be able to raise our own natures to a certain pitch of sublimity '.[20a]   In addition, he scourges relentlessly the false sublimity of bombastic or tasteless writers, and is never deceived by any outward majesty of words which clothe no corresponding elevation of thought, not sparing even to point out the failures of the greatest writers on occasion.

[17] This statement, which used to be made on the bare authority of the commentator Porphyrio on Horace (p. 344, 15, Meyer), has been given new meaning and content by the researches of C. Jensen, *Abhandl. Berlin. Akad.*, 1918, No. 14, who has discovered fragments of Neoptolemos in Philodemos (see p. 410) and approximately determined his date.

[18] So called because it was found in the Codex Coislinianus, a MS. of the tenth century.   It has been published several times (first in Cramer's *Anecdota*), *e.g.*, by Dübner, p. xxvi.

[19] Notice in Suidas, *s.u.* Καικίλιος ; cf. Christ-Schmid, ii, p. 463 *sqq.*

[20] For a temperate and sane discussion, see Roberts, *Longinus*, p. 1 *sqq.* See also G. C. Richards in *C.Q.*, xxxii, p. 133.   [20a] *De sublim.*, 1.

All these good critics, however, although the influence of some of them, notably Dionysios and, it would seem, Caecilius also, on Roman readers was considerable, were unable to check a morbid revival of Asianism blended with the worst affectations of Atticism. Some of the grossest examples of bad taste and artificial puerilities of style were perpetrated in the first three centuries of the Christian era. The sinners were the rhetoricians and their pupils, and the most characteristic form their offence took was the declamation (μελέτη).[21] We have seen (p. 280) that speeches on imaginary topics as a form of rhetorical exercise may be as old as Antiphon ; as exercises, they are perfectly legitimate. But Greek oratory, by the Hellenistic period and still more in the Roman, had lost most of its practical importance, since there were no longer any popular assemblies or great courts of law for a Greek to move to weighty decisions by his eloquence. Apart therefore from loyal addresses, appeals for assistance and other communications with the ruling power, rhetoric became an end in itself, and when not used as an ornament of historical or other books, the declamation was its vehicle. These exhibitions of clever or sensational verbosity were extremely popular with word-loving auditors who no longer had the fine taste of classical Greece, and often were given, not in class-rooms, but before great crowds, in theatres and other public buildings. They were normally of two kinds, *theses* (θέσεις, θετικαὶ ὑποθέσεις), in which, some general question being put forward, one or both sides of a debate on it were maintained by the speaker or speakers (*e.g.*, whether a philosopher ought to take part in politics),[22] and controversies or cases (*causae*) as they were called in Latin, in Greek ὑποθέσεις ἐσχηματισμέναι, where the problem to be debated affected particular persons, real or imaginary. The situation imagined was often most fantastic, as : a certain city offers a reward to tyrannicides. A tyranny having been established, one man hires another to kill the tyrant. Which should have the reward ? Or it might be quasi-historical, thus : Kallimachos the polemarch and Kynegeiros, one of the private soldiers, distinguished themselves at the Battle of Marathon, and were both killed. Supposing that the father of the bravest among the fallen has the right to pronounce the funeral oration over the dead, which of the two fathers concerned should have that privilege now ? POLEMON, who lived, according to Suidas, in and after

---

[21] A good sketch of the revival of Asianism and its relations to Atticism will be found in Schmid, *Atticismus*, i, p. 31 *sqq.*

[22] The definition is from Cicero, *Topica*, 79 ; the controversy is the 382nd of the declamations attributed to Quintilian.

the time of Trajan,[22] has left us speeches for both sides in this case, wherein, so far as brave men dying in a righteous cause can be made tedious and ridiculous, he contrives to do so. His language is meant to be Attic, although his imperfect knowledge betrays him into purely Hellenistic usages now and again.[24] Yet this wretched spouter was considered a most effective speaker, not only by the citizens of Smyrna, where he spent most of his life, but even by Hadrian. He is the earliest surviving representative [25] of the movement generally called the NEW SOPHISTIC, sophist by this time meaning rhetorician. Of its leading authors, concerning whose eloquence Philostratos (see below) gives glowing accounts, but few have come down, and one would willingly exchange them all for one speech of Lysias, save in so far as they here and there throw light on the thought and feeling of their day. Perhaps the most celebrated of them all, for he combined admired eloquence with vast wealth and most public-spirited generosity, was HERODES ATTICUS, or, to give him his full name, VIBULLUS HIPPARCHOS TIBERIUS CLAUDIUS ATTICUS HERODES, of Marathon, 101–177. But one speech ascribed to him survives,[26] and the genuineness of this is not undisputed. Aulus Gellius gives a Latin abstract of another, with a translation of part of it.[27] More has survived of AELIUS ARISTEIDES (died in 189 ; his birth-year may have been 117 or 129),[28] who combined an unusually good knowledge of classical Attic and great diligence in writing speeches (for he was successful neither at extempore orations nor as a teacher) with childish egotism and a singularly un-Greek temperament. The admiration his style excited in later times, when he was regarded almost as one of the classics, has resulted in his works coming down to us fairly complete ; we have in all fifty-five compositions attributed to him, mostly orations, but including some which have the form of letters and half a dozen which are really hymns in prose. He was an invalid

---

[22] Suidas, *s.u.* Πολέμων (b) ; cf. Philostratos, *Vit. Soph.*, i, 25. Polemon was a native of Laodikeia.

[24] As *νῖκος*, *victory*, for *νίκη*, p. 6, 16 Hinck (Teubner ed.) ; θάτερος, τῷ θατέρῳ, pp. 51, 1, 26, 3 ; μή for οὐ with a participle, p. 6, 16.

[25] The earliest that we hear of was Niketes of Smyrna, before and during the time of Nerva, Philostr., *Vit. Soph.*, i, 19.

[26] For the question of authorship, *see* below, p. 424. Text in the Didot *Oratores Attici*, ii, p. 189 *sqq.* For Herodes, see Philostr., *op. cit.*, ii, 1 ; the art. on him by Münscher in Pauly-Wissowa ; Schmid-Stählin, ii, p. 694 *sqq.*

[27] Gellius, xix, 12.

[28] He mentions, *orat.* 50 (Keil), 58, how the planets Jupiter and Mercury and the constellation Leo stood at his birth ; 117 and 129 both fit the data given. For his life, see Philostr., *op. cit.*, ii, 9. Cf. p. 421.

during a great part of his life, and a whole group of his performances describes his long series of attempts to get himself cured by
Asklepios, the dream interviews between himself and the god,
the divine advice as to regimen and medicines, and so forth, in
a fashion which shows him pietistic to the point of superstition,
as well as a hypochondriac.   It is to be noticed that several of his
themes (hymns, laments, rejoicings) are poetical, of kinds once
belonging to the province of Lyric.   His age saw a revival of
Hellenism, partly real, partly the result of governmental encouragement ; Hadrian especially was a great, if somewhat
sentimental Philhellene.   It is unnecessary to pursue the line of
sophists further ; it extends far beyond the limit of this book and
includes such post-classical figures as St. John Chrysostom,
Julian the Apostate, and their teacher Libanios, all of the fourth
century.

   Their biographer, PHILOSTRATOS, claims mention, however.
There were four men of this name, the first absurdly placed by
Suidas [29] in the time of Nero, apparently a mistake arising out
of the attribution to him of the trifling dialogue called *Nero*,
which by a further blunder has come down among the works of
Lucian.   His son, PHILOSTRATOS VERUS, had a son, another
PHILOSTRATOS, also a nephew, Nervianus, whose son, a fourth
PHILOSTRATOS, married the daughter of the third.   The third
lived to the times of Philip the Arab, emperor 244-249 ; he
enjoyed the favour of Julia Domna, wife of Septimius Severus.
Besides the *Lives of the Sophists*, we have a biography, laudatory,
fanciful and quite unreliable, of Apollonios of Tyana, a miracle-
monger and wandering philosopher of the first century A.D.
(*Τὰ ἐς τὸν Τυανέα ᾿Απολλώνιον*) ; two collections of descriptions of
pictures, probably imaginary, prose equivalents of those little
pieces in verse already mentioned (p. 350) ; the *Heroicus*, a
singular performance in which the ghosts of heroes, especially
Protesilaos, favour a respectable old countryman with their
presence and give him remarkable particulars of themselves ;
a collection of *Epistles*, whereof the first sixty-four are not by
Philostratos III, the last nine probably are ; the *Nero*, already
mentioned ; a treatise on gymnastics (*Gymnasticus*), discovered
in 1844 by Menas (Mynas), and now in Paris ; and two lectures
on rhetoric, one of them by Philostratos III.   The proem of the
second collection of picture-descriptions (*Εἰκόνες*) informs us
that it is by Philostratos IV and that the other is by Philostratos I.
Who wrote the sixty-four letters and the other rhetorical lecture

---

[29] Suidas has a notice, none too reliable, of the whole family ; for
a more critical account, see Schmid-Stählin, ii, p. 772 *sqq.*

we do not know ; the *Nero* seems by its style to be the work of Philostratos III, who wrote the rest of the collection.

The chief claim of the non-Philostratean letters to recollection is that they furnished models for Ben Jonson's *Drink to me only* (Nos. 2, 33) and Herrick's *To Anthea* (No. 23). To write letters in the character of a real or imaginary person was a favourite sophistical exercise ; hence not only such frankly fictitious letters as these and the collection of ALKIPHRON (a writer of about Lucian's time, possessed of real ability to express the feelings of the supposed authors of the letters), whose subjects are mostly taken from Attic life of Menander's time, as imagined by him, but also many pretended epistles of notable men, generals, kings, philosophers and so forth. Those of Phalaris are the most notorious, from their famous exposure by Bentley ; some have already been mentioned (pp. 195, 253, 309).

Thoroughly dominated by the sophistic movement and pupil of a sophist of repute, by name Pausanias, was CLAUDIUS AELIANUS, usually known as AELIAN. Though a native of Praeneste, most of whose life was spent in Italy,[30] his literary language at all events was Greek, and he takes a prominent place among the Atticists.[31] He was not an orator, but tried his hand at philosophic and semiphilosophic writing. Two of his works, *On Providence* and *On Special Providences* (Περὶ θείων ἐναργειῶν) are lost ; if we may judge by his surviving treatises, they consisted wholly or chiefly of pious but untrustworthy anecdotes. We have his *Miscellany* (Ποικίλη ἱστορία, *Varia Historia*), partly as he wrote it, partly epitomized, fourteen books of chatty, often silly, always uncritical information, mostly about well-known characters of literary or political history ; a similar work dealing with animals, generally called *De natura animalium*, properly Περὶ ζῴων ἰδιότητος (peculiarity, remarkable feature), which extends to seventeen books and is thought to be somewhat interpolated ; also a few letters supposed to pass between peasants. Since Philostratos gives us to understand that he wrote an invective against Elagabalus, first waiting till that emperor was safely dead, *i.e.*, till 222, his dates would seem to be the late second and first part of the third century.

A contrast to this foolish, if readable anecdote-monger is the really learned ATHENAIOS, the best writer of miscellaneous matter we have left, and the source of an immense amount of information

---

[30] Philostratos, *Vit. soph.*, 31, says Aelian declared he had never left Italy ; Aelian himself, *de nat. anim.*, xi, 40, that he had been in Alexandria, if the passage is not an interpolation or taken verbatim from his (unknown) authority.

[31] Philos., *l.c.* ; Schmid, *Atticismus*, iii, p. 1 *sqq.*

not to be had elsewhere. While it is not to be supposed that he had himself read all the books he quotes, or even a very large proportion of them, his studies must have been extensive. He chose to embody them in a form popular since the fourth century B.C., that of the symposium, and imagines a group of learned men of the day (including Galen and the grammarian Ulpian, him who was nicknamed *Keitoukeitos*, from his habit of inquiring, at every doubtful word, whether it was to be found, κεῖται, or not, οὐ κεῖται, in a classical author, besides some of lesser note) meeting at the house of a friend and dining there. As the meal progresses, they fall to conversing on every subject which can by any stretch of ingenuity be brought into relation with it : fish, vegetables and so forth of every kind ; luxurious habits, especially those of the ancients ; dinner-guests, and so parasites and flatterers, and many other things. All the speakers are credited with prodigious memories, and quote endlessly from a multitude of authors in verse and prose, including many of the lost historians and writers of memoirs and a great number of the lost comedians. The title of the work is Δειπνοσοφισταί, ' the specialists on dining ' (not ' the professors at dinner '). As we have it, there are fifteen books, whereof the first two and part of the third are preserved only in an epitome. His exact date is uncertain, but appears to be about the end of the second century ; his other works, which were partly historical, partly, it would seem, zoological, have not come down to us. He was a native of Naukratis in Egypt.[32]

It is anything but certain that the books we have are as Athenaios wrote them. Apart from slight external evidence (see the *praefatio* to vol. i of Schweighaeuser's edition, p. xv, Schmid-Stählin, ii, p. 791, n. 5) of a fuller form once existing, certain parts of the work as we have it, for instance much of Bk. vii, are so formless as to suggest that they are extracts, not the full text.

Athenaios was by no means alone in his apparently universal curiosity. To name but two others, ALEXANDROS POLYHISTOR, of Miletos, a contemporary of Sulla, got his surname from the width of his knowledge ; his titles (for the text of his work is represented only by fragments) include treatises on the geography and history of various parts of the world, including Judaea, Chaldaea and Rome, also commentaries on poets, including Korinna, an essay on the Pythagorean tabus, another *On the successions of Philosophers*, which Diogenes Laertios used, and a grammatical writing.[33] Hardly less learned was a Gaul, FAVORINUS of Arelate (Arles), the teacher of

---

[32] Athen., 211 a, 329 c ; Suidas, *s.u.* 'Αθήναιος.
[33] His fragments are in *F.H.G.*, iii, p. 206 *sqq*.

Herodes Atticus, a rhetorician of note [34] and also author of two great miscellanies, *Memoirs* ('Ἀπομνημονεύματα) and *The Universal Enquiry* (Παντοδαπὴ ἱστορία) ; the former seems to have consisted of anecdotes concerning philosophers, the latter to have been a kind of encyclopaedia. He may perhaps be regarded as the first of the class of writers to whom Aelian and Athenaios in their different ways belong.

To return to the Second Sophistic, one of its best manifestations was the popular philosophical lecture, a more finished form of the diatribe (see p. 357), of which we have some favourable specimens. Originality is not to be looked for in these works, any more than in the general run of better-class sermons to-day or in the last century ; what we find is a pleasant presentation of views in themselves well-known enough, by men of respectable and amiable character. DION OF PRUSA, surnamed CHRYSOSTOMOS (Golden-Mouth), found Domitian's Rome no place for a philosopher, and set forth on a long series of travels which took him over a great part of the Greek world, including some distant outposts and also the deserted minor towns of Greece proper. He seems to have been received with a good deal of respect, as a learned man and a giver of sound advice. Delivering, in one place after another, popular lectures, sometimes literary, sometimes setting forth a mild type of Stoicism, he was always on the lookout for certain types of virtue which he especially prized, the honesty and simplicity of country people and the Hellenic spirit kept alive in face of barbarism.[35] These activities did not cease after the death of Domitian and the favour which Trajan's government showed him ; until at least 113 (how much longer he lived is not known) he continued to be the apostle of a civilized and, so to speak, Stoicized Cynicism, and also to exert himself for the public good of his own and other Greek cities.

A less important man of similar type was MAXIMUS OF TYRE, the Platonist. His philosophical themes do not differ widely

---

[34] Two speeches attributed to Dion of Prusa, whose pupil he was, are considered to be his, the 37th (the author says he is a Roman knight of Keltic stock, 25, 27, commits a decided Latinism in his syntax, 11, and shows wide reading) and the 64th. Recently a work of his *On exile* has been discovered and published (*Papiro vaticano greco* 11, ed. Norsa and Vitelli, Vatican City, Bibl. apost. vat., 1931). Fragments, *F.H.G.*, iii, 577 *sqq.*

[35] As in the famous *Euboian oration*, No. 7 (13), and the *Borysthenite oration*, No. 36 (19). The standard authority on Dion is J. von Arnim (critical ed., Berlin, Weidmann, 2 vols., 1893 and 1896 ; *Leben und Werke des Dio von Prusa*, Berlin, 1898). For his style, see Schmid, *Atticismus*, i, p. 72 *sqq.*

GREEK LITERATURE IN THE EMPIRE 407

from Dion's, for the differences between the schools do not show strongly in their popular teachings; but he is inferior to him in both style and interest of treatment, while occasional blunders [36] do not give a high idea of the solidity of his learning. Still, there is here and there a note of genuine piety in the man,[37] which, if nothing else, hinders him from being contemptible. His date is the period of the Antonines,[38] and we have forty-one of his ' lectures ' (διαλέξεις) as they are called.

Much more important, however, than any of these philosophizing stylists was a man to whom style was a secondary consideration. PLUTARCH (Πλούταρχος) of Chaironeia [39] (about A.D. 46–120) was born of a good old Boiotian family, several members of which are named affectionately in his works; he married a lady named Timoxena, and was survived, it would seem, by four sons, of whom one, Lamprias, is alleged, but probably falsely, to be the author of a catalogue of his works which survives. A little daughter, named after her mother, died young and gave occasion for one of Plutarch's most touching writings, the *Consolation* addressed to his wife. He was more than once in Rome, partly on public business, and lived there for some years, picking up a smattering [40] of Latin and making good friends among prominent Romans. He made a reputation for himself as a lecturer, especially on philosophical themes; but his best work, so far as it can be dated and placed, was mostly done after

[36] He is of opinion that the Athenian misfortunes in the latter part of the Peloponnesian War were due to their wickedness in putting Sokrates to death (some years after the war was over), *Diss.* 9, end.

[37] Notably *Diss.* 8, end.

[38] Suidas, *s.u. Μάξιμος* (b), says he was in Rome under Commodus.

[39] He represents himself, *de E ap. Delph.*, 385 b, as old enough, when Nero was in Greece (66) to profit by a philosophical discussion; if we suppose him about 20 years old at the time, this will fit the other data well enough. The notice of him in Suidas represents him as having held office under Trajan (98–117), two or three passages in the chroniclers (Eusebios and Synkellos) as being alive in 119. He himself, *de Isid. et Osir.*, 330 b, speaks of armed strife between two Egyptian districts over their respective local cults; if this is the business described, with wild inaccuracies of detail, in Juvenal, *sat.* xv, 27 *sqq.*, as having occurred *consule Iunco, i.e.*, 127, Plutarch must have lived at least till a little after that year, see Parthey, p. 269 of his ed. of the *de Isid.*, where his chronology is vitiated by a false reading in Juvenal, but his general conclusion, that the two events are not the same, is probably right. For his life see, in general, R. Volkmann, *Leben und Schriften des Plutarch von Chaeronea* (2 vols., Berlin, Calvary, 1869); R. Hirzel, *Plutarch*, Leipzig, Dieterich, 1912, chaps. i–x; Christ-Schmid, ii, p. 485 *sqq.* (more literature *ibid.*, n. 6). The principal source is his own works.

[40] For the amount of Latin he knew, see the present writer's *Roman Questions of Plutarch*, Oxford, Univ. Press, 1924, p. 11 *sqq.*

14·

the troublesome reign of Domitian was over, and at Chaironeia, whither he retired, to spend his days quietly in the service of letters, of his country and of his god, for he was one of Apollo's Delphic priesthood and took his duties seriously.

We have a large number of essays, lectures and collectanea, going under the general name of *Moralia*, though by no means all deal with ethics. These include mere debating-themes, as ' Is water or fire the more useful ? ' ; works in the form of question and answer, on the model of the Aristotelian *Problems* (p. 273), of which two, the so-called *Greek Questions* and *Roman Questions*,[41] preserve a great deal of antiquarian knowledge, picked up by Plutarch in the course of his wide reading, while the longest, the Συμποσιακὰ προβλήματα, combines the problem form with the framework of the symposium ; serious discussions of philosophical points, and much else. As might be expected, several works of doubtful authorship, such as a letter of consolation to an unknown Apollonios on the loss of his son, have been included in the collection because of a certain resemblance in tone and subject to Plutarch's own works, while others quite unlike anything he ever wrote have made their way in, the most unlikely being the so-called *Lesser Parallels* (*Parallela Minora*, Συναγωγὴ ἱστοριῶν παραλλήλων), a rubbishy collection of Greek stories, each capped by a Roman one, generally a manifest invention.[42]

Formally, his most famous work belongs to the *Moralia*, for it is a long and elaborate exposition of the theme that, for every Roman that was great either for good or evil, an equally important Greek can be found ; together with the many subsidiary themes which ethical reflections on historical facts must needs suggest. The immortal *Parallel Lives*, addressed to one of his Roman friends, Sosius Senecio, was begun, he tells us (preface to the *Life of Timoleon*), to please others, continued to please himself. He disarms in advance much of the criticism which has been directed against him in modern times by pointing out

---

[41] These two have been commented upon, respectively by Principal W. R. Halliday (*Greek Questions of Plutarch*, Oxford, Univ. Press, 1928) and the author (see last note). Various other of the *Moralia* have been issued separately, more or less well, but on the whole, the collection has been neglected, and a reliable and critical text is but now in process of publication by Teubner.

[42] Latest discussion, I. Schlereth, *de Plutarchi quae feruntur parallelis minoribus*, Freiburg i/B, 1931. He suggests (p. 87) that the compiler happened to begin with an extract from Plutarch, and that the heading of this, ἐκ τῶν Πλουτάρχου διηγήσεων or the like, was mistaken for the title of the whole work.

(preface to the *Life of Alexander*) that he is not writing history, but biography, and that his chief interest is in the characters of those whom he portrays. He might truthfully have added another motive, namely such love of a good story, combined with power to tell it effectively, as had hardly been found since Herodotos. If, then, the reader is looking for exact history, he will often be disappointed ; Plutarch has indeed been at some pains to master the necessary facts, but he had read sympathetically rather than critically, and the value of his narrative, from that point of view, varies with his authority's accuracy and the care with which he has reported him. But if he is content to ask Plutarch for no more than what he professes to give, he will almost certainly join the long line of those who have valued and loved the *Lives* as one of the great books of the world. One advantage to a modern reader who is not well acquainted with Greek is, that being but a moderate stylist, Plutarch is almost as good in a translation as in the original.[43]

The number of the surviving *Lives* is fifty in all, forty-six falling into pairs, each containing a Greek and a Roman, and four others (Artaxerxes II, Aratos, Galba, Otho) which have no counterparts, although the last two probably belong to another series of Lives of the Caesars. These seem to be the result of Plutarch's growing interest in biography. Several are lost (Herakles, Aristomenes, Krates the Cynic, Pindar). The order in which they were written is uncertain,[44] but that they all belong to his maturity or old age seems beyond reasonable doubt.[45]

It will be convenient briefly to mention here the remaining philosophers of this epoch.[46] A very minor writer, once popular in schools because he is highly moral, probably also because it was imagined that he was a contemporary of Sokrates,[47] is KEBES, who has left us a curious little work, *The Painting* (*Πίναξ*), in which human life is set forth in the description of an imaginary allegorical picture. He is guessed to be of about the first century of our era. Somewhat earlier, therefore, is the Epicurean PHILO-

---

[43] For Plutarch's immense posthumous influence, see Hirzel, *op. cit.* chaps. xi *sqq.*

[44] After the rather feeble attempt of Lion, *De ordine quo Plutarchus Vitas scripserit*, Göttingen 1819, two of the most important studies of this subject are Michaelis, *De ordine Vitarum parallelarum Plutarchi*, Berlin, 1875, and Muhl, *Plutarchische Studien*, Augsburg, 1885 ; more in Christ-Schmid, ii, p. 519, n. 8.

[45] He indicates, *Demosth.*, 2, that he was in Chaironeia when he wrote.

[46] Neoplatonism lies outside the scope of this book.

[47] Kebes of Thebes is one of the speakers in the *Phaedo* of Plato.

DEMOS of Gadara, interesting partly because his writings form the
famous library discovered at Herculaneum, and therefore were
among the first papyri studied by modern scholars.   None of
his numerous treatises, dealing with philosophy, music and
literature, is original in contents or has been recovered whole ;
but they preserve a good deal of earlier writings now lost to us,
and have a certain stylistic interest.   The man himself numbered
Vergil and other well-known Augustans among his pupils ; he
probably was born about 110 B.C., and lived till some three years
after Actium.[48]   The Stoics of the Empire are of more importance.
C. MUSONIUS RUFUS, banished under Nero for alleged complicity
in the conspiracy of Piso, A.D. 65, recalled by Galba and banished
again by Titus, wrote nothing that has survived, but we have
fragments, preserved by Stobaios, of notes taken by a listener to
his philosophical lectures.[49]   A treatise on the *Rudiments of
Ethics* ('Ηθική στοιχείωσις) whereof a large part is preserved on a
papyrus, is by a Stoic called HIEROKLES, probably HIEROKLES
OF ALEXANDRIA, about contemporary with Musonius.[50]   A pupil
of Musonius was a certain lame slave, by name EPIKTETOS,
who happened also to be a saint, of the unpretentious and good-
humoured type.   It is fortunate that Arrian (see p. 412) chose
to play Xenophon to his Sokrates, for Epiktetos himself seems
to have written nothing.   From Arrian, however, we have the
teacher's *Diatribes*, setting forth a system in no way original,
for it is popular Stoicism, chiefly ethical, based upon a cheerful
and enthusiastic trust in the Providence in which the lecturer
and his school believed, and abounding in practical advice.
The personality of the author shines through it, and has won
the affection of other Stoics, Neo-Platonists, Christians, Vol-
taireans and men of no particular school, down to the present
day.   Arrian also made, from the *Diatribes*, a little synopsis of
Epiktetos' Stoicism, the *Encheiridion* or Manual, which also is
preserved.[51]   By this time Stoicism had become well established
in Rome, in fact there was a Roman branch, though of no inde-

---

[48] See Christ-Schmid, ii, p. 367, for Kebes, 371 *sqq.* for Philodemos.

[49] The fragments are collected by Hense, Leipzig, 1905.

[50] The papyrus is published in *Berliner Klassikertexte*, vol. iv, 1906.
Stobaios preserves a number of fragments by a Hierokles who is probably
the *Stoicus, uir sanctus et grauis*, of Gellius, ix, 5, 8, and identical with the
author of the στοιχείωσις.   The papyrus being of the second century
A.D., Hierokles the Neo-Platonist (fifth century A.D.) is clearly excluded.

[51] For a list of the diverse readers of Epiktetos, from Herodes Atticus
to the twentieth century, see Christ-Schmid, ii, p. 359 ; it could easily
be made ten times as long, especially as the English readers and translators
of him are not included.

pendent importance, and one member of it, L. ANNAEUS CORNU-
TUS, about contemporary with Musonius and teacher and friend
of the poet Persius, has left us one little work in Greek, a treatise
on the allegorical and etymological interpretation of myths,
bearing the title Ἐπιδρομὴ τῶν κατὰ τὴν Ἑλληνικὴν θεολογίαν
παραδεδομένων or *A sketch of the Greek mythological traditions*.[52]
About a century later, Stoicism produced another saint, an
emperor this time, IMPERATOR CAESAR MARCUS AURELIUS
ANTONINUS AUGUSTUS, to give him his full style. He never
intended, so far as is known, to publish anything on philosophy,
but for his private use he compiled a kind of diary which got about
after his death in 180. It is in no sense a treatise, but simply
what it is perhaps oftenest called in English, *Meditations*, in the
form of addresses to himself on his public and private duties as
seen by the light of Stoicism, sometimes fairly long and orderly,
sometimes hardly more than ejaculations. That he is thought of
along with Epiktetos would not have troubled him, for he was
quite indifferent to the externals of rank, but it probably would
have puzzled him to learn that the Christians whom he despised
and thought it necessary to persecute have ever since furnished
him with admiring readers.[53] The mere fact that both these
Stoic saints have much in common with a religion they had
never studied and owed nothing to shows how the atmosphere
of the world was changing. Classical thought was departing and
giving place to what was to be the medieval mind.

Since the Stoics believed in divination of all kinds and he himself
had some smattering of popular philosophy, ARTEMIDOROS of Daldis
in Lydia (less correctly called an Ephesian) may be mentioned here.
He would appear to have lived some time in the second century A.D.,
and his five books on the interpretation of dreams (*Onirocritica*)
continued to be the foundation of that kind of literature in Europe
from the sixteenth century, when he was translated into modern
languages, till it was discovered that he gave no advice regarding
lotteries.[54]

Although Polybios was the last great historian, history of a
kind was a favourite subject for writers of this period. Some have
incidentally been mentioned ; the fragments of many will be
found in Müller's collection ; the survivors are as follows.

[52] If, that is, the title is his own ; it may quite possibly be added
by some Christian reader, in which case Ἑλληνικὴ θεολογία means ' pagan
theology '.
[53] The title in Greek is usually τῶν εἰς ἑαυτὸν βιβλία.
[54] See the preface to Herscher's edition (Teubner, 1864), and Riess
in Pauly-Wissowa, ii, col. 1334 *sq*.

DIODOROS of Agyrion in Sicily, generally known as DIODORUS
SICULUS, lived under Augustus and set about writing a universal
history, or, as he seems to have called it, a *Historical Library*
(*Bibliotheca*), compiled from the best authorities, both Greek and
Latin, and fitted into a chronological scheme derived from
Apollodoros. Beginning with mythical times—his series of dates
starts with Troy, which fell in 1184 according to his authority—
he brought the work down to 59 B.C.[55] Of the forty books
comprised in the *Bibliotheca* there survive fifteen, with considerable extracts from and fragments of the rest. Diodoros himself
has been well characterized by Macaulay as ' a stupid, credulous,
prosing old ass ';[56] and it goes without saying that the best
which can be expected of him is that he will copy his authorities
correctly, excerpt them not too ill, and arrange events under
the right dates, so far as he knows them. His book is a mine
in which to dig for fragments of better works ; if we had the
older historians, no one would read him.

A much better writer lived in the second century A.D.,
FLAVIUS ARRIANUS, usually called ARRIAN. He was a Roman
citizen, but a native of Nikomedeia in Bithynia ; he served the
State under Hadrian (he was consul suffectus about the twenties
of the century, *legatus Augusti pro praetore* in Kappadokia 131–
137), later retired to Athens, where he was archon in 147 and
died, at latest, about 180.[57] Here he seems to have played
happily at his favourite game of pretending to be Xenophon,
whom he clearly admired beyond measure.[58] We have seen that,
like his model, he wrote memoirs of his philosophical master
(see p. 410) ; these works probably belonged to his early days,
before he became a servant of the State, and his geographical
and tactical writings to the latter period (see pp. 383, 394).
At Athens he set about following his model more closely than
ever. He wrote a treatise on hunting, *Cynegeticus*, evidently
regarding the work on the same subject ascribed to Xenophon
as genuine (p. 309) ; corresponding, presumably, to the *Agesilaus*
were three biographies, two treating of Dion and Timoleon and

[55] This is mostly from Diodoros' own preface ; there is also an article
in Suidas.

[56] Letter to Ellis, Nov. 30, 1836, in Trevelyan's *Life and Letters*,
chap. vi.

[57] Lucian, *Alexandros*, 2, uses language of him which seems to imply
that he is dead ; this work was written not long after 180. This would
give Arrian a long life, for the date of his consulship shows that he must
have been born some time in the first century, possibly about 95.

[58] He actually calls himself Xenophon, *Cyneg.*, 5, 6 ; perhaps also
Ectaxis, 22.

a third, in contrast to his model's unvarying respectability, dealing with a notorious brigand, by name Tilliboros or Tilloboros.[59] These are lost ; but we have Arrian's principal work, the counterpart of the *Anabasis*. Having made no important and venturesome expedition into Asia himself, Arrian was content to describe that of Alexander, giving the work probably the title *'Ανάβασις 'Αλεξάνδρου*.[60] This book, although of course secondary, deriving its facts from writers of Alexander's own date, and not to be followed blindly, is the best account of the matter antiquity has left us, and supremely readable, written in very tolerable imitation Attic. He even produced a counterpart to the *Hellenica, After Alexander (Τὰ μετ' 'Αλέξανδρον)*, in ten books, now lost save for a fragment, also a *History of Parthia* and another of Bithynia (*Παρθικά, Βιθυνιακά*), both lost.

APPIAN (APPIANUS, but his full name is unknown), born in Alexandria, became a civil servant, to use modern terminology, and wrote, about 160,[61] a very respectable history of Rome, in twenty-four books, whereof we have the general preface and eleven books complete, with considerable extracts from some of the rest. His plan was, after three books on the early history of Italy, to take up the rest of the Empire in chronological order of entry into relations with Rome (the Gauls in Book iv, Sicily and the islands in Book v, and so forth), interrupting the series, between the books devoted to Pontos and the Mithridatic War (xii) and to Egypt (xviii–xxi), with five books on the Civil Wars, which still survive and, for want of Appian's authorities, are read. He was in fact yet another compiler, anything but faultless in the use he made of his material, but with sense enough often to follow good, or the best available, authors and usually to be at the trouble of understanding them. His worst defect is that he tries to pack too much into too little space.

Between historian and geographer is PAUSANIAS, author of a work which is still the handbook of every archaeologist. This man must have been born about the end of Trajan's reign and written his book under the early Antonines, to judge by the various chronological references he gives us. He was a native of some place near Mount Sipylos, perhaps Magnesia on the

---

[59] For fragments of his lost works, see *F.H.G.*, iii, p. 586 *sqq*.

[60] The MSS. vary, but the above, being Xenophontic, is much the likeliest for Arrian to have used.

[61] He himself says, about 900 years from the foundation of Rome (753 B.C. + 900 = A.D. 146) and 200 from the foundation of the Empire (if this means Actium, then 31 B.C. + 200 = A.D. 168) ; see his preface 7 and 9.

Maiandros ; [62] he travelled extensively, led, one supposes, by his interest in art and in antiquities, and in particular, he toured the most interesting parts of Greece and described what he saw in the way of ancient monuments, adding historical and mythological disquisitions.[63] The resulting ten books [64] are a storehouse of information, generally accurate as regards the sites, much less so for historical data. The style, Second Sophistic trying to be Herodotean, is none of the best.

This Pausanias is not the same as PAUSANIAS the sophist (see p. 404), who was a native of Caesarea in Kappadokia,[65] although they were contemporaries, nor PAUSANIAS of Damascus (or Antioch), whose date is uncertain ; his fragments are in F.H.G., iv, 467 sqq.

It will have been noticed that some of the historical writers mentioned hitherto were inclined to romance, and certain of the geographers had the same failing. Greek imagination never ceased to be active, and quite late in the history of their literature it found a legitimate outlet in a new form, the novel. This word must be understood rather in the sense of Italian *novella* than in its present-day English acceptation ; the specimens we have are of moderate length, generally amatory, or picaresque, and showing little care for verisimilitude, so long as they remain either exciting or rhetorical. Exactly when they took literary form we do not know. Leading up to them were apparently several tendencies, some of which have already been noticed. There were the rhetorical exercises, which commonly included narrative ; [66] the imaginary voyages, like that of Euhemeros (see p. 368) or the Utopian adventures of IAMBULOS, a writer of uncertain, but Hellenistic date and, to judge by his name, Syrian nationality, who told a tale of happy islands on the Equator where the inhabitants practise a sort of Platonic communism and

[62] Paus., vi, 13, 7.

[63] That all the information is derived from his own observations and inquiries on the spot is highly unlikely ; it has been pointed out that he mentions no monument, however interesting or conspicuous, later than 150 B.C., save recent Imperial benefactions and the like. That he drew upon older descriptions of Greece is nearly as certain as that he did not depend on them solely. See Schmid-Stählin, ii, p. 757.

[64] The first, on Attica, was apparently published separately, see vii, 20, 6. Stephanos of Byzantion, *s.u. Τάμυνα* (p. 600, Meineke), quotes as Παυσανίας ι' περιηγήσεως something which is nowhere in P. ; it is likelier that, as Meineke there suggests, the reference has strayed from another article than that part of P. has been lost.

[65] Philostr., *Vit. soph.*, ii, 13.

[66] Since narrative was an essential part of most forensic speeches it was very natural that it should form a rhetorical exercise, quite apart from the fact that many would-be historians had rhetorical training.

are physically and morally much superior to ourselves ; [67] also the various collections of short amatory narratives of one kind or another, as the mythological compilation of PARTHENIOS, a contemporary and acquaintance of Cornelius Gallus and of Vergil,[68] or the *Milesian Tales* (Μιλησιακά) of ARISTEIDES of Miletos, which became a byword for indecency,[69] we cannot say how justly, for they are lost ; the numerous love-stories in Alexandrian poetry, and the similar episodes, real or fictitious, in historical and quasi-historical works from Herodotos onwards. At all events, by not later than the first century A.D. we find, in a fragmentary form, a romance of a type which is common later, the adventures and reunion of parted lovers. In this case they are Ninos, king of Assyria, and his wife, presumably Semi-ramis, who is a very miracle of chaste modesty ; the cause of their separation is a war which takes him from home and the details of the plot are not recoverable.[70] This tendency to make one of the leading characters semi-historical is found again in CHARITON, whose novel, *Chaireas and Kallirhoe*, seems not to be later than the second century at latest. Kallirhoe is the daughter of the famous Syracusan statesman Hermokrates ; she and Chaireas fall in love with each other at first sight, are married, and then, by a misunderstanding, quarrel violently ; he strikes her, she faints and is supposed dead, but revives in her tomb, is carried off by robbers and sold as a slave, and then follows a series of adventures in which, after showing unheard-of constancy to her husband, she is happily reunited to him in the last of the eight books.[71] XENOPHON OF EPHESOS is probably later, certainly not earlier than Trajan.[72] The hero and heroine of his *Ephesiaca*, Habrokomes and Antheia, are captured by pirates

[67] Preserved in Diod. Sic., ii, 55–60 ; the good Diodoros seems to imagine that it is sober history.

[68] Called Περὶ ἐρωτικῶν παθημάτων, collected from numerous authors in verse and prose, and dedicated to Cornelius Gallus to furnish material for his poems.

[69] See for instance Ovid, *Tristia*, ii, 413–14.

[70] The fragments are preserved on the Berlin papyrus No. 6926 , see Rattenbury in Powell 3, p. 212 *sqq.* ; text and translation at the end of the Loeb ed. of Longus and Parthenios. The papyrus has on the back accounts dating from A.D. 101 ; the style of the writing may very well be of the first century B.C.

[71] The standard work on all these romances (except *Ninos*) is E. Rohde, *Der griechische Roman*, ed. 3, with appendix by Schmid, Leipzig, 1914. Some papyrus fragments indicate a text of Chariton very different from ours ; this may mean (see Schmid-Stählin, ii, p. 809) that the romance had become a chapbook. *See* p. 421.

[72] He mentions (ii, 13, 3) ὁ τῆς εἰρήνης προεστώς, a periphrasis of εἰρηνάρχης, which title is not known before Trajan.

shortly after their wedding, and take but five books to rejoin each other. The story of *Apollonius of Tyre*, the source of the pseudo-Shakesperean *Pericles*, exists for us only in a Latin version of late date and very unclassical style, but resemblances to Xenophon suggest that one was influenced by the other ; the Greek original therefore may have been of about the second century. Another lost romance, that of IAMBLICHOS (not the Neo-Platonic philosopher), is preserved in outline by Photios ; it dates itself (ch. x) as contemporary with Sohaimos king of Armenia, who came to his throne, with Roman help, in 166, and, as it seems to mention Marcus Aurelius as still alive, it presumably was finished before 180. For sheer wild improbability it left the other novels far behind. ANTONIUS DIOGENES is of unknown date ; [73] his characters outdo those of most romancers in the extent of their travels, and he shows a little originality by making his hero and heroine meet each other in Thule, whither the former had gone with his father out of enlightened curiosity, not to escape his enemies. The title was *The marvels beyond Thule*.

Two other romances show very strong influence from the Second Sophistic period, and probably belong to the third century. Of these the better, indeed by far the best of all the Greek novels, is the *Daphnis and Chloe* or *Pastoralia* (Ποιμενικὰ Λεσβιακά) of LONGUS. A boy and a girl, both infants, are found and brought up by kindly rustics living on the island of Lesbos, not far from Mytilene. Named Daphnis and Chloe by their respective foster-parents, they grow up in pastoral surroundings having all the artificial prettiness to be expected of a writer whose ideas of the country probably came for the most part from Theokritos and his successors, and in due course fall in love with each other, but are too innocent to know what love is. Their enlightenment, some not very exciting adventures which befall them, the discovery of their real parents, and their marriage make up the rest of the plot ; but, unlike most of his kind, this novelist had some idea of psychology, and the young lovers are not, like most of these heroes and heroines, simply puppets concerning whom we are to accept the author's assurance that they were swayed by emotions so strong as to resemble a violent illness. The other work which may be assigned to about the same date is the *Aethiopica* of HELIODOROS,[74] a long tale of wonderful adventures,

---

[73] Also preserved in a synopsis by Photios.

[74] That this man was a Christian bishop is a story which Sokrates, *Histor. eccles.*, v, 22, 51 (fifth century) mentions without vouching for it. It has nothing to commend it and would make the novel later than its style warrants ; the tone is wholly pagan.

through which the usual incredibly virtuous heroine passes, sometimes with and sometimes separated from her constant lover Theagenes. She herself is called Charikleia, and is really the long-lost daughter of the king of Ethiopia ; a sage from Egypt, by name Kalasiris, exerts himself to forward their interests, and the tenth and last book ends with the marriage of the much-tried pair.

It is worth mentioning that the Greek original of Dıktys, an alleged contemporary account of the Trojan War, preserved in a much later Latin version,[75] seems to belong to the second century A.D. Whether Diktys' companion author Dares had a Greek original or not is uncertain.

When so much rhetoric was taught, it is not surprising that we find rhetorical treatises surviving. The chief of them are due to Hermogenes of Tarsos, who, after appearing before the public as an infant prodigy, lost most of his talent for declamation in later life. His birth may have been about 160.[76] While still quite young, he began to write on the theory of his art, and there are preserved his works Προγυμνάσματα, Περὶ τῶν στάσεων, Περὶ ἰδεῶν, Περὶ εὑρέσεως, dealing respectively with preliminary exercises in rhetoric, types of argument to be used, especially for the defence, different kinds of style, and choice of subject-matter. These are mostly technical manuals for students, showing little or no originality (much of what he says has been traced to Hermagoras, a rhetorician of the second century B.C.) and of next to no worth for anything they have to say on literary criticism.

Finally, we may conclude this sketch by discussing an author who, although not Greek by birth, summed up in himself a remarkable number of the factors which produced, not only Hellenistic, but to some extent classical Greek literature. Lucian (Lucianus) of Samosata was an extremely clever and witty man, blessed or cursed with a hatred of shams so intense as to incline him strongly, not merely to Cynicism in the ancient sense, but to what we commonly understand by the term. Neither his dates nor the order of all his works can be exactly determined, but he was born probably before 120 and was still alive in 180.[77] His native city being in Syrian Kommagene, presumably his mother tongue

[75] The Greek original, previously suspected to have existed, formed the contents of the roll whereof Tebtunis Papyr., 268, is a fragment.

[76] He exhibited, when 15 years old, before Marcus Aurelius, who was then emperor (Philostr., V.S., ii, 7, cf. Cassius Dio, lxxi, 1, 2) ; a likely date for this would be 176, when Marcus and Commodus were in the East.

[77] He lived ' under Trajan and later ' according to Suidas, which would put his birth not after 117.

was either Syriac or some other Asiatic speech ; [78] at best, a half-Greek patois. Originally intended for a sculptor, he soon left that profession and contrived to secure an extraordinarily good knowledge of Greek (of all the Atticists, he is the one who handles the language most nearly as if it were his own),[79] was trained as a rhetorician [80] and for some time followed that career. Afterwards, his inborn hatred of insincerity filled him with a dislike for the unreal vapourings of the Second Sophistic, and he turned to philosophy, apparently taking up his residence for a while in Athens, when about 40 years old.[81] A really profound philosopher he never was and probably never wished to be ; he felt more or less sympathy with all the less dogmatic schools, notably the Academics, Skeptics and Cynics, and had at least this in common with the Epicureans, that he entertained a most hearty contempt for all forms of supernaturalism, which to him were either superstition or fraud.[82] Later in life, he took up a governmental post in Egypt,[83] which seems not to have carried with it duties so exacting as to leave him no time for writing, for some of his best works belong to this period. His fondness for philosophy, such as it had been, did not last, or at all events did not involve anything but contempt for the philosophers of his own time.

His works cannot be sharply divided into periods ; we may say, however, that those which partake most of the nature of declamations belong generally to the earliest part of his career, those with the most pronouncedly philosophic tone to the middle, and some of his fiercest criticisms of everything to the last phase. We have 132 pieces bearing his name, besides some epigrams ; many are either certainly or probably not his, but subtracting these, the remainder fall into the following classes.

1. *Rhetorical exercises*, such as the two speeches entitled *Phalaris* (I, Phalaris tyrant of Akragas sends his famous bull as

[78] He could not speak Greek in his youth, *bis accus.*, 27 ; for his native place, see *de histor. conscrib.*, 24.

[79] For his early life, see his own account in the *Somnium*, which, however, is not to be taken too literally. For his language, see Schmid, *Atticismus*, i, p. 216 *sqq*.

[80] Suidas, *Λουκιανὸς Σαμοσατεύς*, says he was an advocate in Antioch ; Lucian himself never mentions this.

[81] See *bis accus.*, 31 ; his wife Rhetoric having turned harlot, he was compelled to leave her. For his age, see *Hermotimus*, 13.

[82] This includes Christianity, of which he shows no first-hand knowledge ; see *de morte Peregrini*, 11 *sqq*., a passage which moves his scholiast (p. 216 *sqq*., Rabe) to an amusing burst of indignant eloquence, while Suidas *loc. cit.* is certain Lucian is damned.

[83] This action is the subject of his *Apologia*.

an offering to Delphoi ; II, one of the Delphians advises accepting it), the *Tyrannicide*, the *Disowned Son* ('Aποκηρυττόμενος) and a few more ; one or two are quite late, such as the *Apology for a Wrong Greeting* ('Υπὲρ τοῦ ἐν τῇ προσαγορεύσει πταίσματος ; it is a mock-serious defence of his conduct to a senior official, to whom he had said ' good-bye ' instead of ' good-day '). These differ from the common run of sophistic performances mostly by their greater cleverness.

2. *Works on literary subjects.* These vary a great deal in length and importance. Some are witty trifles, such as the *Trial before the Vowels* (Δίκη φωναέντων), in which Sigma accuses Tau of violent abstraction of property, viz., all those words which are pronounced with *ss* in most dialects, *tt* in Attic,[84] or the *Lexiphanes*, a farcical attack on extreme Atticists who crowded their works with long obsolete words used in forced senses.[85] Others, despite their familiar, even jocular tone, are serious contributions to criticism ; better advice to a would-be historian has seldom been given than that contained in the little tractate *How to write History* (Πῶς δεῖ ἱστορίαν συγγράφειν). Here we may include the parody on such works as that of Iambulos (p. 414), the *True Story* ('Αληθὴς ἱστορία), which justifies its title by informing the reader at the beginning that everything else in it is a lie, and then goes on to take a band of adventurers through most extraordinary and dangerous regions, including the moon and the belly of a prodigious sea-monster.

3. *Quasi-philosophic treatises.* These are perhaps Lucian's most characteristic works. Many of them are in dialogue form, and of these a number confessedly owe much to Menippos (see p. 358), who is introduced into more than one of them. Lucian appears in person in several, thinly disguised as Lykinos, or simply as ' the Syrian '.[86] One, which is not a dialogue, is a biography of the otherwise obscure Cynic Demonax,[87] held up as a pattern of rugged philosophical virtue. In this class we may include the famous *Dialogues of the Dead*, curious and grimly funny little sketches, the moral of which is usually the vanity of human pride and wealth, with their pendants, the *Charon* and the

[84] This was of course due to an Atticist revival of the classical Athenian pronunciation. Steele may have got the idea for his *Humble Petition of Who and Which* (*Spectator*, No. 78) from it.

[85] This served Ben Jonson for the model of one of the funniest scenes in *The Poetaster* (Act V, Scene 1, the vomiting episode).

[86] To go under a Greek name suggesting or translating one's own was a common custom of Hellenized foreigners.

[87] A contemporary, according to Lucian ; he had written the life of another worthy, Sostratos (*Demon.*, 1), which however is lost.

Descent into Hades (Κατάπλους), whereof the former is Charon's comments on the odd doings of mankind, as exhibited by Hermes, the latter shows an average boat-load on its way across the Styx, and the reception of the passengers in the other world. Here also belongs the *Menippos*, otherwise called Νεκυομαντεία, in which the philosopher has visited Hades and comes back to tell a friend what he saw there. One recurrent theme in all these and many other of Lucian's works is the outspoken dislike of the rich and their ways ; this is found, for example, in one of the best of the dialogues, the famous *Cock*, in which Mikyllos the cobbler is instructed, to his great surprise and edification, by his own fowl, which had, in a former existence, been Pythagoras. Other dialogues contain witty negative criticism, for example the *Ikaromenippos* (on the unprofitable disputes of philosophers), the *Confutation of Zeus* (the inconsistency between the doctrines of fate and of the divine free will), the *Sale of Lives* (satire against the various philosophic schools) and its pendant, the *Fisher* (Lucian explains that his quarrel is with the unworthy representatives of philosophy only).

4. *Satirical* dialogues, apart from those of the philosophic group, are numerous, and with them go two remarkable biographies. Some of these are hardly more than sketches of common life, as the *Dialogues of Courtesans*, full, like much that he wrote, of reminiscences of Comedy.[88] Some satirize contemporary life, as the violent attack *Against an ignorant book-buyer* and the savage picture of contemporary Roman society, *Concerning hired companions*, a Juvenalian account of the miseries of hangers-on of great houses. The most notable of this group, however, are the attacks on various religious movements, new and old, ranging from the mild burlesques of conventional mythology in the *Dialogues of the Gods* to the bitterly hostile biographies of two religious innovators, Alexandros of Abonuteichos and Peregrinos. They probably include, for the Lucianic authorship of it is not quite certain, the curious description of an Oriental worship, *Concerning the Syrian Goddess*, written in Ionic and probably meant to be a parody on the many popular accounts (ἀρεταλογίαι) of the miracles of deities.

5. *Miscellaneous* writings, which fall under none of the above classes, include a novel, *Lucius, or the Ass*, apparently a remodelling of an older work by a certain Lucius of Patrai, who seems also to have been the original upon whom Apuleius drew in his *Metamorphoses*.

We thus find in Lucian traces of all the principal tendencies

[88] So he himself claims, *bis accus.*, 33.

of prose writing after the classical epoch ; when it is added that he had a wide knowledge of the earlier literature, especially Homer and the Attic authors, and that he seems, besides his prose, to have written a little verse (two [89] burlesque tragedies, *Tragic Gout, Τραγῳδοποδάγρα*, and *Okypus* [Swiftfoot, a parody on the name of Oidipus], have come down to us), it is clear that this Syrian, besides being the last writer in whom a genuinely Greek spirit is to be found, was a sort of compendium of the literature of his adopted culture.

His is the last age which we need consider. Books in Greek continued and still continue to be written ; but, whatever their merits, their tone is not that of classical Greece, or even a modification of it.

[89] Or two parts of one, see F. Friedrichsmeier, *De Luciani re metrica,* diss., Kiel, 1889, p. 2 *sqq.*

ADDITIONAL NOTE 1

Aristeides (see p. 402) also wrote some verse, of which we have a fragment, see O. Kern, *Religion der Griechen*, III, 265, note 5,267 and refs. there.

ADDITIONAL NOTE 2

The best edition of Chariton is by Warren E. Blake, Oxford 1938.

ADDENDA

P. 7, note 15. Recent investigations by M. Ventris and J. Chadwick make it probable that a Cretan system (Linear B) was used to some extent by the Mycenaeans for writing Greek. See Ventris-Chadwick in *J.H.S.*, lxxiii (1953), 84–103 ; Sterling Dow in *A.J.A.*, lviii (1954), 73–154.

P. 12, note 30a. The conventional name for the author of a Byzantine lexicon, properly ἡ Σοῦδα. See *Oxford Classical Dictionary*, art. *Suidas*.

P. 28, note 24. The lamp in itself would not invalidate the passage. Although lamps were not made in Greece in Homeric times, Minoan examples exist, and it is not unreasonable to suppose that some were preserved and their use known at shrines of so old a goddess as Athena.

P. 62, note 13. The theory several times put forward that the Homeric verse is imitated from the Hesiodic seems to me merely absurd.

P. 71, note 50. Add to Kern's list W. K. C. Guthrie, *Orpheus and Greek Religion* (Methuen, 1935), Rose in *Greek Poetry and Life* (Oxford, 1936), pp. 79–96, I. M. Linforth, *The Arts of Orpheus* (Berkeley, Cal., Univ. of California Press, 1941).

P. 94, note 36. For her (probably Asianic) name see further G. Zuntz in *Museum Helveticum* viii (1951), pp. 12–35.

P. 97. See further D. L. Page, *Sappho and Alcaeus* (Oxford, Clarendon Press, 1955), especially pp. 110–46 for Sappho's character.

P. 105, note 6. See further D. L. Page, *Alcman : the Partheneion* (Oxford, Clarendon Press, 1951).

P. 112, note 35. The same accusation of avarice was brought against Pindar, see, e.g., schol. on *Isth.* v, 2a (iii p. 242, 9 *sqq.* Dr.).

P. 116, note 56. Lobel's views, however, are supported by D. L. Page, *Corinna* (London, Hellenic Society, 1953).

P. 141. For the archaeology of the theatre, see (Sir) A. W. Pickard-Cambridge, *The Theatre of Dionysus in Athens*, Oxford, 1946.

P. 145. For the many uncertainties relating to the dramatic contests at the Great Dionysia, see J. T. Allen, *University of California Publications*, xii (1938), pp. 35–42. For the known facts, see Sir A. W. Pickard-Cambridge, *The Dramatic Festivals of Athens* (Oxford, Clarendon Press, 1953), p. 79 *sqq.*

P. 149, note 63. Much has been made of a recently discovered scrap of papyrus, Oxyrhynchus Papyri No. 2256, frag. 3, which states that under some archon whose name is lost two plays of the *Suppliants* tetralogy were acted with a play or plays known to be much later than the dates above suggested. To me this discovery tells us merely what we knew already, that Aeschylean tragedies were sometimes revived after the poet's death. It is quite outweighed by the overwhelming internal evidence that the *Suppliants* is early and comparatively crude work.

P. 152, note 72. For reasons which I discuss in my *Commentary on the Surviving Plays of Aeschylus*, Vol. i, p. 8 *sqq.*, I now believe the *Prometheus* to be the latest surviving play of Aeschylus, produced during his second visit to Sicily.

P. 156, note 80a. A papyrus fragment of this play is now extant; see D. L. Page, *Greek Literary Papyri I*, pp. 8–11.

P. 157. A considerable fragment of the *Diktyulkoi* is now known, and will be found in D. L. Page, *Greek Literary Papyri* i, p. 10 (part of the former play) and the Appendix to the second and revised edition of the Loeb Aeschylus (fuller text of *Diktyulkoi;* large fragment of *Isthmiastai*). Both are satyr-plays; in the former, Danae and her baby come ashore on Seriphos and are received, among other persons, by Seilenos, who is much attracted by her. In the latter, the Satyrs visit the temple of Poseidon at the Isthmus and resolve to appear as competitors in the Games.

P. 157, note 82a. Papyrus fragments have restored a considerable portion of the *Isthmiastai*, see J. C. Kamerbeek in *Mnemosyne*, S. iv. vol. viii (1955), pp. 1–13.

P. 158. On the new fragment of the *Niobe*, see further Pfeiffer in *Philologus*, 1934, p. 1 *sqq.*; page, *op. cit.*, pp. 2–9.

P. 168, note 116. It is, however, true that a snake of the viperine kind may cause a septic condition which takes a long time to heal; a correspondent instances four months in one case.

P. 175. For a different view of the σφυροκόποι, see M. P. Nilsson in *Arch. f. Religionswissenschaft*, xxxii, p. 134 *sqq.* On the *Skyrians*, see Pfeiffer in *Philologus*, 1933, p. 1 *sqq.*

P. 195, note 40. For proof of this, see Ed. Fraenkel in *Studi in onore di Ugo Enrico Paoli* (Florence, Le Monnier, 1955), pp. 295–304.

P. 218. For Kratinos, see Th. M. F. Pieters, *Cratinus : bijdrage tot de geschiedenis der vroeg-attische comedie* (Leiden, Brill, 1946 ; in Dutch with synopsis in French). On the *Dionysalexandros, see* also G. Méautis in *Rev. ét. anc.*, xxxvii, 462–66.

P. 249. In April 1959 there was published at Geneva a long-awaited play of Menander, found practically complete on a papyrus apparently of the third century A.D., which once formed part of a volume containing several plays by the same author. It is an early work (Lenaia of 317 B.C.) and its plot and action differ a good deal from those of the plays outlined above. Comparison with previously known fragments make it certain that it is the Δύσκολος (*Ill-natured Man*). The scene is the Attic country-side, near a shrine of Pan. On a farm close by lives Knemon, a man of morose temper who shuns all society and lives alone with his daughter and an old slave-woman, Simike. He is separated from his wife, who lives not far off with her son by a former marriage, Gorgias. Pan, pleased with the girl's intelligence and virtue, causes a rich young Athenian, Sostratos, to fall in love with her at sight, but his attempts at honourable advances are frustrated by the savagery of her father. After sundry complications, not very interesting, Knemon falls down his well while attempting to recover a vessel and a mattock which have been dropped into it. Gorgias, aided by Sostratos, who has been trying to pass himself off as a hard-working farm-labourer, and therefore less likely to incur Knemon's wrath than a dandified townsman, hauls him out, very exhausted, whereat he retires to bed. Having, however, a certain amount of gratitude for his preservation, he consents to the marriage of his daughter and Sostratos, whose father meanwhile has appeared and is persuaded to allow a double wedding, Gorgias to marry Sostratos' sister. The play ends with the wedding-feast, in which Knemon, willy-nilly, is obliged to join.

On the whole it is rather a poor play, with no great skill shown in the character-drawing and not much distinction of language or action. Still, it is to be remembered that its author can hardly as yet have come to his full powers.

P. 252. I discuss the new fragment of Sophron in *Eclogues of Vergil* (Berkeley and Los Angeles, 1942), pp. 2, 221. *See* also N. Festa in *Mondo classico*, ii, 476–84.

P. 256. *See* W. H. S. Jones, *Hippocrates and the Corpus Hippocraticum*, in *Proc. Brit. Acad.*, xxxi (1945).

P. 266. Strong arguments against the genuineness of *Alcibiades I* are adduced by J. Bidez, *Eos, ou Platon et l'Orient* (Brussels, 1945), chap. xiii.

P. 280, note 80. There is a recent defence of the genuineness of the *Tetralogies* by G. Zuntz in *Museum Helveticum*, vi (1949), pp. 100–3.

P. 282. The authenticity of this speech is defended by A. Schroff, *Zur Echtheitsfrage d. vierten Rede des Andokides*, diss., Erlangen, 1901. But see A. R. Brown in *Class. Quart.*, N.S. iv (1954), pp. 138–42.

P. 286. For a good exposition of Isokrates, *see* W. Jaeger, *Paideia III* (Oxford, 1945), 45–155.

P. 292. *See* further W. Jaeger, *Demosthenes, the Origin and Growth of his Policy*, Berkeley, California, 1938.

P. 301, note 157. It is pointed out by G. C. J. Daniels, *Religieushistorische studie over Herodotus* (Antwerp-Nijmegen, 1946), p. 31, that Herodotos never in his own person expresses belief in this doctrine.

P. 314. For the cultural level of the Greeks at this epoch, see M. P. Nilsson, *Die hellenistische Schule* (Munich, Beck, 1955).

P. 339. E. Lobel has published (*Proc. Brit. Acad.*, xxxv, 1949, pp. 207–16), a papyrus fragment of a drama on the story of Gyges (Hdt. i, 7), Alexandrian in metre, which may be by one of the Pleiad or a contemporary.

P. 369, note 68. The apologists, Greek and Latin, had for the most part read neither Euhemeros nor Ennius for themselves. See J. W. Schippers, *De Ontwikkeling der Euhemeristische Godencritiek in de Christelijke Latijnse Literatur* (Diss., Groningen, 1952).

P. 396, line 6 from below. Babrios cannot be later than the second century A.D., for Oxyrhynchus Papyrus No. 1249, in Vol. X of that collection, which is part of a copy of the fables, is in a handwriting not later than 200. He may of course be earlier.

P. 402. H. T. Wade-Gery, in *C.Q.*, **xxxix** (1945), p. 19 *sqq.*, reviews the various suggestions regarding the authorship and is inclined to think it may be by Kritias (see pp. 207, 211).

BIBLIOGRAPHY

To give a complete bibliography would be impossible ; all that is attempted here is to list a few works which the author has found particularly useful.

(1) AUTHORS

Practically all the authors mentioned are contained in one or more of the following series : the Didot editions (Firmin Didot, Paris, various dates), with Latin versions. Some of these texts are now antiquated. The *Bibliotheca scriptorum Graecorum et Romanorum Teubneriana* (Teubner, Leipzig and Berlin, various dates). The newer volumes have good critical notes and introductions, and generally represent the latest scholarship. The *Bibliotheca classica Oxoniensis* (Oxford, Clarendon Press, various dates ; usually good). The Loeb series, with English translations (Heinemann, London, and Putnam's Sons, New York ; rapidly adding new volumes. Quality of texts and translations varies greatly). *Collection des Universités de France* (Les Belles Lettres, Paris ; the Budé series) ; texts, usually good, with French translations. Numerous editions and commentaries are mentioned in the footnotes ; the following will be found of service.

Abel, *see* Orphica.

Aeschylus, *see* Wilamowitz-Moellendorff.

Alexandrian poets. *Collectanea Alexandrina: Reliquiae minores Poetarum Graecorum aetatis Ptolemaicae* . . . edidit Iohannes U. Powell. Oxford, Clarendon Press. 1925. (' Powell, *C.A.*')

Alkaios, *see* Lyric.

Aristophanes, scholia on. *Scholia Graeca in Aristophanem, cum prolegomenis grammaticorum.* Fr. Dübner. Didot, 1843. (' Dübner.') W. G. Rutherford, *Scholia Aristophanica*, Macmillan, 1896.

Bergk, *see* Lyric.

Comedians. *Comicorum Atticorum fragmenta*, edidit Theodorus Kock. Teubner, 3 vols., 1880–8. (' Kock.')

Comicorum Graecorum fragmenta, i, 1 (all published). Ed. G. Kaibel. Berlin, 1899. (' Kaibel.')

Supplementum comicum : comoediae Graecae fragmenta post editiones Kockianam et Kaibelianam reperta uel indicata collegit . . . Ioannes Demiańczuk. Cracow, 1912. (' Demiańczuk.')

Critics. *Dionysius of Halicarnassus, The Three Literary Letters* (' L.L.'), 1901 ; *Dion. Hal., On Literary Composition*, 1910 ; *Demetrius, On Style*, 1902 ; *Longinus, On the Sublime*, 1907. All ed. by W. Rhys Roberts ; the second pub. Macmillan, the rest Camb. Univ. Press.

Demiańczuk, *see* Comedians.

Diehl, *see* Lyric.

Diels, *see* Philosophers.

Elegiac poets, *see* Lyric.

Epic (post-Homeric). *Epicorum Graecorum fragmenta, collegit, etc.*, Godefredus Kinkel. Vol. i (all published), Teubner, 1877. *See also* the last volume of Allen's *Homeri Opera* (Bib. class. Oxon.) (' Kinkel ', ' Allen.')

F.H.G., *see* Historians.

F.Ph.G., *see* Philosophers.

Frazer, *see* Pausanias.

G.G.M. Geographi Graeci minores, e codicibus recognouit, prolegomenis, annotatione, indicibus instruxit, &c., Carolus Müllerus. Didot, 1882. 2 vols. (' Müller.')

Halliday, *see* Plutarch.

Hesiod. *Hesiod, Works and Days,* ed. T. A. Sinclair. Macmillan, 1932.

Hesiod, scholia on. In Vol. iii of Gaisford, *Poetae minores Graeci*, Oxford, Clarendon Press, 1820, by the pages of which they are quoted.

Historians. *Fragmenta Historicorum Graecorum, collegit, disposuit, notis et prolegomenis illustrauit* Carolus Müllerus. Didot, various dates ; 4 vols. (' *F.H.G.*', ' Müller.')

Fragmente der griechischen Historiker. Felix Jacoby ; Berlin, Weidmann, 1925— (' F. Gr. Hist.', ' Jacoby.') [1]

Das Marmor Parium, herausgegeben und erklärt von F. Jacoby. Berlin, Weidmann, 1904.

Hudson-Williams, *see* Lyric.

Hunt, *see* Tragedy.

Iambic poets, *see* Lyric.

Jebb, Jebb-Pearson, *see* Tragedians.

Kallimachos (fragments) ; R. Pfeiffer, *Callimachus I*, Oxford, 1949.

Kern, *see* Orphica.

Lobel, *see* Lyric.

Lyric, elegiac and iambic poets.

Poetae lyrici Graeci, recensuit Theodorus Bergk. Fourth ed., Teubner, 1882, reprinted 1914–15. Contains Pindar, Theognis, and the fragments of the others, so far as then known. (' *P.L.G.*', ' Bergk.')

Anthologia Lyrica Graeca, edidit Ernestus Diehl. Teubner, 2 vols., 1924–25. (' Deihl.')

ΑΛΚΑΙΟΥ ΜΕΛΗ. The Fragments of the Lyrical Poems of Alcaeus. Edgar Lobel, Oxford, Clar. Press, 1927. (' Lobel, *A. M.*')

---

[1] Here and elsewhere, a date followed by a dash signifies a work in several volumes, as yet incomplete.

Early Greek Elegy : elegiac fragments of Callinus (&c.) T. Hudson-Williams. Cardiff and London, 1926.

The Elegies of Theognis. T. Hudson-Williams. London, Bell, 1910.

ΣΑΠΦΟΥΣ ΜΕΛΗ. *The Fragments of the Lyrical Poems of Sappho.* Edgar Lobel, Oxford, Clar. Press, 1925 (' Lobel. Σ. Μ.')

Mullach, *see* Philosophers.

Müller, *see* F.H.G., G.G.M., Historians.

Orphica. *Orphica, recensuit* Eugenius Abel. *accedunt Procli hymni, &c.* Leipzig, Freytag, and Prague, Tempsky, 1885.

Orphicorum fragmenta, collegit Otto Kern. Berlin, Weidmann, 1932.

Pausanias. *Pausanias' Description of Greece, translated with a commentary* by (Sir) J. G. Frazer. 6 vols., Macmillan, 1898.

Philosophers.

Fragmenta philosophorum Graecorum, collegit, &c., F. G. A. Mullachius. 3 vols., Didot, 1860–81. (' Mullach.')

Fragmente der Vorsokratiker, griechisch und deutsch, Hermann Diels; 6th ed., 3 vols., Berlin, Weidmann, 1951–52, revised by Walther Kranz. ('F.d.V.', 'Diels.')

See also notes 33 and 43 to chapter xi.

Plutarch. The *Lives* are cited by title and chapter ; the *Moralia,* by the pages (number and letter) of Xylander's edition, reproduced on the margin of the Teubner and other texts. See also notes 40 and 41 to chapter xiii.

Sophokles, *see* Tragedians.

Tragedians.

Tragicorum Graecorum fragmenta recensuit Augustus Nauck. Ed. 2, Teubner 1889. (' Nauck ', ' T.G.F.')

Sophocles, the Plays and Fragments : with critical notes, commentary, and translation in English verse. By (Sir) R. C. Jebb. Cambridge, Univ. Press, 7 vols. (plays only). 1883–1907. (' Jebb.')

The Fragments of Sophocles, edited with additional notes from the papers of Sir R. C. Jebb and Dr. W. G. Headlam, by A. C. Pearson. Same publisher, 1917 ; 3 vols.

Tragicorum Graecorum fragmenta papyracea nuper reperta, recognouit A. S. Hunt. Oxford, Clar. Press, 1912.

(2) MODERN WORKS

Of these, two [2] stand by themselves as indispensable, and reference to them is to be assumed even when not given in the notes. They are : (a) The revision of von Christ's *Geschichte der griechischen Literatur* by W. Schmid, together with the rewriting of it by him

[2] A third of great value has just begun to appear, too late for more than occasional reference in this work. It is : C. Cessi, *Storia della letteratura greca dalle origini all' età di Giustiniano,* vol. i, pte. i, Torino, Società editrice internazionale, 1933. (' Cessi.') The *Oxford Classical Dictionary* (O.C.D.), Oxford 1949, contains many relevant articles.

together with O. Stählin. At present the two supplement each other. *Geschichte der griechischen Literatur*, von Wilhelm Schmid und Otto Stählin, Part. I, Vols. i and ii (separate pagination ; Beck, Munich, 1929 and 1934 respectively), abbreviated to ' Schmid-Stählin I ', is continued by the latter part of *W. von Christ's Gesch. d. gr. Lit., bearbeitet* von W. Schmid, sechste Auflage, (same publisher, 1912 ; ' Christ-Schmid, i ') and the second volume of Christ-Schmid, *die nachklassische Periode d. gr. Lit. von* 320 *vor Christus bis* 100 *nach Christus* (same publisher, 1920) by the final volume of Schmid-Stählin (A.D. 100–530). (*b*) *Paulys Realenzyklopädie der klassischen Altertumswissenschaft, neue Bearbeitung, begonnen von* . . . Georg Wissowa . . . *herausgegeben von* . . . Wilhelm Kroll und Karl Mittelhaus : Stuttgart, Metzler, 1893— (' Pauly-Wissowa ', ' R.-E.'). Other works (as those of Aly, Bowra, Couat, Jebb, Mahaffy, Murray, Susemihl), containing either short accounts of the whole subject or separate treatment of some period, will be found in the catalogue of almost any library.[1] The following treat of matters touched upon in various chapters of this book.

Barber, *see* Powell.

Bentley, Richard. *Dissertation on the Epistles of Phalaris : Dissertations upon the Epistles of Themistocles, Socrates, Euripides, and Others ; and the Fables of Aesop.* Ed. R. Wagner, London, Bohn, 1883 ; cited by Wagner's pages and those of the original editions, from his margin.

Bérard, Victor. *Introduction à l'Odyssée*, Paris, Les Belles Lettres, 3 vols., 1924–5. Large Homeric bibliography. *L'Odyssée, ' poésie homérique '*, same publishers, 3 vols., 1924 (text, translation, notes).

Bowra, (Sir) C. M. *Tradition and Design in the Iliad*, Oxford, Clar. Press, 1930.

Cahen, Emile, *Callimaque et son oeuvre poétique*, Paris, Boccard, 1929. *Les hymnes de Callimaque, commentaire explicatif et critique*, same publisher, 1930. .

Cauer, Paul. *Grundfragen der Homerkritik, dritte* . . . *Auflage*, Leipzig, Hirzel, 2 vols. with continuous pagination, 1921 and 1923. (' Cauer ³.')

C.Q. *Classical Quarterly*, London, 1906—.

C.R. *Classical Review*, London, 1886—.

Deubner, Ludwig. *Attische Feste*, Berlin, Keller, 1932.

Dornseiff, Franz. *Die archaische Mythenerzählungen ; Folgerungen aus dem homerischen Apollonhymnus*, Berlin and Leipzig, de Gruyter, 1933.

Farnell, L. R. *Cults of the Greek States*, Oxford, Clar. Press, 5 vols., 1896–1909. (' C.G.S.') *Greek Hero-Cults and Ideas of Immortality*, same pub., 1921.

Finsler, G. *Homer in der Neuzeit von Dante bis Goethe.* Teubner, 1912.

---

[1] In 1957–58 appeared at Berne (Francke Verlag) an admirable *Geschichte der griechischen Literatur* by Albin Lesky, remarkable for its abundance of information in comparatively little space (827 pp.) and soundness of judgement.

Haigh, A. E. *The Tragic Drama of the Greeks*, Oxford, Clar. Press, 1896.
The Attic Theatre, 3rd ed., revised by Pickard-Cambridge, same
pub., 1907.
Hardie, W. R. *Res Metrica : an Introduction to the study of Greek
and Roman Versification*, Oxford, Clar. Press, 1920.
Heiberg, I. L. *Geschichte der Mathematik und Naturwissenschaften
im Altertum*, Munich, Beck, 1925.
J.H.S. *Journal of Hellenic Studies*, London, 1880—.
J.R.S. *Journal of Roman Studies*, London, 1911—.
Kenyon, Sir F. G. *Books and Readers in Ancient Greece and Rome.*
Oxford, Clar. Press, 1932.
Kern, Otto. *Die Religion der Griechen*, Berlin, Weidmann, 3 vols.,
1926–38.
Kieckers, E. *Historische griechische Grammatik*, Berlin and Leipzig,
de Gruyter, 4 vols., 1925–6.
Kirchhoff, A. *Die homerische Odyssee und ihre Entstehung. Text und
Erläuterungen*, Berlin, Hertz. Ed. 1 (' Kirchhoff ¹ '), 1859 ; ed. 2
(' Kirchhoff ² '), 1879.
Kühner-Blass. *Ausführliche Grammatik der griechischen Sprache*, von
Dr. Raphael Kühner. 3ᵉ Auflage . . . besorgt von Dr. F. Blass.
Hannover, Hahn. 2 vols., 1890–2.
Kühner-Gerth. Vols. 3 and 4 of same, revised by Dr. B. Gerth,
1898 and 1904.
Lachmann, Karl. *Betrachtungen über Homers Ilias, mit zusätzen von
Moritz Haupt*. 2ᵉ Auflage, Berlin, Reimer, 1865.
Lang, Andrew. *The World of Homer*, London, Longmans, Green &
Co., 1910.
Leumann, Ernst. *Zur indischen und indogermanischen Metrik*. In
'*Αντίδωρον, Festschrift Jacob Wackernagel . . . gewidmet*, Gottingen,
Vanderhoeck und Ruprecht, 1924.
Linforth, I. M. *Solon the Athenian*, Berkeley, Cal., 1919.
Lisi, Umbertina. *Poetesse greche*, Catania, Studio editoriale Moderno,
1933/xi.
Lobeck, C. A. *Aglaophamus siue ae theologiae mysticae Graecorum
causis libri tres*, Königsberg, Borntraeger, 1829.
Mahlow, G. H. *Neue Wege durch die griechische Sprache und Dichtung*,
Berlin and Leipzig, 1927.
Meillet, A. *Aperçu d'une histoire de la langue grecque*, Paris, Hachette,
1913.
Les origines indo-européennes des mètres grecs, Paris, Les presses
universitaires de France, 1923.
Nilsson, M. P. *Homer and Mycenae*, London, Methuen, 1933.
Norden, Eduard. *Die antike Kunstprosa vom VI. Jahrhundert v. Chr.
bis in die Zeit der Renaissance*. Teubner, 1898, 2 vols.
Norwood, Gilbert. *Greek Tragedy*, London, Methuen, 1920.
Greek Comedy, same, 1931.
Pernot, H. *D'Homère à nos jours : histoire, écriture, prononciation
du grec*. Paris, Garnier frères, 1921.

Pickard-Cambridge, A. W. *Dithyramb, Tragedy and Comedy*, Oxford, Clar. Press, 1927. *See also* Haigh.

Postgate, J. P. *A short Guide to the Accentuation of Ancient Greek*, London, Hodder and Stoughton, 1924.

Powell, J. U., and Barber, E. A. *New Chapters in the History of Greek Literature*, First Series (' Powell-Barber 1 '), 1921 ; Second Series (' Powell-Barber 2 '), 1929.

Powell, J. U. (alone). Third Series, 1933 (' Powell 3 '). All Oxford, Clar. Press.

Reichel, W. *Homerische Waffen : archäologische Untersuchungen.* 2e, völlig umgearbeitet und erweiterte Auflage. Vienna, Hölder, 1901.

Rose, H. J. *A Handbook of Greek Mythology.* London, Methuen ; and New York, Dutton, 1929; sixth ed., Methuen 1958, and Dutton, 1959.

Sandys, (Sir) J. E. *A History of Classical Scholarship*, Cambridge, Univ. Press, (Vol. i, (ed. 2), 1906 ; Vols. ii and iii, 1908.

Schmid, W. *Der Atticismus in seinem Hauptvertretern von Dionysius von Halikarnass bis auf dem zweiten Philostratus.* Stuttgart, Kohlhammer, 4 vols., 1887–97.

Sheppard, J. T. *The Pattern of the Iliad.* London, Methuen, 1922.

Shewan, A. *The Lay of Dolon . . . with remarks by the way on the canons and methods of Homeric criticism*, London, Macmillan, 1911.

Sturtevant, E. H. *Pronunciation of Greek and Latin*, Chicago, 1920.

Turnbull, H. W. *The Great Mathematicians.* London, Methuen, second ed., 1933.

Vürthheim, J. *Stesichoros' Fragmente und Biographie*, Leiden, Sijthoff, 1919.

Welcker, F. G. *Der epische Cyclus, oder die homerischen Dichter.* Bonn, Weber, 1835.

White, J. W. *The Verse of Greek Comedy*, London, Macmillan, 1912.

Wilamowitz-Moellendorff, U. von. *Sappho und Simonides : untersuchungen über griechische Lyriker*, Berlin, Weidmann, 1913. (' S.S.')

Aischylos, Interpretationen, same pub., 1914. (The second volume of his edition of Aeschylus.)

Die Ilias und Homer, same pub., 1916.

Hellenistische Dichtung in der Zeit des Kallimachos, 2 vols., same pub., 1924.

Der Glaube der Hellenen, same pub., 2 vols., 1931–2.

(Several other works are mentioned in the text and footnotes.)

Wolf, F. A. *Fr. Aug. Wolf's Vorlesungen über die vier ersten Gesänge von Homer's Ilias*, herausgegeben und mit Bemerkungen und zusätzen begleitet von Leonhard Usteri. Bern, Jenni, 1830.

(For his *Prolegomena*, see p. 36.)

ADDENDA TO BIBLIOGRAPHY

Homeric Hymns. T. W. Allen, W. R. Halliday and E. E. Sikes, *The Homeric Hymns*, second edition, Oxford, Clarendon Press, 1936. ('Allen-Halliday').

Lyric. Edgar Lobel et Denys Page, *Poetarum Lesbiorum Fragmenta*, Oxford, Clarendon Press, 1955.

INDEX

(In this index, for assistance in preparing which I wish to thank Mrs. A. Dall, of this University, and my son R. M. Rose, numerals in bold-faced type indicate the principal passages bearing on the subject in question. The abbreviations f[ather], s[on], w[ife], and one or two others easily understood, are used. Accents indicate the pronunciation of the names, which are also given in Greek letters and in the Latin form, where that differs noticeably from the one used in this book.)

---

[1] Milton's 'Irassa' (*P.R.*, iv, 564) is a corrupt form derived from the texts of Pindar then available.